Introduction to
MICROECONOMICS

Introduction to
MICROECONOMICS

David Laidler
University of Western Ontario
and
Saul Estrin
The London School of Economics

Third Edition

PHILIP ALLAN

New York   London   Toronto   Sydney   Tokyo   Singapore

First published 1974 by
Philip Allan
66 Wood Lane End, Hemel Hempstead
Hertfordshire, HP2 4RG
A division of
Simon & Schuster International Group

Second edition 1981
Third edition 1989
© David Laidler 1974, 1981
David Laidler and Saul Estrin 1989

Printed and bound in Great Britain by
Cambridge University Press, Cambridge

British Library Cataloguing in Publication Data
Laidler, David E.W., *1938–*
    Introduction to microeconomics.
    3rd ed
    1. Microeconomics
    I. Title   II. Estrin, Saul
    338.5

    ISBN 0-86003-082-2
    ISBN 0-86003-190-X pbk

4 5 93 92 91

Contents

Preface

Preface to the Third Edition

Like its predecessors, this new edition of *Introduction to Microeconomics* is intended to be read by second-year undergraduates specialising in economics. The book has been extensively revised in this edition, for two reasons. First, the subject matter of microeconomics has changed considerably over the last fifteen years; and second, so has the way in which the topic is taught at the second-year level.

It is nowadays common for students to begin degree courses having already studied a good deal of economics, and in some institutions the level of intermediate courses has risen considerably. This change is not universal, though, and it therefore raises a problem for the authors of any intermediate text, namely, how to challenge advanced students while remaining accessible to others. We have tried to cope with this problem by retaining much of the material contained in earlier editions, which was explicitly aimed at students whose second-year degree course was also their second year of studying economics, and by supplementing this basic content with more advanced material, both technical and economic.

Earlier editions of this book relied almost exclusively on verbal and geometric analysis. Now we make fairly widespread use of calculus, and even of a little game theory. The sections which use such techniques are indicated by *, or, in one or two places where the argument is more difficult, by **. Readers with a strong aversion to algebra who omit these sections will still be left with a coherent treatment of much basic microeconomics, but we urge even non-mathematically inclined readers at least to sample the starred sections. Many of them, particularly at the beginning of the book, begin by repeating analysis presented earlier with words and geometry, so that such readers can gain confidence in handling algebra by seeing it first of all applied to familiar problems. Furthermore, the use of calculus often permits a degree of precision to be achieved, and insights to be revealed, that are simply not available when geometric techniques alone are deployed. Hence our algebraic sections usually extend the geometric analysis as well.

An implicit theme of this book is the unity given to microeconomic theory by the idea of constrained maximisation, and this theme emerges particularly clearly when calculus is applied to economic problems. Here is yet another reason why we urge as many of our readers as possible to work through a few of the starred sections.

But algebra is not used here for its own sake. As we remarked earlier, the subject matter now considered standard in microeconomics has changed and expanded in recent years, and more powerful techniques are needed to deal with many newer topics. Nowhere is this more true than with regard to the idea of duality, where technique and theoretical insight have combined to produce an important advance in economic understanding. This topic turns up twice below, once briefly in the context of consumer theory in Chapter 4, and then in much more detail in the context of cost and production theory in Chapter 12.

Chapter 12 is no doubt the most advanced in this book, and though we make no apology for its presence — a modern micro book which did not deal with duality would be seriously deficient — we are nevertheless aware that many less advanced readers will wish either to omit this chapter, or come to it later in their studies. To this end we have written Chapter 12 as a rather self-contained entity that may comfortably be read out of sequence. Duality is by no means the only topic added in this edition. There is no need to give a detailed list of other additions, since a glance at the table of contents will provide that information. Nevertheless, it is worth noting that a great deal of material in industrial organisation theory — dealing, for example, with oligopoly theory, not to mention the worker-managed firm — has been added; so too has a chapter on trade unions as bargaining agents; as well as a number of topics in general equilibrium theory.

All of this makes for too long a book for a one-term course, and one which offers a considerable challenge for a year-long programme of study. Nevertheless, instructors will find it possible to design shorter courses of their own by omitting particular chapters, say from Part II and Part VI, or by dropping certain areas altogether — a course in partial equilibrium microeconomics would obviously omit the whole of Part VIII, for example. We make no definite recommendations here, for different users will have different tastes. Nevertheless, one of our major objectives in preparing this edition was to bring the book's treatment of other topics up to the same level of comprehensiveness that already marked its treatment of consumer theory. We believe that not the least advantage of such comprehensiveness is that it does indeed permit teachers and students some latitude in designing their own courses.

Another way in which this edition expands on its predecessors is in the provision of problem sets. The number of problems has been considerably expanded, and placed at the end of each part of the book. Problems have been grouped in this way because we felt that many themes worthy of discussion were developed across chapters within one part of the book,

rather than within particular chapters. The problem sets have been expanded in both length and range, covering the new more technical material as well as offering more questions on the subject matter of previous editions. Problems which require a working knowledge of calculus are marked with *.

In preparing this edition we have benefited greatly from the help and advice of Avner Ben-Ber, David de Meza, Peter Holmes, Andrew Oswald and Jan Svejnar. Frank Cowell and Michael Sumner read through the whole manuscript and made numerous helpful suggestions and comments. John Sessions helped in setting the problems and with the numerous stages of proof reading and revisions. Much of the additional material was also first tested on Estrin's first- and second-year microeconomics groups at the LSE. The typing was done by Yvonne Adams, Grace Campbell, Pat Nutt and Lynda Sollazzo, who worked valiantly in the face of a text which was continuously altered in two different handwritings. Thanks also to Philip Allan for encouragement during this long-drawn-out project, to Helen Ramsay and Mary Robinson for editorial assistance and to Tony Bernardo who prepared the index. Finally, mention should be made of our families, whose support and patience have been crucial during the lengthy process of preparing this new edition.

Saul Estrin　　　　　　　　　　　　　　　　　　　*David Laidler*
The London School of Economics　　　*University of Western Ontario*

Preface to the Second Edition

The primary purpose of this second edition of *Introduction to Microeconomics*, like that of the first, is to provide an account of the subject that will be accessible to second year undergraduates taking a single honours degree in economics. The book is still intended to be read slowly and carefully, but in this edition I have reorganised the presentation of the subject matter in order to make it more accessible. There is a little more illustrative material than before, and much more important, chapters are now divided into short, explicitly labelled sections so that readers will have much less trouble finding their way around this edition than they did the first. Moreover, I have added some straightforward numerical exercises to the study questions. A good deal of new material has been incorporated in this edition, particularly on the theory of the firm and those mistakes that I know about in the first edition have been removed.

My colleague James Melvin helped me get certain details of the treatment of returns to scale right this time, and Charles Stuart, now at the University of Lund, offered much helpful advice on the treatment of bilateral monopoly. I am grateful to both of them, as I am to John McInerney of the University of Reading, Michael Sumner of the University of Salford, and Ian Walker of the University of Manchester, who read

earlier drafts of this edition and provided a great deal of helpful advice as to how it could be improved. Most of their advice was gratefully accepted and taken, but considerations of space prevented me from following all their suggestions. Thus I alone am to blame for any errors and omissions that the reader might find in this second edition. Finally, I am grateful to Laurie Bland, Terry Caverhill, and Monica Malkus, all of whom coped ably with various stages of the typing of the manuscript.

DAVID LAIDLER
February 1981

Preface to the First Edition

This book is intended primarily to be used by second year undergraduates taking single honours degrees in economics. It pre-supposes that the reader has already had an introductory course with a significant content of elementary microeconomic analysis. The mathematical techniques used are virtually all geometric. However, the student who has had an elementary mathematics course dealing with basic calculus, and hence with such matters as the inter-relationship between functions and their derivatives, the geometric representations of these inter-relationships, as well as the basic mathematics of constrained maximisation will find the going a lot easier than the reader who has had no exposure to mathematics since GCE ordinary level.

I have not aimed this book specifically at the future specialist in economic theory. Rather, I have tried to present, in one volume, enough microeconomic analysis so that the student who has mastered it will have a background adequate to permit him to take third year applied courses without further specialist study in microeconomics *per se*. Nevertheless, I hope that the future specialist in theory will also find that reading the following pages is helpful. There is probably enough material to keep a second year student busy, but teachers who wish to use it in third year courses are likely to find it a little thin. However, suitably supplemented with references to journal articles and other books, it could be used at the third year level. The suggestions for further reading attached to the text are primarily intended for use at this level, and they often extend, rather than repeat, the subject matter which I have specifically treated. This is particularly so in the case of the theory of the firm, where I have confined my exposition to dealing with the single product neo-classical profit maximising enterprise. Industrial organisation is now so frequently taught as a subject in its own right at the undergraduate level that it seemed wise to avoid producing, in a couple of chapters on alternative theories of the firm, an inevitably inadequate duplication of the subject matter of a fully fledged course in the area. The same may be said of the analysis of labour markets, for here I have left questions of human capital, trade union behaviour and such to be dealt with in a specialist course in labour economics.

Microeconomics is at least as much a way of thinking about problems as it is a coherent body of substantive hypotheses and one does not learn how to think along certain lines without actually doing so. Some microeconomics can be learned by reading about it, but the area can only be mastered by actually doing microeconomic analysis for oneself. With this in mind, I have attempted to pitch my exposition at a level which will force the average reader to work quite hard at mastering the arguments presented. I have also set study questions which sometimes extend the analysis covered in the text rather than call for its mere reproduction. In short, I hope that the reader will find himself involved in a process of 'learning by doing' as he works his way through.

I began writing this book while on a term's leave at Brown University in Providence, Rhode Island, and owe a considerable debt to some of my colleagues there. George Borts, James Hanson, John Kennan, and Mark Shupak all had their brains picked more often than they realised, while I owe special thanks to Allan Feldman who read and commented on an early version of Part I. At Manchester, John McInerney and Michael Sumner read and commented copiously on a first draft of the whole book, placing me considerably in their debt by so doing. Mrs Coral Parrett and Mrs Vicky Whelan coped most patiently with the tedious process of typing and retyping the manuscript, while Mrs Majorie Watts drafted the many diagrams. I am extremely grateful to all three. I would dearly like to implicate everyone I have named in any errors and omissions that the reader might find in the analysis that follows; I can find no sound reason for doing so and am forced, therefore, to accept sole responsibility.

D.L.
February 1974

1

Introduction

Scarcity and Economics

Economics is about scarcity. The word 'scarcity' is used here in a special sense: it refers to a state of affairs in which, given the wants of a society at any particular moment, the means available to satisfy them are not sufficient. If all desires cannot be totally satisfied, then choices have to be made as to which of them are going to be satisfied, and to what extent. To say that economics is about scarcity then is also to say that it is about choice. There is no suggestion here that the scope of the subject is confined to purely material matters, such as the production and distribution of those goods and services that happen to make up such statistical magnitudes as the gross national product. Economics is relevant here to be sure, but its scope is potentially much wider. Any social or private situation which involves a choice of some sort has an economic aspect.

At any time the individuals making up a particular society will desire a wide variety of items — food, clothing, housing, holidays, recreation, access to countryside and seashore, to music, to art, to sporting events, to educational facilities and so on — but the means available to provide all these are limited. The population is of a given size, and possesses a particular mix of skills; a certain given level of technology and mix of capital equipment are available (to say nothing of given amounts of open space and seashore). Thus not everyone can have all that they desire of everything. For any one individual to have more of one thing, he or she must either have less of another thing, or someone else must have less of something.

The scope of the scarcity problem as it faces society is enormous and complex. Given available resources it must somehow be decided how they are to be used, which goods are to be produced and in what amounts. It must also be decided how the resulting output is to be distributed

SCARCITY / CHOICE

Which what How.

1

among the individuals that make up society. Moreover, though at one moment it makes sense to treat resources as given, these can be changed over time both in quality and quantity by devoting part of current output to this end. The provision of productive resources for the future, then, is yet another one of the competing ends to which current production can be devoted. In addition, there is the problem of so organising matters that, at any time, the scarce resources that are available do not lie idle but do, in fact, get used. Thus, questions about the allocation of resources, the distribution of income, economic growth, and the maintenance of full employment are all economic problems, for they all arise from the fact of scarcity. If all wants could be satisfied simultaneously, it would not matter how resources were used, how income was distributed, how the balance was struck between the satisfaction of present and future wants or the extent to which particular resources were utilised.

Different societies organise themselves in different ways to cope with these problems. Capitalist societies invest individuals with property rights in particular productive resources and then allow them to use those resources as they see fit. From the interaction of individual decisions a social solution to the scarcity problem emerges, a solution not in the sense that the problem vanishes, but in the sense that a particular level and pattern of output and resource use emerges, along with a particular distribution of income. A socialist economy deals with the same problem by investing the state rather than individuals with property rights in resources and then attempting to formulate a coherent and consistent plan for their use. Again a solution to the problem is achieved.

It is not only at the social level that scarcity exists and choices have to be made. Individual economic agents face the problem too. Such agents may be individuals, families, capitalist firms, co-operative enterprises or government departments, but all are faced with choices about the use of the scarce resources available to them. An individual or a family must allocate its time between work and leisure, while bearing in mind that the income realised from work is available for the purchase of the various goods and services which it may want to consume. A firm, be it a capitalist enterprise concerned only with its own profits, or some kind of socialist co-operative consciously seeking to contribute to the achievement of socially determined goals, does not have an inexhaustible supply of inputs available to it, nor will it be able to engage in the production of every conceivable output. Somehow it must be decided what goods are to be produced by the enterprise and at what scale, utilising what inputs with what technical processes. A government department in charge of, shall we say, providing education, does not have inexhaustible funds at its disposal. Somehow the resources available to it must be divided between nursery schools, primary education, secondary education and higher education.

The problems facing individual agents are particular manifestations of

the general social problem. The responses of individual agents are interdependent and contribute to the solution of the scarcity problem at the social level. In any planned economy there is still a large area of choice left open to individuals; perhaps the most difficult problem facing any planning bureau is to provide the incentives and instructions to individual agents that will ensure that the choices which they then make will be consistent with the overall plan laid down for the use of the resources available to society. In a capitalist economy the related problem arises as to whether the means by which individuals' choices are linked together and impinge upon each other, the system of contracts and market transactions, are such as to ensure that the plans of all individuals are compatible with one another and with the overall availability of resources.

An Outline of the Book

Quite clearly it is impossible to come to grips with questions such as these without knowing a great deal about the behaviour of individual agents. If one wishes to argue that capitalism results in a satisfactory state of affairs — having, of course, carefully explained what is meant by that deceptively simple word 'satisfactory' in the first place — one must know how individuals behave. But individual behaviour is not just a problem for the apologist for capitalism. As has already been argued, to devise a plan for a socialist economy that will actually work requires that individual agents, whether as workers or consumers, must be persuaded to behave in a manner compatible with that plan. Thus, a knowledge of how individual agents react to particular instructions or incentives must be basic to any kind of planning exercise. Microeconomics is particularly concerned with the behaviour of individual economic agents. Much of this book is concerned with their behaviour towards problems as they arise in capitalist economies, and the authors make no apology for that since this book is intended for readers who live in that kind of economic system. Nevertheless, a good deal of the analysis that follows is of much broader application, as the reader will easily discern.

First, we are going to deal with the behaviour of individual consumers as they face their own version of the scarcity problem — how to allocate a given income between the various goods available. We are going to see how they react to changes in income and the prices of those goods and see what we may say about the way such changes affect their economic wellbeing. Moreover, the same analysis developed to deal with current expenditure decisions can be modified to deal with the question of the determinants of saving behaviour, and choices involving hours of work. These problems will also be discussed, as will certain aspects of choice when the outcomes of particular courses of action are uncertain. We shall outline a new approach to consumer theory which pays particular attention to the complexity of so many modern goods and services and to the

existence of differences between different brands of what are basically the same good.

Second, we shall examine the question of production, in particular in a capitalist economy. We shall mainly deal with the theory of the profit-maximising firm and the principles governing the choices it makes about levels of output, levels of factor utilisation and pricing in the markets for both factors and outputs. We shall also touch upon the analysis of firms that pursue goals other than profit, the maximisation of sales revenue, or the maximisation of revenue per employee. As the reader will discover, the analysis here has a great deal in common with the theory of the profit-maximising firm. The latter is worth close attention, not because it is the only available approach to the problem, but because it is perhaps the most fully developed analysis of the behaviour of business enterprises, and also because it provides a set of predictions about behaviour with which the predictions of other approaches may be compared.

Third, we shall discuss the problems of co-ordinating the choices of firms and consumers in an account of general equilibrium analysis. We shall outline the conditions which must hold if the behaviour of firms and households are to be consistent with one another and with the overall resource constraint on the economy. We will pose the question of whether we can say anything about the desirability of the resulting solution to the scarcity problem, being careful to note those conditions which might hold in an abstract model of capitalist market economy but are unlikely to hold in any actual economy. The problems here are complex and we can only note them at this stage. First, because individuals own resources and obtain their incomes by selling the use of those resources, a particular income distribution is implied by any solution to the allocation problem: does this influence the judgements that we may make about the desirability of a particular allocative scheme? Second, what about the allocation of resources towards satisfying those wants which are not always brought into the range of ordinary market transactions — access to the recreational facilities afforded by a river, for example? How does a capitalist economy deal, or fail to deal, with such problems? The discussion of these and related issues takes up the final section of this book.

Suggested Further Reading

Knight, F.H. 1968. 'Social and Economic Organisation', ch.1 of W. Breit and H.M. Hochman (eds), *Readings in Microeconomics*. New York: Holt Rinehart and Winston.

Radford, R.A. 1945. 'The Economic Organisation of a POW Camp', *Economica*. pp. 519–30.

Robbins, L. 1932. *An Essay on the Nature and Significance of Economic Science*. London: Macmillan.

Von Hayek, F.A. 1945. 'The Use of Knowledge in Society', *American Economic Review*. pp. 189–201.

Part I

ELEMENTS OF THE THEORY OF CONSUMER BEHAVIOUR

2

The Basic Theory of Consumer Choice

Introduction

Economics is about scarcity, about social situations which require that choices be made. The theory of consumer behaviour deals with the way in which scarcity impinges upon the individual consumer and hence deals with the way in which such an individual makes choices. This consumer may, but need not be, an individual person. Families and households also make collective consumption choices on behalf of their members. The theory as we shall present it takes the consumer unit as given. It therefore presents us with an important instance of how other social sciences, such as sociology and social psychology which deal, in part, with the way in which people organise themselves into household and other units, could complement economics.

The theory of consumer choice has many applications. It enables us to deal with the selection of consumption patterns at a particular time and the allocation of consumption over time, and hence with saving. The individual supplying labour can be thought of as simultaneously choosing an amount of leisure time, so the same theory is relevant there as it is when we come to consider behaviour in the face of risk. Moreover, in constructing a theory to deal with problems such as these, we are forced to think carefully about, and to define precisely, such much abused terms as 'real income' and the 'cost of living', so that our theory gives us many valuable insights into matters of potentially considerable practical importance. We shall deal with all these matters, and more, in the chapters that follow.

The Subject Matter of this Chapter

To deal with such problems as these, we need a language of analysis, a general framework in terms of which all these apparently diverse matters can be reduced to their common elements. We shall develop such a framework in this chapter, and then we shall put it to use in deriving two relationships much used in applied economic analysis, namely the *Engel curve* and the *demand curve*. The first of these relates the quantity of a good which a consumer purchases to the consumer's income. The second relates the quantity of a good purchased to its price, and is one of the fundamental building blocks of microeconomics.

Even so, the main emphasis in this chapter is not on these relationships in and of themselves, but rather on the theoretical structure which underlies them. The model of choice-making, from which they are derived, is of much more general interest, and provides the foundation for all of this part of the book, and for Part II as well.

In order to derive this model we need to describe first of all the logical structure of the choice problem which faces any consumer. We will find it helpful to think of that structure as being made up of three components. First, we must consider the items which the consumer finds desirable, the *objects of choice*. Second, since the desirability of an object does not necessarily imply that it is available to be chosen, we must consider any limitations that might be placed on the alternatives available to the consumer, the *constraints upon choice*. Finally, because choice necessarily involves a process of selection among alternatives, we must consider the way in which the consumer ranks the alternatives available, the consumer's *tastes* or *preferences*.

The Objects of Choice

The objects of the consumer's choice are goods and services. In the most general case we may consider patterns of consumption at each particular moment in time and over time. To keep things simple we will now confine ourselves to the choice facing an individual at a particular time, ignoring for the moment the problem of allocating consumption over time. We will also simplify the world by assuming that it contains only two goods, X and Y. This abstraction from a world with many goods to one with two is not quite so restrictive as might appear at first sight, for it is always possible to think of X as being one particular good and Y as being a composite bundle of all other goods.

Now consider Figure 2.1. On the horizontal axis we measure quantities of X per unit of time, let us say per week, and on the vertical axis quantities of Y per week. Any point in the area bounded by these two axes may be interpreted as a pattern of consumption involving a particular mixture of X and Y per week. Thus the point on the X-axis at 5X represents

Figure 2.1

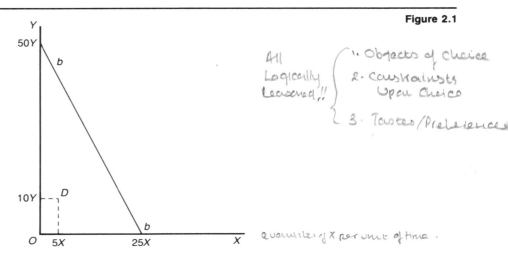

Each point of the diagram represents a bundle of goods. The point D represents a bundle made up of 5X and 10Y. The line bb is a budget constraint drawn on the assumption that a consumer has an income of £50 and faces prices for X and Y of £2 and £1 respectively. The budget constraint divides those bundles of goods that the consumer can obtain, given income and their prices, from those that cannot be obtained.

a consumption pattern of 5X and no Y per week, the point D represents consumption of 5X, 10Y per week, and so on. In short, the objects of choice in this particular simplification of the theory of consumer choice are consumption patterns measured in terms of bundles of goods per week and each such bundle is represented by a particular point on a diagram such as Figure 2.1.

2. The Budget Constraint

Now, in principle, we may extend the axes of Figure 2.1 indefinitely and hence encompass any conceivable bundle of X and Y, but this does not mean that the consumer is in fact able to select any bundle of X and Y found desirable. Goods and services are generally not free and what a consumer can get at a particular moment is limited by available purchasing power. Suppose, for simplicity, that the only source of purchasing power was the consumer's present income. This may be expressed as a certain sum of money per week and it puts an upper limit on consumption. We may represent this in Figure 2.1 in the following way.

X and Y are goods that have prices and it is reasonable enough to suppose that these prices may be taken as constant as far as the individual consumer is concerned. Suppose that the price of X is £2 per unit and that of Y £1 per unit. Suppose also that the consumer's income is £50

per week. Then it is obvious that, if all income is devoted to the consumption of X, the consumer may have not more than 25 units of X per week; alternatively that same consumer may have 50 units of Y per week. However, there is nothing to stop X and Y being combined in the chosen consumption pattern. We can calculate how much is spent on any particular quantity (less than 25) of X, and this sum subtracted from income gives the amount left over to be spent on Y. This amount divided by the price of Y tells us the maximum amount of Y that can be bought, given the quantity of X. If we carry out this calculation for every quantity of X between 0 and 25 and link up the resulting bundles of goods, we derive the line *bb* in Figure 2.1 which represents the consumer's so-called *budget constraint*. This line separates all those consumption bundles that can be afforded from those that cannot be afforded. Given the prices we have assumed, it is clear that for every unit of X given up, two units of Y may be substituted. Hence the slope of this constraint is obviously the inverse of the ratio of the prices we have assumed. If X costs £2 and Y £1, then the ratio of the price of Y to the price of X is 1/2 and the rate at which Y may be substituted for X is 2/1.

Budget line or *Constraint*

More generally, we can specify the equation of the budget constraint as follows. We may define the consumer's money income as M, and retain as the objects of choice in our problem the goods X and Y, which sell at prices p_X and p_Y respectively. If we assume that the consumer spends all his or her income, it will follow by definition that income (M) equals expenditure ($p_X X + p_Y Y$). Hence

$$M = p_X X + p_Y Y \tag{2.1}$$

Rearranging terms to form an equation with Y expressed as a function of X, we derive

$$Y = \frac{M}{p_Y} - \frac{p_X X}{p_Y} \tag{2.2}$$

This equation defines a straight line — the budget constraint — with intercept M/p_Y and slope $-p_X/p_Y$. It should be clear from an inspection of equation (2.2) that increases in money income shift the budget constraint outwards and parallel to itself; changes in M do not affect the slope of the constraint — p_X/p_Y. Changes in the price of X swivel the budget constraint around, pivoting it on the intercept with the Y axis (which equals M/p_Y). An increase in p_X causes it to pivot inwards. Changes in the price of Y lead the budget constraint to pivot around its intercept with the X axis (since M/p_Y alters when p_Y alters), inwards when p_Y increases and outwards when it falls. It should be stressed that in developing this formulation, we do not need to stick with the assumption that income equals expenditure, which of course implies that the consumer does not save. If consumers do not spend all their income, expenditures lie inside the budget constraint rather than on the line itself ($p_X X + p_Y Y < M$). We return to the issue of saving in Chapter 6.

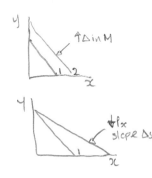

The Consumer's Tastes /Preferences.

We make two assumptions about our consumer's tastes. First we assume that any two bundles of goods can be compared. The consumer can decide if bundle 1 or 2 is preferable, or whether either bundle is equally desirable. In this last eventuality the consumer is said to be *indifferent* between the two bundles. Second we assume that these comparisons are made in a *consistent* fashion. By this we mean that if, when bundles 1 and 2 are compared, 1 is preferred, and when 2 and 3 are compared, 2 is preferred, then, when 1 and 3 are compared, 1 will be preferred.

This assumption of consistent preferences is all that economists imply when they speak of the consumer being 'rational'. However, in constructing the elementary theory of choice, it is usual to make certain subsidiary assumptions in addition to the basic one of consistent preferences. First, having already assumed that the objects of choice are desirable, it is but a small step to the propositions that, when compared with D (the point in Figure 2.1 representing $5X$ and $10Y$), any bundle that has either more X and no less Y or more Y and no less X will be preferred. In terms of Figure 2.2 this means that any point in the shaded area above and to the right of D will be preferred to D, and that D will be preferred to any point in the area below and to the left of it.

It follows from this that if D is one of a set of bundles of goods among which the consumer is indifferent, such bundles must lie in the areas below and to the right of D and above and to the left of D. It is usual to go further than this and argue that all such points must lie on a continuous negatively sloped line, an *indifference curve* such as the line *II* in Figure 2.2, a curve that is convex towards the origin. A smooth convex

① Ass. Comparibility
↳ Indifferent
= equally desirable

② Ass. Consistent
↓
= RATIONAL

These assumptions necessarily lead to:
a) Max Satisfaction.

Figure 2.2

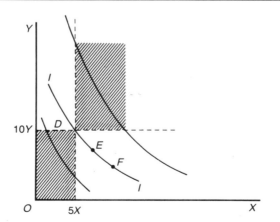

Any point in the area above and to the right of D represents a bundle of goods preferred to D; D is preferred to any point below and to its left. Thus the indifference curve *II* passing through D must have a negative slope. It is generally assumed that such curves are convex to the origin.

Why a curve?
= diminishing
   marginal rate
   of substitution.

Indifference Maps
are everywhere
         dense

Cannot cross
– not using
   rationality.

curve is by no means the only formulation of an indifference curve compatible with the assumption of rationality, but it is both intuitively plausible and, as we shall see below, productive of sensible predictions about behaviour. This particular shape involves what is called a *diminishing marginal rate of substitution* between the goods. This shape implies that the more X there is relative to Y in the bundle to begin with, the more X is required to compensate the consumer for the loss of a given amount of Y. Thus, in Figure 2.2 the movement from E to F involves the same loss of Y as that from D to E, but requires a larger gain in X to keep our consumer on the same indifference curve. The *marginal rate of substitution of X for Y* is the ratio of the amount of X needed to compensate for a small (in the limit infinitesimal) loss of Y to that loss of Y. It is given by the slope of the indifference curve, which is negative; and it becomes less negative (i.e. *diminishes*) as we move down the curve from left to right.

Now II is a particular indifference curve. We may think of the consumption of any bundle of goods on it as yielding a particular level of satisfaction, or *utility,* to the consumer. However there are indifference curves passing through every point of Figure 2.2, each one negatively sloped and each one convex to the origin. Those which pass through points above and to the right of D link up bundles of goods that yield higher levels of satisfaction than those on II; those below and to the left yield lower levels of satisfaction. Such curves can never cross one another, for this would violate the rationality assumption. Consider Figure 2.3 in which two indifference curves have been drawn to cross and consider their interpretation. The consumer is indifferent between points H and J on curve 1 and between R and Q on curve 2. However, bundle H has more of both X and Y than does R and hence must be preferred to it; for exactly the same reason, point Q must be preferred to J. There is clearly an incon-

Figure 2.3

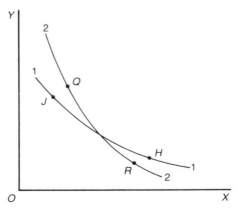

Indifference curves that cross are incompatible with the assumption that consumers order bundles of goods consistently.

sistency here that violates the rationality assumption, and it obviously
arises because the curves cross one another.

More on Tastes — Ordinal and Cardinal Utility

We have characterised the consumer's tastes in an *indifference map* showing how satisfaction (*utility*) varies with (*is a function of*) the consumption
pattern. This *utility function* has two basic properties. Each indifference
curve is convex to the origin, and as we move upwards and to the right
the indifference curves represent higher and higher levels of satisfaction.
Notice that, in constructing this utility function, we have said nothing
about the intensity of the consumer's preferences. We have assumed that
the consumer is able to rank bundles of goods with reference to their
capacity to satisfy desires, but we have assumed nothing about the degree
to which any bundle of goods does so.

To put it another way, in the foregoing analysis we have simply noted
that higher indifference curves represent higher levels of utility; we have
not found it necessary to specify how much higher. We have been deal-
ing with an *ordinal* utility function, that is, a function that tells us the order — not intensity.
in which a consumer ranks bundles of goods, but tells us nothing at all
about the *intensity* of likes or dislikes for particular consumption patterns.
We can only use relative terms such as 'better' and 'worse', 'preferred'
and 'not preferred ' in this context. It is possible, however, at least in
principle, to conceive of a *cardinal* utility function which, in addition to
telling us about how bundles of goods are ordered tells us about the intensity of likes and dislikes, measuring satisfaction, or utility, in precise
units. To argue by analogy for a moment, in the measurement of length,
an ordinal scale would tell us only that some distances were longer or
shorter (or the same length) than others. A cardinal scale would be set
up in units of yards or metres and would tell us how long each distance
was and hence *how much* longer (or shorter) than any other. So long as
we deal with questions about choice under conditions of certainty, the
ordinal utility assumption suffices as a basis for consumer theory but,
as we shall see later, a cardinal utility function is extremely useful in dealing with choice in conditions of risk; indeed the existence of such a function is implicit in the possibility of such a choice. However, for the moment
we are analysing consumer choice in conditions of certainty, and the idea
of ordinary utility is all we require to tackle this problem.

The Solution to the Choice Problem

We now have all the ingredients necessary for the solution of the consumer's choice problem. We have defined the objects of choice. These
are bundles of goods, *consumption patterns*, made up of various quantities

of X and Y. We have also derived the constraint upon choice. The consumer's money income combined with the prices of X and Y have enabled us to draw a line, a *budget constraint*, that separates those bundles of X and Y that are attainable from those that are not. Finally, the consumer's tastes have been summarised in an *indifference map*. In Figure 2.4 we bring these three ingredients together, and the solution to the consumer's choice problem immediately appears.

The consumer wishes to do as well as possible, to select that consumption pattern out of all those available that will yield the highest level of satisfaction — the consumer wishes to *maximise utility*. In terms of Figure 2.4 this involves selecting a consumption pattern on as high an indifference curve as possible. Clearly that pattern is given by the point A with the consumer getting X_1 of X per week and Y_1 of Y.

Consider the properties of this solution, which we call a situation of *equilibrium* for the consumer because there are no forces that would cause a move away from A. First, the point A lies *on* the budget constraint, not inside it. This happens because we have assumed that, when compared to any particular bundle of goods, a bundle with more of one good and no less of another is preferred. For any consumption pattern within the budget constraint, there is at least one on the constraint with just this property. Does this then mean that the analysis of consumer choice rules out saving? It does not, for, as we shall see below, it is possible to characterise saving as an act of devoting current income to future consumption. For our analysis, we made the simplifying assumption that we would not for the time being consider the choice of consumption patterns over time. Hence we have ruled out saving here for the sake of simplicity, not predicted that it cannot take place.

MAXIMISE
UTILITY / satisfaction

Figure 2.4

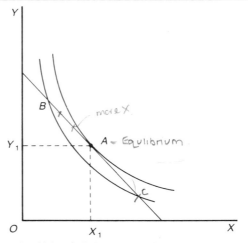

A is the bundle of goods which, of all those available, yields the consumer the highest level of satisfaction. This maximum satisfaction bundle occurs where an indifference curve is tangent to the budget constraint.

The second point to note about the solution depicted in Figure 2.4 is that at *A* an indifference curve is just tangent to the budget constraint. As readers will discover, such tangency solutions continuously occur in geometric representations of economic theory. The slope of the budget constraint tells us, as we saw above, the rate at which our consumer is permitted to substitute *X* for *Y* by the structure of prices. For every amount of *Y* given up some amount of *X* is obtained instead. The slope is equal to the ratio of the price of *Y* to that of *X*. The slope of an indifference curve at any particular point tells us the rate at which the consumer would have to substitute *X* for *Y* in order to maintain a given level of satisfaction, or to enjoy a constant level of utility. This slope is, of course, the marginal rate of substitution of *X* for *Y*. Thus we may characterise a point of tangency between an indifference curve and a budget constraint as a situation in which the marginal rate of substitution of *X* for *Y* is just equal to the ratio of the price of *X* to the price of *Y*.

— A The point of equilibrium

That *A* is indeed a point of maximum satisfaction, or maximum utility, can be seen in another way. Consider the point *B* in Figure 2.4. Suppose the consumer started at this point for some reason. Given available income and the set of prices ruling, the consumer could get more *X* for a particular sacrifice of *Y* than is necessary to stay on the indifference curve that passes through *B*. Thus, by substituting *X* for *Y* along the budget constraint, the consumer can move on to higher and higher indifference curves; until, that is, *A* is reached. With the movement from *B* towards *A*, *Y* becomes progressively more valuable relative to *X* and the rate at which the consumer is willing to give up *Y* in return for *X* falls. At *A* the rate at which the consumer is willing to give up *Y* to get *X* coincides with the rate at which the price structure permits this substitution to be made. Any movement to the right of *A* would involve having to give up more *Y* than is required for the maintenance of a particular level of utility, so further substitution will not be made.

why not B or C

To sum up then, the utility-maximising choice involves selecting the bundle of goods where the budget constraint and the indifference curve touch tangentially. At this point both have the same slope and we can say that the rate at which the consumer is willing to substitute *X* or *Y* to maintain constant utility is equal to the ratio of the price of *X* to the price of *Y*.

*An Algebraic Solution to the Choice Problem

Now instead of formulating our consumer's choice problem in geometric terms, we may use algebra instead. Why, though, should we simply repeat the same result using a different technique? Do we gain anything from doing so? The answer to this perfectly reasonable enquiry is fourfold.

First, as we shall see, the use of algebra enables us to bring out one or two points of economic interpretation more sharply than does the geometric technique.

Second, as will become more apparent as this book progresses, it is easy to be misled into believing that a result that depends entirely on the particular way in which a diagram is drawn is more general in nature. It is much more difficult (but not impossible) unintentionally to bury specific implicit assumptions when algebra is used, and so its application here provides a useful check on the robustness of what has gone before.

Third the use of geometry severely limits the number of goods with which we can deal — usually to two — but algebra enables us to extend the range of the analysis to three, four ... and indeed *n* goods, where *n* is any finite positive number. In what follows here, we shall apply algebra only to a two-good case. That will help the reader unfamiliar with elementary calculus to see clearly the relationship between what is done here and what was done in the preceding geometric analysis. However those who feel at home with these techniques will be able to satisfy themselves easily enough that the results that follow may be easily extended to cases of many goods, and that the essential properties of the results we shall establish remain unchanged when this is done.

Finally, the techniques used here appear now for the first, but by no means the last, time in this book. Their application here is straightforward, and adds only a little to what we have derived with geometry. Later in this book, we shall meet problems whose geometric treatment would be so difficult (or even impossible) that they are much better tackled with algebra. The reader will find working through this section a useful preparation for coming to grips with these later applications.

If we continue to use the notation introduced above, so that M is the consumer's money income, X and Y are goods, and money prices p_X and p_Y, we note that any pattern of expenditure which satisfies the inequality

$$M \geq p_X X + p_Y Y \tag{2.3}$$

is feasible. Our consumer's utility function may be written as

$$U = u(X, Y) \tag{2.4}$$

Though we shall show below that the assumption is not necessary, the reader will find it helpful at this stage to think of this function as relating a cardinally measurable level of utility to the consumption of X and Y, so that its partial derivatives $\partial U / \partial X$ and $\partial U / \partial Y$ often referred to as the *marginal utilities* of X and Y respectively, have well defined quantitative interpretations. Now note that in terms of our diagrammatic representation, each indifference curve represents combinations of X and Y for which utility levels are constant. If we take the total differential of (2.4)

$$dU = \frac{\partial U}{\partial X} \, dX + \frac{\partial U}{\partial Y} \, dY \tag{2.5}$$

then utility is constant when $dU = 0$, namely,

$$\frac{\partial U}{\partial X}dX + \frac{\partial U}{\partial Y}dY = 0 \tag{2.6}$$

The slope of the indifference curve is given by the way in which Y changes when X changes, keeping utility constant, or dY/dX. Rearranging (2.6) yields

$$-\frac{dY}{dX} = \frac{\partial U/\partial X}{\partial U/\partial Y} \tag{2.7}$$

Since we denote the change in utility for an infinitesimal change in X or Y the *marginal utility* of X or Y, equation (2.7) yields the important insight that the slope of the indifference curve, or the *marginal rate of substitution of Y for X, is equal to the ratio of the marginal utilities of the goods.*

The choice problem for the consumer then, is to maximise (2.4) subject to (2.3). If we limit the analysis to situations in which the consumer is *on* the budget constraint, so that (2.3) becomes

$$M - p_X X - p_Y Y = 0 \tag{2.8}$$

we may solve this problem using the method of Lagrange multipliers by forming the function

$$V = u(X,Y) + \lambda(M - p_X X - p_Y Y) \tag{2.9}$$

where λ is the Lagrange multiplier. The first-order conditions for (2.9) to be maximised are

$$\frac{\partial V}{\partial X} = \partial U/\partial X - \lambda p_X = 0 \tag{2.10}$$

$$\frac{\partial V}{\partial Y} = \partial U/\partial Y - \lambda p_Y = 0 \tag{2.11}$$

$$\frac{\partial V}{\partial \lambda} = M - p_X X - p_Y Y = 0 \tag{2.12}$$

Strictly speaking, these conditions might characterise either a maximum or a minimum of (2.4), but the assumptions we have made about tastes, namely that more goods are preferred to fewer, and that a diminishing marginal rate of substitution rules between the two goods, guarantee that second order conditions for a maximum are satisfied in this case. Equation (2.12) tells us that the consumer must choose a bundle of goods on the budget constraint to maximise utility, and certain other properties of this maximum may be revealed by dividing equation (2.10) by (2.11). This yields

$$\frac{\partial U/\partial X}{\partial U/\partial Y} = \frac{p_X}{p_Y} \tag{2.13}$$

See Timbrail cf netes

Clearly the right-hand side of this expression is the ratio of the prices of the two goods. The left-hand side is the ratio of the marginal utility of X to that of Y, and as we saw is an algebraic expression for the marginal rate of substitution between the goods. Hence (2.13) is an algebraic version of the tangency solution of the consumer's choice problem depicted in Figure 2.4. It tells us that utility is maximised when the consumer equates the marginal rate of substitution between the goods to their price ratio.

Now whenever we do constrained maximisation we get a Lagrange multiplier, and that multiplier often has an economic interpretation. To consider the interpretation of λ in this case enables us to sharpen up considerably our understanding of why it sufficed to postulate ordinal utility when carrying out our geometric analysis. (2.10) and (2.11) taken together yield

$$\lambda = \frac{\partial U/\partial X}{p_X} = \frac{\partial U/\partial Y}{p_Y} \tag{2.14}$$

Thus the Lagrange multiplier here tells us how utility changes as money expenditure on either X or Y is increased. It measures, therefore, the *marginal utility of money income*. The fact that λ vanishes from equation (2.13) tells us, however, that the quantitative value of the marginal utility of income is irrelevant to the solution to the consumer's choice problem. Here, then, we have an algebraic confirmation of the assertion we made earlier that we do not need to be able to measure utility cardinally in order to analyse the type of choice under consideration in this chapter. The quantitative value of utility is irrelevant to its outcome.

The Income Consumption Curve

Finding an equilibrium consumption bundle is the starting point of the theory of consumer choice; it is not its end point. We wish to use this analysis to derive predictions about behaviour. We wish to be able to say how the composition of the bundle of goods an individual chooses will change when the observable variables that underlie the budget constraint change in value. There are three such variables: the consumer's income, the price of X and the price of Y.

A different level of income, with the prices of X and Y remaining the same, does not imply a different slope for the budget constraint. This slope tells us the rate at which X may be substituted for Y and, as we have seen, depends only upon the ratio of the two prices. However, a different level of income does involve a different location for the budget constraint. The higher the income, the further up and to the right does the budget constraint lie, for the more bundles of goods can the consumer afford.

There is very little that can be said in general about the consequences for consumption of different levels of income. At higher levels of income the chosen consumption pattern may include more of both X and Y, more X and less Y, or more Y and less X. Any one of these solutions is compatible with an indifference map of the general form we have been assuming, as is apparent from Figure 2.5. All we can do is give labels to the possibilities. Thus, if the quantity of a good consumed falls as income increases, we call that good an *inferior* good. If it rises, we call it a *normal* (or sometimes a *superior*) good. There is no reason why a good must always be in one category or another. We can easily conceive of a good being normal at low levels of income and becoming inferior at higher levels. In Figure 2.6 we consider a variety of income levels in combination with a particular indifference map, and, linking up the points of tangency along what is called an *income consumption curve*, depict just such a case for the commodity X.

Now the analysis carried out so far has been of the behaviour of a consumer at a particular time and Figure 2.6 shows what consumption patterns would be selected at different levels of income *at that time*. This is *not* necessarily the same thing as indicating how, while relative prices remain constant, the consumption pattern will change *over time* as income changes *over time*. However, it is precisely the ability to make predictions about such changes that we seek from economic theory. If we are willing to assume that tastes remain stable over time, in other words that the indifference map does not change, and that there are no factors involved *in the movement* from one preferred consumption pattern to another that influence the consumption pattern being aimed at — and we will meet

Figure 2.5

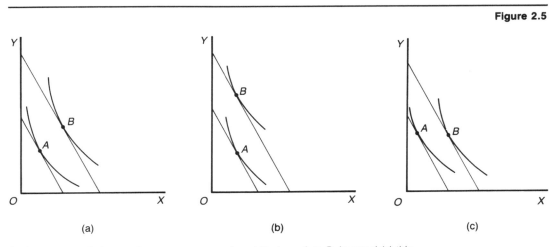

As the consumer's income increases consumption shifts from *A* to *B*. In panel (a) this movement involves an increase in the consumption of both goods: they are both normal. In panel (b) consumption of *X* falls: it is an inferior good, but *Y* is normal. In panel (c), *X* is normal and *Y* is inferior.

Figure 2.6

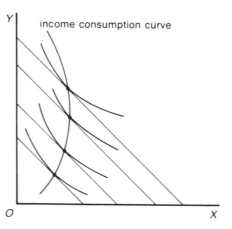

An income consumption curve. As it is drawn, Y is everywhere normal. X is normal at low levels of income, but becomes inferior at higher levels.

cases below where this particular assumption is inappropriate — we may treat the income consumption curve as telling us how the consumer's consumption pattern will respond to changes in income over time.

Price Consumption Curves

In addition to the income consumption curve, we may derive *price consumption curves*, one for variations in the price of X and the other for variations in the price of Y. Since the analysis is the same for each, we need only explicitly consider varying the price of X while holding the price of Y and money income constant. Clearly, when the price of X varies the point at which the budget constraint cuts the Y-axis is unchanged, since this represents the amount of Y that can be bought when all income is devoted to its purchase. What does change is the intercept on the X-axis and the slope of the constraint. As the price of X increases, less X can be bought for the same money and so the point at which the budget constraint cuts the X-axis moves nearer the origin and the slope becomes steeper. In other words, the slope of the budget constraint is given by the ratio of prices of X to that of Y. Raising the price of X increases this ratio and hence the slope of the constraint.

For every price of X there is a preferred consumption bundle and the points representing these may be linked up to a price consumption curve. Figure 2.7 shows three possible situations, all compatible with our assumptions. There is again little to be said about the shape of the curve, but note that the possibility depicted in panel (c), where over a certain range the quantity of X consumed actually falls as the price of X falls,

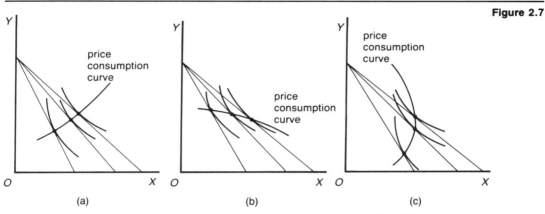

Figure 2.7

As the price of X falls the consumer moves along a price consumption curve. X and Y are complements in panel (a) and substitutes in panel (b), while X is a 'Giffen' good in panel (c).

is more an analytic curiosity than a practically relevant case. It is known as the *Giffen case* after the economist who first noticed the possibility of such behaviour. In panel (b) we have the quantity of Y consumed falling as the price of X declines, while in panel (a) we have a case in which the quantity of both X and Y consumed rises as the price of X declines. In the first of these cases X and Y are termed *substitutes* and in the second *complements*, for obvious reasons.[1]

The Engel Curve

Now from the foregoing analysis we may derive the *Engel curve* and the *demand curve* for X. The Engel curve shows the relationship between a consumer's income and the quantity of a good bought. Figure 2.8 gives an example of the derivation of such a curve, and should be self explanatory. The slope of the Engel curve at any point is known as the *marginal propensity to consume* X and measures, for a small change (in the limiting case an infinitesimal change) in income, the ratio of the resulting change in the consumption of the good to that change in income. We may also define the *average propensity to consume* the good as the ratio of the quantity of it bought at any particular level of income to that level

---

[1] As the student who reads on will discover, the possibility of complementarity can only arise in a two-good world such as we have here, because of an income effect. If we abstract from the income effect, then with normally shaped indifference curves, in a two-good world, the goods in question can only be substitutes. Possibilities for complementarity that do not hinge on an income effect do re-emerge however when there are more than two goods. The meaning of income and substitution effects is discussed below.

Figure 2.8

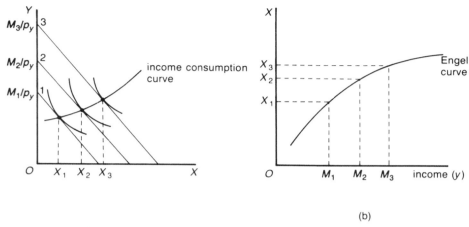

(b)

Increases in income (from M_1/p_y to M_2/p_y to M_3/p_y) shift out the budget constraint in panel (a) (from 1 to 2 to 3). From the income consumption curve we read off the associated levels of consumption of X (X_1, X_2, and X_3). We plot these against income in panel (b) to generate the Engel curve.

of income, or equivalently, given the good's price, as the proportion of income devoted to buying it. The ratio of the marginal propensity to consume the good to the average propensity to consume it is defined as the *income elasticity of demand* for the good, and measures the proportional change in the consumption of the good as a ratio to the *proportional* change in income that causes the variation.

Some extremely simple algebra makes this obvious enough. Let us continue to use the symbol M for income and the symbol ∂ to mean a 'small change in'.[2] It should be clear that the marginal propensity to consume can be written algebraically as $\partial X/\partial M$. Equally clearly, the average propensity to consume X is X/M. The ratio of the marginal propensity to consume X to the average propensity may then be rearranged as follows to give the ratio of a proportional change in the quantity of X demanded to a proportional change in income, the income elasticity of demand for X:

$$e_M = \frac{\partial X/\partial M}{X/M} = \frac{\partial X}{X} \left| \frac{\partial M}{M} \right. \tag{2.15}$$

---

[2] So long as we are dealing with the demand for X, holding the price of all other goods constant, the level of money income and the maximum amount of all other goods that can be bought with money income — the point at which the budget constraint cuts the Y vertical axis — move in perfect harmony with each other. The two differ only in units of measurement. Indeed, it is possible to define arbitrarily the units in terms of which quantities of all other goods are measured so that one unit of money income buys one unit of all other goods. The reader will find that a good deal of the literature on demand theory uses the symbol Y to stand interchangeably for both money income and quantities of other goods. We have used M and Y here to distinguish clearly between the two concepts. Note that in Chapters 5 and 6 below, we shall use Y to stand for income.

Obviously an inferior good, for which the marginal propensity to consume is negative, also has a negative income elasticity of demand, while one for which the marginal propensity to consume is positive, but lower than the average propensity to consume, has an income elasticity of demand between 0 and 1. The proportion of income spent on such a good falls as income increases. Exactly the opposite holds true for a good whose income elasticity of demand is greater than unity.

The Demand Curve

The demand curve, which relates the quantity of X demanded to the price of X, is just as easily derived; this is done in Figure 2.9 for the usual case of a non-Giffen good so that the curve is negatively sloped. Here too there is an elasticity concept to be explained. The inverse slope of the curve, $\partial X/\partial p_X$ divided by the ratio of quantity demanded to price, X/p_X gives us the *own price elasticity of demand* for the good e_p. This measures the ratio of a proportional change in the quantity demanded of the good to the proportional change in price that brought it about. In symbols we have

$$e_p = \frac{\partial X/\partial p_X}{X/p_X} = \frac{\partial X}{X} \left| \frac{\partial p_X}{p_X} \right. \tag{2.16}$$

The own price elasticity of demand is negative, because the demand curve is downward sloping, i.e. $\partial X/\partial p_X$ is negative. However, we often neglect the sign of this parameter in discussing it and talk in terms of its absolute value. There is a relationship between the magnitude of the price elasticity and the volume of expenditure on a good. If the absolute value of the

Figure 2.9

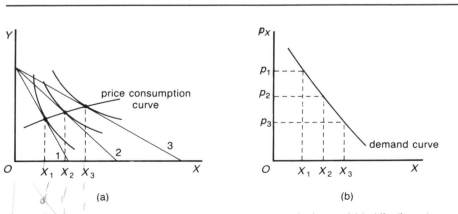

As the price of X falls (from p_1 to p_2 to p_3) the budget constraint in panel (a) shifts (from 1 to 2 to 3). From the price consumption curve we read off the associated quantities of X demanded (X_1, X_2 and X_3) and plot these against the price of X in panel (b), thus generating a demand curve. Here we hold money income and the price of Y constant.

own price elasticity of demand for a good is equal to one, then expenditure on the good does not change as its price changes. The effect on expenditure of a lower price is just offset by the higher quantity bought. If the absolute value is greater than one, then the increase in quantity bought more than offsets the influence of the fall in price and expenditure increases, while the opposite holds true when elasticity is less than one.

Finally, it should be noted that there is a third elasticity concept in demand theory: the *cross elasticity of demand*. This measures the responsiveness of the quantity of X demanded to changes in the price of Y (or vice versa). Thus, the cross elasticity of demand for X with respect to p_Y, the price of Y, is given by,

$$e_c = \frac{\partial X / \partial p_Y}{X / p_Y} = \frac{\partial X}{X} \,\bigg|\, \frac{\partial p_Y}{p_Y} \tag{2.17}$$

The sign of this elasticity will be positive if the goods are substitutes and negative if they are complements, as the reader may readily verify by considering the direction of consumption changes in response to price changes in the two different cases.

The own and cross price elasticity of demand can be related to one another through the budget constraint via another simple piece of algrebra. If we take the differential of the budget constraint (2.1)

$$dM = X dp_X + p_X dX + Y dp_Y + p_Y dY \tag{2.18}$$

and assume that neither money income nor the price of Y change ($dM = dp_Y = 0$), we get

$$X dp_X + p_X dX + p_Y dY = 0 \tag{2.19}$$

Multiplying through by $p_X / M dp_X$ and noting that $1 = X/X = Y/Y$ yields

$$\frac{p_X X}{M} + \left(\frac{dX}{X} \frac{p_X}{dp_X} \right) \left(\frac{p_X X}{M} \right) + \left(\frac{dY}{Y} \frac{p_X}{\partial p_X} \right) \frac{p_Y Y}{M} = 0$$

If we denote the share of X in total expenditure, $p_X X/M$ by α_1 and the share of Y in total expenditure $p_Y Y/M$ by α_2 we may simplify (2.19) to read

$$\alpha_1 (1 + e_p) + \alpha_2 e_c = 0 \tag{2.20}$$

Hence if we know the shares of X and Y in total expenditure, we can use the value of the own price elasticity of demand to estimate the cross price elasticity demand and vice versa.

Concluding Comment

This chapter has largely been devoted to setting out a framework of analysis and defining concepts. These concepts will turn up time and time

again throughout this book and the reader will see that mastering them has not been an end in itself but simply a necessary precondition for applying microeconomic analysis to what it is hoped are interesting and relevant problems. We will not use every idea developed in this chapter in each of the chapters that follows, but all of them will be used again somewhere.

Before moving on the next chapter, the reader should have mastered the following concepts: objects of choice, budget constraint; and utility function; and should understand how to use them in the derivation of income and price consumption curves. The reader should also review the derivation of the Engel curve, and particularly the demand curve, because it is to the further analysis of the latter that the next chapter is devoted.

3

Further Analysis and Applications of the Theory of Consumer Choice

Introduction

In this chapter we continue our exposition of the theory of consumer choice. We shall consider first of all those factors which can cause the demand curve for a particular good, derived in the last chapter, to shift. We shall then go on to look more closely at the relationships among the effects of price and income changes on the consumer's choice of a consumption bundle, in the process elucidating the concepts of the *income* and *substitution effects* of a price change. We shall then show how these concepts in turn help us to achieve a deeper understanding of such ideas as *real income*, the *standard of living*, the *cost of living* and so on, and enable us to construct and interpret various measures of these often elusive concepts.

The Effect of a Change in Income

The demand curve derived towards the end of the previous chapter shows the relationship between the quantity of X demanded and the price of X, given the price of Y and given the consumer's money income. It follows immediately that any change in either of the latter two variables will cause the whole curve to shift. In Figure 3.1, A represents a particular equilibrium at a particular level of income and set of prices. Associated with A is a particular point on the demand curve for X.

Figure 3.1

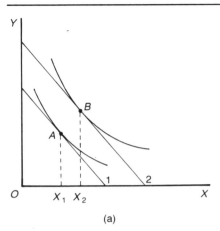

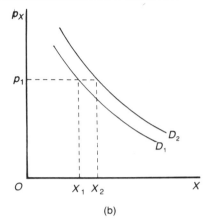

(a)   (b)

For a given price of Y and a given price of X (p_1), an increase in income shifts the budget constraint out from 1 to 2 in panel (a). The consumer's equilibrium shifts from A to B and if X is a normal good, the quantity of it demanded at p_1 increases (from X_1 to X_2). This experiment could be repeated for any price of X and hence panel (b) shows the whole demand curve shifting to the right from D_1 to D_2.

Suppose income increased by a certain proportion. The consumer's equilibrium would shift to B. The indifference map is drawn so that X and Y are normal goods and so, at the higher income level, the consumer buys more X. Thus, with no change in the price of X the quantity demanded has increased. We can carry out this analysis for any point on the demand curve for X, and thereby show that, for a normal good, an increase in income shifts the demand curve to the right. Readers should satisfy themselves that an increase in income shifts the demand curve for an inferior good to the left.

The Effect of a Change in the Price of the Other Good

Now let us analyse the effect of a change in the price of Y. In Figure 3.2 the indifference map is drawn in such a way that X and Y are substitutes. Thus, if we again start at A, we see that a fall in the price of Y shifts the consumer to a new equilibrium at which, with the same level of money income and the same price of X, less X is purchased. Once more this analysis could be carried out for each point on the demand curve for X and we can say that a fall in the price of Y, where Y is a substitute for X, causes the demand curve for X to shift to the left. Clearly, were X and Y complements, the shift would instead be to the right. Readers should derive this result for themselves.

Figure 3.2

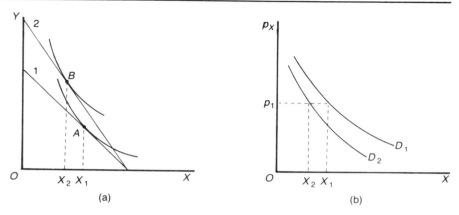

(a)   (b)

For a given level of money income and price of $X(p_1)$, a fall in the price of Y shifts the budget constraint from 1 to 2 in panel (a). The consumer's equilibrium shifts from A to B and if X and Y are substitutes, the quantity of X demanded falls from X_1 to X_2. This experiment could be repeated for any price of X; hence in panel (b) the whole demand curve for X shifts to the left from D_1 to D_2.

The Income Effect and Substitution Effect

The analysis of the immediately preceding section of this chapter, and that developed towards the end of Chapter 2 has all involved movements along price consumption and income consumption curves. It will be obvious to the reader that the shape of the price consumption curve for a given level of income and price of Y depends upon the precise form of the indifference map; and it will be equally obvious that the same may be said of the shape of the income consumption curve at a given set of relative prices. These apparently innocuous statements lead us directly to the next step of our analysis. They point to the *interdependence of the effects of income changes and price changes upon consumption*. Consider Figure 3.3 with the consumer initially in equilibrium at A on a budget constraint given by a line joining X_0 and Y_0. Now let the price of X fall so that the budget constraint pivots on the Y-axis and becomes Y_0X_1; the consumption pattern moves to B.

This is, of course, a movement along a price consumption curve, and it could be readily translated into a movement along a demand curve. However, B is also a point on an income consumption curve and there is another point on the same income consumption curve at C where a budget constraint, Y_2X_2, having the same slope as Y_0X_1, is tangent to the indifference curve I. This is the indifference curve on which A also lies. The movement along the price consumption curve from A to B, and hence along a demand curve for X, may therefore be looked upon as being made up of a movement around a particular indifference curve from A to C and one along an income consumption curve from C to B. The

Figure 3.3

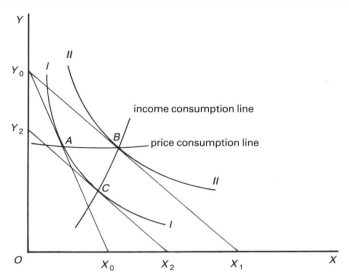

A movement along a price-consumption curve from *A* to *B* may be broken down into a substitution effect around an indifference curve (from *A* to *C*) and income effect along an income consumption curve (from *C* to *B*).

first component of this change is termed the *substitution effect* and the second the *income effect*.

It should be obvious that the substitution effect of a fall in the price of X always involves a movement round an indifference curve to a point below and to the right of A. A *negative* price change leads to a *positive* change in quantity demanded as far as the substitution effect is concerned and this effect is thus said to be *negative* in sign. This must always be the case so long as indifference curves are convex to the origin. The further to the right we move on any given curve, the more shallowly sloped it is. When the price of X falls, we find the point to which the substitution effect takes us by moving to a point at which the indifference curve on which the initial equilibrium bundle is located slopes more shallowly. This must be below and to the right of this initial bundle.

The sign of the income effect depends upon whether or not X is a normal good. If it is, then the *positive* change in income implicit in the fall in the price of X will lead to a *positive* change in the quantity of X demanded. Thus the income effect will be *positive*. This will accentuate the tendency, already implicit in the substitution effect, for the quantity of X demanded to increase as its price falls. If, on the other hand, X is an inferior good, the income effect will be *negative* and will tend to offset the substitution effect since it will work in the opposite direction. Though it is extremely unlikely, it is logically possible that a negative income effect could more than offset a negative substitution effect and lead to a fall

in the quantity of X demanded as its price falls. This would give us a backward-bending price consumption curve. This case was discussed in the previous chapter as that of a Giffen good, and was depicted in Figure 2.7(c). We can now see that a Giffen good *must* be an inferior good, but there is of course no necessity that an inferior good be a Giffen good.

Now if the analysis of income and substitution effects did no more than clarify the nature of a Giffen good, it would be of little interest. However, this analysis turns out to be fundamental to such important practical matters as the distinction between money income and real income, and to the measurement of what is frequently termed the 'cost of living'. The rest of this chapter is devoted to elaborating this claim.

Money Income and Real Income

Consider the following exercise. Suppose that there was a drop in the price of Y by a certain percentage, accompanied by a fall of the same percentage in the price of X. The combined effect of these two changes would be exactly the same as that of an increase of equal proportion in income with the two prices constant. This is yet another example of the interconnectedness of price and income effects in demand theory, and it should prompt us to look more closely at the nature of the demand curve with which we have so far been dealing, particularly with regard to the income concept that underlies it.

The demand curve in question is derived holding *money income* and the price of Y constant. As we move along the curve to lower and lower prices of X, we are also, in terms of an indifference curve diagram, moving to higher and higher levels of utility, to higher and higher levels of what we might call *real income*. Apparently, in order to make an individual better off, all that we need to do is lower the price of one good. Does it follow, therefore, that we could increase the living standards of the whole community by cutting the price of one good? If we simply subsidised X, could we make everyone better off? It would be appealing indeed were it possible, but there is a certain lack of plausibility about the proposal, at least in an economy operating in the region of full employment of a more or less given stock of factors of production with given technology. Yet careless use of our demand curve would suggest that the trick could be carried off.

The problem here involves the things which have been held constant in deriving the demand curve. For one individual it is possible to hold the price of Y and money income constant, lower the price of X and observe a movement along the demand curve for X. However, if the price of X was lowered to the whole community this movement along the demand curve would only represent the first stage in the story, not the end of it. The industry producing X would have to expand, and given

full employment it could only do so by attracting resources from the production of Y. Thus, the expansion in the demand for X would have to be accompanied by a contraction in the supply of Y, a consequent increase in Y's price and a *shift* of the demand curve for X.

All this amounts to saying that, in a fully employed economy, for consumers viewed as a group, it is real income that is fixed, not money income, and the price of all goods save one; it is impossible to analyse the effects of changing the price of one good by a tax or subsidy using a demand curve whose underlying assumptions imply that real income can vary. The 'other things equal' assumptions we made are inconsistent with the problem being analysed. However, it is up to us to decide what things we hold constant in our analysis. There is nothing sacred about holding the price of Y and money income constant and varying the price of X. We can instead, even when dealing with an individual, hold real income constant, or at least we can once we have given precise meaning to the phrase 'constant real income'.

Constant Real Income and the Compensating Variation in Money Income

We have already used a real income concept in our analysis of the income and substitution effect earlier in this chapter. We there referred to the substitution effect as a movement along a given indifference curve and the income effect as a movement to a higher curve. It is reasonable to think of *constant real income* as meaning, for an individual, the ability to gain a particular constant level of satisfaction from consumption. A demand curve holding *real* income and the price of Y constant may then be derived. → Hicksian DC.

Starting from A in Figure 3.4(a), let us lower the price of X, and at the same time vary money income by just enough to keep a budget constraint having the slope implied by the new price ratio in tangency with the original indifference curve (i.e. constraint 3). The required cut in money income just compensates the consumer for the income effect of the fall in the price of X and so the relevant cut in money income is called a *compensating variation*. The resulting demand curve is plotted in Figure 3.4(b) and clearly, has *only* a substitution effect underlying it and hence *must* be negatively sloped. Equally obviously an increase in the consumption of X must be combined with a fall in the consumption of Y. When real income is held constant, X must be a substitute for all other goods taken together (although this does not rule out the possibility of X being complementary to some subset of goods in the overall bundle labelled Y). Now the movement from A to C in Figure 3.4(a) was accomplished by a compensated fall in the price of X. It could equally have been the result of an equiproportional compensated rise in the price of Y, as is shown

Figure 3.4

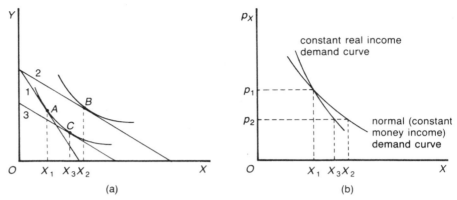

(a)   (b)

In panel (a), holding the price of Y and money income constant, a fall in the price of X from p_1 to p_2 shifts the budget constraint from 1 to 2, and the quantity of X demanded increases from X_1 to X_2. In panel (b) this shift is shown as a movement along a 'constant money income' demand curve. The substitution effect of this price change involves moving from constraint 1 to constraint 3, a change in consumption pattern from A to C and an increase in the demand for X from X_1 to X_3. This change is shown as a shift along a constant real income demand curve in panel (b). Because X is here depicted as a normal good, the income effect of the price change is positive. The constant real income demand curve relies on the substitution effect alone and hence, if X is a normal good, is steeper than the constant money income demand curve that also contains an income effect. If X were an inferior good, the constant real income curve would be the shallower of the two.

in Figure 3.5. When real income is held constant the change in the quantity of X demanded as a result of a change in its price is exactly the same as it is to an equiproportional but opposite change in the price of Y.

This is all very well as far as it goes. We can carry out the compensating variations in income in Figures 3.4 and 3.5 and consider only substitution effects because we have already drawn an indifference map. We know how much we must shift the budget constraint in order to restore our consumer's initial level of real income because we can see the point at which a budget constraint having the slope implied by the new prices is tangent to the old indifference curve. But if we were dealing with an actual consumer we could not do this. We could not 'see' the indifference map and therefore could not know how big a change in money income was needed to maintain the same level of utility and so compensate the consumer for the effects on real income of a particular price change.

Two Measures of Real Income

Our lack of knowledge about the precise shape of the indifference curve would diminish the usefulness of the analysis under discussion were we not able to get around this particular stumbling block by using an approxi-

Figure 3.5

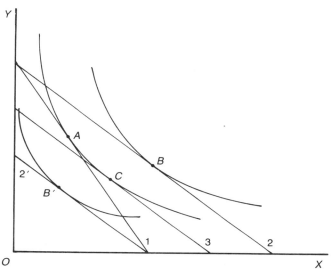

The substitution effect from *A* to *C* may be a component of the effect of one of two price changes: a fall in the price of *X* shifting the budget constraint to 2 and the equilibrium consumption bundle to *B*; or an equiproportional rise in the price of *Y* shifting the constraint to 2' and the equilibrium consumption bundle to *B'*. Recall here that the slope of the budget constraint depends only on the ratio of the prices of *X* and *Y*.

mation. Instead of defining real income as the ability to purchase goods yielding a particular level of utility, let us define it instead as the ability to buy a particular bundle of goods. Thus, instead of treating any budget constraint that is tangent to the indifference curve upon which point *A* lies as representing a given level of real income, treat any budget constraint that passes through point *A* as representing constant real income.

This is an approximation, to be sure, but it has the great merit of being a usable approximation, for, given any price for *X* and *Y*, it is clearly a routine piece of arithmetic to calculate the level of money income that will just permit the bundle of goods represented by *A* to be purchased. The ability to attain a constant level of utility notion of real income is sometimes referred to as *Hicks real income* and the ability to purchase a given bundle of goods concept as *Slutsky real income* after the two pioneers of modern theory who utilised these concepts in their analysis.

It should be stressed that the distinction between Hicks and Slutsky real income is primarily of relevance with regard to applications of the theory of consumer choice which involve discrete changes in the values of prices and quantities. If the analysis were to be undertaken algebraically, using differential calculus and limited to infinitesimal changes, the two concepts would coincide. That is to say the extra income needed to allow a consumer, faced by an infinitesimal price increase, to maintain constant utility is the same required to permit the consumer to continue to buy the quantities of goods initially purchased.

Earlier in this chapter, we analysed what we may now term the Hicks substitution and income effects. In Figure 3.6 we show their Slutsky equivalents. Clearly, the Slutsky substitution effect puts the consumer on a higher indifference curve than the one from which the experiment starts, and does therefore involve some increase in Hicks real income. It should be noted that this is so whether we deal with a price fall or a price increase, though only the former case is explicitly analysed in Figure 3.6. The Slutsky substitution effect is nevertheless unambiguously negative, even for an inferior good. This follows from the smooth convexity of the indifference curves. There can be no point to the left of *A* on budget constraint 3′ that is not on a lower indifference curve than the one passing through *A*. Similarly, there must be points to the right of *A* that are on higher indifference curves. Therefore, the consumer will move to the right of *A*, hence increasing consumption of *X* and decreasing consumption of *Y* when the price of *X* and hence the slope of the budget constraint fall.

The fact that a Slutsky substitution effect encompasses a small increase in Hicks real income means that we can say something about the slope of the demand curve derived holding Slutsky real income constant, as compared to that of the Hicks constant real income demand curve. Consider Figure 3.7. If we begin at a particular price p_1 and quantity X_1, then, whether we lower or raise the price of *X*, holding Slutsky real income constant will put the consumer on a higher indifference curve than the one from which the experiment starts. Thus, where the Slutsky constant real income demand curve that passes through $p_1 X_1$ lies, relative to the Hicks constant real income curve that passes through the same

Figure 3.6

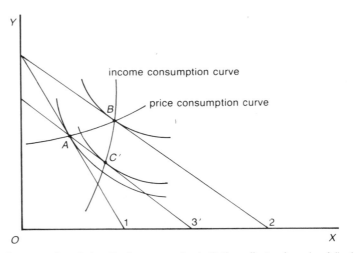

An alternative way of analysing the income and substitution effects of a price fall when 'constant real income' is defined to mean the ability to purchase a given bundle of goods rather than to achieve a given level of satisfaction. Constraint 3′ passes through *A*. The substitution effect is from *A* to *C*′ and the income effect from *C*′ to *B*.

Figure 3.7

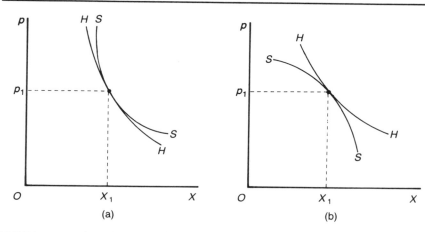

(a) If *X* is a normal good, then the Slutsky constant real income demand curve *SS* passing through p_1X_1 is tangent to the Hicks constant real income curve passing through the same point from above and to the right. (b) If *X* is an inferior good, the tangency in question is from below and to the left.

point, will depend upon the sign of the income effect. If *X* is a normal good, the Slutsky curve will be tangent to the Hicks curve from above and to the right, and if *X* is an inferior good, from below and to the left, as the reader should easily be able to verify.

A market demand curve derived by holding individuals' real incomes constant will more easily enable us to predict the consequences for the quantity of *X* demanded of lowering its price by subsidy — or raising its price by tax — than will one derived from the more orthodox constant money income demand curve. The prediction will still be an approximation, however, because constant real income in the sense of a group of individuals each enjoying a given level of utility is not the same thing as constant real income in the sense of an economy producing output at a given level of productive capacity. It was the existence of an overall constraint on production that gave rise to the difficulty that led us into the foregoing analysis in the first place. However, the ability of consumers to consume a given bundle of goods is obviously not unrelated to an economy's ability to produce a particular composition of output; hence our assertion that a constant real income demand curve, and perhaps particularly if it is real income in the Slutsky sense that is held constant, is likely to be a useful tool in such circumstances.

Constant Real Income and the Equivalent Variation in Money Income

The analysis so far has been based on the breakdown of the response of a consumer to a price change into an income and substitution effect,

the income effect in question being measured in terms of a compensating variation in money income. The response may be broken down in another way. Consider Figure 3.8. Again we start at point *A*, and let the price of *X* fall. However, instead of noting that the point *B* lies on an income consumption curve that must pass through the indifference curve upon which *A* lies, we may with equal justice note that *A* must lie on an income consumption curve that passes through the indifference curve upon which point *B* lies. The income consumption curve in question would do so at a point such as *C ''*. We can, therefore, break down the movement from *A* to *B* as an income effect taking us from *A* to *C ''* and a substitution effect taking us from *C ''* to *B*.

The income effect with which we are dealing here is the result of what is known as an *equivalent variation* in income. It gets this name because the shift of the budget constraint from 1 to 3*''* has an effect on real income *equivalent* to that of the price change whose effects are being analysed. It will not, in general, be quantitatively of the same order of magnitude as the income effect that we get from the compensating variation, and hence the size of the substitution effect will be different also. We will take up this point in more detail in the next chapter.

We may of course construct a Slutsky approximation to the Hicksian analysis contained in Figure 3.8; this is done in Figure 3.9. As with the Hicks analysis there is no need for the income and substitution effects involved here to be of the same size as those produced from an analysis using a compensating variation, but this ought not to worry the reader.

Figure 3.8

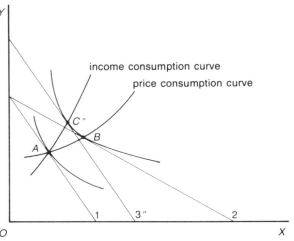

An alternative way of analysing the income and substitution effect of a fall in the price of *X*. The constraint moves from 1 to 2 and the equilibrium bundle from *A* to *B*. We shift the budget constraint at initial prices from 1 to 3*''*. This gives an 'equivalent' gain in real income, measured in terms of satisfaction, to that bestowed by the price fall. The substitution effect is then measured as *C ''* to *B*, while the income effect goes from *A* to *C ''*.

Figure 3.9

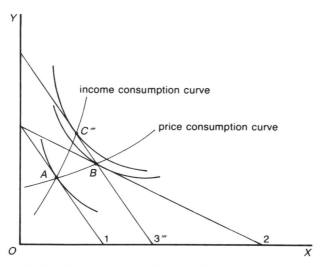

Income and substitution effects of a price fall analysed in terms of an equivalent variation when real income is defined as the ability to purchase a given bundle of goods. Constraint 3‴ goes through *B*. Thus *C*‴ to *B* is the substitution effect and *A* to *C*‴ the income effect of a price fall shifting constraint 1 to 2.

When analysing the substitution effect with a compensating variation, we are dealing with the responsiveness of the demand for *X* to changes in its own price, with real income held constant at the level given by the ability to purchase bundle of goods *A* (or to maintain that level of utility yielded by *A* in the Hicks case). When dealing with the equivalent variation, it is the responsiveness of the demand for *X* to changes in its price at a different higher level of real income that is at stake. There is no reason why the responsiveness of the demand for a good to changes in its own price should be independent of the level of real income, and all that we are observing here is the lack of such independence.

Income and Substitution Effects Without Indifference Curves — the Idea of Revealed Preference

Now the use of indifference curves to characterise the consumer's tastes is an innocuous enough practice as far as pure economic theory is concerned, but such relationships cannot, of course, be directly observed. Thus, it is of some interest that the basis of the foregoing analysis may be established without using them. Instead we may concentrate solely upon directly observable variables, namely prices, income, and the quantities of goods bought by the consumer.

The basic idea needed to carry out this analysis is that of the consis-

tency of consumer choice, discussed in the section on 'The Consumer's Tastes' in the previous chapter. It will be recalled that we argued there that, in the case of a consumer choosing among three bundles of goods, 1, 2 and 3, if 1 was preferred when 1 and 2 were compared, and 2 was preferred when 2 and 3 were compared, then 1 would be preferred when 1 and 3 were compared. This is an example of so-called *strong ordering* of bundles. *Weak ordering* permits the idea of consumer indifference to play a role, and an example of this concept at work would be a state of affairs in which the consumer definitely preferred 1 to 2, but was indifferent between 2 and 3. In this case the idea of consistent choice would enable us to say that the consumer would unambiguously prefer 1 to 3, and would always choose it when offered a choice between this pair of bundles.

Now consider Figure 3.10, where we draw a conventional budget constraint 1. Suppose the consumer faced by this constraint was observed to choose bundle A. Now let the price of X fall so that we get a new budget constraint 2, and then carry out a Slutsky compensating variation to obtain budget constraint 3', which passes through bundle A at the new relative price ruling between X and Y. Consider the segment of 3' above and to the left of A. Obviously our consumer could have chosen any point on this segment at the original set of relative prices underlying constraint 1. From any such point, it would have been possible to move out to constraint 1, consuming more of X for the same amount of Y, more Y for the same amount of X, or more of both; and hence, if both X and Y are

Figure 3.10

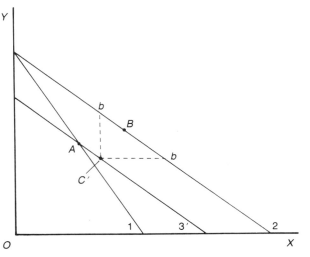

The basic analysis of revealed preference. Starting at point A in constraint 1, the substitution effect of a fall in the price of X will not cause its consumption to fall, and it may increase — say to point C'. The income effect will take consumption to some point such as B on constraint 2. As drawn here, X and Y are normal goods, but note that B might lie outside bb if one of them is inferior. Note finally that Figure 3.10 is essentially the same as Figure 3.6 with the indifference curves omitted.

desirable as we assume them to be (see Ch. 2, p. 11), to reach a preferred position. However, when faced with constraint 1 our consumer chose bundle *A*, thus *revealing a preference* for (or at least a state of indifference between) bundle *A* and any other bundle available on constraint 1. Hence, the postulate of consistency enables us to deduce that the consumer prefers bundle *A* to any bundle on constraint 3' above and to its left.

But what about points on 3' below and to the right of *A*. These were not available when the consumer faced constraint 1, but by reasoning exactly similar to that used in the preceding paragraph, for any bundle below and to the right of *A* on 1, there is a segment of constraint 3' which permits a superior consumption pattern to be attained. We cannot say *for certain* that there exist bundles on 3' below and to the right of *A* which the consumer will prefer to *A*, but it is clearly possible. Hence, we can say, *without reference to indifference curves*, that the Slutsky substitution effect (whose limiting case for an infinitesimal price change is the Hicks substitution effect) will *never* lead to *less* of the good whose relative price has fallen being consumed, and *may* lead to *more* of it being consumed. We can, that is to say, conclude that the substitution effect is *never positive*.

What, though, about the income effect? Suppose the substitution effect took our consumer to bundle *C'*. Then there is clearly an array of bundles on constraint 2 (along the segment *bb*) which will be unambiguously preferred to *C'*. However, if *X* is an inferior good, there may exist even more preferred bundles above and to the left of this segment, and if *Y* is inferior, below and to the right. If both are normal, the ultimate equilibrium will be at some bundle such as *B*, inside this segment, and that is the case we have depicted in Figure 3.10.

Now this last step may seem rather vague, and clearly if we had drawn indifference curves in Figure 3.10, everything could be made more precise. Note, however, that to the extent that we cannot actually observe a consumer's indifference curves, but rather postulate them, the extra precision in question has a spurious overtone to it. As far as the general characterisation of the basic properties of the analysis of consumer choice is concerned, *revealed preference analysis,* as deployed here, establishes all the basic results: namely that the substitution effect is never positive (and is most likely explicitly negative), that the income effect for any particular good may be either positive or negative; but that, in a multi- (including two-) good world, the income effect cannot be negative for every good.

The 'Standard of Living' and the 'Cost of Living'

The compensating variation and the equivalent variation, measured according to Hicks or Slutsky, are alternative measures of the amount by which a consumer's real income changes as a result of a price change; they are alternative ways of measuring the extent to which the purchasing power of a given money income changes when a particular price

changes; or to put the same point a third way, they measure the extent to which the 'cost of living' changes as a result of a change in the price of a particular good. The foregoing analysis, abstract as it is, is therefore of considerable practical relevance. It underlies most attempts to measure variations in that elusive concept, the price level, and is extremely useful in showing just why the concept is such a difficult one to capture. The price level, or cost of living, refers to the money outlay necessary for a consumer to maintain a given standard of living. A natural interpretation of the phrase 'standard of living' is surely a given level of utility, consumption along a particular indifference curve. Figure 3.11 shows yet again the consequences for consumption of changing the price of one good. The consumer has shifted from A to B. How has the cost of living changed? How has the money outlay necessary to maintain a given standard of living been affected by this price change?

There is no unique answer to this question. It all depends upon which standard of living is the given one, which indifference curve we wish to keep the individual on. Suppose it is the curve upon which A lies. Then the cost of living to our consumer has fallen by the amount by which it is possible to reduce income after the fall in the price of X and still keep the consumer on that original indifference curve. The cost of living has fallen by the amount of the Hicks compensating variation which shifts constraint 2 to 3.

Suppose instead, and there is no reason to prefer one to the other, that we decided to take the level of utility at B as the one whose cost of acquisition we were trying to measure. Then the individual's cost of living

Figure 3.11

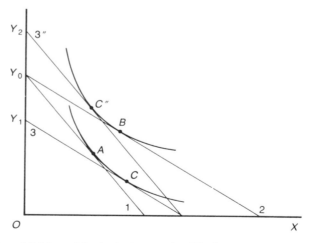

When the price of X falls and the budget constraint shifts from 1 to 2, the consumer's 'cost of living' falls. We may measure this fall in units of money by seeing how much money income must be altered to carry out the compensating variation or the equivalent variation. The first is the amount of income needed to buy $Y_0 - Y_1$ units of Y, the second the amount needed to buy $Y_2 - Y_0$ units.

has fallen by the amount by which it would have been necessary to increase money income in order to permit a point on the same indifference curve as *B* to be attained at the original set of prices, to shift constraint 1 to 3", that is to say by the Hicksian equivalent variation.

There is, as we have seen, no reason why these two measures should be the same. There is, after all, no reason why the effects of a given price change on the cost of maintaining two different standards of living should be the same. In short, the very concept of the cost of living is ambiguous. We must specify the standard of living required before we can measure changes in the cost of maintaining it. Moreover, the extent of such changes for a given change in prices depends upon the shape of the indifference map and hence is specific to a particular individual. There is no such thing as a general cost of living. How a particular set of price changes affects the living standards of particular individuals with given money incomes depends very much upon their tastes, and tastes differ among individuals.

Measuring Changes in the Cost of Living

The problem of measuring price level changes is even more difficult than the above argument would indicate, for indifference curves are not observable. There is no way of assessing quantitatively the variations in money income necessary to maintain a given level of utility, at different sets of prices. This is why the Slutsky method of analysing the income and substitution effects is important. Instead of asking questions about the cost of maintaining a given level of utility, it enables us to ask questions about the cost of obtaining a particular bundle of goods. It should go without saying that our measure of how a particular price change affects the price level will depend upon the bundle of goods we choose to consider.

Suppose we chose bundle of goods *A* as appropriate; then, as is apparent from Figure 3.12, we would have to measure the Slutsky compensating variation if we wished to assess the effect on the cost of living of a fall in the price of *X*. The amount to which we could reduce money income after the fall in the price of *X* would be calculated by multiplying original money income by the ratio of the cost of obtaining bundle *A* at the new set of prices to that of obtaining it at the old set. This ratio is of course a price index, in fact the well-known Laspèyres or *base period* weighted index. Alternatively, we could use bundle *B* as the one whose cost of acquisition we were concerned with. The level of income resulting from carrying out the Slutsky equivalent variation would be given by the original level of money income multiplied by the ratio of the money income necessary to obtain bundle *B* at the old prices, to that necessary at the new prices. This ratio is the *inverse* of another well-know price index, the Paasche or *current period* weighted index. The formulae for these two index numbers are:

Figure 3.12

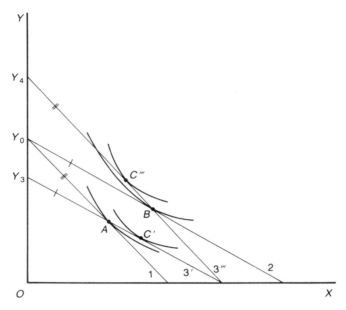

The price of X falls, shifting the constraint from 1 to 2. The change in the cost of living may be measured by the Slutsky compensating variation that shifts 2 to 3', or the equivalent variation that shifts 1 to 3'''. The amounts of income involved would respectively purchase $Y_0 - Y_3$ and $Y_4 - Y_0$ of Y.

$$\text{Laspèyres} = (p_{X1} X_0 + p_{Y1} Y_0)/(p_{X0} X_0 + p_{Y0} Y_0) \tag{3.1}$$

$$\text{Paasche} = (p_{X1} X_1 + p_{Y1} Y_1)/(p_{X0} X_1 + p_{Y0} Y_1) \tag{3.2}$$

where the subscript 0 refers to the base period, the time before the price change, and subscript 1 to the current period, the time after the price change.

These formulae will already be familiar to most readers, as will the fact that the two indices usually give different answers to questions about the cost of living. In fact, they answer questions about what has happened to the cost of acquiring particular and different bundles of goods, not a particular unambiguously defined level of utility. To all the difficulties in the cost of living concept we noted in the context of Hicks' analysis of income effects, we have added an extra problem here by substituting a given bundle of goods for a given level of utility. Whether any index of the price of a particular bundle of goods is relevant to measuring the cost of living for an individual depends very much upon the relationship between that bundle of goods and the consumption pattern of the individual. The implications of this for using allegedly general cost of living indices to measure changes in the purchasing power of the incomes of particular groups with such diverse consumption patterns as, for ex-

ample, the rich, the old, students, poor families with young children, etc., should be obvious.

Both the price indices would give qualitatively the same result in terms of Figure 3.12, both would show that the cost of living had fallen, but this need not always happen. In Figure 3.13 we start off again at A, but now permit the price of X to fall and that of Y to rise simultaneously with the net effect of a shift to B. Has the cost of living risen or fallen? The cost of obtaining bundle A is higher in the second period than in the first, so according to the Laspèyres index a positive compensating variation is required. The cost of living has increased. But initially it would have also required a higher level of income to obtain B than it does after the price changes. From the point of view of the Paasche index and the equivalent variation, the cost of living has fallen.

If we knew about the shape of the indifference map we would not face this particular ambiguity, for it would be possible to tell whether point A or B lay on the higher indifference curve. This kind of problem arises from the use of bundles of goods as approximations to given levels of utility and *may* be encountered whenever two situations are compared in which some prices are lower and others higher.

Figure 3.13

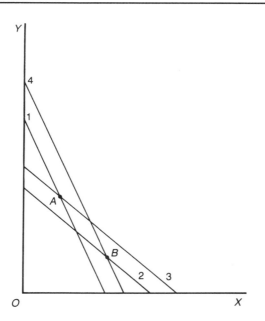

The price of X falls and that of Y rises shifting the budget constraint from 1 to 2. The consumer is observed to shift from consumption pattern A to B. In terms of the Laspèyres index the cost of living has risen, since a compensating increase in income from constraint 2 to 3 would be needed to buy A at the new prices. According to the Paasche index the cost of living has fallen, since bundle B could only have been obtained at the original prices by increasing income from constraint 1 to 4.

Comparisons of living costs across national boundaries, for example, often give rise to such ambiguities. Suppose that, in Figure 3.13, budget constraint 1 was interpreted as reflecting prices in Britain, and constraint 2 as reflecting American prices. Our analysis tells us that we cannot say whether the cost of living is higher in one country or the other. We can, however, conclude that the cost of a British consumption pattern is lower in Britain than in America, and that the cost of an American pattern is lower in America. It is not surprising that such a state of affairs is possible, but willingness to accept this proposition involves acceptance of the fact that international comparisons of such inherently vague notions as the cost of living and the standard of living are capable of yielding ambiguous and sometimes contradictory results that must be handled with the greatest care.

Concluding Comment

The underlying theme of this chapter has been the way in which the nature of a consumer's indifference map renders interdependent the effects of income, the prices of other goods, and its own price on the quantity demanded of a good. Consideration of this interdependence led us to break down movements along a price consumption curve, and therefore along a demand curve too, into income and substitution effects.

We have seen that there is more than one way to make the income−substitution effect distinction, and also how analysis of the possibilities enables us to reach a deeper and more precise understanding of such everyday concepts as 'real income', 'standard of living' and 'cost of living'.

4

Consumer's Surplus and Marshallian Consumer Theory

Introduction

The income effects with which we have dealt in the last chapter measure the change in satisfaction, or utility, that an individual experiences as a result of a change in the price of a particular good. We have seen that, when the price of a good falls, the individual moves onto a higher indifference curve, and that the increase in utility experienced as a result of this is equal to that gained from an 'equivalent' variation in money income. We have also seen that an alternative measure of the same gain is the amount by which money income may be diminished after the price fall in order to leave the consumer just as well off as initially, i.e. the 'compensating' variation in money income. The changes in utility which we are discussing here are often referred to as changes in *consumer's surplus*. The term is an old-fashioned one, but the concept involved is vital in understanding the response of consumers to discriminatory pricing, as it is in understanding what is involved in the application of *cost—benefit analysis* to decision making. In this chapter, we will first of all elucidate the concept in question, and then show how a particular version of consumer theory enables that concept to be analysed in a remarkably simple way. We shall also show how this particular version relates to the general model of consumer choice developed in Chapter 2 of this book.

The Concept of Consumer's Surplus

It is a trivial implication of indifference curve analysis that if we start with the consumer out of equilibrium and permit the substitution of X for Y

until a preferred bundle of goods is reached, this act of substitution makes the consumer better off. More is gained from increasing consumption of X than is given up in reducing consumption of Y. If we start from a situation where no X at all is consumed, as at B in Figure 4.1, where Y_0 is consumed, and move out to A, then the consumer moves from a lower indifference curve to a higher indifference curve. The increase in utility here measures the consumer's surplus obtained from consuming X; it is the maximum gain to be made from being able to trade X for Y at the price ratio underlying the budget constraint, and it is clearly tempting to look for a means of measuring this gain in terms of money.

There are several ways of getting such a measure in terms of Figure 4.1, but we will discuss only two of them. Suppose we began with our consumer facing the price of X that is implicit in the budget constraint of Figure 4.1, and suppose that bundle of goods A was being consumed. Now suppose that we prohibited the consumption of X. We could ask the following question: by how much would we have to increase the consumer's income in order to compensate for this prohibition? Clearly, we would have to raise income by enough to enable a movement from point B to point C, an increase in consumption of Y by $Y_1 - Y_0$. If we know the price of Y, the computation of the amount of income involved here is just a matter of arithmetic. The change in income involved is just enough to *compensate* the consumer for the loss of the ability to consume X. It is one

Figure 4.1

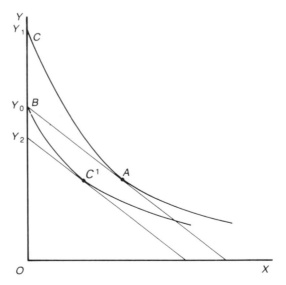

The amount of income needed to buy $Y_1 - Y_0$ of Y gives the consumer a gain in utility equivalent to the one obtained from moving from B to A, since the consumer is indifferent between A and C. The amount necessary to buy $Y_0 - Y_2$ just compensates for this ability to consume X since the consumer is indifferent between point B and C'.

measure of the gain that accrues from being able to consume X at the going price.

On the other hand, we could think in terms of offering the consumer a choice between being forbidden to consume X or accepting a reduction in income. We could then ask how large a reduction in income would leave the consumer just as badly off as the prohibition on the consumption of X. Obviously income could be reduced until consumption was reduced to C', for here the consumer would obtain just that level of utility attainable at B. The change in income here is again easily calculated; it is the amount that would permit the purchase of $Y_0 - Y_2$ of Y. It is in fact that variation in income that has an *equivalent* effect on the consumer's utility to a prohibition on consuming X at the going price.

We have here yet another application of the ideas of compensating and equivalent variation to measuring gains and losses in real income, and there is no reason why the two measures should yield the same answers to the question 'how much does the consumer gain from being able to consume X at the going price? One tells us how much it would take to compensate for a prohibition on consuming X and the other tells us how big a change in income would be equivalent in its effects to such a prohibition. These sound like the same thing at first, perhaps, but they are not, as must be evident from the preceding discussion. Moreover, the reader should note that, as always, which measure is called the 'compensating' and which the 'equivalent' variation depends upon the starting point for the experiment. In the above discussion we have started from point A. If we start instead from point B, as we do in the discussion embodied in the caption to Figure 4.1, the labels attached to these measures are reversed.

An Application of Consumer's Surplus

But why should the concept of the total gain from consuming a good be important? An example will help here. Suppose a government agency was trying to decide whether or not to provide a particular service, for example the operation of a bridge over a river. If the benefits to society of having the bridge outweighed the costs, we might all agree that it should be built. Suppose that a toll was to be charged. Would it be the case that toll revenue could be regarded as measuring the benefits consumers obtained from the bridge, so that, if such revenue did not cover the cost of operating the bridge it should not be built?

Consider Figure 4.2 and suppose that X_1 represents the bridge crossings per week made by a particular consumer at a particular toll per crossing. The actual revenue received from this consumer would be given by whatever sum of money would buy $Y_0 - Y_2$ of Y at going prices, but the *net benefit* to that same consumer of making bridge crossings could be measured by whatever sum of money would buy $Y_1 - Y_0$ of Y. That is

Figure 4.2

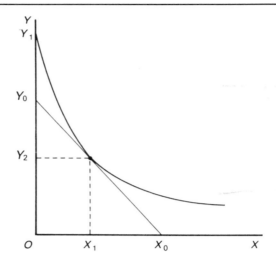

The consumer pays as much income as would purchase $Y_0 - Y_2$ units of Y in order to obtain X_1 units of X. However, consuming X_1 units of X yields the same gain in utility as would have come from consuming $Y_1 - Y_2$ units of Y. The amount of income necessary to buy this amount of Y is therefore one measure of the total benefit that the consumer gets from consuming X.

to say that the total benefit to this consumer from operating the bridge is the *sum* of toll payments *and* consumer's surplus. In terms of Figure 4.2, $Y_1 - Y_2$ is one measure of this total benefit.

This example should suffice for the moment to establish that the concept of consumer's surplus is worth attention. The analysis embodied in Figures 4.1 and 4.2 tells us how it might be measured, but, unfortunately, only in principle. We can only find such distances as $Y_1 - Y_0$ and $Y_1 - Y_2$ if we know the shape of the indifference map. Again we are in need of some quantifiable approximation if the analysis is to be of practical value. It is to the development of one such approximation that we devote the next three sections of this chapter, an approximation that has the great advantage of utilising the shape and location of the demand curve as its analytic basis. In order fully to elucidate this approximation we must return to consider the very foundations of our analysis of consumer choice, paying particular attention to the nature of the utility function.

Marshallian Consumer Theory

Recall that, in Chapter 2, we discussed the concepts of *ordinal* and *cardinal* utility. It was shown there that, as far as deriving demand curves and such was concerned, it sufficed to assume ordinal utility, to postulate that the consumer could make statements about the order of preference in which different bundles of goods were ranked. It was not necessary

to assume that the consumer could perceive the intensity of preferences, and measure the differences in the degree of satisfaction obtained from consuming different bundles.

The idea of cardinal utility is simply redundant in the context of the analysis carried out in Chapter 2. Nevertheless this concept was used in Alfred Marshall's version of demand theory which predates the analysis set out there, and Marshallian demand theory, it turns out, enables us to develop a measure of consumer's surplus that is a usable approximation to the quantities analysed here and earlier. In order to analyse the demand for a particular good X in Marshallian terms, we make three key assumptions. First, we assume that the total utility gained from consuming any quantity of X is independent of the quantity of Y consumed, and vice versa. Second, we assume that the marginal utility of Y is constant, i.e. that the utility gained from consuming Y rises in strict proportion to the quantity of Y so that equal increments of Y yield equal increments of utility. Finally, we assume that the marginal utility of X diminishes as consumption of X increases, i.e. that equal increments in X yield successively smaller increments in utility.

These assumptions are difficult to take literally, to be sure, and we will see what they imply about the nature of the indifference map in a few pages; but for the moment let us pursue their other implications. In Figure 4.3 we measure on the vertical axis utility per unit of X (in terms of some arbitrary unit of measurement such as 'utils') and on the horizontal axis the quantity of X consumed per unit of time. We then plot the relationship between the marginal utility of X per unit of X and the quantity of it consumed. The area under this curve between the vertical axis and one

[handwritten margin notes:]
Alfred Marshall
↓
CARDINAL UTILITY
↓
Demand Theory.
measure of consumer surplus

Figure 4.3

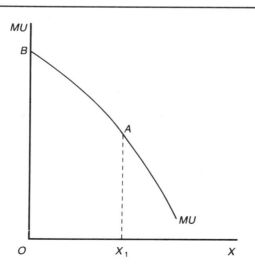

The marginal utility of X declines as the quantity of X consumed increases. The area $OBAX_1$ measures the total utility of consuming X_1 units of X.

unit of X measures the utility per unit of time gained from consuming the first unit, the area under the curve between 1 and 2 units of X measures that gained from consuming the second, and so on. Hence the total utility per unit of time gained from consuming any particular quantity of X per unit of time is found by adding up all these areas. Thus, for X_1 units, for example, this addition yields the area $OBAX_1$ as a measure of the total utility derived from consuming X_1 units of X.

Now X has a price. For each unit of X bought a certain quantity of Y must be given up because money income is given up. This means that a certain amount of utility from consuming Y must be forgone for each unit of X consumed and, since the marginal utility of Y is constant, the amount of utility sacrificed is constant per unit of X obtained. The 'price' to the consumer in terms of utility forgone per unit of X consumed is constant and may be represented by a straight line such as SS on Figure 4.4. The area under the marginal utility curve of X is the total utility gained from consuming it and, by exactly similar reasoning, the area under the line SS is the total cost in terms of utility of acquiring it. The net gain from consuming a particular quantity of X is then the difference in these two areas. For example at X_2 units of X, this net gain is given by the area BCDS.

The utility-maximising consumer obviously wishes to maximise this net gain. Equally obviously in terms of Figure 4.4, this will involve consuming X_1 units of X at which point the marginal gain from consuming it is just equal to its price in terms of utility forgone. The total net gain from consumption of X is, in this case, given by the area SBA and is the consumer's surplus accruing from the consumption of X measured in utils.

Figure 4.4

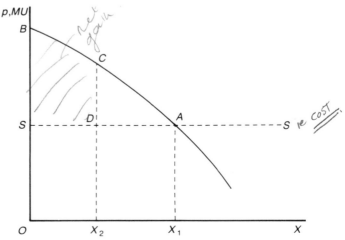

If *OS* measures the amount of utility that must be forgone per unit of X consumed, then utility is maximised by consuming X_1 units of X. The consumer's surplus from so doing is given by the area *SBA*.

It is trivially easy to translate this measure in unobservable utils into one in terms of money. With a given price for *Y*, and a given marginal utility of *Y*, we can freely translate utils into units of money. There is a strictly proportional relationship between every pound spent on *Y*, the volume of *Y* acquired, and the utility yielded by the consumption of the *Y* purchased. Thus, the 'price' in terms of utility forgone of *X* may be transformed into a price measured in pounds and pence. Similarly, the marginal utility of *X* may be measured in terms of the sum of money that would have to be devoted to the purchase of *Y* in order to yield an equivalent flow of utility.

Thus, we may substitute monetary units for utility units on the vertical axis of Figure 4.4; the price of *X* then becomes a money price, and the assumption of utility maximisation ensures that the marginal utility curve will relate the quantity of *X* demanded to its price. Hence the marginal utility curve becomes a demand curve. Consumer's surplus may be measured as the area under the demand curve for *X*, minus total expenditure on *X*: thus we have our monetary measure of consumer's surplus in terms of observable phenomena. We also have monetary measures of the change in utility that arises from changes in the price of *X*. Thus, if the price of *X* falls from p_1 to p_2 in Figure 4.5, consumption increases from X_1 to X_2 and the money value of the gain in utility is given by the area $p_1 A_1 A_2 p_2$.

Now the measure of consumer's surplus in Figure 4.4 is apparently unambiguous, and in Figure 4.5 the measure of the change in consumer's surplus, which is just another name for the effect on real income that arises from a price change, is also unambiguous. Our careful distinction

Figure 4.5

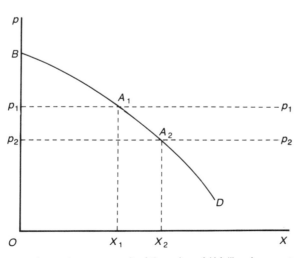

The gain in consumer's surplus as a result of the price of *X* falling from p_1 to p_2 is given by $p_1 A_1 A_2 p_2$.

between compensating and equivalent variations seems to have vanished in the process of producing these measures of consumer's surplus in terms of areas under the demand curve for X. Let us now see how this has come about.

Marshallian Analysis in Terms of Indifference Curves

The nature of the approximations into which our search for an easily quantifiable measure of consumer's surplus has led us, and the reason why the distinction between compensating and equivalent variations has vanished, are easily seen if we translate Marshallian analysis into the language of indifference curves.

In terms of such analysis, to postulate cardinal utility means that we can label each of our indifference curves by the level of utility associated with it. The assumption that the marginal utility of Y is constant means that successive increments in Y, if the quantity of X is constant, lead to equal increments in utility, while the independence of the marginal utilities of X and Y means that these equal increments in utility are the same regardless of the quantity of X being consumed. In Figure 4.6 these assumptions are translated into an indifference map. They involve the indifference curves being equally spaced along *any* line drawn perpendicular to the X-axis; this can only happen if each curve has the same slope where it cuts such a perpendicular. This obviously means that there is a zero income elasticity of demand for X. The quantity of it bought would depend only on the slope and not on the location of the budget constraint. Hence, when prices change, there is no income effect on the demand for X, only on the demand for Y.

The measure of consumer's surplus which we have dealt with in this chapter and the measures of effects on real income of price changes which we dealt with in Chapter 3 all involve measuring the vertical distance between pairs of indifference curves. Measures based on equivalent and compensating variations can differ so long as we impose no requirement that the vertical distance between given indifference curves be the same at every point. The Marshallian assumptions, however, do impose this requirement and hence, in terms of indifference curve analysis, conceptually different measures yield the same estimate of its value.

As we have seen, these same assumptions imply that various areas under the demand curve for a good may be used to measure overall levels of, and changes in, consumer's surplus. Such measurements are quite commonly used in applications of demand theory to concrete problems, but they are approximations to the much more slippery, and ambiguous, quantities analysed earlier. As the reader might expect, the closer to zero the income elasticity of demand for X, and the smaller the effect on income of whatever change is under analysis, then the better is the approximation and the more accurate will be the predictions based upon its use.

Figure 4.6

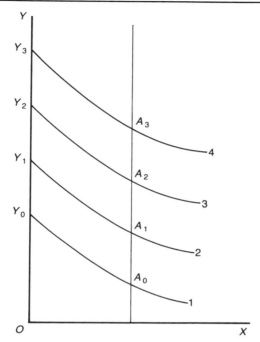

The indifference map implicit in Marshallian utility theory. Up any line perpendicular to the
X-axis (including the Y-axis itself) the indifference curves are parallel to each other. Thus
the slope of each curve is the same at Y_0, Y_1, Y_2 and Y_3, and, for example, at A_0, A_1, A_2
and A_3. At any quantity of X, successive equal increments in the amount of Y yield equal
increments in utility from 1 to 2, 2 to 3, etc. The curves become more shallow as we
move to the right; hence successive equal increments in the amount of X consumed for
any given quantity of Y yield successively smaller increases in utility.

The demand curve is one of the basic relationships of economic theory,
and as we have already noted, Marshall's derivation of it predates the
indifference curve approach upon which this book concentrates. That is
one reason why many real-world applications of the consumer's surplus
concept use the demand curve, and areas under it, as their basic ingredients. It is, however, only in the limiting zero income effect special case
that the area under the demand curve yields an accurate estimate of the
more fundamental measures of consumer surplus given by equivalent
and compensating variations. More generally, though, there is in fact a
systematic relationship among these three measures of consumer's
surplus whose nature depends, as the reader might guess, upon the
magnitude of the income effect.

A precise understanding of the nature of these relationships is worth
having for anyone interested in real-world applications of consumer's
surplus, where, as we have said, the demand curve is often used as a
starting point. However, to analyse these relationships using geometry
alone is very complex, but once geometry is supplemented by a little

algebra matters become more straightforward. Readers who go on to the starred sections of this chapter will find this matter taken up again in more detail in the second of them.

The Impossibility of Comparing Utility between Persons

The problems in measuring consumer's surplus which we have discussed so far have all been concerned with the ambiguity of this concept when analysing the individual consumer's situation. We have, however, seen that we may produce an apparently unambiguous monetary measure of an individual's satisfaction from consuming a particular good if we make the special assumptions set out in the two previous sections of this chapter. It must be noted, however, that even making these assumptions provides no basis in economic theory for adding these measures of satisfaction over individuals to produce some global measure of the gain to the community from consuming a particular good. Even if we are willing to postulate the existence of a cardinal utility function for each member of the community, there is no basis for comparing these functions between people and hence no way of adding them up. A pound's worth of satisfaction to one person and a pound's worth of satisfaction to another may or may not be the same amount of satisfaction. There is no way of knowing. Thus, though getting a measure of consumer's surplus is one of the major problems in cost–benefit analysis, it is by no means the only one. Equally important is finding a means of comparing consumer's surplus between individuals when, as is inevitably the case, the benefits (and costs) that must be measured accrue to different individuals. This section of the book has nothing to say on this score.

Thus, to return to our bridge-building example, we now know much more that we did about the extent to which the benefits to individuals from having the services of a bridge might be measured, but we have learned nothing about how to sum these individual benefits in order to get a global measure of 'the benefit to the community' of the bridge. The problem here is one involving the distribution of economic benefits between individuals, and it is raised now only to warn the reader that it has not yet been treated in this book. We shall deal with it in a more general framework in Part VIII when we take up problems involving the interaction of individuals in the economic system.

*The Algebra of Marshallian Analysis

We may apply the simple algebra of constrained maximisation developed in Chapter 2 to elucidating the nature of Marshallian consumer theory. The key here is to find a specific form of the utility function which has the required characteristics, that is independence of the marginal utilities

of X and Y, constancy of the marginal utility of Y, and a tendency of the marginal utility of X to decline with its quantity.

Such a utility function is given by

$$U = aX^\alpha + bY, \quad \alpha < 1 \tag{4.1}$$

As in Chapter 2, we may write the budget constraint as

$$M - p_X X - p_Y Y = 0 \tag{4.2}$$

Forming the Lagrangian expression gives us

$$V = aX^\alpha + bY + \lambda(M - p_X X - p_Y Y) \tag{4.3}$$

Taking the partial derivatives of (4.3) with respect to X, Y and λ, and setting these equal to zero gives us the first-order conditions characterising a maximum. These are

$$\frac{\partial V}{\partial X} = \alpha a X^{\alpha-1} - \lambda p_X = 0 \tag{4.4}$$

$$\frac{\partial V}{\partial Y} = b - \lambda p_Y = 0 \tag{4.5}$$

$$\frac{\partial V}{\partial \lambda} = M - p_X X - p_Y Y = 0 \tag{4.6}$$

Now (4.5) may be arranged to yield

$$\lambda = \frac{b}{p_Y} \tag{4.7}$$

If we hold the price of Y constant, we may define it as being equal to unity and (4.4) becomes

$$\alpha a X^{\alpha-1} - b p_X = 0 \tag{4.8}$$

We can now solve equations (4.6) and (4.8) for the unknowns Y and X as functions M and p_X, but let us concentrate here on the demand function for X, which is the one underlying the analysis carried out in this chapter.

Equation (4.6) may be rearranged as

$$X = \frac{M - Y}{p_X} \tag{4.9}$$

and (4.8) as

$$X = R p_X^{1/(\alpha-1)} \tag{4.10}$$

where

$$R = \frac{b}{\alpha a}^{1/(\alpha-1)} \tag{4.11}$$

Substituting (4.9) into (4.10) gives us the demand for Y as a function of M and p_X

$$Y = M - Rp_X^{\alpha/(\alpha-1)} \tag{4.12}$$

and substituting this back into (4.9) gives us the demand function for X

$$X = [M - M + Rp_X^{\alpha/(\alpha-1)}]/p_X = Rp_X^{1/(\alpha-1)} \tag{4.13}$$

Thus we have confirmed that Marshallian assumptions eliminate the income effect from the demand for X, but produce a function in which quantity demanded varies inversely with price.

**A More General Treatment of Equivalent Variation, Compensating Variation and Consumer's Surplus — the Idea of Duality

Now the Marshallian analysis is simple enough, but the assumptions about the nature of the utility function which we made to achieve that simplicity are very special indeed. At the price of extra analytic complexity, it is possible to analyse more generally the relationship between equivalent variation, compensating variation and consumer's surplus, linking them to total expenditures, and the compensated demand curve introduced in the previous chapter. It will be remembered that the (Hicksian) equivalent variation measures the impact of a change in price upon real income, measured from the new indifference curve. The (Hicksian) compensating variation measures the impact of a change on real income, measured from the old indifference curve. Changes in consumer's surplus, on the other hand, refer to triangles under the (uncompensated) demand curve.

To develop the relationship between these apparently distinct concepts formally, it is useful to specify an *expenditure function*, in which the consumer's outlay, E, varies with prices and the level of utility. We saw in Chapter 2 that consumer choice could be modelled in terms of maximising utility subject to a budget constraint. In terms of diagrams, the consumer is assumed to choose a bundle of commodities on the highest possible indifference curve, subject to the constraint that this equilibrium must lie within the feasible set of expenditures, delineated by the budget constraint. Outcomes therefore occur at the tangency between indifference curves and budget lines.

One can think of an exact *dual* to this problem, in which we predetermine the level of utility, say $\bar{u}$, and search for the minimum level of expenditure at given prices required to achieve this level of utility. Expenditures are of course indicated by the intercept of the budget constraint to the Y axis, so the problem becomes to find the bundle of X and Y on indifference curve V at which, for the given p_X and p_Y, expenditure

is minimised. As before, the solution lies at the tangency of the indifference curve, $\bar{u}$, and the budget constraint. It is this minimum level of expenditure, dependent on prices and the utility level, which is expressed through the *expenditure function*. The expenditure function is written as

$$E = E(p_X, p_Y, \bar{u}) \tag{4.14}$$

which must be interpreted as the minimum of

$$E = p_X X + p_Y Y \tag{4.15}$$

subject to $V(X, Y) \geq \bar{u}$. (4.16)

The solution to this problem is illustrated in Figure 4.7 which, apart from the notation employed, is of course identical to our previous representations of consumer choice.

Many of the standard results of consumer theory developed in earlier chapters can also be derived in terms of this specification. We can for example establish that the ratio of marginal utility to price must be equalised across goods $((\partial V/\partial X)/p_X = (\partial V/\partial Y/p_Y))$ — see equation 2.14; and that the ratio itself must equal the cost of obtaining utility at the margin. Moreover the ratio of prices (p_X/p_Y) must equal the marginal rate of substitution $((\partial V/\partial X)/(\partial V/\partial Y))$; this is, of course, the familiar tangency condition. Perhaps most importantly, we can derive compensated demand functions directly from the expenditure function, by differentiating with respect to price. Thus it can be established that

$$\frac{\partial E}{\partial p_Y} = Y^*(p_X, p_Y, \bar{u}) \tag{4.17}$$

Figure 4.7

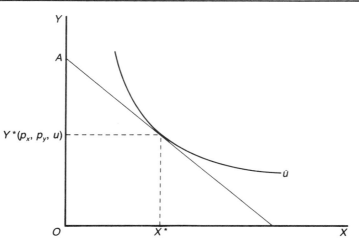

Consumer choice of X and Y around the indifference curve $\bar{u}$. Expenditure to achieve a level of utility $\bar{u}$ at prices p_x and p_y is minimised at (Y^*, X^*). Expenditure measured in terms of Y, $E(p_x, p_y, \bar{u})$, is given by OA.

where Y^* represents the quantity demanded, as in Figure 4.7. A simple example will help the reader grasp the intuition of the argument. Suppose we are buying 10 bars of chocolate per week and the price rises by 1 penny per bar. It is approximately true that one needs to spend 10 pence more in order to maintain the same level of utility. The compensated demand function for each is therefore the derivative of the expenditure function with respect to prices.

The reader will have noted that this formulation of the consumer's choice problem in terms of minimum expenditures is consistent with the one adopted earlier when dealing with the compensated and equivalent variations, each of which represents changes in expenditures around a given indifference curve. Let us look at this more closely, considering once again the adjustments analysed in the previous chapter in terms of Figure 3.11. There are two possible ways of measuring the impact of a fall in the price of X, say from p_X^1 to p_X^2. The equivalent variation indicates the change in expenditure around the new indifference curve I_2, and can be written algebraically as

$$EV = E(p_X^2, p_Y, I_2) - E(p_X^1, p_Y, I_2) \tag{4.18}$$

In Figure 3.11, the equivalent variation equals $Y_2–Y_0$. The compensating variation indicates the change in expenditure around the old indifference curve I, and can be written algebraically as

$$CV = E(p_X^2, p_Y, I_1) - E(p_X^1, p_Y, I_1) \tag{4.19}$$

In Figure 3.11, the compensating variation is $Y_0–Y_1$.

Inspection of equations (4.18) and (4.19) makes clear that as the change in price from p_X^1 to p_X^2 becomes smaller, they approach *integrals* of the expenditure function with respect to price. Hence we can rewrite them as

$$EV = \int_{p_X^1}^{p_X^2} \frac{\partial E(p_X, p_Y, I_2)}{\partial p_X} \, dp_X \tag{4.20}$$

$$CV = \int_{p_X^1}^{p_X^2} \frac{\partial E(p_X, p_Y, I_1)}{\partial p_X} \, dp_X \tag{4.21}$$

and similarly for changes in the price of Y. But we know from equation (4.17) that derivatives of the expenditure function with respect to price are the compensated demand function for that good. Hence

$$EV = \int_{p_X^1}^{p_X^2} X^*(p_X, p_Y, I_2) \, dp_X \tag{4.22}$$

and

$$CV = \int_{p_X^1}^{p_X^2} X^*(p_X, p_Y, I_1) \, dp_X \tag{4.23}$$

The compensated and equivalent variations therefore represent areas under compensated demand curves, the former going through the uncompensated demand curve at the old price and the latter going through the uncompensated demand curve at the new price.

With the aid of this conceptual apparatus we can now turn to the issue of the relationship between equivalent variation, compensating variation and consumer's surplus. Consider the demand curve for the normal good X illustrated in Figure 4.8. We initially start at the price p_X^1 which falls to p_X^2. The (uncompensated) demand curve passes through $X_1{}^*$ and $X_2{}^*$, the levels of demand associated with each price. The change in consumer's surplus resulting from the price fall is given by initial expenditure ($ABCD$) plus the triangle under the uncompensated demand curve, CDF. The equivalent variation is the area under the compensated demand curve around the new price, p_X^2, between the two prices p_X^1, and p_X^2. It is given by the initial expenditure ($ABCD$) plus the rectangle $CDFG$; and is larger than the consumer's surplus. The compensating variation is the area under the compensated demand curve at the original price p_X^1 between the prices p_X^1 and p_X^2. It equals the initial expenditure ($ABCD$) plus the triangle DCE, and is less than both consumer's surplus and equivalent variation. (Note that CV and EV necessarily have a different sign; we here

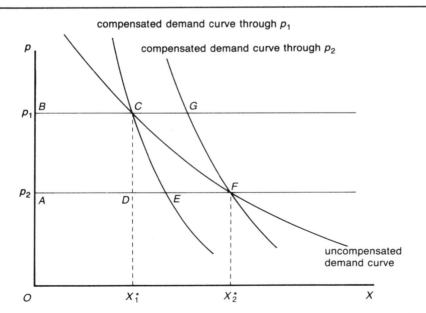

Figure 4.8

The effect of a fall in the price of X on welfare. The change in consumer's surplus coming from a fall in the price of X from p_1 to p_2 is given by $ABCD$ (the transfer from producers to consumers given by the price fall) plus DCF. It is less than the equivalent variation ($ABCD + DCGF$) and more than the compensating variation ($ABCD + DCE$).

refer to their absolute values). The change in consumer's surplus thus has an interpretation as a rough average of the equivalent and compensating variation.

This analysis has been undertaken on the assumption that the good in question is normal. As we know from Chapter 3, compensated demand curves cut normal demand curves from below when the good in question is inferior. It is left to readers to prove for themselves that the relative size of equivalent variation, consumer surplus and compensating variation is reversed when the good is inferior.

Concluding Comment

This chapter has dealt with the manner in which consumer theory may be extended to deal with measuring the benefits a typical consumer obtains from consuming a particular good. The example of the toll-bridge was used to illustrate the potential importance of this problem, and the concepts of equivalent and compensating income variations were deployed to illustrate some of the difficulties inherent in it. Marshallian consumer theory, it turns out, yields benefit measures that may be derived directly from the consumer's demand curve, and hence, to the extent that demand curves are themselves measurable, are immediately applicable to real-world data. However, we have also seen that this demand theory rests on very special assumptions about the consumer's underlying utility function, assumptions which eliminate the income effect from the demand for a good and hence remove differences between the equivalent and compensating variations. Finally, readers who have worked through the final starred section of this chapter have seen in a more general way how the ideas of consumer's surplus, equivalent and compensating variations are related to one another.

Now it would be easy to conclude from all this that the measurement of economic benefits is so fraught with difficulties that it should not be undertaken. Though some might take this position we do not. Our tools are imperfect, to be sure, but they are the only ones available, and the tasks for which we need them are important. Hence we would urge, not that they never be deployed, but that when they are used it is with caution, and in full understanding of their shortcomings.

The analysis set out here, and in the preceding two chapters, constitutes in and of itself a good grounding for further work in economics, but it by no means exhausts the possibilities of consumer theory. The next section of this book, therefore, deals with further extensions of the ideas developed so far, and it is our hope that the reader will be tempted to study at least some of this material before proceeding to the theory of production.

Questions for Study and Discussion for Part I

1. Discuss which of the following statements is true or false and explain why:

    (a) a good is inferior if the quantity demanded of it falls as the price falls;
    (b) a good is inferior only if the quantity of it falls as the price falls;
    (c) a good is inferior if the Hicks compensated demand curve cuts the normal (money income) demand curve from above;
    (d) a good is inferior if the Slutsky compensated demand curve cuts the normal (money income) demand curve from below;
    (e) a good is inferior if the Hicks compensated demand curve cuts the Slutsky compensated demand curve from above.

2. Can an individual's demand curve be upward sloping at all prices?
3. The indifference curves shown in the following diagrams do not conform with those drawn earlier in this part of the book, though they do not necessarily illustrate unrealistic preferences. Explain the underlying assumptions made in each case and illustrate your answer with examples of commodities which you believe are consistent with these preferences.

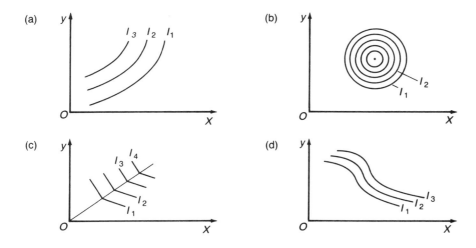

4. Person *A* buys one unit of a good when its price is 10 pence and two units when its price is 5 pence. Would that person be willing to pay 13 pence for two units of the good, rather than forgo it in its entirety? What is the most that person *A* would pay for two units of the good, rather than forgo consuming it altogether?

5. Draw the budget constraint implied by the following information:

    consumer's income   £500 per week
    price of X   £1 per unit
    price of Y   £2 per unit

    Would the consumer be able to attain any of the following consumption patterns?

    100 Y and   200 X per week
    100 Y and   20 X per week
    200 Y and   100 X per week
    200 Y and   1600 X per month
    300 Y and   1200 X per month

    How much would be left over per week from purchasing those bundles within reach?
    Suppose that the budget constraint instead were given by:

    consumer's income   £500 per week
    price of X   £1 per unit for the first 150 per week,
                                            thereafter £2 per unit
    price of Y   £2 per unit

    How would this affect your answers to the above questions?
6. Draw the indifference curves between X and Y where:

    (a) An extra unit of X adds nothing to a consumer's satisfaction unless accompanied by an extra unit of Y.
    (b) The consumer may always be compensated for the loss of one unit of X by being given two units of Y, regardless of the proportions in which he or she is originally consuming them.
    (c) The consumer must be compensated for consuming extra units of X by being given extra units of Y, the amount of Y needed to compensate for consuming one unit of X increasing as the level of consumption of X increases.

7. Derive the relationship between the quantity of X demanded and the price of X if the consumer's indifference map *vis-à-vis* X and Y has curves concave to the origin.
    Let X be games of golf per annum and Y all other goods. Draw the indifference map and budget constraint of:

    (a) an amateur who pays to play golf;
    (b) a professional who is paid to play golf.

    May we conclude that golfers turn professional because they dislike the game?
8. Draw the budget constraints and indifference map implicit in the following observations made in two different weeks on two different consumers. Assume in each case that all income has been spent on X and Y.

Consumer *A*

week 1   price of *X*   £2
                   price of *Y*   £1
                   income   £500 per week
                   quantity of *X* bought   100 units per week

week 2   price of *X*   £2
                   price of *Y*   £1
                   income   £600 per week
                   quantity of *X* bought   80 units per week

Consumer *B*

week 1   price of *X*   £2
                   price of *Y*   £1
                   income   £300 per week
                   quantity of *X* bought   110 units per week

week 2   price of *X*   £2
                   price of *Y*   £1
                   income   £250 per week
                   quantity of *X* bought   110 units per week

Is *X* an inferior good for consumer *A* or *B*? If someone told you that consumers *A* and *B* had identical tastes *vis-à-vis* *X* and *Y* would you be able to contradict them on the basis of the above information?

9.   We observe the same consumer in two successive weeks:

week 1   price of *X*   £10
                   price of *Y*   £10
                   quantity of *X* bought   10 units per week
                   quantity of *Y* bought   10 units per week

week 2   price of *X*   £5
                   price of *Y*   £15
                   quantity of *X* bought   7 units per week
                   quantity of *Y* bought   11 units per week

Calculate her income in the two weeks on the assumption that she spends it all on goods *X* and *Y*. Do the above observations enable you to conclude that her tastes have changed between the two weeks?

10. Is it possible when there are only two goods, *X* and *Y* (a) for *Y* to be both a substitute for *X* and a normal good (b) for *Y* to be both a complement to *X* and an inferior good?

11. An individual is faced with a choice of buying housing in one of two markets; the private market where he may buy any amount of housing he pleases at the going price, and the public housing market where he will be offered, on a take-it-or-leave-it-basis, a particular amount of housing at a price lower than that which he would pay for it on the private market. Will he necessarily choose the public housing? If so, may we conclude that he will consume more housing than he would have purchased had he been forced to buy it on the private market? (With thanks to Dr Leslie Rosenthal).

12. The following observations are taken on a consumer's behaviour on two successive weeks:

   week 1   price of X   £10
   price of Y   £10
   quantity of X bought   10 units per week
   quantity of Y bought   10 units per week

   week 2   price of X   £5
   price of Y   £20
   quantity of X bought   20 units per week
   quantity of Y bought   5 units per week

   Has the consumer's money income changed between the two weeks?
   Calculate the Laspèyres price index for week 2 taking its value in week 1 to be 100.
   Calculate the Paasche price index for week 2 taking its value in week 1 to be 100.
   Has the 'cost of living' risen between week 1 and week 2?

13. Suppose that it costs 12 pence a mile in *direct* operating costs to run a car.
   Let X be miles per week and p be measured in pence, and an individual's demand curve for car transport be given by

   $$p = 400 - 4Q$$

   (a) how many miles per week will be driven?
   (b) how much consumer's surplus will be gained from operating the car?
   (c) would the individual be willing to pay a fixed cost, over and above variable costs, of £60 per week to operate the car?
   (d) suppose the direct cost of operating a car rose to £2 per mile because of an increase in the price of petrol. How would your answers to questions (a), (b) and (c) change?

   Use the Marshallian demand curve assumptions in answering this question.

14. Starting with an individual's Marshallian demand curve for hours of television watching and the knowledge that each hour's watching uses a given amount of electricity, show how a fall in the price of electricity will affect:

   (a) the amount an individual is willing to pay to rent a television;
   (b) the market demand curve for rented television.

15. Suppose that good X is an inferior good. Use diagrams to illustrate the relationship between the equivalent variation, the compensating variation and the change in consumer surplus when the price of X rises from p_X^1 to p_X^2. Does the change in consumer's surplus equal the equivalent variation?

16. The price of food falls by 30 per cent and disposable income by 10 per cent. If a person spends one third of income on food, is it the case that he would be neither better off nor worse off as a result of these changes?

**17. A consumer chooses weekly quantities of X and Y in order to maximise the utility function

$$U = X^{1/2}Y^{1/2}$$

Total income over the week is £100, and the prices of X and Y are £5 and £10 respectively.

  (a) How much of X and Y will the consumer buy?
  (b) What happens to the demand for X if the price of X rises to £10?
  (c) What happens to the demand for Y if the price of X rises to £10?
  (d) What is the equivalent variation and the compensating variation resulting from the increase in the price of X from £5 to £10? (Hint: calculate the utility levels at each price combination and apply the formulae in equations (4.22) and (4.23)).

Suggested Further Reading to Part I

Bailey, M.J. 1954. 'The Marshallian Demand Curve', *Journal of Political Economy*. Reprinted in Breit and Hochman (*op.cit.*).

Brown, A. and Deaton, A.S. 1972. 'Models of Consumer Behaviour: A Survey', *Economic Journal*.

Currie, J.M., Murphy, J.A. and Schmitz, A. 1971. 'The Concept of Economic Surplus and its Use in Economic Analysis', *Economic Journal*.

Deaton, A.S. and Muellbauer, J. 1980. *Economics and Consumer Behaviour*. Cambridge: Cambridge University Press.

Friedman, M. 1949. 'The Marshallian Demand Curve', *Journal of Political Economy*, 1971, reprinted in Breit and Hochman (*op.cit.*).

Green, H.A.J. 1971. *Consumer Theory*. London: Penguin.

Hicks, J.R. 1941. 'The Rehabilitation of Consumer's Surplus', *Review of Economic Studies*. Reprinted in K.J. Arrow and T. Scitovsky (eds) on behalf of the American Economic Association), *Readings in Welfare Economics*. Homewood, III: Irwin.

Hicks, J.R. 1946. *Value and Capital* (2nd edition). New York: Oxford University Press, Chs 1–3.

Marshall, A. 1920. *Principles of Economics* (8th edition). London: Macmillan. Book 3.

Phlips, L. 1974. *Applied Consumption Analysis*. Amsterdam: North-Holland.

Samuelson, P.A. 1947. *Foundations of Economic Analysis*. Harvard: Harvard University Press.

Sen, A.K. 1979. 'The Welfare Basis of Real Income Comparisons: A Survey', *Journal of Economic Literature*.

Part II

CONSUMER THEORY: FURTHER TOPICS

5

The Individual's Supply of Labour

Introduction

In this chapter we apply the theory of choice to aspects of the supply of a productive service — labour. In particular, we consider the choice of an individual member of the labour force as to how many hours of work per week will be undertaken. As always, we need to know about three factors in order to set the problem up in manageable form — the objects of choice, the constraints upon choice, and the tastes which govern the choice.

The analysis that follows will concentrate upon investigating the consequences for the outcome of this choice problem of variations in the nature of the constraint that faces the individual. We shall show how the constraint's form varies when such complications as overtime payments, a fixed length working week, and the possibility of household production are taken account of, and we shall examine the effects of such variations on the individual's labour supply behaviour.

The Nature of the Choice Problem

Consider first the objects of choice involved in the labour supply decision. At first glance one might think of each member of the labour force being faced with a choice between work and leisure, but a moment's reflection makes it apparant that only one item is in fact being chosen. When hours to be worked have been selected, the number of hours available for leisure are already determined and vice versa. In mentioning work and leisure we are specifying only *one* of the objects of choice,

and in our analysis it is convenient to deal explicitly with leisure and hence implicitly with work. Our individual gives up leisure, and receives wage payments in recompense. Income — the ability to purchase consumption goods — is gained and leisure is sacrificed. The objects of choice here are therefore income and leisure.

We measure income along the vertical axis of Figure 5.1 and leisure along the horizontal axis. Now let us consider the constraint upon the individual's choice. First of all there is the obvious physical constraint that limits the number of hours of leisure available in a week to the number of hours that there are in a week. This point is given by L_0 on the horizontal axis of Figure 5.1.

Working is only one source of income, and there is no reason why any person cannot also receive unearned income. Such income receipts are common indeed in a modern economy in which the state provides a number of services to individuals. Free education for children, health insurance — the benefits of which are unrelated to contributions — and so forth, are all part of income, but receipt of them does not depend in any way upon hours worked. More traditional forms of unearned income accruing from ownership of wealth belong here as well. Thus, there is no reason to suppose in general that the level of income associated with not working, i.e. with L_0 hours of leisure per week, is zero. In Figure 5.1 it is assumed to be Y_0 and the budget constraint is drawn vertically up to this level of income. Beyond this point, however, more income can only be obtained by working and hence by sacrificing leisure.

Each hour worked increases income by the hourly wage that the individual can command. Hence the slope of the budget constraint above

Figure 5.1

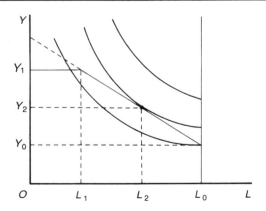

The choice between combinations of income, Y, and leisure, L. Note that hours worked may be measured moving to the left from L_0. If we read the diagram from right to left in this way, it depicts the choice of the best available combination of a 'good' (income), and a 'bad' (work). The individual here chooses to work $L_0 - L_2$ hours for a wage income of $Y_2 - Y_0$. See p. 22, fn 2 on the use of Y to denote income.

point $L_0 Y_0$ is given by the wage rate, with a negative sign of course, showing the rate at which income can be substituted for leisure. It is clearly not possible to continue the constraint to cut the vertical axis since no individual can work every hour of the week without some 'leisure' time being devoted to eating and sleeping. Thus there is a cut-off at some minimum amount of leisure L_1 and an associated maximum income level of Y_1. Thus, the constraint on the choice we are analysing is characterised as a kinked relationship such as shown in Figure 5.1. The continuity of the constraint over the range $L_0 Y_0 - L_1 Y_1$ implies that the individual may choose the length of the work week. This is obviously too simple for direct application to modern labour market institutions. Despite this degree of simplification, however, the analysis is of considerable interest.

As to the individual's tastes, if income and leisure are both goods in the sense that more of one of them, without sacrifice of the other, increases satisfaction, then we are safe in characterising them by a conventional indifference map. One may object to this on the grounds that perhaps the first few hours work a week may actually be a pleasant alternative to the boredom implicit in complete idleness, and prefer indifference curves that actually become upward sloping at high levels of leisure as in Figure 5.2. But reflection on the results in Chapter 2 makes clear that this extra complication adds nothing to the analysis that follows, so we ignore it from now on. This is not to say, though, that the assumption underlying it lacks plausibility.

The formal solution to the choice problem portrayed in Figure 5.1 is obvious enough. Our worker will consume L_2 hours of leisure per week at the going wage, hence working $L_0 - L_2$ hours for an income of Y_2.

Figure 5.2

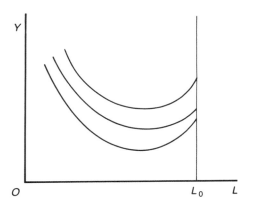

The indifference map implicit in the assumption that, after a certain point, leisure becomes a 'bad'. Moving to the left from L_0 the individual would be willing to pay for permission to work for the first few hours.

Variations in the Wage Rate

We are now in a position to see how the individual's supply of working hours changes in response to changes in the constraints under which they are chosen. First let us derive the supply curve of effort as a function of the wage rate. As the wage rate rises the mid-sector of the budget constraint becomes steeper, pivoting on point $Y_0 L_0$, as in Figure 5.3(a). The 'price' of income falls, and, provided only that it is a normal good — hardly a proviso to argue about — the amount of it demanded rises as our individual moves from A to B. However, we are mainly interested in what happens to the demand for leisure and hence the supply of hours worked. To put the matter in the language of consumer theory, this is a cross effect rather than an own price effect. If income and leisure are substitutes, then hours worked will increase with the wage rate, but if they are complements, hours worked will actually fall. The former case, with its upward-sloping supply curve of hours worked is shown in Figure 5.3; the latter with a backward bending supply curve is shown in Figure 5.4.

Now if there were only a substitution effect to consider here there would be no problem. A fall in the price of income would be synonymous with a rise in the price of leisure. It is because there is an income effect at work that we run into ambiguity. We examine this matter more closely in Figure 5.5. After the wage rate rises, we carry out a Slutsky compensating variation on our individual's budget constraint by lowering unearned income until we reach constraint 3. Clearly, the overall response to this rise in the wage rate can be broken down into a movement from A to C, a substitution effect, and a movement from C to B, an income effect. If leisure were an inferior good, there would be no ambiguity in the in-

Figure 5.3

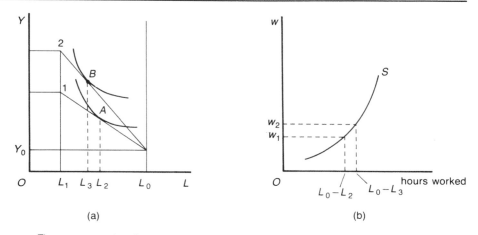

(a)

(b)

The wage rate rises from w_1 to w_2 and the equilibrium moves from A to B. More income is demanded but less leisure. If income and leisure are indeed substitutes, the supply curve of labour slopes upwards as shown in panel (b).

Figure 5.4

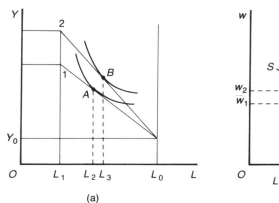

(a)   (b)

The wage rate rises from w_1 to w_2 and the equilibrium moves from A to B. More income is demanded, but in this case the indifference map is drawn so that income and leisure are complements. Thus we get the backward-bending supply curve of labour depicted in panel (b).

Figure 5.5

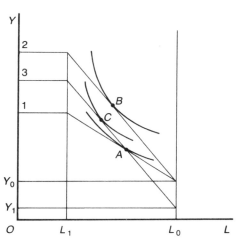

The movement from A to B involves a substitution effect from A to C and an 'income effect' from C to B. The compensating variation to get from constraint 2 to 3 may be thought of as involving a cut in unearned income from Y_0 to Y_1.

dividual's response: the negative income effect and the negative substitution effect would reinforce one another to produce an upward-sloping supply curve of labour. However, to think of leisure as being an inferior good is implausible, to say the least. If it was such a good, we would expect to observe the longest hours being worked for wages by those whose unearned incomes were highest! If leisure is a normal good though, the income effect on hours worked of an increase in the wage rate operates in the opposite direction to the substitution effect and may or may not

outweigh it. This is why an individual's supply curve of labour services as a function of the wage rate may either be upward sloping or backward bending.

Overtime Payments

We may look at overtime payment arrangements in the light of the foregoing analysis. They are a form of price discrimination, by which we mean that a different price is paid for different units of the same item (see Chapter 15), and can prevent the supply of labour from falling as its price rises. Consider Figure 5.6 and suppose that our typical individual, at the going wage rate on constraint 1, was supplying $L_0 - L_2$ hours of work. Now suppose that the employer wished to induce our individual to work longer hours. One course of action would be to offer the same wage rate for all hours worked up to $L_0 - L_2$ and a higher rate thereafter.

In terms of Figure 5.6, the effect of this is to kink the budget constraint at A, making it more steeply sloped above and to the left of this point (constraint 3). But if A was initially an equilibrium point, there must exist a point on a higher indifference curve, such as C, which also lies on the more steeply sloped segment of the constraint, the movement to which is motivated by a pure Slutsky substitition effect.

The price discrimination involved here clearly reduces the real income of the wage earner relative to what it would have been had the same wage rate been received for every hour worked. This is easily shown. In Figure

Figure 5.6

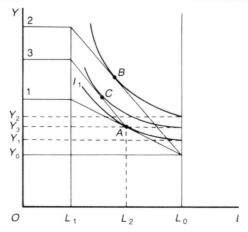

If the wage rate rises, the individual moves from A to B with a gain in utility equal to that yielded by an increase of $Y_2 - Y_1$ in unearned income. Such a movement as that from A to B may or may not involve an increase in hours worked. If the new wage rate is introduced as an overtime only rate, we have a pure substitution effect from A to C, an unambiguous increase in hours worked, but the gain in utility is here only equivalent to $Y_3 - Y_1$.

5.6, at the original wage rate, the individual is on indifference curve I_1, and hence at a level of utility exactly equivalent to that which would have been attained with an unearned income of Y_1. The difference between this and Y_0 measures the surplus that accrues from working at the wage rate in question. Were the wage rate simply to go up so that a new budget constraint was given by 2, then this change would be equivalent to an increase of $Y_2 - Y_1$ in unearned income. However, if the new rate is an overtime only rate, the gain is reduced. It is equivalent to an increase in unearned income of only $Y_3 - Y_1$. It is perhaps small wonder, therefore, that the length of the basic working week is so often a bone of contention in wage negotiations between unions and employers.

Now overtime payments are by no means the only arrangement that can introduce a kink into the budget constraint. National Insurance contributions levied as a proportion of income up to a maximum amount, an income tax which begins to bite above a certain threshold income level, to give but two other examples, also have this effect. Readers who wish to be sure that they have mastered the material just presented might find it helpful to analyse these cases for themselves.

The Effect of Fixing the Length of the Working Week

Now the reader will no doubt have been somewhat concerned that our analysis so far has dealt with an individual who is able to choose the length of the working week to the very minute. In fact, of course, the length of the basic working week tends to be institutionally determined. The effect of this is to present the individual with an all or nothing choice. He or she can work $L_0 - L_2$ hours at the going rate or not at all. Such a choice is depicted in Figure 5.7. Our individual will work if the point L_2, Y_2 lies on a higher indifference curve than the point L_0, Y_0, otherwise not. If the length of the basic working week is given at a fixed wage, but there is flexibility in the worker's choice of overtime hours, then we may be back with the analysis of marginal choices. Figure 5.8 deals with this case.

Household Production: the Simple Case

Our analysis has so far taken it for granted that an individual's opportunities to sacrifice leisure in order to generate income all lie in the labour market. This is a gross oversimplification. Work carried on within the home, including housework, does not generate cash income but it surely generates income in kind. The tools we have developed in this chapter may be extended easily enough to encompass the important phenomenon of household production.

Figure 5.7

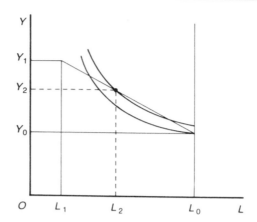

If the length of the working week is fixed by the employer along with the wage offered, the individual is faced with a choice between two income leisure combinations L_0, Y_0 and L_2, Y_2. As this figure is drawn, the latter is on the higher indifference curve and will choose to work.

Figure 5.8

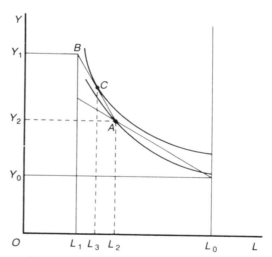

If the individual is permitted a free choice of overtime hours beyond $L_0 - L_2$ at an increased wage rate, the constraint is given by the point L_0, Y_0, and any point along the line AB linking L_2, Y_2 and L_1, Y_1. As the indifference map is drawn here, the individual moves to point C and works $L_3 - L_2$ overtime hours. Note though, that if the indifference curve passing through A had been drawn to slope more steeply than the continuous section AB of the constraint, our individual would have refused to work overtime.

Consider Figure 5.9. As before we endow our individual with a certain amount of unearned income Y_0, and recognise the existence of some minimum requirement of leisure L_1. Suppose, however, that our individual is excluded from any organised labour market, but is permitted

Figure 5.9

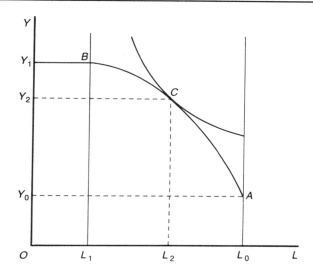

Household production. If leisure may be transformed into income by devoting time to household production, and the individual has no access to the labour market, then $L_0 - L_2$ hours of work will be carried out at home to produce $Y_2 - Y_0$ of income.

to trade off leisure in return for income by engaging in household production along the curve *AB*. This curve is known as a *production opportunity locus*. It is drawn concave to the origin, thus implying that the first units of time devoted to household production are more productive than later ones, that our agent's productivity in household activity falls as more time is devoted to it, that the activity is subject to *diminishing returns* (see Chapter 10). If we superimpose our individual's indifference map on Figure 5.9, we may solve for the utility-maximising allocation of time between leisure and household production at point *C*.

Household Production and the Labour Market

Let us now remove the restrictions that keep this individual out of the organised labour market, while leaving open as before the opportunities for household production characterised by *AB*. How should we now construct the budget constraint? Note first that any point along *AB* is still available to be chosen. Note secondly, and crucially, that the agent is not compelled to make an 'either−or' choice between household production and participation in the labour market. Working time can be divided among these two activities and leisure. These two observations imply that our individual may choose a level of household production, say that given by point *D'* in Figure 5.10, and starting at that point, begin to supply

Figure 5.10

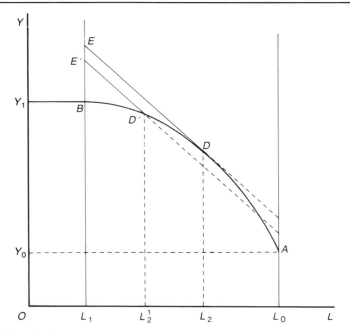

Household production in the presence of market opportunities. If the individual engaged in household production also has access to the labour market, then there is a market opportunity locus such as E' passing through every point, such as D' on the production locus AB. The market opportunity loci here have the slope of minus the wage rate, and the highest available one E is just tangent to AB at D.

labour in the organised market along a straight line such as $D'E'$ whose slope is given by the market wage rate. This line is known as a *market opportunity locus*, and it will be apparent that the analysis of previous sections has already made extensive use of this device drawn for what now appears as the special case in which the agent under analysis devotes no time to household production. In that case the market opportunity locus does in fact originate at point A.

Now if the agent can select any point along the production opportunity locus AB, there is, for a given market wage rate, a market opportunity locus beginning at every point along AB. The agent's utility-maximisation problem involves choosing the best combination of leisure, household production and work in the organised market, and part of its solution must involve the choice of a level of household activity that permits the most satisfactory market opportunity locus to be attained. Since our individual attains higher and higher levels of satisfaction as we move upwards and to the right in Figure 5.10, that market opportunity locus must be the one that lies furthest out from the diagram's origin. In turn that must be DE, the market opportunity locus just tangent to the production opportunity locus. Any other market opportunity locus having the same

slope as *DE*, and starting at a point on the convex production opportunity locus *AB* must lie below and to the left of *DE*. Our individual will devote no more than $L_0 - L_2$ of time to household production, because moving to the left beyond L_2, more income can be generated by supplying services in the organised labour market than by devoting them to further household production. Thus, for our individual, whose household production opportunities are described by *AB*, and who faces a market wage ratio given by the slope of *DE* (or *D'E'*), the overall budget constraint on the labour–leisure choice is given by *ADE*.

The individual's tastes may be such that, at the given wage rate, the best available choice lies somewhere along the segment *AD*, and hence involves staying at home. However, if we were then to allow the market wage rate to rise, a critical level would eventually be reached at which the individual would be tempted to enter the labour market. Moreover, once in the market, if the experiment of increasing the market wage is continued, the individual will respond by systematically reducing the

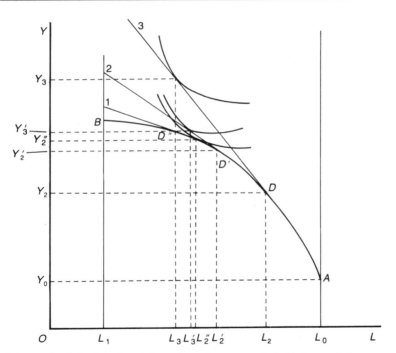

Figure 5.11

Market opportunity loci, 1, 2 and 3 are drawn for successively higher market wage rates. 1 is tangent to *AB* at *D"*, and the individual's tastes are such that $L_0 - L_2''$ is devoted to producing $Y_2'' - Y_0$ at home and no time is supplied to the market. At the wage underlying 2, tangency occurs at *D'*, $L_0 - L_2'$ is devoted to producing $Y_2' - Y_0$ at home, and $L_2' - L_3'$ in the labour market generates $Y_3' - Y_2'$ of income. At the wage underlying 3, tangency occurs at *D*, $L_0 - L_2$ yields $Y_2 - Y_0$ from household production, and $L_2 - L_3$ of labour time is sufficient on the labour market to generate $Y_3 - Y_2$ of income.

amount of time devoted to household production. This effect occurs because, as the market wage rate increases, the market opportunity locus gets steeper, so that the point (*D* in Figure 5.10) at which it is tangent to the production opportunity locus moves down the latter to the right. Figure 5.11 shows what is involved here.

Household Production and the Labour Supply Function

Now this analysis of household production is of considerable empirical importance because of the implications it yields for the form of the individual's supply function of labour to the organised labour market. The earlier analysis of this chapter ignored household production. That analysis yielded the prediction that, given the plausible assumption that leisure is a normal good, the individual's labour supply function might well be backward bending, and more generally was likely to display considerable insensitivity to the wage rate. Consideration of household production softens this conclusion. When the market wage rate is in the region at which an individual engaged only in household production will be induced to enter the labour market by a small increase in that variable, the supply of labour (to the organised market) is unambiguously positively related to the market wage. Moreover, as the market wage rate increases beyond that level, the individual may substitute market-oriented labour against household production activities, as well as against leisure. Thus the likelihood of an increase in the wage rate inducing an increase in the supply of labour to the formal market is increased by the availability of household production opportunities. Indeed it is quite possible for both the supply of labour outside the household, and the consumption of leisure, to increase at the expense of household production as the market wage rises. Figure 5.12 is drawn to depict this possibility.

Concluding Comment

It should be noted that the concept of the 'utility of income' used throughout the foregoing discussion is a summary measure of the utility that can be had from the goods that income will buy, or indeed of the goods that may be created by household production. Though the analysis of this chapter has treated the income—leisure choice as if it is made without explicit consideration of the allocation of income among consumption goods, this is a simplifying assumption rather than one that is generally valid. A fuller analysis of these matters, which is beyond the technical scope of this book, would have leisure, income, and the allocation of income among consumption goods all chosen simultaneously. Nevertheless, it is to be hoped sufficient has now been done to show the reader that the theory of consumer behaviour may readily be applied to problems

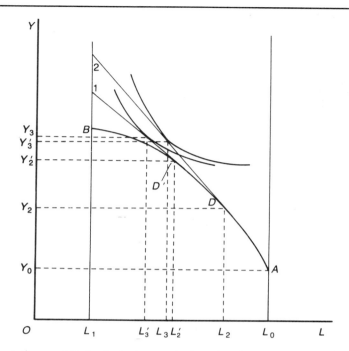

Figure 5.12

As the market wage shifts the budget constraint from 1 to 2, this individual's tastes are such that consumption of leisure rises from $O-L_3'$ to $O-L_3$. Nevertheless, because household production time is reduced from $L_0 - L_2'$ to $L_0 - L_2$, the amount of time offered on the labour market increases from $L_2' - L_3'$ to $L_2 - L_3$.

involving the labour market and is indeed quite a flexible analytic device in this context. We return to the issue of labour supply at the market level in Part VI, and in particular to the way that unions affect labour supply decisions, in Chapter 22.

One final technical point should be stressed. The reader who intends to go on to study the further topics discussed in this book should be sure that the technique of combining a relationship describing household production opportunities with a market opportunity locus to produce a budget constraint has been understood. This technique will be deployed, in another guise, in Chapter 6.

6

Capital Market Decisions: The Allocation of Consumption over Time

Introduction

We now apply the theory of consumer choice to the allocation of consumption over time. First, we shall deal with a situation in which the individual may lend and borrow on the capital market and set out the analysis that underlies much modern work on saving decisions and the consumption function. Then we shall extend the framework to permit the individual the opportunity of transforming currently available goods into future goods by way of production. This extension of the basic analysis is the foundation for a great deal of work on investment theory.

The basic postulate of consumer theory is that consumption alone yields satisfaction. The objects of choice in the analysis that follows are consumption now and in the future. Obviously a full characterisation of this choice problem would have us considering the time path of consumption over an individual's planning horizon, a horizon which might well be as long as a lifetime, or longer still if the individual cares about the welfare of descendents. However, we make the drastic simplification of dividing the planning period into two discrete chunks, the current period and the next period, t and $t + 1$, and consider the allocation of consumption between them.

The Framework of Choice Without Production

To begin with, we will rule out the possibility that our individual is able to engage in production. If we make this simplifying assumption, we may

characterise the individual's choice problem in Figure 6.1. There, we plot consumption in period t on the horizontal axis and consumption in period $t+1$ on the vertical. The objects of choice in the analysis that follows are allocations of consumption between the two periods. The constraint upon choice is constructed as follows. We assume that the individual receives a particular amount of income, Y_t, in time t and expects, as if with certainty, to receive a particular amount of income, Y_{t+1}, in time $t+1$ as well. There is no reason for us to treat these two amounts of income as equal, and in Figure 6.1 we have made Y_{t+1} greater than Y_t. Now if our individual consumes all current income in each period, the consumption pattern will also be given by Y_t, Y_{t+1}, but the individual can, by borrowing or lending, reallocate consumption between periods. If we assume that the capital market is perfect, that the single rate of interest (r) at which borrowing and lending takes place is completely uninfluenced by the amounts in which the individual does so, then the budget constraint, known once again as the *market opportunity curve*, is a straight line having the slope $-(1+r)$ and passing through Y_t, Y_{t+1}.[1]

To see this, neglect questions about what might be biologically feasible and consider what would happen if the individual decided to undertake no consumption at all in the current period. All current income could then be set aside to earn interest at rate r and in the next period consumption could be equal to $Y_{t+1}+(1+r)Y_t$. Alternatively, the individual might decide to carry out all consumption for the two periods in the current

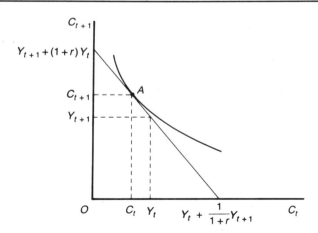

Figure 6.1

The level of saving is the result of a choice of consumption levels for now and the future. Given Y_t of income now and the certainty of receiving Y_{t+1} in the future and faced with an interest rate of r, the individual depicted saves $Y_t - C_t$.

[1] The reader should note that, though the phrase 'market opportunity' used here was also used in earlier discussions of the labour-supply decision, the opportunities referred to differ. In Chapter 5 they were labour market opportunities, and here they are capital market opportunities.

period, devoting all of next period's income to paying off the debts thereby incurred. At an interest rate of r, the maximum that can be borrowed against future income is equal to $Y_{t+1}/(1+r)$ and maximum current consumption is $Y_t + [Y_{t+1}/(1+r)]$. For every pound saved out of current income, $1+r$ pounds of future consumption is obtained, and for every pound of future income devoted to repaying debts, $1/(1+r)$ pounds of current consumption can be obtained: hence the market opportunity curve in Figure 6.1.

A conventional indifference map describes tastes and completes the picture set out in Figure 6.1, the slope of any indifference curve at any point defining the marginal rate of substitution between current and future goods.

Time Preference and the Solution to the Choice Problem

It is worth pausing for a moment to ask why, if the consumption goods available are identical in the two periods, the marginal rate of substitution between them should ever differ from -1, one unit of future goods for one unit of current goods. There are two distinct factors at work here. First, if the quantities of goods available in the two periods are not the same, there is no reason to suppose that an extra unit will be equally valued in both periods — one would expect an extra unit of goods to become relatively more highly prized the smaller was the bundle to which it was being added. This argument just restates the reasons for expecting there to be a convex indifference map in any application of the theory of consumer behaviour.

The second factor at work in this particular application is the fact that the goods in question are available at different times and for this reason alone are not the 'same' in every respect. Neglect all other differences between bundles of goods, and consider situations in which equal quantities are available in each period. Consider, that is, bundles along a $45°$ line drawn through the origin of an intertemporal indifference map such as we have in Figure 6.2. It is not obvious that the marginal rate of substitution between present and future consumption will be -1 here; indeed many arguments, that may be summarised in the word 'impatience', have been adduced for suggesting that present goods will be valued more highly on the margin when they are available in the same quantities as future goods.

Now the marginal rate of substitution between present and future goods is frequently referred to as being equal to $-(1+\rho)$, where ρ is defined as the *rate of time preference*, i.e. the amount by which future goods are discounted on the margin relative to present goods for all reasons. The marginal rate of substitution between present and future goods *when equal quantities of them are available in each period* involves a particular value for ρ known as the *rate of time preference proper*, which measures the amount by which future goods are discounted on the margin simply by virtue

Figure 6.2

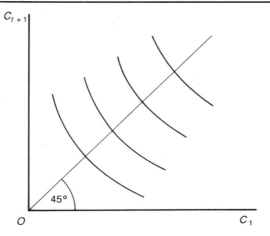

The marginal rate of substitution between present and future consumption is defined as $-(1+\rho)$, where ρ is known as the 'rate of time preference.' The 'rate of time preference proper' is the rate of time preference where equal amounts of consumption are available in each period. If the rate of time preference proper is zero, then the indifference curves in this diagram will all cut a line drawn at 45° from the origin at right angles, since they will have a slope of -1 at that point.

of their being available in the future. A zero rate of time preference proper implies that the indifference curves all cut a 45° line drawn from the origin with a slope of -1.

In any event, the solution to our choice problem depicted in Figure 6.1 occurs at A with a saving out of current income equal to $Y_t - C_t$. This is a point at which, to adopt the terminology just introduced, *the rate of interest and the rate of time preference are equal to one another.* The solution has a number of characteristics worth noting.

For one thing, it tells us that current saving, and hence current consumption, depend not just upon current income but also upon future income and the rate of interest. If we use the word 'wealth' to describe the total purchasing power currently available to an individual (in this case current income plus the present value of future income) then the point at which the market opportunity curve of Figure 6.1 cuts the horizontal axis clearly measures wealth, and we may equivalently say that current consumption depends upon wealth and the rate of interest; these two variables are sufficient to locate the budget constraint. The implications of this for analysis which uses a simple consumption function that makes consumption depend only on current income should be obvious.

Saving and the Level of the Rate of Interest

We may use the framework set out in Figure 6.1 to answer questions about the effect on consumption, and hence on saving, of variations in the rate

of interest, being careful to distinguish between the implications of *different values of the rate of interest considered as alternatives* on the one hand and the consequences of *changes in the interest rate* on the other. Consider Figure 6.3, which is based on Figure 6.1. If the individual's income pattern in the two periods is given by Y_t, Y_{t+1} and the rate of interest is equal to r_1, then the market opportunity curve is determined and we have equilibrium at A, just as in Figure 6.1. If the rate of interest had been higher at r_2, the budget constraint would instead be given by the market opportunity line labelled 2. Clearly, our individual would, in this second case, select point B, given the nature of the indifference map. As we have drawn it, the individual would consume fewer current and more future goods at this higher rate of interest. In other words, at a higher rate of interest more is saved. Obviously, as we show in Figure 6.4, preferences could equally easily have been such as to lead to a lower savings level at a higher interest rate; the influence of the rate of interest on the level of savings is therefore ambiguous.

We do not have to look too far for the source of this ambiguity. If we carry out a compensating variation in wealth to enable us to break down the difference between A and B into a substitution effect and an analogue to an income effect — call it a *windfall effect* — we get the constraint labelled 3 in Figure 6.4. The substitution effect of a higher rate of interest from A to D clearly involves an increase in saving. It is the windfall effect from D to B that offsets this substitution effect more than completely when

Figure 6.3

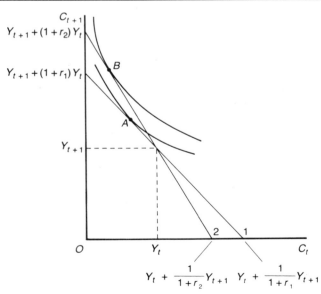

A higher rate of interest, r_2, shifts the market opportunity curve from 1 to 2, pivoting it at point Y_t, Y_{t+1} because this endowment of goods is available as a consumption bundle without borrowing or lending. At the higher rate of interest our individual will select point B rather than A.

Figure 6.4

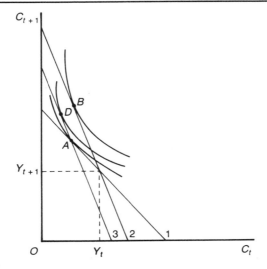

The movement from *A* to *B* at a higher interest rate may involve an increase or decrease in saving. The substitution effect, from *A* to *D*, unambiguously points to more saving but the 'windfall' effect from *D* to *B* may offset this tendency because it is reasonable to suppose that current consumption is a normal good.

a higher interest rate leads to less saving. In Figure 6.3 the windfall effect was not enough to offset the substitution effect. The windfall effect works against the substitution effect because the indifference map is drawn so that both current and future consumption are normal goods.

Saving and Changes in the Rate of Interest

So far we have been careful to talk about the rate of interest being higher and lower, rather than rising and falling. What then does the foregoing analysis tell us about the effects of *changes* in the rate of interest on the savings rate? If savings are channelled into an institution such as a building society, in which the borrower pays a given rate of return, variations in which do not alter the capital value of savings to the lender, then the foregoing analysis is applicable without modification. However, if lending takes the form of purchasing a bond — a promise to pay *a given sum of money* in the next period — then it requires a little further thought, for here variations in interest rate do affect the current capital value of savings.

Consider Figure 6.5. Our individual starts out at Y_t, Y_{t+1} with the market rate of interest such that the budget constraint is given by 1. The preferred allocation of consumption is at *A*, just as in Figures 6.1, 6.2 and 6.3. However, now let the individual buy a bond in order to accomplish this reallocation, thereby moving to point *A*. In purchasing the bond the individual has given up $Y_t - C_t$ of current income in return for a

Figure 6.5

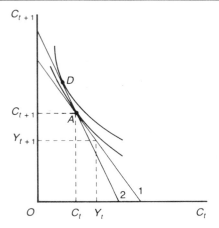

When an individual saves by buying a bond, the ability to consume at point *A* no matter what should subsequently happen to the rate of interest is ensured. Thus a rise in the interest rate pivots the market opportunity curve from 1 to 2 at *A*. The result is a pure substitution effect from *A* to *D* and an unambiguous increase in saving.

guaranteed receipt of $C_{t+1} - Y_{t+1}$ in the next period. The issuer of the bond has promised to provide this volume of extra consumption. Thus, no matter what now happens to the rate of interest, our individual saver can still stay at *A*. Now suppose, after the bond has been bought, but still during the first time period, the rate of interest rises. The individual can now move away from *A* along a more steeply sloped budget constraint than the original one. Since the constraint has pivoted at *A*, our individual is no longer in equilibrium there, and will move to *D*, buying another bond in the process on new, now more favourable, terms. Saving will unambiguously increase, for the change that we have been analysing here is clearly the outcome of a Slutsky substitution effect. Thus, in this case we can conclude that there is a positive relationship between the amount of saving and the rate of interest.

Intertemporal Choice with Production Opportunities

So far in this chapter we have considered the behaviour of an individual who is able to reallocate consumption over time by borrowing or lending in a *perfect* capital market. However, instead of being limited to taking currently available resources and lending them out with a view to consuming the proceeds of the loan in the future, the individual may also have the opportunity of using those resources in a production process that yields output consumable in the future. Let us now analyse the factors that will determine whether, and to what extent, the individual will

take advantage of access to such a production process, and, in doing so, develop the basis of what, in macroeconomics, is known as 'neo-classical' investment theory.

In the analysis that follows, the objects of choice facing the individual remain the same as they were above, namely consumption in the present period, C_t, and consumption in the next period C_{t+1}. The criteria in terms of which the choice is made are also the same and are summarised in exactly the same indifference map as was used there. The availability of access to a productive process (or processes) as opposed to, or in addition to, a capital market does, however, change the constraint upon choice. In this respect, the analysis we are about to carry out, which is mainly due to Jack Hirshleifer, differs from that described above.

The Production Opportunity Curve and the Internal Rate of Return

It is convenient to begin by considering an individual who for some reason has no access to a market in which borrowing and lending are possible and who can only transform currently available goods into goods available in the future by devoting them to production. A situation such as might face such an individual is described in Figure 6.6. First, we assume for simplicity's sake, that our individual's entire endowment of consumption goods for the two periods is available in time t. Hence, at the outset, the individual is at point Y_t on the horizontal axis in Figure 6.6. Second, we assume that there are available a whole array of opportunities for transforming current goods into future goods by way of production, and that as many, or as few, of these may be undertaken, and in any order.

Figure 6.6

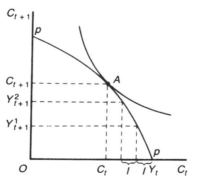

Intertemporal choice with production, *pp* is a production opportunity curve. Starting with an initial endowment of Y_t, successive equal investment of I in production yield diminishing increments in output. The utility-maximising investment–production–consumption plan occurs at point *A*, where the rate of time preference equals the internal rate of return in production.

That is, we assume that production opportunities are *divisible* and *independent*. A simple example of such a state of affairs would involve an individual whose endowment of goods came in the shape of corn, which could either be consumed today, or planted in a field with a view to consuming the resulting crop. The assumption of divisible production opportunities would here mean the individual could plant just as much or as little corn as seemed appropriate, and the assumption of independence that corn could be planted in any part, or parts, of the field without the yields being in any way affected.

This assumption of independence is important because there is no reason to suppose that all oppportunities facing an individual will be equally productive; in terms of our primitive example, some parts of the field might be more fertile than others. However, if production opportunities may be taken up in any order, the individual can begin with the most productive one, move on to the next most productive one, and so on. The concave to the origin shape of the curve labelled pp in Figure 6.6, which we may call a *production opportunity curve*, follows from the assumption that production opportunities are undertaken in diminishing order of productivity.[2] Thus, if, starting from point Y_t an amount of resources I is devoted to production, the resulting output will be Y^1_{t+1}. If another equal amount I is added to production, the resulting output overall will be Y^2_{t+1}. However, the *increment* in output in this second case will be smaller than the initial one, the increment in output resulting from a third equal increment of amount I to the resources devoted to production would be yet smaller again, and so on.

Let us consider the slope of the production opportunity curve a little more closely. As we move up it from right to left, resources are being withdrawn from current consumption and devoted to production. These *investments* yield a payoff in terms of consumption goods in the next period in amounts that may be read off the vertical axis, and this payoff may be thought of as having two components, the first just replacing the initial outlay, and the second presenting a net return on the investment. Earlier in this chapter we showed that the slope of the market opportunity curve was $-(1+r)$ where r is the market rate of interest, and defined the slope of a typical indifference curve as $-(1+\rho)$ where ρ is the rate of time preference. By exact analogy with these arguments, we may define the slope of our production opportunity curve at any point as $-(1+R)$ where R is the marginal rate of return on investment, or as it is usually called in the context of the analysis we are developing here, the *internal rate of return*.

The solution to the choice problem depicted in Figure 6.6 is straightforward. As in previous sections of this chapter, the objects of choice are

---

[2] Once again note that the phrase 'production opportunity' refers to a different phenomenon to that discussed in Chapter 5. There the opportunity involved transforming leisure into income. Here it refers to transforming present consumption goods into future consumption goods.

consumption in time t and $t+1$, and the indifference map is identical to that used there. Because we have assumed that our individual has no access to a capital market, but does face a set of production opportunities, the production opportunity locus becomes the relevant constraint upon choice. The utility-maximising solution to our individual's choice problem clearly lies at point A, where the production opportunity curve carries the individual onto, and is just tangent to, the highest attainable indifference curve. Here the individual consumes C_t of goods in the current period, and invests $Y_t - C_t$, thus producing C_{t+1} of consumption goods for the next period. The reader might note that the fact that point A is one of tangency between an indifference curve and the production opportunity curve means that this equilibrium occurs where there is equality between the rate of time preference ρ, and the internal rate of return on investment R.

Access to a Perfect Capital Market

Now there is really nothing very startling about the analysis just presented. What we have said is that, when excluded from borrowing and lending on the capital market, the amount that any individual will devote to productive investment will be determined by the tangency of an indifference curve to a production opportunity curve, and hence will depend upon tastes. If we don't have specific information about tastes, there doesn't seem to be anything very concrete that we can say about our individual's behaviour. As we shall now see, if we change the assumptions of our analysis to permit our individual to have access to a perfect capital market of the type which we analysed earlier in this chapter, in addition to having access to the kind of productive opportunities we have just discussed, this conclusion changes radically. We find that we are able to make precise predictions about investment decisions without having to know anything at all about tastes beyond the usual assumption that they may be characterised by a convex to the origin indifference map.

To see why this is so, consider what would happen if we suddenly were to allow the individual whose behaviour we have been analysing to have access to a perfect capital market where one can borrow and lend at a given interest rate. Consider Figure 6.7. Suppose first of all that the individual had already moved up to point A, when access to the capital market was granted. By moving from point Y_t to point A the endowment of goods available is changed, and the first question to be settled when access to the capital market opens up these borrowing and lending opportunities is whether a further improvement upon point A is possible.

Suppose for the sake of argument that the rate of interest ruling in the capital market is higher than the internal rate of return on investment at A. Then, passing through point A is a market opportunity curve, MM, a straight line with a slope of $-(1+r)$ which is by assumption steeper

Figure 6.7

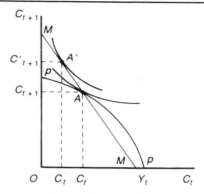

Intertemporal choice when access to a perfect capital market is made available after the individual is committed to investment—production plan A. the market rate of interest is assumed to be higher than the internal rate of return at A, so the individual rearranges consumption by further lending, moving to point A '.

than that of the production opportunity locus at A. Clearly, if our individual insists on investing $Y_t - C_t$ in production, and hence on moving to point A on the production opportunity locus, matters can now be further improved by moving from point A up to the left along the market opportunity curve as far as point A'. An amount $C_t - C'_t$ is now lent out on the capital market, earning in return $C'_{t+1} - C_{t+1}$. This yields a higher level of satisfaction than that achieved by investment alone.

However, this is the best that can be done *only if* the individual is already tied to the original investment—production decision at A when access is gained to the capital market. If the individual is not tied to that decision, then, by revising investment plans, an even greater gain in utility can be achieved than that depicted in Figure 6.7. The reason for this is straightforward. Wherever our individual may choose to settle on the production opportunity curve, borrowing or lending activities in the capital market may be started from that point. There is, that is to say, an attainable market opportunity curve passing through every point on the production opportunity curve. As we have drawn it, Figure 6.7 depicts a state of affairs in which the market rate of interest is higher than the internal rate of return ruling at point A, so that there is a segment of the production opportunity curve below and to the right of A that lies outside of the market opportunity curve passing through that point. This means that our individual, by cutting back on the original investment plan and moving downwards to the right along the production opportunity curve, is able to move onto higher and higher market opportunity curves, and hence open up the possibility of achieving higher and higher levels of utility. Now it is obvious that the further out to the right lies the market opportunity curve onto which our individual moves, the higher is the level of utility that can be attained. Hence a utility-maximising individual is going to plan production activities in such a way as to move onto the highest possible market opportunity curve, and that in turn will be the one that is just tangent to the production opportunity curve.

The Separation of Investment and Consumption Decisions

The state of affairs just described is depicted in Figure 6.8. Here, as before, we start with an initial endowment of Y_t and face our individual with production opportunities described by the curve PP. In the absence of access to the capital market, our individual chose that combination of present and future consumption denoted by point A as the solution to both production and consumption plans; given that the individual has access to the capital market, point B is instead chosen as a solution to the production plan. $Y_t - \bar{Y}_t$ is invested in order to produce $\bar{Y}_{t+1}$, and the individual then moves along the market opportunity locus $M'M'$ to point D, which denotes the utility-maximising solution to the consumption plan. As the reader will see, this involves lending out $\bar{Y}_t - \bar{C}_t$ on the capital market in order to obtain $\bar{C}_{t+1} - \bar{Y}_{t+1}$ as a return.

Now Figure 6.8 shows that having access to a perfect capital market enables a maximising individual to separate production and consumption decisions, but it shows more than that. A moment or two spent examining the diagram in question should convince the reader that, although the solution to the consumption plan — the choice of point D — certainly depends upon our individual's tastes as depicted in the indifference map, the solution to the production plan — the choice of point B — depends solely upon the shape of the production opportunity curve and the slope of the market opportunity curve and is completely independent of tastes. That is to say, the individual's investment–production

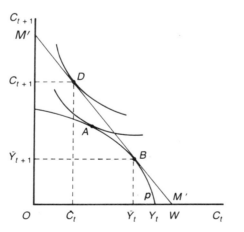

Figure 6.8

Intertemporal choice when all production opportunities are available, and access to a perfect capital market exists. The preferred investment production plan is now at point B, rather than at A, and the utility-maximising consumption plan is at point D. The choice of point B is independent of the individual's tastes and may be described as the result either of equating the internal rate of return in production to the market rate of interest, or of choosing the production plan with the highest present value, denoted by W, at the market rate of interest.

decision depends entirely upon factors that are given exogenously, these factors being the nature of the production opportunities available and the market rate of interest. Thus we can make statements about the rules that a utility-maximising individual will follow in making investment—production decisions, without referring to the precise properties of the indifference map.

Rules for Selecting the Optimal Investment—Production Plan

We have seen that, in order to maximise utility from consumption, our individual must first choose an investment—production plan that makes attainable the highest market opportunity locus. One way of characterising the outcome of this production choice involves noting that the highest attainable market opportunity curve is one whose intercept with the horizontal axis of a diagram such as Figure 6.8 lies as far to the right as possible. As we showed earlier in this chapter, this horizontal intercept has an economic interpretation. It measures the maximum quantity of current consumption goods that our individual can command, i.e. the *present value* of the income stream, or *wealth*. That is why it is labelled W. Thus the proposition that a utility-maximising individual will choose an investment—production plan so as to get onto the highest market opportunity curve available to the individual may be rephrased to say that the individual will choose that plan which *yields the highest present value,* or which *maximises wealth* at the current rate of interest. The same proposition may be rephrased to say that a production plan will be chosen at which the slopes of the production opportunity curve and the market opportunity curve are equal, at which *the internal rate of return in production is equal to the market rate of interest*. These two alternative ways of characterising the rule whereby a utility-maximising individual will formulate investment—production plans seems at first sight to be equivalent, and indeed in terms of the case considered in Figure 6.8 they are. However, the first of them is in fact more general and yields the 'right' solution in a wider variety of cases than the second, as we shall now show.

Interdependent Production Opportunities

The key characteristic of the situation depicted in Figure 6.8 that makes the two decision rules seem equivalent is the assumption of *independence* among production opportunities that we made at the very outset. This assumption implies that our individual is able to take up the available production opportunities in any order, and so enables us to arrange them in order of decreasing productivity and hence to construct a production opportunity curve everywhere concave to the origin. However there are

many ways in which this assumption of independence may be violated, and Figure 6.9 depicts two of them.

In panel (a) of that figure we show what would happen if there were some indivisibility in production opportunities such that the individual was forced to choose between two sets of productive opportunities, and was unable to mix them together in any way. Such a state of affairs would arise in the context of our earlier example if for some reason our corn planting individual had to choose between two fields for the crop and, having chosen one of them to be planted, was excluded from any use of the other. If one field had some extremely fertile patches, and some not so fertile, its use might face our individual with a production opportunity curve such as $p'p'$, and if the other was of more even fertility, but with its best patches inferior to those of the first field and its worst patches better, the curve relevant to it would be the less concave one labelled $p''p''$. Our individual must now choose which production opportunity locus to be on, as well as where to locate on it. As the reader

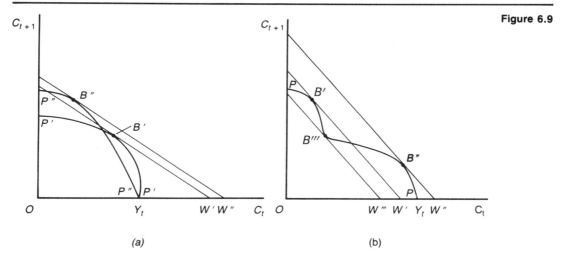

Figure 6.9

(a) (b)

Two situations in which the rule 'equate the internal rate of return to the market rate of interest' will not necessarily find the best investment–production plan, but in which the rule 'maximise the present value of the plan at the market rate of interest' will do so:
(a) The production opportunity curves $P'P'$ and $P''P''$ are mutually exclusive. Points B' and B'' both satisfy the internal rate of return rule, but B'' has a higher present value, W'', than does B' whose present value at the market rate of interest is W'.
(b) The production opportunity curve PP has a convex section that results from a lack of independence among the production opportunities available. Here, the internal rate of return rule cannot distinguish between any of the three tangencies shown, though B''' whose present value is W''' is clearly a utility-*minimising* rather than maximising plan. Application of the present value rule enables plan B'' whose present value is W'' to be identified as superior to B' whose present value is W'. The reader with some knowledge of calculus will recognise that the 'internal rate of return' rule corresponds to the application of first-order conditions for a maximum, that the application of second-order conditions would rule out B''' in panel (b), and that the application of the 'present value' rule involves the application of conditions capable of finding a global, as opposed to merely local, maximum.

will see from inspecting Figure 6.9(a), the rule 'maximise present value' does enable the individual to select both the better production opportunity locus, and the best point on it, while the rule 'equate the internal rate of return to the market rate of interest' enables the individual to find only the best point on each production opportunity curve but not to choose between them.

Panel (b) of Figure 6.9 depicts a situation in which the individual faces only one set of production opportunities, but is not free to take them up in any order, being forced to undertake some rather low productivity opportunities (the flatter central section of the curve) before certain high productivity opportunities become available. Such a situation might arise in our example if, for reasons of fertility maintenance, a particular balance of production had to be adopted, so that, in order to go beyond a certain acreage of corn, it was first necessary to grow some less productive, but fertility restoring, crop such as grass, if additional corn plantings were to be undertaken. Such a situation as we are here describing gives rise to a production opportunity curve that is convex rather than concave to the origin over that segment where lower productivity opportunities must be taken before those with higher productivity. Again, simple inspection of the diagram will enable the reader to see that the 'maximise present value' rule will enable the individual to find the best investment—production plan, while the other rule will select three possible plans. One of these (at point B''') is the *worst* available rather than the best, and the other two are the best available on their own particular concave segment of the curve. However, the rule 'equate the internal rate of return to the rate of interest' gives no guidance as to how the choice between the latter two should be made.

Capital Market Imperfection

The qualifications to our analysis that we have just discussed do not affect the basic conclusion established earlier that it is possible to discuss the factors affecting the choice of the best investment—production decision independently of the consumption decision, and hence to analyse investment decisions in terms of such objective factors as the market rate of interest and the nature of available productive opportunities. However, we did note that this conclusion was conditional upon the individual being faced with a perfect capital market, and it is now time to consider this important qualification in more depth. A perfect capital market is one in which the individual can borrow and lend, up to limits imposed only by the need to remain solvent, at a given rate of interest, which is the same regardless of whether the individual is borrowing or lending and regardless of the scale at which either is being done. Only with capital market perfection can we draw the market opportunity curve as a straight line in the way that we have done throughout this chapter. If we drop

this assumption, the independence of consumption and production decisions vanishes, as we shall now see.

There are many types of capital market imperfection that we could introduce into our model, but to make the point it will suffice to deal only with one quite simple case. Let us therefore assume that the market interest rate faced differs, depending upon whether the individual is a borrower or a lender, and that it is higher in the former case. To keep the analysis simple, let us also assume that the rate of interest at which the individual who chooses to lend can do so, does not vary with the amount involved, and that the borrowing rate faced is similarly constant (albeit at a higher level). Finally, and again purely for the sake of simplicity, let us assume that the production opportunities facing the individual are independent of one another so that the production opportunity curve is concave to the origin.

Figure 6.10 depicts the state of affairs implicit in these assumptions. Once more the individual starts with Y_t of resources and faces a production opportunity curve PP. However, instead of one market opportunity curve (or rather one set of market opportunity curves each passing through a different point on PP) we now have two. One set has a slope determined by the rate of interest at which the individual can borrow, and the other set has a slope fixed by the rate at which the individual can lend. BB represents the highest borrowing opportunity curve that

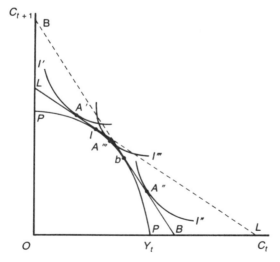

Figure 6.10

Intertemporal choice with production opportunities given by *PP*, but with access to an imperfect capital market where the borrowing rate of interest exceeds the lending rate. Here the optimal investment production plan for a would-be borrower will be point *b*, for a lender it will be point *l*, or for an individual who chooses neither to borrow nor lend it will be at point such as *A'''*, *I'*, *I''*, *I'''* are *alternative* indifference curves typical of these three possible cases, and *A'*, *A''* and *A'''*, represent the corresponding alternative consumption plans. Thus, when the capital market is imperfect, the choice of an investment–production plan comes to depend upon the individual's tastes.

can be reached, and it is tangent to the production opportunity curve at *b*, while *LL* is the highest lending market opportunity curve, being tangent to the production curve at *l*. Because the individual can only borrow at the rate of interest underlying *BB*, points above and to the left of *b* on that line are not available. By similar reasoning, the inability to borrow at the same low interest rate at which lending is possible rules out all points on *LL* below and to the right of *l*. These unattainable segments are drawn as dotted lines, and the effective constraint upon our individual's choice is made up of the discontinuous line consisting of the lower (solid) part of *BB*, the segment *bl* of the production opportunity curve and the upper (solid) part of *LL*.

What production plan will this individual choose? If the indifference map is characterised by shallowly sloped curves such as *I'*, then being a lender on the capital market will appear desirable and the production—investment decision will be at point *l*. If the relevant indifferent curves are steep, like *I"*, and the individual wishes to be a borrower, then the investment—production plan will have point *b* being chosen. If they are of some intermediate slope like that of *I'''*, and are tangent to the production opportunity curve somewhere in the segment *bl*, then a point such as *A'''* will characterise both the production and consumption plans, and the individual will be neither a borrower nor a lender in the capital market. In any event, however, the investment—production decision that our individual makes depends upon the nature of tastes in the cases we have analysed here in a way that it does not when the capital market is perfect.

Concluding Comments

We have by no means exhausted the analysis of the allocation of consumption over time in this chapter. We have said nothing about the problems involved when there are durable goods; in this case the utility yielding act of *consumption* analysed in this chapter becomes separated from the act of *consumer expenditure* which is relevant for a macro theory of income determination. Nor have we said anything about how individuals might learn from each other so that their consumption patterns become interdependent, or about how they may take time to adjust their consumption patterns when the constraints facing them shift. Thus, the analysis presented here, though it is fundamental to modern macro theories of consumption, does not tell the whole story about this problem area.

In the field of production choices, we have said nothing about what happens when the individual is able to hire other productive services, for example labour, to co-operate in production plans, or about what happens when production is undertaken for the market rather than home consumption. Moreover, we have said nothing about how this analysis

relates to those special types of investment in 'human' capital known as 'training' and/or education. Nevertheless we have done quite enough to show what a powerful tool our basic theory of consumer behaviour can be in this context. We have seen that a maximising individual will relate consumption plans to wealth rather than income and that they will also vary in a predictable fashion with the rate of interest. This must mean that the simple relationship between consumption and income so frequently used in elementary macroeconomics is very much a first approximation to be defended only on the grounds of its simplicity. As far as investment decisions are concerned, we have seen how important is the assumption of a perfect capital market to the conclusion that they do not depend on an individual's tastes.

7

Uncertainty and Information: Choice in the Face of Risk

Introduction

The subject of this chapter is not so much an application of our basic consumer theory as it is an extension of it. Up to now we have analysed choice-making behaviour on the assumption that the individual making the choices is certain about the outcome of any choice, or at least acts as if such certainty ruled. This is clearly a highly simplifying assumption and if we continue to make it we will be completely unable to analyse some important economic phenomena. For example, if the outcome of every choice was certain, there would be no role for insurance companies to play. After all, the basic service they provide is that of taking risks on behalf of their customers. Thus, we now go on to examine the question of choice in risky situations. Our first step will be to show that the ability to make consistent choices in conditions of risk implies the existence of a form of cardinal utility function; when this has been established, we will use this function to analyse choice-making behaviour.

The Idea of Expected Utility

Let us consider as simple a choice involving risk as it is possible to conceive of. Suppose we face an individual with the choice between receiving either the sum of £1 with certainty or a chance or winning £100 in a draw of some sort. Which alternative is chosen will depend upon the probability of winning the £100; a very small chance of winning will tend to make the individual select the certain alternative, while a very large chance of winning will point to the selection of the risky alternative. It

is equally plausible that there is some value for the probability of winning £100 that just makes the individual indifferent between the certain and the risky alternative. It is the consequences of assuming that such a probability does exist that we now examine.

If our choice maker is able to express indifference between £1 with certainty and winning £100 with a particular probability, this is equivalent to saying that the alternatives will yield the same gain in satisfaction, the same increase in utility. The notion of one pound yielding a given increase in utility is relatively straightforward, but what do we mean by the utility associated with an uncertain situation?

To say that the probability of winning a particular draw is, for example, 0.2 implies that if the draw were repeated an indefinitely large number of times then two out of ten outcomes would be wins and eight out of ten would be losses. If it were a draw for £100, then £100 would be obtained two times in ten, and nothing would be gained eight times in ten. Hence the utility of a gain of £100 would accrue to the person involved in the draw two times in ten. On average, 0.2 times the utility of £100 would be obtained per repetition (on the assumption that a zero gain yields zero utility). The assumption that we make about behaviour is that our individual treats the average utility that would be obtained from many repeated tries of the risky alternative as the gain in utility to be assigned to participating in it on any one occasion. This is an *ex-ante* idea. Once the draw is made the individual either gets the utility of £100 or of nothing, and so it is only before the draw is made that the *ex-ante* average or *expected* utility concept is relevant. We did not need to distinguish between *ex-ante* and *ex-post* utility levels in dealing with choice under conditions of certainty, for there the two were always the same. The consequences of making a particular choice were fully known before any choice was made. However, the distinction is obviously a vital one in dealing with situations involving risk.

Probability and Cardinal Utility

If our choice maker is able to say that there is a particular probability of winning £100 exactly equivalent to receiving £1 with certainty, that individual is also saying that the utility of one extra pound is equal to the expected utility of the risky alternative. Mathematically speaking, expected utilities are calculated by multiplying the utility of each possible outcome by the probability of its occurrence, and then adding these products together. This process yields a *probability weighted average of utilities*. In the particular case being analysed here, this expected utility is equal to the probability of winning one hundred pounds times the utility of a gain of £100 plus the probability of winning nothing times the utility of a zero gain. If we let $U(£1)$ be the utility of £1 extra and p_1 be the probability of winning £100 then we have:

$$U(£) = p_1 U(£100) + (1-p_1) U(0) \qquad (7.1)$$

Now if it is possible to find a probability value that satisfies the above equation, it is presumably equally possible to find a value, call it p_2, that would make the utility of a chance at the draw equivalent to the utility of £2 extra with certainty, and so on all the way up to £100 (at which point the value of p would clearly have to be equal to one).

We could write down a whole array of equations as follows:

$$U(£1) = p_1 U(£100) + (1-p_1) U(0)$$

$$U(£2) = p_2 U(£100) + (1-p_2) U(0) \qquad (7.2)$$

. . . .

. . . .

$$U(£99) = p_{99} U(£100) + (1-p_{99}) U(0)$$

$$U(£100) = 1 U(£100) + (0) U(0)$$

If there is no gain in utility attached to getting zero extra pounds, then $U(0)$ is equal to zero and these expressions can be rearranged to read

$$U(£1) \, \frac{1}{U(£100)} = p_1$$

$$U(£2) \, \frac{1}{U(£100)} = p_2$$

. . . . (7.3)

$$U(£99) \, \frac{1}{U(£100)} = p_{99}$$

$$U(£100) \, \frac{1}{U(£100)} = 1$$

When we put it this way, it is clear that the probability indices on the right may be used as cardinal indicators of the utility of various sums of money. To be sure, everying is here being measured relative to the utility of gaining £100 with certainty; the analysis implies no absolute scale for measuring utility. We could equally well conceive of experiments that would measure the utility of gaining various sums of money relative to the utility of gaining £200 or £300 or any other amount. We are in no position to say that one sum of money yields twice the utility of some other sum, for such a statement could only be made if we knew where to put zero on our utility scale; but we can say that the *difference* in the utilities yielded by two amounts of money is twice the *difference* in utilities of two other amounts.

The measurement of utility is thus rather like the measurement of temperature. A temperature which is twice the number of degrees of some

other temperature on the centigrade scale will not be twice the number of degrees on the fahrenheit scale: 'twice as hot' doesn't mean anything. However, the relative size of differences between particular levels of heat is the same on the two scales. The difference between 30°C (86°F) and 20°C (68°F) is twice the difference between 10°C (50°F) and 5°C (41°F) no matter which scale is used. Utility and temperature are measurable in the same sort of way and to exactly the same extent.

Diminishing Marginal Utility and Expected Utility

Now the purpose of the foregoing analysis is to show that it is legitimate for us to draw a diagram such as Figure 7.1 in which the utility accruing to an individual is related to wealth. The units of measurement on the vertical axis are arbitrary, as is the location of the origin, but to exactly the same extent as if temperature were being measured there. This arbitrariness is irrelevant to the analysis that follows. The relationship is drawn on the assumption that successive equal increments of wealth yield diminishing increments in utility. It displays *diminishing marginal utility* of wealth. The consequences of making alternative assumptions will be considered later. We may use this utility of wealth function to analyse the nature of the choice facing an individual who must decide in a risky situation deciding whether or not to insure against the risk in question. Suppose that the individual faces a 50–50 chance of losing a certain amount of wealth $(W_1 - W_0)$ within a particular time period. In terms of Figure 7.2, given an initial level of wealth, W_1, our choice maker will end the period in question either at W_1 with an associated utility level of $U(W_1)$ or at W_0 with an associated utility level of $U(W_0)$. *Ex ante* there is a 50 per cent chance of ending up in either situation. The expected value of wealth therefore is $\frac{1}{2}W_0 + \frac{1}{2}W_1 = W_2$, but it is not wealth *per*

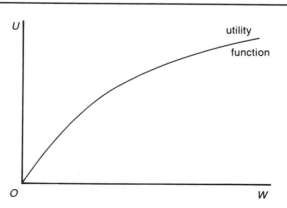

Figure 7.1

A utility function displaying diminishing marginal utility (U) of wealth (W)

Figure 7.2

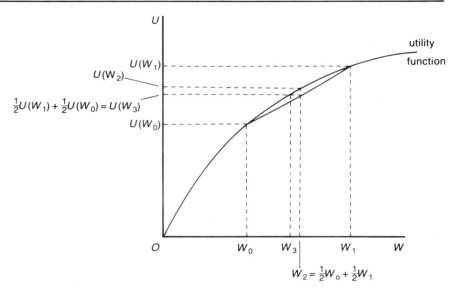

Ex ante, the individual faces a choice between a 50–50 chance of W_0 and W_1, and the certainty of W_2 which lies half-way between them. The expected wealth involved in the two alternatives is the same, but the expected utility of the certain alternative is higher by $U(W_2) - [\frac{1}{2}U(W_1) + \frac{1}{2}U(W_0)]$. A measure of the consumer's surplus gained by selecting the certain alternative by insuring is $W_2 - W_3$.

se that is relevant to our individual but the utility that this wealth yields. Expected utility in the risky situation is given by $\frac{1}{2}U(W_0) + \frac{1}{2}U(W_1)$. This measures the utility accruing to our individual, seen *ex ante*, at the beginning of the time period under consideration.

Insurance and Gambling

Now suppose that the individual can buy insurance against risk. Suppose that, in return for a premium paid at the beginning of the period, some agent guarantees to reimburse the individual completely for any loss incurred during the period. For payment of a fee a situation of certainty can be obtained. By reducing the level of wealth with which the period is begun by the amount of this fee, our individual can be guaranteed to end the period with that same level of wealth. The utility of this alternative is clearly the utility of having W_1 minus the premium with certainty. Faced with the choice of insuring or not insuring, the individual will presumably choose the alternative that will yield the highest level of *ex-ante* utility. In terms of Figure 7.2, so long as the insurance premium is less than $W_1 - W_3$ the individual would prefer to buy in-

surance. W_3 is the level of wealth which, if available with certainty, yields the same utility as a 50—50 chance of W_0 or W_1.

If we ignore the administrative costs of actually buying and selling insurance — we will return to these costs later — the maximum amount that this individual will pay for insurance is more than the minimum the agent providing insurance will accept by way of premium, always provided that the agent in question has a large number of customers, each facing similar, but independent risks. The minimum acceptable premium is one that will enable the insurer just to break even. If a large number of 50—50 risks are being covered, then half of the clients will have claims and a premium set at 50 per cent of the loss on any one claim will just cover the insurer's outgoings. That is to say, *if we ignore any costs that the insurance agent incurs in running the business,* that agent will be able to offer the client what is usually called 'a fair bet'. A fair bet is one on which, were it to be repeated an indefinitely large number of times, both participants would expect, in the long run, to break even. The agent selling insurance to many people is in fact facing a large number of trials of the same situation, not over time, but over different clients at the same time. Provided that there is no connection between one client incurring a loss and another doing so as well, provided also that the risks taken by the insurance agent are *independent* to use a statistical term, the agent is enabled to offer clients fair bets.

This implies in turn that the minimum premium that an insurer will charge will be such as to permit the insured to enjoy with certainty the level of wealth that, in the risky situation, was the expected value of that person's wealth. Because the individual may enjoy that wealth with certainty when insured, the utility level now is $U(W_2)$ and the difference between this and $\frac{1}{2}U(W_1) + \frac{1}{2}U(W_0)$, the utility when not insured, measures the gain of being in a situation of certainty; it is the consumer's surplus that arises from buying insurance at the minimum rate at which it can be provided. Another way of looking at the same point is to note that the difference between the minimum premium that is acceptable and the maximum premium that would be paid $(W_2 - W_3)$ measures the money value of this consumer's surplus and hence the scope available to a monopolistic seller of insurance to make a positive profit from dealing with this individual and to cover the administrative costs of the transaction.

Now the assumption of diminishing marginal utility of wealth is crucial to the foregoing analysis. As Figure 7.3 shows, a linear utility function — constant marginal utility of wealth — implies that the individual is indifferent between insuring and not insuring at the minimum premium that an insurer would offer, and would prefer not to insure at any higher premium. It is equally clear from Figure 7.4 that increasing marginal utility of wealth will involve the individual in refusing insurance at any feasible premium. The risky alternative will be chosen rather than the safe one and hence the individual may be said to 'gamble'.

Figure 7.3

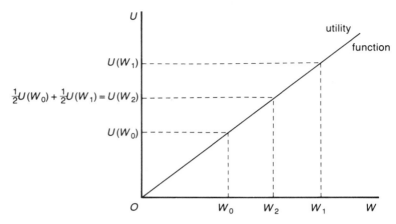

When the marginal utility of wealth is constant, not only the expected values of wealth involved in the certain and uncertain situations are the same, but also the expected utility. The alternatives here are a 50–50 chance of W_0 or W_1, or W_2 with certainty.

Figure 7.4

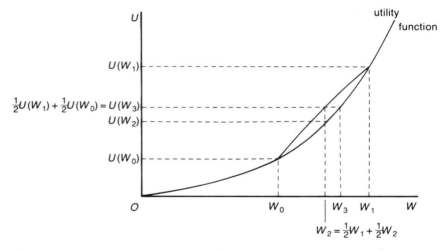

Increasing marginal utility of wealth makes the risky alternative preferable. Only the utility function distinguishes the analysis contained in this diagram from that depicted in Figure 7.2 and 7.3. Here a gain of $W_1 - W_2$ would add more to utility than an equal sized loss ($W_2 - W_0$) would subtract from it. Thus a 50–50 chance of such a gain or loss has a higher expected utility than the certainty of W_2. $W_3 - W_2$ measures the money value of the extent to which the uncertain alternative is preferred.

Insurance and Gambling: Further Analysis

If it is the case that increasing marginal utility of wealth implies gambling behaviour and decreasing marginal utility implies insuring, it would appear that an individual would always do one or the other. That is to

say, a person who insures against large risks will also insure against small risks; a person who insures a house will insure every other risk as well, and will not fill in football coupons; a person who backs horses will carry only the minimum legal motorcar insurance. Such predictions are contrary to even casually observable facts and present something of a problem for the analysis which we have just described. One way of dealing with such awkward facts proposed by Friedman and Savage is to suggest that though, in general, the marginal utility of wealth diminishes overall, it may increase locally.

The shape of the utility function implicit here is displayed in Figure 7.5. An individual might experience increasing marginal utility of wealth in the region of W_2 and hence gamble small amounts — this includes not insuring against small risks — and yet find that, for risks involving the possibility of large losses, the tendency of the utility function to display diminishing marginal utility of wealth was the dominant factor in the decision. The difficulty with this solution is that there seems to be no particular tendency for people at one particular level of wealth to gamble

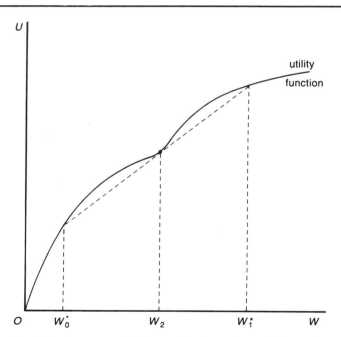

Figure 7.5

A utility function displaying successively decreasing, increasing and decreasing marginal utility of wealth. If an individual who has such a utility function is faced with the choice between W_2 with certainty and the 50–50 chance of W_0 and W_1, where the expected value of the uncertain outcome is W_2, then the risky alternative will be selected so long as W_0 and W_1 fall within the bounds given by W_0^* W_1^*. The individual will prefer the certain alternatives if they lie outside these bounds. This is a special case of a general tendency of individuals with such a utility function to take risks when the variations in wealth involved are relatively small and to insure when the variations are relatively large.

more on small amounts than do those who are better or worse off. It would be quite a coincidence if the workings of the economic system produced a distribution of wealth which gave each individual just that level of wealth at which its marginal utility was increasing. Virtually everyone, at every level of wealth, insures against some risks but not against others — hence gambling by default — nor does there appear to be any marked relationship between wealth and a propensity to engage in active gambling on the outcome of sporting events and games of chance.

Perhaps a more satisfactory approach to one aspect of this problem is to look more closely at the costs of running an insurance business. There obviously are administrative costs involved in selling insurance policies, and an insurance agent must cover these out of premium income. Thus, the agent can, in fact, never quite offer a fair bet to a customer. A premium must be charged that takes some of the consumer's surplus that would accrue to the customer were a completely fair bet offered. Now as the reader ought to be able to see easily enough, the smaller the loss which a particular consumer might face, the smaller the surplus accruing from buying insurance at a 'fair' premium. Thus, the less that consumer will be willing to pay above that fair premium to cover the insurance agent's costs of handling the transaction. But there is no reason to suppose that these costs decline in any kind of simple proportion as the value of the loss against which insurance is being sought declines. It might easily take the same amount of time and trouble to deal with the paperwork on a small policy as on a large one, and the same amount of work to assess the risk involved and calculate the fair premium. For insurance involving small amounts, these administrative costs might well exceed the consumer's surplus available to cover them.

In short, for some risks the gain from having the insurance at a 'fair' premium is outweighed by the administrative costs. Hence, it is not bought and the consumer gambles. This possibility is illustrated in Figure 7.6. The argument here is surely a plausible explanation of why individuals who insure against large risks nevertheless gamble by failing to buy cover against smaller ones. However, the argument does not explain why people *actively* undertake gambles. One avoids transaction costs by not filling in football coupons, and by not placing bets on horses. One incurs them by doing so, and they are, of course, covered by the football pool company or bookmaker shading the odds they offer in their own favour and away from a fair bet. Hence, to take account of transactions costs is to make it even more difficult to explain this type of gambling in terms of the analysis presented in this chapter. Only if one postulates that active gambling yields satisfaction to the individual who undertakes it over and above that which obtained from consuming winnings (if any) can one explain its occurring. This amounts to saying that some people gamble because they like gambling and is perilously close to being no explanation at all of the phenomenon.

Figure 7.6

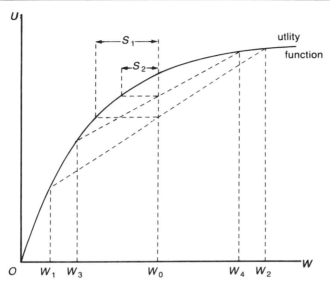

The gain from buying insurance at a fair premium against a 'large' risk: that of losing W_2 − W_1 with a 50 per cent probability is given by S_1. For a 'small' risk, that of losing W_4 − W_3 with a 50 per cent probability, the gain from insuring at a fair premium is S_2. For the smaller risk, the surplus available to pay administrative costs associated with taking out insurance is also smaller. Hence the individual is less likely to insure against small risks.

A Note on Moral Hazard and Adverse Selection

Other problems arise in the economics of insurance because the information held by the two parties to the trade is *asymmetric*; the insurance company does not have the same information as the individuals being insured. Two examples will serve to establish the point. Suppose individuals have some influence over the probability that the unfavourable outcome will occur. When they are insured, they will pay inadequate attention to ensuring that the insured-against outcome does not occur. This problem is called *moral hazard*, and can severely restrict the formation of a free market in insurance. For example, we may drive relatively more carelessly if we are insured against the consequences of a crash, and may be relatively less security conscious in the home if we are insured against burglary. Insurance companies obviously respond to this problem by specifying more precisely the responsibilities of the people purchasing insurance, for example, by making the first £100 of damage in the event of a car crash the responsibility of the insured, or by requiring them to fit window locks.

A second problem in insurance markets is known as *adverse selection*, which arises where the very act of selling insurance leads to demand for it by bad risks. Suppose there are two types of drivers: 'safe' and

'dangerous', with the latter having a higher probability of crashing. Clearly the insurance company would like to identify each separately and to sell insurance to the more risky group at a higher price. However, suppose there is no way for the insurance company to distinguish between the two groups of individuals, and that it offers to sell insurance at prices appropriate for low-risk individuals or for an average of dangerous and safe drivers. This price would be cheap for high-risk individuals, who would try to buy insurance and thereby lead the company to make a loss. The solution here of course is for the company to investigate the characteristics of 'dangerous' drivers, and to associate these with easily distinguishable features — age, gender, region of the country where they live, and so forth — which can form a basis for dispersion in insurance prices.

Concluding Comment

The analysis set out in this chapter has many applications to the behaviour of capital markets and insurance markets as well as firms and individuals. We therefore return to these issues in the later chapters of this book. It also underlies much of the modern work on inventory theory and on the monetary aspects of macroeconomics. As the reader will appreciate, then, this chapter has provided only the briefest introduction to a most important branch of modern micro theory.

8

Goods and their Attributes

Introduction

Our final examination of consumer behaviour involves an extension and reformulation of the theory of consumer choice rather than another application of it. We can by no means give a complete exposition of this alternative way of coming to grips with the problems we have already considered. We simply do not have the space to do so. Nevertheless, this view has provided insights into a number of problem areas in which the more conventional approach is rather unhelpful and even a brief exposition of its salient features enables this to be seen. The approach is mainly due to Kelvin Lancaster.

We still analyse the choice-making situation in terms of three basic components — the objects of choice, the constraint upon choice and the tastes in terms of which the choice is made — but we consider them in a rather different way. We have thought in terms of the consumer deriving utility from the consumption of goods, and the constraint upon consumption being a financial one given by income and the prices of goods. The key to the new approach lies in looking more closely at the connection between the possession of goods and the derivation of satisfaction from their consumption.

Goods, Attributes and Choice

The 'goods' which are bought by consumers on the market are virtually never commodities that yield a single well-defined service to their purchaser. Instead, they have a number of attributes and it is reasonable to

argue that it is these attributes which yield satisfaction in consumption, not the goods themselves. Thus a particular house or flat provides a whole variety of services to its occupier. It has a certain amount of floor space, a definite number of rooms, a particular quality of finish, a specific location relative to transport and recreational facilities, and so on; the list that one could draw up is virtually endless. Housing is a particularly complicated commodity to be sure, but even something as simple as a loaf of bread may be described in terms of attributes: its flavour, texture, colour, to say nothing of its nutritional characteristics, which are themselves a complex mixture of attributes.

Thus this approach to consumer theory views the objects of choice as being not the commodities which are available on the market, but their attributes. The utility function in terms of which choices are made deals not with bundles of goods, but with bundles of these attributes. What about the third ingredient of choice-making behaviour, the constraint upon choice? Instead of it being defined solely in terms of income and prices, it now must be defined in terms of income, prices and the technical characteristics of particular commodities available on the market. The demand for market goods and services is no longer to be regarded as the direct result of choice-making behaviour among bundles of such goods and services, but an indirect result of a more fundamental choice-making process.

The Basic Framework

Let us now look briefly at the way in which this new approach helps us to understand particular problems in economics. The reader will by now be used to our simplifying problems so as to render them tractable, and in this case we must simplify ruthlessly. We shall consider the case of a particular commodity, and shall assume that it has but two attributes. We shall also consider a highly artificial situation in which the consumer's volume of expenditure on that particular good is predetermined. In this way we can easily depict our problem in a two-dimensional diagram.

Let us then consider good X and treat it as having two attributes, R and S. The reader who wishes to give rather more concrete content to the analysis that follows, may think of X as being baked beans, and R measuring the number of beans and S the amount of tomato sauce, or of X as nut chocolate with the two attributes being an amount of chocolate and a quantity of nuts. In Figure 8.1 we measure not quantities of a good along the axes, but quantities of a particular attribute: any point on Figure 8.1 denotes a particular combination of attributes of good X. Now suppose that there were three brands of X available to the customer, each of which mixed the attributes in different proportions, with the first brand

Figure 8.1

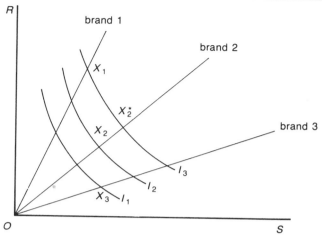

R and S are attributes of good X and the indifference curves describe a consumer's tastes *vis-à-vis* those attributes. Three brands of X are available, each combining the attributes in different proportions. X_1, X_2 and X_3 represent quantities of these different brands of X that can be bought for a given outlay. If constrained to spend just that amount, our consumer will choose to buy X_1 of brand 1, since I_3 is a higher indifference curve than I_2 or I_1.

having mostly attribute R and the third having mostly attribute S. Our consumer then can increase consumption of R and S in fixed proportions by moving out from the origin along any one of the three rays.

Associated with each point on any one of these rays is a price that must be paid to acquire just that combination of R and S. Tins of baked beans, if you like, have a price and, depending on the brand, contain different amounts of beans and sauce. In the artificial example which we are considering, we have endowed our individual with a fixed sum of money to spend on X, and with this sum that individual can just reach a particular point on each of the three rays. Let these points be X_1, X_2 and X_3 respectively. If our consumer is restricted to buying only one of the brands and is restricted to spending a fixed sum on that brand, then these three points represent the alternatives among which a choice must be made. They represent a highly discontinuous budget constraint. However, the important characteristic of the budget constraint as it is viewed in this approach is not its discontinuity, but the fact that it is no longer constructed on the basis simply of market data such as income and prices; the technical characteristics of particular goods also enter into it.

Tastes may be treated quite conventionally. We may draw an indifference map of the usual form which shows the consumer's preferences between bundles of attributes. Such a map, displaying a diminishing marginal rate of substitution between the attributes R and S, is drawn

in Figure 8.1, and the consumer, as always, goes to the point on the budget constraint that yields the highest level of satisfaction. In this case the consumer has but three points to choose among, and as Figure 8.1 is constructed, it is point X_1 that is on the highest indifference curve.

A Simple Application — Brand Loyalty

All this seems innocuous enough, and yet this analysis both makes predictions that are not given by the more conventional approach, and enables us to formulate questions about which that approach is silent. Consider first of all the simple question of the individual consumer's response to a fall in the price of a particular good. Conventional analysis predicts that as the price falls, more of the good in question will be bought, and that the bigger the price fall, the bigger will be the consumer's response. Consider, however, the consequences for the individual's behaviour of a fall in the price of just one brand of good X, say brand 2. The lower the price of this brand, the further out along the relevant ray does X_2 lie. However, unless it gets as far as X_2^* — the point at which the indifference curve passing through X_1 cuts ray 2 — there will be no effect whatsoever on our consumer's behaviour. Any price fall that enables the consumer to get beyond X_2^* will cause the entire consumption of X to be switched to this second brand.

Clearly, this is a very different kind of individual response to that predicted by orthodox demand theory. Instead of a smooth and continuous movement from the relatively expensive good towards consumption of one whose price is falling, there is an all or nothing shift the size of which is quite unrelated to the extent of the price fall. However, it should be noted at once that though the notion of a smooth downward-sloping demand curve is undermined here, it is only undermined at the level of the individual's behaviour. The aggregate demand for a particular brand of a good may still be smoothly downward sloping, but this property would come from the likelihood of different individuals having different tastes, and hence switching at different prices, to a brand whose price is falling.

Now the reader will have noted that in the foregoing discussion we referred to different 'brands' of X. The word did not crop up at all in our discussion of more conventional consumer theory. We derived demand curve for X on the assumption that it could be treated as a homogeneous product. However, product differentiation and the closely associated phenomenon of the use of brand names are wide-spread and conventional consumer theory has considerable difficulty in dealing with them. To try to apply such analysis to the empirical study of the market, even for so uncomplicated a product as baked beans, immediately leads one to ask questions about whether it is satisfactory to treat all brands

as if they were one homogeneous good, or whether each brand should be treated as a separate good. Only *ad hoc* answers are available to this question because the very notion of product differentiation has no place in conventional analysis. It starts after all by taking the product as given, as the basic object of choice. By treating the attributes of products as the basic objects of choice, the new approach enables us to talk about product differentiation as involving goods mixing basic attributes in different proportions. In using it to analyse a consumer's choice between three brands of a particular good, we have shown that there is no reason to expect that smooth substitution relationships will exist between brands of the same good. There is a range of price variation over which the individual will continue to consume a particular brand of X; we have thus given the notion of 'brand loyalty' — the phenomenon of continuing to buy a particular brand even though its price may have risen relative to others — a basis in economic theory, a basis which it does not have in the more conventional approach.

An Elaboration — Combining Brands

One assumption underlying the choice analysed in Figure 8.1 was that the consumer was unable to get any mix of attributes other than those made available by consuming one or another brand of X. The consumer was not able to mix brands. For some goods this is a reasonable enough assumption, but not for others. If the only difference between brands of baked beans was the ratio of beans to sauce in the tin, then by mixing the contents of different manufacturers' tins in different proportions, a much wider variety of combinations of attributes can be obtained. Indeed, in terms of Figure 8.2, a constant outlay could obtain any combination of attributes R and S along a straight line drawn between X_1 and X_2 by combining the first and second brand, between X_2 and X_3 by combining the second and third, and between X_1 and X_3 by combining the first and third. As the figure is constructed, however, the first and third brands would never be combined, since more of the good in question is always available in combinations involving brand 2. Given the tastes depicted in Figure 8.2, our individual will in fact combine brands 1 and 2 and settle at A. Should the price of brand 2 fall, a smooth substitution towards S will ensue, so long as this is not a Giffen attribute, but this may involve *either more or less* of brand 2 being purchased as is also shown in the figure.

This analysis is of interest for two reasons. First, it shows that the all or nothing nature of the response to a price change predicted in the previous section of this chapter is dependent upon the individual being unable to combine different brands of the same good in order to reach a personally preferred mixture of attributes, or at least unable to do so without incurring costs — which may be merely in terms of time and trou-

Figure 8.2

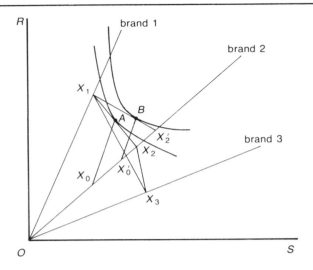

If brands can be mixed in order to obtain intermediate combinations of attributes, then a constant outlay on X enables our consumer to obtain R and S anywhere along the lines $X_1 X_2$, $X_2 X_3$ and $X_1 X_3$. Given tastes, the consumer will select combination A. If the price of brand 2 falls this is equivalent to a fall in the price of attribute S, since brand 2 contains relatively more of S than does brand 1. The consumer moves to point B and, for a given outlay, unambiguously increases outlay on S. Whether this also involves buying more of brand 2 is uncertain. Point A is reached by purchasing X_0 units of brand 2 and $A - X_0$ units of brand 1. Point B is reached by buying X_0' units of brand 2 and $B - X_0'$ units of brand 1. As the indifference curves are drawn, X_0' clearly exceeds X_0 so that more of brand 2 is bought. However, an indifference curve could easily be drawn tangent to $X_1 X_2'$ at a point which would involve X_0' being less than X_0.

ble — that more than offset any advantage that might be gained from so doing. Second, in showing that the demand for a particular brand of a good might fall as its own price falls, even though none of the attributes that make it up are inferior, the analysis warns us that the phenomenon of an upward-sloping demand curve might not be quite the practically irrelevant analytic curiosity that orthodox analysis of the Giffen good case might suggest.

Product Differentiation and Market Research

The foregoing considerations lead us immediately into another problem area. It is not unreasonable to suppose that manufacturers of particular goods will find it much easier to vary the proportions in which their output combines various attributes than will individual consumers. Consider Figure 8.3. Our consumer with a given outlay to make on X will buy brand 1 so long as only three versions of the product are there to be chosen

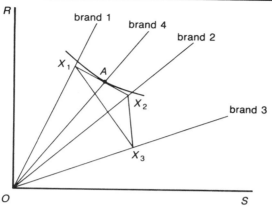

Figure 8.3

If, at going prices, enough consumers prefer *R* and *S* combined in the proportion given by *A*, it might pay a firm to introduce a brand 4 that would appeal to such consumers.

among. However, consider that combination of attributes that lies along the ray labelled 4. If some manufacturer can produce a new brand of *X* that combines *R* and *S* in these proportions, and offer it for sale at a price that enables our consumer to reach a point above and to the right of *A* for the given outlay, the consumer will switch to that brand. Given the particular tastes depicted in Figure 8.3, the consumer will be better off in so doing. If there are enough consumers with such tastes, and if it is technically feasible, there is a strong incentive for some firm, or firms, to produce brand 4.

The line of reasoning implicit in this very simple example helps us to understand two pervasive phenomena in everyday economic life. First, not every consumer will have the same tastes and hence we can begin to see why it will pay firms, and indeed even the same firm, to produce an array of brands of the same good, each one having slightly different attributes. Moreoever, there is no reason to suppose that any firm can possibly know *a priori* just how many of its potential customers prefer particular combinations of attributes in a particular product; but without such knowledge it would be all too easy to 'miss the market'. The importance of market research to firms becomes much easier to understand when we look at it in this light.

Advertising

If product differentiation and market research are phenomena that are illuminated by this new approach to consumer theory, it will come as no surprise to the reader to learn that it is also helpful in the analysis

of advertising. Consider what the conventional analysis set out in previous chapters enables us to say about advertising. Consumers have given tastes *vis-à-vis* goods, and, given these tastes, do the best they can for themselves in the light of their incomes and the market prices that rule. Traditional analysis makes it difficult indeed to deal with advertising, for everything is presumed to be known to the consumer, but it does not take too much of a stretch of the imagination to realise that consumers in fact do not have perfect information. There is no reason to suppose that a consumer knows either the full array of prices ruling in the market at any time, or just who has what to sell. Clearly, there is room for an industry that specialises in conveying such information, so that there is room for 'informative advertising' in conventional analysis. But even quite casual observation soon convinces one that there is a lot more to contemporary advertising practices than conveying information about who has what to sell at what price. Estate agents' advertisements in local newspapers perform this role, but what about detergent advertisements on television? Prices and names of stockists are seldom, if ever, mentioned.

Such advertising is obviously aimed at persuading consumers to purchase one brand of a good rather than another, and since it hardly makes sense to suggest that consumers do not know their own tastes, the only way to fit such advertising into conventional analysis is to suggest that it is designed to change tastes, to shift the consumers' indifference maps. There is no need to dwell on the social and political implications of this interpretation. However, given conventional consumer theory, there is no other way of interpreting such advertising. The approach outlined in this chapter does leave room for an alternative interpretation without however ruling out the possibility that one of advertising's roles is to mould tastes.

If consumers do know their own tastes and advertising does not in fact change those tastes, then it must inform consumers about the objects of choice and about the constraints upon choice. Think of consumers having tastes for the attributes of goods, rather than directly for the goods themselves. Think also of different brands of a particular good combining attributes in different proportions so that the technical characteristics of particular brands are components of the constraint on the consumer's choice. There is no reason for us to suppose that consumers are familiar with the technical characteristics of each particular brand. We may then view advertising as informing consumers about what brands of a particular good are available, where, and at what price, and we can also think of it as informing them about the attributes of particular brands.

Thus, advertising that does not stress information about market prices and such, and which, in terms of conventional consumer choice theory, must be interpreted as having to do with an attempt to change tastes, may, in terms of this approach, be interpreted as informative. Consider, for example, car advertising that typically stresses such characteristics as

fuel economy, passenger carrying capacity, manoeuverability, acceleration, and so on. This is not to say that such advertising *must* be so interpreted, or that it is necessarily correct to interpret it so; only that an alternative hypothesis is available in the context of this new analysis. Which is correct is an empirical question that must await the formulation and performance of empirical tests designed to distinguish between them, but it is a strong point in favour of looking at goods in terms of their attributes that it opens up the possibility of formulating such tests.

Concluding Comment

In this chapter we have outlined a different approach to the analysis of consumer choice, based on the attributes of goods rather than the commodities themselves. This approach is rather more complex than that taken in our previous discussion, and suggests that individual demand curves may not be smoothly downward sloping after all. It also helps us to understand a number of 'real-world' phenomena not well explained by conventional consumer theory; brand loyalty, product differentiation and advertising. We shall discuss some of these issues from the perspective of the supplier in Chapter 16.

Questions for Study and Discussion for Part II

1. Suppose that income and leisure are perfect substitutes. Use indifference curve and budget line diagrams to illustrate the cases when

    (a) the individual will work for every hour available;
    (b) the individual will not work at all;
    (c) the individual will work an indeterminate number of hours.

2. An individual is known to increase the hours per week worked when non-wage income is decreased. What will happen to the hours worked if (a) a proportional income tax is levied on wage income; (b) a proportional income tax is levied on total income; and (c) a proportional tax on wage income is used solely to finance an increase in non-wage income?
    Would any of your answers differ if the individual were known to decrease working hours when non-wage income decreased?
3. Discuss the impact of an increase in the marginal rate of income tax on the individual's supply of labour, on the assumption that leisure is a Giffen good. What are the implications for the market wage rate

and employment level? Under what conditions will the labour market be unstable?

4. Draw the two-period budget constraints implied by the following information:

   (a) income this period $50
        income next period $50
        rate of interest   10%

   (b) income this period $50
        income next period $50
        rate of interest   5%

   (c) income this period $0
        income next period $105
        rate of interest   10%

   (d) income this period $0
        income next period $105
        rate of interest   5%

   (e) income this period $100
        income next period $100
        rate of interest   10%

   (f) income this period $100
        income next period $100
        rate of interest   5%

   (g) income this period $50
        income next period $165
        rate of interest   10%

   (h) income this period $50
        income next period $165
        rate of interest   5%

5. Show that (a) if an individual borrows by selling bonds at a particular value of the rate of interest, a fall in the rate of interest will lead to more borrowing; (b) if current and future consumption are both normal goods, then if the individual borrows by taking out a fixed capital value loan, a fall in the rate of interest will also lead to more borrowing.

6. It is known that, were the current period's income increased by £100, an individual would increase current consumption by £80. If the rate of interest is 10 per cent, what will be the effect on the same individual's current consumption of a guaranteed increase in next period's income of £110?

7. Two individuals have the same tastes *vis-à-vis* consumption now and in the future, and the same endowment of resources. One of them can engage in home production at a constant rate of return of 5 per cent, but is excluded from the capital market to which the other has access and where the rate of interest is 6 per cent. Can

we predict which one will enjoy the higher level of consumption in the initial period?

8. Draw the budget constraints on the work/leisure choice implied by the following information.

    (a) non-wage income $100 per week
        wage rate $4 per hour
    (b) non-wage income $200 per week
        wage rate $2 per hour
    (c) non-wage income $200 per week
        wage rate for first
        40 hours $2 per hour
        wage rate for hours
        above 40 $4 per hour
    (d) non-wage income   0
        wage for 40-hour
        week with no hours
        less than 40 $120 per week
        permitted
        overtime rate $5 per hour

9. We have information on the consumption choices between X and Y of an individual in two successive time periods. In each she spends all of her income. In the first time period, the price of X is £100, the price of Y is £100 and she consumes 10 units of X and Y respectively. In the second time period, the price of X is £150 and of Y is £150. She consumes 7 units of X and 11 units of Y respectively. Do we have enough information to conclude that here tastes have changed between the two periods?

*10. An individual, A, survives for two time periods, 1 and 2. In the first, he works, earns W and consumes C_1. In the second, he is retired and receives a pension, out of which he consumes C_2. We assume that the pension is non-contributory, and the rate is set to ensure that post-retirement earnings equal half of wages during his working life. The individual's utility function is $U(C_1, C_2) = C_1^{\frac{1}{2}} C_2^{\frac{1}{2}}$, and the rate of interest is 10 per cent.

    (a) How much does individual A save during his working life (period 1)?

    (b) What is the impact on A's savings during period 1 of an increase in the rate of interest to 15 per cent?

    (c) What is the impact on A's savings during period 1 of an increase in the non-contributory pension rate to three-quarters of the wage in period 1?

    (d) Suppose that there were another individual, B, who attached relatively less weight to consumption during the retirement period, so $U(C_1, C_2) = C_1^{\frac{2}{3}} C_2^{\frac{1}{3}}$. If we return to an interest rate

of 10 per cent and a 50 per cent non-contributory pension in period 2, does person *B* save more than person *A*?

12. Consider the following lottery tickets:

   (a) ticket 1 gives a return of £600 with a probability of 0.03 and a zero return otherwise;
   (b) ticket 2 gives a return of £100 with a probability of 0.18 and a zero return otherwise;
   (c) ticket 3 gives a return of £36 with a probability of 0.5 and a zero return otherwise.

   Individual *A* is willing to pay prices P_1, P_2 and P_3 for tickets 1, 2 and 3 respectively.

   Suppose that individual *A* is risk averse. What can we say about the absolute and relative values of P_1, P_2 and P_3? In what ways will the answer be different if the individual is risk neutral?

13. An individual has the utility function, $U = W^{1/2}$, where *W* denotes wealth, and is considering a bet in which there is a 30 per cent chance of winning £49 clear, and a 70 per cent chance of winning nothing.

   (a) Will the individual take the bet if it costs £5?
   (b) Will he or she take it if it costs £2?
   (c) Will he or she take it at a cost of £5 if utility function takes the form $U = W$?
   (d) Will he or she take it at a cost of £20 if the utility function takes the form $U = W$?
   (e) Will he or she take it at a cost of £20 if the utility function takes the form $U = W^2$?

14. Discuss why people typically choose to underinsure the contents of their houses in their domestic insurance policies.

15. It was asserted in chapter 8 that a fall in the price of a particular brand of good could lead to less of it being demanded. Where the good in question has two attributes, *R* and *S* (a) could this happen if *R* and *S* were substitutes for each other; and (b) must it happen if they are complements?

Suggested Further Reading to Part II

Alchian, A. 1953. 'The Meaning of Utility Measurement', *American Economic Review.* Reprinted in Breit and Hochman (*op. cit.*).

Arrow, K.J. 1971. *Essays in the Theory of Risk Bearing.* Amsterdam, North-Holland.

Auld, D. 1972. 'Imperfect Knowledge and the New Theory of Demand', *Journal of Political Economy.*

Becker, G. 1965. 'A Theory of the Allocation of Time', *Economic Journal.*

Ehrenberg, R.G. and Smith, R.S. 1982. *Modern Labor Economics.* Glenview, Ill: Scott, Foresman.

Friedman, M. 1957. *A Theory of the Consumption Function*. Princeton, NJ: Princeton University Press for the NBER, chs 1–3.

Friedman, M. and Savage, L.J. 1953. 'The Utility Analysis of Choices Involving Risks', *Journal of Political Economy*, 1948. Reprinted in Stigler, G.J. and Boulding K.E. (eds) on behalf of the American Economic Association *Readings in Price Theory*. London: Allen & Unwin.

Hey, J.D. 1979. *Uncertainty in Microeconomics*. Oxford: Martin Robertson.

Hirschleifer, J. 1958. 'On the Theory of Optimal Investment Decision', *Journal of Political Economy*.

Killingsworth, M.R. 1983. *Labour Supply*. Cambridge: Cambridge University Press.

Lancaster, K. 1966. 'A New Approach to Consumer Theory', *Journal of Political Economy*.

Lancaster, K. 1971. *Consumer Demand: A New Approach*. New York: Columbia University Press.

Robbins, L.C. 1946. 'On the Elasticity of Demand for Income in Terms of Effort', *Economica*, 1930. Reprinted in Fellner, W. and Haley, B.F. (eds) on behalf of the American Economic Association, *Readings in the Theory of Income Distribution*. Philadelphia: Blakiston.

Tobin, J. 1965. 'Liquidity Preference as Behaviour Towards Risk', *Review of Economic Studies*, 1958. Reprinted in Mueller, M.J. (ed.) *Readings in Macroeconomics*. New York: Holt Rinehart and Winston.

Von Neumann, J. and Morgenstern, O. 1944. *Theory of Games and Economic Behaviour*. Princeton: Princeton University Press.

Part III

PRODUCTION AND COSTS

9

Production and the Firm

Introduction

Up to now, the analysis presented in this book has concerned itself with consumer choice, and in particular with the allocation of income among expenditures on various goods and services. It hardly needs pointing out that the goods and services which consumers purchase do not simply materialise out of the blue. In large measure they have to be produced. Moreover, we have also seen that important elements in consumer decision making involve, not the purchase of goods and services, but the sale of productive services, not least labour services. Of course, it is these very services that are used in the production of goods which in turn become the objects of the consumer's demand. In short, the analysis of consumer behaviour, vital though it is to an understanding of economic life, cannot tell us the whole story. The study of consumption needs to be supplemented by a study of production and it is to the analysis of production that the next five sections of this book are devoted.

Production

The essential fact about production is so obvious that it hardly needs stating: it involves the use of services of various sorts to generate output. However, productive services do not usually come together spontaneously, their use is typically organised in some way. Clearly, the manner in which production is organised has important social and political, as well as economic aspects, and much of what follows is relevant to more than one form of social and economic organisation. For example, the technical relationships between flows of inputs of productive services and flows of outputs are just as relevant to the student of

production processes organised by socialist planners as they are to the student of the private profit-making firm, as indeed is the relationship between such technical relationships and the analysis of costs of production. Production costs are, after all, as relevant to the manager of a collectively owned enterprise as to the manager of a privately owned firm. Indeed, the reader who pursues studies of microeconomics into the area of the economics of socialism will find that many of the principles which we shall develop below in the context of studying the behaviour of the profit-maximising firm also have important applications to questions about how to organise an economy where the means of production are collectively owned.

Nevertheless, the following chapters do take certain social and political conditions for granted inasmuch as they are overwhelmingly concerned with decisions about the production of goods and services as they arise in the context of an economy where such decisions are taken by privately owned, and (in the main) profit-oriented firms. We have already noted that production involves the organisation of flows of inputs in order to generate flows of output, and we are going to analyse the decisions that underlie such organisation as they are taken by privately owned firms. Now of course, in the real world, firms come in many shapes and sizes ranging from the family owned corner business all the way to the giant multinational, multiproduct corporation, and there is no way in which a book as brief as this one could come to grips with all the manifold details of the organisation and operation of such a wide variety of concerns. Thus, the theory of the firm as we shall present it will be abstract and will concentrate on certain properties, one hopes the essential ones, that all such enterprises have in common.

The Firm and the Entrepreneur

The firm, as we shall analyse it, is a social entity that carries out three activities. It buys productive services, organises them so as to produce output, and then sells the output. Its task is to take the decisions upon which the organisation of production depend, and economists have often found it useful to personify this decision-making role in the form of being called the *entrepreneur*. There is no need literally to postulate that any one human being in a particular firm takes all the decisions about input purchases, the choice of technology, and the marketing of output, to make the concept of an entrepreneur a useful one. It is sufficient to realise that in any undertaking such decisions must be made in a mutually consistent way in order to see that it might be a useful abstraction to think about those decisions 'as if' they were all taken by one individual.

One thing that the reader should be careful about here is not to confuse the entrepreneur with another personification of a particular social

function who sometimes turns up in discussions of the behaviour of market economies, namely the 'capitalist'. 'Capitalists' certainly exist as far as the following analysis is concerned, but only in the background. It is their role to own the capital equipment used by the firm in the production process, and to sell its services to the entrepreneur. Their income is derived from their ownership of capital, and is just as distinct from the entrepreneur's income as is their function in the organisation of production. The entrepreneur's 'profit' is what is left from the proceeds of sales after the labour force has been paid for its services and capitalists have been paid for the use of their equipment.

To say that it is the task of the entrepreneur to plan and oversee the execution of the productive activities undertaken by the firm against the background of a market economy raises the following issue. It is often argued that a market economy operates so as to organise in a harmonious way the activities of numerous individual agents without any person or institution having to formulate an overall plan for the economy as a whole. The information and incentives conveyed to individual agents by prices are supposed to be sufficient to ensure that each one of them, pursuing their own self-interests, act in a way that is compatible with the activities of everyone else without supervision of any sort. We analyse this proposition in Part VIII. Such an argument, taken to an extreme, would seem to rule out the existence of firms as social institutions and to give no scope for entrepreneurial activity. It is after all of the very essence of a firm that those who provide productive services to it act under supervision, in accordance with a plan laid down by the entrepreneur, rather than as free agents making voluntary choices about their activities at each and every instant in response to price signals.

The apparent paradox involved here was first noted by Karl Marx who used it to help justify the usefulness of what we would now call socialist planning for an industrial economy. He argued that if planning is useful at the level of the firm, it must be useful at the level of the economy as a whole as well. Much modern work in the field of industrial organisation, particularly that pioneered by Ronald Coase, rests upon an alternative response to this same paradox. The basis of that response is to note that whether any particular set of activities will be co-ordinated within a firm on a planning basis or between individual agents by the use of market mechanisms, will depend on the relative costs of doing so in one way or the other. According to this view, market transactions *per se* are costly to undertake, so that if an entrepreneur can plan and co-ordinate aspects of individuals' behaviour more cheaply than they can be organised by market mechanisms, they can be compensated in the incomes they receive for the sacrifice of freedom they make in committing themselves in advance to obeying orders for the period of time for which they agree to work. In short, production activities come to be organised within firms when it is economical to do so.

This line of reasoning has enabled economists to begin to come to grips with a whole range of problems having to do with the factors that determine the extent of vertical and horizontal integration within industries and the way in which mergers between firms come about, not to mention many aspects of the behaviour of bureaucratic organisations both in the private and the public sectors. To deal with this wide range of subject matter would take us far beyond the scope of this book, but as they work through the analysis of the behaviour of the firm that follows, readers should constantly bear in mind that the analysis in question simply takes it for granted that firms exist. A deeper treatment of the way in which firms operate might go into the question of why they exist, and how they might evolve over time, along the lines so briefly described in the last few paragraphs. As we have already noted, such analysis does exist, and the material that follows in this book should therefore be regarded as constituting an introduction to the analysis of the behaviour of firms and industries, rather than as being anything approaching a comprehensive account of this branch of microeconomics.

Concluding Comment

As has already been remarked, there are certain technical matters inevitably involved in the analysis of production that involve the processes whereby inputs are transformed into outputs, and the properties of the relationships involved here impinge upon all aspects of the behaviour of the firm. Thus, in the next chapter, we begin our detailed analysis by considering the *production function* in terms of which these relationships are summarised, and having done that will then proceed to analyse the nature of production costs. Only when we have laid this groundwork will it be possible to proceed to consider the decisions that the entrepreneur will take for the firm *vis-à-vis* its activities in the markets for its outputs and its inputs. These matters form the subject matter of Parts V, VI, VII and VIII of this book.

10

Properties of the Production Function

Introduction

Just as market prices and income constrain the behaviour of households, so the technological possibilities of production constrain the decisions taken by the entrepreneur about the behaviour of the firm. The basic framework of the theory of the firm must concern itself to an important degree with the technical relationships involved in the transformation of such inputs as the services of labour and capital equipment into outputs of goods and services. That is why we devote this and the next part of this book to dealing with these production relationships.

The notion of production is very general. Not only are physical goods produced, but also services, such as transportation, education, insurance and so forth. Any process which involves the transformation of one kind (or kinds) of good or service into another may be thought of as a process of production. However, as with consumption, so with production we can reduce the situation to an extremely basic and simple form and deal in detail with a fairly special case in order to get to grips with fundamental issues.

Therefore, in this chapter we will consider the production of good X, and will presume that there are but two inputs to its production. We will refer to these inputs, *factors of production* as they are usually called, as capital (K) and labour (L). It should be noted at the outset that just as the production of X is to be thought of as a *flow* of output, so the inputs into the production process should also be thought of in flow terms: K and L represent machine-hours and man-hours of productive services, not a stock of capital and a labour force.

The reader should not infer that it is possible to add together the services of all the manifold types of equipment and inventories used in a modern production process to give one unambiguous index number that measures the 'quantity of capital services' employed. Nor may one necessarily aggregate the hours worked by people of many different skills directly involved in production, to say nothing of those indirectly involved in a management or sales promotion role, into some unambiguously measurable quantity called 'the services of the labour force'. Nevertheless, the results of the two input/one output special case are both useful and often capable of being generalised, and are therefore well worth the reader's attention.

Activities and the Isoquant

We start with the most primitive concept in the analysis of production, an 'activity'. Carrying on an activity means combining flows of factor services per unit of time in a particular proportion and getting a rate of flow of output from doing so. Thus, in Figure 10.1 we depict an activity that involves combining machine services and labour services in the ratio 2/1 by a line labelled 1, and another that combines them in equal proportions by a line labelled 2. It is a reasonable initial simplifying assumption that if one doubles the quantities of inputs in any particular activity one will also double output, or, to put it more generally, that equiproportional increases in inputs will lead to equiproportional increases in output. This is the assumption of *constant returns to scale*. An equal distance moved

Figure 10.1

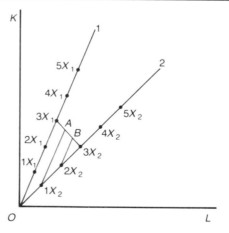

Inputs K and L are combined in given proportions along rays 1 and 2 in 'activities' that yield equal increments in the output of X for equal increments to inputs. Activity 1 and activity 2 may be combined at level of output $3X$ (or at any other level of output) to make any combination of capital and labour along the line $3X_1$, $3X_2$ available as a means of producing that level of output.

along each activity line in Figure 10.1 thus represents an equal increase in both inputs and output.

Now there is no obvious reason why a firm should be confined exclusively to one production activity or another. It could presumably mix them. Thus, in Figure 10.1 it could produce an output of say 3X units of X by using all activity 1, all activity 2, or, by combining these activities in different proportions, it could obtain that level of output by combining capital and labour services anywhere along the line joining $3X_1$ and $3X_2$. For example, 3X units of X could be achieved by producing 2X units by activity 1 and 1X by activity 2, thus ending up at point A. The same output could be reached by producing 1X unit with activity 1 and 2X units with activity 2 thus ending up at point B. Readers who have worked through Chapter 8 will recognise the similarity between this analysis and that set out there where we considered the possibilities of mixing different brands of a particular good in order to obtain a mixture of attributes between those available from exclusive consumption of one brand or another.

There is no reason to confine the analysis to the case of a firm having just two activities available to it. In principle, the analysis can be extended to an indefinitely large number of activities, but, for the sake of clarity alone, in Figure 10.2 we depict the case of four available activities, each using capital and labour services in different proportions. Any pair of activities may be used together, and so we have linked up each available pair of activities with straight lines as we did in Figure 10.1.

At this point in the argument, even when apparently dealing with purely technological matters, we must introduce an assumption about the firm's motivation and behaviour if we are to proceed further. This

---

Figure 10.2

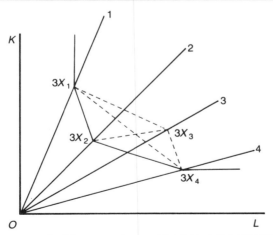

With four activities, any pair of them may be combined. Here the solid kinked line passing through $3X_1$, $3X_2$ and $3X_4$ shows the minimum combinations of capital and labour that will produce 3X units of output. Above activity line 1, this isoquant becomes vertical and to the right of activity line 4 it becomes horizontal, because further additions to inputs in these directions add nothing to output.

assumption is that, whatever motivates those running the firm, they will never use more units of input than are necessary to get a given output. As we have drawn Figure 10.2, any output plan that utilises activity 3 requires more inputs for a given output than any plan that does not use it. This activity is said to be *technically* inefficient and will not be used by a firm seeking to minimise the inputs used for any output. Moreover, any combination of 1 and 4 uses more inputs than combinations of 1 and 2 and 3 and 4, or 1, 2 and 4 alone. Thus, the kinked line linking the points $3X_1$, $3X_2$ and $3X_4$ gives the locus of the minimum combinations of factor inputs required for an output of $3X$ given prevailing technology. The line becomes vertical beyond $3X_1$ and horizontal beyond $3X_4$ to indicate that further increases of capital and labour beyond these points add nothing to output.

This kinked line is a simple special case of a much used analytic device in the economics of production. The output of X is the same at any point on it, and hence it is known as an 'equal product curve' or an 'iso-product curve' or, most frequently, an *isoquant*. The most important property of an isoquant is already implicit in the simple analysis carried out in Figure 10.2. It will never be concave towards the origin, and will in general be convex. In terms of Figure 10.2, the isoquant would have been concave to the origin if activity 3 had been used in its construction, for it would have contained the segment $3X_2\ 3X_3\ 3X_4$, but this segment is not part of the isoquant, because for any point on it there is a point on the line $3X_2\ 3X_4$ at which the same amount of output could be produced using fewer inputs.

In Figure 10.1, with two technically efficient activities we have a straight line isoquant; in Figure 10.2, with three such activities we have an isoquant that is kinked convexly to the origin. But we have already remarked that there is no need to confine ourselves to considering small numbers of activities. The more technically efficient activities there are, each using capital and labour services in different proportions, the more kinks there will be in the isoquant, and the more will it come to resemble a smooth curve, convex to the origin. Just as along a particular consumer's indifference curve we plot all those bundles of goods the consumption of which will yield equal satisfaction, so along a smooth isoquant we plot all those combinations of factor services that will yield an equal level of output. A great deal of analysis is considerably simplified, with no important loss of accuracy, if we treat the various technically efficient factor combinations that will produce a given level of output as lying along a smooth curve such as, for example, $3X$ in Figure 10.3.

The Production Function

The previous section of this chapter was concerned with the various ways in which a particular level of output, $3X$ units of X, could be produced.

Figure 10.3

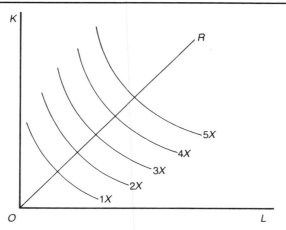

A smooth production function. The isoquants show the maximum level of output to be had for each combination of inputs. As we move out along any ray (such as *OR*) drawn from the origin, inputs of capital and labour increase in equal proportions.

The choice of this output level was, of course, quite arbitrary, and we could have carried out exactly the same analysis for any other level of output. Hence, there is not just one isoquant implicit in the foregoing analysis, but a whole family thereof, one for each conceivable level of output. A map of such isoquants is shown in Figure 10.3, which is a geometric representation of a *production function*. The output of X depends on — that is to say, is a *function* of — inputs of capital and labour services into the process. The isoquant map of Figure 10.3 tells us, for any combination of factor inputs, what the maximum attainable output of X will be. Equivalently, it also tells us, for any given level of output of X, what are the minimum combinations of inputs necessary to produce it. Provided that we are willing to think of inputs as being divisible into infinitely small units and of output as being similarly divisible, then we may also think of there being a smooth continuous isoquant passing through every point in Figure 10.3. However, as with the indifference map in consumer theory, it suffices for analytic purposes to draw only a selection of these. The rest of this chapter is devoted to looking at the properties of the production function in more detail.

Long-Run and Short-Run Analysis

To begin with, it will be useful to distinguish in general terms between two types of analysis: *'long-run'* analysis, which concerns the period when all inputs can be varied simultaneously, and *'short-run'* analysis, when some factors are assumed to be fixed and increments to output are assumed to derive solely from changes to variable factors. If the inputs

are assumed to be capital and labour, then capital is taken to be the fixed factor in the short run, and labour the variable one. If we consider Figure 10.3 as a contour map for a three-dimensional diagram, with output rising vertically from the origin *O*, the long-run properties of the production function describe the shape of the whole hill. Within that context, we will be concerned with *returns to scale*, which describe the slope of the hill along a fixed capital—labour ratio (such as *OR*) from the origin, and the degree of *substitutability* between inputs, which has to do with the curvature around the hill at a given level of output, or the shape of the isoquant. The *short-run production function* describes the relationship between output and labour input for a given level of capital, and can be imagined as being characterised by a slice through the hill at any given level of capital $\bar{K}$. The relevant property of the short-run production function concerns how output varies with labour input alone or, more generally, *returns to a factor*.

The Long-Run Production Function: Some Preliminaries

Algebraically, we specify the two input production function depicted in Figure 10.3 as

$$X = f(L,K) \tag{10.1}$$

We typically assume $f(\cdot)$ to be a *monotonic* function, one in which X rises as either L or K, or both, rise. It should always be possible to produce at least as much output as in an initial situation by using at least as much of each input as in that situation. This proposition implies that the firm can always dispose costlessly of inputs which are surplus to the minimum required to produce a given level of output, a characteristic sometimes referred to as *free disposal*.

Much of the analysis which follows will draw on the relationship between two variables which characterise the production function (10.1). First, the *average product* of a factor is output per unit of time divided by factor input per unit of time: X/L for labour and X/K for capital. These ratios are sometimes referred to, rather loosely, as labour and capital *productivity* respectively. Second, the *marginal product* of a factor is the increment to output per unit of time for an increment of a factor input per unit of time, holding the other factor input constant. In the limit, when the increments become infinitesimal, they are therefore the partial derivatives of the production function (10.1). Hence $\partial X/\partial L$ is the marginal product of labour and $\partial X/\partial K$ is the marginal product of capital.

Returns to Scale

The concept of 'returns to scale' refers to what happens to output when every input is increased in equal proportion. In terms of a diagram such

as Figure 10.3, equiproportional increases in both inputs involve moving out along a straight line, a ray, drawn from the origin. In general, we may speak of production functions displaying decreasing returns to scale, constant returns to scale, and increasing returns to scale. If successive equal increments of all factor inputs yield successively smaller increases in output, we have decreasing (or diminishing) returns to scale, if they yield equal increments in output we have constant returns to scale, and if they yield successively increasing increments in output we have increasing returns to scale.

The notion of returns to scale can be related to the production function (10.1) in the following way. Take equation (10.1) and note that if we start with a given level of inputs K and L, we will have some level of output X. Now, multiply K and L by some factor t, and note that output will change by some related multiplicative factor α. Thus we may write

$$\alpha X = f(tL, tK) \tag{10.2}$$

If, as we vary t, α varies in the same proportion, we have constant returns to scale; if it varies proportionately more, we have increasing returns; and if it varies proportionately less, we have decreasing returns.

Strictly speaking, statements about returns to scale characterise what happens over a particular range along a given ray through the origin, and do not necessarily describe the whole production function. If all we require of our isoquants is that they be smooth and convex to the origin, then it is easy indeed to construct a production function which yields constant returns along some rays and diminishing (or increasing) returns along others, or which yields successively increasing, constant and diminishing returns along the same ray. Nevertheless, there are special types of functional relationships for which what is true of one section of one ray through the origin is true of all sections of all rays. One class of such functions is called *homogeneous functions*.

Mathematically speaking a production function is homogeneous of degree k if

$$t^k X = t^k f(L,K) = f(tL, tK) \tag{10.3}$$

where k is a constant, $t > 0$ and, in terms of the notation used in (10.2), $t^k \equiv \alpha$. Homogeneity implies two characteristics in the two input case. The first is that *all* the isoquants that cut *any one* ray through the origin do so with the same slope. This characteristic is known as *homotheticity*. Homothetic isoquants which are equidistant from one another along any one ray are also equidistant along any other. To move from one isoquant to another represents a definite cardinally measurable change in the level of output. The second characteristic of a homogeneous production function is that it displays the same returns to scale characteristics along any ray regardless of the input combination represented by that ray. Figure 10.4, in fact, depicts a special case of such a relationship: the constant returns to scale special case. Such a production function displays

Figure 10.4

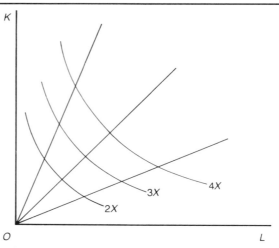

A 'homogeneous of degree one' production function. As we move out along any ray
through the origin, equal increments in input yield equal increments in output. All
isoquants have the same slope as they pass through any particular ray.

homogeneity of degree one. As the reader will see by comparing equations
(10.2) and (10.3), $\alpha = t^k = t$ where k = 1, so that $d\alpha/dt = 1$.

If we return to thinking of the production function diagrammatically
as a contour map of a hill, we can see that the assumption of homogeneity makes life a lot easier for us in describing the shape of the hill. It means
that, as we walk up the hill in any fixed direction (along *OR*, for example,
Figure 10.3), the slope is changing at a constant rate. If we have constant
returns to scale, that constant rate of change of the slope is in fact zero;
that is a slice through the hill from the origin along a *K/L* ray plots a
straight line. Constant returns to scale are therefore a characteristic of what
is often called *linear* production technology. The property of homotheticity
implied by homogeneity means that the rate of change of the slope of
the hill is not just constant but is the same along every possible *K/L* ray
from the origin. The convenience of the assumption of homogeneity is
this. It enables us to provide a simple summary statistic, a single number
measuring the degree of homogeneity of the function, that describes the
way in which output changes with all inputs. This statistic is independent of both the level of output used and of the capital—labour ratio. These
properties are so convenient that homogeneity is a commonly made
assumption in applied work on production functions.

Homogeneity is a very strong assumption to make about the nature
of technology, however. It is not hard to think of examples where returns
to scale are initially increasing with output, and then become either constant or diminishing beyond a certain point. In the former case the output level where increasing returns change into constant returns is called
minimum efficient scale of production. We will return to this notion again

when we consider the shape of *cost functions*, the nature of which will be shown to be directly associated with the returns to scale characteristics of the production function. The point to note at this stage is that though homogeneity implies homotheticity as a characteristic of a production function, homotheticity does not require homogeneity. To put it precisely, homogeneity is sufficient for homotheticity, but it is not necessary. Homotheticity is in fact a weaker assumption, which can be retained even after the assumption of homogeneity has been relaxed.

Factors Leading to Variable Returns to Scale

Now the production function derived from activity analysis obviously displays constant returns to scale and the question must arise as to how any production function could display any other characteristic? The key simplifying assumption that yields this property is that it is possible to carry on any activity, with equal efficiency, at any level of output. This need not always be so. In agriculture, for example, it is not the case that, simply by halving all inputs, including the size of the field, one also halves output, nor that output can be doubled merely by doubling all inputs. There are technical indivisibilities here that make it impossible to utilise certain types of technology at small output levels and that make it preferable to switch from one technical process to another as the scale of output changes. The type of harvesting equipment used on large North American type farms cannot be used effectively on the small farms that at one time dominated British agriculture, and are still widespread on the Continent of Europe. Or, to give another example, in the battery production of eggs, if one wishes to double the number of hens housed, it is far from clear that it is technically most efficient to double the air space of the buildings in which they are housed. There is no reason to suppose that the amount of inputs needed to heat the henhouses in question will be doubled for, even if one did just double the airspace of the building by, for example, doubling its floor area one would not double the area of its outside surfaces, nor would one double its propensity to heat loss. Nor, of course, would one double the building materials required to erect the building by doubling its air space.

We could multiply examples like this *ad nauseam*, but enough ought now to have been said to convince the reader that a production function that everywhere displays constant returns to scale is a special case, albeit, perhaps, a useful and relevant special case. *A priori*, there is nothing in general that can be said about the returns to scale characteristics of production functions. One can have decreasing, constant or increasing returns to scale, or indeed a combination of all three in any production function. It depends upon the nature of the technology that is available to a particular industry.

Substitutability

Substitutability, the second key property of production functions to which we referred earlier, characterises the rate at which capital can be used to replace, or can be *substituted* for, labour (or vice versa) in the production process, while holding output constant. Two limiting cases of substitutability can easily be identified.

Suppose first that the firm only has one production activity available to it. For example, suppose we require 3 machines and 5 people to produce one unit of X; 6 machines and 10 people to produce two units of X; and so on. If we have only 6 machines, the maximum attainable output level is therefore $6X$, regardless the number of workers available. Additional workers can produce nothing without equipment to operate. Similarly, if the labour force is 25, output has a fixed maximum of 5, even if we have 30 or 40 machines. Additional capital cannot increase output without additional labour made available in *fixed proportion* to capital. In this case there is no possibility of substituting workers for capital or vice versa, in the production process. The degree of substitutability between the factors is zero. Assuming constant returns, the isoquant map for this case is illustrated in Figure 10.5a. The production function for fixed proportions technology, sometimes called *Leontief* technology in reference to the economist who first analysed it in detail, may be written as

$$X = f(L,K) = \min(L,K) \tag{10.4}$$

Suppose, on the other hand, that technology is such that a unit of the capital equipment used can do exactly the same job as a certain number of workers. Such a case might arise if capital equipment took the form of robots. From the point of view of output, we could therefore either use an additional robot or a certain number of additional people to produce a given increment of production. In this case, capital and labour are said to be *perfect substitutes* for each other, and the isoquants of a production technology characterised by perfect substitutability are illustrated in Figure 10.5b. The relevant production function may be written in the following general form

$$X = f(L,K) = aL + bK \tag{10.5}$$

In the special case where inputs can be substituted at a ratio of 1:1, $a = b = 1$, and the isoquants will cut the L and K axes with an angle of 45°.

Figures 10.5a and 10.5b illustrate the limiting cases of zero and perfect (infinite) substitutability respectively. As we have seen, if production possibilities are adequately described by an array of activities which can be operated independently, then weighed averages of pairs of activities provide feasible ways of producing output, as well as the use of a single activity. It is this possibility which underlies the common assumption that isoquants are *convex* to the origin, as they are drawn in Figure 10.3. Such a technology is characterised by less than perfect, but more than zero, substitutability between factors.

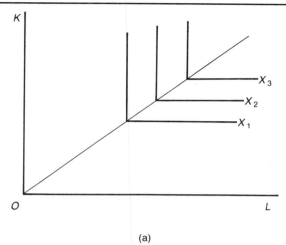

Figure 10.5a

(a)

Fixed proportions technology, with constant returns to scale.

Figure 10.5b

(b)

Inputs are perfect substitutes, with constant returns to scale.

The Elasticity of Substitution

To investigate the concept of substitutability further, consider the slope of the isoquant. This slope is referred to as the *marginal rate of technical substitution (mrts)* between inputs. The *mrts* between labour and capital is denoted $mrts_{LK}$. It measures the rate at which the firm will have to substitute one input for another in order to keep output constant. A precise measure of the *mrts* can be derived by first of all taking the total differential of production function (10.1)

$$dX = \frac{\partial X}{\partial L} dL + \frac{\partial X}{\partial K} dK \qquad (10.6)$$

Note that, along any isoquant, inputs are varied while the level of output is fixed. The slope of the isoquant is thus $\partial L/\partial K$ when $dX = 0$. Rearranging (10.6) with $dX = 0$ yields

$$mrts_{KL} = \frac{dL}{dK} = \frac{\partial X/\partial K}{\partial X/\partial L} \qquad (10.7)$$

The marginal rate of technical substitution of labour for capital at any point therefore equals the ratio of the marginal product of capital to that of labour, and vice versa. For the case of fixed proportions, the marginal products are not defined and the discontinuous *mrts* is therefore also not defined. For the case of perfect substitutes, from (10.5), $\partial X/\partial L = a$ and $\partial X/\partial K = b$. The slope of the isoquant (dL/dK) is therefore given by the constant ratio $-b/a$.

As we noted in our discussion of the demand curve in Chapter 2, the slope of a curve is an unsatisfactory number with which to characterise the sensitivity of quantity demanded to price, because it is not independent of the units of measurement. This problem arises also when we characterise the degree of substitutability between factors. In the case of the demand curve, the concept of the *elasticity* of demand provided us with a useful and unit-free measure of the sensitivity of quantity demanded to price. In the case of the isoquant, there is an analogous notion, the *elasticity of substitution*.

Assuming that isoquants are convex, the marginal rate of technical substitution of labour for capital will decline in algebraic terms, and increase in absolute value, as labour is substituted for capital along the isoquant. At the same time, of course, the capital–labour ratio will be diminishing. The *elasticity of substitution* is a pure number which is defined as the proportionate change in factor proportions (K/L) that takes place as we move around an isoquant, divided by the proportionate change in the marginal rate of technical substitution that simultaneously occurs. Hence denoting the elasticity of substitution by σ, we have

$$\sigma \equiv \frac{\partial(K/L)}{K/L} \bigg/ \frac{\partial(mrts_{LK})}{mrts_{LK}} \equiv \frac{\partial(K/L)}{K/L} \bigg/ \frac{\partial(\partial K/\partial L)}{\partial K/\partial L} \qquad (10.8)$$

As the reader will intuitively see, the more easily capital is replaced by labour, the less will be the proportional change in the *mrts* of labour for capital as the capital–labour ratio falls, and the greater in absolute value will our measure of the elasticity of substitution be. In the limiting case of perfect substitutability, the *mrts* will not change at all, and the elasticity of substitution will be infinite.

The Short-Run Production Function and Returns to a Factor

In the short run, we assume capital to be held constant while only labour and output can vary. The short-run production function, which describes the interaction of labour input and output, is thus two dimensional and is easier to analyse. It is depicted in Figure 10.6 geometrically. Denoting fixed capital stock by $\bar{K}$, the short-run production function may be written

$$X = f(L, \bar{K}) \tag{10.9}$$

We typically assume that increments to the fixed capital stock *increase* the average product of labour, or shift the short-run production function upwards. (The reasons for and implications of this assumption are discussed in Chapter 19.) More important than this characteristic however is the upward convex shape we have given to the function in Figure 10.6, which we shall now discuss in some detail.

The production function, whether long-run or short-run, is basically a technical relationship; economics takes it as given and classifies the characteristics it may display. However, this does not mean that it displays no dominant characteristics of particular importance to economics. When it comes to *returns to a factor*, which characterise the short-run production function, we may say something very definite about its nature, namely that, in the region that is relevant for analysing the behaviour

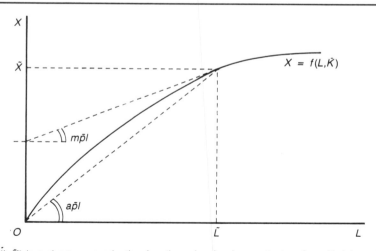

Figure 10.6

$X = f(L, \bar{K})$ is a short-run production function, showing how output varies with labour input when capital is held constant at $\bar{K}$. The average product of labour at each level of employment is given by the slope of a line from the point on the production function to the origin. When $L = \bar{L}$, $X = \bar{X}$ and hence the average product of labour, $a\bar{p}l$ is given by $\bar{X}/\bar{L}$. The marginal product of labour is the slope at the tangent to the production function at each level of employment. When $L = \bar{L}$, $\partial X/\partial L = m\bar{p}l$. Concavity of the short-run production function implies that the average product always exceeds the marginal product of labour.

of competitive firms, the short-run production function displays *decreasing* or *diminishing returns to a factor*. The concept of returns to a factor refers to what happens to output as successively equal increments of one input are combined with a fixed quantity of other inputs; about what happens as we move along the short-run production function. It is this characteristic of diminishing returns which is embodied in the convex shape of the relationship portrayed in Figure 10.6.

This property of diminishing returns relates the way that the marginal product of labour changes with the level of employment. More formally it may be described in terms of the sign of the derivative of the marginal product, which is the second derivative of the short-run production function and second partial derivative of the long-run one. What is sometimes called 'the law of diminishing returns' therefore refers to the assumption that

$$\frac{\partial}{\partial L}\left(\frac{\partial X}{\partial L}\right) = \frac{\partial^2 X}{\partial L^2} < 0 \tag{10.10}$$

This assumption is satisfied when the short-run production function is upwards convex, as in Figure 10.6. In terms of Figure 10.7, we use an isoquant map to illustrate diminishing returns. We ask what happens to output as we move along a line drawn perpendicular to the capital axis,

Figure 10.7

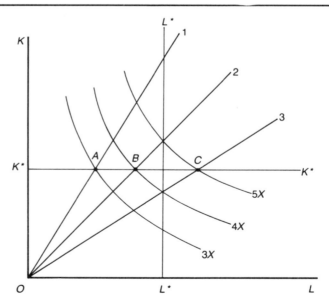

This homogeneous of degree one production function displays constant returns to scale but diminishing returns to a factor. Thus, as we move along K^*K^*, the movement from A to B to C involves successively greater increases in labour input for equal increments in output. Note that this movement takes us from ray 1 to 2 to 3, so that the isoquants become progressively less steep as we move to the right.

and hence what happens to output as we vary labour and hold capital constant. To postulate diminishing returns to labour (indeed to either factor) involves postulating successively decreasing increments in output for equal increments in the factor in question, labour in this case.

More on Diminishing Returns

To say that diminishing returns to a factor always exist in the region that is relevant for analysing the behaviour of the firm is to say two things: first, that it is usual for production functions to display in some region diminishing returns to a factor regardless of their returns to scale characteristics; second, that firms behave in such a way as to ensure that tendency exists in the region of the production function upon which they choose to operate. Since we have not yet said anything about what motivates this behaviour of firms, we cannot take up this second point at this stage, but it is easy to show that the tendency to diminishing returns is present in almost any production function.

In Figure 10.7 the production function which we have drawn displays constant returns to scale along any ray drawn out from the origin, and the isoquants that describe it are convex to the origin. These two properties are enough to ensure diminishing returns to both capital (as we move along L^*L^*) and to labour (as we move along K^*K^*) because along either of these lines isoquants showing successively equal increases in output are growing further and further apart. That this must be the case is easily seen. Let us consider the case of increasing labour inputs. The isoquant that cuts K^*K^* at C is more shallowly sloped than that which cuts it at B, which in turn is more shallowly sloped than A. The further to the right we move along K^*K^* the more rapidly is each isoquant moving away from the one to the left of it, and the wider the horizontal gap between successive curves. Only if the isoquants were straight lines touching both axes would there be no tendency for diminishing returns to a factor when returns to scale are constant.

Even the simple isoquant map based on the existence of two activities presented in Figure 10.1, and drawn here as Figure 10.8, would display diminishing returns, and in a dramatic way. With a given quantity of capital of K^* we would have constant returns to labour up to output $3X$. Here there is enough labour to make activity 1 fully viable. We would then have constant positive returns to labour (but at a lower rate) between level of output $3X$ and level of output $5X$. At the latter point, activity 2 would be the only one in use and further increments of labour could not be productively employed without adding to the capital stock. In short, returns to labour, holding capital constant, would suddenly diminish to zero at output level $5X$.

If returns to a factor always end up diminishing when returns to scale are constant, it should be obvious that they also diminish when returns

Figure 10.8

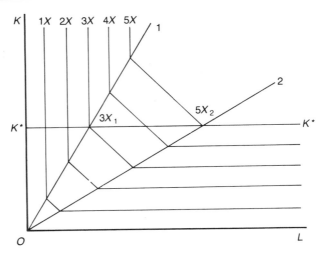

Diminishing returns to labour with but two constant returns to scale activities. Equal increments in labour yield equal increments in output along K^*K^* until point $3X_1$. Thereafter increments to output continue but at a smaller size until point $5X_2$. Thereafter, further increments to labour inputs add nothing to output.

to scale decrease. If, in terms of Figure 10.7, successive increments of capital or labour, holding the other factor constant, lead to successively smaller increases in output when equal movements along any ray through the origin yield equal increments in output, they must also do so when equidistant movements out from the origin yield successively smaller increments in output. Diminishing returns to scale accentuate the tendency of a production function to display diminishing returns to a factor. If a production function displays increasing returns to scale this can offset the tendency to diminishing returns to a factor, and indeed as we show below it is mathematically possible to write down formulae for production functions in which returns to scale increase so rapidly that returns to a factor never begin to diminish. However, what is mathematically possible is not always empirically plausible, and such cases are logical curiosities rather than practically relevant examples.

In the real world, it is clear that the tendency to diminishing returns to a factor is ubiquitous. No matter what the technical process of production is like, and no matter what might happen to its productivity if all inputs into it are increased in proportion, if only one input is increased, sooner or later that input is going to find it harder and harder to find units of other inputs to co-operate with; it may even begin to get in the way of production simply by its physical presence. The contribution of extra units of this factor to production is then inevitably going to diminish. One cannot indefinitely cram more and more machines into a given building with a given labour force; one cannot indefinitely add men to

a production line; one cannot put more and more hens into a given hen-house; one cannot put more and more fertiliser on a given plot of land, and not expect to see the extra units of the input that is being varied make a diminishing contribution in terms of additions to output.

*A Specific Production Function: The Cobb–Douglas Case

In this chapter we have developed a large number of categories and defini-tions of relevance to producer theory, which have wide theoretical use and considerable empirical relevance. In both theoretical and empirical work, analysts frequently simplify matters by assuming that technology takes a specific form. A particularly convenient specification of the pro-duction function is the *Cobb–Douglas*, named after its originators. Our purpose in this section is to use the Cobb–Douglas function as an exam-ple to illustrate the material which went before, and to derive the key parameters of interest in production theory.

The Cobb–Douglas production function takes the form,

$$X = f(L,K) = AL^\alpha K^\beta \tag{10.11}$$

The parameter A translates units of inputs into units of output, while α and β determine the responsiveness of output to increments in factor inputs. The Cobb–Douglas function has been widely used in empirical work. By taking logs of (10.11) we obtain

$$lnX = lnA + \alpha lnL + \beta lnK \tag{10.12}$$

The Cobb–Douglas function thus specifies technology as linear in the logarithms of variables, and this property renders it particularly amenable to econometric analysis.

Let us investigate the returns to scale characteristics of this function. Let us suppose first that

$$\alpha + \beta = 1, \text{ so } \beta = 1 - \alpha$$

In this case (10.11) becomes

$$X = A\left(\frac{L}{K}\right)^\alpha K \tag{10.13}$$

If we increase L and K in equal proportions, their ratio does not change, so the term $A(L/K)^\alpha$ remains the same. However K has changed by a given proportion, and equation (10.13) implies that X will change in the same proportion. For example, a doubling of both inputs will exactly double output. Hence the assumption $\alpha + \beta = 1$ implies that the Cobb–Douglas function displays constant returns to scale.

More generally, we may take the differential of (10.11)

$$dX = \alpha A L^{\alpha-1} K^{\beta} dL + \beta A L^{\alpha} K^{\beta-1} dK \tag{10.14}$$

which, substituting from (10.11), can be rewritten as

$$dX = \alpha \frac{X}{L} dL + \beta \frac{X}{K} dK \tag{10.15}$$

The notion of returns to scale refers to the way in which output changes as both inputs vary, holding factor proportions, the ratio K/L, constant. Suppose then, that

$$\frac{dL}{L} = \frac{dK}{K} \tag{10.16}$$

Hence (10.15) becomes

$$dX = X \frac{dL}{L} (\alpha + \beta) = X \frac{dK}{K} (\alpha + \beta) \tag{10.17}$$

or

$$\frac{dX}{X} = \frac{dL}{L} (\alpha + \beta) = \frac{dK}{K} (\alpha + \beta) \tag{10.18}$$

If $\alpha + \beta = 1$, as we have already seen, output increases in strict proportion to labour (or capital) input so long as the capital–labour ratio is held constant, and we have constant returns to scale. If $\alpha + \beta > 1$, output increases proportionately more than labour (or capital) input and we have increasing returns to scale. On the other hand, $\alpha + \beta < 1$ implies diminishing returns to scale.

In the Cobb–Douglas case, so long as α and β are each less than one, the marginal products of factors decline as their use increases, and bear a constant proportion to average products. From (10.15), when $dK = 0$, we have, as the marginal product of labour,

$$\frac{\partial X}{\partial L} = \alpha \frac{X}{L} \tag{10.19}$$

Similarly when $dL = 0$,

$$\frac{\partial X}{\partial K} = \beta \frac{X}{K} \tag{10.20}$$

Note that X/L and X/K are the average products of labour and capital respectively. The second derivatives are

$$\frac{\partial^2 X}{\partial L^2} = \alpha(\alpha - 1) \frac{X}{L^2} \tag{10.21}$$

and

$$\frac{\partial^2 X}{\partial K^2} = \beta(\beta - 1)\frac{X}{K^2} \tag{10.22}$$

respectively. Hence, if α and β are less than 1, these second derivatives are negative and so marginal products (the first derivatives) diminish. We therefore confirm that diminishing returns to a factor can coexist with constant returns ($\alpha + \beta = 1$) and diminishing ($\alpha + \beta < 1$) returns to scale, and may coexist with increasing ($\alpha + \beta > 1$) returns to scale. Note, however, that if α or β were to be greater than 1, labour or capital respectively would yield increasing returns as it was varied, holding the other input constant. Thus the 'law of diminishing returns' is an economic proposition about the empirical properties of real world production processes. It is not a mathematically necessary property of any logically conceivable production function.

Now let us consider the elasticity of substitution (see 10.7). The marginal rate of technical substitution in the Cobb–Douglas case is given by

$$mrts = \frac{\partial L}{\partial K} = -\frac{\partial X / \partial K}{\partial X / \partial L} = \frac{-\beta X}{K} \bigg/ \frac{\alpha X}{L} = \frac{-\beta}{\alpha}\frac{L}{K} \tag{10.23}$$

Convexity of the isoquant implies that the slope of the isoquant ($-dL/dK$) increases as L/K increases. This will hold provided $\alpha, \beta > 0$.

The elasticity of substitution can be derived as follows. Recall that

$$\sigma \equiv \frac{\partial (K/L)}{K/L} \bigg/ \frac{\partial (\partial K / \partial L)}{\partial K / \partial L} \tag{10.8}$$

From (10.23) we have

$$\partial K / \partial L = -\frac{\alpha}{\beta}\frac{K}{L} \tag{10.24}$$

so

$$(\partial K / \partial L)/(K/L) = -\frac{\alpha}{\beta} \tag{10.25}$$

Differentiating $\partial K / \partial L$ with respect to K/L yields

$$\partial(\partial K / \partial L)/\partial(K/L) = -\frac{\alpha}{\beta} \tag{10.26}$$

Hence, substituting (10.25) and (10.26) into (10.8) we have

$$\sigma \equiv -\frac{-\alpha}{\beta} \bigg/ \frac{-\alpha}{\beta} = 1 \tag{10.27}$$

The Cobb–Douglas production function therefore is always characterised by an elasticity of substitution of unity. This holds regardless of its

returns to scale characteristics, or, more generally, of the values attached to the parameters α and β.

We have already noted that the short-run Cobb–Douglas production function, $X = AL^{\alpha}\bar{K}^{\beta}$ displays a diminishing average and marginal product of labour provided $\alpha < 1$. The marginal product is as we have seen $\alpha X/L$ and the average product is of course X/L. We noted previously that diminishing returns to a factor implies that the marginal product is regularly less than the average product. In this case,

$$\frac{X/L}{\partial X/\partial L} = \frac{1}{\alpha} \tag{10.28}$$

so

$$\frac{X}{L} > \frac{\partial X}{\partial L} \text{ provided that } \alpha < 1 \tag{10.29}$$

Finally note that the effect of an increase in the capital stock on the marginal product of labour is given by substituting (10.11) into (10.19) and differentiating with respect to K, to obtain,

$$\frac{\partial^2 X}{\partial L \partial K} = \frac{\alpha \beta X}{LK} > 0 \text{ provided that } \alpha, \beta > 0 \tag{10.30}$$

Hence in the Cobb–Douglas case, increases in capital shift the short-run production function upwards, and increases the marginal (and average) product of labour. It is also the case that

$$\frac{\partial^2 X}{\partial K \partial L} = \frac{\beta \alpha X}{KL} > 0 \text{ provided that } \alpha, \beta > 0 \tag{10.31}$$

which establishes that the cross derivatives of the Cobb–Douglas function are symmetric. An increase in labour input has the same impact on the marginal and average products of capital as does an increase in capital inputs on the marginal and average products of labour.

Concluding Comment

It might be helpful to summarise the points developed in this chapter. We have argued that the production function is a technical relationship between the rate of flow of factor services put into a production process and the rate of flow of output emerging from it. When inputs are increased in equal proportion, we describe the consequences for output in terms of the concept of returns to scale, and we have seen that a production function may be characterised by decreasing, constant, or increasing returns to scale. Indeed, it may exhibit a combination of these characteristics as output increases over different ranges.

A second important property of the long-run production function is the degree of substitutability between the inputs required to produce a given level of output. Technology can display a range of degrees of substitutability from zero to perfect substitutability. This property of substitutability is measured by the 'elasticity of substitution'.

When we analyse the short-run production function, and only one factor is varied, holding constant the quantities of all the others, we speak of the consequences in terms of returns to that factor. Though certain production functions *may*, logically speaking, display a tendency to increasing returns to a factor, the overwhelming general tendency here is for returns to a factor to diminish, and as we shall see below, competitive firms always operate in the region of the production function where they do diminish. The importance of all this, as far as the behaviour of firms is concerned, is that the production function provides a vital link between their behaviour in goods markets with that in markets for factors of production. We shall begin to investigate this link in the next chapter, and return to it in Chapter 19.

11

Cost Functions

Introduction

The production function is central to the economics of the firm because it is the relationship that enables us to translate market prices of individual factors of production into costs of production for output, and to derive from market prices of output the costs which firms are willing to incur in order to obtain factors of production. This chapter uses the production function to clarify the way in which production costs vary with the level of output.

As the reader might guess, it is always logically possible to construct peculiar special case production functions that in turn yield peculiar relationships between output levels and costs. In what follows, we normally stick to dealing with homogeneous (or at least homothetic) production functions (described in Ch. 10) in order to keep the analysis manageable, and so some results are not quite general. Nevertheless, they are sufficiently widely applicable that they serve quite adequately as a basis for the analysis of firm behaviour that is dealt with subsequently. Results are generalised in the more technical treatment of the subject contained in the chapter which follows.

We said earlier that a firm would seek to produce any given output utilising no more inputs than were necessary. Such behaviour is a consequence of a more basic proposition about the behaviour of firms, namely that whatever level of output they choose to produce, they will do so at the minimum possible cost. This in turn is an implication of the basic assumption of the so-called neo-classical theory of the firm, that the entrepreneur's motive is to maximise profit. We will discuss this assumption at some length below but, for the moment, the reader need only accept the weaker cost minimisation hypothesis as a basis for the following analysis.

Expenditure on Inputs and the Cost Function

Let us continue to assume that the firm whose behaviour we are to study produces only good X, and uses the services of labour and capital in its production. Let us further assume that, in relation to the markets for these inputs, the firm stands in very much the same way as did the consumer of Part I in relation to the markets for X and Y. That is to say, the prices the firm must pay for labour services and for capital services do not vary with the amounts bought. Input prices are therefore exogenous to the firm.

The measurement of input prices, though straightforward, is worth explicit attention. As we have seen, inputs are measured in flow terms — in hours worked per week or per month as far as labour is concerned; as to capital, the appropriate input measure is also a flow, for example, hours or weeks per week or month. Thus, the relevant price for labour is the wage per hour worked, denoted w, and the relevant price of capital is emphatically *not* the price of a new machine. Rather it is the weekly or hourly rental price of a machine, denoted r. Though machinery is sometimes leased, it is more typically owned by the firm that uses it, but the reader might find it helpful to think of the firm renting the machine from itself. The rental price of the machine is given by what the firm forgoes, per hour, or per week, by owning the machine, that is clearly the interest that the firm could earn per hour or per week on the funds tied up in the machine (the normal net rate of return on capital in the economy times the value of the machine) plus any depreciation (or minus any appreciation) in its value. It is the *opportunity cost* of owning the machine.

Total costs can be defined as the sum of outlays on labour, L and capital K.

$$C = wL + rK \qquad (11.1)$$

A *cost function*, however, describes how the *minimum* total costs of production C change with the volume of output and with input prices.

$$C = C(X,w,r) \qquad (11.2)$$

Even with input prices given, the move from (11.1) to (11.2) requires us to know two things: firstly, the quantities of factor inputs chosen by the firm, which we assume is done on the basis of cost minimisation; secondly, the way those quantities of inputs, optimally chosen in the long-run case where all inputs are variable and denoted K^* and L^*, are transformed into output via the production function,

$$X = f(L,K) \qquad (11.3)$$

We shall be particularly interested in whether or not properties of the production function described in the previous chapter have implications for the shape of the cost function (11.2).

Long-Run Cost Minimisation

Formally, the long-run cost function (11.2) is the solution to the minimisation problem;

$$\min_{L,K} C = wL + rK \qquad (11.4)$$

subject to

$$X = f(L,K) \qquad (11.3)$$

This procedure of cost minimisation subject to the constraint imposed by the production function is analogous to the constrained utility maximisation of Chapter 2. We provide an algebraic solution to this problem in Chapter 12, and in this chapter we largely confine our attention to results which we can derive on the basis of geometry. We can get most of the conclusions in which we are interested at this level geometrically, so non-technical readers will not necessarily be seriously penalised by skipping Chapter 12. Nonetheless, those who want to go further in their study of economics should be aware that algebra is more powerful and general in its application, and Chapter 12 is therefore worth their attention.

We can obtain an intuitive understanding of the solution to the cost minimisation problem by using a diagram which illustrates both the firm's tradeoffs in the choice of inputs, and the underlying technological constraints which it faces. The latter we characterise in terms of an isoquant map, such as Figure 10.3. Tradeoffs between inputs available to the firm are formalised in terms of *isocost* curves. These describe the quantities of capital and labour services that can be bought per unit of time for a given cost outlay. For example, let the price of capital and labour be £100 and £50 respectively. Then for an outlay of £1,000 per week, we see that the firm can acquire 10 units of capital, 20 units of labour, or any combination of inputs along the line joining $10K$ and $20L$. This is illustrated in Figure 11.1.

Algebraically, we may rearrange equation (11.1) to read

$$K = \frac{C}{r} - \frac{w}{r}L \qquad (11.5)$$

For any given outlay, $\bar{C}$, this equation defines a straight line with intercept $\bar{C}/r$ and slope $-w/r$ ($\partial K/\partial L = -w/r$). In terms of our previous numerical example, we would have $C = 1000$, $r = 100$. Hence $C/r = 10$, and the slope of the isocost line is given by $-50/100 = -0.5$. From equation (11.5) we note that the isocost curve shifts up parallel to itself as outlays rise, that changes in labour's price alters the slope of the curve, but not its intercept with the capital axis, while changes in capital's rental price r, changes both its slope and intercept with the capital axis.

Minimising the cost of production of X means two equivalent things.

Figure 11.1

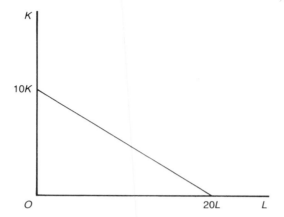

An isocost curve, showing the quantities of capital and labour services that can be bought per unit of time for an outlay of £1,000 per unit of time when their prices are £100 and £50 per unit respectively.

One may say that the firm, for a given outlay on factors, maximises production of X or, that for a given level of output, minimises the cost of obtaining the factors necessary to produce that level of output. In geometric terms, cost minimisation takes place where an isoquant representing a particular level of output is just tangent to an isocost curve. By exact analogy with arguments developed in Chapter 2, we may say that *costs are minimised where the marginal rate of substitution between inputs in production*, the slope of the isoquant, is equal to the ratio of factor prices, the slope of the isocost curve. Any other combination of factors along the isoquant in question, other than that at which this condition holds, will result in more expense for no extra output, and any other point on the same isocost curve will mean the same expense for less output. So much should be obvious from inspection of Figure 11.2.

Long-Run Total Cost and the Expansion Path

We are now in a position to derive a curve relating the total cost of producing X to its level of output: *a total cost curve*. As we have seen, the assumption of cost minimisation ensures that, in these circumstances, the outlay on factors incurred in producing a given output level will be that underlying the isocost curve that is tangent to the relevant isoquant.

Each equilibrium point in KL space, such as A, B or C in Figure 11.2 is a point on the firm's *expansion path*. This path is defined as the locus of equalities between *mrts* and input price ratios, or tangencies between isoquants and isocost curves at different levels of cost outlay, and therefore output.

Figure 11.2

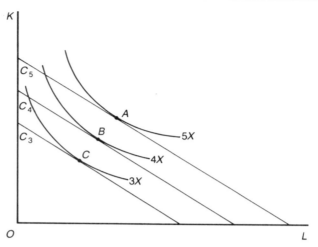

A family of isocost curves superimposed upon the production function. At point A we have the cheapest way of producing output $5X$ since any other point on that isoquant must be above isocost curve C_5. Equivalently, an output of $5X$ is the maximum output that can be had for an outlay of C_5 on factors of production. Any point other than A on isocost line C_5 is on a lower isoquant than $5X$. Similarly, C_3 and C_4 are the minimum costs of producing $3X$ and $4X$ units of output.

The long-run total cost function links cost outlay with output on the assumption that factor proportions have been chosen in such a way as to minimise costs. We therefore relate cost outlay with corresponding output levels *along the expansion path* in order to derive this function.

Figure 11.3(a) shows the long-run total cost curve (LTC) when returns to scale are constant. It is derived from Figure 11.2 where the production function was drawn to display this property. Equiproportional increases in outlay on factors lead to equiproportional increases in their quantity devoted to producing X, and hence in equiproportional increases in output. The long-run total cost curve is, therefore, an upward-sloping straight line. Readers should satisfy themselves that a production function that everywhere displays decreasing returns to scale produces a long-run total cost curve that slopes upwards at a rate that increases with output, Figure 11.3(b), and one that displays increasing returns to scale produces a long-run total cost curve that slopes upwards at a rate that decreases with output, Figure 11.3(c).

*The Cobb–Douglas Case Again

To understand the long-run total cost curve's properties better, consider the example of the Cobb–Douglas production function, which is homogeneous and therefore homothetic. We established earlier that for

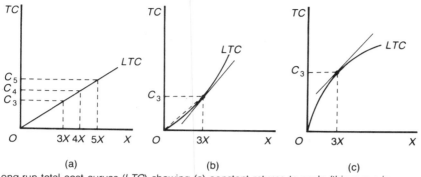

(a)   (b)   (c)

Long-run total cost curves (*LTC*) showing (a) constant returns to scale (this curve is explicitly derived from Figure 11.2 by relating the value of each isocost curve to that of the isoquant tangential to it), (b) decreasing returns to scale, (c) increasing returns to scale. As a particular level of output, average cost is given by dividing total cost by output (e.g. $C_3/3X$) Long-run marginal cost at any level of output is given by the slope of the total cost curve at the level of output.

such a function, the marginal rate of technical substitution between labour and capital is $-\beta/\alpha$ (L/K) (see equation 10.19). The ratio of prices is exogenous for the firm, and fixed at w/r. Hence in equilibrium

$$\frac{-\beta}{\alpha}\frac{L}{K} = w/r \tag{11.6}$$

and $\quad \dfrac{K}{L} = \dfrac{-\beta r}{w\alpha} \tag{11.7}$

Equation (11.6) implies that, for given input prices, w, r, the capital–labour ratio is, in this Cobb–Douglas case, the same at every tangency between isoquants and isocost lines. The expansion path is therefore a straight line for a Cobb–Douglas function, and, more generally, for all homothetic production functions. In the particular Cobb–Douglas case, where $\alpha + \beta = 1$ and the production function is homogeneous of degree one, factor outlays will rise in proportion to output along this expansion path, and the long-run total cost curve will be linear.

Average and Marginal Costs in the Long Run

Two other cost/output relationships are implicit in Figure 11.3. There is a relationship between *average cost* and output and between *marginal cost* and output. Average cost is simply the total cost of producing a given volume of output divided by the volume of output. In terms of Figure 11.3, it is measured by the height of the total cost curve at any point divided by its distance from the vertical axis or, in other words, by the

slope of a straight line drawn from the origin to that point on the total cost curve. As the reader will readily discern, when returns to scale are constant, average cost does not vary with output; when they diminish, average cost increases with output; when they increase, average cost systematically falls with output.

Now consider the relationship between marginal cost and output. Marginal cost per unit of output is the ratio of the additional cost incurred by making a small (in the limit, infinitesimal) addition to output, to that addition to total output. In terms of calculus it is the derivative of the cost function (11.2). It is thus measured by the slope of the total cost curve — in just the same way as the marginal propensity to consume a good is given by the slope of an Engel curve (Chapter 2), the marginal utility of wealth is given by the slope of the total utility of wealth function (Chapter 7), and labour marginal productivity is given by the slope of the short-run production function. It should be obvious from Figure 11.3(a) that when returns to scale are constant, marginal cost is equal to average cost and does not vary with output. Figure 11.3(b) implies that decreasing returns to scale involves marginal cost increasing with output and exceeding average cost, while in Figure 11.3(c) we find marginal cost falling with output and being below average cost.

Long-Run Costs with Varying Returns to Scale

Now we remarked in the previous chapter that there was no need to confine our attention to production functions that everywhere display the same returns to scale characteristics; that it was quite conceivable that the technical conditions of producing a particular good were such as to result in increasing returns to scale at low output levels and decreasing returns at higher output levels. Such a production function is, in fact, most useful in the analysis of the behaviour of the competitive firm, as we shall see in Chapter 13 and the long-run cost curves implicit in it are worth consideration at this point.

In Figure 11.4, we draw the long-run total cost curve implied by such a production function, still assuming that factor prices are fixed to the firm. Total costs first increase with output at a decreasing rate and then at an increasing rate. Long-run average cost at first falls with output, and then rises; it reaches a minimum at level of output X^* where a straight line from the origin is tangent to *LTC*. As we have already said, long-run marginal cost at any level of output is given by the slope of the total cost curve. At first this too falls with output, and at levels of output lower than X^* is below average cost — as the reader should easily be able to verify by inspecting Figure 11.4. However, marginal cost begins to rise at X^{**} before output X^* is reached and becomes equal to average cost at X^*; at this level of output the slope of a straight line from the origin to the total cost curve is just equal to the slope of the total cost curve.

Figure 11.4

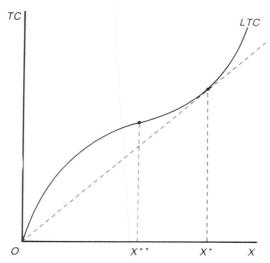

A long-run total cost curve showing first increasing and then decreasing returns to scale. Average cost is given by the slope of a straight line drawn from the origin to the curve. The slope of such a line, and hence average cost, is at a minimum at output X^* where the relevant line is tangent to the total cost curve. This straight line through the origin has the same slope as the total cost curve and hence, at output X^*, average cost and marginal cost are equal to each other. The slope of the total cost curve, and hence marginal cost, is at a minimum at output X^{**}, which is lower than X^*.

Beyond X^* marginal cost continues to rise, and readers should satisfy themselves that marginal cost is above average cost at higher output levels than X^*. The relationships between long-run marginal cost, long-run average cost, and output implicit in Figure 11.4 are displayed in Figure 11.5. The average cost curve (LAC) takes a form that is often called U-shaped, and is cut at its minimum point by a rising marginal cost curve (LMC). The reader will become very familiar with curves of this general shape in the chapters that follow.

The Concept of the Short Run

We can now investigate further the distinction between short and long run introduced in the last chapter. The curves with which we have been dealing so far are long run. They tell us how costs vary with output on the assumption that the firm may move freely to any point on its production function, that it may use any combination of inputs with equal ease, and that it always chooses the minimum cost combination. Movements such as this take time; the use of some inputs can be varied more rapidly than that of others. It is easier to hire more hourly paid labour than it is to order and install new machinery. It is easier to cut back on outlays on hourly paid labour than it is for the firm to rid itself of

Figure 11.5

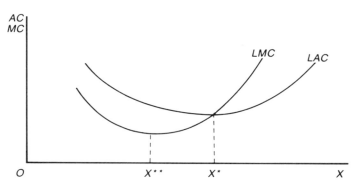

Long-run average and marginal cost curves implicit in Figure 11.4. Marginal cost cuts average cost from below at the minimum point of the average cost curve.

machinery once acquired. In ignoring such problems we were implicitly assuming that the firm had sufficient time to overcome them.

In contrast, we may define the 'short run' as that period of time over which the services of at least one factor input flowing to the firm are fixed as a result of past decisions. For the two-factor case it is usual to think of this fixed factor as being capital. Inasmuch as capital consists of machinery, it is physically fixed in place, owned or leased by the firm and it is by no means straightforward to vary the amount of it. The labour force, on the other hand, is more likely to be on short-term contract, weekly or monthly, easily reduced by short-time working and dismissals and just as easily expanded by overtime and new hiring. Thus, we assume that, in the short run, only labour can be varied and capital is fixed.

This is nevertheless a naive assumption made, in the main, to keep the analysis simple. There is no particular reason why in any actual firm every type of capital should be only slowly variable and every type of labour rapidly variable. It is true that some types of labour are on short-term contract and easily hired and fired, but by no means all types. Equally, plant and equipment may be difficult to expand and contract quickly, but inventories of raw materials are just as much a part of capital and in some cases they may easily be adjusted. For any firm, there is a time horizon over which all inputs may be varied, but there are many, not just one, shorter horizons over which some inputs are fixed. Moreover, it is not necessarily the case that any type of labour may be varied more rapidly than any type of capital.

When in the following analysis we define the short run as the period over which labour but not capital inputs can be varied, we are not attempting directly to describe any kind of empirical reality. We are constructing a simplified special case in order to make certain analytic notions clear. Any attempt to apply the short-run/long-run distinction to a real world problem that simply takes it for granted that there is a factor called

labour whose services can be varied more rapidly than those of capital, and does not instead look carefully at the whole array of inputs involved in the particular situation to see which is the most easily varied is likely to be misleading.

Short-Run Cost Functions

With the above caveat in mind, let us proceed to the analysis of short-run costs and their relationship to long-run costs. Just as the returns to scale characteristics of the production function underlie the shape of the long-run cost curves, so the nature of short-run cost curves depends upon the returns to the variable factor (labour in this simplified example) characteristics that it displays. We will explicitly analyse only the relatively complex case of a production function that displays increasing, followed by decreasing, returns to scale, but the reader will find it helpful to carry out the same analysis for at least one simpler case — say that of constant returns to scale.

We fix K at some historically given level K^* in Figure 11.6 and note that, given the prices of labour and capital, long-run cost minimisation would involve the firm producing at A. If it wishes to vary its output over short periods it must move along the line K^*K^* rather than along the ray through the origin. We may construct a short-term total cost curve from

Figure 11.6

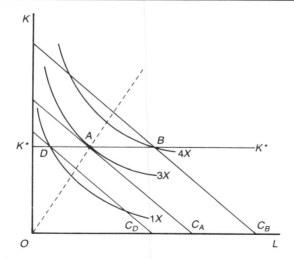

Given factor prices, the firm would produce level of output 3X at point A, using K* units of capital services, even if it was free to vary the capital stock. With capital fixed at K* any other level of output (e.g. 4X produced at B or 1X produced at D) will be produced at greater cost than it would be were the firm free to vary its capital input. C_D and C_B are the minimum short-run costs of producing 1X and 4X. Note that the isoquants are here drawn to display first increasing and then decreasing returns to scale.

Figure 11.6 by relating to one another the values of the isoquants and isocost lines that intersect K^*K^*. In this case, as we have drawn Figure 11.7, like the long-run curve, the short-run total cost curve displays first increasing and then decreasing returns, but these are returns *to the factor* and not returns *to scale*.

Now A represents a point that is both on the short-run total cost curve (STC) and on the long-run curve (LTC) as drawn in Figure 11.7. The level of output here is the only one for which short-run and long-run total costs of production are equal. The short-run total cost of producing any other level of output is higher than the long-run cost, for at any other point on K^*K^* the isocost lines *intersect* the isoquant and are not tangent to it. If, at level of output $3X$, the long-run curve and the short-run curve coincide, and at all other levels of output short-run costs are higher, there is obviously a tangency between the two curves at level of output $3X$.

The derivation of the short-run average cost curve and the short-run marginal cost curve from the short-run total cost curve is, analytically speaking, exactly the same exercise as the derivation of the relevant long-run curves and there is no point in repeating it explicitly. Because the long-run and short-run total cost curves touch tangentially at output $3X$ we may make inferences about the relationship between short-run and long-run average costs at that output, and between the two marginal cost curves. The average and marginal cost curves are drawn in Figure 11.8. First, the slopes of the two total cost curves are equal at A, in Figure 11.7, so short- and long-run marginal cost are equal at output $3X$. Immediately to the left of A the short-run total cost curve is less steeply sloped than the long-run curve, and to the right of A it is more steeply sloped. Hence, the short-run marginal cost curve (SMC) cuts the long-run curve (LMC) from below and to the left at level of output $3X$.

Figure 11.7

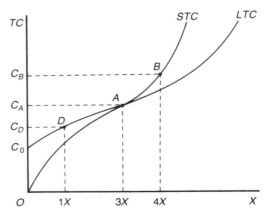

A short-run total cost curve for a particular level of the capital stock will be tangent to the long-run curve at A — coresponding to point A in Figure 11.6. C_0 here represents outlay on the services of K^* units of capital. It is a cost that must be met in the short run, even if output is zero.

Figure 11.8

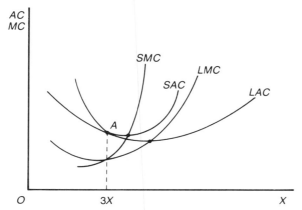

The relationship between long- and short-run average and marginal costs. The two average cost curves are tangent to each other at A — corresponding to point A in Figure 11.7, while the two marginal cost curves intersect at the same level of output ($3X$).

Short- and long-run average costs coincide at this level of output, $3X$, too, but here we have *tangency* between the two rather than an *intersection*. At any other level of output, total and hence average costs are higher in the short run than in the long run. Note that this does *not* mean that short-run average cost (SAC) is at a minimum at level of output $3X$. The tangency of the two total cost curves means only that short-run average costs will fall *less rapidly* or rise *more rapidly* than long-run average costs as output expands, or contracts, not that they will necessarily rise in absolute terms. As Figures 11.7 and 11.8 are drawn, both short-run and long-run average costs are, in fact, falling at level of output $3X$.

Short- and Long-Run Average Cost — The 'Envelope'

Now we carried out the foregoing analysis on the assumption that there was a given level of capital that could not be varied. The amount we chose was quite arbitrary. There is in fact a different array of short-run curves for every level of the capital stock and, as the reader should see from Figure 11.9, the higher the level of the capital stock, the higher is the level of output at which the lines representing this stock (K^*K^* and $K^{**}K^{**}$) intersect the ray through the origin along which the long-run cost curves are derived. Hence the higher the level of output at which the two total cost curves coincide. For every level of the capital stock there is a short-run average cost curve tangent to the long-run curve, and a short-term marginal cost curve intersecting the long-run curve. Figure 11.10 depicts a few of these curves, and its very appearance explains why the long-run average cost curve is often referred to as being the 'envelope' of the short-run curves. As should be clear from the analysis presented earlier,

Figure 11.9

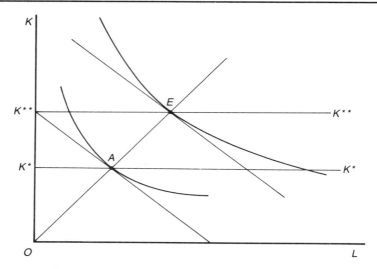

The higher the given level of the capital stock, the higher the level of labour input, and of output associated with the firm having the long-run cost minimising ratio of inputs. Point *A* here corresponds to point *A* in Figure 11.6. Point *E* is a similar point; it would yield a tangency between long-run and particular short-run total and average cost curves, the latter derived for a higher fixed level of capital services (K^{**}).

Figure 11.10

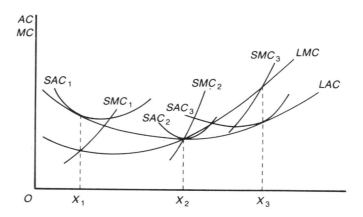

The long-run average cost curve is an 'envelope' of short-run average cost curves, each of the latter being derived for a different, fixed, level of capital services. There is a short-run marginal cost curve associated with each short-run average cost curve. It cuts the latter at its minimum point. It intersects the long-run marginal cost curve at the same level of output at which the short-run average cost curve is tangent to the long-run average cost curve. X_1, X_2 and X_3 are the output levels at which this happens for the three sets of short-run curves shown here. The curves labelled SAC_2 and SMC_2 are associated with a level of the capital stock which permits long-run average costs to be minimised. Hence SAC_2 equals LAC at the lowest point in the latter curve and SMC_2 intersects LMC where each curve cuts its associated average cost curve.

the 'U' shape of the long-run average cost curve in Figure 11.10 depends upon the assumption that we are dealing with a production function characterised by increasing returns to scale at low levels of output and decreasing returns to scale at higher levels. Such a production function was presented in Figure 11.6.

Fixed and Variable Costs

Now we have included outlays on capital services in the short-run costs with which we have been dealing. However, because capital input is fixed, outlay on it is fixed. It is often helpful to distinguish between the fixed and variable components of short-run costs. In the long run, of course, all costs are variable because, by definition, the level of all inputs can be varied as the firm desires. To obtain total variable costs from total short-run costs one simply subtracts the fixed outlay on capital. The short-run total cost curve depicted in Figure 11.7 and reproduced in Figure 11.11 cuts the vertical axis at C_0, for in the short-run, at zero output, the firm must still pay this amount for capital services even if they are not utilised. To get the total variable cost curve (*TVC*), one simply shifts the short-run total cost curve (*STC*) down until it cuts through the origin, as shown in Figure 11.11. Since marginal cost measures the slope of the total cost curve, the distinction between variable and total cost does not affect the short-run marginal cost curve. After all, if fixed costs are fixed, then they do not vary with increments to output.

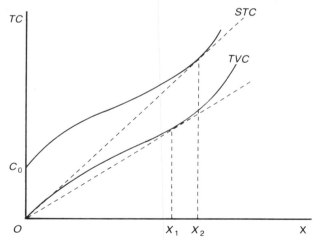

Figure 11.11

Total variable cost is equal to short-run total cost minus fixed costs (C_0). Average variable cost (the slope of a line drawn from the origin to *TVC*) is at a minimum at a lower level of output, X_1, than is short-run average cost (the slope of a line drawn to *STC*). The latter is minimised at X_2.

However, the distinction between fixed and variable costs is relevant to the discussion of average costs. If we average fixed costs over an increasing level of output, their contribution to overall average cost diminishes, as is shown in Figure 11.12. Average variable cost may be obtained from average overall cost by subtracting average fixed cost (*AFC*). Alternatively, the slope of a line drawn from the origin to the total variable cost curve in Figure 11.11 measures average variable cost. These two methods of obtaining the average variable cost curve are, of course, equivalent and the minimum point of the average variable cost curve lies to the left of that of the overall short-run average cost curve. The marginal cost curve, of course, cuts both average cost curves at their minimum points. All this is shown in Figure 11.12. Readers who doubt any of the foregoing propositions will find it helpful to derive them for themselves.

*From Production to Cost Functions in the Short Run — A Formal Treatment

The relationship between production and cost functions in the short run can be brought out even more simply with the aid of calculus. In the short run, with capital costs fixed at Co ($r\bar{K} = Co$), the total cost of function (11.1) becomes

$$C = wL + Co \tag{11.8}$$

and variable costs (*VC*) are given by wL.

The short-run production function is of course

Figure 11.12

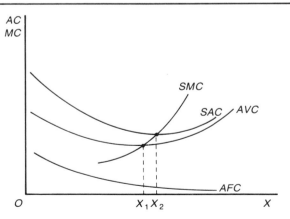

Average variable cost (*AVC*) is equal to short-run average cost (*SAC*) minus average fixed cost (*AFC*). The latter is simply a constant divided by an increasing level of output and hence declines systematically with output. Thus *AVC* and *SAC* move closer together as output increases. The short-run marginal cost curve cuts both of these two curves at their minimum points at X_1 and X_2.

$$X = f(L, \bar{K}) \tag{11.9}$$

which, since there is only one variable factor, can be respecified as

$$L = f^{-1}(X, \bar{K}) \tag{11.10}$$

In other words, with capital fixed, the level of output is unambiguously determined by employment only and vice versa. For given w, average variable cost (AVC) is therefore inversely associated with average product.

$$AVC = \frac{VC}{X} = \frac{wL}{X} \tag{11.10}$$

while short-run marginal cost is also specified as depending on the wage and the marginal product of labour.

$$\partial C/\partial X = w\frac{\partial L}{\partial X} \tag{11.12}$$

On this basis, we can discuss the relationship between average and marginal product and average and marginal costs. As we saw in Chapter 10, diminishing returns to a factor implies that average and marginal products both decline as output increases, with the former being *greater* than the latter. Diminishing returns thus also implies that average and marginal costs increase with output, with the former being everywhere *less* than the latter. Short-run curves such as those illustrated in Figures 11.8, 11.10 and 11.12, therefore, are all based on the assumption that returns to a factor are initially increasing, then constant, then diminishing as output increases.

The relationship between average and marginal cost will not in general remain constant as output changes. However, in the Cobb–Douglas case, marginal costs are a constant multiple of average costs, with

$$\frac{VC}{X} = \frac{wL}{X} \quad \text{and} \quad \frac{\partial C}{\partial X} = \frac{wL}{\alpha X}$$

so that

$$\frac{\partial C}{\partial X} \bigg/ \frac{VC}{X} = \frac{wL}{\alpha X} \bigg/ \frac{wL}{X} = \frac{1}{\alpha} \tag{11.13}$$

Concluding Comment

Now the analysis of cost curves is quite tricky and if it was being carried out only for its own sake, it would be tedious as well. However, cost/output relationships such as those we have discussed here are a basic ingredient to the price and output decisions of the firm. We have now dealt with them in sufficient detail to begin discussing, in Part V of this book, the entrepreneur's decision making about the quantity of output

to be produced and the price at which it is to be sold. Readers who seek a deeper understanding of cost functions should read Chapter 12 next, but those who wish to defer mastering this material may proceed directly to Part V at this stage, and return to Chapter 12 later.

Questions for Study and Discussion for Part III

1. A firm uses capital and labour to produce a single output, and its production function displays increasing returns to scale at all levels of ouput.

    (a) Does this imply that the average products of labour and capital are increasing?
    (b) Does this imply that the marginal products of labour and capital are increasing?
    (c) Does this imply that the short-run average cost curve is downward sloping?
    (d) Does this imply that the long-run average cost curve is necessarily downward sloping?

2. Explain why

    (a) Short-run marginal cost is greater than or equal to long-run marginal cost.
    (b) Short-run average total cost is greater than or equal to long-run average total cost.

3. United Widgets plc has a production function which displays increasing returns in the output range from zero to X_1, constant returns from X_1 to X_2 and diminishing returns thereafter. What is the shape of the firms' long-run total cost curve? What is the relationship between long-run average and long-run marginal cost at levels of output between X_1 and X_2? Draw the long-run average and marginal cost curves for United Widgets.

4. (a) Do diminishing marginal returns to a factor imply diminishing average returns to a factor?
    (b) Do diminishing marginal returns to a factor imply diminishing returns to scale?
    (c) If every factor generates diminishing marginal returns to a factor, does that imply factors are perfect substitutes for each other?
    (d) If every factor generates diminishing marginal returns to a factor, does that imply that factors are perfect complements?

5. 'Since an entrepreneur can always build the same factory next door, there is no reason to believe that long-run average costs will actually ever increase as output rises.' Discuss.

6. A firm has the following short-run production functions:

employment per week	output per week
0	0
1	3
2	7
3	11.5
4	16
5	19
6	21

(a) Plot the average and marginal products of labour on a graph. Does this production function display diminishing marginal returns to labour eventually?

(b) If the wage is £5 per week, plot the short-run variable and marginal cost curves.

(c) If fixed costs are £10 per week, plot the short-run average and marginal cost curves.

7. A firm uses labour and capital to produce output, X. A new manager is appointed, who notes that, while each worker costs £5 per week and that the weekly rental price of capital is £10, the marginal product of capital is 200 units of output per week. Can the manager conclude that the firm is minimising costs? If not, what actions should she take with regard to employment, the capital stock and output in order to rectify the situation?

8. Analyse the effect of an increase in the rental price of capital on average costs in the short run and in the long run? Is the impact greater in the short run or the long run? Why?

9. Suppose that the long-run production function which describes how labour and capital generate output is homothetic and displays constant returns to scale.

(a) Will the expansion path be upward sloping and convex for given input prices?

(b) Under what conditions will the long-run average cost curve be downward sloping?

Suggested Further Reading to Part III

Arrow, K.J. 1974. *The Limits of Organisation*. New York: Norton.

Coase, R.H. 1937. 'The Nature of the Firm', *Economica*. Reprinted in Stigler and Boulding (eds) (*op. cit.*).

Ferguson, C.E. 1969. *The Neoclassical Theory of Production and Distribution*. Cambridge: Cambridge University Press.

Heathfield, D.F. 1974. *Production Functions*. London: Macmillan.

Henderson, J.M. and Quandt, R.E. 1971. *Microeconomic Theory: A Mathematical Approach*. (2nd edn) New York: McGraw-Hill, Ch. 3.

Leontief, W.W. 1966. *Input–Output Economics*. Oxford: Oxford University Press.

Robinson, J. 1971. 'Rising Supply Price', *Economica*. Reprinted in Stigler and Boulding (eds) (*op. cit.*).

Viner, J. 1931. 'Cost Curves and Supply Curves', *Zeitschrift für Nationalökonomie*. Reprinted in Stigler and Boulding (eds) (*op.cit.*).

Part IV

PRODUCTION AND COSTS — FURTHER TOPICS

12

Production Functions, Cost Functions and the Demand for Factors of Production

Introduction

The foregoing analysis of costs, cast in terms of the production function and factor prices, is reasonably straightforward. Moreover it yields, as we have already seen, and will later see below, many useful insights into the economic analysis of production, not least into the many parallels that exist between this topic and the theory of consumer choice. Nevertheless, when it comes to explicitly empirical work, there can be problems; and though this book deals only with economic theory, we are concerned that its readers learn economic theory which is helpful in analysing and understanding the real world.

The problems to which we refer here arise because the data on the characteristics of actual production functions are always hard, and often impossible, to obtain. They run parallel to the problems caused for applications of the theory of consumer choice by our inability to measure consumers' utility functions directly. Here, as with the theory of consumer choice, that body of analysis known as *duality theory* is extremely helpful. We saw briefly in Chapter 4 that the application of this idea enabled us to obtain useful results directly from data on consumer income and expenditure volumes on particular goods, without having any knowledge of the utility function. In the production function area, the analogous variables are output levels and outlays on factor purchases. Just as analysis of the expenditure function pays large dividends when dealing with consumer behaviour, so too does analysis of the cost function when producer behaviour is under study.

Now the mathematical techniques underlying duality theory are more complicated than others used in this book, and so this chapter, which sets out the basics of this theory as it applies to production, is more difficult than those which have come before it. Moreover, the real benefits from mastering the techniques in question arise in empirical work, or in the treatment of certain theoretical questions, only a few of which are treated below (mainly in Chapter 19). Hence though the material dealt with here is a vital part of the training of any economist, and should therefore command the attention of readers who intend to carry their studies further, we have written this chapter so that, if readers so choose, they may omit it without detracting in any large measure from their ability to read the rest of the book. This chapter can also be read out of sequence, for example following Chapters 19 and 20 rather than Chapters 10 and 11.

The essence of duality theory is that all aspects of a firm's production technology which are relevant to the economist can be summarised in a simple way in its cost function. This deceptively simple and apparently purely technical statement has important implications for the way we analyse firms' output and input choices. For example, optimal factor inputs can be derived directly from the cost function, without reference to the cumbersome isoquant—isocost apparatus that we developed in the previous chapter. Input demands at a given level of output, and given input prices, can instead be derived by differentiating the cost function with respect to these input prices. Moreover, we shall also see that the slopes of input demand curves are themselves given by the second derivatives of the cost functions with respect to their prices, and that average and marginal cost curves can be shown to shift with input prices according to the derivatives of the cost function with respect to output and input prices. These points are fairly hard to establish, and we rely to some extent on specific examples rather than general proofs to present them in this chapter.

As we have already noted, a further reason for taking duality theory seriously is its usefulness in empirical work. Applied economists working, for example, on problems of public policy, frequently find that the policy prescription depends on the shape of production technology. However, it is often hard to get reliable information on factor inputs, at least in an appropriate form. For example, the available data on labour inputs may cover the number of workers, but not control for skill level, hours worked or the intensity of effort. Problems are even more serious in the case of capital, where the evaluation of the flow of services yielded by a capital stock is particularly tricky. The value of capital is often hard to measure, and information about capacity utilisation is hard to obtain. Firms typically have more information about costs. Duality theory shows us how to make inferences about the shape of production technology, for which data are sparse and poor, using cost relationships, where data are more readily available and reliable.

*From Production to Cost Functions in the Long Run

Before coming to grips with duality theory proper, we first run through the formal analysis, analogous to that of utility theory in Chapter 2, in which we deduce the implications of cost minimisation for enterprise choice of output and input volumes.

It will be remembered that costs are defined as

$$C = wL + rK \tag{12.1}$$

The cost *function* relates costs of production to input prices and the volume of output on the assumption that the firm's choice of inputs, K^* and L^*, is optimal, i.e. cost minimising. The cost function,

$$C = C(X,w,r) \tag{12.2}$$

is therefore derived as the solution to a formal cost minimisation problem.

We can think about linking costs to output for given input prices in two ways. The first is to fix the level of cost at, for example, $\bar{C}$, and then to find the maximum output which can be produced at that level of cost. Alternatively one can fix output at, say, $\bar{X}$ and find the minimum level of cost, given input prices, at which that quantity can be produced. The two methods are analogous and provide an identical solution, at the tangency between the isocost and isoquant curves. This is illustrated in Figure 12.1. As we noted in Chapter 11, every point on the long-run cost curve is associated with an optimal capital–labour ratio, or *choice of technique*, which occurs at the tangency point. Here, the ratio of input prices equals the marginal rate of technical substitution (*mrts*) between the inputs.

Starting with our first method, if we fix the level of cost at $\bar{C}$, the cost-minimisation problem becomes an output-maximisation problem, namely to maximise

$$X = f(L,K) \tag{12.3}$$

subject to

$$\bar{C} = wL + rK \tag{12.4}$$

We can therefore form the Lagrangian

$$H_1 = f(L,K) + \lambda_1 (\bar{C} - wL - rK) \tag{12.5}$$

where λ_1 is the Lagrange multiplier. The first-order conditions are

$$\frac{\partial H_1}{\partial L} = \frac{\partial X}{\partial L} - \lambda_1 w = 0 \tag{12.6}$$

$$\frac{\partial H_1}{\partial K} = \frac{\partial X}{\partial K} - \lambda_1 r = 0 \tag{12.7}$$

Figure 12.1

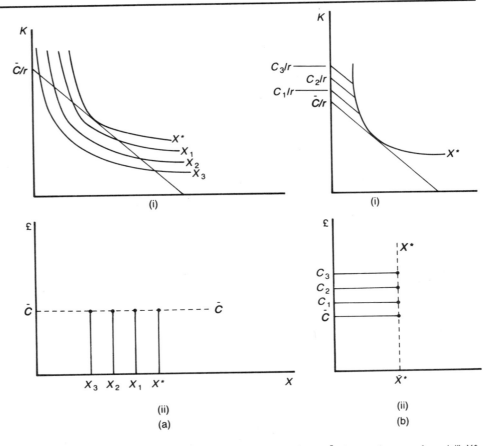

(ai) illustrates output maximisation for a given level of cost $\bar{C}$. As can be seen from (aii) X^* represents the greatest output that can be obtained for $\bar{C}$; X_1, X_2 and X_3 are outputs produced with inefficient capital–labour ratios. (bi) illustrates cost minimisation for a given level of output. There are numerous factor combinations available to produce X^*, costing C_1, C_2 and C_3 for example. The cheapest is $\bar{C}$, the lowest point in (bii).

$$\frac{\partial H_1}{\partial \lambda_1} = \bar{C} - wL - rK = 0 \tag{12.8}$$

From (12.6) and (12.7),

$$\frac{1}{\lambda_1} = \frac{w}{\partial X/\partial L} = \frac{r}{\partial X/\partial K} \tag{12.9}$$

We know from the previous chapter that the expression $(w/(\partial X/\partial L))$ defines marginal cost in the short run (see equation (11.12)). Hence the

Lagrange multiplier, λ_1, is equal to short-run marginal cost. We may interpret equation (12.9) as telling us that, if the firm is cost minimising, the marginal cost of increasing output must be the same whether it does so by using additional units of labour or additional units of capital $(r/(\partial X/\partial K))$. This result is intuitively appealing; if it did not hold, we could always in the long run increase output while holding costs constant, by switching to the input with lower marginal cost while reducing our use of the input with the higher marginal cost. In short, for a maximum, the contribution of the last unit of cost outlay to output must equal λ_1 for both inputs.

Rearranging terms in (12.9), we have

$$\frac{\partial X/\partial L}{\partial X/\partial K} = w/r \tag{12.10}$$

We know from Chapter 10 that the ratio of marginal products equals the slope of the isoquant, the *mrts* (see equation (10.7)). Hence since

$$\frac{\partial K}{\partial L} = -\frac{\partial X/\partial L}{\partial X/\partial K} \tag{12.11}$$

we have established that

$$\frac{\partial K}{\partial L} = -w/r \tag{12.12}$$

Output maximisation for a given cost requires that the ratio of relative input prices equals the marginal rate of technical substitution between them. This is the result we deduced geometrically in Chapter 11 (see p. 156).

Precisely the same result can of course be obtained by minimising cost for a given level of output X. The problem here is to choose capital and labour inputs to

$$\text{Min}_{L,K} \; C = wL + rK \tag{12.13}$$

subject to

$$X = f(L,K) \tag{12.14}$$

The Lagrangian is

$$H_2 = wL + rK + \lambda_2 (X - f(L,K)) \tag{12.15}$$

with first-order conditions

$$\frac{\partial H_2}{\partial L} = w - \lambda_2 \frac{\partial X}{\partial L} = 0 \tag{12.16}$$

$$\frac{\partial H_2}{\partial K} = r - \lambda_2 \frac{\partial X}{\partial K} = 0 \tag{12.17}$$

$$\frac{\partial H_2}{\partial \lambda_2} = X - f(L,K) = 0 \qquad (12.18)$$

From (12.16) and (12.17) we derive

$$\lambda_2 = \frac{w}{\partial X/\partial L} = \frac{r}{\partial X/\partial K} \qquad (12.19)$$

from which (12.12) can be derived as before. The results of deriving the cost function from an output-maximising problem, subject to a cost constraint, are identical to those which emerge if the cost function is instead derived from a cost-minimising problem, subject to an output constraint.

*Fixed Proportions Technology

We have already discussed in the previous chapter how the shape of the cost function is influenced by the returns to scale characteristics of the production function. In particular, constant, rising and falling long-run average costs are associated with, respectively, constant, diminishing and increasing returns to scale. We now begin to consider this relationship more formally, as well as the relationship between the degree of substitutability between factors and the shape of the cost function.

Consider first the case of zero substitutability between inputs, which was illustrated in Chapter 10, Figure 10.5a. Suppose that the level of output is given by the minimum of γL and θK, where γ and θ are exogenous parameters which jointly determine the capital–labour ratio. That is, the ratio at which it would be impossible to reduce the input of either factor without reducing output, or, to put it in terms of Figure 12.2, the ratio at which the right angle in a representative isoquant occurs. The production function is therefore

$$X = \min (\gamma L, \theta K) \qquad (12.20)$$

and the isoquants are L-shaped as in Figure 12.2. To produce each unit of X, we therefore need both X/γ of labour and X/θ of capital, at a cost of w and r respectively. The minimum cost is therefore

$$C = \frac{Xw}{\gamma} + \frac{Xr}{\theta} \qquad (12.21)$$

which can be rearranged as

$$C = X\left(\frac{w}{\gamma} + \frac{r}{\theta}\right)$$

This cost function can be used to illustrate formally the points made in Figure 12.2. The fixed coefficient technology we have envisaged here

Figure 12.2

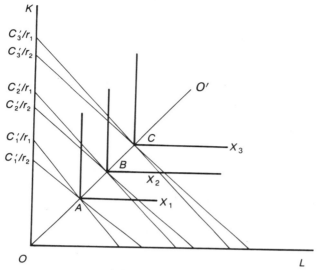

Fixed proportions and the choice of technique. Fixed coefficient technology implies that the 'tangency' between the isoquant and isocost line always occurs at the kink, at *ABC* along the optimal capital–labour ratio ray 00′. The resulting long-run cost function is therefore linear because the production function displays constant returns to scale, and the choice of technique is not affected by input prices. However, costs themselves increase with input prices. For example if capital costs rise from r_1 to r_2, the cost of producing *X*, rises. This can be seen by noting that, at the higher rental price of capital, the isocost curves passing through *A*, *B* and *C*, cut the horizontal (labour) axis further to the right. Since wages are constant by assumption, this implies that factor outlays are higher.

has constant returns to scale, so we expect the total cost function to be linear from the origin with respect to output, with average cost equal to marginal cost. From (12.21), we derive the marginal cost by taking the derivative with respect to output. This yields

$$\frac{\partial C}{\partial X} = \frac{w}{\gamma} + \frac{r}{\theta} \tag{12.22}$$

which is *constant* for given input prices. Dividing (12.21) by X generates average cost (C/X) which gives exactly the same expression as in equation (12.22). Hence, as expected, marginal and average costs are equal, and do not vary with output. We have therefore established formally that for a constant returns fixed coefficient technology, the total cost curve is indeed linear.

We can also examine the relationship between costs and input prices at a given level of output. Differentiating (12.21) by each input price,

$$\frac{\partial C}{\partial w} = \frac{X}{\gamma} = L > 0 \tag{12.23}$$

$$\frac{\partial C}{\partial r} = \frac{X}{\theta} = K > 0 \tag{12.24}$$

We know from the production function that X/γ is the amount of labour services, L, and X/θ is the amount of capital services, K, being used to produce X units of output. Hence differentiating the cost function with respect to input prices reveals that an increase in the price of an input increases the minimum cost of producing a given level of output by the amount of the input being used. Minimum costs *always* rise when input prices increase. The increase in the minimum cost of producing X_1, when wages rise, is the employment level L_1 times the wage increase. Similarly, when capital costs rise the increase is given by that rise times the capital stock, K_1. This important result is an application of *Shephard's lemma*, which is one of the central findings of the so-called 'duality' literature. It establishes that the firm's demand for a factor at a given level of output can be expressed as the derivative of the cost function with respect to that input's price. This result is not, therefore, specific to the special case of fixed proportions.

*Perfect Substitutability

Let us now repeat the foregoing exercise on the assumption that labour and capital are perfect substitutes in the production process. As we saw in Chapter 10, the production function in this case takes the form

$$X = aL + bK \tag{12.25}$$

and the isoquants are straight lines, as illustrated in Figure 12.3. Since the inputs are perfect substitutes, a cost-minimising firm will choose that input which is cheapest per unit of output. If only labour is used, we require X/a units of employment to produce X units of output. Employment per unit of output is therefore $1/a$; the cost per unit of output is w/a. Similarly, if only capital is used, we require X/b units of capital to produce X units of output and the cost per unit is r/b.

The cost-minimising firm will, as we have said, choose the cheaper option, so the cost function is

$$C = \min\left(\frac{w}{a}, \frac{r}{b}\right) X \tag{12.26}$$

In defining technology here, we have once more assumed constant returns to scale, so, as with fixed coefficient technology, average costs and marginal costs are equal and constant, with given input prices. Thus, it is easy to show, by differentiating equation (12.26) with respect to X and by dividing it through by X, respectively, that

Figure 12.3

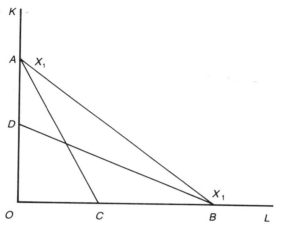

Perfect substitutes and the choice of technique. The isoquant X_1X_1 is given by the straight line AB. DB, AC and AB also represent three different isocost curves. When the (negative) slope of the isocost curve is less than that of the isoquant, as in AC, the cost-minimising firm uses only capital, and produces X_1 at A. When the (negative) slope of the isocost curve is greater, as in DB, the firm produces using only labour, at B. When the slopes of the isoquant and the isocost curve are the same, as in AB, the firm produces anywhere along the isoquant AB.

$$\frac{\partial C}{\partial X} = \min\left(\frac{w}{a}, \frac{r}{b}\right) = \frac{C}{X} \qquad (12.27)$$

Moreover, the 'derivative property' of the cost function which associates input demand functions at constant levels of output with the derivative of the cost function with respect to input prices — Shephard's lemma — holds for this functional form. Thus assuming no induced changes in technique, if the firm chooses to use only labour we have

$$\frac{\partial C}{\partial w} = \frac{X}{a} = L \qquad (12.28)$$

and if it chooses only capital, we have

$$\frac{\partial C}{\partial r} = \frac{X}{b} = K \qquad (12.29)$$

In this case too, therefore, we have established that the minimum cost of producing a given output increases when a factor price increases, by the amount of the input used times the change in its price.

**Cobb–Douglas Technology

Let us now consider, as a final illustration, the case where production technology is described by a Cobb–Douglas function

$$X = AL^\alpha K^\beta \tag{12.30}$$

The properties of this functional form were discussed at greater length in Chapter 10. Let us simplify the analysis without losing any of its content, by choosing the units in which inputs and output are measured so that $A = 1$ and let us maintain the assumption of constant returns to scale, so that $\alpha + \beta = 1$. The production function then becomes $X = L^\alpha K^{1-\alpha}$. Interested readers may wish to resolve the problem which follows with $(\alpha + \beta)$ not equal to one in order to establish for themselves the relationship between returns to scale and the shape of the cost function.

Let us now solve the minimisation problem,

$$\min_{L,K} C = wL + rK \tag{12.31}$$

subject to

$$X = L^\alpha K^{1-\alpha} \tag{12.32}$$

by forming the Lagrangian

$$H_3 = wL + rK + \lambda_3 [X - L^\alpha K^{1-\alpha}] \tag{12.33}$$

Differentiating,

$$\frac{\partial H_3}{\partial L} = w - \lambda_3 [\alpha L^{\alpha-1} K^{1-\alpha}] = 0 \tag{12.34}$$

$$\frac{\partial H_3}{\partial K} = r - \lambda_3 [(1-\alpha) L^\alpha K^{-\alpha}] = 0 \tag{12.35}$$

$$\frac{\partial H_3}{\partial \lambda_3} = X - L^\alpha K^{1-\alpha} = 0 \tag{12.36}$$

Rearranging terms

$$\lambda_3 = \frac{wL}{\alpha X} = \frac{rK}{(1-\alpha)X} \tag{12.37}$$

so that

$$L = \frac{r}{w} \frac{\alpha}{1-\alpha} K \tag{12.38}$$

and $\quad K = \dfrac{w}{r} \dfrac{1-\alpha}{\alpha} L \tag{12.39}$

Substituting (12.38) into the production function

$$X = \left(\frac{r}{w}\right)^\alpha \left(\frac{\alpha}{1-\alpha}\right)^\alpha K^\alpha K^{1-\alpha}$$

so
$$K = \left(\frac{r}{w}\right)^{-\alpha}\left(\frac{\alpha}{1-\alpha}\right)^{-\alpha}X \tag{12.40}$$

Similarly, substituting (12.39) into the production function

$$X = L^{\alpha}\left(\frac{w}{r}\right)^{1-\alpha}\left(\frac{1-\alpha}{\alpha}\right)^{1-\alpha}L^{1-\alpha}$$

so
$$L = \left(\frac{w}{r}\right)^{\alpha-1}\left(\frac{1-\alpha}{\alpha}\right)^{\alpha-1}X \tag{12.41}$$

Substituting these values for optimal L and K into the cost function, we obtain

$$C = wL + rK$$
$$= wXw^{\alpha-1}r^{1-\alpha}(1-\alpha)^{\alpha-1}\alpha^{1-\alpha} + rXr^{-\alpha}w^{\alpha}\alpha^{-\alpha}(1-\alpha)^{\alpha}$$
$$= Xw^{\alpha}r^{1-\alpha}(1-\alpha)^{\alpha}\alpha^{-\alpha}\left(\frac{\alpha}{1-\alpha} + 1\right)$$
$$= Xw^{\alpha}r^{1-\alpha}(1-\alpha)^{\alpha}\alpha^{-\alpha}\left(\frac{1}{1-\alpha}\right)$$
$$= Xw^{\alpha}r^{1-\alpha}(1-\alpha)^{\alpha-1}\alpha^{-\alpha} \tag{12.42}$$

At first sight, the cost function, equation (12.42), for the Cobb–Douglas production function seems complicated. However, it can be simplified to,

$$C = Xw^{\alpha}r^{1-\alpha}B \tag{12.42'}$$

(where $B = (1-\alpha)^{\alpha-1}\alpha^{-\alpha}$), which is the dual of the original production function form. Studying (12.42), it comes as no surprise that if the output level doubles, the cost of production doubles, since we have assumed constant returns to scale. As in our previous two examples, if we derive the average and marginal costs, they are equal for given input prices, taking the value $w^{\alpha}r^{1-\alpha}B$.

To analyse the demand for inputs as their prices change, we take the derivatives of the cost function with respect to factor prices. Thus

$$\frac{\partial C}{\partial w} = \alpha Xw^{\alpha-1}r^{\alpha-1}B$$
$$= \frac{\alpha C}{w} \tag{12.43a}$$

Similarly,

$$\frac{\partial C}{\partial r} = (1-\alpha)Xw^{\alpha}r^{-\alpha}B$$

$$= \frac{(1-\alpha)C}{r} \tag{12.43b}$$

To establish the relevance of (12.43a) and (12.43b), we need to draw on material proved formally only in Chapter 19. Readers willing to take our word at this point can simply accept that the factor weights, α and $(1-\alpha)$, in equation (12.43a) and (12.43b) represent the proportions in which the value of total output is distributed between wage payments to labour and rental payments to capital if the firm makes zero profits. To see how this result might arise, accept that λ_2 in our cost-minimisation problem at the start of the chapter is in fact equal to the product price p. Then equations (12.16) and (12.17) show that in equilibrium the firm equalises the input price to the marginal product times the output price for each input. In the Cobb–Douglas case, this implies that $w = p\alpha X/L$, and $r = p(1-\alpha)X/K$. Provided profits equal zero, so the entire value of output is exhausted by payment to factors of their marginal product; these can be rearranged to equal

$$\alpha = \frac{wL}{pX}; \ (1-\alpha) = \frac{rK}{pX}$$

Hence, the Cobb–Douglas weights represent the shares of each factor in the value of output.

Returning to equations (12.43a) and (12.43b), αC is labour's share of costs, and $(1-\alpha)C$ is capital's share of costs. As in our previous examples, $\alpha C/w$ therefore equals the number of workers and $(1-\alpha)C/r$ the stock of capital used to produce total output. In fixed coefficients and perfect substitutability, therefore, the minimum cost of producing a given output alters in response to change in input price by exactly the amount of the input used.

The Idea of Conditional Factor Demand Functions

We have so far illustrated how minimum costs change with output and with changes in factor prices on the basis of special assumptions about the nature of technology. Results on the first relationship have been associated with returns to scale, and results on the latter are associated with factor demands. The relationship between input prices and factor demands is potentially complicated because substitution effects away from relatively more expensive inputs (analogous to substitution effects in consumer theory) may be offset by scale effects via output adjustments resulting from changes in the relationship between cost and price (analogous to income effects in consumer theory). The duality approach

allows us to avoid all this complexity and derive factor demands directly from the cost function, without having to worry about changes in output and the choice of technique (factor proportions). Given output, the value of the derivative of the cost function with respect to wages turns out to give us the optimal level of employment, and the derivative with respect to the rental price of capital yields the optimal level of the capital stock. These factor demand functions we shall refer to as *conditional factor demands*. In the balance of this chapter we outline more generally results on cost functions, input prices, and conditional factor demands. Profit-maximising factor demands, which take account of changes in output, are analysed in Chapter 19. Students who seek formal proofs of the arguments which follow or wish to see the ideas developed further are referred to the readings listed at the end of the chapter.

Costs When Input Prices Change

The general cost function, $C = C(\bar{X}, \hat{w}, \hat{r})$, gives the minimum cost of producing output $\bar{X}$ when input prices are $\hat{w}, \hat{r}$, and L^*, K^* are the optimal values of factor inputs given those input prices. The first important property of this cost function is that the total cost of a given output will increase in proportion to a simultaneous equiproportional increase in both wages and the rental price of capital. For example, if the factor prices both double, the cost of producing $\bar{X}$ doubles, because the relative cost of the inputs remain constant and therefore the choice of technique does not alter. The only effect of proportional increases in input prices is therefore on costs; they do not influence relative factor demands at a given output level. We can say that the cost function is *linearly homogeneous* (or homogeneous of degree one) in factor prices in the same way as we spoke of linearly homogeneous production functions in Chapter 10. Similarly, since input demands are not affected by proportionate changes in wages and the rental price of capital, we can say that input demands (L^*, K^*) are homogeneous of degree *zero* in input prices.

A second important result, linking optimal input demand at a given level of output to the derivative of the cost function, has already been derived for special cases earlier in this chapter. *Shephard's lemma* tells us that

$$\frac{\partial C}{\partial w} = L^*; \ \frac{\partial C}{\partial r} = K^* \tag{12.44}$$

When wage rates increase by one penny, the minimum cost of producing the given level of output increases by L^* pence, and for an increase of r of one penny it increases by K^* pence. This result is of course equivalent to that developed on the demand side in Chapter 4 (see equation 4.17) where we established that the compensated demand curve was the derivative of the expenditure function with respect to price.

This result is convenient because it enables us to analyse how costs change with input prices without direct reference to changes in the choice of technique and the underlying shape of the production function. Consider for example the extent to which costs change as wages alter. One might expect to have to take account of how capital is substituted for labour around the isoquant and therefore, to take account of the elasticity of substitution of labour for capital, but this turns out to be unnecessary. We define the elasticity of total cost with respect to wages in the normal way as

$$\varepsilon_w^C = \left(\frac{dC}{C}\right) \bigg/ \left(\frac{dw}{w}\right)$$

$$= \frac{\partial C}{\partial w} \frac{w}{C} \tag{12.45}$$

Substituting from equation (12.44),

$$\varepsilon_w^C = \frac{wL^*}{C} \tag{12.46}$$

Hence total costs vary with wages according to the percentage of costs accounted for by the labour input. If the share of labour input in total costs is 50 per cent, total costs increase by 0.5 per cent if wages increase by 1 per cent. As the share of labour costs in total costs increase, the impact of a rise in wages on total costs increases proportionately.

The mathematics of duality therefore allows us to analyse extremely simply the underlying relationships between input prices and costs, without reference to the production function or a formal minimisation problem.

The Cost Function and Conditional Factor Demand Functions

As we noted above, it is important to stress the distinction between two sorts of factor demand functions. The first, which is the topic of this section, relates optimal employment of labour and capital services to the wage rate and the cost of capital, *conditional* on the assumption that output is fixed. Hence the name given to factor demand functions of this sort: *conditional factor demand functions*. The second sort of input demand function takes account of changes in output as well as changes in the choice of technique when considering factor demand responses to changes in their price. We shall refer to this as a *profit-maximising factor demand function* and analyse it in detail in Chapter 19.

In this section, we are therefore concerned with how optimal input quantities and proportions alter with input prices as we move around

an isoquant. The analysis is analogous to our discussion of Hicks' compensated demand curves in consumer theory, when we analysed how the quantity demanded of our two goods changed with their relative price as we moved around the indifference curve (see Ch. 3, pp. 28–37). The slope of the isocost curve is the (negative) ratio of wages to capital costs, which increases with the wage rate. As the cost of labour relative to capital increases, cost-minimising firms substitute capital for labour around the isoquant; as in the case of consumer theory, so here too the substitution effect is always negative. This is illustrated in Figure 12.4.

Some Properties of Conditional Factor Demand Functions

The degree to which input demands respond to changes in their relative prices, conditional on output, may be expressed as the elasticity of factor demand. As before, it is helpful to begin the discussion with reference to the two special cases of zero and infinite substitutability between the inputs.

Consider first the case of fixed coefficients, illustrated in Figure 12.2. Since the 'tangency' between the isocost line and the isoquant always occurs at the kink of the latter, whatever the slope of the isocost line, factor proportions and input demands are not affected by input prices. Since we cannot substitute between labour and capital, the demand for factors at each level of output is independent of input prices. In the example of production function (12.20), the optimal capital–labour ratio

Figure 12.4

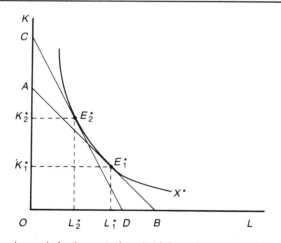

Conditional factor demand. As the cost of capital falls or the wage rate increases the isocost line shifts around the isoquant from AB to CD. The equilibrium choice of technique becomes more capital-intensive, moving from E_1^* to E_2^* with optimal employment falling from L_1^* to L_2^* and optimal capital rising from K_1^* to K_2^*.

is always θ/γ, and the elasticity of conditional factor demand is zero. (Interested readers can derive this formally from the conditional input demand functions, (12.23) and (12.24).)

The results in the perfect substitutes case are equally transparent. The firm will either use only capital, or only labour in its production process, unless the slope of the isocost line equals the slope of the isoquant, in which case the outcome is indeterminate. The impact of factor prices on the capital–labour ratio, and hence the elasticity of factor demand, is thus discontinuous in this case. Consider an instance when input prices yield isocost line AC in Figure 12.3, with isoquant AB. As the cost of capital rises (as the cost of labour falls so the *relative* cost of capital rises), the isocost line AC swivels outwards. At a certain point, the slope of the isocost line equals that of AB, and the firm may start to hire some labour, though the actual choice of technique is indeterminate. If the cost of capital rises any further, the firm switches to using labour only in its production process, at the corner B in Figure 12.3. The resulting conditional demand for capital curve for a given level of output is drawn in Figure 12.5. Its elasticity is either zero at a rental rate below $\hat{r}$, or infinite at $\hat{r}$.

These zero and infinite substitutability cases are, of course, highly restrictive. In general, one might expect a smoothly downward-sloping conditional input demand curve, analogous to the compensated demand curve of Chapter 3. It is fairly straightforward to show this for the case of the Cobb–Douglas function. It is useful to start with the elasticity of substitution, defined in Chapter 10. Equation (10.8), provides a unit free measure of the curvature of the isoquant, and therefore the extent to which factor proportions adjust with input prices. This elasticity is defined as

Figure 12.5

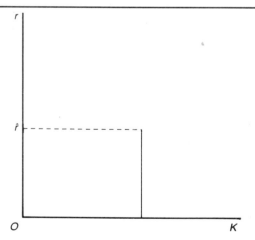

Demand for capital when inputs are perfect substitutes and output is given. The rental price of capital, $\hat{r}$ is such that, for the given wage rate $\hat{w}$, the slope of the isocost curve $\hat{w}/\hat{r}$ exactly equals the slope of the linear isoquant, as along AB in Figure 12.3.

the ratio of the proportionate change in factor proportions to proportionate changes in the marginal rate of technical substitution that occur as we move around the isoquant. Since cost minimisation implies equality between the marginal rate of technical substitution and the input price ratio, w/r, the elasticity of substitution also measures the proportionate change in the capital–labour ratio for a proportionate change in the ratio of input prices,

$$\sigma = \frac{\% \text{ change in } K/L}{\% \text{ change in } w/r} = \frac{\partial(K/L)}{\partial(w/r)} \frac{w/r}{K/L} \tag{12.47}$$

In this case of Cobb–Douglas production function, where isoquants are smoothly convex to the origin as in Figure 12.4 and where, crucially, the elasticity of subsitution is unity (see equation 10.27), we may immediately see that a 1 per cent increase in the relative cost of labour leads to a 1 per cent rise in the capital–labour ratio. As we might expect from the conditional demand functions (12.43a) and (12.43b) optimal inputs therefore smoothly decline with input prices for a given output in the Cobb–Douglas case.

We may establish these results more formally. Recall that we showed in equation (12.44) that the derivative of the cost function with respect to the input prices yield input demands. We have also established that, provided isoquants are convex to the origin, conditional input demands diminish with input prices, or

$$\frac{\partial L}{\partial w}, \frac{\partial K}{\partial r} < 0 \tag{12.48}$$

But by the standard rules of differentiation,

$$\frac{\partial L}{\partial w} = \frac{\partial(\partial C/\partial w)}{\partial w} = \frac{\partial^2 C}{\partial w^2} \tag{12.49}$$

and $\quad \dfrac{\partial K}{\partial r} = \dfrac{\partial(\partial C/\partial r)}{\partial r} = \dfrac{\partial^2 C}{\partial r^2} \tag{12.50}$

Hence we may say that, if the cost function is concave with respect to input prices, then the conditional input demand functions must be downward sloping with respect to input prices; $\partial L/\partial w$ and $\partial K/\partial r < 0$ if $\partial^2 C/\partial w^2$ and $\partial^2 C/\partial r^2 < 0$.

The information summarised in equations (12.49) and (12.50) implies that we may derive the conditional input demand *functions* with respect to input prices directly from the cost function in an extremely straightforward way. They are merely the second derivatives of the cost function with respect to the input price. Thus, returning to the examples given at the start of this chapter, if technology has fixed coefficients, so that

the relevant cost function takes the form of (12.22) with optimal employment given by equation (12.23) and optimal capital by (12.24), we may derive the conditional input demand equation from the second derivatives of the cost function,

$$\frac{\partial L}{\partial w} = \frac{\partial^2 C}{\partial w^2} = 0 \tag{12.51}$$

$$\frac{\partial K}{\partial r} = \frac{\partial^2 C}{\partial r^2} = 0 \tag{12.52}$$

Hence we establish formally the point made earlier, and more discursively, via Figure 12.2 that the demand for factors is independent of input prices when there is perfect complementarity between inputs.

The conditional input demand functions cannot be determined using differential calculus for the case when capital and labour are perfect substitutes because the cost function is not continuous, and we have seen in Figure 12.5, the conditional input demand functions are also discontinuous. However, for the Cobb–Douglas case, the cost function is given by equation (12.42) and optimal employment and capital by equations (12.43a) and (12.43b). The conditional input demand functions are therefore given by

$$\frac{\partial^2 C}{\partial w^2} = \frac{\alpha(\alpha-1)C}{w^2} < 0 \tag{12.53}$$

$$\frac{\partial^2 C}{\partial r^2} = \frac{(1-\alpha)(-\alpha)C}{r^2} < 0 \tag{12.54}$$

As we noted above, conditional factor demands decline as factor prices increase when isoquants are convex to the origin, as they are in the case of Cobb–Douglas technology.

*The Effect of Changes in Input Prices on Average and Marginal Costs

From the perspective of output supply decisions, to be discussed in the next two parts of this book, the long-run average and marginal cost curves reflect the most important characteristics of the cost function. The bulk of this chapter has been spent investigating the ways in which total costs and conditional factor demands vary with wages and the rental price of capital, but the implications of this analysis for marginal and average costs are also worth considering. We shall now discuss these matters.

We have already established that the elasticity of total costs with respect to wages, for example, is given by the share of the wage bill in total costs

(see equation (12.46)). The same result must clearly hold for average costs, since the level of output enters both the top and bottom of the elasticity formula. Hence, if the elasticity of average costs with respect to wages is ε_w^{ac}, at a given level of output, X^*,

$$\varepsilon_w^{ac} = \frac{\partial(C/X)}{\partial w} \cdot \frac{wX^*}{C} = \frac{1}{X^*} \frac{\partial C}{\partial w} \frac{wX^*}{C}$$

$$= \frac{\partial C}{\partial w} \frac{w}{C}$$

$$= \frac{wL^*}{C} \qquad\qquad (12.55)$$

The same argument holds for a change in capital costs, $\varepsilon_r^{ac} = rK^*/C$. Hence an increase in either input price always shifts the average cost curve upwards because the share of each input in total costs is clearly positive.

However, the upward shift will only be a proportionate one if the share of labour costs in total costs is constant as output changes. This will occur if technology is *homothetic*, and expansion paths are therefore linear in capital—labour space. In this case, the vertical upward shift in the long-run average cost curve will be in the same proportion for every level of output. Hence the output level at which average costs reach a minimum will remain unchanged. In other cases the upward shift will not necessarily be proportionate and the level of output at which average costs reach a minimum may alter.

The effects of a change in input price on long-run marginal cost can, logically speaking, be positive or negative, depending on a further property of the production function; whether the input whose price has changed is 'normal' or 'inferior'. (As we shall see, the terms are used here exactly as they are in consumer theory.) Consider the effect of an increase in the wage on marginal cost, *mc*. We know that

$$\frac{\partial(mc)}{\partial w} = \frac{\partial^2 C}{\partial X \partial w} \qquad\qquad (12.56)$$

By the rules of differentiation

$$\frac{\partial^2 C}{\partial X \partial w} = \frac{\partial^2 C}{\partial w \partial X}$$

and we also know from Shephard's lemma that

$$\frac{\partial C}{\partial w} = L^*$$

Hence $\dfrac{\partial(mc)}{\partial w} = \dfrac{\partial L^*}{\partial X}$ $\qquad\qquad$ (12.57)

The direction of the change in marginal cost at a given level of output when wages increase therefore depends on how optimal employment adjusts as output changes, starting at that initial level of output. There are two possible cases. If labour is a *normal input*, in the sense that optimal employment increases when output increases, then $\partial L^*/\partial X>0$ and marginal cost rises with wages.

However, this is not the only logically possible case. Suppose we have a production process in which it is efficient to reduce the labour input as output expands. Labour is in this case an *inferior input* in precisely the same sense as a good whose demand falls with income is an inferior good. In these circumstances $\partial L^*/\partial X$ will be negative and marginal cost will fall as the wage increases. Precisely the same line of argument applies to an increase in the cost of capital. Marginal cost will rise if capital is a normal input, but fall if it is an inferior input.

The results just established may once again be illustrated by referring to two of the three special case technologies which we have analysed throughout this chapter. If the production function displays fixed proportions technology, the cost function is given in equation (12.21) and marginal cost in (12.22). The change in marginal cost when wages rise is given by

$$\frac{\partial(mc)}{\partial w} = \frac{\partial^2 C}{\partial X \partial w} = \frac{1}{\gamma} > 0 \qquad\qquad (12.58)$$

This is an intuitively obvious result. Since labour is a normal input with fixed coefficient technology, marginal costs must clearly increase with the cost of labour. In the case of perfect substitutes the discontinuity of the cost function once again leaves us unable to analyse changes in marginal cost using differential calculus. With the Cobb–Douglas production function, and therefore a cost function as given by (12.42), marginal costs are

$$\frac{\partial C}{\partial X} = w^\alpha r^{1-\alpha}(1-\alpha)^{\alpha-1}\alpha^{-\alpha} = \frac{C}{X} \qquad\qquad (12.59)$$

and the change in marginal cost with respect to wages is given by

$$\frac{\partial^2 C}{\partial X \partial w} = \alpha w^{\alpha-1} r^{1-\alpha}(1-\alpha)^{\alpha-1}\alpha^{-\alpha} = \frac{\alpha C}{wX} > 0 \qquad\qquad (12.60)$$

As we would expect with smooth isoquants, convex to the origin, and an elasticity of subsitution of unity, labour is here a normal input and increased wages raise marginal cost.

Conclusions

We have sought in this chapter to give readers an introduction to recent developments in production and cost theory. In particular, we have focused on the way that traditional propositions in the theory of supply, for example that input demand curves slope downwards, can be derived directly from the cost function without reference to the underlying shape of production technology. While recognizing that many of the arguments we have presented are subtle and difficult, it is hoped that they give an insight into economists' methods and into the assumptions underlying the traditional relationships we postulate when analysing questions about production decisions and costs.

Questions for Study and Discussion for Part IV

1. Examine the effect of an increase in the cost of labour on marginal costs in the short run and in the long run. Under what conditions will the long-run marginal cost curve shift down?
2. Suppose that the production function takes the form $X = \min(10L, 5K)$ and that a competitive firm faces a wage rate of £60 per week and a weekly capital rental of £32.

    (a) How much must the firm spend to produce 100 units of output, and what is the average cost of production when $X = 100$?
    (b) What is the incremental cost of producing the 101st unit of output?
    (c) What happens to the cost of producing 100 units of output if the wage rate and the rental cost of capital rise by 25 per cent each? What happens to the average and marginal cost?
    (d) What happens to the cost of producing 100 units of output if the wage rate increases by £1, or if the cost of capital increases by £1.
3. Suppose that the weekly production function takes the form $X = 2L + K$, with the firm facing a weekly wage rate of £100 and capital rentals of £300.

    (a) Will the firm use any labour at all in the production process?
    (b) Suppose that output of X is 500 units per week. What are marginal costs? What are average costs?
    (c) Suppose that the wage rate increases by 60 per cent. What happens to the cost of production? What happens to average and marginal cost?
4. The firm faces a long-run production function (for output per week)

    $$X = 10L^{\frac{1}{2}}K^{\frac{1}{2}}$$

and input prices of £100 per week for labour and £200 per week for capital rental.

(a) What are the firm's cost-minimising levels of employment and capital stock if it produces 200 units of output?

(b) What if it produces 400 units of output? What are long-run average and marginal costs in each case (i.e. if output = 200 and 400)?

(c) Suppose that the firm becomes more efficient technically, so that the production function becomes

$$X = 11L^{1/2} K^{1/2}$$

What happens to total, average and marginal costs if output equals 200? If output equals 400?

(d) What happens to the capital—labour ratio if output equals 200 and the wage rate increases by 10 per cent? What happens to total and marginal costs?

Suggested Further Reading to Part IV

Diewert, W.E. 1971. 'An Application of the Shephard Duality Thoerem: A Generalised Leontief Production Function', *Journal of Political Economy.*

Diewert, W.E. 1974. 'Applications of Duality Theory', in *Frontiers of Quantitative Economics.* Vol. 2, M. Instilligator and P. Kendrick (eds) Amsterdam: North-Holland.

Fuss, M. and McFadden, D. 1978. *Production Economics: A Dual Approach to Theory and Applications.* Amsterdam: North-Holland.

Shephard, R. 1953. *Cost and Production Functions.* Princeton: Princeton University Press.

Part V

INDUSTRIAL ORGANISATION THEORY: COMPETITION AND MONOPOLY

13

Perfect Competition

Introduction

We shall be concerned, in this and the following part of the book, with the decisions of firms about how much to supply to the product market. One of our major interests will be the relationship between the demand for a product, associated with its price in competitive markets, and the quantity that a firm chooses to produce. This can be contrasted with the focus, in Part VII of the book, on the relationship between product demand and factor demand. The precise relationship between product demand and production can be shown to depend on the structure of the market in which the enterprise operates and upon the motivation of those who take the relevant decisions. In this part of the book we shall concentrate on perfect competition and monopoly, before going on to discuss a variety of forms of imperfect competition and alternative company objectives in the following part. In what follows, we shall assume that firms are motivated to maximise profits, except in Chapter 19 where we examine the implications for supply behaviour of certain alternative assumptions about enterprise objectives.

This and the following chapter outline the theory of supply in a competitive industry. In this chapter we derive supply curves at the level of the firm and that of the competitive industry under some rather special assumptions about technology and factor price behaviour. In Chapter 14 a more general treatment of these same topics is provided, while in Chapter 15 we deal with the price and output decisions of a monopolist.

The Profit-Maximisation Hypothesis

The maximisation of profits is not the only conceivable motive for the operator of a firm, whom we designated earlier as the 'entrepreneur'.

However, if the entrepreneur is a utility-maximising individual who gains utility solely from the consumption of goods and services obtained on the market, then maximising profit is consistent with achieving that end. To the extent that an individual draws satisfaction from less tangible factors, such as power, the esteem of friends and neighbours and so forth, it is possible to construct arguments that suggest that the size of the firm (perhaps measured by the value of sales) or the rate of growth of the firm would be more appropriate variables to maximise. Moreover, when one recognises that the world in which any actual firm operates is far from being a certain one, so that it is seldom clear which particular decision among the alternatives available will indeed result in maximum profits, motives based upon acquiring security, cutting down the effort put into decision making and such, also begin to look appealing.

A large part of the literature of that field of economics known as *industrial organisation* is devoted to careful analysis of the questions just raised about motivation. It is not our purpose in an intermediate text to go into this, even superficially. Because we assumed that consumption alone yielded utility when dealing with the consumer, and because we are going to adopt, albeit usually implicitly, the assumption that uncertainty about the future does not exist when dealing with the firm, consistency suggests that we adopt profit maximisation as well. It is not an uncontroversial assumption about motivation, but it does yield relatively simple and useful analysis. Its implications are worth pursuing for that reason alone. Moreover, in the last analysis, any firm, whatever the motivation of its owners and managers, must earn profits if it is to survive. There must always be an element of profit seeking in the behaviour of any firm and it is not perhaps unreasonable to approximate this with the simplifying assumption of profit maximisation. Remember, though, that the following pages do not represent a comprehensive survey of the theory of the firm, dealing as they do mainly with the theory of the profit-maximising firm operating in conditions of certainty.

The Perfectly Competitive Firm's Demand Function

We will now analyse the so-called perfectly competitive firm, sometimes called a *price-taking* firm. As the latter name implies, the firm is one that takes the price of its output and of its inputs as given and makes decisions only about the volume of its output and the quantities of inputs it will employ.

It is usual to think of the price-taking firm as being a sufficiently small part of the industry of which it is a member that its own activities could not possibly have a noticeable effect on the price of the industry's output. A single farm producing a particular crop is the archetypal example here, which is one of the reasons why agricultural economists find the perfect competition model so attractive and useful. The demand curve

for output that such a firm faces takes the form of a horizontal line at a given price such as that depicted in Figure 13.1. The curve shows an infinite price elasticity of demand, since the smallest fall in its selling price will lead to an infinite increase in the quantity that the firm can apparently sell.

Competitiveness is often associated not only with a very large, and potentially infinite, number of suppliers, but also with each operating under broadly the same conditions. By this last phrase we mean that information about technology is freely accessible, so that everyone can in principle choose the same techniques of production, and that there are no restrictions on new firms starting to trade on the market, nor on existing firms leaving the market if they are unable to earn an adequate return. In the real world, of course, these conditions are rarely satisfied in full, but the perfectly competitive model is nevertheless useful. It provides both a standard by which outcomes in other market structures can be judged and an idea of the outcome to which a market with large numbers of firms, free entry and exit of traders, and free access to information and technology would tend.

Total, Average and Marginal Revenue

The revenue function faced by the firm describes the relationship between total revenue (or the total value of sales) and output. Calculus is particularly useful in bringing out the relationship between revenue, revenue

Figure 13.1

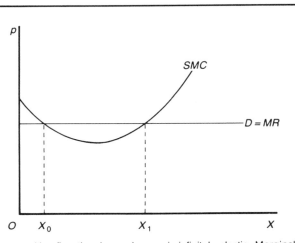

For a perfectly competitive firm the demand curve is infinitely elastic. Marginal revenue therefore equals price. Profits are maximised in the short run where marginal cost cuts the marginal revenue curve from below (at output X_1). At output X_0 marginal cost cuts the marginal revenue curve from above and losses are maximised. Figure 13.2 presents the same analysis in terms of total revenue and total cost functions.

per unit of production and incremental, or marginal, revenue. Revenue, R, depends upon the quantity of output sold and its price,

$$R = R(X) = pX \tag{13.1}$$

We define *average revenue* as revenue per unit of output (R/X), which obviously equals price. The average revenue curve therefore relates price to output, and is the firm's *demand curve*. *Marginal revenue* is the increment to revenue generated by the sale of an additional unit of output, and can therefore be derived formally as the derivative of the revenue function with respect to output. In the general case, where we allow for price to vary with output along the demand curve, marginal revenue is given by

$$mr = \frac{\partial R}{\partial X} = p + X\frac{\partial p}{\partial X} \tag{13.2}$$

where $\partial p/\partial X$ is the slope of the demand curve faced by the firm. However, in a perfectly competitive market, the demand curve is horizontal, as in Figure 13.1. The slope of the demand curve is zero and marginal revenue equals price. Hence for perfect competition, *and for perfect competition only*, the marginal and average revenue curves coincide, as in Figure 13.1. Since in competition, $\partial R/\partial X = p$, which is a constant by assumption, the revenue curve, denoted TR in Figure 13.2, is a straight line with slope p. If we wish to think of this analysis in terms of the elasticity of demand, we may note that the elasticity of demand, e, is defined as $(\partial X/\partial p)(p/X)$ so that we can derive one of the fundamental relationships in the theory of the firm, that

$$mr = \frac{\partial R}{\partial X} = p\left(1 + \frac{1}{e}\right) \tag{13.3}$$

This equation gives another way of thinking about the perfectly competetive firm's demand curve. In competition e is infinite and therefore marginal revenue equals price.

It is worth repeating explicitly that average and marginal revenue are not in general the same concept; they just happen to be equal when the demand curve that the firm faces is horizontal. When price does not vary with the volume of sales, then marginal revenue (the amount added to total revenue per unit of output when a small addition is made to output — and hence to sales) is simply price per unit of output. If the price the firm received did vary with output, this would not be the case. The behaviour of firms differs with market structure precisely because market structure can affect the slope of the demand curve faced by each individual firm, and therefore the impact of particular output decisions on the revenue to be earned by it. We shall begin to take up such issues in Chapter 15.

Figure 13.2

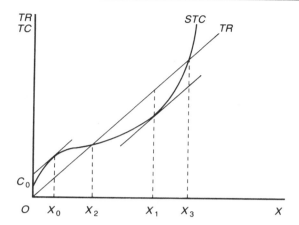

Short-run profits are maximised where short-run total cost is at a maximum distance below total revenue. This is at level of output X_1 where the slopes of the two curves are equal (i.e. where marginal cost equals marginal revenue) where the slope of the total cost curve is increasing. At X_0 the slopes of the two curves are equal, but here costs exceed revenue and the slope of the total cost curve is falling. Hence short-run losses are maximised here.

The Firm's Short-Run Supply Curve

What, then, about profit maximisation? First, let us consider the *short-run* situation. There are two equivalent geometrical ways of finding the level of output at which profits are maximised in the short run. They are depicted in Figures 13.1 and 13.2. Consider first Figure 13.2 where a short-run total cost curve that displays at first increasing and then decreasing returns to labour, is set alongside the total revenue curve. Profits are equal to total revenue minus total costs which, in terms of Figure 13.2, is the vertical distance between the two curves. This distance is obviously at a maximum at output level X_1, where the total cost curve is below the total revenue curve and their slopes are parallel to each other. At any lower level of output, revenue is rising faster than cost, and at any higher level it is rising more slowly. Note that, by a similar argument, maximum losses would be made at output X_0.

Now we know that the slope of a 'total' curve defines a 'marginal' curve. If it is a condition of profit maximisation that the slope of the total revenue curve be equal to that of the total cost curve, then this also means that *marginal cost should be equal to marginal revenue*. This could take place at either X_0 or X_1 in Figure 13.1, but output X_0 is one that maximises losses. It is also a condition of profit maximisation then that the *marginal cost curve cuts the marginal revenue curve from below*. This, of course, is at a level of output at which there are diminishing returns to labour. We

have here an example of the condition asserted in Chapter 10, that the firm will always operate in the region of the production function characterised by diminishing returns to a factor.

Now for a price-taking firm, marginal revenue and price are equal to one another. Thus, in the short run, a profit maximising price-taking firm will fix output at that level whose marginal cost of production (on the upward-sloping segment of the marginal cost curve) is equal to market price, with one qualification that we must now discuss.

It is always open to the firm to produce nothing at all, and there are circumstances where this is the most profitable (in the sense of being the least costly) thing it can do. In the short run, the firm must always pay its fixed costs, regardless of its level of output. It incurs variable costs only if it produces output, and it is easy to construct a case in which both the total cost curve and the total variable cost curve lie above the total revenue curve at every level of output. In such a case price is below both overall average cost and average variable cost at any positive level of output. Figure 13.3 depicts just such a situation. If this firm *must* produce something then it will certainly maximise profits (that is minimise losses; the terms are synonymous) at output X_1 where marginal cost and marginal revenue are equal. However, by producing X_1, it would make greater losses than it would incur if it produced nothing at all. If it produced nothing, it would lose only its fixed costs, whereas by producing X_1 it is making a loss on its variable costs also. Unless a firm can reduce its losses by producing, it will not produce, and it can do this only if the price it receives for its output exceeds the minimum value of average variable cost.

Figure 13.3

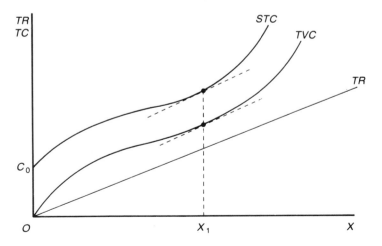

If total revenue is everywhere below total variable cost, then losses are greater at output X_1 (where they are nevertheless minimised for any positive level of output), than they would be if the firm produced nothing and incurred a loss of C_0 — its fixed costs.

At any price above this level, which just covers average variable cost, profit-maximising output is found by inspecting the marginal cost curve, but below this level the firm will produce no output at all. Notice what has just been said: above the minimum point of the average variable cost curve the marginal cost curve relates the firm's profit-maximising output to price. Since the firm is a profit maximiser, this will be its actual output. Hence, for the individual competitive firm in the short run, *the marginal cost curve is its supply curve.*

*A Formal Treatment

Supply decisions for competitive firms can be analysed particularly simply with the aid of calculus, which also offers a more general interpretation than our previous geometric approach. Algebraically, the firm chooses output to maximise profits, which equal revenue minus costs. Profits are given by

$$\pi = pX - wL - rK \qquad (13.4)$$

which, because of our work on cost functions in Chapters 11 and 12 and on revenue functions above, we can respecify as

$$\pi = \pi(X) = R(X) - C(X) \qquad (13.5)$$

The first-order condition for maximisation is

$$\frac{\partial R}{\partial X} - \frac{\partial C}{\partial X} = 0 \qquad (13.6)$$

which, in the case of competition when marginal revenue equals price, is

$$p - \frac{\partial C}{\partial X} = 0 \qquad (13.7)$$

The first-order condition states that profits are maximised at a level of output where marginal cost $(\partial C/\partial X)$ equals price. This is, however, only a *necessary* condition for profit maximisation. We derive the *sufficient* condition from the second derivative of the profit function (13.5). The second-order condition is

$$\frac{\partial^2 \pi}{\partial X^2} = \frac{\partial^2 R}{\partial X^2} - \frac{\partial^2 C}{\partial X^2} < 0 \qquad (13.8)$$

In competition, the slope of the demand curve faced by the firm is a constant so $\partial^2 R/\partial X^2 = 0$. Sufficiency therefore hinges on the sign of the second derivative of the cost function, which must be positive, as we saw in Figures 13.1 and 13.2. Hence profits reach a maximum provided, at the point where price equals marginal cost, marginal costs are increasing with output. If we interpret our cost functions as relating to the short

run, when only labour input is variable, we will remember, following the analysis of Chapter 10, that rising marginal cost implies diminishing returns to labour. Note also that we can also think about the firm's output decision directly in terms of the impact of a changing production level on profits. An example is illustrated in Figure 13.4 of the quadratic profit function implied by the revenue and cost functions of Figure 13.2.

Price Determination in the Short Run

We are now in a position to investigate how the price, taken as given by the individual firm, is in fact determined, at least in the short run. The market demand curve for X may be obtained by summing up the individual demand curves derived in Part I (using the constant real income rather than constant money income curves if we wish to deal with a fully employed economy). Just as the individual's demand curve tells us how much that agent will buy at a given price, so the market demand curve tells us how much all the individuals in the market for X will together buy at a given price. By analogous reasoning, we may derive the short-run market supply curve for X on the assumption that input prices are constant for all producing firms, regardless of their output. The short-run marginal cost curve above the minimum point of the average variable cost curve tells us how much X any individual firm will supply at a given price. Adding up the amounts of X over all firms tells us how much the whole industry will supply. Figure 13.5(b) portrays the relevant market supply and demand curves. Their intersection at p^*, X^* determines the overall output of X and its price. This is the price which is given to the individual firm whose situation is depicted in Figure 13.5(a). At this price,

Figure 13.4

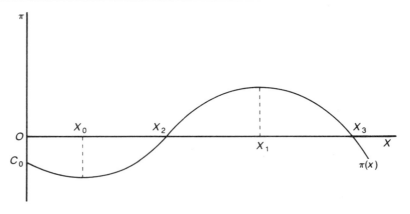

The profit function implied by the cost and revenue functions of Figure 13.2. Profits reach a minimum at X_0, and maximum at X_1 and equal zero at X_2 and X_3. Profit maximisation implies that the firm chooses X_1, where marginal revenue equals marginal cost.

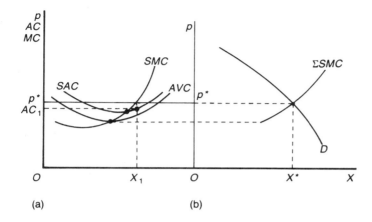

The short-run industry supply curve, when factor prices are given, is the horizontal sum of each firm's marginal cost curve above the minimum point of each firm's average variable cost curve (ΣSMC). The interaction of supply and demand at the industry level determines industry output at X^* and price at p^*. At this price the individual firm produces X_1 units of output and makes a total profit of $(p^* - AC_1)X_1$. Note that, to keep the diagram manageable, the scale on the horizontal axis of panel (b) is greatly reduced from that which is used on the same axis panel (a), so that a given horizontal distance from the origin of (b) represents a greater volume of X.

the consumption plans of consumers and the output plans of firms are just compatible. We have an *equilibrium* situation.

Now the situation for the particular firm shown in Figure 13.5(a) has it producing X_1 at the going market price. Since the average cost of producing that level of output is AC_1, the firm is clearly making a total profit of $(p^* - AC_1)X_1$. A number of questions now arise. First, suppose we look at the behaviour of this firm over a rather longer time period. Would it still be the case that this is the level of output it would choose? Once it is free to vary its capital inputs, might there not be some other level of output that was more profitable at that price? Second, the supply curve used to determine the market price was obtained by adding up the marginal cost curves of all firms in the industry. It is only valid to aggregate individual short-run marginal cost curves in this way if we assume that input prices do not vary even when all firms in the industry vary their output levels. We have also been assuming that there is a given number of firms in the industry. Now, over a time period where the individual firm cannot vary its capital stock, it is quite reasonable to make this latter assumption. But what determined how many firms were in the industry in the first place? When we consider a horizon long enough to make all factors of production variable, we must also consider the possibility of firms entering and leaving the industry. In short, we must consider the determination of price and output in the long run.

The Firm and the Industry in the Long Run

The foregoing analysis showed, with input prices constant, that the short-run supply curve of the perfectly competitive firm is that section of its marginal cost curve which lies above its average cost curve. For purely expositional purposes, let us first consider the supply behaviour of already existing firms in the long run, though in practice it will be impossible to distinguish between capital expansion by existing firms and entry of new ones. If, still holding factor prices constant, we assume that entry is impossible and simply substitute the long-run total cost, average cost, and marginal cost curves for their short-run counterparts in the arguments embodied in Figures 13.1, 13.2, and 13.5, the firm's long-run supply curve is given by that section of its long-run marginal cost curve that lies above the minimum point of the long-run average cost curve. This conclusion also follows from a straightforward reinterpretation of the cost function embedded in equation (13.5) as a long-run relationship. However, it does not follow from this that the industry's long-run supply curve is simply some horizontal summation of the individual firms' supply curves. The reason is that, in the long run, each firm is free to vary the quantities of all the inputs that it uses, and if existing firms can do that, then they can, if they choose, leave the industry, while new firms can enter it. In the long run, therefore, the number of firms in the industry is variable. As we noted above, this is a second crucial characteristic of a competitive market structure.

In order to carry our analysis further, suppose that there are no special resources or limited skills necessary to produce X, so that the production function underlying the cost curves of the particular firm we have been considering is available to any firm. Suppose also that each firm is able to buy its inputs at the same price as any other. It then follows that the short-run and long-run cost curves for any firm will be identical to those for any other. For the remainder of this chapter, we assume that technology displays increasing, then constant, then diminishing returns to scale, so that the *long-run average cost curve is U-shaped*.

In order to appreciate the importance of the possibility of entry by new firms to the behaviour of a competitive industry in the long run, it is helpful to consider first a hypothetical situation in which entry is not possible. Consider, in the light of this assumption, Figure 13.6. Here we show the short- and long-run cost and supply curves for a typical firm in the industry. It is assumed in drawing this figure that the firm is in a situation in which price is equated to both long-run and short-run marginal cost, so that, given the price ruling in the market, the firm has the right sized plant. If this is true of each firm, there will be no internal tendency for it to change its output at all: each one will be making profits of $(p^* - AC_1)X_1$ — the maximum available. Such a situation as we have depicted in Figure 13.6 could exist only if there were no entry into the industry. If the technology underlying the production function is readily

Figure 13.6

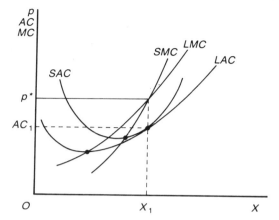

Suppose that price is given by p^*. At this price the typical firm will, in the long run, wish to sell X_1 of X. At this scale of output there are associated short-run average and marginal cost curves, the latter cutting the long-run marginal cost curve from below at output level X_1. As this figure is drawn, the firm makes positive profits at an output of X_1. From the point of view of the industry, this cannot be a long-run equilibrium situation.

available to all-comers, and if anyone may enter the industry, existing firms would not be allowed to remain undisturbed in that situation, if they were ever in it in the first place.

The profit which each firm is depicted as making is the difference between revenue and outlay on both the wage bill and on the rental of all its capital equipment. It is a pure surplus, because any 'normal rate of return' is already included in the rental price of capital, as we pointed out in Chapter 11. This profit is a rate of flow of extra income that is available simply as a result of being in the industry. If we start with barriers to entry, and then remove them, new firms will obviously be attracted by the existence of this profit and will set up in the production of X. By assumption, they can now costlessly enter the industry. Only when such profit is completely competed away will there be no further entry.

The means by which such profit is competed away are easily analysed. As each new firm enters the industry its output must be added to the output of the firms already in the industry. Because the market demand curve for X slopes downwards, the market price of X will fall as industry output is increased in this way. Firms will continue to enter the industry until market price has fallen to such an extent that no profits are being made by any firm. At this point, with neither entry nor exit, each firm may be said to be of equilibrium size and the industry to contain an equilibrium number of firms. As readers should be able to satisfy themselves, when the industry is of equilibrium size, the output of each firm in it will be lower than in what we now know to be the non-equilibrium situation depicted in Figure 13.6.

Now the foregoing description of profits being competed away after the removal of some unspecified barrier to entry of new firms serves the purpose of emphasising the important role played by the number of firms in the industry in determining the properties of the long-run competitive supply curve. It should not be taken literally as a description of a process often encountered in the real world. In an industry in which entry was always possible, it is unlikely that any firm would put itself in a position as that depicted in Figure 13.6. If market price was ever high enough to create positive profits, the firm would realise that they would attract other firms into the industry and that they would be competed away. Hence the firm would not expand its capacity along its long-run marginal cost curve. It would foresee the arrival of new entrants and realise that it would be left with too much capacity to produce efficiently its share of the industry's long-run equilibrium output once they started producing. Hence the firm would avoid getting itself into this overcapacity situation in the first place, and at most would move along its short-run supply curve in order to take advantage of any temporary rise in output price above its long-run equilibrium level. We analyse the role of firms' expectations about the behaviour of others, upon which we merely touch here, in more detail in Chapter 17 below.

Now the industry's long-run equilibrium output level, at which there is neither entry nor exit, must be such that the price facing each firm in the industry just enables it to cover its costs while maximising profits. Maximum profits mean that marginal cost must equal price and zero profits mean that average cost must equal price. Marginal and average cost are only equal to one another at the minimum point of the average cost curve. Thus, if firms are free to come and go in the industry, the

Figure 13.7

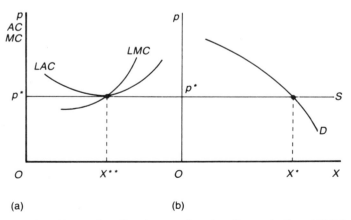

(a)   (b)

The existence of positive profits will entice new firms into the production of X. If factor prices are constant and all firms are equally efficient, price will always tend, in the long run, to be equal to the minimum attainable level of long-run average cost. Hence the long-run industry supply curve will be horizontal at this price. Each firm will produce X^{**} at price p^*.

price of output will always return to this same level in the long run. The long-run supply curve for the industry will be a horizontal line at the minimum value of long-run average cost for any firm in the industry, as we show in Figure 13.7 and each firm will produce an output of X^{**}.

Concluding Comment — the Properties of the Competitive Industry

In this chapter, we have assumed that each firm has identical technology with increasing, constant and then diminishing returns to both labour and to scale. Each firm therefore faces identically shaped long-run and short-run U-shaped average cost curves. Each firm also faces the infinite elasticity of demand which means that in perfect competition, price equals marginal revenue. On these assumptions, we have deduced that profit maximisation leads each firm to select the level of output at which marginal cost equals price. The price of goods sold on competitive markets therefore reflects the incremental costs of producing the last unit of output. It will be shown in Part IX of this book that this sort of output rule can be associated with efficiency in the allocation of resources.

14

More on the Theory of Supply in Perfect Competition

Introduction

So far, our analysis of supply under competitive conditions has been confined to a rather special case: namely an industry of equally efficient firms each one having a U-shaped long-run average cost curve, and each one facing the same, invariant, set of prices for its inputs. Now we shall look at the special assumptions involved here in more detail. Only the assumption of the U-shaped cost curve plays more than a simplifying role in the analysis of perfect competition, and so we shall take up this matter first.

Alternative Assumptions about Returns to Scale

The returns to scale characteristics of the firm's production function that underlie the U-shaped long-run average cost curve assumed above play an important role in the theory of perfect competition, and this is best seen by examining what would happen if these characteristics were different.

Consider, first of all, the long-run average and marginal cost curves of a firm that faces diminishing returns to scale at every level of output. They will be as depicted in Figure 14.1. Clearly, at any price above p^*, say p_1, this firm will be making positive profits. If every firm, actual and potential, faces the same cost conditions, the existence of positive profits will lead to an expansion of the industry. This expansion should go on until each firm is producing at the lowest point on its long-run average cost curve, but that would be at a level of output approaching zero. The prediction that an industry will end up in the long-run situation of hav-

Figure 14.1

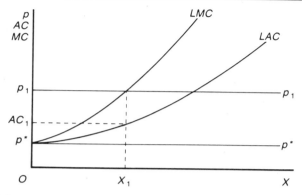

For a firm which experiences diminishing returns to scale at every level of output, the minimum point on its average cost curve is arbitrarily close to the vertical axis. In perfect competition with all firms equally efficient, then each such firm would end up making zero profits at an output approaching zero. The assumptions of consistently decreasing returns to scale together with that of equally efficient firms are not useful in the context of perfect competition.

ing a number of firms approaching the infinite, each producing an output verging on zero, does not make much empirical sense, and we may rule this case out on these grounds alone. If the perfectly competitive firm is to have a finite equilibrium size in the long run, then the minimum point on its average cost curve must not coincide with the vertical axis.

When the firm's production function is everywhere characterised by constant returns to scale, its long-run average and marginal cost curves coincide and are horizontal lines. This case produces indeterminate rather than nonsensical results at the level of the analysis of the individual firm. In Figure 14.2 the long-run equilibrium price at the industry level is given at p^*, and the demand curve faced by the individual firm will be horizontal at that price, coinciding at every point with the firm's marginal and average cost curves. Thus, the number of firms in the industry and their sizes are left indeterminate in this case. One firm or many could equally efficiently produce the whole industry's output. Constant returns to scale at the level of the firm cannot be reconciled with a useful analysis of the behaviour of the individual perfectly competitive firm, at least not in terms of the simple analysis upon which we base this chapter.

Finally, consider the case of the individual firm benefiting from continuously increasing returns to scale. The appropriate cost curves are depicted in Figure 14.3(a). This case, though empirically plausible, is incompatible with the existence of perfect competition. When there are continuously increasing returns to scale up to the level of output that will satisfy the entire market demand for the industry's output, one firm can produce the whole industry's output at a lower average cost than can two or more firms, and that firm could therefore always undercut and drive out any smaller firms that tried to compete with it.

Figure 14.2

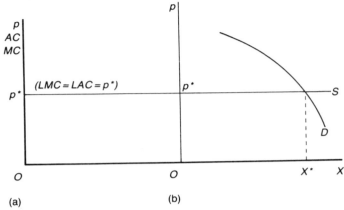

(a)   (b)

If all firms are equally efficient and experience constant returns to scale, industry output is determinate at X^*. However, the firm's output is indeterminate since the marginal cost, average cost and marginal revenue curves coincide when zero profits are being made.

Figure 14.3a

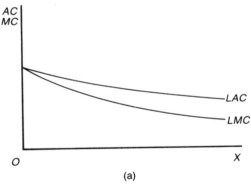

(a)

When returns to scale are always increasing, long-run average cost falls continuously and marginal cost is below it. There is no meaningful price and output equilibrium to this case in the context of perfect competition. Increasing returns to scale naturally lead to monopoly.

Figure 14.3b

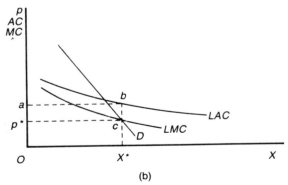

(b)

If a natural monopoly is forced to set price equal to marginal cost it makes a loss of $abcp^*$.

We have here what is known as *natural monopoly* and the perfectly competitive model may not be applied in this case. The theory of monopoly, dealt with in the next chapter, is the appropriate device to use in its analysis. It should be noted however that any attempt to force a natural monopoly to mimic competitive behaviour, for example by the imposition of a price equals marginal cost rule along the lines discussed in the previous chapter, will lead the firm in question to make losses. The point is illustrated in Figure 14.3(b). Suppose that the regulatory authorities calculate that, given the demand curve for output D, the market will clear when price equals p^*. If these same authorities also enforce the output rule for the natural monopoly that output must be chosen to equalise price and marginal cost. In this case, output will be X^*. Increasing returns to scale imply that the firm will always make a *loss* under these circumstances, equal to the hatched area under *LAC* in Figure 14.3(b). This happens because, with increasing returns to scale, the long-run average cost curve lies everywhere above the long-run marginal cost curve. This technical consideration, rather than inherent inefficiency, will lead even well-run natural monopolies regulated by price equals marginal cost rules to make losses.

*Returns to Scale and Profitability in the Cobb–Douglas Case

The relationship between returns to scale, equilibrium output and profits in the long run for perfectly competitive firms can be illustrated formally using the example of the Cobb–Douglas production function. We therefore assume that the firm maximises profits,

$$\pi = pX - rK - wL \tag{14.1}$$

where $X = AL^{\alpha}K^{\beta}$ \hfill (14.2)

but impose no restrictions on the degree of homogeneity of the production function (given by the sum of α and β).

Recall from Chapter 12 that $\lambda_1 = w/(\partial X/\partial L) = r/(\partial X/\partial K) = \lambda_2$ where λ_1 and λ_2 are the Lagrange multipliers for the output maximisation (for a given cost outlay) and cost minimisation (for a given level of output) problems respectively (see equations (12.9) and (12.19)). The Lagrange multipliers were shown to equal marginal cost. The analysis in the previous chapter established that price must equal marginal cost in both the short and long run. Our analysis of the output decision, based on the comparison of marginal cost with price, can therefore be turned into a model of *labour and capital demand* decisions by substituting price for λ_1 and λ_2 in the above equalities and rearranging terms. This implies that firms hire labour until

$$p\,\frac{\partial X}{\partial L} = w \qquad\qquad (14.3)$$

and hire capital until

$$p\,\frac{\partial X}{\partial K} = r \qquad\qquad (14.4)$$

These 'marginal productivity' conditions are studied in much greater detail in Chapter 19. For current purposes, we merely note that factor inputs are hired provided that the amount they add to revenue (marginal product times price) exceeds their cost.

Substituting equations (14.3) and (14.4) in (14.1), and remembering from Chapter 10 that in the Cobb–Douglas case $\partial X/\partial L = \alpha X/L$ and $\partial X/\partial K = \beta X/K$, we can derive

$$\pi = pX - \frac{p\alpha X}{L}\,L - \frac{p\beta X}{K}\,K$$

$$\pi = pX(1 - \alpha - \beta) \qquad\qquad (14.5)$$

Then we may see at once that

$$\pi \gtreqless 0 \text{ as } \alpha + \beta \lesseqgtr 1 \qquad\qquad (14.6)$$

With diminishing returns to scale ($\alpha + \beta < 1$), (14.5) shows that profits in a competitive firm are always positive. With increasing returns to scale on the other hand, ($\alpha + \beta > 1$), long-run losses are technologically guaranteed for price-taking enterprises at any level of output. Perhaps the most interesting case is when the production function is linearly homogeneous, $\alpha + \beta = 1$. In this case the firm earns zero profits regardless of the level of output. These results are essentially those developed above in Figures 14.1, 14.3, and 14.2 respectively.

The profit function itself is *linearly homogeneous*, as defined in Chapter 10, when the production function is homogeneous of degree one. This can be checked by noting that multiplying the right-hand side of (14.2) through by a constant factor, k, raises profits by that same factor k; i.e.

$$pf(kL,kK) - rkK - wkL = k\pi, \qquad\qquad (14.7)$$

when the production function is linearly homogeneous.

Three outcomes are formally possible in this case, only one of which we illustrated in Figure 14.2. In the first place, price could be higher than long-run marginal and average cost. Here the firm will have an incentive to increase its size indefinitely. Second, price could be below long-run marginal and average costs, and the firm would make losses at every conceivable level of production. Equilibrium output in this case is zero. Finally, we have the case illustrated in Figure 14.2, where market price is such that it equals long-run marginal and average cost. Equilibrium output in this case is indeterminate for the firm.

Factor proportions used in production are nevertheless determinate when technology is linearly homogeneous. Consider again the Cobb–Douglas production function. With linear homogeneity, i.e. $\alpha + \beta = 1$, then $\beta = 1 - \alpha$ and the function can be rewritten in the form

$$\frac{X}{L} = A\left(\frac{K}{L}\right)^{1-\alpha} \tag{14.8}$$

which is drawn to be concave in Figure 14.4. If the firm earns zero profits, dividing both sides of (14.1) through by L and setting profits equal to zero yields

$$0 = p\frac{X}{L} - r\frac{K}{L} - w \tag{14.9}$$

or $$\frac{X}{L} = \frac{w}{p} + \frac{r}{p}\frac{K}{L} \tag{14.9'}$$

This equation is drawn, for given p, r and w, as a straight line in Figure 14.4. Its slope is given by the rental price of capital divided by the product price, referred to as the *real rental price of capital*. Profits are maximised (at zero) where the line is just tangent to the transformed production function, that is where the *marginal product of capital is equal to the real rental price of capital*. This solution yields a determinate value for output per unit of labour $(X/L)^*$ and for the capital–labour ratio $(K/L)^*$.

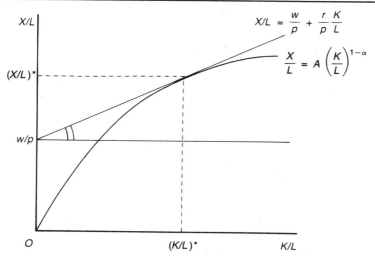

Figure 14.4

The choice of technique when production technology is linearly homogeneous. Even though the level of output is indeterminate (see Figure 14.2), the firm can still choose optimal factor proportions $(K/L)^*$ and labour productivity $(X/L)^*$ to maximise profit subject to production technology, which is assumed to be concave in $(X/L, K/L)$ space. Note that (X/L^*), or equilibrium output per unit of labour, minus the real wage is equal to the total return to capital per unit of labour.

Linearly homogeneous production functions are often used in empirical work despite the fact that they leave the size of the individual firm's output indeterminate, because one is still able to use them to analyse the choice of factor proportions, the *choice of technique* as it is often called, in competitive markets.

The U-Shaped Average Cost Curve and Managerial Inputs

The reader will by now appreciate the importance of postulating a U-shaped long-run average cost curve in the context of the theory of the perfectly competitive firm. It is only when the curve takes this form that the individual firm's output level is finite, positive and determinate. The following argument is often advanced as a plausible justification for using this type of cost function.

The production process is not solely an engineering matter; there are also administrative problems involved in getting goods produced. Someone has to organise the factors of production to ensure that they do end up co-operating in the technically most efficient manner, and someone must decide upon output levels and so forth. There is, in effect, a third input into our production process, namely the managerial skill of the organiser of the firm, the entrepreneur. Thus, when a firm expands output by equiproportional increases in labour and capital services, this does not represent equiproportional increases in *all* inputs. Managerial skill is being held constant. If, at very low levels of output, this skill is under-utilised, the firm will be able to do an increasingly effective job of organising capital and labour as output expands — to get, that is, decreasing average costs of production — up to a certain level. But, as output expands further, this same amount of organisational skill is likely to become increasingly overtaxed: hence at higher output levels there arises a tendency to rising average costs.

Once we treat managerial skill as an input, there is a need to discuss how the entrepreneur is rewarded. The answer here, as we noted in Chapter 9, is that the reward comes out of the firm's profits. Competition is no longer assumed to bid these down to zero, but down to some minimal acceptable level known as *normal profits*. One can reconcile the existence of normal profits with the analysis set out in the previous chapter in two equally acceptable ways. First, one can note that the entrepreneur, if not working in one industry, would be in some other. Hence, to engage in organising a firm in the production of X, the profit that could have been earned by organising a firm in some other industry is being forgone. The normal profits available elsewhere are then a cost of production of X in addition to outlays on capital and labour. It then becomes reasonable to think of these as being included in the factors lying behind the firm's long-run cost curves. Alternatively, one may simply suppose that these

normal profits, when spread over a sufficiently large equilibrium volume of output, make such a small difference between the minimum point on the firm's average cost curve and the price of output as to be negligible.

The notion of normal profits is not devoid of problems of its own, however. Two points in particular should be noted. Their basis is that entrepreneurial capacity represents an indivisible factor of production, but the 'entrepreneur' may just as well be a management team as an individual person. Once that is realised, the case for treating entrepreneurial capacity as indivisible begins to lose much of its initial appeal. Furthermore, the management decisions that need to be undertaken by those in charge of a firm operating in the kind of perfectly competitive industry we are envisaging here, are trivial to the point of being negligible. Our analysis abstracts from all the uncertainty about markets, about technical change, about the behaviour of competitors, and so on, that make entrepreneurial activity so taxing in the real world. Thus, arguments to the effect that the indivisibility of entrepreneurial inputs lies at the root of the U-shaped long-run average cost curves that we attribute to perfectly competitive firms are better regarded as attempts to extend the logical completeness of an already rather abstract, but not for that reason irrelevant, model than as attempts to bring that model closer to reality.

Inter-Firm Differences in Efficiency

Let us now turn to relaxing certain other assumptions made in the previous chapter. As we shall see, these are by no means as critical for the perfectly competitive model as is that of a U-shaped long-run average cost curve. When we made the assumption that all firms in the industry are equally efficient, the long-run industry supply curve turned out to be infinitely elastic at a price given by the minimum point of the typical firm's long-run average cost curve. One way of looking at this case is to note that, by adding firms to the industry, one is adding to the production process units of the third input, the skill of the entrepreneur, and that constant returns to scale are emerging at the level of the industry rather than at the level of the firm. This solves the indeterminacy of output problem at the level of the firm which arises when we postulate a linearly homogeneous production function, while retaining the result that long-run supply curves are horizontal.

But it may not be reasonable to assume that firms are in fact equally efficient. In practice some firms may be more efficient than others, and may be able to maintain their technological advantage, for example by keeping details of their production process secret, or because they have some locational advantage which other firms cannot obtain. Such efficiency differentials affect the shape of the industry supply curve, as we shall now see.

Assume that every firm already in a particular industry is observed to

be making positive — or above normal — profits, so new firms will still be attracted into that industry. If the factors that make existing firms more efficient are specific to the particular industry in which they find themselves, rather than arising from general advantages that could be exploited in any industry, and if they are not available to newcomers, then the new entrants will be less efficient in the sense that the minimum long-run average cost of production that they can achieve will be higher than that incurred by those already there, even though they pay the same price for other inputs. The entry of new firms will bid down the price of output, and this will continue to fall until the least efficient firm in the industry is producing at the minimum point of its long-run average cost curve. This least efficient firm is often called the *marginal firm*, for obvious reasons. All other firms in the industry will operate with average costs lower than price.

The long-run equilibrium described here is depicted in Figure 14.5, and this diagram should be self-explanatory. The important implication of the analysis set out in the figure is that in this case the industry's long-run supply curve slopes upwards even when the number of firms varies. This is because as output expands, less and less efficient firms, with higher and higher average costs of production, enter the industry. At each level of output, equilibrium price is given by the minimum average cost of the marginal firm, and the higher the level of output, the less efficient is that marginal firm.

It might seem to follow from the foregoing argument that differences in technical efficiency will necessarily produce a dispersion of profits across firms in a competitive industry, with only the marginal firm earning zero profits. One must be careful here though. The advantage in

Figure 14.5

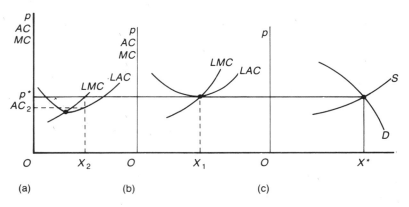

When all firms are not equally efficient, even when factor prices are constant, the industry's long-run supply curve with the number of firms variable (S) slopes upwards. Only the marginal firm, panel (b), makes no profits at its equlibrium output of X_1. Any intra-marginal (i.e. more efficient) firm such as that depicted in panel (a) will make positive profits at its profit-maximising level of output (X_2). Note that the intra-marginal firm does not produce at a scale of output that minimises long-run average cost, but at a larger scale with an average cost of AC_2.

technical efficiency enjoyed by a particular firm might arise because it has access to some particularly advantageous technology embodied in a trade secret, or some advantage in the location of its plant. If access to the secret, or the favourable plant site, is open to competitive bidding, the surplus of revenue over costs due to its being exploited will be paid to its owner, and not to the firm which uses it (unless that firm, fortuitously, happens to be the owner). In this case, even though the industry supply curve slopes upwards, each firm in the industry will make normal profits. Certain specific inputs, too short in supply to be available to all firms will, however, be paid what are often termed rents, equal to the market value of the contribution they make to the value of the output of the firms that enjoy them. A fuller discussion of the concept of rent is contained in Chapter 21 below.

Finally, it should be noted that if some firms are more efficient than others because the entrepreneurs running them are in general more skilful, and if their greater skill could be utilised effectively in any industry, then the extra return that it yields in the X industry should properly be regarded as a cost, because that extra return could also be earned elsewhere. In this case the industry long-run supply curve is a horizontal straight line, and there is no uniquely identified marginal firm.

Variations in Factor Prices in the Short Run

So far we have dealt with the effects on supply conditions of the technical characteristics of production within the industry and within firms. We have, throughout the analysis, held input prices constant. Let us now relax this particular assumption, and deal with the consequence of what are frequently called *pecuniary economies* and *diseconomies of scale*, which impinge upon firms' behaviour through the variations that they produce in factor prices. They are so called to distinguish them from real economies and diseconomies internal to the firm that, being the consequence of increasing and decreasing returns to scale in the production function, are under the control of the firm itself, i.e. are internal to its decision-making process. We will explicitly analyse pecuniary effects only in the case of an industry made up of equally efficient firms, but the reader might find it helpful to reproduce the analysis modified to fit the case of an industry where the firms vary in efficiency.

Consider first of all the effects of factor prices rising as the whole industry expands. If any particular firm is sufficiently small that no variations it makes in its scale of operations can influence factor prices, but if the industry as a whole is large enough relative to factor markets to bid up input prices when it expands, and bid them down when it contracts, then such factor price variations are outside the control of the firm, and hence are indeed external to its decision making. Because such variations result from changes in the industry's size, they may be referred to as internal to the industry.

Let us analyse an industry's short-run response to an increase in the demand for its product at any given price. In Figure 14.6 the industry demand curve shifts; each firm moves up its short-run marginal cost curve, and the industry as a whole moves up its short-run supply curve, which is of course just the sum of these short-run marginal cost curves. Now suppose that the effect of the increased demand for labour implicit in this move is to increase the price of labour. This might occur if the industry were a relatively large employer so that an increase in this demand for labour would lead to a tightening of the labour market overall. Then the short-run average and marginal cost curves of each firm are obviously shifted vertically upwards, as is the industry's short-run supply curve. We know this from Chapter 11 (and 12), where it was established that the short-run marginal cost was the wage divided by the marginal product of labour. An increase in the wage therefore increases marginal cost proportionately.

The movement to a new short-run equilibrium in this case involves in part a movement along, and in part a shift upwards, of marginal cost curves, and the new equilibrium is to be found at a point such as $p^*X_2^*$ in Figure 14.6. Now we can perform the experiment of shifting the demand curve many times and the consequence will always be this combination of movements along curves and shifts of curves, the resulting

Figure 14.6

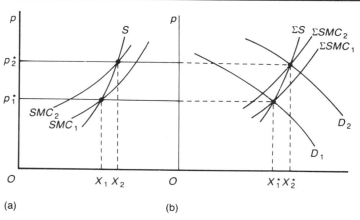

(a)   (b)

The short-run supply curve when prices of factors increase with an increase in their employment: industry demand increases from D_1 to D_2, each firm attempts to move out along SMC_1, and hence industry supply tends to shift along ΣSMC_1. However, the price of the variable factor rises as output expands shifting every firm's short-run marginal cost curve upwards. Equilibrium is re-established at X_2^* and p_2^*, as opposed to the initial equilibrium of X_1^*, p_1^*. Here the price of the variable factor is higher, so that each firm is on SMC_2 and that industry is on ΣSMC_2. The supply response of the firm from X_1 to X_2 is a mixture of a movement along a marginal cost curve and shift of such a curve; which may be summarised into a movement along a curve such as S, which is the firm's short-run supply curve of X when the whole industry is expanding its output of X and the price of the variable factor of production increases with its utilisation. The industry's short-run supply curve is the sum over all firms of curves such as S, ΣS. It is more steeply sloped than the supply curve derived holding factor prices constant.

equilibrium price and output combinations for the industry lying along
a line such as ΣS, which may then be interpreted as the industry's short-
run supply curve *when factor prices rise with output*. Such a curve will clearly
be more steeply sloped than the summed marginal cost curves at any
given level of factor prices. The reader can check that, were the price of
labour to fall as output increased, the resulting short-run supply curve
would have a shallower slope.

Factor Price Variations in the Long Run

Long-run supply relationships must be modified in a way similar to the
short-run response when factor prices are allowed to vary. Output increases, the prices of both capital and labour services tend to increase,
and so the minimum level of average cost attainable by any firm in the
industry shifts upwards. Thus, the long-run supply curve derived from
permitting the number of firms to vary acquires an upward slope. All
this is shown, at the industry level, in Figure 14.7.

What happens at the level of the particular firm when, in the long run,
factor prices increase as the industry expands is not altogether clear-cut.
It is certain that each firm's cost curves shift upwards and also that, when
the industry is in long-run equilibrium with an expanded number of firms,
each firm will once more be producing at the minimum point of its long-
run average cost curve. This much is clear, but what cannot in general

Figure 14.7

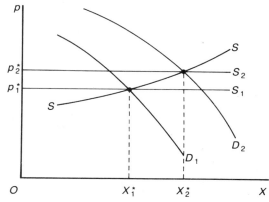

When all firms are equally efficient, but inputs prices vary positively with the industry's
demand for them, a shift from D_1 to D_2 in the demand for X leads in the long run to an
increase in the number of firms in the industry, and an increase in factor prices that shifts
up the minimum point on each firm's average cost curve. Hence the long-run supply
curve permitting the number of firms to vary, but holding factor prices constant, shifts up
from S_1 to S_2. The industry's supply response is thus a mixture of a shift along such a
curve and a shift up of such a curve and may be summarised in a movement from $p_1^* X_1^*$
to $p_2^* X_2^*$ along a curve such as S. This is the industry's long-run supply curve, when we
permit the number of firms in the industry to vary and the prices of factors of production
to rise systematically with output.

be predicted is what will happen to the individual firm's scale of output. This is because one would not in general expect the prices of capital and labour to increase equiproportionately as the industry expands. As we saw in Chapter 11, the firm will change the proportions in which it employs labour and capital, sometimes called its *choice of technique*, towards the relatively cheaper factor. When factor proportions are thus changed it is not necessarily the case that the minimum point on the long-run average cost curve will occur at the same level of output at the two different sets of factor prices. It may, or may not. Everything here depends upon the specific nature of the production function.

Factor prices may fall rather than rise as output increases. This would happen if there existed some economies of scale in other industries producing inputs, or if the quality of inputs increased with their scale of use. If all firms are equally efficient, the long-run supply curve would then slope downwards. This is a point of some interest because it enables us to be precise about the extent to which average costs that fall as the level of output increases are compatible with competition. We have already seen earlier that falling average costs produced by increasing technical returns to scale — *economies internal to the firm* — lead to monopoly. So it is only when average costs fall as a result of declining input prices — as a result of *economies external to the firm* — that competition and decreasing costs are compatible.

Such external economies as these most often arise when we have a regionally localised industry requiring specialised skills on the part of its labour force. Thus, in the case of Britain, the localisation of the cotton industry in Lancashire, lace-making around Nottingham, and the pottery industry around Stoke, for example, led to a tradition among the local labour force that perhaps reduced the costs of training labour — hence effectively lowering the price of the services of skilled labour to individual firms. Moreover, the importance of this phenomemon tends to vary with the size of the industry, so that, for example, the advantages to a textile firm of locating in Lancashire now, as compared to say 80 years ago, have probably considerably diminished, as the scale of the industry in that area has diminished.

Perfect Competition and the Supply Curve

Now in this chapter we have been discussing various aspects of the supply curve. We have seen that, as for the demand curve, there is no unique way of deriving a supply curve. Just as we could have demand curves for individuals and market demand curves, so we have here had firm and industry supply curves. Moreover, just as one gets different demand curves depending upon what it is that is conceptually held constant, so we have had different supply curves for the short run, for the long run, for constant factor prices and for variable factor prices.

Again, as with the demand curve, there is no uniquely correct way to define a supply curve; the appropriate choice must always depend upon the situation under analysis and hence upon one's assessment of which factors it is appropriate to hold constant in a particular instance. Nevertheless, the ability to generate a relationship between quantity supplied and price, to complement that between quantity demanded and price, so that the tools of supply and demand may be utilised, is an important one. *Of all the forms of industrial organisation that we will consider in this book, perfect competition is the only one that enables us to generate this relationship.*

15

Monopoly and Discriminating Monopoly

Introduction

The perfectly competitive firm with which we dealt in the last two chapters faced a horizontal demand curve and was able to sell all it pleased at the going market price. The monopolistic firms we shall analyse in this chapter face downward-sloping demand curves. As we shall see, there is no unique set of influences which ensures that the demand curve faced by every monopolist is the market demand curve for its product, but for the moment it will suffice if the reader thinks of such a firm as being the sole seller of a good in an industry where, for one reason or another, the entry of competitors is quite impossible. In such a situation the market demand curve for the good does indeed become the demand curve that faces the monopolist.

The Demand Curve, Total Revenue and Marginal Revenue

The monopolist's demand curve is downward sloping, so the total revenue function is *not* an upward-sloping straight line along which revenue is proportional to sales. As we saw in Chapter 13, a demand curve is, by definition, an average revenue curve, and if all we know about that curve is that it slopes downward, a wide variety of shapes is available for the total revenue function. The property we require for the total revenue function is that straight lines drawn to it from the origin slope less steeply at higher and higher levels of output; the slope of such lines measures average revenue, which is, of course, demand price. Figure 15.1

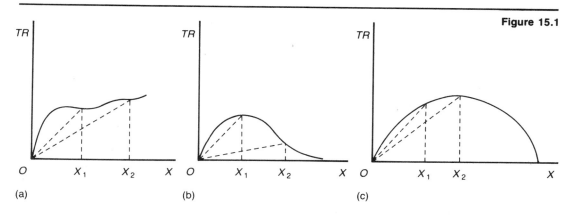

Figure 15.1

Three possible shapes for a total revenue curve associated with a downward sloping demand (average revenue) curve. The slope of a straight line from the origin to any one of these curves falls systematically as output increases. The movement from X_1 to X_2 gives an example of this. Panel (c) shows the total revenue curve associated with a straight line demand curve. Around level of output X_2, total revenue is constant as output varies. Thus, price must be changing in equal but opposite proportion to quantity and the elasticity of the demand curve must be unity at this point. At lower levels of output than X_2 demand must be elastic, and at higher levels inelastic.

displays a number of such curves and, curiously shaped though some of them are, all are compatible with a downward-sloping demand curve. The curve in Figure 15.1(c) is the one upon which we shall concentrate since it is derived from a straight-line demand curve, and the use of such a demand curve will make the exposition simpler. Simplicity is the only reason for preferring a straight line demand curve, however; there is no theoretical or empirical reason for preferring it.

Now the reader will recall that as price falls and quantity demanded increases, total expenditure by consumers increases when the price elasticity of demand is in excess of unity: expenditure remains the same at unit demand elasticity and falls when elasticity is less than unity. Note that total expenditure by consumers is just the monopolistic firm's total revenue by another name and consider the linear demand curve of Figure 15.2, which has a constant slope $\partial p/\partial X$. As we discussed previously, elasticity e_1 is defined as $(\partial X/\partial p/(X/p))$. At point A it is clear that X/p is smaller than $\partial X/\partial p$. Hence elasticity is greater than one and total revenue is increasing with quantity. By similar argument, at C, it is clear that X/p is greater than $\partial X/\partial p$. At this point elasticity is smaller than unity and total revenue is decreasing. At B which lies halfway along the curve, $\partial X/\partial p$ and X/p are equal. Elasticity is unity and total revenue is not changing with quantity. The straight-line demand curve encompasses all elasticities from infinity at its intersection with the vertical axis to zero at the horizontal, and the shape of the total revenue curve in Figure 15.1(c) reflects this.

The relationship between the demand curve, the marginal revenue

curve and the elasticity of demand can be established formally as follows. We noted in Chapter 13 that the slope of the total revenue function, marginal revenue, was given by

$$mr = \frac{\partial R}{\partial X} = p + X \frac{\partial p}{\partial X} \qquad (15.1)$$

Since $\partial p / \partial X$ is always negative because demand curves slope down (provided the good in question is not a Giffen good), we know from (15.1) that *marginal revenue is less than price* at every level of output greater than zero. The marginal revenue curve therefore lies below the average revenue curve in Figure 15.2. We also saw that an alternative formulation of marginal revenue, in terms of the elasticity of demand, e, is

$$mr = \frac{\partial R}{\partial X} = p \left[1 + \frac{1}{e} \right] \qquad (15.2)$$

This expression is obtained from (15.1) by multiplying the right-hand side through by $1 = p/p$ to obtain

$$mr = \frac{\partial R}{\partial X} = p \left(1 + \frac{X}{p} \frac{\partial p}{\partial X} \right)$$

and noting that $\frac{1}{e}$ equals $X/p(\partial p/\partial X)$.

Marginal revenue is therefore positive if the elasticity of demand is less than -1 (greater in absolute value than 1), negative if it is greater than -1 (less in absolute value than 1), and zero if the elasticity of demand is (minus) unity.

Figure 15.2

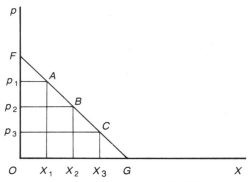

A straight-line demand curve. Its slope is constant at OG/OF. Halfway between F and G, at point B, the ratio OX_2 to Op_2 is equal to the slope of the curve, so its elasticity is equal to unity at this point. (OFG, p_2FB and X_2BG are similar triangles; FB equals BG and is half of FG. Thus X_2B which equals Op_2 is half of OF, and similarly OX_2 is half of OG.)

Profit-Maximising Price and Output

There is no reason to suppose that a monopolist's cost functions differ in any qualitative way from those of a competitive firm and, with the exception that entry of new firms is ruled out, our previous analysis of the long-run/short-run dichotomy still holds.

There is no need for us to repeat all this then, and we may immediately analyse monopoly pricing in the long run. The analysis of short-run behaviour simply involves the substitution of short- for long-run cost curves in what follows. Figure 15.3 superimposes a long-run total cost curve upon the total revenue curve. Profits will be maximised where the vertical distance between the two curves is at its greatest (with revenue in excess of costs) and this occurs at output X_1, where the two functions have equal slopes. This statement about equality of slopes is another way of saying that profits are maximised where marginal cost equals marginal revenue. Figure 15.4 depicts the same profit-maximising solution in terms of explicitly drawn marginal cost and marginal revenue functions. As we have seen, for a monopolist, marginal revenue and price are not equal because the total revenue function is not a straight line through the origin. Indeed, if we call price by its other name, average revenue, it becomes obvious that a downward-sloping demand curve implies continually falling average revenue, with the marginal revenue curve everywhere below average revenue. This, be it noted, is *not* the same as saying that marginal revenue is always falling, as readers may prove for themselves

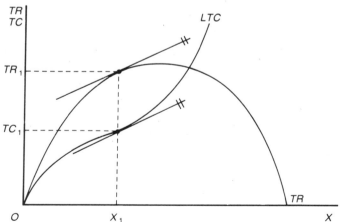

Figure 15.3

Long-run profit maximisation for a monopolist facing a straight-line demand curve, and endowed with a long-run cost function characterised by increasing followed by decreasing returns to scale. Maximum profits occur where the slopes of the two curves are equal (i.e. where marginal cost equals marginal revenue). Profit is equal to $TR_1 - TC_1$. So long as total costs increase with output, profit maximisation requires that output be fixed on the rising section of the total revenue curve, i.e. where the elasticity of demand for the product is greater than 1 in absolute value.

Figure 15.4

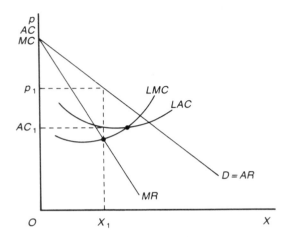

The profit-maximising monopolist will fix output where marginal cost equals marginal revenue at X_1 and charge the maximum price the market will bear for that quantity of output, p_1. This diagram repeats, in more familiar terms, the analysis set out in Figure 13.3. Profits are given by $(p_1 - AC_1)X_1$, which is equal to $TR_1 - TC_1$ in Figure 15.3.

by reproducing the relevant panels from Figure 15.1 and deriving the average and marginal revenue curves implicit in them; and as we establish more formally in a subsequent starred section of this chapter. These exercises clarify our reason for sticking for the most part to the special case of the straight-line demand curve for purposes of exposition, and the dangers inherent in overgeneralising from analysis based upon it. In this case the marginal revenue curve is always downward sloping.

Now, what can we say about the properties of the long-run price and output decision of the monopolist set out in Figures 15.3 and 15.4? First, it shows positive profits being made equal to $TR_1 - TC_1$ as measured in Figure 15.3, or $(P_1 - AC_1)X_1$ as measured in Figure 15.4. That positive profits are earned is not a necessary consequence of monopolistic behaviour. It results from the assumption about costs and revenues which we have built into the diagrams and nothing else. Thus, in Figure 15.5(a) we have a situation in which the cost and revenue functions are such that the maximum available profit is zero, and in Figure 15.5(b) a situation in which losses would be made at any level of output, so that in fact no production would take place in the long run.

The second characteristic of Figure 15.4 worth noting is, however, a general property of monopoly behaviour (unless certain types of price discrimination to be dealt with below take place): the price charged is greater than marginal cost. Now, in perfect competition we noted that, in the long run, price is equal to long-run marginal cost. If it is the case that the monopolist's marginal cost curve is the same as that which would

Figure 15.5

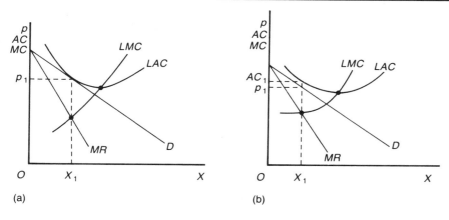

(a)　　　　　　　　　　　　　　　　(b)

A monopolist whose profit-maximising level of output X_1 yields (a) zero profit, and (b) a loss of $(AC_1 - p_1)X_1$. In panel (a), if LAC is just tangent to D, then MR equals LMC at this level of output, for at this level of output the total revenue curve would just be tangent to the total cost curve from below.

yield the long-run supply curve of a competitive industry, then the monopolist will charge more and produce less than a competitive industry.

This implication explains why economists often argue that a monopolistic market structure is *inefficient* relative to that of a competitive industry. The price of the good sold exceeds the incremental cost of producing it. We can perceive monopolists exploiting their 'monopoly power' (as sole source of supply) to restrict output and thereby drive up the price by creating an artificial scarcity. Moreover, monopolists do not generally produce at the minimum point on their long-run average cost curve, though such an output is not *logically* impossible. For example, in Figures 15.3 and 15.4, the monopolist restricts supply below minimum efficient scale. One cannot rule out the possibility, however, that revenue and cost functions take a shape such that equilibrium output is to the right of the minimum point on the long-run average cost curve, or is even at the minimum itself. Readers might like to illustrate these cases for themselves.

We stress again that, because the monopolist produces where marginal cost equals marginal revenue, so long as marginal cost is positive, price and output will be at a level such that total revenue increases as output increases — a point where *the elasticity of demand for output is greater than unity.* It is a common misconception that monopolists are particularly likely to exist where demand for products is inelastic. Any monopolist in such a situation can increase profits by curtailing output and raising price until an elastic segment of the demand curve is reached. Inelastic demand and profit-maximising monopoly (at least non-discriminating monopoly) are incompatible. The formula given above as equation (15.2) confirms this point. If elasticity lies between 0 and -1, it yields a negative value for

Figure 15.6

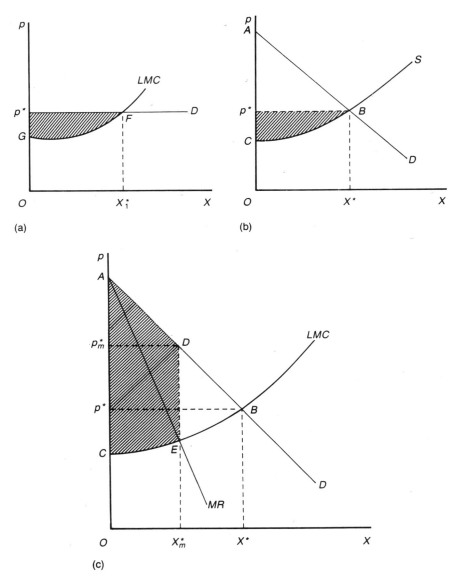

(a)

(b)

(c)

(a) The individual firm produces X_1^* at p^* and generates producer surplus equal to the shaded area p^*FG.

(b) At the level of the industry as a whole, producer surplus is given by p^*BC, and consumer surplus by ABp^*, and the total gain to utility by devoting resources the production of X is given by ABC.

(c) When the production of X is monopolised, output falls from X^* to X_m^*, and price rises from p^* to p_m^*. Consumer surplus falls from ABp^* to ADp_m^*, producer surplus increases from p^*BC to p_m^*DEC, and the total gain from producing X shrinks by DBE. This decline in total. surplus is referred to as a *deadweight loss*.

marginal revenue, and so long as marginal costs are positive, the profit-maximising level of output cannot lie in such a region of the demand curve.

Producer's Surplus and the Cost of Monopoly

The negative impact of monopoly on what economists refer to as economic *welfare* is directly measurable in a rough and ready way with the aid of the concept of consumer's surplus introduced in Chapter 4 and the closely related concept of *producer's surplus*. It will be remembered that consumer's surplus was measured by the area under the demand curve above and to the left of the equilibrium price—quantity point. We can construct an equivalent measure of welfare for the supply side of the market. This is producer's surplus.

Consider first a typical competitive firm in long-run equilibrium, as depicted in Figure 15.6(a). The total cost that it generates to produce its output is given by the area under its long-run marginal cost curve, and its total revenue is given by the area under its marginal revenue curve, which is in this case its horizontal demand curve. The difference between the two is the surplus the firm generates, its profit, or producer's surplus (which might, if the firm in question was producing at the minimum point of its long-run average cost curve, be zero). For the industry as a whole, producer's surplus is simply the sum of these surpluses generated by individual firms. The case we have depicted in Figure 15.6(b) to illustrate the concept is of an industry with firms of varying degrees of efficiency (discussed in Chapter 14) and the industry measure of producer's surplus is given by the area above the long-run supply curve, and below equilibrium price, the area p^*BC.

Now consumer's surplus in this case is given by the area ABp^*, (provided that we do not scrutinise too carefully the problems inherent in adding up the utilities of individual agents, and are willing to treat the market demand curve as the sum of individual 'Marshallian' demand curves). The total benefit conferred on society by the activities of this industry may be thought of as the difference between the total utility derived by consumers from its products — the area under the demand curve to the left of X^*, and the total costs imposed by producing its output, or the area under the supply curve to the left of X^*. This difference is the sum of producer's and consumer's surplus.

Now suppose that this industry was monopolised, with, however, a long-run marginal cost curve identical to the competitive industry supply curve. This case is illustrated in Figure 15.6(c). Output would be cut to X_m^*, price would rise to p_m^*, producers surplus would increase to p_m^*DEC, but consumer's surplus would fall to ADp_m^*. The total benefit conferred by this industry would now be $ADEC$, an amount unambiguously smaller

than that operated in the competitive case, and an amount which measures the monopoly's negative impact on welfare. This decline in total surplus is sometimes referred to as a *deadweight loss*.

Now the welfare measure we have developed here has the great advantage of being related to observable functional relationships such as demand curves and cost curves, but we had to cut some analytic corners to develop it. Some of these we noted during our exposition, for example the use of Marshallian demand curve assumptions and our willingness to add up the utilities of different individuals, but there are other problems buried behind the analysis which we have left hidden. We defer further discussion of welfare issues until Chapter 25, but readers might like to come back to the analysis of this section when they have read those chapters to make up their own minds about how serious its shortcomings actually are.

*A Formal Treatment of the Relationship between Demand and Marginal Revenue: Some Examples

To formalise the analysis depicted in Figure 15.2, consider the linear demand curve

$$p = a - bX \tag{15.3}$$

for which $\partial p / \partial X = -b$. From (15.1), we can calculate that marginal revenue is $(a - 2bX)$. The same result can be derived directly by differentiating the revenue function,

$$R = pX = aX - bX^2 \tag{15.4}$$

$$mr = \frac{\partial R}{\partial X} = a - 2bX \tag{15.5}$$

The total revenue function in this case reaches a maximum when $\partial R / \partial X = 0$, and therefore where $X = a/2b$. This is the point X_2 in Figure 15.1(c). It should be noted that, since the average revenue curve is $p = a - bX$ and the marginal revenue curve is $p = a - 2bX$, the marginal revenue curve always slopes twice as steeply as the demand curve when the latter is linear.

As to the elasticity of demand, if we use (15.3), to substitute for p in the usual formula, and recall that $\partial p / \partial X = -b$ we get

$$\frac{a - bX}{-bX} \tag{15.6}$$

When $X = a/2b$, the simple substitution into (15.6) confirms that the quantity at which total revenue is maximised in Figure 15.1(c) occurs where the elasticity of demand is -1. Similarly it can be seen that when output is less than $a/2b$, the elasticity of demand is less than -1, and when X exceeds $a/2b$, the elasticity is greater than -1.

An alternative form for the demand curve addresses the need in much applied work to make the simplifying assumption that the elasticity of demand is a constant. We use this form in our analysis of monopolistic competition in Chapter 16. The family of demand curves with this convenient property takes the general form that

$$p = AX^{-\alpha} \tag{15.3'}$$

Where A and α are positive, the slope of the demand curve $(\partial p/\partial X)$, equals $-\alpha p/X$. The elasticity of demand is therefore given by

$$e = \frac{p}{X} \frac{\partial X}{\partial p} = -\frac{X}{\alpha p} \frac{p}{X} = -\frac{1}{\alpha} \tag{15.6'}$$

which is, of course, a constant. Marginal revenue can be derived from the revenue function,

$$R = pX = AX^{1-\alpha} \tag{15.4'}$$

so

$$mr = \frac{\partial R}{\partial X} = (1-\alpha)AX^{-\alpha} = (1-\alpha)p \tag{15.5'}$$

The same result (15.5') can be deduced by substituting the value of the elasticity of demand $(e = -1/\alpha)$ in equation (15.2). Hence, though the elasticity of demand is a constant, marginal revenue is still everywhere below price.

A particular special case of the constant elasticity demand function is sometimes encountered, namely when the elasticity of demand is assumed to be unity for every level of output. If we set $\alpha = 1$, we derive the demand curve

$$p = \frac{A}{X} \tag{15.3''}$$

with slope $(\partial p/\partial X)$, equal to $-A/X^2$. The elasticity is therefore

$$e = \frac{p}{X} \frac{\partial X}{\partial p} = -\frac{X^2}{A} \cdot \frac{A}{X^2} = -1 \tag{15.6''}$$

It is clear from substituting the value of α in equation (15.5') that marginal revenue in this case is zero.

*A Formal Treatment of Monopoly Equilibrium

The formal maximisation problem faced by the monopolist has a similar structure to that of the competitive counterpart but, as we saw in the geometric sections, has rather different results because we can no longer

assume that marginal revenue equals price. The firm chooses output as before to maximise

$$\pi = pX - wL - rK \tag{15.7}$$

subject to

$$X = f(L,K) \tag{15.8}$$

and, in addition, the demand curve

$$p = p(X), \, \partial p/\partial X < 0 \tag{15.9}$$

Equation (15.7) can be reformulated in terms of revenues and costs

$$\pi = R(X) - C(X) \tag{15.10}$$

where $C(X)$ can be either a short-run or long-run cost function. We assume the latter henceforth and derive first-order conditions

$$\frac{\partial \pi}{\partial X} = \frac{\partial R}{\partial X} - \frac{\partial C}{\partial X} = 0 \tag{15.11}$$

and second-order conditions for a maximum

$$\frac{\partial^2 \pi}{\partial X^2} = \frac{\partial^2 R}{\partial X^2} - \frac{d^2 C}{dX^2} < 0 \tag{15.12}$$

Equation (15.11) is simply the conventional marginal revenue equals marginal cost condition which we have been using in our geometric exposition, and is formally identical to that derived for the competitive case.

The second-order conditions, however, are less restrictive here than under competition because we no longer require the marginal cost curve to be upward sloping at equilibrium. The slope of the marginal cost curve can be negative, provided that its value is more than offset by the negative slope of the marginal revenue curve. Given that marginal revenue is always diminishing with output ($\partial^2 R/\partial X^2 < 0$), an upward-sloping marginal cost curve ($\partial^2 C/\partial X^2$) is *sufficient* to ensure that inequality (15.12), the second-order condition, is satisfied, but it is not *necessary*.

Price Discrimination

Twice in the previous discussion we have referred to the idea of price discrimination, which is closely associated with monopoly power. We will now investigate this characteristic of monopoly in more detail. Price discrimination involves nothing more than selling different units of the same good at different prices. It is a widespread phenomenon and we will consider it in two forms: first, charging different prices to different consumers and second, charging the same consumers different prices for different units of the good. Obviously these are not mutually exclusive

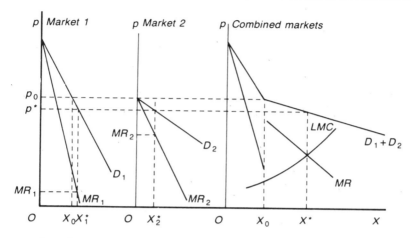

A monopolist sells in two different markets, but being unable to separate them sells at the same price p^* in both of them, X_1^* in market 1 and X_2^* in market 2. Thus marginal revenue is different in the two markets and profits could be increased by charging different prices in the two markets and equalising marginal revenues. A unit of output withdrawn from market 1 and transferred to market 2 would add more to revenue in the second market than it subtracted from revenue in the first since at p^*, MR_1 is below MR_2.

practices — more complicated cases do indeed exist and may be analysed with the tools we shall now develop.

Suppose that, for some reason, the market for X facing the monopolist with whom we have so far been dealing were to expand by having a new group of consumers added to it. We would analyse the results of this by adding the demand of our new consumers to that of those already in the market, deriving the new marginal revenue curve and thereby solving for price and output. We do this in Figure 15.7. The only point here that is new to the reader is the discontinuity in the marginal revenue curve for the aggregate market. This arises because, at p_0, the price at which the new group of consumers comes into the market, there is a kink in the summed demand curve. There will therefore be a kink in the total revenue curve, as shown in Figure 15.8, and that implies a discontinuity in that curve's slope, in marginal revenue.

The profit-maximising solution depicted in Figure 15.7, where marginal cost equals marginal revenue in the aggregate market, is an output of X^* sold at a price of p^*. Both groups of consumers are paying the same price for X; note that this implies that the marginal revenue accruing from selling to each group is different except in the special case where each group's elasticity of demand for X at that price is the same. Now marginal revenue is the addition to be made to total revenue from a small increment in the quantity sold (or the loss accruing from reducing quantity sold). As we have constructed Figure 15.7, holding output, and hence costs, constant, one could increase revenue by withdrawing units of X

Figure 15.8

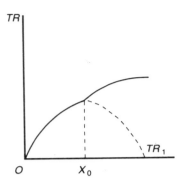

The total revenue curve implicit in summing the individual market demand curves of panels (a) and (b) of Figure 15.7 to get a total market demand curve. Up to output X_0, goods are sold only in market 1 and hence only TR_1 is relevant. However, at X_0, price is sufficiently low that purchasers in market 2 begin to buy the good. Hence total revenue is now that earned in both markets and there is a kink in the total revenue curve at this level of output that corresponds to the kink in the total demand curve. The slope of the total revenue curve (marginal revenue) thus increases discontinuously at output X_0. Note that this total revenue curve is derived on the assumption that the good X is sold at the same price in both markets. It is not relevant to the analysis that follows when different prices are charged in the two markets.

yielding a low marginal revenue from market 1 and selling them in market 2 where marginal revenue is higher. Gains would arise from doing this up to the point where marginal revenue was equated in the two markets. Such equating of marginal revenues, though, would involve charging different prices to the two groups of consumers, in short, there would be *price discrimination* between them.

Demand Elasticity and Price Discrimination

A monopolist does not necessarily have the power to charge different prices to different people. It depends what good is being sold and how easy it is to identify and keep separate members of the two (or more) groups. If the good is such that one consumer can sell it to another after purchase at trivial cost in time and trouble, then discrimination is not possible, for any attempt to charge a higher price to one group would result in them having members of the lower price group make their purchases for them. Thus a cinema might offer a price discount to old age pensioners, but not a bookshop; a football ground might offer a discount to school children, but not a sweet shop. Readers can readily construct further examples of their own. If we assume that our two groups can be identified, and that the good is such that they can be kept from retrading it between them, it will pay the monopolist to charge them different prices. Moreover, we may predict who will pay the higher price.

The reader will find it helpful to recall at this point that, just as the slope of the total revenue curve is equal to marginal revenue and just as the slope of the long-run total cost curve is equal to long-run marginal cost, so the area under the marginal revenue curve measures total revenue and the area under the long-run marginal cost curve measures long-run total cost. The reader should also recall the relationship between marginal revenue, price, and the elasticity of demand, equation (15.2).

If to maximise profits a discriminating monopolist is to equate marginal revenue between two markets, then the higher the absolute value of the elasticity of demand in either one of them, the lower will be the price. In terms of Figure 15.9 which reproduces Figure 15.7 and extends the analysis, the gain in profits from price discrimination is given by the area $CDX_2^*X_2$ minus the area $ABX_1X_1^*$. This is the gain in revenue from lowering price in market 2, minus the loss from raising it in market 1. Equivalently, it is given by the area GEF which is the difference between the area under the curve that is marginal to the summed demand curves of markets 1 and 2, and that under the summed marginal revenue curves of these markets. These two curves are *not* the same. The first is $HGFEJ$ and the second is $HGEJ$. The first marginal revenue curve tells us how marginal revenue changes with quantity when *that quantity is sold to yield an equal price* in each market. The second deals with a situation when *that quantity is sold so as to yield the same marginal revenue* . The summed demand curve is irrelevant in the second case: it is the sum of the marginal revenue curves in the individual markets that is important.

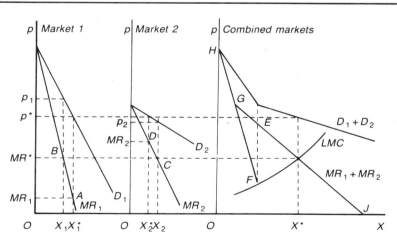

Figure 15.9

Price discrimination between two markets. Prices are set in the two markets so as to equalise marginal revenue, so that p_1 is above p_2. The higher the elasticity of demand in a particular market, the lower the price charged. The increase in profits relative to charging the same price (p^*) in both markets is given equivalently by the areas ($CDX_2^*X_2 - ABX_1X_1^*$) or GEF. Sales in the first market contract from X_1^* to X_1 and those in the second market expand from X_2^* to X_2. There is no change in overall output X^* from the no price discrimination case and hence no change in costs of production. That is why revenue changes may be used to measure profit changes in this case.

This distinction is crucial when analysing the special case where the firm's marginal cost curve just passes through the discontinuity on the curve that is marginal to the summed demand curves. Here the inability to discriminate might lead to a price being set at which one group of consumers buys nothing. The ability to discriminate allows the latter group to be charged a lower price, and actually results in output increasing from the no discrimination situation. Readers will find it instructive explicitly to carry out the analysis for themselves.

Perfect Price Discrimination

To charge different prices to different groups of consumers is only one form that price discrimination can take. As we saw when we dealt with the theory of consumer's surplus, it is of the very essence that a consumer faced with a single price for a commodity gains from being able to purchase it; it is only marginal units purchased that are worth no more to consumers than they are asked to pay for them. Consider Figure 15.10 where a typical consumer's demand curve has been drawn, and let us make the Marshallian assumptions that permit us to treat the area under that curve as an approximate measure of the maximum amount that an individual would be willing to pay to obtain any particular quantity of the good. If the price is p_1, our consumer buys X_1 units of X spending in total $p_1 X_1$, but would be willing to spend up to ABX_1O to obtain this quantity.

If the firm selling X was able to charge a different price for each unit bought, it could charge the area under the curve between A and C for

Figure 15.10

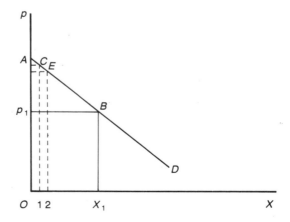

An individual's demand curve for X derived on Marshallian assumptions (*cf.* Chapter 4). A perfectly discriminating monopolist could acquire revenue of $OABX_1$ if it sold X_1 units of X to this consumer.

the first unit, that between C and E for the second and so on. It would obtain a total revenue of $OABX_1$ from the sale of X_1 units, and would thereby increase its profits by ABp_1. Such 'perfect price discrimination', as it is called, would obviously be adopted by the profit-maximising firm if it was able to do so. Figure 15.11 shows what the situation would be from the point of view of the total market for X, rather than from that of the individual consumer (but still dealing with a demand curve based on Marshallian assumptions).

If the monopoly depicted there were able to price discriminate to perfection, its total revenue would be given by the area under the market demand curve for X, its total costs by the area under the long-run marginal cost curve; profits, the difference between the two, would obviously be maximised where the price of the last unit sold was just equal to long-run marginal cost. In this case, the market demand curve in effect becomes the firm's marginal revenue curve, rather than its average revenue curve. Now such perfect price discrimination as this is a limiting case of a very general phenomenon. Any consumer who faces a multi-part tariff for the use of electricity or gas, or who pays a cover charge at a restaurant, is on the receiving end of a discriminatory pricing scheme.

Multi-Part Tariffs

Perfect price discrimination appropriates to the seller of a good all the consumer's surplus that each consumer would get from buying it at a

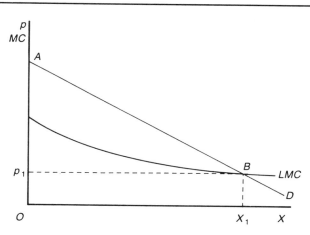

Figure 15.11

A profit-maximising perfectly discriminating monopolist would charge p_1 for the last unit of X that it sold and get a total revenue of ABX_1O. Equivalently, if it could operate a multipart tariff scheme it would charge p_1, i.e. long-run marginal cost per unit of X and have available the area Ap_1B as the maximum amount it could collect by way of a fixed charge for the privilege of buying X at price p_1. Note that the downward slope of LMC in this diagram makes the firm a natural monopoly (cf. Figure 14.3 above).

constant price. A two-part tariff for gas or electricity, whereby a consumer can choose any quantity at a given price, after paying a rent for the right to receive any supply at all, takes some consumer's surplus in the form of this rental payment. If a profit-maximising seller knew the exact form of the consumer's demand curve, the rental could be fixed equal to the area ABp_1 in Figure 15.11 and obtain exactly the effect of perfect price discrimination. Similarly for the restaurant that imposes a cover charge. Lack of perfect knowledge about the exact form of each customer's demand curve and the fact that it is expensive to acquire such knowledge even imperfectly — to say nothing of the administrative costs of running a different pricing scheme for every customer — leads such firms to set a uniform fixed charge which leaves some consumers with a surplus, some with none and persuades others to refrain from consuming the good at all where the charge is in excess of this surplus.

Price discrimination of the type just analysed can occur wherever it is possible for the seller to identify an individual consumer and to offer a two-part choice: whether to consume the good at all, and how much of it to consume, given that some is to be consumed. The possibility of imposing such a choice depends very much on the technical nature of the good being supplied. Electricity and gas consumption require the installation of supply facilities in individual houses and factories, the consumption of a restaurant meal requires that a particular table be occupied. Hence rental, or cover, charges may be imposed. Readers are invited to think up further examples of their own where discrimination is possible. Doing so will not only help in understanding the foregoing analysis but establish the ubiquity of the practice.

How much output will a discriminating monopolist of the type just described sell, and at what kind of price structure? To maximise profits, the first step is to set the price on the margin in such a way as to maximise the possible gain from charging a higher price for intra-marginal units. The possible gain in question is of course equal to the profits that would be made by a perfect price discriminator and these are maximised, as we have seen, by setting price on the margin equal to marginal cost. In terms of Figure 15.11 output would still be equal to X_1 and price on the margin would be set at p_1, even if perfect discrimination were not feasible. How much of the consumer's surplus existing in the area ABp_1 the monopolist would appropriate, and with what kind of price structure, would depend upon how much was known about the shape of the demand curve and how ingenious the monopolist was at devising a suitable pricing scheme. The important implication here is that the monopolist who is able to price discriminate by using multi-part tariffs will produce exactly the same output as a perfectly competitive industry, if the long-run marginal cost curve is indeed the same curve that would be such an industry's long-run supply curve. It is only monopolists who do not have the power to discriminate who will restrict output below its competitive level. Where price discrimination of the type just analysed

is possible it is the amount of profits obtained (or consumer's surplus lost) and not the level of output, that differentiates the consequences of monopoly from those of competition.

Concluding Comment

Perfect competition and monopoly between them do not provide a complete theory of firm's supply behaviour because they do not touch on problems arising from firms' interactions. Taking the demand curve that faces the firms as being given exogenously, the supply problem for each firm is to pick the point on that curve which will maximise profits; for the perfect competitor this involves choosing output alone, and for the monopolist it involves choosing a combination of price and output.

Lying behind the demand curve, whether of a monopolist or a perfect competitor, are the prices of other goods. An implicit assumption behind the theories we have so far discussed is that the decisions taken by the firm under analysis have very diffuse effects on the demand curves facing other firms. If this assumption is granted, there is no need to consider the possibility of other firms reacting to the actions taken by the firm under analysis in such a way as to cause the demand conditions under which it is operating to change, and the theories of perfect competition and monopoly are adequate tools of analysis. However, if this assumption does not hold and firms' demand curves do in fact become significantly interdependent in any circumstances, then these theories begin to break down. Oligopoly theory, certain aspects of which we will discuss in sections of the following chapters, represents an attempt to come to grips with such matters.

Questions for Study and Discussion for Part V

1. You are a consultant offering firms advice on how to maximise profits. Each firm operates as a price taker in its product and factor markets. What do you recommend from the options below, in each of the cases in the table on the following page?

   1 firm is now in correct position;
   2 firm should raise price;
   3 firm should lower price;
   4 firm should increase output;
   5 firm should decrease output;
   6 firm should close.

2. 'The introduction of microtechnology will raise output and real wages.' 'The introduction of microtechnology will cause unemployment.' How does our analysis of the perfectly competitive market lead us to respond to these statements?

Question 1

Case	Price	Quantity of output	Total revenue $	Total cost $	Total fixed cost $	Total variable cost $	Average cost $	Average variable cost $	Marginal cost $	Increase in output: MC would
a			10,000	9,000			1.80		2.00	rise
b		1,000	5,000		1,500			5.50	5.00	rise
c			8,000		1,000		3.50	3.00	4.50	
d			12,000	12,000		9,000	At minimum level	1.50		
e	3.00				6,000	8,000	3.50	At minimum level		
f	4.00	2,000				7,000	4.50		4.00	rise
g		1,000	3,000		1,500			3.50	3.00	rise
h	1.00	10,000		8,000			At minimum level			
i	3.00	2,000			3,000	7,000			3.00	fall

*3. A firm in perfect competition faces the following total cost function:

$$C = 250X - 20X^2 = 2X^3$$

(a) What is the firm's supply function?
(b) At what output is marginal cost minimised?
(c) What is the firm's long-run equilibrium output and, assuming that every firm has the same cost function, price?
(d) In this long-run equilibrium, what is the value of profits?
(e) The firm is now a monopolist, with demand curve $p = 550 - 10X$. What are equilibrium price, output and profit?

4. With price measured in $ per thousand units, and X being measured as thousands of units per week, a perfectly competitive industry faces a demand curve given by

$$p = 20 - 2X$$

and produces output at constant supply price of $1 per thousand units

(a) Find, on the assumption that the area under the demand curve measures the total benefit accruing to consumers of X, the consumers' surplus accruing to purchases of X.
(b) Now suppose that a single firm takes over the whole industry, and that $1 per thousand units now represents its long-run marginal and average cost of producing X.

Find   (i) its output;
       (ii) the price of that output;

      (iii)   the firm's profits; and

      (iv)   the consumer's surplus accruing to purchasers of X.

  (c) Suppose a sales tax of 10 cents per thousand units is levied on X. Recompute your answers to parts (a) and (b).

  (d) Suppose a maximum price of $1.20 per thousand units is imposed by government decree. Recompute your answers to part (b).

5. How will the imposition on firms of a fixed charge per annum for the privilege of operating affect (a) the price and output set by a monopolist; (b) the price and output of a competitive industry where all firms are equally efficient; (c) the price and output of a typical firm in that industry; (d) the price and output of an intra-marginal firm in a competitive industry in which some firms are more efficient than others? In each case analyse short- and long-run responses.

6. A law is passed fixing, below the level currently prevailing, the maximum price that can be charged by a monopolist who produces good X. It responds by increasing output. Is this behaviour compatible with profit maximisation?

7. With price measured in £ per thousand units and X being measured in thousands of units per week, consider a monopolist producing X at a constant long-run marginal and average cost of £2 per thousand units, and selling to two groups of consumers whose demand curves are given by:

Group 1 $p = 40 - 2X$
Group 2 $p = 20 - 2X$

On the assumption that the monopolist cannot discriminate between the two groups find:

  (a) overall output;
  (b) the price of output;
  (c) the amount sold to each group of consumers; and
  (d) profits.

Calculate all outputs to the nearest 10 units and prices and profits to the nearest penny. On the assumption that the monopolist can discriminate between the two groups, recompute your answers to (a), (c) and (d), and also find the prices at which it sells to the two samples of consumers.

8. Suppose a firm had a natural monopoly in the production of electricity and could impose an annual rental charge at a rate chosen by itself for the use of a meter without which no electricity could be used. (a) If the firm wished to maximise profits should it set the price of electricity at marginal cost? (b) Suppose the firm was prevented by law from charging a meter rental charge. Should this affect the profit-maximising price and output of electricity?

9. Consider a firm that sells as a monopolist in its home market and as a perfect competitor in export markets. Show (a) how its price and output will be determined in each market; and (b) how they will change if the currency of the home country is devalued.

10. Explain how technical advance which raises output per unit of labour affects equilibrium price and output in competition. What happens in a monopoly? Why might a competitive industry fail to develop these techniques?

11. Under what conditions will the long-run supply curve of the perfectly competitive industry be upward sloping?

*12. A firm is operating in a perfectly competitive industry which contains a fixed number of identical firms in the short run, namely 1000. The industry demand curve is $p = 1000 - 5X$ and each firm has the cost curve

$$C = 5 + 20X + 10X^2$$

(a) What is the equilibrium price and output for the industry?
(b) Suppose that there is now free entry and exit. How many firms will produce and what is the long-run price?
(c) Suppose that the original 1000 firms merge to form a monopoly. What are industry output and price? What is the change in consumer's surplus?

*13. The short-run average cost curve of every firm in the industry is

$$C = 50 + (X - 50)^2$$

The firms sell to two types of consumer, type 1 and type 2. The demand curve for type 1 is $p_1 = 250 + 2X$, and for type 2 is $p_2 = 200 - X_2$. Calculate (a) output and price if the market as a whole is assumed to behave according to the assumptions of perfect competition; (b) output, price and profit under pure monopoly; (c) output, prices and profit under discriminating monopoly.

Suggested Further Reading to Part V

Atkinson, A.B. and Stiglitz, J.E. 1980. *Lectures on Public Economics*. Maidenhead: McGraw-Hill.

Cohen, K.J. and Cyert, R.M. 1965. *Theory of the Firm*, Englewood Cliffs, NJ: Prentice-Hall, Chs 4–6, 10–12, 15–17.

Friedman, M. 1953. 'The Methodology of Positive Economics', *Essays in Positive Economics*. Chicago: University of Chicago Press.

Frisch, R. 1950. 'Alfred Marshall's Theory of Value', *Quarterly Journal of Economics*.

Harberger, A.C. 1957. 'Monopoly and Resource Allocation', *American Economic Review*.

Heidensohn, K. and Robinson, J.N. 1974. *Business Behaviour*. Deddington, Oxford: Philip Allan.

Lerner, A.P. 1934. 'The Concept of Monopoly and the Measurement of Monopoly Power', *Review of Economic Studies*.

Sharkey, W.W. 1982, *The Theory of Natural Monopoly*. Cambridge: Cambridge University Press.

Part VI

INDUSTRIAL ORGANISATION THEORY: FURTHER TOPICS

16

An Introduction to Imperfect Competition: Monopolistic Competition and Oligopoly

Introduction

The theories of monopoly and perfect competition set out in the last three chapters are the basic building blocks of the traditional theory of the firm. But as we have already hinted, there is a rich literature in the field of industrial organisation, which encompasses a wide variety of other models of firm and industry behaviour. In this part of the book we shall deal with a selection of these models, in order to give readers at least a flavour of this extensive literature. In this chapter, we consider some traditional models of imperfect competition: monopolistic competition, and in the area of oligopoly, theories based on kinked demand curves and price leadership. Much recent analysis of oligopoly, discussed in the following chapter, draws on game theory to analyse the behaviour of a small number of firms playing strategically for market position. We make no claim to comprehensiveness in our treatment of these issues. It would take a textbook by itself to survey the material currently available, and some further reading is suggested at the end of this part of the book. However, it is hoped that the following pages will provide a useful introduction for those who plan to carry their studies of this area further.

The Idea of Monopolistic Competition

It is a widely held view that perfect competition and monopoly represent two extreme ends of what might be termed a spectrum of different

forms of market organisation. This view has spawned a whole literature on alternative models of the behaviour of the firm, under conditions that lie between these two alleged extremes, and one of the best known of these models deals with a situation known as *monopolistic competition*.

We saw in the last chapter that the monopolist has the possibility of making positive profits in long-run equilibrium. We did not consider the question of why competitive firms did not spring up to compete these profits away. There are abundant reasons why a monopolist may be able to remain a monopolist at least for a significant time. There may be legal barriers to other firms producing the same good as the monopolist; patent protection for the product; access to some trade secret that gives a significant cost advantage in producing the product; technology is characterised by increasing returns to scale; and so on. At the opposite extreme, if other firms can reproduce the product to perfection at no cost disadvantage, the industry becomes perfectly competitive. What about intermediate cases in which a similar, but not identical, product can be produced by other firms at no cost advantage? It is precisely with such a case that the theory of monopolistic competition seeks to deal.

However, the theory was built up at a time before economists had available to them that approach to the theory of demand, some of whose rudimentary characteristics are set out in Chapter 8. It was not clear at that time that goods could be looked upon as constituting bundles of attributes, an approach to their definition that opens up the possibility of giving some sort of precision to ideas like 'similar but not identical goods'. Thus, there has always been an element of imprecision to this particular theory of firm behaviour that has limited its direct empirical applicability. Despite this, the theory remains of analytic interest, as we shall now see.

Differentiated Products

Consider a market with a large number of identical firms, each producing a slightly *differentiated product*. By this we mean products which are similar, but not identical, at least in the mind of the consumer. An example of such products would be soap powders, of which numerous different but highly substitutable brands compete for broadly the same market. This example is misleading in one important respect, however, because the theory of monopolistic competition treats each brand as being produced by a separate firm, while in the real world there are in fact only a few producers of soap powders. Product differentiation here is thus a consequence of oligopolistic strategies and the monopolistic competition model does not fit the soap-powder industry too well. Even so, the example serves to illustrate the concept of differentiated products; similar goods, perhaps distinguished by brand names which are viewed as close substitutes by consumers.

Spatial economics — which deals with the location of consumers and

producers — provides another example of product differentiation and one that better motivates the monopolistic competition model that we shall soon discuss. Imagine that all consumers and producers of a particular good are located at different geographical locations. The consumer will buy from the producer who offers the lowest price, net of transport costs, to the consumer's specific location. By varying prices, producers can capture the custom of consumers located at different distances away from them. As one producer's price falls, the number of consumers who find that product the cheapest increases. As that producer's price increases, consumers from further away will begin to shop elsewhere, but the producer remains a relatively cheap supplier to consumers who are close by. Hence in such a spatial economy each firm faces a downward-sloping demand curve, even though there are numerous suppliers of an identical (except for the location of its production) product to the market.

The situation of each monopolistically competitive firm may be portrayed just like that of a monopolist, except that the demand curve facing the firm represents that for its own output and not the market demand for the output of the whole industry. Spatial product differentiation is not the only potential source of a downward-sloping demand curve for the individual firm in an otherwise competitive industry, but it is an example that the reader may find helpful to keep in the back of the mind as the analysis of this section proceeds.

The Firm in Monopolistic Competition

Figure 16.1 shows a firm in monopolistic competition in an initial long-run equilibrium position, producing where marginal revenue equals marginal cost and making profits equal to $(p_1 - AC_1)X_1$. Now suppose that it was possible for other firms to set up and produce a different brand of the same product under the same cost conditions as this firm. The effect of this would be both to make the demand curve for this firm's product more elastic at any particular price, and to shift the curve in to the left as customers are lost to these other firms. If there are no barriers to entry of new firms, this process would continue until there were no profits being made to attract new entrants. Thus, our original firm and all its competitors would find themselves in an equilibrium such as portrayed in Figure 16.2.

This equilibrium for the monopolistically competitive firm has the property that firms are constrained on the demand side of the market. By this, we mean that firms would like to sell more at the going price, but, because they have a downward-sloping demand curve, they can make additional sales only if price is reduced. This contrasts with the equilibrium for competitive firms, which are characterised as being able to sell as much as they want at the going price, and are constrained only by their willingness to supply. This property of the monopolistically competitive model,

Figure 16.1

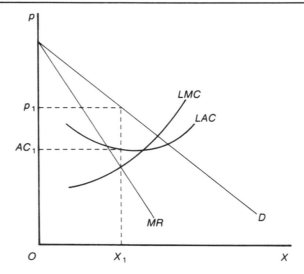

A monopolistic competitor in long-run equilibrium earning profits of $(p_1 - AC_1)X_1$. This diagram is similar in all respects to Figure 15.4.

Figure 16.2

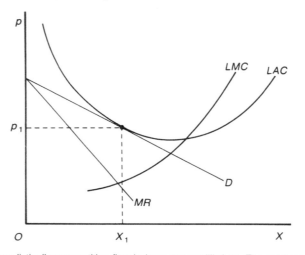

A typical monopolistically competitive firm in long-run equilibrium. The existence of positive profits attracts new firms which produce a similar but not identical product to X. The expansion of such firms results in the demand curve for X shifting until it is just tangent to the firm's long-run average cost curve at p_1X_1. This figure is similar in every essential respect to the zero profit special case of a monopolistic firm portrayed in Figure 15.5(a).

as well as its ability to describe the process of price formation, has made it attractive to macroeconomists working in the 'Keynesian' tradition seeking microfoundations for their analysis of the influence of the aggregate demand for output on the level of output and that of employment too.

Monopolistic Competition and Efficiency

A characteristic of the equilibrium portrayed in Figure 16.2 is that the firm is making no profits. It is in equilibrium at a level of output at which long-run average cost and price are equal. Because competitors are producing 'similar' but not identical products, the demand curve facing each firm slopes downwards so that with price being equal to average cost where profits are maximised, each firm is necessarily producing on the downward-sloping segment of its long-run average cost curve.

It is sometimes argued that a firm involved in monopolistic competition is inherently less efficient than its perfectly competitive counterpart, since it ends up producing output at more than minimum average cost. This finding does not necessarily hold in the case of pure monopoly, because, as will be remembered from the previous chapter, a monopolist simply produces where marginal revenue equals marginal cost without reference to the average cost curve. Monopolists could, in principle, produce at the minimum point of the long-run average cost curve therefore. A rough and ready intuition for this finding of 'excess capacity' under monopolistic competition is that there are 'too many firms' in long-run equilibrium. Since long-run average cost curves are U-shaped by assumption, and in perfectly competitive equilibrium every firm produces at the minimum of long-run average costs, an excess of firms implies that, in monopolistic competition, each firm produces less than its counterpart under perfect competition, and is therefore constrained to the downward-sloping part of the long-run average cost curve.

*A More Formal Analysis

We can illustrate the above discussion with some simple calculus. We also draw on our formal analysis of the monopolistic firm to obtain a representation of the model of monopolistic competition using the example of a Cobb–Douglas production function.

We assume that the firm in monopolistic competition maximises profits

$$\pi = pX - rK - wL \tag{16.1}$$

subject to a Cobb–Douglas production function

$$X = AL^\alpha L^\beta \tag{16.2}$$

and downward-sloping output demand curve

$$p = p(X), \ \partial p / \partial X < 0 \tag{16.3}$$

We make no restrictions on returns to scale $(\alpha + \beta)$, *a priori*. We established in Chapter 14 that, in competition, the price equals marginal cost condition could be rearranged to the labour hiring rule that price times the marginal product of labour, known as the marginal revenue product of

labour, equals the wage (see equation (14.3)). Similarly we can derive the capital hiring rule for competitive product markets that the price times the marginal product of capital, known as the marginal revenue product of capital, equals the rental price of capital (see equation (14.4)).

These conditions, which are examined in more detail in Chapter 19, have to be modified somewhat when product markets are imperfectly competitive (see Chapter 20). In particular, the marginal revenue product terms ($p\partial X/\partial L$ and $p\partial X/\partial K$) must be specified differently because the addition to revenue from an additional unit of output is *marginal revenue*, not price, when competition is imperfect.

Hence the marginal revenue product of labour is marginal revenue times the marginal product of labour $(p + X(\partial p/\partial X))(\partial X/\partial L)$. Denoting marginal revenue for the moment as mr, the equilibrium conditions are

$$mr\, \frac{\partial X}{\partial L} = mr\, \frac{\alpha X}{L} = w \qquad (16.4)$$

$$mr\, \frac{\partial X}{\partial K} = mr\, \frac{\beta X}{K} = r \qquad (16.5)$$

Substituting equations (16.4) and (16.5) into (16.1) yields

$$\pi = pX - \frac{mr(\alpha XL)}{L} - \frac{mr(\beta XK)}{K} \qquad (16.6)$$

$$\pi = pX - mr(\alpha + \beta)X \qquad (16.7)$$

As we have seen, firms in monopolistic competition which make positive profits are subject to competitive pressures which shift product demand curves inwards and make them more elastic. This process ceases when every (technologically identical) firm earns zero profits. Hence full market equilibrium requires that each firm's situation is characterised by

$$\pi = 0 \qquad (16.8)$$

The two equations (16.7 and 16.8) therefore describe the equilibrium for the firm in monopolistic competition after entry has ceased. Combining them and rearranging terms yields

$$\frac{p}{mr} = \alpha + \beta \qquad (16.9)$$

Thus, the firm must produce where $(\alpha+\beta)$, which is an index of returns to scale, equals the ratio of price to marginal revenue. We have already noted that, since demand curves slope downwards, marginal revenue is everywhere less than price (see Chapter 15, in particular equations (15.1) and (15.2)). Hence the left-hand side of equation (16.9) is greater than 1. This means that for (16.9) to hold, $\alpha+\beta>1$; the firm must produce in

the range of increasing returns to scale. We have therefore established that the firm's own equilibrium conditions in the face of a downward-sloping demand curve — the marginal revenue product equals the cost of the factor input — and the zero profit condition from free entry and exit, can only be satisfied simultaneously if the equilibrium occurs in the range of increasing returns to scale, when long-run average costs are diminishing. This result carries over to the case where production technology is not homogeneous, and as we have seen is illustrated in Figure 16.2.

Mark-Up Pricing

A great attraction of the model of monopolistic competition is that it allows us to think about firms' pricing policies rather more explicitly than do the models of market structure dealt with earlier. In particular, it allows us to derive formally a 'mark-up' model of pricing, in which prices are set as a multiple of average costs. This model is worth readers' attention for two reasons. First, much applied work in industrial organisation has dealt with the idea that output price is often set by adding a fixed mark-up to average costs, and it is by no means clear at first sight that such behaviour is compatible with profit maximisation. Certainly, the models of firm behaviour that we have considered so far give us no reason in general to predict such behaviour. It is therefore of some interest to see that, on certain specific assumptions, profit maximisation does indeed lead to fixed mark-up pricing. The analysis that follows will enable readers to see just what those assumptions are, and to form their own opinions about their plausibility.

Second, many macroeconomic models of the inflationary process see the link between labour-market conditions and the behaviour of money wages as being a crucial element in that process. Nevertheless, it is only one element, and must be supplemented by a theory of the relationship between labour-costs and price if the so-called 'wage—price spiral' is to be analysed. The idea of mark-up pricing has often been pressed into service to provide such a theory.

The analysis in question is most simply undertaken with the aid of a number of restrictive assumptions some of which conflict with those made elsewhere in this chapter. In particular, it is helpful to focus on a monopolistically competitive industry made up of identical firms, each with constant average and marginal costs.

In order to make sense of this assumption, we are forced to assume also that some barrier to the entry of new firms into the industry exists, for under such cost conditions, the typical monopolistically competitive firm will make positive profits at any positive level of output. Free entry would ensure that the 'zero profit' equilibrium depicted in Figure 16.2, where the demand curve is tangent to the average cost curve, would

degenerate into a 'corner solution' in which the typical firm sold an infinitessimally small (in the limit zero) level of output at a price just equal to average and marginal cost.

Nevertheless, if we are willing to assume that the number of firms in the monopolistically competitive industry is exogenously given, we may then assume constant average and marginal costs of production and proceed to develop a model of mark-up pricing. In terms of the Cobb–Douglas production function, such as we set out above, constant returns to scale implies $\alpha + \beta = 1$. Unlike in perfect competition, where enterprise equilibrium is indeterminate with constant returns (see Chapter 14), the monopolistically competitive firm can achieve a determinate equilibrium level of output with constant average costs because the demand curve is downward sloping. As we know from Chapter 11, constant returns to scale means that long-run average costs equal long-run marginal costs, and we denote them by C. Let us assume that each firm faces a constant elasticity demand curve (see Chapter 15). We know from equation (15.2) that

$$mr = p\left(1 + \frac{1}{e}\right) \tag{16.10}$$

We also know that the monopolistically competitive firm produces where $mr = mc$. Hence in this case it produces where

$$p\left(1 + \frac{1}{e}\right) = LMC = LAC \equiv c \tag{16.11}$$

or $$p = \left(\frac{1}{1 + \dfrac{1}{e}}\right) LAC \tag{16.12}$$

As we have assumed e is a constant, we can denote $(1/(1 + 1/e))$ as a constant $(1 + m)$. Hence

$$p = (1 + m)\, c \tag{16.13}$$

Equation (16.13) states that price is a mark-up (m) of long-run average cost, the size of the mark-up depending on the elasticity of demand. The more inelastic demand is, the greater the mark-up on costs to reach the selling price. The model of monopolistic competition, with some strong assumptions about entry conditions, not to mention demand and technology, therefore allows us to derive a simple *behavioural* model of how prices are set.

Criticisms of Monopolistic Competition

The foregoing analysis is appealing and popular, not least, as we have noted earlier, among economists seeking microfoundations for Keynesian

macroeconomics, and among those looking for a theoretical framework within which to cast empirical studies of firms' pricing policies. It is not beyond criticism, however. In particular, its critics ask whether it adds anything to the monopoly model with which we dealt earlier. Monopoly differs from perfect competition in its analysis of the behaviour of the firm in one respect only: the monopolist's demand curve slopes downward. So also does that of the monopolistically competitive firm, and in long-run equilibrium with freedom of entry it is just a special case of monopoly where zero profits are being made. The version of the model used to analyse mark-up pricing is yet another special case of monopoly, this one with constant returns to scale. If this analysis does add anything to our understanding of firms' behaviour, then, it must be because it tells us something about the interactions between firms in an industry, for it tells us nothing new about the individual firm.

But according to the critics there is a problem at this level too. The monopolistically competitive industry is made up of firms producing 'similar', though not identical, products that are therefore 'close', but not perfect, substitutes for each other. The question upon which, so they claim, the analysis founders is 'how close is close?' Are different brands of tea 'similar' products? And if they are, is coffee a sufficiently 'close' substitute that we should talk about a 'beverage' industry? And if we do, are cocoa producing firms part of it? The model does not tell us how to draw the boundary around an industry and hence leaves it up to the individual economist carrying out the analysis to decide whether to treat a particular group of firms as individual monopolies or as members of a monopolistically competitive industry. Since no one has ever suggested that there are no substitutes for an individual monopolist's output, and that changes in the price of those substitutes will not shift the demand curve, the critics argue that the notion of the monopolistically competitive industry adds little to our ability to understand firms' behaviour that is not already inherent in the theory of pure monopoly.

The Concept of Oligopoly

The theories of perfect competition and monopoly have in common the assumption that the decisions taken by any particular firm have such diffuse effects on the environment in which other firms operate that the individual firm can safely neglect this reaction to its behaviour in making its own decisions. However, it is easy to think of circumstances in which this is not a sensible assumption. In particular, when a small number of large firms dominate a particular industry producing identical or closely substitutable products, one would expect the likely response of other firms to be a major factor influencing any price/output decision. Such a state of affairs is central to the form of industrial organisation known as *oligopoly* — competition among a few firms.

The study of oligopolistic markets is rather more difficult than of competitive and monopolistic markets because we have to specify ways in which firms interact with each other, as well as with consumers. Profit maximisation has been a fairly straightforward affair until now: given their demand and cost functions, firms chose output to equalise marginal revenue and marginal cost. The cost side is assumed not to be affected by product market structure but it is, as we shall see, of the essence of oligopoly that firms cannot know their demand curves, at least not without making assumptions about the way in which competitors will react to their own actions. Suppliers' quantity and pricing decisions are therefore interdependent. There are a number of ways of analysing oligopolistic markets, each based on a different set of behavioural assumptions. In the remainder of this chapter we focus on two traditional models of oligopolistic behaviour — the kinked demand curve and price leadership models. Neither model stresses 'strategic interaction' among firms, though the latter points towards a game theoretic approach to analysing firms' behaviour. Such game-theoretic analysis, however, is not developed formally here; it is taken up at the end of the next chapter.

The Kinked Demand Curve

This model was originally devised, not as a tool to analyse price and output determination, but to explain the apparent fact that, in oligopolistic markets, prices once set as a mark-up on average costs (see the previous section) tend not to change. However, the model deals in a simple way with the manner in which expectations about the behaviour of competitors might influence decision making in oligopolistic markets, and it is this aspect of it upon which we focus.

The basic properties of the model are set out in Figure 16.3, and are derived in the following way. We deal with a firm, one of a small group of firms producing closely related products, which produces output X_1 and sells it at price p_1. Consider the demand curve for this product. If the prices charged by competing firms are held constant, then we have a conventional demand curve such as DD. This curve has been drawn with a relatively shallow slope to reflect the fact that some of the other goods whose prices are being held constant are close substitutes for X. It is by no means obvious that the producers of these close substitutes will set their prices independently of the price of X. We can draw another demand curve for X that reflects the response of quantity demanded to price, on the assumption that other firms would also alter their prices in the same direction as the price of X when it was varied. Such a curve would obviously be more steeply sloped than DD and in Figure 16.3 it is drawn as dd. There is a marginal revenue curve for each of these demand curves, and they are labelled as MR and mr respectively.

Figure 16.3

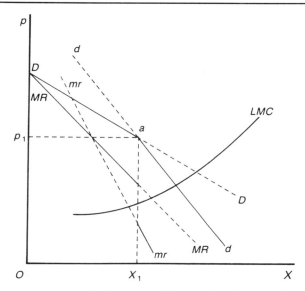

The kinked demand curve model of oligopoly. With price fixed at p_1 the firm believes that if it raises price, other firms will not follow suit. Hence the response of quantity demanded of X to such a move will be relatively large. However, the firm believes that others will follow a price cut so that the response of quantity demanded to such a move will be relatively small. Thus the firm thinks itself confronted by a demand curve kinked at point a, and hence as facing the discontinuous marginal revenue curve $MR - mr$. Note that cost fluctuations that do not shift LMC outside of the discontinuity in the marginal revenue curve will not result in the firm changing either price or output.

Now suppose that the firm takes the view that its competitors will react asymmetrically to a price change, that they will follow a price cut but will not follow a price increase. Then the demand curve that faces the firm will appear to be given by Dad, a kinked relationship. There is an element of *a priori* plausibility about this demand curve because, if one firm out of a small group of firms raises its price, all the others who at the old price were happy with the volume of sales they were enjoying, would see that volume of sales increase without their doing anything. Hence they might be expected to be reluctant to follow a price increase. On the other hand, one firm lowering its price would take customers from them if they did not respond. Hence, to avoid this possibility, these other firms would be likely to follow a price cut. And not only is there *a priori* plausibility here; there is also a certain amount of evidence from questionnaires circulated to firms that they do indeed tend to expect their competitors to react this way — not following a price increase, but following a price cut.

If the demand curve which a particular firm thinks it faces does indeed take the form of *Dad*, then it will also think of the marginal revenue curve

which it faces being a discontinuous relationship. Readers who are uncertain as to why there should be this discontinuity in the marginal revenue curve should construct for themselves the total revenue curve implicit in a kinked demand curve such as *Dad*. They will find that, at the level of output corresponding to the kink, there is a kink in the total revenue curve. Its slope will discontinuously become less at that level of output and this is equivalent to saying that marginal revenue will discontinuously become lower.

As we have drawn Figure 16.3, the firm's long-run marginal cost curve passes through the discontinuity in the marginal revenue curve and so the firm is in equilibrium at price p_1 and X_1. Note that, in this situation, fluctuations in costs that do not take the marginal cost curve out of the range of discontinuity in the marginal revenue curve will not result in price changes.

The analysis looks appealing then, and yields the prediction that for an oligopolist, the price of output will be relatively rigid in the face of cost changes. The model does not, however, explain how that particular price and quantity, rather than any other, happened to get established. Nor is there any way of knowing where equilibrium will be re-established if the marginal cost curve moves out of the discontinuity in the marginal revenue curve. In other words, Figure 16.3 gives us a portrait of a particular situation in which a firm might find itself, but contains no information as to how the situation in question arose in the first place. For this reason, the kinked demand curve model is best regarded as an illustration of the oligopoly problem, rather than a systematic solution to price and output determination in such a market structure.

Price Leadership

Our second oligopoly model also deals with the interdependence problem by making assumptions about how firms will behave. However, it is a rather richer framework which draws on special assumptions about the structure of a particular type of oligopolistic market, in which there is one *dominant firm* from which all others take the lead as far as pricing policy is concerned. The dominant firm takes the reactions of the other firms into account when making its decision about price and output, but they take the dominant firm's price as given in settling on their own behaviour. The phenomenon involved here is therefore called *price leadership*.

Consider Figure 16.4. In panel (a) we have the market demand curve for X, and a long-run market supply curve derived from the behaviour of a group of perfectly competitive firms. For simplicity we assume that given factor prices lie behind this curve and that it derives its upward slope from declining efficiency of new firms as supply expands. Now suppose that a new relatively large (and hence 'dominant') firm was con-

Figure 16.4

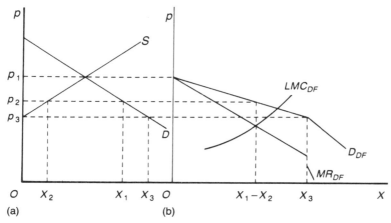

Price leadership. The industry demand curve, combined with the supply curve of a number of perfectly competitive firms is depicted in panel (a). The demand curve of the dominant firm D_{DF} is derived by subtracting the competitive supply curve from the industry demand curve. Faced with this demand curve in the long run the dominant firm equates marginal cost (LMC) to marginal revenue (MR_{DF}). Price is determined at p_2, competitive firms supply X_2, total demand is given by X_1 and the dominant firm sells $X_1 - X_2$. Note that, unless it can produce a positive output at price less than p_1, the equilibrium price in its absence, the dominant firm will not exist. Thus a firm can only achieve dominance if it has a significant cost advantage. If its profit-maximising price was p_3 or below, the dominant firm would be the only firm in the industry.

sidering entering the market for X. How would it view the demand conditions it faced? Clearly at a price p_1, the already existing competitive firms would supply the entire market and the dominant firm would be able to sell nothing. However, were it to set its price at p_2, below p_1, less efficient competitive firms would drop out of the market. Those remaining would supply X_2, leaving $X_1 - X_2$ to be sold by the large firm. In other words, the quantity demanded from the dominant firm at any particular price, is found by taking the market demand at that price and subtracting from it the quantity that would be supplied by the competitive firms. Obviously, at price p_3 the resulting demand curve becomes the market demand curve. There is a kink in the dominant firm's demand curve at this point and hence a discontinuity in its marginal revenue curve. This is *not*, however, the same type of kinked demand curve as we met in the previous analysis, as ought to be obvious. As we have drawn Figure 16.4 the price/quantity solution that emerges is one at which price is fixed at p_2 by the large firm. The total amount demanded is X_1, of which the dominant firm supplies $X_1 - X_2$, leaving X_2 to be supplied by small firms at the going price.

As well as explaining how price is determined, this model yields several interesting insights. First, a dominant firm can only emerge if it is capable of producing a 'substantial' proportion of the industry's output at a lower price than would emerge under competition among relatively small firms.

The example of the supermarket in comparison to small groceries as a purveyor of retailing services comes to mind here. Second, it is not just existing competitors that affect the elasticity of a demand curve facing a firm, but potential competitors as well. Thus, a downward-sloping demand curve facing a firm is by no means necessarily synonymous with the market demand curve for the good in question — *even if that firm is the sole producer of the good in question.*

To make this point quite clear consider Figure 16.5 which is a variation on the theme developed in Figure 16.4. It differs from Figure 16.4 in two ways only. First it is assumed that all small firms are equally efficient and second it is assumed in drawing its marginal cost curve as LMC that the large firm's cost advantage is such as to permit it to take the whole market for X. Nevertheless, this firm, even as the sole producer of X, has no power to raise its price above p_1. That is to say, a sole seller of a good who is in that position simply by virtue of a cost advantage is far less a 'monopolist' than one whose advantage stems from some legal barrier to competition. The latter but not the former, can treat the market demand curve as the relevant one.

Another variation on Figure 16.5 is also worth considering. Suppose the large firm's marginal cost curve lay at LMC_1. It would produce a large part of the industry's output, but would in fact be a perfect competitor as far as its pricing behaviour was concerned.

Concluding Comment

The analysis of earlier chapters seemed to indicate that the nature of price–quantity outcomes would depend upon the number of firms in an

Figure 16.5

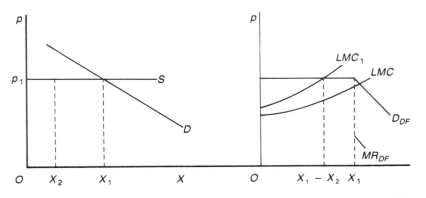

Price leadership when the long-run competitive industry supply curve is horizontal. If the dominant firm's marginal cost curve is given by LMC it produces the whole industry's output, but sells it at the competitive price p_1. If it is given by LMC_1 it sells a proportion of the industry's output, $X_1 - X_2$, at the competitive price with competitive firms selling X_2. In neither case does the dominant firm have any monopoly power, even when it is the only firm in the industry.

industry. Thus equilibrium in perfect competition, with a large number of firms, was characterised by price equalling the minimum of long-run average costs. In contrast, monopolistic markets had higher prices and smaller levels of output; output was set where marginal revenues equalled marginal cost and price, given quantity, was determined on the demand curve.

One might have expected that 'intermediate market structures', with relatively few firms, would generate outcomes somewhere between these extremes. One important implication of the material presented in this chapter as well as that dealing with discriminating monopoly is that this perspective simplifies to the point of being misleading. The model of monopolistic competition suggests that market imperfections involve phenomena other than the number of firms in an industry: analysis must also take account of the degree of product differentiation and the ease or difficulty of entry. The simplest of oligopoly theories, such as that based on the kinked demand curve, highlights the crucial impact for how we model price—quantity determination of assumptions about the behaviour of other suppliers when decision making is interdependent. Finally, our discussion of the price leadership model has established, among other things, that when the long-run competitive industry's potential supply curve is horizontal, the number of firms in an industry is not, *in and of itself*, any indicator of the competitiveness of that industry.

17

Models of Oligopoly and the Theory of Games

Introduction

In this chapter we extend our treatment of price and output determination under imperfect competition to consider a more thorough analysis of the interaction of producers. We also set out a brief introduction to the theory of games, a technique which is particularly helpful in this context. Because inter-firm interactions in imperfect markets take many forms, oligopoly theory lacks unambiguous results of the sort we developed for competition and monopoly. Instead, we have a variety of results derived from different behavioural assumptions, with each model potentially relevant to certain real world situations, but not to others. Our aim in this chapter is to provide an introduction to some of the more important models available, and a unifying framework which helps to highlight the sources of their differences, as well as to offer a strategic interpretation of the behaviour of interdependent producers through the theory of games.

As we saw in the previous chapter, models of enterprise decision making in oligopoly derive their special character from the fact that firms in an oligopolistic industry are, and know that they are interdependent. In competitive markets, there are enough other producers that each firm can safely ignore the reactions of rivals to its decisions when it makes its own output choices. This is not necessarily the case where there are only a few producers; and two broad approaches may be taken to solve the problem created by this fact. First the oligopolist can be thought of as making assumptions about the variables to which competitors will react and about the nature of their reactions. Models dealing with such behaviour are referred to as *non-collusive* because, though in equilibrium the expectations of each firm about the reactions of rivals are realised,

264

the two sides never communicate with each other directly about their likely reactions. Alternatively, firms can be thought of as agreeing to co-operate in setting price and quantity from the outset. *Collusive* models deal with such behaviour. In these models firms form a *cartel*, and output-price combinations equivalent to those which would emerge under monopoly are chosen for the industry as a whole. The question then arises as to how the monopoly profits are divided between the participating firms. The likelihood of arguments arising over profit shares has led economists to predict that cartels will be inherently unstable.

In order to simplify the analysis which follows, we will usually assume that there are only two firms in the industry — a situation usually called *duopoly*. Results will be extended to the case of more than two firms where such generalisation yields additional insight. We commence with the best known non-collusive model, derived by Augustin Cournot in 1838. In this formulation, the strategic variable to which the firm reacts is the out-put of its rival, and the firm is assumed to take its rival's output choice as given. The resulting equilibrium will be contrasted with the output decisions which result when the two sides collude by forming a cartel. Then we shall consider an alternative modelling strategy offered by Joseph Bertrand who argued that, in the context of non-collusive behaviour, price rather than quantity should be the relevant variable for strategic interac-tion. Some of the ideas contained in the price leadership model set out in the previous chapter were formalised by Heinrich von Stackelberg, who in the context of a Cournot model allows one firm to exploit a leadership position. We shall also discuss this analysis. The results of several of the above-mentioned models can be derived from, or illuminated and extended by, the theory of games. In the final section of this chapter we therefore introduce some simple notions of game theory and illustrate their application.

The Cournot Model   — 1838.

As we saw in the last chapter, the central problem faced by a firm in a duopoly is that its decisions affect the price or quantity choices of its rival. The kinked demand curve model depicted this problem, and made the *ad hoc* assumption that the firm believes that its competitors will follow a price cut but not follow a price increase. The Cournot model focuses instead on quantities, and is based on the assumption that the firm is expected *not to respond at all* to changes in the output decisions of its rival. Thus firm 1 chooses its output, say X_1, on the assumption that the out-put level of firm 2, X_2, is fixed. Similarly, X_2 is chosen on the assump-tion that X_1 can be treated by firm 2 as given. This is analogous to the assumption made in competitive markets that firms make their decisions without reference to the reactions of their rivals, and makes some sense in oligopolistic markets where there are a relatively large number of firms.

The assumption appears rather strange in the limiting case of duopoly, but it must be remembered that in the *Cournot equilibrium*, when quantities are not changing, the expectations of each firm about the reactions of its rival will in fact always be realised.

Iso-Profit Curves and Reaction Functions

The Cournot model is best explained diagrammatically with reference to isoprofit curves and reaction functions. An *isoprofit curve* for firm 1 is the locus of points in (X_1, X_2) space defined by different levels of output for both firm 1 and firm 2 which yield the same level of profit to firm 1. In duopoly, the profits of each firm depend on the output decision of its rival because the price obtained for the good depends on industry output $(X_1 + X_2)$. Isoprofit curves are concave to the axis of the firm to which they relate, with the level of profits declining with the height of the isoprofit curve above the horizontal axis. A family of isoprofit curves is illustrated in Figure 17.1. Note that, if firm 2 produces nothing, firm

Figure 17.1

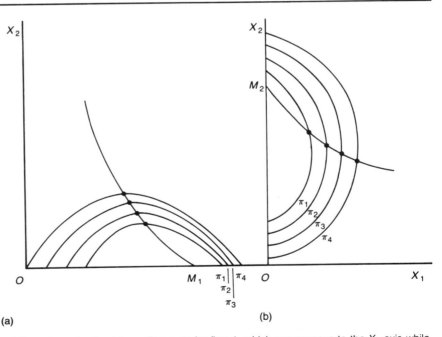

(a)   (b)

(a) illustrates a family of isoprofit curves for firm 1, which are concave to the X_1 axis while (b) illustrates analagous curves for firm 2. The level of firm 1's profits rises as we move closer towards the X_1 axis ($\pi_1 > \pi_2 > \pi_3 > \pi_4$) and correspondingly for firm 2's isoprofit map. The output of X_1 at which profit is maximised for firm 1 increases as the output of firm 2 is reduced, and vice versa. At M_1 (M_2) the output of X_2 (X_1) is zero, and firm 1 (firm 2) makes monopoly profits. These points of maximum profit, given the other firm's output, define a reaction function, see Figure 17.2.

1 is a monopolist, output is M_1 and the isoprofit curve corresponding to monopoly profits is, in essence, a point on the axis at M_1. Similarly, M_2 represents monopoly output for firm 2.

In order to analyse the Cournot equilibrium, we need to consider the impact of a change in firm 2's output upon the quantity produced by firm 1, and vice versa. The relationships through which we summarise these interactions are called *reaction functions*: firm 1's reaction function tells us how firm 1 will change output in response to a change in X_2, and firm 2's reaction function will tell us how firm 2 will respond to a change in X_1. We assume that both firms seek to maximise profits and that the industry as a whole faces a downward-sloping demand curve along which price varies with the quantities produced by both firms, that is the sum of X_1 and X_2. With the Cournot behavioural assumption that firms take the output of their rival as given, an increase in X_2 lowers the price both firms receive from the market, lowers the marginal revenue obtained by firm 1 at each level of output and therefore, for given marginal cost, leads firm 1 to reduce output; and similarly for firm 2, which suggests that the reaction functions for both firms are backward bending.

The argument is illustrated in Figure 17.2. For a given level of output in firm 2, say X_2^1, firm 1 seeks to maximise profits, which entails choosing an output level X_1^1 which yields the lowest isoprofit curve consistent with X_2^1 at the tangency between π_1^1 and X_2^1. If firm 2 increases its output level to X_2^2, the highest level of profit attainable is at output level X_1^2 at the tangency between π_1^2 and X_2^2. The locus of the tangencies between given values of X_2 and isoprofit lines therefore plots out the reaction function for firm 1. This is of course the locus of maxima of the isoprofit curves and as we saw is backward bending. If one does the same analysis for firm 2, starting by taking output of firm 1 as constant at, say, X_1^3, we derive firm 2's reaction function as the locus of maxima of firm 2's isoprofit curves.

Each reaction function therefore plots the profit-maximising level of output for each firm given every conceivable expected value of production which could be chosen by its rival. The *Cournot equilibrium* is reached when the expectation of each firm about its rival's output choice proves to be correct. Clearly, this occurs at the intersection of the two reaction functions, where each firm is choosing to produce exactly the level of output which its rival expects. This mutual realisation of output expectations is illustrated at output levels (X_1^*, X_2^*) in Figure 17.3. Readers should note that industry output $X = (X_1^* + X_2^*)$ is greater than under pure monopoly $(M_1$ or $M_2)$, and therefore price must be lower than the monopoly price.

We can also illustrate the path of adjustment towards equilibrium implied by Cournot behaviour in Figure 17.3. If we arbitrarily start with the assumption that firm 1 chooses X_1^1, profits are maximised for firm 2 at the point where X_1^1 intersects firm 2's reaction function at X_2^1. But this output pair, (X_1^1, X_2^1) is not a Cournot equilibrium because firm 1's expectation of firm 2's behaviour is not confirmed by firm 2. Firm 1 chose

Figure 17.2

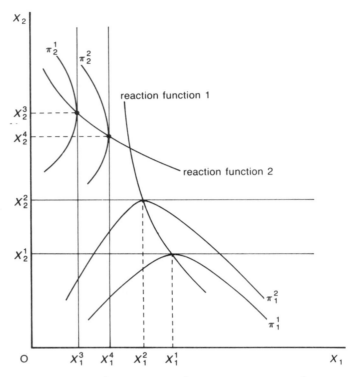

Firm 1 maximises profits at π_1^1, by choosing X_1^1 when firm 2 chooses X_2^1. Its optimal output declines to X_1^2, yielding π_1^2, when firm 2 increases output to X_2^2. The locus of these maxima of the isoprofit function is therefore firm 1's reaction function. Symmetrically, firm 2 maximises profits at π_2^1 by choosing X_2^3 when firm 1 chooses X_1^3 and will reduce output to X_2^4 in response to firm 1's increase of output to X_1^4.

X_1 because it expected firm 2 to produce X_2^0, but in fact it produced X_2^1. The process of adjusting output in order to maximise profits (i.e. along the reaction function) in response to unrealised expectations about the output choice of rivals will stop when expectations are mutually consistent, at (X_1^*, X_2^*) where the reaction functions cross.

The process described here is *stable*, in the sense that, from any initial starting point on either firm 1 or firm 2's reaction function, it will lead to the Cournot equilibrium. This will be so, provided that firm 1's reaction function is steeper than firm 2's reaction function. Readers can prove for themselves, however, that when the relative slopes of the two curves are reversed, Cournot behaviour and profit maximisation lead away from the point of intersection of the two reaction functions from any initial starting point, except the intersection itself. In this case, the equilibrium is said to be unstable.

Figure 17.3

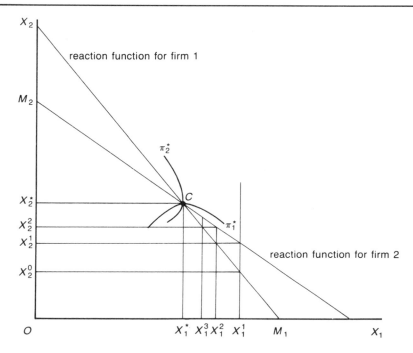

The Cournot equilibrium point C, at the intersection of the two reaction functions. At this point, the expectations of each firm about the behaviour of its rival are confirmed. Suppose instead that firm 1 chooses X_1^1. Firm 2 responds with X_2^1, but at that output level, firm 1 would choose X_1^2. Expectations are therefore not confirmed, 2 chooses X_2^2 and 1 responds with X_1^3. The process continues until X_1^*, X_2^* is reached. The process is stable provided that 1's reaction curve is steeper than 2's. Note that in this case the reaction functions are drawn as straight lines mainly to keep the diagrammatic analysis manageable; but see the following formal analysis.

*A More Formal Treatment of the Cournot Model

The more mathematically inclined student can obtain a better understanding of the subtleties of the Cournot model from the following general formalisation and example. In the duopoly case, the profits of each firm depend on the level of output of both because output price is given by the industry demand curve. Hence if the industry demand curve is

$$p = p(X) = p(X_1 + X_2) \tag{17.1}$$

where X is industry output, the profits of the two firms are given by

$$\pi_1 = p(X_1+X_2)X_1 - C(X_1) \tag{17.2}$$

and

$$\pi_2 = p(X_1+X_2)X_2 - C(X_2) \tag{17.3}$$

where $C(\cdot)$ represents each firm's cost function.

The Cournot assumption is that each firm chooses its output level taking the output of its rival as given. Hence firm 1 chooses X_1 to maximise π_1 given X_2, and firm 2 chooses X_2 to maximise π_2 given X_1. In each case, this maximum occurs where

$$\partial \pi_i / \partial X_i = 0, \ i = 1,2 \tag{17.4}$$

There is a different value of X_i for every assumed value of $X_j (i \neq j)$, each representing the maximum of a particular isoprofit line as illustrated in Figure 17.1.

In this example, let us make the particularly simple assumptions that the demand curve is linear; that costs have a fixed element F and a constant marginal cost, c per unit of output. Hence, the demand curve is

$$p = a - b(X_1 + X_2) \tag{17.5}$$

and $\quad C(X_1) = F + cX_1; \ C(X_2) = F + cX_2 \tag{17.6}$

Then the profit functions are

$$\pi_1 = aX_1 - bX_1^2 - bX_2X_1 - F - cX_1 \tag{17.7}$$

$$\pi_2 = aX_2 - bX_1X_2 - bX_2^2 - F - cX_2 \tag{17.8}$$

Rearranging equation (17.7) yields the equation for firm 1's isoprofit curve

$$X_2 = \frac{a-c}{b} - X_1 - \left(\frac{\pi_1 + F}{bX_1}\right) \tag{17.9}$$

which for each value of π_1, yields an inverse U-shaped line concave to the X_1 axis. This is firm 1's isoprofit curve as depicted in Figure 17.1. Similarly for firm 2, the equation of the isoprofit line is

$$X_1 = \frac{a-c}{b} - X_2 - \left(\frac{\pi_2 + F}{bX_2}\right) \tag{17.10}$$

We can derive firm 1's reaction function by maximising π_1 in equation (17.7) taking X_2 as given. Profits are maximised where

$$\frac{\partial \pi_1}{\partial X_1} = a - 2bX_1 - bX_2 - c = 0 \tag{17.11}$$

which can be rearranged to yield the familar marginal revenue (a $-bX_1 - bX_2$) equals marginal cost (c) relationship. From equation (17.11) we can derive the relationship between X_1 and X_2 when profits are maximised,

$$X_1 = \frac{a-c}{2b} - \frac{X_2}{2} \tag{17.12}$$

This is firm 1's reaction function and in the range where profits are positive it is linear when demand and marginal cost curves are linear. Similarly,

we can derive firm 2's reaction function by maximising π_2 in equation (17.8) taking X_1 as given. Hence

$$\frac{\partial \pi_2}{\partial X_2} = a - 2bX_2 - bX_1 - c = 0 \qquad (17.13)$$

which gives us a relationship between X_2 and X_1,

$$X_2 = \frac{a-c}{2b} - \frac{X_1}{2} \qquad (17.14)$$

This is firm 2's reaction function. The two reaction functions are *symmetric* because we have assumed that the firms face the same structure of demand and cost equations.

The Cournot equilibrium occurs where the two reaction functions intersect, or at the solution to the simultaneous equation system (17.12) and (17.14). Substituting (17.12) into (17.14) yields

$$X_2 = \frac{a-c}{2b} - \frac{a-c}{4b} + \frac{X_2}{4} \qquad (17.15)$$

so that

$$X_2 = \frac{a-c}{3b} \qquad (17.16)$$

Substituting back into equation (17.12) yields

$$X_1 = \frac{a-c}{3b} \qquad (17.17)$$

Since demand and cost conditions are assumed to be identical in this example, and the reaction functions are symmetric, the firms divide the industry output between themselves equally. The equilibrium is also stable. The slope of firm 2's reaction function $(\partial X_2/\partial X_1 = -\frac{1}{2})$ is less in absolute value than the slope of firm 1's reaction function $(1/(\partial X_1/\partial X_2) = -2)$. Industry output is $X = X_1 + X_2 = (2(a-c)/3b)$, while price is $(a+2c)/3$.

This equilibrium solution can be compared with the result under pure monopoly, where there is only one producer, say firm 1, producing X_1. Setting $X_2 = 0$ in equation (17.5) gives industry output as $X_1 = ((a-c)/2b)$ from equation (17.12) and the monopoly price as $p = (c+a)/2$. Hence output is greater and price lower in the Cournot equilibrium as compared with the pure monopoly outcome. Moreover, it will be shown at the end of the chapter that, if we assume additional producers to have the same cost structure as those already in the industry, industry output expands and price falls as the number of firms increases. For example, readers can prove for themselves that if there are three producers in the industry,

each will supply $((a-c)/4b)$ and market supply will be $(3(a-c)/4b)$. The larger the number of firms, the closer are output and price to the competitive level.

Collusive Behaviour — Cartels

The Cournot model analyses one possible way in which firms might interact in oligopolistic markets. However, as we have seen, while each firm maximises its own profit at the Cournot equilibrium (given its assumptions about the output choice of its rival) industry profit is not maximised. Output is greater, and price lower, than it would be if the industry were monopolised. This is shown diagrammatically in Figure 17.3, where the isoprofit curves of the two firms (π_1^*, π_2^*) cut each other at the Cournot equilibrium, point C. Each firm could increase profits (move to an isoprofit curve closer to its own axis) by moving in a south-westerly direction (reducing output), provided that its rival responded in kind. But outcomes of this sort cannot be attained if Cournot behaviour is assumed. An alternative behavioural assumption is that firms collude in setting quantity and price in order to maximise joint profits. Collusive behaviour of this sort is, as we have already noted, referred to as forming a cartel.

In the Cournot model, firms do not communicate with each directly about their production plans, but instead make assumptions about their rivals' behaviour, assumptions which in equilibrium are satisfied. As we have seen, production choices will always lie on each firm's reaction function under these circumstances. However, suppose these two firms agree not to compete with one another; rather they set price and output that maximise the profits accruing to the industry as a whole and then share those profits out according to some formula or other. In such a case, the industry as a whole comes to act like a single monopolistic firm. Figure 17.4 depicts the essentials of the behaviour of such an industry.

Suppose that the market demand curve for X is given by the curve DD in Figure 17.4(c). If industry profits are to be maximised, then industry marginal revenue must be equated to industry marginal cost, just as in the case of the conventional single firm monopolised industry. The curve labelled MR is the relevant marginal revenue curve, while the industry long-run marginal cost curve is obtained by horizontally summing the long-run marginal cost curves of the individual firms depicted in Figure 17.4(a) and (b). Hence, industry profit-maximising output is determined at X^*, while price is given by p_1. Each firm then agrees to produce that quantity of output at which its marginal cost is equal to that of the industry at the aggregate profit-maximising level of output, so that firm 1 produces X_1 and firm 2 produces X_2.

Suppose that the industry's rule for dividing up profits was simply that each firm kept the revenue raised from its own sales. Though there is no logical necessity that such a rule be adopted, it does have the merit

Figure 17.4

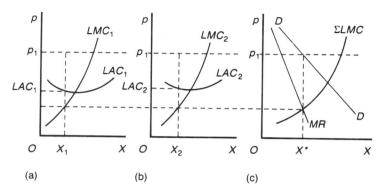

A two-firm cartel. Firm 1, panel (a), and Firm 2, panel (b) collude to fix price and output at the industry level to maximise their joint profits, panel (c). Each firm takes p_1 as given, and hence has an incentive to cheat on the cartel arrangement by expanding its output up to the point at which its long-run marginal cost equals p_1.

of requiring no machinery to administer it and hence would be a likely one for a cartel to adopt. In that case, the profits accruing to firm 1 would be given by $(p_1 - LAC_1)X_1$ and to firm 2 by $(p_1 - LAC_2)X_2$.

Notice that the essential property of the agreement between the firms which we are discussing here is that each one of them takes as given to it the industry's output price which is determined by a joint profit-maximising output decision taken in collusion. Each individual firm, from its own narrow vantage point, becomes a price taker, and hence p_1 becomes its marginal revenue. Inspection of Figure 17.4 will confirm that p_1 is obviously and necessarily greater than the marginal cost of production to either firm at the levels of output which each of them must maintain if industry-wide profits are to be maximised. Hence, each firm has an incentive to increase its output a little in order to increase its profits at the expense of the other; in other words *each firm has an incentive to cheat.*

More on Collusive Behaviour — the Contract Curve

When two firms collude, it is reasonable to suppose that they will reach an agreement under the terms of which it will be impossible to make one of them better off without making the other worse off. If they were not in such a situation, at least one of them could propose a change in the terms of the contract between them which would make the proposer better off without harming the other. It is hard to see why such a proposal should be resisted. The fundamental principle of voluntary contracts underlies much of our analysis of trade unions in Chapter 22, and the economy as a whole in Chapter 24, as well as the theory of collusive oligopolies

which follows. In each case, equilibria which satisfy the conditions outlined above are said to lie on a *contract curve*.

For the case of collusive firms we construct the contract curve by considering the isoprofit curves and reaction functions developed earlier. We noted there that, starting in a Cournot equilibrium, say C in Figure 17.3, both firms could increase their profits by moving in a south-westerly direction. The potential advantages of collusion will be exhausted, and such moves cease, when they are unable to find another combination of outputs which would allow for an improvement in the profits of one while not reducing the profits of another. This is satisfied only when the isoprofit curves are tangential. The locus of all such tangencies, is the contract curve for the two firms, and is illustrated in Figure 17.5.

Collusive equilibria always lie somewhere on the contract curve, though their precise location depends on the agreement about the allocation of

Figure 17.5

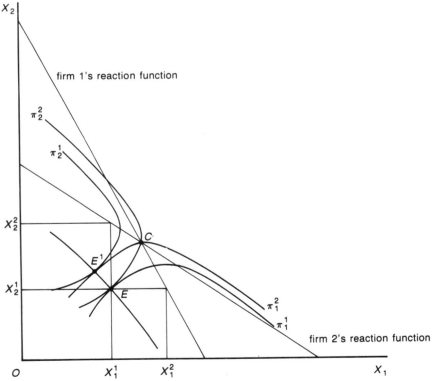

Isoprofit curves cross at the Cournot equilibrium (C) so profits can be increased for both parties by moves in a south westerly direction. Profit-enhancing output changes are exhausted for both parties when isoprofit curves are tangential, along the contract curve EE^1. Collusive equilibria therefore lie along the contract curve, their precise location depending on the allocation of profits between the two parties to the bargain. As we move from E to E^1, the profits of firm 2 increase and those of firm 1 fall.

profits made when the cartel is formed. For example, suppose we start at the Cournot equilibrium, C, and the two firms agree to collude on the basis that firm 2 receives exactly the profits that it would earn under the Cournot solution (π_2^2), while all the incremental profits from the cartel accrue to firm 1 (which gains $\pi_1^1 - \pi_1^2$). The collusive equilibrium will be on the contract curve at E. If firm 2 shares in the gains that cartelisation brings to the producers (though not of course to consumers), the actual equilibrium will lie somewhere to the north-west of E. It seems unlikely that any bargain would be struck which took the outcome beyond E^1, however, since beyond that point incremental moves along the contract curve reduce the profits of firm 1 below those that it would make in Cournot equilibrium.

[handwritten margin note: Between the two Cournot eq]

Cheating and Retaliation

The problem of cheating in a cartel can also be illustrated in this framework. Suppose that the cartel has agreed to distribute profits at (π_2^2, π_1^1) at point E on the contract curve. We know from the shape of the reaction function that, provided firm 1 believes that firm 2 will keep its output constant at the agreed level, X_2^1, it can increase its profits by expanding output. Indeed, firm 1's profits are maximised if firm 2 sticks to X_2^1, when firm 1 moves to X_1^2 on its reaction function. Similarly, if firm 2 believes firm 1 will keep its output constant at X_1^1, it will maximise its own profits on its reaction function at X_2^2. Hence while the cartel maximises *joint* profits, each individual firm can hope to do better by cheating on the bargain, provided that their rival does not respond.

There is nothing in general that economics can say about such a state of affairs. If the industry under analysis is one in which it is very easy for each firm to monitor the output and the pricing policies of the other (or others for this result holds when the number of firms is greater than two), then of course any attempt at cheating would be met by prompt retaliation, and each firm would know this in advance. If the retaliation was likely to involve price cutting by its competitors, then each firm would come to think of itself as facing a kink in its demand curve at its current price and output level, and the analysis of the previous chapter would become relevant to its behaviour. Note though that the analysis in question is now modified and expanded because we now have a way of explaining how price and output are determined in the first place. Even so, many other kinds of retaliation aimed at keeping cartel members in line — other than simple price cutting — are possible in the real world, depending upon the nature of the particular industry. A price-cutting airline might well find itself having difficulty in obtaining landing rights at key airports; or, under private medical care systems, the doctor who charges less than the medical association's 'recommended' fees sometimes loses hospital privileges. These are but two examples of the way in which

[handwritten margin note: Ease of monitoring output.]

[handwritten margin note: other pressures to keep Cartels in line]

cartel pricing arrangements may be enforced without resort to retaliatory price cutting.

Of course, to consider retaliatory action at all presupposes that the cheater gets caught, and not in every industry does each firm find it easy to police its competitors. Surreptitious discounts to particular customers, preferential after sales service involving for example 'secret warranties', priority delivery dates to particular favoured customers, are but a few of the more obvious ways in which firms who wish to cheat on cartel agreements may act in order to keep hidden what they are doing. All economic theory can say in general about these matters is that an agreement among firms to collude so as to maximise industry profits *automatically* creates an incentive for participants to cheat if they can. Whether they will do so, by what methods, and to what extent, whether their cheating will be detected, and if so by what means it will be punished — all these matters depend upon the nature of the specific case under analysis.

Extensions to the Non-Collusive Approach — An Overview

Two widely discussed alternatives to the Cournot model of non-collusive equilibrium have emerged in the literature. The first is due to Bertrand, who argued that if price rather than quantity is the strategic variable to which firms react, and if their product is homogeneous, then price will fall to the competitive level, even if the market is duopolistic. The firm charging the lower price will always end up supplying the whole market, and therefore, so the argument goes, firms will continue to undercut each other while price exceeds marginal costs. Such price competition ceases only when profits have fallen to zero, at the competitive price which equals marginal cost.

The second alternative is due to Stackelberg, who classifies duopolists in a Cournot model as either leaders or followers, with the former maximising profit subject to the reaction function of the latter. In effect, in this model, the leader bluffs the follower into believing that he is behaving according to Cournot principles, but in fact produces more output than would be produced in a Cournot equilibrium. The follower is thereby misled into producing less than in the Cournot equilibrium, and earns lower profits. Under certain conditions, industry output is greater than that of the Cournot equilibrium, however.

Both of these models are subject to the comment, made in the context of the Cournot model, that joint profits for the two firms are not maximised in their equilibria. Indeed, Bertrand interprets his finding that price interaction leads to zero profits as pointing to the likelihood of collusive rather than non-collusive equilibria emerging. The Stackelberg model also raises the possibility of a conflict between the two firms as to who is the leader and who is the follower. If both seek to be a leader, there is dis-

equilibrium until either one party backs down, or the two sides agree to collude. We shall now discuss these models in detail.

The Bertrand Model

Bertrand's approach is similar to that of Cournot, except that he assumes each firm chooses price rather than output, and makes that decision on the assumption that its rival will keep its price constant. Three fairly straightforward assumptions of the Cournot model, taken over by Bertrand, have considerable significance for the results generated by his model. The assumption of product homogeneity is crucial in the Bertrand framework, and the results change when it is altered. In particular, product differentiation allows positive profits to be sustained in equilibrium. The Bertrand model also requires the assumption that each firm has sufficient capacity to supply the entire market; there may be no equilibrium if each of the two firms does not have sufficient spare capacity. Finally it is critical to assume that firms face identical cost curves; otherwise the one which faces lower marginal costs will always end up supplying the entire market. Here we assume that, at given input prices, marginal cost is constant and equal to average cost.

Bertrand's analysis can be developed with the use of isoprofit curves and reaction functions. However, prices, rather than quantities are on the two axes. Also, as illustrated in Figure 17.6, isoprofit maps for each firm are convex rather than concave to the axis of the firm in question. This is the case because, starting at the right of the minimum of any isoprofit line, say π_1 in Figure 17.6, firm 1 must cut price in order to maintain profits in response to its rivals' price reductions. Profits decline as we move to lower and lower isoprofit curves. The reaction function for each firm is the locus of points at which profits are maximised for firm 1 when the price of firm 2 is taken as given, and vice versa for firm 2. It is therefore the locus through the minimum of the relevant U-shaped isoprofit curves, and is upward sloping for both firms.

The *Bertrand equilibrium* is achieved when each firm's expectations about the price behaviour of its rival are realised. Hence in Figure 17.6, if firm 1 expects firm 2 to charge p_2^1, it will choose p_1^1 on its reaction function in order to maximise its profits at that price. But at p_1^1, firm 2 will actually charge p_2^2, on its own reaction function. Provided that firm 1's reaction function has a steeper slope than that of firm 2, this iterative procedure will lead the firms to the Bertrand equilibrium, which is where the two reaction functions intersect. This is labelled as point B in Figure 17.6. Since their products are assumed to be homogeneous, each firm must charge the same price in equilibrium. If they did not, the one offering the lower price would actually get all the demand. Hence the equilibrium must be characterised by equal prices, and therefore lie on a 45° line beginning at the origin.

Moreover, the equilibrium price must equal the (assumed identical)

Figure 17.6

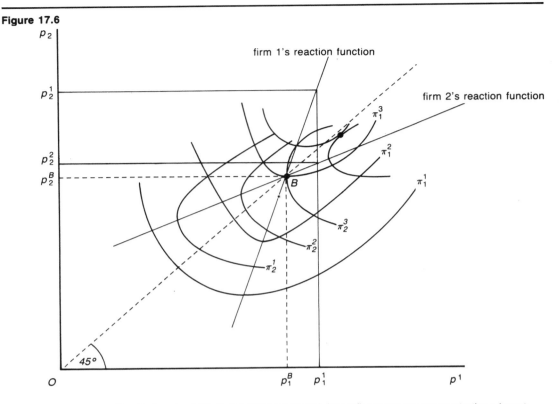

The Bertrand model. In the Bertrand model, isoprofit curves are convex to the relevant firm's axis with profits increasing as we move out. The reaction functions are the loci of minima of each firm's isoprofit curves and are upward sloping. The Bertrand equilibrium is at the intersection of the two reaction functions, at B, yielding equal (competitive) prices p_1^B and p_2^B along the 45° line.

marginal cost of each producer. This is because, if the equilibrium price exceeds marginal cost, and firm 1 believes that firm 2 will not alter its price in response to a price cut by firm 1 (the Bertrand behavioural assumption), then firm 1 will always cut its price, because in doing so it will capture the entire market. Exactly the same argument applies to firm 2. This incentive to cut price is eliminated only when the two firms charge an identical price equal to marginal cost, and industry profits are zero.

Bertrand competition therefore leads us to the perfectly competitive solution despite the small numbers of firms in the industry. This is a formalisation of an important, if hotly contested, argument in economics, to the effect that competition over price can lead to zero profits, even if there are very few firms in the industry. Its relevance to real world situations depends in part on one's evaluation of the assumptions of the model—price rather than quantity competition, product homogeneity, no

capacity constraints, identical firms and the Bertrand behavioural assumption that the rivals' price is taken as given — but that relevance is ultimately an empirical question, the discussion of which lies beyond the scope of this chapter.

It should be noted that the Bertrand model is also open to the criticism that firms will collude to avoid its zero profit equilibrium. Clearly if non-collusion and competition lead firms to a zero profit outcome, the formation of cartels will seem even more attractive to the two parties than in the Cournot case, where, though each party earns less than when joint profits are maximised, it does at least earn positive profits. The point is illustrated in Figure 17.6, where we note that at the Bertrand equilibrium, B, the firms' isoprofit curves intersect. The two firms depicted could both raise profits by moving in a north-easterly direction, that is by agreeing to raise price. As before, one can derive a contract curve as the locus of points of tangency between isoprofit curves along which industry profits are maximised. There is also the same tendency to cheat in a price collusive equilibrium since, if a firm believes that its rival will keep price constant while it reduces price, it can thereby capture the entire market. Collusive equilibrium in prices therefore tends to be unstable in the same way as in output-based cartels. However, to the extent that price is a more easily monitored variable than output, cartel arrangements that involve price fixing may be easier for their members to monitor.

Stackelberg Equilibrium

The Cournot model is based on the idea that each firm takes its rival's output as given when choosing its level of production. Stackelberg analysed what would happen if one firm understood the structure of the Cournot model sufficiently well to work out how the other firm would react, and then used this information to improve upon its position in the equilibrium. We shall term this sophisticated firm the 'leader' and its more naive rival the 'follower'.

The Stackelberg model can then be developed as an extension of the Cournot framework. Firm 1, which we shall take to be the leader, seeks to maximise profits in the knowledge that firm 2, the follower, will treat firm 1's output decision as given. Hence firm 2 will always make decisions along its reaction function, while firm 1 maximises profits subject to firm 2's reaction function. The resulting Stackelberg equilibrium is at the tangency between firm 1's isoprofit curve and firm 2's reaction function, point S on Figure 17.7.

A comparison of the Cournot and Stackelberg equilibria gives us some intuition about how the leader firm uses its better knowledge to its own advantage. In the Cournot model, each party takes the behaviour of the other as given and adjusts output in response to disappointed expectations until an equilibrium of consistent expectations is reached (point C

Figure 17.7

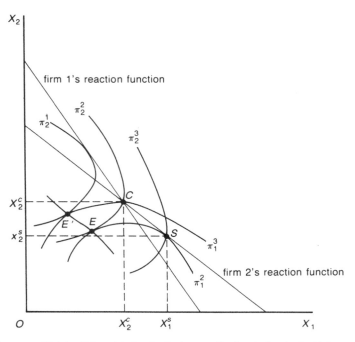

Stackelberg equilibrium. If firm 1 is leader it chooses the level of output which maximises profit given firm 2's reaction function, at X^s_1, where its isoprofit curve (π^s_1) is tangent to firm 2's reaction function. Firm 2 responds to this choice with X^s_2, and has profits of π^3_2. Firm 1 produces more output and correspondingly has higher profits, firm 2 less output and correspondingly lower profits, than at the Cournot equilibrium C.

in Figure 17.7.). In the Stackelberg model, firm 1 knows that firm 2 behaves in this way. It therefore chooses its output level, X^S_1, above that implied by its own Cournot reaction function in order to maximise profits subject to firm 2's reaction function. Given its expectation of X^S_1, firm 2 then responds with X^S_2, as firm 1 calculated that it would. Firm 2 in turn finds that its expectation of firm 1's behaviour is confirmed. Firm 2 is therefore misled into thinking that it is in a Cournot equilibrium, though it is producing less than X^c_2 and therefore has lower profits ($\pi^3_2 < \pi^2_2$). Firm 1 on the other hand is producing more than the Cournot equilibrium ($X^S_1 > X^c_1$) and is therefore earning higher profits ($\pi^2_1 > \pi^3_1$).

Industry profits are still not maximised at the Stackelberg equilibrium — both sides could gain from a move to a collusive equilibrium along EE^1 in Figure 17.7. However, one suspects that the leader might be less sympathetic to the formation of a cartel in these circumstances than it would be under Cournot or Bertrand conditions, particularly if the rival's behaviour is hard to monitor.

Finally, note that, if both firms seek to be leaders, the Stackelberg model cannot yield an equilibrium. If both firms understand the other's Cournot

behaviour, then they will either agree to collude or will enter a price war
to determine who will act as leader and who as follower. The incentives
for them to seek the former solution are obvious.

*A Formal Treatment of the Stackelberg Model

The difference between the Cournot and Stackelberg models and the consequences for industry output and price can be illustrated formally. We
return to the example we used for the Cournot model, with a linear
demand curve, equation (17.5), and a linear cost function (equation (17.6)).
Firm 1's profit function is therefore,

$$\pi_1 = aX_1 - bX_1^2 - bX_2X_1 - F - cX_1 \qquad (17.7)$$

while firm 2's reaction function is

$$X_2 = \frac{a-c}{2b} - \frac{X_1}{2} \qquad (17.14)$$

In the Stackelberg equilibrium, firm 1 chooses X_1 to maximise (17.7)
subject to the constraint that firm 2 chooses X_2 on its reaction function
(17.14). We therefore substitute (17.14) into (17.7) and maximise profits,

$$\frac{\partial \pi}{\partial X_1} = a - 2bX_1 - \left(\frac{a-c}{2}\right) + bX_1 - c = 0$$

$$X_1 = \frac{a-c}{2b} \qquad (17.18)$$

Substituting into equation (17.14), we derive X_2 as,

$$X_2 = \frac{a-c}{4b} \qquad (17.19)$$

If we compare this with our solution to the example of the Cournot model
(equations (17.16) and (17.17)), we note that the leader is producing more
and the follower less than at the Cournot equilibrium. Interested readers
are invited to prove for themselves that firm 1 also earns higher profits,
and firm 2 lower profits, than at the Cournot equilibrium. In this particular example, industry output is also higher and price lower than in
the Cournot equilibrium. A more general case is analysed in the following
section.

*Further Analysis of the Oligopoly Models

Algebra allows us to derive most of the results obtained in previous sections, and some important generalisations of them, a good deal more
simply than diagrams. It also allows us to categorise the various models
in a unified framework based on assumptions about the reactions of a

firm to the behaviour of its rivals. Our attention in this section is devoted to the models in which behaviour is directly concerned with quantities rather than prices.

For most of our discussion so far, we have assumed that firms have identical cost functions and that the number of firms (n) is two, but the analysis can be readily generalised to cover many firms, each with different costs. In general terms, a typical firm in the industry, denoted i, maximises the profit function,

$$\pi_i = p(X)X_i - C_i(X_i) \tag{17.20}$$

where

$$\sum_{i=1}^{n} X_i = X \tag{17.21}$$

Profit maximisation implies that

$$\frac{\partial \pi_i}{\partial X_i} = p + X_i \frac{\partial p}{\partial X} \frac{\partial X}{\partial X_i} - \frac{\partial C_i}{\partial X_i} = 0 \tag{17.22}$$

We assume that the second-order conditions are satisfied ($\partial^2 \pi_i / \partial X_i^2 < 0$ for every firm), and note that equation (17.22) is a version of the familiar marginal revenue equals marginal cost condition, with the complication that marginal revenue depends upon both the slope of the industry demand curve ($\partial p / \partial X$) and the adjustment of industry output to the firm's output level ($\partial X / \partial X_i$). It is by considering alternative specifications of expectations about this latter term, $\partial X / \partial X_i$, that we can classify oligopoly models.

To get an intuitive grasp of the approach we shall use, start with the simple two-firm case where

$$X = X_1 + X_2 \tag{17.23}$$

so

$$\frac{\partial X}{\partial X_1} = \frac{\partial X_1}{\partial X_1} + \frac{\partial X_2}{\partial X_1} = 1 + \frac{\partial X_2}{\partial X_1} \tag{17.24}$$

The adjustment of industry output to firm 1's output, $\partial X / \partial X_1$, can therefore be broken into two parts, $\partial X_1 / \partial X_1$ which of course equals unity, and the response of X_2 to a change in X_1 ($\partial X_2 / \partial X_1$). The same reasoning in the more general case (equation (17.21)) leads us to the equation

$$\frac{\partial X}{\partial X_i} = \frac{\partial X_i}{\partial X_i} + \frac{\partial X_j}{\partial X_i} = 1 + \lambda_i \tag{17.24}$$

where X_j refers to the sum of the output of all firms other than i. If there are only two firms, $X_j = X_2$ and $\lambda_i = \partial X_2 / \partial X_i$.

In order to choose an output level using equation (17.22), each firm must evaluate $\partial X / \partial X_i$, which we now see involves making an estimate of, or a 'conjecture' about, the value of the term λ_i (or $\partial X_2 / \partial X_1$ in the two-firm case). λ_i is therefore referred to as the *conjectural variation* term. This term captures a key property of the various models which we have discussed, and derives directly from the interdependence of firms in an oligopolistic market. If we divide equation (17.22) through by price and rearrange terms, we obtain

$$\frac{p - \partial C_i / \partial X_i}{p} = -\frac{x_i}{X} \frac{X}{p} \frac{\partial p}{\partial X} (1 + \lambda_i) = \frac{s_i (1 + \lambda_i)}{e} \qquad (17.25)$$

where s_i is the share of firm i in industry output (X_i / X) and e is the price elasticity of demand ($-X/p/\partial p/\partial X$). The term on the left-hand side of the equation is the difference between price and marginal cost expressed as a ratio to price. It is often referred to as the *price—cost margin* and used as an indicator of monopoly power. Equation (17.25) therefore tells us that the proportional mark-up of price to marginal cost increases with a firm's market share and λ_i, and decreases with the (negative) elasticity of demand.

The conjectural variation term in equation (17.25) can be used to categorise outcomes in terms of various market structures. In order to set our frame of reference, let us start with the case of perfect competition, where the market price is given to each firm and demand equals supply at zero profit. If one firm considers reducing its level of output, it does so on the assumption that market price remains unchanged. This can only occur if the industry output remains unchanged, which implies that other firms will make up its output reduction exactly. The derivative $\partial X_j / \partial X_i$ therefore equals -1, and this is the value of conjectural variation term for every competitive firm. When $\lambda_i = -1$ for all firms, equation (17.25) reduces to

$$p - \partial C_i / \partial X_i = 0 \qquad (17.26)$$

which is the familiar price equals marginal cost condition for firms in a competitive industry.

The Cournot model is based on the opposite to competitive assumption that each firm believes that its rivals will *not* respond to its own quantity adjustments. Hence, in this case the conjectural variation is assumed to be zero for all firms. From equation (17.25), we can derive the price—cost margin in the Cournot case as

$$\frac{p - \partial C_i / \partial X_i}{p} = \frac{s_i}{e} \qquad (17.27)$$

If we go on to assume that firms have the same cost curves ($C_1(X_1) = C_2(X_2) = \ldots = C_n(X_n)$), we know that firms will be of the same size

because they each face an identical profit-maximising condition, equation (17.22). Hence if there are n in firms in the industry, the market share of each is $1/n$ and (17.27) can be further simplified to

$$\frac{p - \partial C_i / \partial X_i}{p} = \frac{1}{ne} \qquad (17.28)$$

From this formula we note the point asserted above, that the price–cost margin in the Cournot equilibrium declines as the number of firms increases. We can also establish formally from (17.28) that the outcome approximates the competitive equilibrium as n increases towards infinity.

In the case of collusion, each firm knows that its rivals will follow suit if it increases or decreases output, by an amount sufficient to leave market shares constant. This implies that the rival will react by altering output exactly in proportion to the current ratio of their market shares. Hence if there are only 2 firms, $\partial X_2 / \partial X_1$ is simply the ratio of their current market shares, X_2 / X_1. More generally, in a collusive market

$$\lambda_i = \frac{1 - s_i}{s_i} \qquad (17.29)$$

If we substitute this into equation (17.25), we find for identical firms that

$$\frac{p - \partial C_i / \partial X_i}{p} = \frac{1}{e} \qquad (17.30)$$

which rearranges to the simple monopoly condition, marginal revenue equals marginal cost. Thus as we saw earlier collusive outcomes yield the monopoly output and price.

Finally, the Stackelberg model is characterised by the fact that the leader and the followers have different conjectural variations. The followers behave as do all firms in the Cournot model, and therefore the conjectural variation term for them is zero. The situation for the leader is more complicated because it builds its knowledge about the followers' reactions into its decision making. If we consider the two-firm case, firm 1 as leader knows that the follower, firm 2, will adjust output in response to its level of production according to the second firm's reaction function. The conjectural variation term for the leader is therefore given by the slope of firm 2's reaction function. This took the value of $-\frac{1}{2}$ in the worked example of the previous section (see equation (17.14) where $\partial X_2 / \partial X_1 = -\frac{1}{2}$), and more generally, depends on the sum of each follower's reaction to the leader's output change.

The Theory of Games — Some Basic Terminology

As we have seen, traditional or 'classical' oligopoly theory yields a variety of answers to the question of how firms choose output and price when

there are only a few interdependent suppliers. Even with the unified framework of the last section, this situation is ultimately an unsatisfactory one because we still do not know which is the best model to use in various circumstances. A possible way out of this dilemma has recently been offered by the application of the *theory of games* to the problem of oligopoly. This theory provides an alternative framework in which to analyse the strategic interactions among firms, and in this section we give a brief introduction to some of the issues dealt with by game theory, and their application to oligopoly theory. We return to these questions again in Chapter 22 on trade unions.

Game theory is concerned with the strategic elements of economic agents' behaviour and the rewards or *payoffs* that they expect to obtain. It can be used to analyse any sort of interaction which involves playing to a strategy, from chess or card games to arms limitation negotiations. For simplicity, we confine ourselves to games in which there are only two players (a *two-person game*) and where the returns to playing the game are not fixed in advance (a *non-constant sum* game). An important classification of games is between games in which the players cannot make binding agreements among themselves, termed *non-co-operative* games, and games in which they can, termed *co-operative games*. As the reader might guess, this classification parallels the distinction between non-collusive and collusive models made in previous sections of this chapter. In this chapter we focus on non-co-operative games, and spend more time on co-operative games in Chapter 22.

Dominant Strategies

The first concept needed in order to grasp the essential features of game theory is that of a *payoff matrix*. Suppose two players, firms 1 and 2, play some game according to certain moves, or *strategies*, for example by choosing various levels of output or price. If we restrict our attention to output choices, we can consider the payoff matrix in Figure 17.8, where strategies *A* and *B* for each firm represent different output choices given known demand and cost conditions and the numbers in the boxes represent the payoffs, in this case profits, to each firm from following each strategy.

The payoffs in Figure 17.8 have been chosen because they provide the game with an obvious solution. Let us consider the choices of firm 2. If firm 1 plays strategy *A*, it will choose to play strategy *A* as well because its payoff is greater (500 > 300). Moreover if firm 1 plays strategy *B*, firm 2 will still choose strategy *A* because its payoff is still greater (250 > 125). So firm 2 will always choose strategy *A*. Turning to firm 1, if firm 2 plays strategy *A* firm 1 will receive higher profits by playing strategy *A* as well (500 > 250). If firm 2 chooses strategy *B* firm 1 will also choose strategy *A* to maximise its payoffs. Hence both firms always choose strategy *A*, which is therefore termed the *dominant* strategy, and the game has a unique equilibrium.

Figure 17.8   Payoff matrix with dominant strategy

		Firm 2	
		Strategy A	Strategy B
Firm 1	Strategy A	500,500	300,300
	Strategy B	250,250	125,125

It is in fact fairly rare that payoffs take a form such that rival firms each have a single dominant strategy. For example, if we consider the payoff matrix set out in Figure 17.9, firm 1 chooses strategy C in response to firm 2's strategy C, but strategy D in response to strategy D. Firm 2, on the other hand, has a dominant strategy, always preferring strategy C (because if firm 1 chooses strategy C, C yields firm 2 350 > 300 and if firm 1 chooses strategy D, C yields firm 2 450 > 400). There is therefore no dominant strategy outcome with this pattern of payoffs; firm 1's decision is contingent on firm 2's choice of strategy.

Nash Equilibrium

The American mathematician John Nash developed an equilibrium concept which is weaker than that of the dominant strategy to deal with cases of the sort just described. The strategies of the two players are said to yield a *Nash equilibrium* if each strategy chosen maximises payoffs given the other player's choice. There can be more than one Nash equilibrium, even in a two-person, two-strategy game. It is easy to see that the pair of strategies (C,C) yield a Nash equilibrium for the payoff matrix in Figure 17.9. If firm 1 plays strategy C, firm 2 will choose strategy C (350 > 300). Similarly, if firm 2 plays strategy C, firm 1 will respond with C (350 > 300). Hence strategies (C,C) are mutually consistent given the choice of the other player, and are therefore a Nash equilibrium.

There are no other Nash equilibria in Figure 17.9. For example, consider the strategy pair (D,D). If firm 1 plays strategy D, firm 2 responds with strategy C. But we know that if firm 2 plays strategy C, firm 1 will also choose strategy C instead of confirming firm 2's expectations at D. Hence the strategy pair (D,D) is not a Nash equilibrium. We can think of a Nash equilibrium as involving expectations on the part of each player about strategies of the other with the characteristic that, once each rival

Figure 17.9   Payoff matrix for Nash equilibrium

		Firm 2	
		Strategy C	Strategy D
Firm 1	Strategy C	350,350	350,300
	Strategy D	300,450	400,400

has played its own choice, neither wishes to change its strategy because the expectations upon which its choice depended have been realised.

If we think in terms of output strategies, a Nash equilibrium involves a pair of production levels for which each rival's expectation about the behaviour of the other is confirmed. When we characterise a Nash equilibrium for output strategies in this way, we immediately recognise that we have described the Cournot equilibrium discussed earlier. Recall that, in the Cournot duopoly model, firms choose output on the basis of expectations about their rival's production, and that equilibrium occurs where both sets of expectations are mutually consistent. The notion of the mutual consistency of optimal strategies, we have now seen, is also at the heart of the Nash equilibrium. The formal equivalence of these equilibrium concepts has led analysts in recent years to conflate them, referring to the equilibrium of the Cournot model as the Cournot–Nash equilibrium. This analysis also establishes that the Cournot equilibrium, contrary to the view formed from the rather naive behavioural interpretation of the classical oligopoly model, is firmly grounded as the optimal outcome of strategic interaction.

The Prisoner's Dilemma

We can also use game theory to investigate questions about cheating in a cartel. The appropriate analytical framework here is a game known as the prisoner's dilemma, which was originally illustrated with reference to the behaviour of two suspects being interviewed in separate rooms about their involvement in a major and a minor crime. Each is given the option of confessing and thereby implicating the other, or of refusing to confess. The two suspects are forbidden to communicate with each other. If both suspects stay silent, they will be convicted of the minor offence but without a confession there is not enough evidence to convict either the major crime. If either talks while the other does not, the one who remains silent will get a long sentence for the major crime, and the one who talks a lighter one for 'good behaviour'. They both get a long sentence (although still with some remission) if they both confess.

The game is called the prisoner's *dilemma* because, even though both suspects are better off (i.e. receive shorter jail sentences) if *neither* confesses, the incentives of the game are such that *both will confess*. This result arises from the fact that, if one looks at the suspects' individual strategies, each is separately better off to confess whether or not the other does likewise. The Nash equilibrium of this game (and in this case the dominant strategy) leads to an outcome — of both confessing — in which welfare could be increased if the players were allowed to communicate and collude. In that case they would agree to remain silent.

The general structure of the prisoner's dilemma game is applied to the case of a cartel in Figure 17.10. Suppose firms 1 and 2 have entered a

Figure 17.10

The prisoner's dilemma

		Firm 2	
		Cheat on cartel	Stick to cartel
Firm 1	Cheat on cartel	300,300	800,200
	Stick to cartel	200,800	600,600

cartel which yields monopoly profits of £1200, which they divide equally. This payoff is entered in the bottom right-hand box of the payoff matrix. Now let each firm realise that, if its rival keeps its production constant, it can raise its own profit, say to £800, by expanding production and assume also that, if the rival stuck to the agreement and kept its production constant, it would then receive £200 in profits. Assume also, however, that if the rival responded by increasing production as well, the two firms would ultimately reach a Cournot–Nash equilibrium where profits to each are lower, at £300. This payoff is entered in the top left-hand box.

The game set out in Figure 17.10 has exactly the perverse properties that we previously described for the prisoner's dilemma. Industry profits are maximised when both firms stick to the cartel. However, each perceives itself as being potentially able to do better by cheating, provided that its rival does not respond. Indeed, cheating is the dominant strategy in this case. For example, firm 1 makes higher profits by cheating, whether firm 2 responds by cheating or not. The same is true for firm 2. This is because the rewards perceived to be available when both parties cheat are greater than those accruing to the firm which sticks to the cartel agreement when the other cheats. Mutual cheating is thus the dominant strategy, though of course both parties would be better off staying in the cartel. Our analysis of these sorts of pressures formalises and clarifies our conclusions about the tendency for cartels to be unstable.

Conclusions

Our aim in this chapter has been to provide an introduction to classical oligopoly theory and to its more modern interpretation in terms of the theory of games. As we have seen, there is no single answer to what industry output and price will be when firms are interdependent. The possibilities range from the competitive outcome of the Bertrand model to the monopolistic equilibrium of the cartel. We have concentrated on the Cournot equilibrium as the principal example of a non-collusive equilibrium because of the formal equivalence between this equilibrium and the Nash equilibrium concept of game theory. This equivalence suggests that the Cournot model has an appealing intellectual basis, while the analysis of the prisoner's dilemma suggests that the pressures for

cartels to disintegrate are very strong. We shall use some of the ideas set out here as a basis for our discussion of union bargaining in Chapter 22, and the idea of 'the contract curve' will reappear in our discussion of general equilibrium in Chapter 24.

18

Alternative Objectives for the Firm

Introduction

The material on the theory of the firm dealt with so far in this book has assumed that the objective of the enterprise is to maximise profits. This assumption is justified with reference to the motives of individual entrepreneurs who seek to maximise their personal returns from carrying on business. But, as has been hinted on several occasions, this is not necessarily the most appropriate assumption about enterprise motivation in all circumstances. Even within capitalist firms, the relevance of profit maximisation is less obvious for large modern corporations where ownership and control of the firm are separated: the former in the hands of potentially diffuse shareholders and the latter vested in professional management. Many analysts have suggested that this separation provides a considerable degree of decision-making autonomy for managers, whose behaviour may in consequence deviate significantly from that implied by profit maximisation. In the first part of this chapter, we follow the lead of William Baumol in investigating the consequences of assuming that firms seek to maximise their size, measured by their sales revenue, rather than profits. Other models analysing the implications of the separation of ownership from control on company behaviour are cited in the references at the end of the chapter.

Capitalist firms are not the only form of productive enterprise, even within capitalist economies. Numerous other forms of enterprise coexist — public corporations, consumer co-operatives, partnerships and workers co-operatives — though typically these play a secondary role in the economy as a whole. Once we broaden our interest to non-Western economies, the range of enterprises is even larger, including the socialist

corporations and state farms of the Soviet Union, Eastern Europe and China, and less well-known institutions like the Kibbutz in Israel and worker-managed firms in Yugoslavia. The assumption of profit maximisation is implausible for all of these organisations, though for a variety of different reasons. It is beyond the scope of the book to analyse fully the implications of different behavioural assumptions in all of these cases; the interested reader is referred to Comparative Systems texts at the end of the chapter. (There are reasons to believe that state-owned firms, like their managerially controlled capitalist counterparts, may be interested in maximising their size, in which case our discussion of sales revenue maximisation will also be relevant to them.) We focus instead, in the second part of the chapter, on what is perhaps analytically the most interesting example of the non-capitalist firm — referred to in the literature as the labour-managed firm. Such enterprises are run by, or at least in the interests of, their workers, and the framework we develop below therefore analyses behaviour of potential relevance to a wide variety of organisations, from the producer co-operatives of the West to the worker-managed firms of Yugoslavia.

We could argue indefinitely as to whether particular assumptions about enterprise objectives are appropriate or 'realistic' in various circumstances, but *a priori* debate about assumptions is rarely fruitful. It is more helpful to see whether alternative hypotheses about firms' objectives enable us to say anything about the way in which they might behave which is different from what is implied by profit maximisation. As we shall see, particularly in the case of labour-managed firms, differences in behaviour tend to be highly sensitive to differences in assumptions about enterprise objectives.

Revenue Maximisation in a Competitive Market

There are several reasons why revenue maximisation may be a plausible alternative to profit maximisation as an objective for certain types of firms. If managers are not the same people as owners, and the latter have only limited control over the former, we might expect to see the objectives of managers to some extent supplementing the goal of profit maximisation. Baumol has suggested that, while managerial rewards may not be closely associated with company profits, managers' power, authority and status in society will be related to the size of the firm which they control. Hence they will seek to maximise the size of the company. Note that this has the rather subtle implication that we are addressing issues which are implicitly dynamic — the growth of the firm — in the sales-maximisation approach, though the framework remains formally static.

Whatever the justification, it is unreasonable to postulate that the firm seeks to maximise its revenue and to leave it at that. A perfectly competitive firm, which faces a given price for its output can always increase

its revenue simply by increasing output, at least up to the level of taking over the whole industry. However, we have already seen that when the perfectly competitive industry is in equilibrium with each firm maximising profits, the actual level of profits that will be made by a particular firm, unless it happens to have some special advantage not available to its competitors, will be zero. Thus, to expand output beyond this profit-maximising level for the sake of increasing revenue would involve the perfectly competitive firm in making losses.

The above argument has two important implications. First, because no privately owned firm can stay in business if it continually makes losses, the revenue-maximisation hypothesis does not, when taken by itself, make sense. It must be qualified by saying that firms seeks to maximise sales revenue up to a level of output that ensures some minimum acceptable level of profits, which cannot be negative. The second implication follows immediately from this first one. The perfectly competitive profit-maximising firm is, as a result of market forces, put in a position of producing its output at a level which in the long run yields zero profits. Hence, it is already up against a minimum acceptable profit constraint, and its behaviour is going to be no different from a firm that seeks to maximise its sales revenue subject to that same constraint in perfectly competitive conditions.

This conclusion is of considerable interest. The conventional theory of the firm has often been criticised for the 'unrealistic' nature of its underlying assumptions, and the profit maximisation hypothesis in particular has been singled out for criticism along these lines. There are many who would regard the revenue-maximisation postulate as more acceptable, and yet we have now seen that, in the important case of perfect competition, without which we could not derive the supply curve which is so widely used in applications of simple microeconomics, the 'realistic' revenue-maximising hypothesis leads us to exactly the same conclusions about behaviour as does that of profit maximisation. Revenue-maximising firms behave 'as if' they were interested only in maximising profits, and may safely be analysed on the basis of this latter 'unrealistic' assumption. This illustrates a general principle first explicitly proposed by Milton Friedman and often invoked by economists in defence of their highly abstract models; namely that debate about whether or not a model's assumptions are 'unrealistic' or descriptively 'inaccurate' is usually futile; the degree of conformity to reality of the conclusions it yields provides a more constructive basis for criticising a model.

The Revenue-Maximising Hypothesis under Monopoly

Now as it happens the revenue-maximisation hypothesis does not always yield the same results as does profit maximisation. Consider the case of monopoly. We have already seen that a profit-maximising monopolist

whose marginal production costs are positive will choose a point on the demand curve for output where the absolute value of the elasticity of demand is greater than one. This means that such a firm could increase its revenue by lowering price and increasing output. So long as we are dealing with a typical case, in which maximum attainable profits were positive, the firm could do so without violating the requirement that it make some minimum level of profits. Thus, under conditions of monopoly, the revenue-maximising firm would produce a greater output than the profit-maximising firm. Just how much greater depends upon the cost conditions facing the firm.

Recall that sales revenue will be maximised at a level of output at which the elasticity of demand is equal to -1, and consider Figure 18.1 which depicts two possible cases. In panel (a) we depict a firm whose long-run average production costs are rather 'low' so that they are still below price at the level of output at which the elasticity of demand is equal to -1. This firm will settle at this level of output and will make positive profits. In panel (b) we depict a firm with rather 'high' average costs which become equal to price while output is still in the elastic range of the demand curve. If minimum acceptable profits are zero, this firm will settle at a level of output at which price equals average cost, and profits are zero. The literature on this topic has tended to concentrate on the latter case, in which the firm's output decisions are constrained by the minimum acceptable level of profit.

Figure 18.1

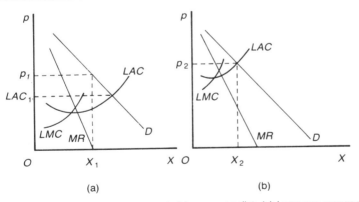

(a)   (b)

Two possible solutions for the revenue-maximising monopolist. (a) Long-run average costs are 'low' so the firm produces X_1 and sells it at p_1; at this point the elasticity of demand is -1 and profits are positive at $(p_1 - LAC_1)X_1$. (b) Long-run average costs are 'high' so the firm produces X_2 for sale at a price of p_2. At this output profits are zero, and because demand is still in the price elastic range, revenue is not at its unconstrained maximum. In either case, output is higher than the profit-maximising $(LMC = MR)$ level.

The imposition of a lump-sum tax shifts the long-run average cost curve upwards by the amount of the tax divided by output, but does not shift the marginal cost curve. So long as the tax is less than $(p_1 - LAC_1)X_1$, its imposition will not affect the price and output of the firm (a); if the tax is greater than this amount firm (a) will come to act like firm (b) and set its price equal to long-run average cost including the tax. The imposition of such a tax on firm (b), regardless of its amount, will shift the *LAC* upwards and will cause output to fall and price to rise.

The Effects of Lump Sum Taxes

It is worth noting that, in either case described above, the reaction of the firm to a lump sum tax levied on its profits may be different from that of a profit maximiser, who will not react to the imposition of such a tax. After all, the price and output that maximise profits will also maximise profits net of some constant deduction unless the tax is greater than maximum profits, in which case the firm will simply go out of business. (More formally, lump sum impositions which are independent at the level of output and inputs do not affect the first-order conditions for maximisation.) In the case of the revenue-maximising firm depicted in panel (a) of Figure 18.1, the imposition of such a tax, depending upon its size, will either leave its price and output unchanged if net of tax profits are still positive, or cause it to lower its output to a point of higher profit if the amount of the tax is greater than the profit it was making at revenue-maximising price and output. In the case of the firm depicted in panel (b), the imposition of any such tax will cause it to lower output and to raise price. As with the profit-maximising firm, of course, it is possible to set the tax in question sufficiently high that the revenue maximiser will be driven entirely out of business by its imposition.

Now the point here, as in the previous two sections has been to show that the equivalence of the sales revenue-maximisation hypothesis and the profit-maximisation postulate that exists under assumptions of perfect competition does not exist under conditions of monopoly. Readers should note that this lack of equivalence was established, not by arguing about the relative degrees of 'realism' that might be attributed to the alternative *assumptions*, but rather by showing that there are circumstances under which they lead to *different conclusions* about the way in which we would expect to see firms behave. Whether the circumstances in question are sufficiently widely observed in the real world as to make the revenue-maximisation hypothesis an important alternative to profit maximisation is perhaps a moot point. Lump sum taxes are something of a rarity and real world 'profit' taxes are typically levied on the rental rate earned by capital equipment owned by the firm as well as on any pure monopoly profit that it might be earning, and hence are not quite equivalent to the profits tax we postulated.

Nevertheless, if the foregoing analysis convinces the reader that there is an alternative theory of what it is that motivates firms to the simple pursuit of profit, that the theory in question does not always yield the same predictions about behaviour, that the profit-maximisation hypothesis should not therefore be taken for granted as a foundation for the theory of the firm, and that the ultimate test here is the empirical truth or falsity of the predictions yielded by competing hypotheses, its presentation will have served its purpose.

*A Formal Treatment of Revenue Maximisation

For completeness, and to illustrate maximisation of a non-profit objective subject to a profit constraint we end our discussion of sales revenue maximisation with a formal derivation of the result established geometrically in Figure 18.1(b). In Chapter 13 above, we showed that revenue, pX, depends upon output X. The revenue function may therefore be written compactly as $R = R(X)$. This function will be maximised where its derivative (marginal revenue) is zero, $\partial R/\partial X = 0$, and we already know (again from Chapter 13) that since $\partial R/\partial X = p(1+1/e)$, this maximum will be achieved when the elasticity of demand equals -1.

It is easy to establish formally the point illustrated above: that the level of output with revenue maximisation will be greater than with profit maximisation. Profits are maximised where marginal revenue equals marginal cost. Marginal costs are positive and marginal revenue will thus be higher at the profit-maximising level of output, where it equals marginal cost, than at the revenue-maximising level of output, where it equals zero. If marginal revenue is a decreasing function of output, which we usually assume it to be (but see Chapter 15 for possible exceptions to this usual case), production will be greater when revenue is maximised than when profits are maximised.

The argument can be extended to the case of a monopolist who maximises revenue subject to a minimum profit constraint, say π_0. The objective is to

$$\text{Max } R = R(X) \tag{18.1}$$

subject to

$$\pi = R(X) - C(X) \geq \pi_0 \tag{18.2}$$

The formal analysis which follows requires that revenue maximisation drives profits to the minimum set by the constraint, as occurs in Figure 18.1(b). This assumption means that (18.2) holds with equality, so we can use our previous constrained maximisation approach and form the Lagrangian

$$Z = R(X) + \mu(R(X) - C(X) - \pi_0) \tag{18.3}$$

where μ is the Lagrange multiplier. The first-order conditions are

$$\frac{\partial Z}{\partial X} = \frac{\partial R}{\partial X} + \mu \left(\frac{\partial R}{\partial X} - \frac{\partial C}{\partial X} \right) = 0 \tag{18.4}$$

$$\frac{\partial Z}{\partial \mu} = R(X) - C(X) - \pi_0 = 0 \tag{18.5}$$

From these we have

$$\frac{\partial C}{\partial X} = \frac{1+\mu}{\mu} \frac{\partial R}{\partial X} = 1 + \frac{1}{\mu} \frac{\partial R}{\partial X} \tag{18.6}$$

Since the shadow price of the profit constraint on revenue is positive ($\mu > 0$), (18.6) implies that *marginal cost exceeds marginal revenue* in the equilibrium of the constrained revenue-maximising monopolist. Of course, marginal cost equals marginal revenue in the profit-maximising case, so provided that marginal revenue falls faster than marginal cost as output increases, we can deduce that output is greater in the case of the constrained revenue-maximising monopolist than in the profit-maximising case. Interested readers may go on to use this framework to analyse the effect of a lump sum tax on a sales revenue-maximising firm.

The Competitive Labour-Managed Firm — An Introduction

When one thinks about institutions on the supply side of the product market, one of the most enduring (if economically somewhat marginal), is the producer co-operative. Such organisations, owned and run by their workforce, have existed in Western economies since the 1840s. There are more than fifteen hundred of them producing in the United Kingdom today, most of them small and concentrated in service activities. They are rather more common in France, Spain (clustered around the Basque town of Mondragon) and particularly in Italy, where around one employed person in 50 works in one of the more than 10,000 producer co-operatives. Workers' decision making combined with *public* ownership has also represented a significant tradition in the socialist economies of Eastern Europe, and particularly in Yugoslavia where, since the early 1950s, all manufacturing industry is, at least nominally, 'self-managed'. Self-management now offers a potential route for the reformers of Eastern Europe and China to follow. Our aim in this section of the chapter is to illustrate how economic theory can offer important insights into how this different form of productive organisation will make its supply decisions.

From a theoretical perspective, a labour-managed firm is an enterprise in which the labour force as a whole takes the economic decisions. This group undertakes the entrepreneurial role, and receives the surplus of revenue over cost, which they distribute amongst themselves according to some prearranged mechanism. We will assume that every worker has the same skills, and that the collective of workers has agreed to distribute the surplus, or pure profit, equally amongst the membership. The collective of workers is also assumed not to own the capital stock, but rather to be renting it at a market determined price. In the labour-managed firm, labour hires capital rather than capital hiring labour or an entrepreneur hiring both.

It should be noted that the analysis which follows focuses exclusively

on the competitive case, so that the firm is assumed to be a price taker. The differences between the labour-managed and profit-maximising firms which we analyse below are not very different as we move from competitive to non-competitive market structures. Interested readers can establish this for themselves by studying some of the references given at the end of the chapter.

Maximising Income per Worker

For the economic analyst, one of the most important distinctions between labour-managed firms and their capitalist counterparts arises from the postulated objective of the organisation — to maximise average earnings per head rather than profits. This maximand was first proposed by Benjamin Ward and may be defended by the argument that worker-members would always prefer outcomes with higher income to those with lower incomes. The case for income maximisation in labour-managed firms is straightforward. Economists usually assume that the group of entrepreneurs in charge of a firm (the group may have but one member) maximise their residual income. But since, in a capitalist enterprise, the size of this residual income, the firm's profit, does not depend upon the number of entrepreneurs in the group running the firm, the objective of maximising the amount of profit per entrepreneur can be reduced to the simpler objective of maximising profit. However, under labour management, the labour force undertakes the entrepreneurial role, the quantity of output produced, and hence the amount of profit, varies with the size of the labour force. Hence the above mentioned simplification is no longer possible. The assignment of the entrepreneurial role to a productive factor, namely labour, implies that the maximisation of profit per member of the entrepreneurial group cannot be simplified to the maximisation of the enterprise's profits, pure and simple. The number of workers varies with output and, therefore, maximising income per worker is not the same as maximising profits. It is the former which is the natural goal for the labour-managed firm.

In the case of a labour-managed firm, it is normally assumed that the workers' collective exerts its control over economic decisions through a 'democratic process', but the nature of this process is here left deliberately vague. Critics point out that such a mechanism could be seriously inefficient in practice if internal dissension slows or prevents rational economic choices being made. We avoid these issues by assuming that authority can be divided between executive and policy-making powers. Our approach is consistent with the enterprise being run in accordance with the following arrangements. In the first instance, all members of the collective are assumed to be identical, in that they desire the labour-managed firm to maximise the same objective, average earnings per head. The collective appoints a director who is given completely autonomous powers to execute this policy, subject to dismissal for failure. The labour force

therefore exercises its control of the enterprise by determining the maximand, but the price and output decisions required to achieve this goal are taken in exactly the same way as in the capitalist firm.

Each labour-managed firm chooses simultaneously its own level of earnings and factor demands, including employment, subject to the constraints set by its own technology and the economic environment. For the most part, our attention in this book has been focused on the analysis of the firm in the long run. We did consider a short-run framework at the beginning of our study of the theory of competitive supply in Chapter 13, but it was quickly established that the pattern of results for the short run was duplicated in the long run, at least at the industry level. Since long-run models are more general than short-run ones, we concentrated on the former. In our analysis of the labour-managed firm, however, we adopt the short run as the principal 'period' of analysis, even though the main result which we shall establish — that the labour-managed firm always adjusts to a given product price change less than its capitalist counterpart — also carries through in the long run. Nevertheless, we use a short-run framework for much of what follows because it permits the main results to emerge in a particularly striking form, and one that is capable of both geometric representation and simple economic interpretation. The argument is generalised for the long run at the end of the chapter. In the analysis which follows we therefore assume, in the first instance, that the capital stock is fixed at a value, say $\bar{K}$. We also make the simplifying assumption that, in the short run, average and marginal products of labour *everywhere* decline with output. This assumption differs from that of an inverse U-shaped average and marginal product curve underlying the U-shaped short-run average cost curve derived in Chapter 11 and deployed in Chapter 13, but can be made at this point because, as for its capitalist counterpart, equilibrium for the labour-managed firm always occurs where technology displays diminishing returns to a factor.

Enterprise Choices in the Short Run

In order to maximise average earnings in the short run, the labour-managed firm chooses output and employment subject to the constraints set by technology and the economic environment. If we denote earnings per head by y, these can be seen as comprising a notional wage per worker, w, and an (assumed) equal share of profit, π/L. Hence

$$y = w + \frac{\pi}{L} \tag{18.7}$$

where $\pi = pX - wL - rK$ $\qquad$ (18.8)

From this we derive the traditional maximand of the labour-managed firm,

$$y = \frac{pX - rK}{L} \tag{18.9}$$

and average earnings are revealed to be average net product, or average revenue minus fixed costs per unit of labour. It can be seen by comparing (18.7) with (18.9) that the notional wage, w, plays no role in the economic decision making of the labour-managed firm.

The firm's choice is illustrated in Figure 18.2. The slope from the intersection of fixed costs ($r\bar{K}$) on the vertical axis to a point on the revenue function (which in the short run given price depends only on the level of employment) is average earnings for that level of employment. The labour-managed firm wishes to maximise this average, and clearly will do so if it chooses level of labour input L^*, at the tangency between the production function and the average earnings line. At this point the slope from the intersection of fixed costs on the vertical axis to the revenue function is maximised. Here AB is revenue net of fixed costs, and y^* is earnings per worker. In equilibrium, earnings per worker equal the slope of the revenue function, which is in turn the marginal revenue product of labour.

*A More Formal Treatment

The algebra of income per head maximisation is subtly different from that of conventional profit maximisation, and helps us to develop additional

---

Figure 18.2

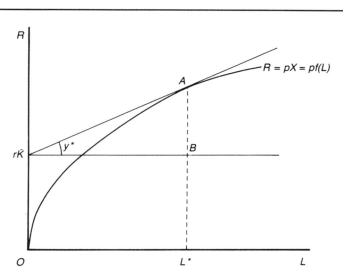

The labour managed firm chooses employment to maximise average earnings, which equal revenue minus fixed costs ($r\bar{K}$) per worker. Earnings at each level of employment are therefore the slope of the line from the revenue function to the $r\bar{K}$ intercept. They are maximised at L^*, where earnings, y^*, equal the marginal revenue product of labour.

geometric representations of the problem. The labour-managed firm chooses employment to maximise

$$y = \frac{pX - r\bar{K}}{L} \tag{18.9'}$$

subject to a short-run production function $X = f(L, \bar{K})$. Substituting $f(L, \bar{K})$ for X in equation (18.9), the first-order condition is

$$\frac{\partial y}{\partial L} = \frac{1}{L^2} \left(Lp \frac{\partial X}{\partial L} - pX + r\bar{K} \right) = 0 \tag{18.10}$$

which can be rearranged as

$$p \frac{\partial X}{\partial L} = (pX - r\bar{K})/L = y \tag{18.11}$$

Equation (18.11) appears at first sight to be the same as the labour hiring rule under capitalism, requiring the collective to add members until the marginal value product $(p \partial X/\partial L)$ of the last recruit equals the income that recruit generates. But appearances are misleading in this case. Wages, like other factor prices, are determined in the labour market under capitalism, and are therefore taken as given by the competitive profit maximisers. Average earnings are a choice variable for the labour-managed firm, however. The collective can choose the number of members it employs, and the rule governing this choice, and summarised in (18.11), is to increase the labour force only when this raises everyone's income. It is this maximum of income per head which occurs where earnings equal the marginal revenue product of labour.

Looking at it another way, the labour-managed firm will increase employment when a new member adds more to revenue per head than to cost per head. Denoting revenue per head by $G(=pX/L)$ and costs per head by $F(=r\bar{K}/L)$, the collective adds to the membership until $\partial G/\partial L = \partial F/\partial L$. We could draw G and F in value-employment space, in which case the equilibrium level of employment would be chosen where the slopes of the two curves were equal. A rearrangement of terms reveals that the slopes are in fact equal at the point where earnings equal the value marginal product of labour. Thus

$$\frac{\partial G}{\partial L} = \frac{Lp \partial X/\partial L - pX}{L^2} = \frac{1}{L} \left(p \frac{\partial X}{\partial L} - p \frac{X}{L} \right) \tag{18.12}$$

while

$$\frac{\partial F}{\partial L} = \frac{-rK}{L^2} \tag{18.13}$$

Equation (18.12) tells us that the slope of the revenue per head function depends on the relationship between marginal revenue product and the

average revenue product of labour at each level of employment. It will be negative given our assumption of diminishing returns to labour (see Chapter 10). Equation (18.13) indicates that fixed costs per head vary with employment along a rectangular hyperbola.

Income per head is maximised when increments to revenue per head from hiring one additional worker equal increments to fixed costs per head. If we therefore set $\partial G/\partial L = \partial F/\partial L$, this implies

$$\frac{1}{L}\left(p\,\frac{\partial X}{\partial L} - p\,\frac{X}{L}\right) = \frac{-rK}{L^2} \tag{18.14}$$

or

$$p\,\frac{\partial X}{\partial L} = y \tag{18.11}$$

A Comparison of Income-per-Worker-Maximising and Profit-Maximising Firms

To compare the behaviour of income- and profit-maximising firms, we directly plot in Figure 18.3 the slope of the short-run earnings function (18.9′) as a function of employment. Inspection of Figure 18.2 should convince readers that this function will have an inverse U-shape. When the marginal revenue product of labour exceeds average earnings, average earnings will increase with employment, and the curve relating these two variables will be upward sloping. When the reverse holds, average earnings will be a declining function of employment. When marginal revenue product equals average earnings, earnings will have reached their maximum. All this is shown in Figure 18.3, which can now be used to compare the behaviour of the labour-managed firm with that of its profit-maximising counterpart.

We know that the labour-managed firm chooses the income–employment combination to maximise the income per head of its labour force (y^*, L^* in Figure 18.3). In contrast, a profit-maximising firm hires labour until the marginal revenue product of labour equals the wage (see Chapters 13 and 14). We can now show that the profit maximiser which has the same technology and faces the same market determined prices, makes exactly the same short-run output decisions as the labour-managed firm *if profits are zero*. We know from equation (18.7) that if profits in the capitalist firm equal zero, earnings must equal the market wage. But if wages are the same as average earnings (for example, $w = w_2$ in Figure 18.3), the profit-maximising firm hires the same number of workers as its labour-managed counterpart because, at that point only, maximum earnings and the marginal revenue product line coincide. Thus, if labour management is introduced into a fully competitive economy where zero profits are being earned, this will have no effect on the allocation of

Figure 18.3

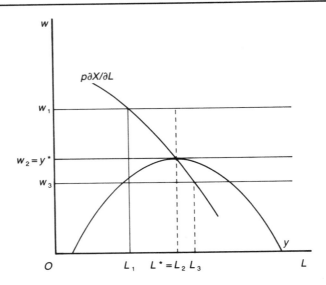

Average earnings for the labour-managed firm. With income maximisation, the firm always chooses (y^*, L^*). The profit-maximising firm chooses more, less, or the same level of employment (L_3, L_1, or L_2) depending whether market wages are less than, more than or the same (w_3, w_1 or w_2) as average earnings (y^*).

resources (at least in the short run). This sort of result has led some economists to argue that competitive market forces are more important than specific institutional arrangements in determining the allocation of resources.

But the foregoing conclusion arises only in the zero profit case. If the equivalent profit-maximising firm was operating at a loss ($\pi < 0$), equation (18.7) indicates that wages must exceed the maximum feasible average earnings (when wages are $w_1 > y^*$ in Figure 18.3). If demand and cost conditions are such that the capitalist firm makes losses in the short run, these must be borne collectively by the worker entrepreneurs after the introduction of labour management and this will depress earnings. The labour-managed firm will then shift to producing a relatively greater output with a larger labour force than its profit-maximising counterpart ($L_1 < L^*$ in Figure 18.3), in order to spread the losses over a larger number of workers. This result may help to explain the tendency for labour-managed firms to emerge in declining sectors. In such conditions, labour-managed firms often give the impression of being overmanned relative to capitalist enterprises.

Finally, consider what would happen if labour management were to be introduced into a profitable capitalist firm. In this case, output would be reduced and wages increased. Positive profits imply that earnings will exceed the market wage after the introduction of labour management.

(If $\pi > 0$ in equation (18.7), we have the case where $w = w_3 < y^*$ in Figure 18.3). In this case, labour-managed firms are employment restrictive, relative to their profit- maximising counterparts. In Figure 18.3 when $w = w_3$ we find $L^* < L_3$. Since positive or zero profits seem the most likely outcome for most industries most of the time, this analysis suggests that labour management will either have no effect on output and employment, or lead to reductions in output and employment relative to profit maximisation.

The Short-run Supply Curve

We cannot derive the short-run supply curve for the labour-managed firm using its marginal cost curve, as we do in the competitive profit-maximising case because, as we have stressed above, in this instance, the opportunity cost of labour is not determined in the labour market, and therefore independent of the level of output, as it is in the profit-maximising perfectly competitive case. We must instead investigate the impact of changes in product price on output via its effect on employment decisions. We continue to make the assumption that the capital stock is fixed.

The adjustments of output to an increase in product price is illustrated in Figure 18.4. The labour-managed firm is shown to respond to an increase in product price by reducing output and employment in order to increase average earnings. Its short-run supply curve is therefore *backward bending*. This striking result has no counterpart in the case of the profit-maximising firm. With profit maximisation, an increase in price raises the value marginal product of labour relative to the market determined wage, which leads the firm to hire *more* workers in order to increase profits. In the labour-managed firm, the increase in price increases earnings more than it increases the marginal revenue product of labour because, given our assumption of diminishing returns to labour, the marginal product of labour (the slope of the revenue function) is always exceeded by the average product. This effect gives the firm an incentive to reduce its output.

The intuition behind the backward-bending supply curve under labour management is as follows. The average revenue per head of the labour-managed firm will increase as the membership declines because of diminishing returns to labour. It should be stressed that the assumption of diminishing returns to a factor, at least in the range of output and employment around the equilibrium, is required in order for average earnings to reach a maximum at all. Hence, the enterprise would seek to become as small as possible, say, in the limit one worker, to raise earnings if there were not a constraint imposed by fixed costs. These fixed costs force the firm to settle for a larger membership because, per capita, they are inversely related to employment. Any equilibrium must reflect

Figure 18.4

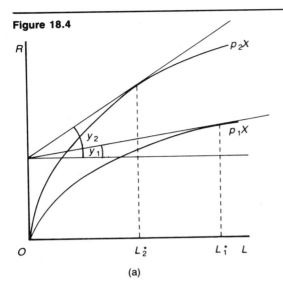

(a)

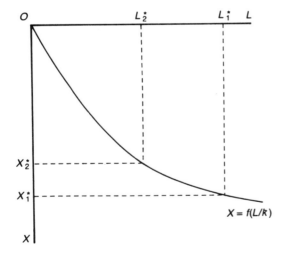

(b)

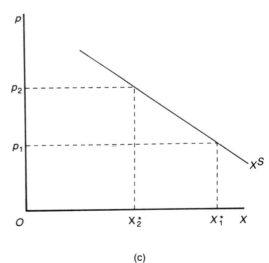

(c)

Supply under labour management: The supply curve of the income-maximising labour managed firm is backward sloping (see 18.4c). In Figure 18.4(a) we start at price p_1, with earnings of y_1, employment L_1^*, and therefore output X_1^* via the short-run production function $x = f(L, \bar{K})$ of Figure 18.4b. If product price rises to p_2, maximum earnings rise to y_2 and employment declines to L_2^*. Via the production function (Figure 18.4b) output, also declines, to X_2^*. The locus of price-output combinations — the supply curve — is illustrated in Figure 18.4c and is backward bending by derivation.

a balance between these forces: where the marginal gain to the collective, in terms of revenue per head, of reducing membership exactly
balances the marginal loss, in terms of fixed costs per head. An increase
in product price does not affect the marginal loss from reducing membership. However, it increases the marginal benefit by raising revenue per
capita at each level of employment. Thus the relaxation of the constraint
imposed by fixed costs leads the co-operative to reduce membership, and
therefore production, in order to raise average earnings.

A further difference between labour-managed firms and their profit-
maximising counterparts in the short run concerns the impact of changes
in fixed capital costs on output. Changes in fixed costs under labour
management have an immediate effect on employment and therefore output in the short run, whereas under profit maximisation they have no
effect. This result is illustrated in Figure 18.5. In terms of our previous
intuition, an increase in fixed costs, for example via a lump sum tax, raises
the marginal loss to the firm of reducing employment without affecting
the marginal gain. The collective therefore recruits more members in order
to spread the new higher fixed costs over more workers. This result can
be contrasted with that for the sales revenue-maximising monopolist.

Figure 18.5

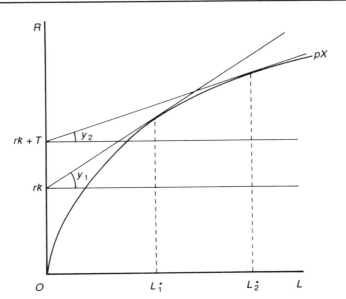

The response of the labour-managed firm to an increase in fixed costs because of the
imposition of a lump-sum tax, T. By shifting the intercept with the vertical axis upward, the
increase in fixed costs increases employment from L_1^* to L_2^* while reducing incomes from
y_1 to y_2.

*A More Formal Treatment of the Short-run Supply Curve Under Labour Management

The backward-bending supply curve can be derived more formally from the first-order condition for income maximisation, equation (18.10). In doing so we illustrate the role of the implicit function rule in simplifying the formal derivation of comparative static results. Let us set the slope of earnings function, $(y = (pX - r\bar{K})/L)$, equal to zero,

$$\frac{\partial y}{\partial L} = \frac{1}{L^2}\left(Lp\,\frac{\partial X}{\partial L} - pX + r\bar{K}\right) = 0 \qquad (18.10)$$

Using the implicit function rule, we get

$$\frac{\partial L}{\partial p} = \frac{-\partial^2 y}{\partial L\,\partial p}\,\frac{\partial^2 y}{\partial L^2} \qquad (18.15)$$

where

$$\frac{\partial^2 y}{\partial L\,\partial p} = \frac{1}{L}\left(\frac{\partial X}{\partial L} - \frac{X}{L}\right) \qquad (18.16)$$

and

$$\frac{\partial^2 y}{\partial L^2} = \frac{p}{L}\,\frac{\partial^2 X}{\partial L^2} \quad \text{since} \quad \frac{\partial y}{\partial L} = 0 \qquad (18.17)$$

Hence our assumptions about technology imply that

$$\frac{\partial L}{\partial p} = \frac{(X/L - \partial X/\partial L)}{p\,\partial^2 X/\partial L^2} < 0 \qquad (18.18)$$

because with diminishing returns to labour, $X/L > \partial X/\partial L$, and $\partial^2 X/\partial L^2 < 0$.

The slope of the supply curve, $\partial X/\partial p$, is determined (given $\partial L/\partial p$) via the short-run production function, and with $\partial X/\partial L > 0$,

$$\frac{\partial X}{\partial p} = \frac{\partial X}{\partial L}\cdot\frac{\partial L}{\partial p} = \frac{\partial X/\partial L(X/L - \partial X/\partial L)}{p\,\partial^2 X/\partial L^2} < 0 \qquad (18.19)$$

This result highlights the role played by diminishing returns to labour in generating the backward-bending supply curve.

The Labour-Managed Firm in the Long Run

Our analysis of the labour-managed firm in the short run suggests that such organisations may respond 'perversely' in the supply of output, reducing production as price increases and vice versa. This rather startling

result is, in fact, an extreme version of the general argument, for the case of multiple inputs and outputs, that labour-managed firms always vary output by a smaller amount in response to given price changes than do their capitalist counterparts. We can see this by considering the behaviour of the labour-managed firm in the long run, when both labour and capital inputs can be varied simultaneously. For the moment, we maintain the assumption that there is neither entry into nor exit from the industry in question, whether firms are profit-maximising or labour-managed. This crucial assumption is relaxed in the following section.

Let us assume as before that the labour-managed firm maximises average earnings, in this case though, subject to the long-run production function. The formal problem is to maximise

$$y = \frac{pX - rK}{L} \tag{18.9}$$

subject to

$$X = f(L,K) \tag{18.20}$$

We can derive first-order conditions by substituting equation (18.20) into (18.9), and setting equal to zero the partial derivatives of the resulting expression with respect to employment and capital.

$$\frac{\partial y}{\partial L} = \frac{1}{L^2}\left(Lp\,\frac{\partial X}{\partial L} - pX + rK\right) = 0 \tag{18.10'}$$

$$\frac{\partial y}{\partial K} = \frac{1}{L}\left(p\,\frac{\partial X}{\partial K} - r\right) = 0 \tag{18.21}$$

Equation (18.10') is the labour hiring rule analysed above for the situation when the capital stock is variable, and equation (18.21) tells us that the labour-managed firm hires capital until its marginal value product $(p\partial X/\partial K)$ equals its rental cost (r). This latter condition is identical to that governing the behaviour of conventional competitive profit-maximising enterprises (see Chapter 19). The change in maximand from profits to average earnings per head therefore affects the way in which the enterprise chooses employment but not the way in which it selects its capital stock.

It will be remembered that, since the labour force has undertaken the role of entrepreneur in labour-managed firms, it receives the entire flow of profits in its pay-packet (see equation (18.7)). Hence there is no pure surplus remaining in the labour-managed firm. First-order conditions (18.10') and (18.21), on the other hand, tell us that on the margin the remuneration of each factor, including its share of the profit in the case of labour, exactly equals its marginal revenue product. As we noted in Chapter 14, when factors are paid their marginal products, pure surplus, or profits, can equal zero only when the production function is linearly

homogeneous at the equilibrium. Thus the labour-managed firm will achieve a long-run equilibrium only where the production function displays constant returns to scale.

The bulk of our analysis in this part of the book has been conducted under the assumption that the production function in the long run displays first increasing, then constant, then diminishing returns to scale. This assumption generates the by now familiar U-shaped long-run average cost curves used in Chapters 13, 14 and 15. The argument above has established, assuming that the returns to scale characteristics of the production function do not vary with factor proportions, that *the labour-managed firm always operates at the level of production at which long-run average costs would be minimised if the enterprise were profit maximising.* The actual level of average payments to inputs (including the profits distributed to workers as part of average earnings) might be higher, lower, or the same as that achieved by the profit-maximising counterpart, depending on whether the latter organisation makes a profit, a loss, or just breaks even; but the labour-managed firm always produces at the output level at which the long-run average cost curve of the equivalent profit maximiser is at its minimum. The profit maximiser, of course, can produce anywhere to the right of that minimum point, depending on the relationship between marginal cost and price. This result is illustrated in Figure 18.6.

Figure 18.6

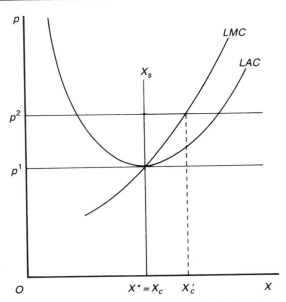

The labour-managed firm always produces at the output level where the production function displays constant returns to scale, denoted X^*. When price equals p_x^1 the competitive profit-maximising firm produces the same output, X_c with profits equal to zero ($p_x^1 = LAC$). However, if the price is higher, say p^2, the profit maximiser produces at x_c^1 while the labour-managed firm continues to produce at X^*. The higher profits in the latter are paid to employees, raising earnings and therefore average payments to inputs. The labour-managed firm's long-run supply curve is therefore vertical at X^*.

Our analysis of the competitive profit-maximising firm showed that in the absence of entry its supply curve is the long-run marginal cost curve, which is upward sloping in the relevant range. For the labour-managed firm, however, supply in the absence of entry is fixed at the point of constant returns, independently of the price which output fetches. Provided that returns to scale do not vary with the capital—labour ratio, the firm's long-run supply curve is therefore perfectly inelastic, rather than being backward bending as was the case in the short run.

Labour-Managed and Profit-Maximising Firms with Free Entry

In our discussions of the long-run theory of competitive supply in Chapter 14, we noted that while it was logically possible to think of an industry supply curve *from* incumbent producers' long-run marginal cost curves on the assumption that there could be no entry, it was of no practical relevance. This was because firms would not make decisions about their scale of operations, the profitability of which would be undermined by the entry of new competitors. Hence a proper analysis of long-run industry supply required that account be taken of entry and exit.

In the light of this, it is important to stress that the analysis of the previous section, concerning the labour-managed firm in the long run in the absence of entry, was not undertaken in order to reach general conclusions about the shape of the industry supply curve. It was rather intended to illustrate that the perverse supply behaviour which we derived initially in our short-run analysis was not merely a consequence of special assumptions, in particular the assumption that the labour-managed firm had a fixed capital stock. We now see that such perversity was in fact a specific example of a quite general property of the behaviour of labour-managed firms, namely, their tendency to restrict employment relative to their profit-maximising counterparts whenever profits are positive.

In order to derive the long-run industry supply curve under labour management when entry is possible, we need to consider in more detail the motivations of worker-entrepreneurs. The discussion takes place on the assumption that all firms have identical technology. We have seen that the objective of the labour-managed firm is to maximise average earnings per head. On that basis, it is reasonable to suppose that individual worker-entrepreneurs will also be motivated by average earnings. They will therefore seek to form new labour-managed firms in activities where average earnings available exceed those that they are currently receiving, and to leave enterprises in which remuneration is below the rate available elsewhere in the economy. If we assume costless enterprise formation and closure, this means that there will be entry of new labour-managed firms into industries in which average earnings exceed remuneration elsewhere, and exit in industries for which the converse is true.

But we saw at the start of our discussion of labour-managed firms that there is a relationship between average earnings paid under labour management and the level of profits which would pertain in a capitalist environment. This relationship is given by equation (18.7) and states that average earnings exceed (are lower than) the wages which would be paid by the profit-maximising firm according to whether profits are positive (negative). Hence entry will take place into industries which would, if the firms were profit maximisers, be earning a positive profit, while exit will occur in industries which would, under profit maximisation, be loss-makers. These are precisely the same conditions for entry and exit that rule in the long run under capitalism.

Moreover, the process which drives the system as a whole to equilibrium is also the same as under capitalism. Consider an industry in which earnings for some reason, say a favourable demand shift, exceed those available elsewhere in the economy. As we have argued above, supply adjustments by incumbent firms to such a new higher level of demand will be smaller than those of their profit-maximising counterparts, and may even be perverse. However, this increase in demand and its consequent higher output price creates incentives for worker-entrepreneurs in other, lower paying sectors, to form new firms in the industry. As market supply is increased by their entry, price falls and the earnings of all firms in the industry decline. The process of entry, declining price and reductions in average earnings ceases when earnings in the sector are once again the same as those earned elsewhere in the economy.

The supply curve for a competitive labour-managed industry of identical firms is therefore perfectly horizontal, for exactly the same reasons as is the industry supply curve of profit-maximising firms. The previous discussion suggests, however, that the labour-managed economy may have to rely relatively more on entry and exit to ensure adequate supply responses to changes in demand than its profit-maximising counterpart. This will not cause problems if, as we assumed above, the process of entry and exit is costless. The adjustment of supply to demand or cost disturbances will be sluggish, however, which may cause problems if the process of entry and exit by worker enterprises is in fact a costly one.

Conclusions

The discussion of the behaviour of firms in this book concentrates on examining the implications of profit maximisation under alternative assumptions about market structure. Our aim in this chapter has been to give a brief introduction to a parallel line of enquiry: examining the implications of alternative objectives for enterprise behaviour. For the most part, we have undertaken this analysis on the assumption that product markets are competitive, but as our discussion of revenue maximisation suggests, one can combine assumptions about alternative objectives and

market structures to reproduce a set of results for these new organisations that parallel all those analysed in the literature on conventional firms.

One proposition that we have illustrated in this chapter is that the
behaviour of firms in the market-place depends on their objectives as well
as on the structure of the market in which they operate. Firms that seek
to maximise their revenue will be larger than conventional profit maximisers provided that they are monopolists. Labour-managed firms may
respond perversely to an increase in their product price in the short run,
and will in general adjust quantity in response to a change in price less
than their capitalist counterparts. These results arise because in each case
the new objective alters economic incentives on the margin. Even so, the
equivalence of the equilibria of labour-managed and zero-profit capitalist
firms shows that, at least in the competitive case, market forces can be
as important as enterprise objectives in determining output decisions.

Questions for Study and Discussion for Part VI

1. 'The theory of supply suggests that, as a rough and ready rule, the
   public authorities should keep their eye on the number of producers
   in an industry. When this becomes too small, public intervention
   will become necessary'. Discuss.
2. Are there any circumstances in which the firm in monopolistic competition can produce at a level of output at which the average cost
   curve is upward sloping? What do you conclude from your answer
   about the efficiency of monopolistically competitive industries?
3. With p measured as $ per thousand units and X measured as
   thousands of units per week, the market demand for X is given by

   $$p = 20 - X$$

   A group of small firms are able to provide X along a supply curve
   given by

   $$p = 2 + 2X$$

   (a) Find:
       (i) the price of X; and
       (ii) the quantity of X.
   (b) A large firm appears on the market which can produce X at
       a constant long-run marginal and average cost of $8 per thou-
       sand units.

       Find:
       (i) the demand curve facing that firm;
       (ii) the price and output of the firm;
       (iii) the firm's profit;
       (iv) the overall output of X; and

(v) the quantity of X produced by the small competitive firms.

4. Consider a situation in which only one firm in a country produces a good X but in which foreign firms also provide X to the market under perfectly competitive conditions. How will the imposition of (a) a flat rate tariff, and (b) a ban on imports, affect the price, output and profits of the domestic firm?

5. Consider the industry described in question 3. Suppose that the monopolist who takes it over is a revenue maximiser instead of a profit maximiser. Recompute your answers to parts (b) and (c) of question 3.

6. Increases in demand always bring forth increases in the total amount supplied where the market structure is competitive. However, this does not necessarily hold when supply is in the hands of one or very few producers. Discuss with reference to the Cournot and Bertrand duopoly model, as well as monopoly.

*7. Suppose that a firm in monopolistic competition faces a demand curve, $p = 10/X^2$ and cost curve $C = 50 + 30X$. What is the mark-up of price on average cost? Suppose that the demand curve now shifts out, so $p = 20/X^2$. What happens to the mark-up?

8. Suppose that a duopolist holds the following beliefs about the behaviour of a rival.

   (i) If the duopolist makes 'small' changes in price, say within 10 per cent of the current price, either up or down, the rival will not react.

   (ii) If the duopolist makes 'large' changes in price, the rival will match the changes exactly.

   Derive the average and marginal revenue curves implied by these beliefs. What are the implications of these beliefs for output and price setting?

9. Consider an industry with five suppliers. One is very large relative to total supply, with the capacity, in the relevant price range, to supply a significant proportion of market supply on its own. The remaining suppliers comprise two middle size firms and two that are relatively small. The largest and smallest firms each have relatively low (constant) unit costs, but average costs are somewhat higher for two middle size firms. Discuss the problems that the five suppliers will face in forming and maintaining a cartel.

*10. There are two identical firms in an industry, 1 and 2, each with cost function $C_i = 10X_i$, $i = 1,2$. The industry demand curve is $P = 100 - 5X$ where industry output, X is the sum of the two firms outputs $(X_1 + X_2)$.

   (i) If each firm makes its output decisions on the assumption that the other will not react to its choices (the Cournot assump-

tion), what is the equilibrium output for each firm. What is the equilibrium price?

(ii) Suppose that each firm takes it in turn to choose its level of output, on the assumption that the other's output level is fixed. Would the process of adjustment be stable?

(iii) Suppose that firm 1 introduces a cost saving innovation, so that its cost curve becomes $C_1 = 8X_1$. Firm 2's cost curve and the industry demand curve are unchanged. What happens to equilibrium quantity produced by each firm and to market price?

*11. Suppose the two firms in question 9 are now playing a Stackelberg game, with firm 1 as leader and firm 2 as follower. What are the equilibrium levels of output and industry price? How does your answer change if firm 1 has the cost function given in 7 (iii)?

12. 'Since we know that firms compete over price rather than quantity, the theory of oligopoly suggests that outcomes will approximate those of perfect competition, even when there are only a few suppliers in the industry.' Discuss.

13. The prisoners' dilemma game offers insights into the incentives to cheat of agents who will not be placed in the same situation again, such as two criminals whom we can presume will not again be partners in crime. These insights carry over to the case where two suppliers are operating temporarily in a particular market, and have formed a cartel in order to maximise their short-term joint profits. Discuss the ways in which the argument will have to be modified if the two parties to the cartel know that they will be facing each other on the same market for many periods to come.

14. 'The common characteristic of the Cournot model is that it assumes a common pattern of reaction by competitors in each period which, despite the fact that the expected reaction does not in fact materialise, is never altered. This assumption that firms never learn from their past experience is excessively naive.' Discuss with reference to the distinction between Cournot behaviour and the Cournot equilibrium, and in the light of the insights that game theory yields about the character of the Cournot equilibrium.

15. Analyse the consequences of imposing a profits tax on a revenue-maximising monopolist if the tax also changes the minimum profit constraint faced by the firm. In what ways does this reaction differ from that of the profit maximiser?

16. Suppose technology is such that the labour-managed firm in the short run faces an average earnings curve which is inverse U-shaped, as in Figure 18.2. Use this short-run diagram to illustrate

(i) the change in the level of earnings after an increase in price at the initial equilibrium level of employment;

(ii) the change in the marginal revenue product of labour after

an increase in price at the initial equilibrium level of employment;

(iii)   the new equilibrium level of earnings and employment after an increase in price;

(iv)   the new equilibrium level of earnings and employment after an increase in capital rentals.

*17.   A competitive labour-managed firm in the short run faces fixed costs of £100 per week and a weekly short-run production function, $X = 5L^{1/2}$. The market price of the output is £10.

(i)   What is the level of employment which maximises average earnings per head? What do workers earn at that equilibrium?

(ii)   Suppose that price increases to £15. What happens to employment and to earnings?

(iii)   Suppose that capital costs increase to £150 per week. What happens to employment and to earnings?

(iv)   Suppose that the firm introduces new technology which increases average and marginal labour productivity, so that $X = 8L^{1/2}$. What happens to employment and to earnings?

*18.   Suppose that the competitive labour-managed firm uses two inputs in the short run (when capital is fixed at K_0), labour and material inputs M. The firm purchases materials at their market price, p_m. The objective of the firm is therefore to maximise

$$y = \frac{pX - rK_0 - p_m M}{L}$$

subject to the short-run production function $X = f(L, K_0, M)$ where $\partial X/\partial M > 0$, $\partial^2 X/\partial M^2 < 0$.

(i)   What rule does the labour-managed firm use in determining its optimal level of material input? In what way does it differ from that of a profit-maximising firm?

(ii)   What is the effect of an increase in the price of material inputs on the demand for material inputs, on employment and on average earnings?

(iii)   Suppose the firm now faces an increase in product price. Is the short-run supply curve necessarily backward bending?

Suggested Further Reading to Part VI

Arrow, K.J. *op. cit.*

Bain, J.S. 1962, *Barriers to New Competition*. Cambridge, MA: Harvard University Press.

Baumol, W.J. 1959. *Business Behaviour, Value and Growth*. New York: Macmillan.

Baumol, W.J., Panzar, J.C. and Willig, R.D. 1982. *Contestable Markets and the Theory of Industry Structure*. New York: Harcourt, Brace, Jovanovich.

Chamberlain, E. 1956. *The Theory of Monopolistic Competition*. Cambridge, MA: Harvard University Press.

Cowling, K.G. and Waterson, M. 1976. 'Price Cost Margins and Market Structure', *Economica*.

Cyert, R.M. and March, T.G. 1963. *A Behavioural Theory of the Firm*. Englewood Cliffs, NJ: Prentice-Hall.

Demsetz, H. 1959. 'The Nature of Equilibrium in Monopolistic Competition', *Journal of Political Economy*.

Dixit, A.K. 1982. 'Recent Development in Oligopoly Theory', *American Economic Review*. (papers and proceedings).

Estrin, S., Jones, D.C. and Sjevnar, J. 1987. 'The Productivity Effects of Worker Participation in the Producers Cooperatives of Western Economies', *Journal of Comparative Economics*.

Friedman, M. 1953. 'The Methodology of Positive Economics', in *Studies in Positive Economics*. Chicago: University of Chicago Press.

Friedman, J.W. 1977. *Oligopoly and the Theory of Games*. Amsterdam, North-Holland.

Hall, R.L. and Hitch, C.J. 1939. 'Price Theory and Business Behaviour', *Oxford Economic Papers*.

Ireland, N.J. and Law, P.J. 1982. *The Economics of Labour-Managed Enterprise*. London: Croom Helm.

Machlup, F., 1967. 'Theories of the Firm, Marginalist, Managerialist, Behavioural', *American Economic Review*.

Marris, R. 1964. *The Economic Theory of 'Managerial' Capitalism*. London: Macmillan.

Nash, J. 1950. 'The Bargaining Problem', *Econometrica*.

Scherer, F.M. 1980. *Industrial Market Structure and Economic Performance*. Chicago: Rand-McNally.

Simon, H.A. 1957. *Models of Man*. New York: Wiley.

Stigler, G.J. 1947. 'The Kinky Oligopoly Demand Curve and Rigid Prices', *Journal of Political Economy*. Reprinted in Stigler and Boulding (eds) *op. cit.*

Svejnar, J. 1982. 'On the Theory of a Participatory Firm', *Journal of Economic Theory*.

Sweezy, F.M. 1939. 'Demand Under Conditions of Oligopoly', *Journal of Political Economy*. Reprinted in Stigler and Boulding (eds) *op.cit.*

Vanek, J. 1970. *The General Theory of Labour-Managed Market Economies*. New York: Cornell University Press

Ward, B. 1957. 'The Firm in Illyria: Market Syndicalism', *American Economic Review*.

Waterson, M. 1984. *Economic Theory of Industry*. Cambridge: Cambridge University Press.

Williamson, O.E. 1964. *The Economics of Discretionary Behaviour*. Englewood Cliffs, NJ: Prentice-Hall.

Part VII

FACTOR MARKETS

19

The Demand for Factors of Production in Competition

Introduction

In previous chapters, we used revenue and cost functions to analyse the way in which profit-maximising firms choose the price and quantity of their output. Those readers who worked through Chapter 12 will already be well aware that implicit in these output market choices are decisions about the demand for factor inputs. In that chapter we analysed, in considerable detail, *conditional* factor demand curves, a conceptual construct which examines the change in factor demand which occurs as input prices vary, on the assumption that output is fixed. In this chapter we turn to the full input (or factor) demand problem, allowing changes in output as well as the choice of technique (or choice of factor proportions) to influence factor demands when input prices vary. Input demand curves of this sort may be termed *profit-maximising* factor demand curves. Let it be clear that we are not here analysing new or different decisions taken by the firm. We are looking at exactly the same decisions with which we dealt earlier when analysing the output market, but from a different perspective; from the point of view of the market for the inputs used by the firm. We start by analysing input demand on the assumption that product markets are perfectly competitive. We shall consider the consequences for factor markets of product market imperfections in the next chapter.

Physical Products and Revenue Products

It is convenient to begin where we began before, with the two input production function (Figure 19.1), but this time with the aim of deriving

Figure 19.1

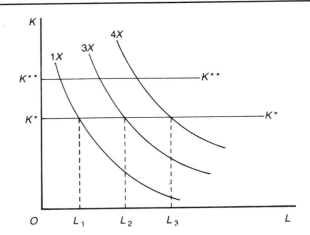

A production function displaying first increasing then decreasing returns to scale and two short-run paths along which output can be expanded holding capital fixed $-K^*K^*$ and $K^{**}K^{**}$.

the demand curve for a factor of production rather than with the aim of deriving cost functions and from them a supply curve for output. The relationship between price and quantity is not uniquely defined merely by the term 'demand curve'. We must specify what other things there are that we are holding constant before we can be precise in this respect. We will concern ourselves initially with deriving the demand curve for labour of a perfectly competitive firm *in the short run*; that is to say when the amount of capital services in the production process is given and when the price of output is given. Thus, we are concerned with what happens to the price that the firm is willing to pay for labour as it moves along a path such as K^*K^* in Figure 19.1.

The first step in the analysis involves investigating what happens to the 'physical productivity' of labour as its quantity is varied; the marginal product of labour, $\partial X/\partial L$. If the short-run production function is assumed to display increasing, then constant, then diminishing returns *to a factor*, as in Figure 19.2(a), the average (physical) and marginal (physical) product curves will take the shapes illustrated in Figure 19.2(b). As we noted in Chapter 11, these short-run average and marginal (physical) product curves are exact (inverse) analogs of the short-run average and marginal cost curves. Thus L_2, the employment level at which the average product is at its maximum in Figure 19.2(b) generates an output level of $3X$ in Figure 19.2(a), which is the level of output, given output prices, at which short-run average costs are minimised, for example X_2 in Figure 11.12.

We assume that the firm is not concerned with physical productivity for its own sake, but rather with the profits it can make from its productive activities. It is therefore the *revenue* that a factor generates, rather than

Figure 19.2

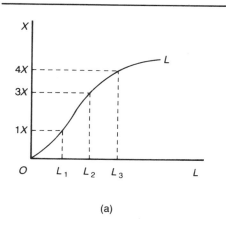

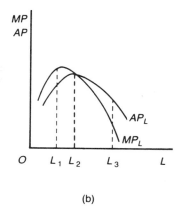

(a)

(b)

(a) The short-run production function implied by Figure 19.1. (b) The average and marginal (physical) product of labour curves (AP_L and MP_L) implicit in panel (a).

the physical output it creates, which is ultimately of interest. Our productivity measures therefore have to be changed from physical to value terms. *Physical products* must be transformed into *revenue products*. This is done in Figure 19.3, where we multiply units of output, X, by the price, p, which is a constant since we are considering a perfectly competitive firm. Given that the level of capital inputs, and hence cash outlay on capital inputs, is constant, profits will be maximised if total revenue minus total outlay on labour is maximised. If we assume a constant price for labour, total outlay on that output is proportional to the quantity of it employed, and we may draw a straight line *total factor outlay* (or cost) *curve* in Figure 19.3.

Profits are then maximised where the *slope* of the total factor cost curve is equal to the *slope* of the total revenue curve, that is, where marginal revenue product is equal to marginal factor cost. In this case, constancy of the price of X means that we may also refer to the marginal revenue product of labour as the *value of the marginal product* of labour.

Now readers will no doubt have been struck by the similarity between this analysis and that by which the short-run supply curve of the individual firm was derived in Chapter 13. What we have been doing here is to look at exactly the same set of conditions which we discussed there from a different point of view. We said in Chapter 13 that profits would be maximised where marginal cost was set equal to marginal revenue. Short-run marginal cost of production is given by the extra outlay on labour per unit of output necessary to produce a small addition to output. As we saw, it therefore equals the marginal outlay on labour per unit of labour divided by the marginal product of labour; or, to put the same point in other words, short-run marginal cost is the additional cost of employing an extra unit of labour divided by the amount that that unit will add to output.

Figure 19.3

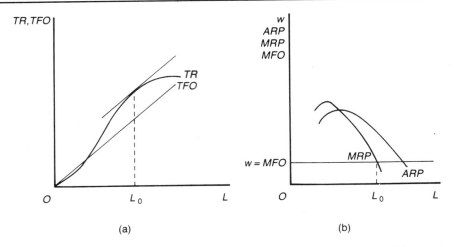

(a) Profits are maximised where the vertical distance between the total revenue (*TR*) and total outlay on the factor (*TFO*) is maximised, that is at the level of employment L_0 where their slopes are equal. (b) An alternative portrayal of the profit-maximising level of employment. Here the marginal revenue product of labour (*MRP*) is equal to marginal outlay on labour (*MFO*). Since the wage rate is given at *w*, *MFO* is constant and equal to *w*.

The point can be made much more simply with algebra. Using our previous notation, the condition that price equals marginal cost for the competitive firm can be written as

$$p = mc \equiv \frac{w}{\partial X/\partial L} \tag{19.1}$$

But we have just shown that, when looking at the factor market, profit maximisation requires that marginal factor outlay, the wage in a competitive labour market, must equal the marginal revenue product of labour, i.e.

$$w = p\frac{\partial X}{\partial L} \tag{19.2}$$

Obviously (19.2) is equivalent to (19.1), and can be derived from it by multiplying both sides of (19.1) by $\partial X/\partial L$.

Factor Demand in the Short Run

If the perfectly competitive firm will always set its employment of the variable factor at a point where its marginal revenue product equals the price of that factor, then this curve becomes the firm's short-run demand

curve for the factor. This is a mirror image of the proposition that the firm's short-run supply curve of output is its short-run marginal cost curve. The firm's shut-down condition, namely that the firm will not produce at all if the product price is less than average cost also has a corollary for the demand for labour curve; the firm will not hire a factor if its average revenue product is less than the price of the factor divided by the product price. Note also that, for the equality of marginal factor outlay and marginal revenue product to be consistent with profit maximisation, the latter curve must cut the former from above. Thus, the firm will always be operating at a level of output where returns to labour are diminishing. This point was made earlier in Chapter 13, during our discussion of the firm's short-run supply decision.

The *industry's* short-run demand curve for labour will not just be the sum of the firm's demand curves. When analysing the individual firm, it makes sense to hold the price of output constant, but when we consider the whole industry expanding its labour input, and hence its output of X, we must remember that this will affect the price of X. This price will fall as output expands so long as the demand curve for X does not shift. Hence, the *industry's* demand curve for labour in the short run will be more steeply sloped than the sum of the *firms'* marginal revenue product curves. The latter slopes downwards only because the marginal productivity of labour diminishes. The industry's demand curve slopes more steeply because, in addition, the price of X falls as the industry's output increases. Figure 19.4 illustrates this.

The Firm's Factor Demand in the Long Run

The interesting question remains of how the demand for a particular factor changes in the long run, when both inputs can vary simultaneously. A higher level of the capital stock, say K^{**} in Figure 19.1, may involve, at any given level of labour input, a higher total, average and marginal physical productivity for labour. If it does, then as a consequence, in the long run the firm's demand for labour will be more elastic than it is in the short run, provided that ouput price is held constant.

As we have seen, a fall in the price of labour involves more labour being employed by the firm, even if capital cannot be varied: costs of production unambiguously fall and at a given price output expands. However, as we saw in Chapter 10, an increase in the employment of labour is usually assumed to *raise* the physical productivity of capital. In other words, the derivative of the marginal product of capital with respect to labour is positive, i.e.

$$\frac{\partial^2 X}{\partial K \partial L} > 0 \tag{19.3}$$

Figure 19.4

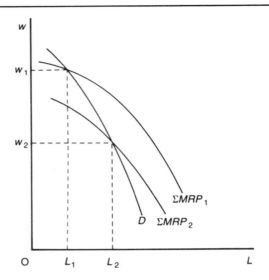

A short-run industry demand curve for labour. It is more steeply sloped than the sum over all firms in the industry of their marginal revenue product curves at a constant output price because, as employment and hence output increases, the price of output falls. Thus, when the wage rate falls from w_1 to w_2, the summed marginal revenue product curve shifts down from ΣMRP_1 to ΣMRP_2 and employment increases from L_1 to L_2. The industry's demand curve for labour is given by D.

By the rules of calculus, the other cross partial derivative $(\partial^2 X/\partial L\partial K)$ must also be positive and identical to (19.3). The converse case, when the cross partial derivatives are both negative, is also conceivable in principle, and is referred to as a case in which the factors of production are 'inferior'. This latter case is empirically unlikely, however, for if we had inferior factors of production, this would, for example, imply that an increase in the capital stock *reduces* the marginal product of labour. We henceforth rule out this analytic curiousity by assumption. A fall in the price of labour, with the output price given, therefore leads to an increase in the marginal revenue product of capital.

With a given supply price for capital services, employment of capital will increase in the long run, and the short-run marginal revenue product curve of labour will shift to the right. The long-run demand curve for labour, then, is the result of movements along and shifts in the same direction of the short-run curve, and hence is more shallowly sloped. This is illustrated in Figure 19.5.

Industry Demand for Labour

The analysis of the industry's long-run demand for labour is less clear-cut than that of the firm because we must drop the assumption that output price is given. Two considerations now affect the marginal revenue

Figure 19.5

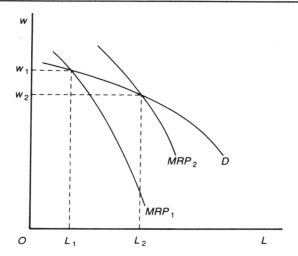

The firm's long-run demand for labour, holding the price of output constant. An increase in employment of labour following a fall in its price from w_1 to w_2 increases the productivity of capital and hence leads to an increase in its employment in the long run, thus shifting the *MRP* of labour to the right. The firm's long-run demand curve, *D*, is a compound of a shift along and a shift of the *MRP* curve and hence is more shallowly sloped, generating a change in the demand for labour from L_1 to L_2.

product of capital services when the quantity of labour employed varies, and these operate in opposite directions. Increased labour input increases capital's *physical productivity*, but expanding industry output lowers the price of output and hence drives its *productivity in revenue terms* downwards. The net effect of these two tendencies may go either way. We may end up with more capital employed and hence have a long-run industry demand curve for labour that, though more steeply sloped than the simple summation of firm's demand curves, is nevertheless more shallowly sloped than the short-run industry demand curve. On the other hand, it is possible for the demand for capital actually to fall, and for the long-run demand curve for labour to be less elastic than the short-run curve. Figure 19.6 illustrates both cases.

The effect of a fall in the price of labour on the demand for capital depends on the relative importance of two offsetting tendencies. First, there is a tendency for labour to be substituted for capital and hence for the demand for capital to decrease, but second, there is a tendency for output to increase and the demand for capital to increase. If the first tendency dominates, the amount of capital used will fall in the long run, the physical productivity of labour at any scale of input will diminish, and the industry's long-run demand for labour will be less elastic than the short-run curve along which the level of capital utilisation is held constant. Such a situation will be associated with a degree of substitutability between factors that is high relative to the elasticity of demand for output. Cases where the long-run demand curve for labour is more

Figure 19.6

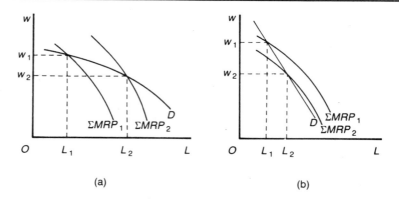

D is the industry's long-run demand curve for labour. (a) *D* will slope more shallowly than *ΣMRP* if, when the wage rate falls from w_1 to w_2, the consequent expansion of employment and output and the fall in output price on balance increase the revenue productivity of a given stock of capital. More capital inputs will be used, *ΣMRP* of labour will shift to the right and employment will increase from L_1 to L_2. (b) *D* will slope more steeply than *ΣMRP* if a fall in the wage rate from w_1 to w_2 produces responses that lead to a fall in the revenue productivity of a given stock of capital. In this case, a cut in capital input shifts *ΣMRP* of labour to the left, though employment still increases from L_1 to L_2.

elastic than the short-run curve will occur where substitutability between factors is relatively low and the elasticity of demand for output is relatively high.

Influences on the Elasticity of Factor Demand

As we saw in Chapter 10, substitutability has to do with the extent to which the ratio in which capital and labour will be used changes in the long run when the ratio of their prices changes. A higher degree of substitutability involves a greater change in the capital—labour ratio for a given change in the price ratio of inputs. In terms of isoquants, the flatter they are, the less convex towards the origin, the greater is the degree of substitutability between factors. The concept of substitutability is important because the extent to which factors are substitutes for one another has a great deal to do with determining the degree to which the long-run industry demand for a particular input is sensitive to its own price.

It should be immediately obvious that, other things being equal, the greater the degree of substitutability between factors of production, the more elastic will be the demand for a particular factor. However, as we have seen, the long-run response of the demand for a particular factor — let us take the case of labour — to a change in its price does not consist solely of a substitution of labour for capital at a given level of output. A fall in wages leads to a fall in marginal production costs and hence to

a fall in output price and an increase in the volume of output. Clearly, the larger the increase in output as a result of a given fall in the wage rate, the greater will be the resulting change in the demand for labour for a given degree of substitutability between labour and capital. There are two steps between a change in the wage rate and a change in output. The first step is a fall in output price, and the larger is that part of production costs made up of payments to labour, the larger will be the fall in output price as a result of a given fall in the wage rate. The second step is the response of the demand for output to a change in its price, and the more elastic the demand for output the greater will this response be.

Thus, for a given price of other inputs, the greater the degree of substitutability between labour and these other inputs, the greater is the proportion of production costs made up of wages, and the more elastic the demand for the final output, the more elastic will be the demand for labour. However, there is no reason to treat the price of other inputs as necessarily remaining constant. If a fall in the price of labour causes the demand for other inputs to increase in the long run, then the less effect this increase in demand has on the prices of other inputs, the smaller will be the extent to which the effect of a fall in wages on output price will be offset by price increases of other inputs. If the fall in wages leads to a fall in demand for the other factor, then the smaller the effect this has on their prices the less tendency is there for substitution towards labour as a result of the initial fall in wages to be offset. In short, to the three influences on the elasticity of demand for labour already derived, we must add a fourth, namely the elasticity of supply of other factors. The higher this is, holding other influences constant, the higher will be the elasticity of demand for labour.

Factor Payments, the Value of Output and the Euler Theorem

Lying behind the various demand curves for labour whose properties we have been considering in this chapter is the marginal productivity of labour. We could, of course, just as easily have concerned ourselves with the demand for capital, for from a formal point of view the two pieces of analysis are absolutely identical. This observation leads us into a problem area that at one time much concerned economists and even now is worth some brief discussion. Consider again the firm in the long run. Suppose that in terms of Figure 19.7 the firm is in long-run equilibrium employing L_1 units of labour services at a wage rate of w_1. Implicit in the assumption that the firm is in long-run equilibrium is the proposition that a certain flow of capital services is also being utilised, the marginal revenue product of which is also equal to the price of capital services. In terms of a production function diagram, the firm is at a position such

Figure 19.7

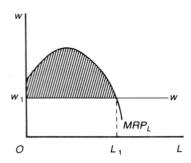

The marginal revenue product of labour. The wage bill is given by w_1L_1 leaving the shaded area available for payments to capital. If factor payments exhaust the value of output this area should equal r_1K_1 in Figure 19.9.

Figure 19.8

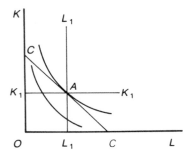

The firm in long-run equilibrium at point A, with employment of labour at L_1 and of capital at K_1. The ratio of factor prices is given by the slope of the isocost line CC and equals the ratio of the marginal productivities of the inputs given by the slope of the isoquant at point A.

as A in Figure 19.8 where the marginal rate of substitution between factors is equal to the ratio of their prices.

Associated with the employment of capital services at a rate K_1 is a marginal revenue product curve for labour that passes through the long-run demand curve at L_1w_1 and is derived by moving along the line K_1-K_1 in Figure 19.8. Now, the area under this marginal revenue product curve between the vertical axis and L_1 measures the total revenue accruing to the firm at its equilibrium output level. (If output at L_1 is X_1, then the area under the marginal revenue product of labour curve is the integral from zero to L_1 of $p\partial X/\partial L$, which equals revenue at X_1, pX_1). Since payments to labour amount to w_1L_1, it is clear that an amount equal to the shaded area in Figure 19.7 is left over to make payments to capital. (The return to the factor that is fixed in the short run is often called a *quasi-rent* for reasons that we shall go into below.) An exactly parallel argument may be developed in terms of the demand

for capital services. Variations in the marginal revenue product of capital as one moves along a line such as $L_1 - L_1$ in Figure 19.8 may be plotted in a diagram exactly similar to Figure 19.7. Figure 19.9 is such a diagram; here the area r_1K_1 represents payments to capital and the shaded area then becomes what is left over to meet the wage bill. Now we may put an interesting question: are the alternative measures of wage payments and capital payments depicted in Figures 19.7 and 19.9 consistent with one another? Do factor payments exhaust the value of output?

This is a question which bothered economists for many years. It seemed to boil down to a technical question about what kind of production function had the properties which would, in general, ensure that the sum of the marginal revenue product of each factor of production multiplied by the quantity of that factor being utilised, when added up over factors, would just turn out equal to the value of output. To put it in symbols for the two-input case, under what circumstances will it be the case for a competitive firm engaged in producing X that

$$pX = p\frac{\partial X}{\partial K} K + p\frac{\partial X}{\partial L} L \qquad (19.24)$$

or, dividing through by output price,

$$K\frac{\partial X}{\partial K} + L\frac{\partial X}{\partial L} = X \qquad (19.25)$$

If we ask what are the mathematical properties of a production function that will guarantee that the above equality always holds, the answer given by the so-called *Euler Theorem* turns out to be a production function which is *homogeneous of degree one*. Among its other properties such a function everywhere displays constant returns to scale — as we mentioned in Chapter 10.

Figure 19.9

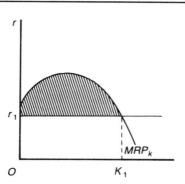

The marginal revenue product of capital. Where r is the rental price of capital, outlay on capital is r_1K_1, leaving the shaded area available to meet the wage bill. If factor payments exhaust revenue this area should be equal to w_1L_1, in Figure 19.7.

If we were forced to require that the production function take on the rather restrictive mathematical characteristic of homogeneity of degree one before payments to factors add up to the value of output, we might regard a theory of the demand for factors of production based on perfectly competitive profit-maximising behaviour with a certain amount of scepticism. However, notice that the question 'do factor payments exhaust the value of output?' is the same question as 'do total costs equal total revenue?' When the question is put this way it becomes apparent that it does not concern only the production function but also the way in which firms behave. Suppose that the area under the marginal revenue product curve of labour is less than total expenditure on factors of production at that scale of output. The firm of which this was true would leave the industry since it would be making long-run losses. Firms would continue to leave the industry until such long-run losses had been eliminated. Similarly, if the area under the marginal revenue product curve of labour were to exceed total factor payments as measured by their prices times the quantity of them employed, then this would imply the existence of positive profits, price would be above long-run average cost, and firms would enter the industry until these profits were eliminated.

So long as each firm has the same production function, then profit-maximising behaviour ensures that each firm will achieve just that level of output at which factor payments do indeed exhaust revenue. That is to say, each firm will produce at zero profits at the minimum point of its long-run average cost curve, but that is precisely a point at which cost per unit of output is neither rising nor falling, a point at which returns to scale may be said to be constant.

In an industry in which different firms are of different levels of efficiency this will be true only of the marginal firm, of course. All others will be earning positive profits and factor payments will not exhaust their revenues. There is no need to elaborate further on all this. We have already been through the analysis in some detail in Chapter 14. The important point to notice here is that whether or not factor payments exhaust the revenue of a perfectly competitive firm is a question that must be answered with reference to market behaviour and not just to the technical nature of the production function.

*The Firm's Factor Demand in the Long Run — A Formal Analysis

At several points in previous chapters (see for example Chapters 14, 16 and 18), we have referred to the solution of an enterprise's general maximisation problem, in which the firm chooses the level of production and the factors to be employed on the basis of output and input prices and its knowledge of production technology. In this section we provide an

algebraic representation of this problem and its solution, analogous to our previous uses of constrained optimisation to describe utility maximisation.
  The firm seeks to maximise

$$\pi = pX - rK - wL \tag{19.4}$$

subject to the production function

$$x = f(L,K) \tag{19.5}$$

We can therefore form the Lagrangian,

$$H_3 = pX - rK - wL + \lambda_3(f(L,K) - X) \tag{19.6}$$

with first-order conditions

$$\frac{\partial H_3}{\partial L} = -w + \lambda_3 \frac{\partial X}{\partial L} = 0 \tag{19.7}$$

$$\frac{\partial H_3}{\partial K} = -r + \lambda_3 \frac{\partial X}{\partial K} = 0 \tag{19.8}$$

$$\frac{\partial H_3}{\partial X} = p - \lambda_3 = 0 \tag{19.9}$$

$$\frac{\partial H_3}{\partial \lambda_3} = f(L,K) - X = 0 \tag{19.10}$$

From equation (19.9) we note that the Lagrange multiplier λ_3 is in fact equal to the output price. Substituting into (19.7) and (19.8) yields the conditions discussed less formally earlier.

$$p \frac{\partial X}{\partial L} = w \tag{19.11}$$

$$p \frac{\partial X}{\partial K} = r \tag{19.12}$$

Equation (19.11) is of course the same as (19.2), and with (19.12) states that profit-maximising competitive firms will hire inputs until the marginal revenue product of that input equals its price. To link the solution of the profit-maximisation problem ((19.4) and (19.5)) back to our previous formulation in terms of cost minimisation (see Chapter 12), we note that

$$\lambda_3 = \frac{r}{\partial X/\partial K} = \frac{w}{\partial X/\partial L} \tag{19.13}$$

which is identical to (12.9) and (12.19).

Equations (19.11) and (19.12) are implicit factor demand functions. We can make these functions explicit if we consider the special case of the Cobb–Douglas production function. Rather than re-solve the whole problem with $X = AL^{\alpha}K^{\beta}$ replacing $X = f(L,K)$ as equation (19.5), we can instead simply substitute the partial derivatives with respect to labour and capital into the first-order conditions (19.11) and (19.12). Since we know from Chapter 10 that $\partial X/\partial L = \alpha X/L$ and $\partial X/\partial K = \beta X/K$ if the production function is Cobb–Douglas, these two equations can be rewritten

$$p\frac{\alpha X}{L} = w$$

and $$p\frac{\beta X}{K} = r$$

which yield

$$L = p\frac{\alpha X}{w} \tag{19.14}$$

$$K = p\frac{\beta X}{r} \tag{19.15}$$

the labour and capital input demand equations. It can be seen by inspection that with this specification of technology, the demand for both factors *increases* with output and with output price, but *declines* with the price of the input. Previous chapters have stressed the first two relationships but here we shall concentrate on the third. Hence, denoting optimal values with a star, we can deduce that

$$\frac{\partial L^{\star}}{\partial w}, \ \frac{\partial K^{\star}}{\partial r} < 0 \tag{19.16}$$

i.e. that factor demands fall with their prices, holding output price and the volume of output constant. As we established previously, this point generalises to any production technology, provided only that the marginal physical product of the input diminishes as the input increases.

We now offer a formal analysis of how the firm adjusts inputs in response to a change in their price — the comparative statics of factor demand. Consider the two first-order conditions,

$$p\frac{\partial X}{\partial L} - w = 0 \tag{19.11'}$$

$$p\frac{\partial X}{\partial K} - r = 0 \tag{19.12'}$$

If we take a total differential of these two equations, allowing both capital and labour to vary, we derive

$$\frac{\partial X}{\partial L} dp + p \frac{\partial^2 X}{\partial L^2} dL + p \frac{\partial^2 X}{\partial L \partial K} dK - dw = 0 \qquad (19.17)$$

$$\frac{\partial X}{\partial K} dp + p \frac{\partial^2 X}{\partial K \partial L} dL + p \frac{\partial^2 X}{\partial K^2} dK - dr = 0 \qquad (19.18)$$

From (19.18)

$$dK = \frac{dr - \dfrac{\partial X}{\partial K} dp - p \dfrac{\partial^2 X}{\partial K \partial L} dL}{p \partial^2 X / \partial K^2}$$

Substituting for dK in (19.17),

$$\frac{\partial X}{\partial L} dp + p \frac{\partial^2 X}{\partial L^2} dL - dw + \frac{\partial^2 X}{\partial L \partial K} \frac{\partial K^2}{\partial^2 X} dr - \frac{\partial^2 X}{\partial L \partial K} \frac{\partial K^2}{\partial^2 X} \frac{\partial X}{\partial K} dp$$

$$- p \frac{\partial^2 X}{\partial L \partial K} p \frac{\partial^2 X}{\partial L \partial K} \frac{\partial K^2}{p \partial^2 X} dL = 0$$

yields

$$dp \left(\frac{\partial X}{\partial L} - \frac{\partial^2 X}{\partial L \partial K} \frac{\partial K^2}{\partial^2 X} \frac{\partial X}{\partial K} \right) - dw + \left(\frac{\partial^2 X}{\partial L \partial K} \frac{\partial K^2}{\partial^2 X} \right) dr$$

$$+ dL \left(p \frac{\partial^2 X}{\partial L^2} - p \left(\frac{\partial^2 X}{\partial L \partial K} \right)^2 \frac{\partial K^2}{p \partial^2 X} \right) = 0$$

Multiplying through by $p \partial^2 X / \partial K^2$ yields

$$p \frac{\partial^2 X}{\partial K^2} \left(\frac{\partial X}{\partial L} - \frac{\partial^2 X}{\partial L \partial K} \frac{\partial K^2}{\partial^2 X} \frac{\partial X}{\partial K} \right) dp - p \frac{\partial^2 X}{\partial K^2} dw + p \frac{\partial^2 X}{\partial L \partial K} dr$$

$$+ \left(p^2 \cdot \frac{\partial^2 X}{\partial L^2} \frac{\partial^2 X}{\partial K^2} - p^2 \left(\frac{\partial^2 X}{\partial L \partial K} \right)^2 \right) \partial L = 0 \qquad (19.19)$$

If we first consider the effect of an increase in wages on employment in the long run, on the assumption that prices and capital costs remain constant, i.e. $dp = dr = 0$, (19.9) simplifies to

$$p \frac{\partial^2 X}{\partial K^2} dw - \left(p^2 \frac{\partial^2 X}{\partial L^2} \frac{\partial^2 X}{\partial K^2} - p^2 \left(\frac{\partial^2 X}{\partial L \partial K} \right)^2 \right) dL = 0$$

so that

$$\frac{dL}{dw} = p \frac{\partial^2 X / \partial K^2}{D} \tag{19.20}$$

where $D = \left(p^2 \frac{\partial^2 X}{\partial L^2} \frac{\partial^2 X}{\partial K^2} - p^2 \left(\frac{\partial^2 X}{\partial L \partial K} \right)^2 \right)$

Equation (19.20), describing the behaviour of the competitive firm in response to a change in wages, can be given a simple intuition. Starting with the term D in equation (19.20), we know that if there are diminishing returns to any factor, its marginal product declines with output. Hence, since second-order conditions require diminishing returns to each factor, we know that $\partial^2 X / \partial K^2$, $\partial^2 X / \partial L^2 < 0$ and their product, $(\partial^2 X / \partial L^2)$ $(\partial^2 X / \partial K^2)$ must therefore always be positive. But, whatever the sign of the cross partial derivative $(\partial^2 X / \partial L \partial K)$, its square must always be positive, and output price too is always assumed to be greater than zero, so the sign of D is thus at first sight indeterminate. However, as is established in most texts in mathematical economics (see the references at the end of this part of the book), and as mathematically inclined readers may wish to prove for themselves, second-order conditions imply that,

$$D > 0 \tag{19.21}$$

This condition can be interpreted as showing that in equilibrium, profits must be decreasing with respect to changes in both capital and labour. Hence, given (19.20), we know that employment will always be decreased if the wage is increased, provided only that the production function is concave. Hence we have deduced that if equilibrium employment is L^*,

$$\frac{dL^*}{dW} < 0$$

provided

$$\partial^2 X / \partial K^2 < 0 \text{ and } D > 0$$

The impact on the demand for one input of a change in the price of another can be evaluated by considering dL/dr from equation (19.19) on the assumption that $dp = dw = 0$. We therefore derive

$$p \frac{\partial^2 X}{\partial L \partial K} dr + \left(p^2 \frac{\partial^2 X}{\partial L^2} \frac{\partial^2 X}{\partial K^2} - p^2 \left(\frac{\partial^2 X}{\partial L \partial K} \right)^2 \right) dL = 0 \tag{19.22}$$

Hence

$$\frac{dL}{dr} = \frac{-p(\partial^2 X)/(\partial L \partial K)}{D} \gtrless 0 \text{ as } \frac{\partial^2 X}{\partial L \partial K} \gtrless 0 \tag{19.23}$$

This ties down our previous informal discussion of 'inferior inputs', where we identified the determining role of the cross partial derivative on the

effect of an increase in one input price on the demand for another input. If we assume that an increase in the quantity of one input increases the marginal product of the other, i.e. $\partial^2 X/\partial L \partial K > 0$, then increases in the first input price will reduce the demand for the second input. However, in the case of an 'inferior' input, when $\partial^2 X/\partial L \partial K < 0$ and the marginal product of one factor declines with increasing usage of the other, input demand will actually increase with increases in the price of the other.

Concluding Comment

We have so far discussed the theory of the demand for factors of production solely from the point of view of perfect competition. Just as dropping the assumption of perfect competition led us to modify our analysis of price/output behaviour, so our analysis of the demand for factors of production changes somewhat when we depart from perfectly competitive assumptions. We will take up some of the major problems involved here in the next chapter.

20

The Demand for Factors of Production: Monopoly and Monopsony

Factor Demand under Monopoly

For the product market monopolist, just as for the perfectly competitive firm, the demand for factors arises as a corollary of profit-maximising price and output decisions, and not as the solution to some separate and distinct set of problems. Moreoever, the basic nature of the decision is the same as that of the competitive firm. The employment of any factor of production will be expanded just as long as profits are increased by so doing, that is to say, as long as the expansion adds more to revenue than it does to costs. In short, the condition that marginal revenue product be equal to marginal factor costs underlies the monopolist's demand for factors just as it does that of the competitive firm, and is but another way of stating the product market condition that marginal cost should be equal to marginal revenue.

The Monopolist's Factor Demand Curves

However, this is not to say that the monopolist's behaviour does not differ at all from that of a competitive firm. If the monopolist is a price taker in the market for factor inputs, and their supply price does not vary with the quantity purchased, then the market price of the input is equal to marginal factor cost, and this side of the market is the same as it was in our analysis of the competitive firm. To the competitive firm though, the price of output and marginal revenue are identical. Thus the short-run

demand curve for the factor which related its marginal revenue product to the quantity of it utilised was obtained by multiplying the factor's marginal physical product by a constant output price. Marginal revenue product was equivalent to the value of the factor's marginal product. To the monopolist, price declines with output, and marginal revenue is less than price. The value of the marginal product of a factor of production employed by a monopolist is obviously marginal product multiplied by price, but marginal revenue product is obtained by multiplying marginal physical product by marginal revenue. The two magnitudes are different for a monopolist, marginal revenue product being always the lower of the two.

Figure 20.1 shows the two relationships, the difference between them reflecting in the factor market the gap between the price of output and the marginal revenue accruing from the sale of one extra unit of output. If the demand curve for output faced by the monopolist was the same as that which would be faced by a competitive industry, the production function was the same as would characterise that industry; and the wage rate w_1 was the same as would face a competitive industry, then such a competitive industry's short-run demand curve for labour would be given by the value of the marginal product curve in Figure 20.1 and its employment of labour would be equal to L_2 instead of L_1, the quantity employed by the monopolist. This tendency of the monopolist to curtail the use of factor inputs relative to what might be demanded by a competitive industry is simply a reflection in the factor market of the tendency to restrict output relative to a level that would be realised by a competitive industry, noted in Chapter 15.

Figure 20.1

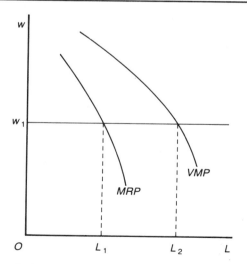

For a monopolist, marginal revenue is below output price. Hence the marginal revenue product or *MRP* (marginal physical product times marginal revenue) of a factor is below the value of its marginal product or *VMP* (marginal physical product times output price).

There is little to be said about the monopolist in the long run. The demand for a particular factor may be more or less elastic in the long run than in the short run, depending upon the outcome of two competing tendencies. A fall in the price of one factor leads to more of it being used and hence raises the marginal physical product of the other factor. It also leads to increased output and lower marginal revenue. The net effect of these competing tendencies can lead either to an increase or a decrease in the quantity of the other factor employed. Thus a monopolist's long-run demand curve for a factor of production may either be more or less elastic than the short-run relationship.

Finally, it should be noted that the question of factor payments exhausting revenue does not arise in the context of monopoly. If it just happens that the monopolist's profit-maximising price for output equals long-run average cost of production, then factor payments will equal revenue. If positive profits are made then they obviously will not. As with perfect competition, what happens in this regard is a matter of the firm's behaviour and not simply of the nature of the production function.

*A Formal Treatment

In Chapter 16, we referred to the general maximisation problem for the firm in imperfect competition choosing its factor inputs simultaneously with its output. In this section we offer a formal treatment of that problem, analogous to that undertaken for the competitive firm in the previous chapter. Instead of choosing output levels to maximise profits, as in equations (15.7)−(15.12), we focus instead on the choice of inputs, K and L. The optimisation problem is therefore to maximise

$$\pi = pX - wL - rK \tag{20.1}$$

subject to

$$X = f(L, K) \tag{20.2}$$

and $$p = p(X) \tag{20.3}$$

Rather than once again solving the full constrained optimisation problem by forming a Lagrangian, in this case we illustrate an important simplification. The constrained problem can be simplified to an unconstrained problem by substituting equations (20.2) and (20.3) into (20.1), yielding

$$\pi = p(X)f(L, K) - wL - rK \tag{20.4}$$

This can be maximised with respect to L and K, without reference to the output decision. In effect this is the approach we used in our formal treatment of the labour-managed firm in Chapter 18. This approach yields first-order conditions

$$\frac{\partial \pi}{\partial L} = \frac{\partial p}{\partial X}\frac{\partial X}{\partial L}X + p\frac{\partial X}{\partial L} - w = 0 \tag{20.5}$$

and

$$\frac{\partial \pi}{\partial K} = \frac{\partial p}{\partial X}\frac{\partial X}{\partial K} X + p\frac{\partial X}{\partial K} - r = 0 \tag{20.6}$$

Hence $\left(p + X\frac{\partial p}{\partial X}\right)\frac{\partial X}{\partial L} = w$ (20.7)

and $\left(p + X\frac{\partial p}{\partial X}\right)\frac{\partial X}{\partial K} = r$ (20.8)

are the hiring equations for labour and capital respectively. As noted in Chapter 13, the expression $(p+X\partial p/\partial X)$ is marginal revenue, which is everywhere less than price because the demand curve slopes down $(\partial p/\partial X < 0)$. Equations (20.7) and (20.8) are therefore the counterparts for the monopolistic case of the competitive first-order conditions derived in the last chapter, namely equations (19.11) and (19.12). They state that factors will be hired until their marginal revenue product is equal to the cost of hiring them. Because $(p+X\partial p/\partial X) < p$ for all X, the factor demand implied by a given value of the input price is always less under monopoly than competition.

Monopsony

The analysis carried out so far has been of the demand side of the market for a factor of production; and whether the firm under consideration is a competitor (as in the last chapter) or a monopolist (as in this one), as far as the market for output is concerned, the assumption has been made throughout that factor inputs are purchased competitively. That is to say, each firm we have considered has been assumed able to buy as much as it pleases of any factor of production at a given price, a price presumably determined in some broader market for the factor in question of which the firm under analysis makes up a small part. In other words the firm faces a horizontal supply curve of the factor.

There is no need to restrict our analysis of factor markets to such a situation any more than, when discussing product markets, it was necessary to restrict ourselves to dealing with a firm which could sell all it pleased at a given price. Just as we can think of a particular seller of a product being faced with a downward-sloping demand curve for output, so we can think of a particular purchaser of a factor of production being faced with an upward-sloping supply curve for that input, so that the price paid for the input varies with the quantity purchased. Such a purchaser is called a *monopsonist*.

Faced with an upward-sloping factor supply curve, the firm must distinguish between the price (i.e. the average cost) of the factor on the one hand, and the marginal cost of obtaining it on the other. The total factor outlay curve associated with the horizontal supply curve that

underlay the analysis of the last chapter would clearly be a straight line through the origin. Figure 20.2 shows an upward-sloping factor supply curve (a straight line for simplicity) — which may be termed an *average factor outlay* (or *average factor cost*) curve — as well as the associated total factor outlay curve. Total factor cost here increases at an increasing rate with the quantity of the input purchased, and the slope of the total factor cost curve is everywhere steeper than the slope of a straight line drawn to it from the origin. That is to say, *marginal factor cost* everywhere lies above the market price of the factor. Though Figures 20.2 and 20.3 show the relationship in question for the special case of an upward-sloping, but linear, factor supply curve, the reader must bear in mind that its properties, though analytically very convenient, are those of a case that is every bit as special as the straight line demand curve which we used in Chapter 15 when we considered the behaviour of a monopoly seller of a good.

The profit-maximising firm will purchase that flow of inputs for which marginal revenue product equals marginal factor outlay and will choose the price which it pays for that quantity as the minimum which it needs to pay in order to obtain it; that is to say, the price it pays will be given by the factor supply curve. All this is shown in Figure 20.3 with L_1 units of labour being employed at a wage rate of w_1. Just as it is inappropriate to refer to the monopolist's marginal cost curve as a supply curve since it does not relate quantity supplied to price, so it is inappropriate to refer to the monopsonist's marginal revenue product curve as a demand curve for a factor. A further parallel with monopoly in the product market is worth noting here: as compared to perfect competition, monopsony leads to a restriction of input use just as monopoly leads to a restriction of output. Figure 20.4 shows the combined effects of these tendencies for a firm that is both monopolist in its product market and monopsonist

Figure 20.2

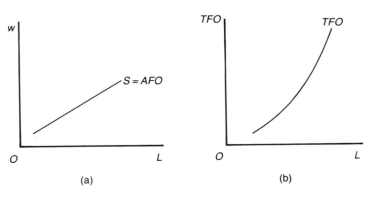

(a)   (b)

(a) An upward-sloping supply curve of labour yields (b) a total factor outlay curve that slopes upwards at an increasing rate. Hence, marginal factor outlay lies above the factor supply curve.

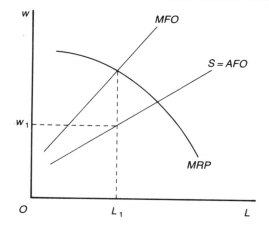

Figure 20.3

A monopsonist equates marginal factor outlay to marginal revenue product in order to determine the profit-maximising level of employment for a factor, L_1 in this case, paying it the wage rate given for that quantity by the supply curve, w_1 in this case.

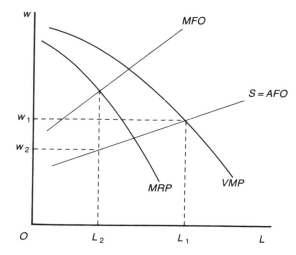

Figure 20.4

A monopsonist in a factor market who is also a monopolist in the product market employs less labour at a lower wage than would a competitive industry. The latter would equate the value of labour's marginal product to the wage rate and would employ L_1 at a wage rate of w_1, while the former equates marginal factor outlay to marginal revenue product, thus employing L_2 of labour at w_2.

in its factor market. Perfect competition in both markets would result in the market price of the factor being set at w_1 and L_1 of it being employed. The combination of monopoly and monopsony results in a lower price of the factor (w_2) and a smaller quantity of it being utilised (L_2).

Discriminating Monopsony

As readers may well have suspected, the parallels between product market monopoly and factor market monopsony run further than we have so far taken them. Thus, we can have discriminating monopsony in the factor market. Consider a situation in which a monopsonist has two sources of supply for a particular factor input, sources of supply that can be kept separate in the sense that it is impossible for the owners of the services from one source to begin to provide them instead by way of the other source. Then, as we show in Figure 20.5, it will pay our monopsonist to equate the marginal costs of obtaining the factor from each source of supply and this will result in different prices being paid to factors obtained from the two sources.

The argument here is exactly parallel to that already set out when we discussed the price and output behaviour of a discriminating monopolist. Suppose our monopsonist initially was unable to discriminate between the two sources of supply. The same price would then have to be paid to each unit of the factor regardless of where it was bought. But the marginal cost of obtaining an extra unit of input from market 1 is, in these circumstances, higher than it is in market 2. If the monopsonist acquires the power to pay different prices in the two markets, profits can be increased by reducing purchases in the first market and increasing purchases in the second, thus cutting down on the total outlay on this

Figure 20.5

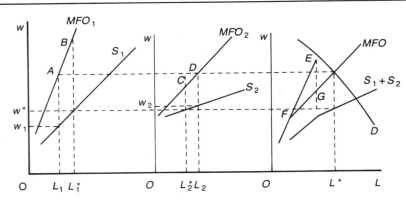

A firm which buys its labour in two markets will employ L^* units of it at a wage of w^* if it cannot discriminate between markets. If it can discriminate, it will equate marginal factor outlay in the two markets. The wage rate will fall to w_1 in the first market with employment falling from L_1^* to L_1; in the second market, wages will rise to w_2 and employment will expand from L_2^* to L_2. The overall level of employment will remain the same, the increase in expenditure on labour in the second market is given by $CDL_2L_2^*$, and the cut in expenditure in the first market is $ABL_1^*L_1$. The gain in profits from being able to discriminate is given by the difference between these two areas, or equivalently by the area EFG which is the difference between the area under the marginal factor outlay curve that corresponds to the summed factor supply curves of the two markets — which is relevant in the no discrimination case — and the area under the summed marginal factor cost curves of the two markets, which is relevant when discrimination takes place.

particular factor without reducing the quantity of it available for employment. As readers will see from Figure 20.5, this results in the factor price being lower in the market where the elasticity of supply is lower.

It is often asserted that discriminatory wage fixing in the labour market between men and women may be explained by the fact that women, having fewer alternatives for employment than men, face any potential employer with a less elastic supply curve for their services. However, other factors contributing to lower productivity on the part of female workers must also be taken into account before concluding that wage differentials between men and women in the same occupation are to be taken as *prima facie* evidence of the existence of discriminating monopsony.

Now the price discrimination in the factor market just discussed is a particular kind of price discrimination. Factor markets apparently provide scope for paying a particular provider of a factor service a different price for different units of it. Overtime payment arrangements for workers are an example of such behaviour. We have already analysed certain aspects of such behaviour in Chapter 5. As with perfect price discrimination in the product market (see Chapter 15), the more finely monopsonists can separate from one another the services they are buying, and pay a different price for each of them, the more closely will the quantity of the input bought approach the competitive solution. In terms of Figure 20.4, a perfectly discriminating monopsonist would buy L_1 of labour, paying w_1 for only the last unit of it, and lower prices for each intermediate unit, always provided the output market was competitive.

Concluding Comment

In this and the previous chapter we have been concerned with the demand for factors of production, and the determination of their prices, and have simply taken supply conditions for granted. Of course we have already said something about supply-side considerations in Part II. The general decision as to whether to work or not, and for how long (Chapter 5) is clearly one element that underlies the supply of labour to a particular firm or industry. Similarly, capital equipment cannot be made available for leasing out to firms unless someone refrains from current consumption in order to acquire such equipment. Thus, the analysis of saving behaviour set out in Chapter 6 is of some relevance in dealing with the supply of capital equipment to particular firms or industries. However, when the decision to work has been taken, or the decision to acquire savings, and hence perhaps capital equipment, there still remains the issue of whom to work for, and to whom to rent capital equipment. Thus, we still need to say something about influences on the supply of factors of production to particular firms and industries. This topic provides the subject matter of the next chapter. We consider institutions on the supply side of the labour market in more detail in Chapter 22.

21

Some Aspects of the Theory of Factor Supply

Introduction

In the last two chapters we have analysed various aspects of the theory of the demand for factors of production. Of course the price of a particular productive input, just like that of any output, is determined by the interaction of both demand and supply-side considerations. We have dealt with the firm's demand and the industry's demand for factors of production, very much taking the supply side of the market for granted. In this chapter we consider the supply side of the factor market in more detail.

Flows, Stocks and their Relationship

Recall at the outset the nature of the units in which we measure factor inputs. The production function relates a flow of output to a flow of inputs. Labour is measured in units such as man-hours per week, capital in terms of machine-hours per week, and so on. The demand for factors discussed in the last two chapters has also been for inputs measured in such units. However, when we think of the level of employment of labour in a firm or industry, or the amount of capital it utilises, we usually think in terms of stocks: the number of men and women on the payroll, or the number of machines of particular types that the firm has on hand. Clearly, a given increase in inputs to production may be realised in many ways: by working the existing stock, be it capital or labour, more intensively; by increasing the stock and working each unit at the same rate as before; or by some combination of the two. Similarly, the flow of inputs can be reduced by short-time working, by reduction of the number of employees

344

and machines, or by a combination of these methods. The analysis of the last two chapters, which implicitly assumed that there was one and only one way to increase or decrease the quantity of any input, and one price — or marginal factor cost — at which this was possible, greatly simplified the nature of the problem that any firm has to solve.

There is no reason why the costs of obtaining more inputs by taking on more employees, or by buying more machines, should be the same as those involved in lengthening working hours. For example, to get more capital services by utilising a given stock of machines more intensively might involve maintenance difficulties; buying new machines might involve the firm in costs of ordering and installing them. On the labour side, the cost involved in inducing workers to put in more hours may be a higher overtime wage rate, but associated with an addition to the labour force in a firm are administrative costs having to do with each employee's tax and social security contributions etc.

We raise these problems now although we are not going to go on and analyse them. Nevertheless, the reader ought to be aware that a whole set of interesting economic problems is involved if one is to proceed carefully from an analysis of the demand for the services of factors of production to conclusions about the level of employment, in any firm or industry, of labour or of machines or indeed of any other stock that yields a flow of productive services. As before, so in this chapter we will make the simplifying assumption that there is a unique relationship between the number of employees which a firm or industry has and the hours of labour services which go into its production process, and we shall make a similar assumption about the relationship between capital inputs and the stock of machines. Thus, when we talk about the supply and demand for labour, we talk of both hours and people, and when we talk about capital we talk about machine-hours and machines. This will greatly simplify the exposition of the following analysis without, it is hoped, making it also too misleading. Nevertheless, a whole set of interesting problems is bypassed by making this assumption.

Supply to the Firm and the Industry

With this caveat in mind then, let us consider the factors that determine the nature of the supply curve of a productive input. The first question that must come to mind is surely 'supply to whom?' We must distinguish between the supply curve of an input as it appears from the point of view of a particular firm, of an industry and, indeed, of the economy in general, given that not working is a viable alternative for some inputs.

The more narrowly we define the entity to which factor services are being supplied, the more alternatives there are open to their owners and hence, one would suppose, the more elastic the supply curve. Thus, if we consider by way of example the supply curve of a particular type of

labour to a typical perfectly competitive firm, each worker has the alternative of working for some other firm in the same industry at the going wage rate. If the firm is indeed 'typical' of the industry, there is no reason why any worker should have a preference for working for this firm rather than any other, and hence there is no reason to accept a lower wage in order to work for it. Nor, of course, is there any reason why any worker in the industry should remain with any other firm if the one whose supply curve we are studying were to be paying even slightly more than the going wage rate. In short, one would expect the supply curve of labour to this particular firm, and to every other in the industry, to be perfectly elastic at the going market wage rate.

There is nothing specific to the behaviour of labour in this analysis. One can equally well think of the owners of machines, or factory buildings, or land, or any other productive resource, deciding to whom to lease that resource and, if they have no reason to prefer one firm in the industry to another, a perfectly elastic supply curve at the going payment rate for the resource will be the result in the long run. The argument here is, as the reader will have realised, exactly parallel to the reasoning that underlies the perfect elasticity of the demand curve that faces the perfectly competitive firm in the output market. In the short run, obviously, such inputs cannot so readily be transferred from one firm to another, so that the short-run supply curve of inputs even to a single firm might have a positive slope to it (indeed, being vertical in the limit), this supply curve becoming horizontal as time passes.

When we come to look at factor supply from the point of view of the industry, matters immediately become more complex. We cannot easily ignore the possibility that the owners of a particular resource might have a personal preference for having it used in one industry rather than in another. The most obvious reasons for such preferences arise when we consider labour, for conditions of work may be more pleasant in one industry than in another; though such differences can exist between firms in the same industry, they are likely to be greater and hence more important across industrial boundaries. Moreover, what are or are not 'pleasant' working conditions is to some degree a matter of taste for the individual worker, involving preferences for the type of work, etc., and tastes are likely to differ in this respect.

Though differences of taste about employment are most obviously relevant in the case of labour, they can also affect the choices made by owners of other factors when they decide to which industry they might be allocated. Thus, the owners of a hall (to pick a less usual example) may have a taste for the performing arts that would lead to them permitting it to be used for live performances of plays or classical music at a lower rent than would be required for it to be used as a cinema or a bingo hall.

Furthermore, differences in the alternatives available elsewhere, to what, from the point to view of one particular industry, are different units of the same input, might affect its elasticity of supply. Just because two

units of a resource are equally productive in one industry does not mean that they are equally productive in alternative uses. Two halls may be equally suitable for bingo, but because of their acoustic properties only one might be a viable theatre. Two people may be equally productive as pop singers, but because of differences in education may have completely different alternative job opportunities: one might otherwise be a lawyer, and the other a lorry driver.

Transfer Price and Rent

Thus, some resources are more specific to a particular industry than others, and some will work in a particular industry at a lower rate of payment than others, either because of a subjective preference for employment in that industry on the part of their owners, or as a result of an objective inability to work more productively elsewhere. We call the price at which a particular unit of a resource will come into industry its *transfer price* or *transfer earnings* to that industry. We would expect this price to rise *on the margin* as more resources are brought in to any particular industry, those whose owners find it particularly congenial to be in that industry being available at a lower price than those for which there are more attractive alternatives.

Now given a competitive industry demand curve, the equilibrium price of any factor in a particular use is determined. As should be apparent from Figure 21.1, at this equilibrium price only the marginal unit of the resource is being paid its transfer price — indeed this statement is just a way of defining the term *marginal unit*. Every other unit is being paid more than would be necessary to keep it in this particular use. The amount

Figure 21.1

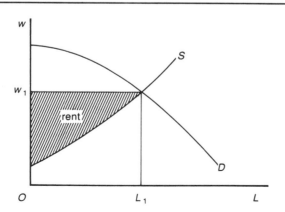

The demand for and supply of labour to a particular competitive industry. The L_1th worker is being paid exactly transfer earnings. At any wage below w_1 he or she would leave the industry, and is the marginal worker at that wage. The shaded area represents the total amount of payments to labour that represent rents, payments above transfer earnings.

by which the price it receives exceeds its transfer price is called a 'rent'. There is a close relationship between such a 'rent' and the notion of consumer's surplus which we explored earlier in this book. Consumers of a good receives a 'surplus' from being able to obtain all but the last unit of it at a price below the maximum which they would be willing to pay to obtain them; the owners of a productive resource receives a rent because they are paid more for the services of that resource than the minimum price at which they would be willing to provide them to a particular industry. Just as discriminating monopolists appropriate some or all of the available consumer surplus to themselves, so clearly would a discriminating monopsonist be appropriating rents to itself.

Now how much of the payment to a particular factor of production is made up to transfer earnings and how much of rent clearly depends upon the elasticity of its supply curve. As we have seen in our analysis of the firm, a perfectly elastic supply curve involves all factor payments being transfer earnings; and at the opposite extreme, a perfectly inelastic supply curve would mean that all payments are rents, for the resource would be available in the same quantity even at zero price. These two extreme cases are depicted in Figure 21.2.

Quasi-Rent

When might a resource be in completely inelastic supply to a particular industry? Only when it is specific to the technology of that industry and has no alternative use elsewhere. Readers will recall that in the short run, the quantities of some productive resources available to any particular firm are fixed. From the point of view of their owners then, they cannot be moved elsewhere and hence have no alternative use. In the short run,

Figure 21.2

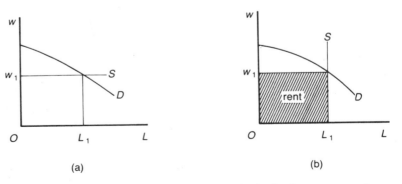

(a) When the supply of labour to an industry is perfectly elastic all wage payments are transfer earnings. (b) When the supply is perfectly inelastic all payments are rents since a perfectly inelastic supply curve implies that all workers in the industry would be there even for zero wages.

the income accruing to them has the character of a rent. In the long run, of course, the owners of such resources can move them in and out of particular uses and considerations of transfer earnings enter into the determination of their earnings in any use. Hence, returns to factors fixed in the short run are often referred to as *quasi-rents*. As far as capital equipment is concerned, the rental price to be paid for it is a fixed cost in the short run, and a firm whose quasi-rents are insufficient to meet this fixed cost is making a loss. To the extent that the rental price of capital equipment represents a 'normal' rate of return to the owner of the equipment, then it is apparent that 'making a loss' and 'making less than a normal rate of return' are synonymous phrases.

Though it is usual to think of such factors as machinery as being the inputs whose services yield quasi-rents in the short run, the same concept is also helpful in dealing with labour income. Labour services, after all, are not some kind of homogeneous raw input. They consist of the application of many different kinds of skills to the production process, skills that can only be acquired by the worker making an investment of time and trouble, to say nothing in some cases of forgone income, in their acquisition.

To the extent that a worker's skills are specific to the production process of a particular firm, the return to that skill in the short run is just as much a quasi-rent as is the return to a machine; the alternative is not to utilise the skill. Thus the difference between earnings as a skilled worker and as an unskilled worker is a quasi-rent accruing to the specific skill. If that skill is specific to a particular industry and there is short-run mobility of workers between firms then, from the point of view of any firm, the wages represent transfer earnings, though from the point of view of the industry they contain an element of a quasi-rent. Now all this amounts to is saying that for some problems it is illuminating to treat the ownership of skills by a worker as analogous to the ownership of machines: to treat these skills as *human capital* and to view their acquisition as an act of investment.

Factor Prices and the Distribution of Income

In this chapter, we have been concerned with the supply of factors of production to firms and industries. In the last chapter we dealt with the demand for factors of production. Hence we have the ingredients of a theory of factor prices and hence of factor incomes. Is this theory sufficient to tell us about the distribution of income? The brief answer to this question is: between factors, yes, but between people, no. We have the ingredients of a theory of the *functional* distribution of income, but not of the *personal* distribution. Before one can say anything about the distribution of income among people on the basis of a theory of factor pricing,

we must have a theory which explains how the ownership of factors of production is distributed among people.

The theory alluded to above that treats the acquisition of particular productive skills as investment in human capital tells us something about the way in which the ownership of labour services might be acquired. Moreover, the acquisition of machinery and such, as well as that of human capital, requires that current consumption be deferred. Hence the elementary analysis of saving behaviour set out in Chapter 6 is also relevant to the theory of factor ownership. Though we may have acquired some insights into some of the matters which will influence it, we are far from being able to produce a coherent overall model for the distribution of income between people. Readers should not expect too much from the analysis developed in this book in attempting to understand the overall distribution of income among people in any economy.

However, this is not to say that distribution is an unimportant matter for economics, just that it is not thoroughly understood. As we shall see in the final part of this book, where we deal with the workings of the economic system as a whole, questions concerning distribution are an important element to be taken into account when we try to appraise the success or otherwise of the way in which a market economy works, and put an important limit on the amount that we can say about such matters.

22

The Economic Analysis of Trade Unions

Introduction

In previous chapters we have analysed factor markets in general, but have not considered in any practical detail the operation of actual input markets, either for capital or for labour. Some issues concerning the functioning of the capital market have, however, already been raised in Chapter 6. Our purpose in this chapter is to focus on the labour market, taking explicitly into account from the outset the existence of one of its more notable institutions, trade unions. The supply and demand apparatus that we have built up in previous chapters will form the basis for our analysis of how trade unions − institutions operating on the supply side of the labour market − influence the determination of wages and employment.

Alongside firms, trade unions are among the most pervasive institutions formed by economic agents in pursuit of their economic interests. In 1980, some 50 per cent of the labour force was unionised in the United Kingdom, 40 per cent in West Germany, 31 per cent in Japan and 50 per cent in Italy, though it had declined to below 40 per cent in the UK by 1987. As with firms, our analysis will concentrate on what unions do, rather than why people form them, though the positive wage differential paid to unionised workers which we derive in the models which follow might give a clue here. Our main purpose in this chapter is to analyse the determination of employment and wages in the presence of unions. Since unions are such an important feature of most Western economies, our analysis of factor markets would be seriously incomplete without such a discussion.

Trade unions are of course complex organisations operating at many

levels and with objectives in the social and political as well as the economic sphere. It may therefore at first appear that, while trade unions are too important a form of economic organisation to ignore, they are also too complicated to analyse with the narrow tools of economics. One thing we hope to show in this chapter is just how far even simple tools of economic analysis can in fact take our understanding of relatively sophisticated (and to some extent non-economic) organisations such as unions.

An Overview of Union Behaviour

Unions are formed by workers to influence the rates of pay and the level of employment in a firm, an industry or even perhaps the economy as a whole. In a competitive industry made up of identical firms, however, we know that, if they operate at the level of the firm, unions will be unable to affect the competitive equilibrium. If technology is freely available, any firms which agree to higher pay for unionised workers will be driven out of business because they will face higher costs than their competitors. Hence, unions can influence equilibrium outcomes only if there are intra-marginal profits (or rents as they are sometimes called) available to be distributed. For example, if a competitive industry's output supply curve is upward sloping because the lowest cost technology is not freely available to every entrant, rents will be available in intra-marginal firms. Perhaps more realistically for our purposes, rents will also be available when product markets are imperfect and in particular when they are monopolised. It will be helpful to begin with the case in which a trade union faces a single employer in an industry, but it must be stressed that the essential feature sustaining the emergence and existence of the union is the existence of rents in the industry, initially appropriated entirely by the producer, but in principle partially available to workers through the exercise of bargaining power by their trade union. A product market monopoly simply provides a special case of this general situation.

In our analysis of output markets, we distinguished between traditional models of imperfect competition, and more recent treatments of oligopoly which have arisen from the application of game theory. As we shall explain below, a parallel dichotomy arises in the economic analysis of trade unions. Traditional models begin with the perception of the union as a monopolist on the supply side of the labour market, while more recent models based on game theory explicitly take account of the bargaining process between management and unions. The former approach extends the analysis of Chapters 19 and 20; the latter parallels the analysis set out in Chapter 17.

As we mentioned above, one way to view a union is as analogous on the labour supply side to a monopolist in the product market who faces a given demand curve. The resulting model is referred to as the *monopoly*

union model, and provides the framework of analysis for the first part of this chapter. The traditional model of the monopoly firm has it setting output price, and permitting output to be determined on the demand curve. A monopoly union is thought of as setting the wage, and allowing the employer to choose labour input as its profit-maximising level. In contrast, *bargaining models* assume that unions have control over employment as well as wages, and are therefore able to push firms off their labour demand curves in order to achieve mutually beneficial collusive outcomes. Wage and employment determination in bargaining models are discussed in the second part of this chapter.

Basic Analysis of the Monopoly Union Model

In the monopoly model the union is assumed to operate by restricting the supply of labour to the firm so as to ensure that, in order to obtain labour, the firm must pay the union determined wage. The mechanisms whereby the supply of labour can be restricted by a union range from direct control of employment, as in the cases of doctors, actors and, until recently printers, through the exercise of social pressure which prevents workers from offering to supply labour at below the union rate, to strike activity. Whatever the mechanism, in the monopoly union framework the union sets the wage, and the firm in effect faces a supply of labour curve which is perfectly elastic at that wage.

Now of course a union could not attract members if the *union wage*, let us call it w_u, was not higher than workers could obtain elsewhere. This latter level of pay we term the *alternative wage*, w_a. Depending on the nature of the broader economy in which the union operates, this alternative wage could represent the level of pay available to workers in non-unionised sectors, or, if the entire economy is unionised, the level of unemployment benefit. For present purposes, the key point is that we presume the union is always able to maintain pay above the alternative wage,

$$w_u > w_a \tag{22.1}$$

How then, does the union choose its desired wage level, w_u? If a monopoly union was interested in the level of wages alone, it would be able to raise them to any value that it wished (subject to the constraint imposed by the employer's demand for labour). Simple wage maximisation would lead to the absurd outcome of the industry employing only one worker for an essentially infinitessimal period of time per week, with the wage paid equalling the intercept of the labour demand curve with the wage axis. Here, though, the benefits to prospective members in terms of wages are obviously more than offset by losses in terms of employment. This argument tells us that union will be interested in employment

as well as pay targets, and that they might be viewed as maximising a utility function (U^u) in wages and employment, of the form

$$U^u = U(w,L) \tag{22.2}$$

Here we assume that the marginal utility the union gains from both wages and employment is positive but diminishing in the conventional way (see Chapter 2). This preference function can be represented by standard convex-to-the-origin indifference curves, such as I_1, I_2 and I_3 in Figure 22.1. The monopolist's demand for labour curve, which as we showed in Chapter 20 is its marginal revenue product curve (*mrp*), represents the constraint on the union's wage–employment choice. The outcome of the union's maximisation problem is at the tangency between the union's indifference curve and the firm's labour demand curve. The union will therefore fix its wage at w_u which is, by assumption, higher than the alternative wage w_a. The effective labour supply curve faced by the firm is $w_u w_u$, and it chooses employment L_u, just the amount desired by the union.

Wage Bill Maximisation

The foregoing analysis is interesting as far as it goes, but it does not go very far. In particular it says next to nothing about the shape of the union's

Figure 22.1

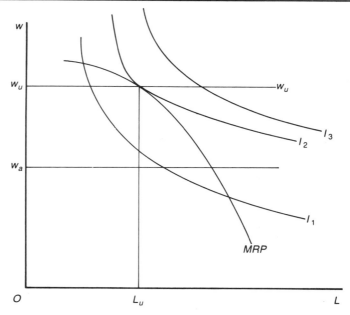

The monopoly union equilibrium is (w_u, L_u) at the tangency of the union indifference curve between wages and employment and the monopolist's labour demand curve, *MRP*. The union wage is assumed to exceed the alternative wage, w_a.

preferences. A number of attempts have been made to specify the union's objectives more precisely. Thus John Dunlop proposed, as a rough and ready approximation, that unions seek to maximise the wage bill paid to their members. The utility function in this case takes the form

$$U^u = w_u L \tag{22.3}$$

The implications of this hypothesis are illustrated in Figure 22.2. The rectangle formed by the choice of any wage—employment combination on the labour demand curve, *mrp*, gives the wage bill (wL) for that level of output. The labour demand curve is therefore analogous to the demand, or *average revenue* curve, in product market monopoly theory, where the rectangle formed under the demand curve gives total revenue. Associated with this labour demand or 'average wage bill' (*awb*) line is therefore a marginal wage bill line (*mwb*) which plots the increment to the total wage bill created by reducing the wage sufficiently to lead the firm to employ an additional worker. The marginal wage bill line is exactly analogous to the marginal revenue curve in monopoly theory, and lies everywhere below the average wage bill line because the fall in wage required to permit an additional worker to be employed reduces the wage for all other employees as well.

As we have drawn it in Figure 22.2, with a linear labour demand curve, the marginal wage bill line bisects the angle made by the average wage bill line with the vertical axis. The wage bill is maximised where the marginal wage bill is zero, at (w_{wb}, L_{wb}). At this point, wages are half the level of their maximum value (w_{max}), the level that would be chosen in the absurd case in which the union was concerned with wages alone.

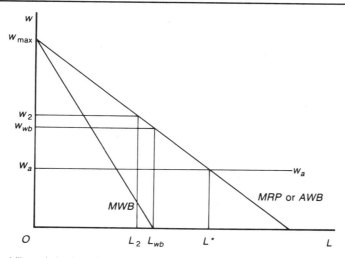

Figure 22.2

For wage bill maximisation when the labour demand curve is linear, the union chooses the wage rate, w_{wb}, at which the marginal wage bill equals zero, at the point where the wages are half the maximum available (w_{max}). The firm then chooses employment to be L_{wb}. We assume that $w_{wb} > w_a$. If the wage were raised to w_2, employment would fall to L_2.

While the wage bill maximisation idea enables us to be more precise than general utility maximisation, its arbitrary nature can be easily illustrated. First, there are no forces within the model to ensure that the wage consistent with wage bill maximisation actually exceeds the alternative wage. It is therefore conceivable that, if pursued, this maximand would lead unions to a choice as unlikely as that of wage maximisation — setting the union wage below the alternative wage. It is hard to see how the union could attract members in such a case.

Nor is this the only problem with wage bill maximisation. Figure 22.2 illustrates clearly the gains and losses from unionisation. Suppose that there existed a market clearing equilibrium wage of w_a in the absence of the union, at which employment would be L^*. The wage-bill maximising union would restrict the supply of labour by $L^* - L_{wb}$ workers, forcing up the wage by $(w_{wb} - w_a)$ in Figure 22.2. Thus OL_{wb} workers gain $(w_{wb} - w_a)$ each, while $(L_{wb} - L^*)$ workers lose their jobs. The gainers and losers here are not the same people, and there is no reason to suppose that wage bill maximisation leads to a balancing of the opposing gains and losses from unionisation to which workers would agree. Furthermore, there is no way of knowing whether a further reduction in employment, from L_{wb} to L_2, would be sufficiently beneficial to the L_2 workers who retain their jobs at the new higher wage w_2 to compensate them for the relatively low probability $(L_{wb} - L_2)/L$, of losing their job if they agree to such a new union policy. In short, wage bill maximisation is, upon close inspection, an *ad hoc* and unsatisfactory hypothesis about union motivation.

Rent Maximisation

Our first criticism of the wage bill maximisation model hinged on the fact that, in order to justify their existence to their members, unions had to provide a *mark-up* on the alternative wage. A simple way to ensure this outcome is to build it into the wage bill maximisation objective, to assume that the union maximises the total rents earned by its members, net of the alternative wage. This gives us a union utility function

$$U_u = (w_u - w_a)L \tag{22.4}$$

In effect, this function has the union maximising the value of its monetary 'profits', where the alternative wage can be viewed as the 'marginal cost' to the union of supplying an incremental worker to the firm. The outcome here is exactly analogous to the standard profit-maximising result for the monopolistic firm. The union will maximise rents when the 'marginal revenue' from supplying an additional worker, which we have already seen is the *mwb*, equals the 'marginal cost', the alternative wage. This equilibrium is illustrated in Figure 22.3 using the same labour demand curve and alternative wage as in Figure 22.2. Rents are maximised at

Figure 22.3

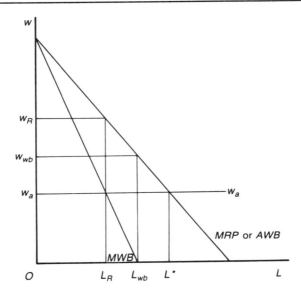

With rent maximisation, the union chooses the wage (w_R) at which the increment to the wage bill exactly equals the incremental cost of supplying an additional worker, which is the alternative wage. The firm then chooses the level of employment to be L_R. In this model, w_R is always greater than w_a. Moreover, rent maximisation always implies a higher level of pay and lower level of employment than wage bill maximisation.

(w_R, L_R), at the level of employment where the marginal wage bill equals the alternative wage. Because the alternative wage is positive, rent maximisation always implies a lower level of employment and a higher rate of pay than wage bill maximisation. (This result is exactly parallel to that yielded by the product market monopolist model which has the firm unambiguously producing on the elastic segment of its demand curve.)

*Maximising Expected Utility of the Representative Worker

Our second criticism of the wage bill maximisation hypothesis was that it gave us no framework for analysing how to weigh the losses of workers who lose their jobs when the union begins to operate against the gains of those who receive higher wages. At first sight, it would appear that this argument applies with even more force to the hypothesis of rent maximisation, because the number of losers and the benefits to the gainers are always greater in this case than under wage bill maximisation. In fact, we will establish that rent maximisation is a perfectly rational objective for workers who weigh up potential income gains against possible job

loss, provided that workers are assumed to be *risk neutral*, in the sense defined in Chapter 7. (Risk neutrality, it will be remembered, refers to the case when the individual is indifferent between a sure payment and a risky one which yields the same expected value. Risk aversion, in contrast, refers to the case when the individual prefers the sure payment to a risky one yielding the same expected value.)

Our approach in this section will be to derive an objective for the union by building from assumptions about individual preferences concerning wages and employment. The model explicitly takes account of the potential benefits and costs of joining a union as viewed by workers before the union begins to operate. Potential members are thought of as weighting possible outcomes by the probabilities of their occurring, and treating the resulting sum of expected payoffs as the utility to be gained from joining the union. The approach therefore is an application of the ideas set out in Chapter 7, and, as there, is called *expected utility maximisation*.

We start by assuming that every employed worker in a non-unionised industry is required to join the union, which fixes the maximum membership of the union at L^*, in terms of Figures 22.2 and 22.3. We also make the simplifying assumptions that individual workers obtain utility (with respect to the activities of their union) solely through the rate at which they are paid, and that all workers are identical in this regard. Hence, as far as the union is concerned, the preferences of a *representative* worker can be described by a utility function in wages, $U(w)$.

The job of the union is to ensure that, for every worker, the expected value of this utility function across different employment states is maximised. There are two possible outcomes for the worker as a consequence of the union's activity. He or she can be employed in the industry at the union rate, w_u, or can be displaced and forced to move to another industry in which the ruling rate for the job is the alternative wage. As we argued above, if we denote employment in the unionised industry by L_u, the probability that the representative worker remains employed is L_u/L^* and the expected return from his or her employment is $(L_u/L^*)U(w_u)$. The activities of the union could instead force the worker to work in another industry at the alternative wage. The probability of this occurring is $(L^* - L_u)/L^*$ and the expected return for this outcome is $(L^* - L_u)/L^*(U(w_a))$.

The expected utility function of the representative worker (U_r^u) can therefore be represented by

$$U_r^u = \frac{L_u}{L^*} U(w_u) + \left(\frac{L^* - L_u}{L^*} \right) U(w_a) \tag{22.5}$$

We can rearrange terms to yield

$$U_r^u = \frac{L_u}{L^*} (U(w_u) - U(w_a)) + U(w_a) \tag{22.6}$$

This allows a particularly simple representation of the effect of the union, because it will be remembered that in the absence of the union, $w = w_a$ and the representative worker has a probability of employment at the alternative wage equal to one. The second term on the right-hand side of equation (22.6) thus represents the representative worker's level of utility attainable in the absence of the union. The *gains* for the representative worker in joining the union are described by the first term on the right-hand side of equation (22.6), the expected value of the utility surplus resulting from the union mark-up of wages above the alternate wage. It is this which we assume that the union seeks to maximise for each worker.

The objective for the union is therefore to maximise the representative worker's expected gain from unionisation, $U_r^u - U(w_a)$, for each worker. We therefore multiply the representative worker's utility function net of the base level of utility by L^* to derive the *union's expected utility function*,

$$U_u = L_u(U(w_u) - U(w_a)) \tag{22.7}$$

Recall our general analysis of equilibrium in the monopoly union model (see Figure 22.1). We there established that equilibrium levels of pay and employment in a monopoly union model are determined at the tangency between the union's indifference curve and the firm's demand for labour curve. This in turn implies that, in equilibrium, the slope of the labour demand curve, $\partial L / \partial w$, must equal the slope of the union's indifference curve. The union's utility function contains wages and employment, and we know from Chapter 2 that the marginal rate of substitution between them will equal the ratio of their marginal utilities $(\partial U / \partial w) / (\partial U / \partial L)$.

We can establish this result formally by viewing the union as choosing wages and employment to maximise the general utility function

$$U^u = U(w, L) \tag{22.2}$$

subject to the labour demand curve which we can write for this purpose in the form

$$L = L(w) \tag{22.8}$$

where we know that employment falls as the wage declines ($\partial L / \partial w < 0$). Maximisation yields the general first-order condition that

$$-\frac{\partial U / \partial w}{\partial U / \partial L} = \frac{\partial L}{\partial w} \tag{22.9}$$

which of course describes an equilibrium of the sort illustrated in Figure 22.1.

We now apply this general approach to the case when the union's utility function takes the expected utility form. If we assume that union preferences are described by equation (22.7), the specification of the left-hand side of the general first-order condition (22.9) may be made more precise as follows. The derivative of the expected utility function with respect

to wages is $L\partial U/\partial w$ and with respect to employment is the bracketed term $(U(w_u) - U(w_a))$. Hence in this case the first-order condition (22.9) takes the form

$$- \frac{L\partial U/\partial w}{U(w_u) - U(w_a)} = \frac{\partial L}{\partial w} \tag{22.10}$$

The equilibrium level of employment and wages therefore depends on the specification of the representative worker's utility function with respect to wages $U(w)$. In this probabilistic context, this function indicates the worker's attitude to risk. We can illustrate this argument with an example.

Suppose that the marginal utility of incremental wages is constant, which would imply that the underlying utility function is linear in income. This means that the individual is risk neutral. If the representative individual's utility function, U_r^u, takes this simple linear form,

$$U_r^u = w \tag{22.11}$$

then the expected utility function (22.7) becomes

$$U^u = L_u(w_u - w_a) \tag{22.12}$$

This is of course identical to the utility function under rent maximisation (see equation (22.4)). Maximising rents yields the equilibrium described in Figure 22.3, in which the marginal wage bill equals the alternative wage. The marginal wage bill is the derivative of the wage bill with respect to employment $(\partial(wL)/\partial L)$. Thus in equilibrium

$$mwb = \frac{\partial(wL)}{\partial L} = w_u + \frac{L\partial w}{\partial L} = w_a$$

which holds when

$$w_u - w_a = -L\partial w/\partial L \tag{22.13}$$

Rather than using the formal condition implied by Figure 22.3, we can instead derive (22.13) directly from the first-order condition (22.10), as follows. If the individual's utility function is just the wage (equation (22.11)), $\partial U/\partial w = 1$, $U(w_u) = w_u$ and $U(w_a) = w_a$. Hence the first-order condition can be rewritten

$$\frac{-L}{w_u - w_a} = \frac{\partial L}{\partial w}$$

which rearranges to

$$w_u - w_a = -L\frac{\partial w}{\partial L} \tag{22.13}$$

This establishes that, if we had explicitly drawn the union's rent-maximising utility function in Figure 22.3, it would have been tangent

to the average wage bill at exactly the equilibrium point (w_R, L_R). We therefore obtain a formal link between the two diagrammatic approaches used above: the utility-maximisation approach of Figure 22.1, in which equilibrium is located at the tangency between the labour demand curve and the union's indifference curve, and the monopoly union approach of Figures 22.2 and 22.3, in which the union appears to choose the wage and employment level without direct reference to the utility function.

As we noted in discussing Figure 22.3, the objective of rent maximisation implies lower employment and higher wages than the objective of wage bill maximisation. We can now see that this is because workers who are risk neutral are willing to risk their jobs relatively more in return for a higher wage differential than they would if they are risk averse. If we assume some degree of risk aversion, the slope of the indifference curves will become relatively steeper at any wage—employment combination, and we move to an equilibrium with higher employment and lower wages, such as point B in Figure 22.4. In the limit, where workers are unwilling to bear any risk of job loss in order to obtain a higher wage, the union's indifference curve will yield a tangency at the alternative market clearing wage. The expected utility framework therefore suggests

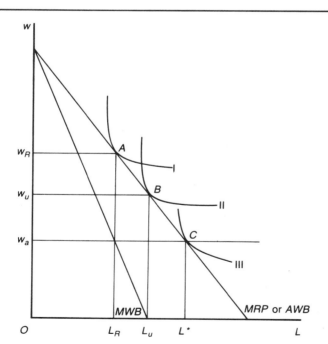

Figure 22.4

Expected utility maximisation with a variety of attitudes to risk. Risk neutrality yields indifference curves such as I, and the rent-maximising outcome at A. Some degree of risk aversion in individual utility functions implies indifference curves such as II, with an equilibrium at B. Finally, if the workers are unwilling to accept any risk of job loss, the union's indifference curve must be at III and the union is unable to attain any increase in wages.

that the extent of the union—non-union wage differential and the resulting loss of jobs, for a given labour demand curve, depends on the attitude of individual workers to risk.

The Monopoly Union Model — A Final Comment

The monopoly union model sheds some light on how unions are likely to operate, and the conditions under which their actions are most likely to be successful. While we have been unable to tie down union objectives precisely, the previous section has yielded insights into one likely important determinant of those preferences, namely the attitude of individual union members to employment and wage risks. The expected utility approach argues that the union will seek to attain a positive differential between the union and alternative wages, while keeping the resulting loss in employment as low as possible given that differential. This suggests that the unions will be more successful, the more *inelastic* is the demand for labour curve in the region at which the market would clear in the absence of the union. (In the region where the rent-maximising union will set the wage, of course, the demand for labour will, as we have seen, always be elastic, for exactly the same reasons as a product market monopolist always operates on the elastic part of the demand curve (see Chapter 15 above). As we saw in Chapters 19 and 20, the demand for labour is derived from product demand, and will be more inelastic, the more inelastic the demand for the product, and the lower the degree of substitutability between labour and capital. When we combine this result with the incentives for unions to restrict factor supplies, and the requirement that they operate in sectors where product markets are imperfect (so that there are rents to be shared), we get a surprisingly rich set of insights into how and where unions will be most effective.

Bargaining between Unions and Firms

The monopoly union model starts from the premise that unions can control the supply of labour at their chosen wage rate (in particular, preventing workers offering to work for less than the union rate) but are unable to influence the level of employment directly. That is assumed to be chosen by the firm in order to maximise its profits given the union wage. This framework has the obvious attractive feature that outcomes always lie on the labour demand curve. However, it has the less obvious drawback that such outcomes fail to offer the best available wage—employment combination, in terms of the utility yielded to the two parties. As we shall now see, for any given point on the labour demand curve, one can find an outcome with lower wages and higher employment at which the union's utility is increased and the firm's profitability is not

affected. Alternatively, we can find outcomes at which the firm's profitability is increased while the union's utility remains unchanged. The essential characteristic of these outcomes is that they result from the union and the firm bargaining over wages and employment *simultaneously*, with each agreeing to stick by the negotiated wage–employment contract. Such outcomes cannot be achieved in the monopoly union framework because it is assumed that unions fix wages and firms the level of employment in separate decisions.

It is not necessary to alter our analysis of the union to any great extent in order to model a more general bargaining process. We shall simply revert to the general assumption that the union maximises some utility function in wages and employment such as (22.2), without recourse in the first instance to specific functional forms. The big difference in bargaining models comes in the treatment of the firm, which is now assumed to be an active participant in the bargaining process rather than simply choosing employment at a wage unilaterally set by the union. As we saw in Chapters 19 and 20, the firm's labour demand curve is derived from a profit-maximising exercise with respect to employment. For a given wage, we deduce a particular level of employment at which profits are maximised. Suppose instead that we take as given the level of profit, say π_0, and consider the combinations of wages and employment which would yield the same level of profit. We can plot these combinations in wage–employment space to produce what is termed an *isoprofit curve* analogous to those derived in Chapter 17 in the duopolists' output space. A family of such curves is plotted in Figure 22.5. Because, for a given level of employment, and hence output, profits will rise as wages fall, these curves represent higher and higher levels of profit as we move down the diagram. Moreover, each curve is at its maximum height where it cuts the labour demand curve. Starting at the maximum point on the curve, to increase employment at a given wage will certainly reduce profit. Therefore to hold profits constant, the wage must fall as employment rises. Similarly to cut employment and output at a given wage also reduces profits, hence to keep profits constant, the wage must fall as we move to the left of the demand curve.

Efficient Bargaining

The analysis of *efficient bargaining* is now straightforward, and parallels our formulation of joint profit maximisation by cartels in Chapter 17. If we look back to Figure 22.1, we can remind ouselves that in the monopoly union framework, wages and employment are determined at the point of tangency between the union's indifference curve and the labour demand curve, point A on Figure 22.6. We can clearly achieve wage–employment outcomes which raise either the firm's profits (by moving to a lower isoprofit curve) or the union's welfare, or both, by moving

Figure 22.5

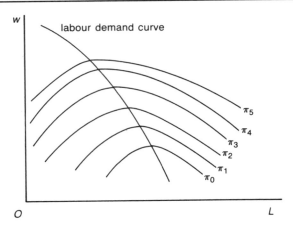

Each point on the labour demand curve is associated with an isoprofit curve, such as π_0, π_1, π_2 etc., which plots the levels of wages and employment at a given level of profit, i.e. π_0, π_1, π_2, etc. The isoprofit curve reaches its maximum height at the wage–employment combination on the labour demand curve. Higher and higher points on the labour demand curve are associated with lower and lower levels of profit ($\pi_0 > \pi_1, > \pi_2$ etc.).

Figure 22.6

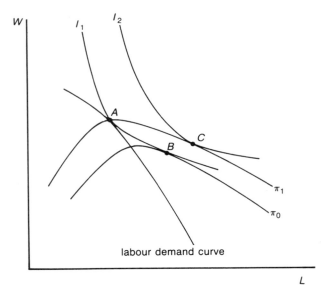

Bargaining as against monopoly union outcomes. If we suppose the union's indifference curves to take the form l_1, l_2, the monopoly union equilibrium occurs at point A. However, this is not the best conceivable bargain for either party. The union could attain the same level of satisfaction while the firm earned higher profits at B, while the converse is true at point C. In general, bargaining equilibria are characterised by tangency between the firm's isoprofit curve and the union's indifference curve.

to a point at which the level of employment is higher and the wage rate lower than under the monopoly union outcome. Such equilibria are indicated by points such as B or C in Figure 22.6. We cannot say exactly which outcome bargaining will lead us to. However, we do know that the situations in which neither the firm nor the union can be made better off without the other party to the negotiations being made worse off are all characterised by the fact that the slope of the union's relevant indifference curve is equal to the slope of the firm's relevant isoprofit curve. Points B and C in Figure 22.6 characterise such situations. The locus of all such points we again refer to as the *contract curve* and we now develop its analysis for firm—union bargains below. (See also Chapter 17 and Chapter 25 for further applications of the contract curve idea.)

Consider first the determination of the union—firm curve's end points. In our discussion of the monopoly union case, we indicated that unions would be unable to attract members, and hence to control the supply of labour, at any wage below that available in alternative lines of work. This sets a floor to the wage level to which firms can push unions, at the alternative wage, w_a. This wage level is depicted in Figure 22.7. Conversely, however powerful the union, it cannot raise wages and employment so high that the firm is driven out of business. We can denote the firm's minimum acceptable level of profit by π_{min}. There is of course an isoprofit line associated with this minimum profit level, π_{min}, and we draw it in Figure 22.7. The part of the contract curve along which bargains between unions and firms can be struck therefore lies above w_a and below the isoprofit curve π_{min}. This is the segment XY in Figure 22.7.

In order to press our analysis further, we need to know about the relative bargaining power of the union and the firm. As the firm becomes relatively more powerful, it can force the union to accept lower levels of utility, towards point X in Figure 22.7. Similarly, as the union becomes more powerful it can extract an increasing proportion of the firm's profit for its members, shifting the outcome of bargaining along the contract curve toward point Y in Figure 22.7. To say more about the outcome than this requires an explicit theory of the bargaining process which we shall introduce in the following section.

For the moment, let us assume that relative bargaining powers are fixed so that the union is unable to obtain utility greater than I_1 in Figure 22.7. In the monopoly union framework we developed earlier, to obtain this utility level, the union would fix a wage of w_u, and the firm would set employment on the demand curve at L_u. Now suppose we move to efficient bargaining. Since we have fixed the union's utility level at I_1, the benefits from efficient bargaining must by assumption then accrue entirely to the firm, which can raise its profits from π_2 to π_1. The efficient bargaining equilibrium is characterised by a higher level of employment and lower pay, at (L_b, w_b), than obtained in the monopoly union case. This result arises because the union is assumed to gain higher utility from greater levels of employment as well as higher wages. In this bargaining

Figure 22.7

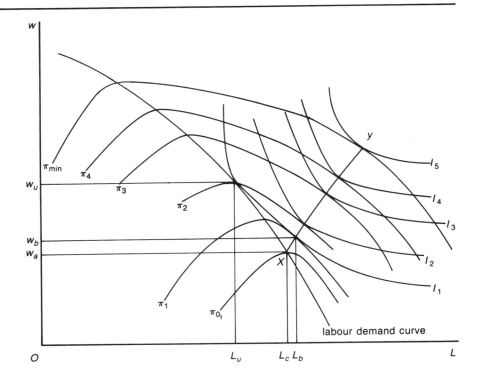

Union—firm bargaining. The contract curve is the locus of tangencies between the union's indifference curves (l_1, l_2, ...) and the firm's isoprofit curves (π_0, π_1, ...) between the minimum acceptable level of pay for the union (w_a) and the minimum acceptable level of profits for the firm (π_{min}); the segment *XY*. The precise point on the contract curve chosen depends on the relative bargaining power of the two sides. As the firm becomes relatively more powerful, outcomes move along the contract curve towards *X*. In the monopoly union model unions decrease employment and raise wages relative to the competitive outcome (w_a, L_c), attaining an equilibrium such as (w_u, L_u). If we suppose the attainment of l_1 represents the union's relative bargaining power, employment is greater and wages less with efficient bargaining (w_b, L_b). Indeed employment exceeds that attained under competition.

framework which allows the union to trade employment against wages, it will therefore agree with firms to settle on an outcome beyond their labour demand curve.

It should be noted that in Figure 22.7 we have drawn the relevant section of the contract curve, *XY*, as upward sloping in wage—employment space. As a result, the equilibrium level of employment in efficient bargaining exceeds that which would arise from a competitive labour market ($L_b > L_c$). Firms earn less profit under efficient bargaining than in the competitive case, however, because wages as well as employment are higher ($w_b > w_a$, $\pi_1 < \pi_0$ in Figure 22.7). For this reason, efficient bargaining models are often seen as describing the 'labour hoarding' or

'feather bedding' considered characteristic of unionised industries, which are said to overemploy labour and therefore to have relatively lower labour productivity. In this framework, overemployment arises from the union's interest in employment as well as wages and its assumed ability to enforce agreed levels of employment as well as pay on the firm.

However, contract curves are not necessarily always upward sloping. A backward bending contract curve is illustrated in Figure 22.8. As we shall show more formally in the next section, the slope of the contract curve can be associated with the relative weights attached by the union to wages and employment in its utility function. Roughly speaking, if the union weights employment heavily relative to wages on the margin, the contract curve will be upward sloping, as in Figure 22.7. In this case, increased union power leads to higher employment. Conversely, if the union weights wages relatively more highly, the contract curve will be backward bending as in Figure 22.8 and equilibrium employment under efficient bargaining will be less than the competitive level ($L_b' < L_c'$). With backward-sloping contract curves, increased union power acts to reduce employment and to increase wages.

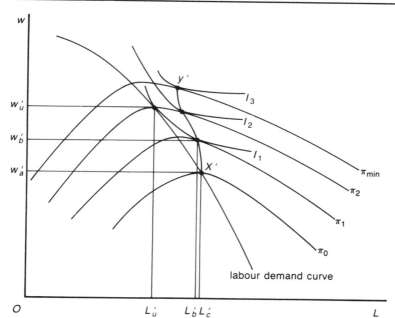

Figure 22.8

The contract curve is the locus of tangencies between the union's indifference curves (I_1, I_2) and the firm's isoprofit curves (π_0, π_1). In contrast to Figure 22.7, the union is here assumed to attach relatively more weight to wages than employment, so the contract curve $X'Y'$ is backward bending. If the union's utility level is fixed at I_1, that which would be attained at the monopoly union solution w_u', L_u', efficient bargaining will increase employment to L_b' and reduce the wage to w_b'. However, with a backward-bending contract curve, employment is less than L_a', the amount that would rule at the alternative wage, w_a'.

*A Formalisation of the Efficient Bargaining Model

As with our analysis of oligopoly, game theory can yield considerable additional insights into the interactions between unions and firms. The monopoly union model closely parallels the non-collusive games developed in Chapter 17. Indeed, alert readers will have recognised precisely the structure of a Stackelberg game in the premise that unions can control the supply of labour at a given wage but the firm chooses the level of employment. It is our intention in this chapter, however, to extend our use of game theory in order to formalise the outcome of *collusive* bargaining processes. We therefore concentrate our attention on how firms and unions combine to choose wages and employment jointly through efficient bargaining. We use the Nash bargaining solution, or the *Nash* fixed threat point model in this analysis, an approach which could equally well be applied to the discussion of cartels in Chapter 17.

The game which we assume that unions and firms play takes the following form. The two players *co-operate* in order to achieve the highest possible joint rewards, which they then divide between themselves according to their relative bargaining powers. 'Rewards' in this context, are defined relative to *threat points*, the payments which each party would receive in the absence of any binding agreement. If we follow our previous notation, the firm's threat point is therefore its shutdown level of profit, $\pi_{\min}$, while the union's threat point is the utility derived at the competitive outcome (w_a, L_c), termed $U^u_{\min}$. Nash deduced, from axioms about the outcome, that the solution to a game of this type is provided by the *maximisation of the product of the union's and the firm's utility increments above their respective threat points*. We can therefore investigate the properties of Nash equilibrium by analysing the first-order conditions of the joint maximisation problem.

Let us suppose we can represent the relative bargaining power of the firm as against the union by the parameter μ. The Nash approach leads the union and the firm to maximise the product of their respective gains above the threat points.

$$N = [\pi - \pi_{\min}]^\mu \, [U^u(w,L) - U^u_{\min}] \tag{22.14}$$

Maximisation with respect to wages and employment yields two first-order conditions which can be rearranged to yield

$$-\frac{\partial U/\partial L}{\partial U/\partial w} = \frac{1}{L}((mrp) - w) \tag{22.15}$$

where (mrp) is the marginal revenue product of labour. Equation (22.15) defines the contract curve. The left-hand side defines the slope of the union's indifference curve in wage–employment space. To understand the right-hand side, we must consider the firm's profit-maximising behaviour. If, in order to keep the analysis simple, we abstract from fixed costs, we can define profits as

$$\pi = pX - wL \tag{22.16}$$

so that for a given level of profits, $\bar{\pi}$, the equation of an isoprofit curve for a monopolist on the product market is given by

$$w = \frac{pX - \bar{\pi}}{L} \tag{22.17}$$

The slope of the isoprofit curve is given by

$$\frac{\partial w}{\partial L} = \frac{L(mrp) - (pX - \bar{\pi})}{L^2}$$

$$= \frac{L(mrp) - wL}{L^2}$$

$$= \frac{1}{L}((mrp) - w) \tag{22.18}$$

The right-hand side of equation (22.15) is therefore the slope of the isoprofit curve. Interested readers will note the parallels with the analysis of the labour-managed firm in Chapter 18. Equation (22.15) is the algebraic version of the condition we deduced geometrically in Figure 22.7, that the contract curve is the locus of points at which the union's indifference curve is tangent to the firm's isoprofit curve. As we can see by inspection of (22.15), in general, we cannot say whether the contract curve is upward sloping or backward bending.

*Different Union Objectives and Efficient Bargaining

A fairly simple representation of union and firm preferences allows us to examine the impact of different assumptions about the union utility function on the shape of the contract curve. We will first assume that firms go out of business if profits become negative, so that the firm's threat point, π_{min}, equals zero. The firm's relative bargaining power we continue to represent with the parameter μ. In specifying union preferences we adopt a version of a functional form widely used in demand theory, namely the *Stone–Geary* function in which utility is the weighted product of the arguments of the function. Thus,

$$[U^u(w,L) - U^u_{min}] = (w - w_a)^\gamma L^\theta \tag{22.19}$$

Alert readers will note the similarities between the functional form of equation (22.19) and the Cobb–Douglas function which we have employed extensively in the analysis of production.

The Nash product of utility increments under these conditions can be written as

$$N^1 = [\pi]^\mu (w - w_a)^\gamma L^\theta \tag{22.20}$$

This of course is merely a particular specification of the general Nash product (22.14), given (22.19) when $\pi_{min} = 0$. Maximising N^1 with respect to wages and employment and simplifying yields first-order condition

$$w = w_a + \left(\frac{\gamma}{\mu}\right) \frac{\pi}{L} \tag{22.21}$$

$$(mrp) - w = - \left(\frac{\theta}{\mu}\right) \frac{\pi}{L} \tag{22.22}$$

Combining these equations yields the contract curve

$$[(mrp) - w] = - \frac{\theta}{\gamma} (w - w_a) \tag{22.23}$$

which can be rearranged to the convenient form

$$w = \frac{\gamma}{\gamma - \theta} (mrp) - \frac{\theta}{\gamma - \theta} w_a \tag{22.24}$$

The slope of this curve depends on the relationship between the weight attached in the union's utility function to wages (γ) and that attached to employment (θ). We can distinguish three cases, each of which are illustrated in Figure 22.9. If the union attaches more weight to employment than wages ($\theta > \gamma$), since mrp is a decreasing function of employment, equation (22.24) establishes that the contract curve will be upward sloping, such as the locus AC in Figure 22.9. More formally, differentiating (22.24) with respect to employment, we derive its slope, $\partial w / \partial L$,

$$\frac{\partial w}{\partial L} = \frac{\gamma}{\gamma - \theta} \left(\frac{\partial (mrp)}{\partial L}\right) \tag{22.25}$$

$\partial (mrp)/\partial L$ is negative because of diminishing returns to a factor and downward-sloping product demand curves. Hence if ($\gamma - \theta$) is less than zero, the slope of the contract curve is positive. Conversely, if the union attaches more weight to wages than to employment ($\gamma > \theta$), equation (22.25) tells us that the contract curve will be backward sloping, for example, the locus AC' in Figure 22.9.

Finally, the case of rent maximisation discussed above is also yielded by a special case of utility function (22.19), namely when $\theta = \gamma = 1$ (see equation 22.12). Under this assumption, the slope of the contract curve is infinity and this locus is therefore vertical. If we refer back to the original formulation of the contract curve under this specification, equation (22.23), when $\theta = \gamma = 1$, it reduces to

$$(mrp) = w_a \tag{22.26}$$

Hence if the union's objective is to maximise rents and the framework for negotiation is efficient bargaining, employment will be fixed independently of the wage rate at the level where the marginal revenue product of labour equals the alternative wage at the competitive employment level

Figure 22.9

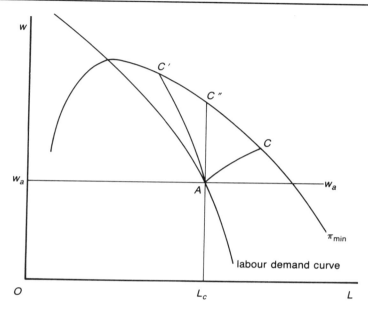

If the union's utility function takes the form $U^u = (w - w_a)^\gamma L^\theta$, the slope of the contract curve depends on the relative magnitudes of γ and θ. If $\theta > \gamma$, the contract curve is upward sloping, locus AC. If $\gamma > \theta$, it is backward bending, locus AC'. If $\theta = \gamma$, which holds if the union maximises rents, the locus is vertical at employment level L_c between the alternative wage and the minimum profit level, locus AC''.

L_c. The wage will be determined along the vertical contract curve above w_a according to relative bargaining powers, as illustrated by the locus AC'' in Figure 22.9.

Concluding Comment

In this chapter, we have shown that the simple framework which we derived to analyse the behaviour of single economic agents, be they consumers or firms, can be extended to more complex organisations such as trade unions. Moreoever, the fact that we were unable to identify with any degree of precision an objective for such organisations proved to be only a limited drawback for our analysis.

A number of unambiguous predictions have emerged from this work, of which the most important is that unions act to push wages above the level which would pertain in a competitive market. This result holds for all sensible specifications of the union's objectives, including formulations which explicitly take account of the possibility that such wage-increasing activities may reduce the level of employment. In general, the greater the stress placed on the level of remuneration by the union, the greater will

be the mark-up over the competitive wage that the organisation will achieve.

We were unable, however, to conclude unambiguously that wage increases also act to reduce employment. Rather, it emerged that the outcome here depends on the bargaining framework in which unions and firms operate. If the union is unable to control the determination of employment, their wage-increasing activities must reduce the level of employment. If employment as well as wages are open to negotiation, we enter a bargaining framework in which sufficiently high stress on employment in the union's preferences can lead to a greater level of employment than would pertain under competition.

Questions for Study and Discussion for Part VII

1. Discuss the assertion that input demand of the firm is merely the mirror image of output supply.
2. 'In competitive equilibrium, workers always earn less than their average product.' Discuss.
3. A firm uses 8 units of labour and 24 units of capital to produce 24 units of output. If there are constant returns to scale and the marginal product of labour is 1.5, what is the marginal product of capital? Will it be greater or smaller if technology instead displays diminishing returns to scale?
4. Analyse the effect of an increase in the price of capital on the demand for labour when the elasticity of substitution between labour and capital is low and the elasticity of the demand for output is high.
*5. Use a Cobb–Douglas production function $(X = L^\alpha K^\beta)$ to illustrate the propositions that, provided the firm can reach an equilibrium,

   (i)   Euler's Theorem (equation 19.25)) holds when a homogeneous production function displays constant returns to scale;
   (ii) there will always be a positive profit in a competitive firm which has a homogeneous production function with returns to scale less than one, and which pays its inputs their marginal products;
   (iii) there will always be a positive profit in a monopoly which faces a linearly homogeneous production function.

6. What will be the effect on the following of fixing a minimum wage above the market equilibrium level: (a) employment in a perfectly competitive industry in which all firms are equally efficient; (b) the number of firms operating in that industry; (c) employment in a particular firm in that industry; and (d) employment in a firm that, prior to the fixing of the minimum wage, faced an upward-sloping supply curve of labour?

7. A monopsonist in the labour market faces a relatively inelastic supply of female labour and hence pays its female employees a lower wage than its male employees even though the two groups are equally productive. What will be the effect on (a) the wage level paid to women; (b) the number of women employed; (c) the wage level of men; and (d) the number of men employed, of legislation forcing the firm to pay the same wage to all employees?

8. Suppose, at a given wage rate, there is unemployment in a particular competitive industry of a certain type of labour. Will government policies of (a) subsidising its wage, and (b) subsidising the rental price of capital equipment, result in an increase in the employment of that type of labour?

9. What is the relationship between

   (i)   the elasticity of factor substitution and the elasticity of demand for labour?
   (ii) the elasticity of demand for the product and the elasticity of demand for labour?
   (iii) the ratio of labour costs to total costs and the elasticity of demand for labour?
   (iv) the elasticity of supply of other inputs and the elasticity of demand for labour?

10. Discuss what the 4 propositions derived in question 9 (Marshall's laws of derived demand) tell us about the factors likely to influence the relative success or failure of unions in attaining wage increases for their members without causing substantial job losses.

11. Suppose that in a monopoly union framework, the union maximises its wage bill and the firm's labour demand curve can be approximated by a straight line.

   (i)   What happens to the level of employment and the wage paid if demand in the product market increases? What happens to profits?
   (ii) What happens to the level of employment and the wage paid if the firm introduces a technical innovation which increases the marginal physical product of labour at each level of output?
   (iii) Are these results altered if we assume that the firm maximises rents rather than the wage bill?

*12. Suppose that the representative worker's utility function takes the form $U_r^u = w^\gamma$. Show that, if the union maximises expected utility and unions and firms bargain according to the monopoly union model, the equilibrium level of employment declines as the value of the parameter γ increases.

13. Suppose in an efficient bargaining framework, the union and firm have attained a particular equilibrium on the contract curve.

(i)   What is the effect on wages and employment of an increase in the alternative wage?

(ii) What is the effect on wages and employment of an increase in product demand?

*14. Suppose that a union and a firm operate in an efficient bargaining framework, with equal bargaining powers (so the term for bargaining power in the Nash product equals one). The union is assumed to have a utility function, specified net of its threat point, of the form $U = (w - w_a)L$. The firm gains satisfaction from profits according to the utility function $U(\pi) = \pi$ with the threat point, π_{min} equal to zero.

(i)   Derive the equation for the contract curve.

(ii) Show that the level of employment is determined independently of the equilibrium value of wages.

(iii) Show that changes in the degree of bargaining power affect wages but not employment.

Suggested Further Reading to Part VII

Becker, G.S. 'Investment in on the Job Training', in Blaug, M. (ed.) (*op. cit.*).

Becker, G.S. 1975. *Human Capital*. (2nd edn). New York: Columbia University Press.

Bishop, R.L. 1964. 'A Zeuthen–Hicks Model of the Bargaining Process', *Econometrica*.

Dunlop, J.T. (ed) 1957. *The Theory of Wage Determination*. London: Macmillan.

Farber, H, 1986. 'The Analysis of Union Behaviour', in Ashenfelter, O. and Layard R. (eds), *Handbook of Labour Economics*. Amersterdam: North-Holland.

Ferguson, C. E. 1969. *The Neoclassical Theory of Production and Distribution*. Cambridge: Cambridge University Press.

Henderson, J.M. and Quandt, R.E. (*op. cit.*).

Hicks, J.R. 1963. *The Theory of Wages* (2nd edn). New York: St. Martin's Press.

Hirsch, B.T. and Addison, J.T. 1986. *The Economic Analysis of Unions*. Boston, Allen & Unwin.

McDonald, I.M. and Solow, R.M. 1981. 'Wage Bargaining and Employment', *American Economic Review*.

Oswald, A. 1982. 'The Microeconomic Theory of the Trade Union', *Economic Journal*.

Robinson, J. 1934. 'Euler's Theorem and the Problem of Distribution', *Economic Journal*. Reprinted in Breit and Hochman (eds) (*op. cit.*).

Schultz, T.W. 1961. 'Human Capital', *American Economic Review*.

Part VIII
GENERAL EQUILIBRIUM AND WELFARE

23

An Overview

Scarcity and the Co-ordination of Choices

We stressed at the very outset of this book that economics is about scarcity, and that scarcity implies that people must make choices. The relationship between this proposition and the analysis we have presented so far is surely clear to readers. Consumer theory deals with the choices of individual households and their consequences for behaviour. Similarly, production theory and the theory of industrial organisation have much to say about the choices of individual firms. Scarcity, however, is not merely a private phenomenon. It has a social aspect as well. Individuals can formulate plans about how to make the best use of the resources available to them, but unless those plans are compatible with those made by others, they will not be able to execute them. Hence a coherent solution at the level of the economy as a whole to the problems posed by scarcity requires that the choices made by individuals be co-ordinated with one another.

In the preceding chapters we have had a good deal to say about the interaction of households and firms in markets, and many of the mechanisms we have analysed may usefully be thought of as operating to co-ordinate the choices which individual agents make. Thus, to cite the most obvious example, we have shown that equilibrium exists in a perfectly competitive market for a particular good where its supply and demand curves intersect; this state of affairs is one in which the plans of agents to buy the good in question are just compatible with those of firms to sell it, this compatibility being achieved by varying the price at which the good is traded. If, at some initial price, consumers plan to buy more of it than firms plan to supply, this incompatability between choices may be removed by raising the price, and vice versa. In this example, then, it is the price of the good being traded which moves to co-ordinate the choices of buyers and sellers.

Partial and General Equilibrium

Now the analysis of markets for particular goods and services is certainly interesting and useful but, when it comes to helping us to develop an understanding of the way in which individual choices are co-ordinated on an economy-wide basis, it does not go far enough. The theory of consumer behaviour shows that the consumer's decision about how much of any particular good to buy is not taken in isolation, but as part of an overall plan about how to allocate income over an array of available goods and services. At the same time the theory of the firm shows that the firm's output decision is taken simultaneously with others concerning the purchase of factors of production. Moreoever, if the typical consumer's income is derived from the sale of productive services to a firm, then firms' factor market decisions will affect consumers' incomes and hence their choices about the purchase of goods and services. Clearly, there must be much more to the co-ordination of the choices of individual householders and firms than the interaction of supply and demand in a particular market.

The analysis developed so far in this book is usually referred to as *partial equilibrium* analysis. It concentrates upon the way in which choices in certain parts of the economy are made and co-ordinated, while neglecting the way in which solutions achieved in one market impinge upon others. Underlying it is the assumption that these interactions are sufficiently minor that to neglect them does not undermine the validity of the conclusions reached. If this assumption holds, then it is well worth making, for to neglect such interactions certainly enables us to achieve a degree of simplicity in our theorising that would not otherwise be attainable. In general though, there are no rules which can blindly guarantee that partial equilibrium analysis may be validly applied to a particular issue. It is a matter for the judgement of the individual economist to decide when it is appropriate to hold 'other things equal', and indeed to choose which 'other things' they should be. There is, however, as we have just noted, one set of issues at least, where partial equilibrium analysis will not do. If one is concerned to understand the way in which market mechanisms do, or do not, work in order to achieve compatibility of agents' choices on an economy-wide basis, a *general equilibrium* analysis which focuses on the interaction of markets is required.

General Equilibrium Analysis — An Outline of Subsequent Chapters

As readers may have already guessed, general equilibrium theory, the very purpose of which is to analyse the way in which the choices of individual consumers and firms are co-ordinated across markets on an

economy-wide basis is potentially very complicated. Such analysis must do everything that partial equilibrium analysis does, and more. It must deal with consumers' decisions about the demand for goods and services, and the supply of factors of production, show how those choices impinge upon one another, and are rendered compatible among consumers. It must deal with firms' output supply and input demand decisions, and show how these are co-ordinated among firms. Moreoever, since factor sales are the source of consumers' incomes, it must also show how the output market decisions of firms and consumers interact with their factor market decisions. Finally, and crucially, it must deal with all of these matters *simultaneously*. The fact that a particular market can reach an equilibrium, taking the prices from all other markets as given, tells us little about the possibilities for all markets to reach a state of general equilibrium.

A body of theory dealing with general equilibrium does indeed exist, and the next chapters of this book will be devoted to expounding its essential properties. We shall develop the properties one step at a time. First, because many of its complexities arise from the interactions among consumption and production decisions, we shall abstract from these by considering an economy with no production, an *exchange economy* in which consumers trade with one another exogenously given endowments of goods. In this context we shall analyse the nature of a situation in which all agents' trading and consumption plans are compatible with one another, and say something about the mechanisms whereby such a state of general equilibrium might be achieved. We shall then complicate the analysis by introducing production, and having first analysed the nature of equilibrium in production, will proceed to bring the two sides of the economy together in order to display the characteristics of general equilibrium in an economy with production.

Once the properties of a production economy in general equilibrium have been set out we shall discuss the application of such analysis to so-called *welfare economics*, which confronts questions about the ethical desirability of various solutions to the scarcity problem. We shall ask whether the solution implied by our analysis is a desirable one, and discuss ways in which particular problems arising in the private sector of the economy might impinge upon its desirability. Finally, we shall also have some things to say about the way in which government action might deal with the problems of *market failures*, and also say something about issues having to do with the distribution of income.

24

General Equilibrium in an Exchange Economy

Introduction

In this chapter we shall develop some of the essential properties of general equilibrium theory. In order to keep our analysis as clear as possible we shall initially confine our discussion to an exchange economy, so-called; one in which agents are endowed with particular quantities of goods and services and trade them, but in which there is no production. We shall discuss the key characteristics of equilibrium in such an economy and also say something about the means whereby it might be achieved. In particular we shall discuss the role played by competitively determined prices in our economy and the activities of a somewhat mysterious entity usually referred to as the *auctioneer* in setting and changing them. As it happens, considerable simplicity can be obtained if we deal with an economy in which only two agents trade two goods. Though a two person two good economy with no production is far removed from anything one might conceivably encounter in the real world, it turns out that the critical features of general equilibrium in such an economy also occur in much more complex production economies with many goods, many agents and many inputs. Hence we surrender realism here in order to obtain a great deal of simplicity. Nevertheless, proofs of many of the key propositions in the chapters which follow rely on the assumption that there are a large number of traders, so it should always be remembered that our treatment here is meant to achieve clarity of exposition, not theoretical rigour.

A Simple Exchange Economy — the Box Diagram

Consider an economy in which two goods are made available to two consumers at constant rates per unit of time. There is no production, the

goods in question simply being delivered from the outside, but our two consumers are allowed to exchange goods. The essential properties of this economy may be set out in a diagram, Figure 24.1. Let the goods with which the economy is endowed be called X and Y, and let us refer to the two consumers as A and B. In Figure 24.1 we measure quantities of X on the horizontal axis and of Y on the vertical. There is available to the economy a given-amount, an endowment, of X, X_0, and a given endowment of Y, Y_0, so let us close off the space above and to the right of the axes at these quantities, thus drawing what is usually referred to as a 'box'.

Let us measure the quantity of X available to consumer A (X_A) from left to right along the horizontal axis, and the quantity of Y available to that same consumer (Y_A) from bottom to top of the vertical axis. If we do this, it is immediately apparent that X_0 minus A's consumption of X gives us the amount of the economy's endowment of X left over for B to consume, and that Y_0 minus A's consumption of Y gives us the amount of Y left over for B. In other words, if we treat the bottom left-hand corner of the box as the origin relative to which A's consumption is measured, the top right-hand corner becomes the origin relative to which B's consumption may be measured. If we further impose the condition that A and B between them must consume the economy's entire endowment of goods, then we may interpret any single point within the box as representing simultaneously a combination of X and Y consumed by A and a combination of X and Y consumed by B. Thus, if A consumes X_A of X and Y_A of Y, then Y will consume $X_0 - X_A$ and $Y_0 - Y_A$, so that

Figure 24.1

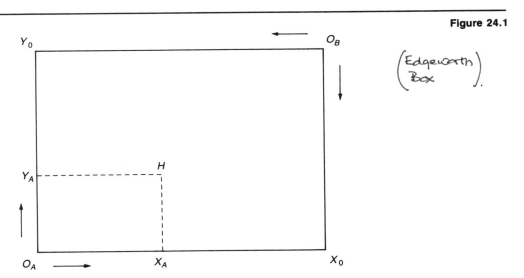

X_0 and Y_0 are the total quantities of X and Y available. Consumer A's consumption of the goods is measured from the bottom left-hand corner O_A and B's from the top right-hand corner O_B. Any point such as H represents a division of X and Y between the consumers that results in the available quantities of both goods being entirely consumed.

the point labelled H will represent this joint consumption pattern. Any point within the box, including those lying on the axes, represents a feasible joint consumption pattern for our two agents, given the economy's endowments of X and Y.

The Contract Curve, Trade and the Core

We draw our two agents' preference patterns for X and Y in Figure 24.2. A's satisfaction increases as we move from bottom left to top right in this box diagram and B's increases as we move from top right to bottom left. We also draw a line linking the two origins of the box and passing through all the points within it where indifference curves of our two agents are tangent to one another. As we saw in Chapters 17 and 22, loci of this sort are called *contract curves*. We have already remarked that any point within our box, including those on the axes, represents a feasible joint consumption pattern of X and Y that A and B could undertake. We may now subdivide these points into two groups, those which lie on the contract curve and those which do not, and it is helpful to do this because the economic significance of the two sets of points differs in an important way.

Figure 24.2

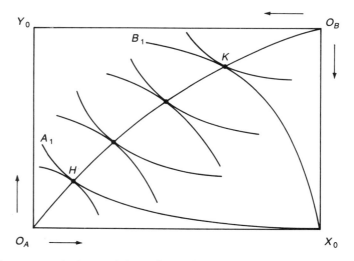

A's indifference map is drawn relative to O_A and B's relative to O_B. The contract curve $O_A O_B$ is a locus of points of tangency between the two indifference maps. At any point on it, it would be impossible to make one consumer better off without reducing the satisfaction of the other. If A begins with all the X and B with all the Y, voluntary trade will never move A below indifference curve A_1 or B below B_1. The equilibrium outcome of their trading would thus lie between H and K. This segment of the contract curve is known as the core of the economy.

Consider first a typical point on the contract curve such as H in Figure 24.2. Suppose that, when the economy's endowment of X and Y arrived it·was distributed between A and B so as to locate them at this point. Would there be any way of redistributing the economy's endowment of X and Y between A and B to which they would both consent? Clearly not, because if the redistribution in question involved a movement along the contract curve, one of our two agents would be moved to a lower level of satisfaction as the other gained, while if it involved a movement off the contract curve at least one, and perhaps both agents would see their level of satisfaction reduced. Now consider some point not on the contract curve, say X_0 in Figure 24.2 at which A has all the X and B has all the Y, and ask the same question. Here the answer is just as clearly yes, for A would consent to any redistribution of goods that involved a movement along indifference curve A_1 or to a curve that lay above it. Similarly B would consent to any redistribution that involved a movement along B_1 or to a curve lying above it. Clearly there is much scope within the area bounded by these two indifference curves to redistribute goods among our consumers so that both gain. Being maximising agents, they would both consent to such a redistribution.

Now note that, in the foregoing argument, point H stood for any point on the contract curve, and X_0 for any point off it. We have shown, therefore, that if goods are distributed between our consumers in such a way that they are not at a point at which their indifference curves are tangent to one another, are not on the contract curve, they can both gain from a redistribution of goods between them. W~ have also shown that, if they are at a point on the contract curve, no gains are available to both of them simultaneously. Hence if, when they receive their initial endowments, we permit our two agents to trade with one another until all mutually beneficial trades are exhausted, we may conclude that their activities will be such as to place them on the contract curve.

The contract curve therefore links up all those distributions of goods between our two consumers which could be attained if they freely contracted with one another to exchange goods, starting from any arbitrary distribution of goods within the box. Now in any particular instance we can, if we specify the initial distribution of the economy's endowment, find the segment of the contract curve to which voluntary trade would lead. The distribution of goods actually reached in any instance would have to result in a gain (or at least no loss) in satisfaction to both parties. Thus, to refer back to Figure 24.2 again, there is a segment of the contract curve below and to the left of point H, and another above and to the right of point K, which would not be attainable if our agents were to start their trading from point X_0. Any point between H and K could, however, be reached by mutually agreeable trades beginning from X_0. This segment of the contract curve is usually referred to as the *core* of the economy, and its location must be defined not just with respect to the tastes of agents inhabiting the economy, and its overall endowment

of goods, as is the whole contract curve, but also with respect to the initial distribution of that endowment between the two agents from which trading activity begins.

Competitive Prices and the Auctioneer

Readers will have been struck by the vagueness of our description, in the foregoing section, of the trading process underlying the movement from a point off the contract curve to a point on it, and we now turn to clarifying this matter. In principle one could conceive of a wide variety of rules under which two agents could bargain with one another, but here we shall consider what happens when the agents trade with one another at competitively determined prices, It is true, of course, that we normally associate competition with large numbers of traders being at work in a market, but the reader who treats our application of competitive notions to the highly artificial two agent case as a simplification designed clearly to reveal the key properties of a market made up of many traders, will not be misled.

We must begin our exposition by drawing attention to a puzzle. It is of the very essence of a competitive market that every agent operating in it has no control over prices. These are taken by every individual as given by 'the market' and treated as the basis for that agent's decisions about quantities. Consider our treatment of consumer theory in Chapter 2 above. There the typical consumer was treated as taking the prices of goods as given, and the demand curve we derived told us how the consumer's demand for a particular good would vary as its market price changed. Similarly, our analysis of the perfectly competitive firm in Chapter 13 treated it as a price taker choosing its quantity of output. But suppose that every market in an economy is to be treated as perfectly competitive. This implies that every agent in that economy is a price taker and, therefore, that no one within the economy sets prices. Who then sets prices? How do they change? This gap in the theory of competitive markets is a real one, and the standard way of filling it, which we shall now set out, though logically viable, leaves many economists extremely uncomfortable about the validity of blindly applying competitive market theories to the real world. The discomfort in question figures particularly prominently in debates about macroeconomic issues, and so we simply note it here rather than discussing it at any length.

The problem of price setting in a perfectly competitive market economy is usually dealt with by postulating that the system works as if it was presided over by an *auctioneer* who neither consumes nor produces goods, and whose sole job it is to set prices according to certain rules and to inform traders about them. The rules in question involve the auctioneer operating what is usually referred to as a process of *tâtonnement*, which in a pure exchange economy may be thought of as working as follows.

When they receive their endowments of goods, agents come to a 'market' presided over by the auctioneer, and this entity suggests to them a list of prices for all the goods in the economy. Each agent then submits to the auctioneer a list consisting of the quantities of goods to be supplied and demanded by that individual at those prices. It is then the auctioneer's task to check these lists to see if the trades offered can all go through. If they cannot, if more (or less) of some good is being demanded than is available, then the auctioneer recognises that the market is not in equilibrium, that all agents' plans are not mutually compatible, and tries another set of prices. The new set of prices is not chosen at random, however. The auctioneer raises the prices of those goods for which the sum of agents' demands exceeds the economy's endowment, and lowers the prices of those for which demand falls short of the endowment.

This process of groping for an appropriate set of prices continues until one is found at which the sum of agents' demand for each and every good just equals the economy's endowment of it, at which the so-called *excess demand* for each good is zero. At this point the auctioneer permits trading to begin at this equilibrium set of prices, and agents may do so confident that all of their planned exchanges can indeed go through. It should be stressed that in our model of the perfectly competitive economy, the auctioneer never permits anyone to trade until equilibrium prices have been established. This assumption is crucial in the analysis which follows. One derives markedly different results if we assume that agents actually exchange goods at disequilibrium prices, referred to as *trading at false prices*, though models of this sort are beyond the scope of this book (see the Suggested Further Reading at the end of this part of the book).

Properties of Competitive Equilibrium

The process of *tâtonnement* we have described leads to a state of competitive equilibrium, and we can learn something about its properties by considering a two person two good exchange economy in which trade takes place according to the rules just set out. Figure 24.3 depicts such an economy, indeed the same economy described in Figure 24.2, in which its initial endowment of goods is distributed so that A has all the X and B has all the Y. Now let the auctioneer suggest a price for X in terms of Y which implies that our two agents can trade along a line such as I. Faced with such a budget constraint, A would wish to move to point L, consuming X_1 of X and Y_1 of Y. B on the other hand would wish to move to point M, consuming X_2 of X and Y_2 of Y. Obviously in this case the economy-wide planned consumption of X $[(O_A - X_1) + (O_B - X_2)]$ falls short of its total endowment $(O_A - X_0)$, and planned consumption of Y $[(O_A - Y_1) + (O_B - Y_2)]$ exceeds its total endowment $(O_A - Y_0)$. In these circumstances the auctioneer would not permit our agents to attempt to trade with one another, but would instead try another lower relative price

Figure 24.3

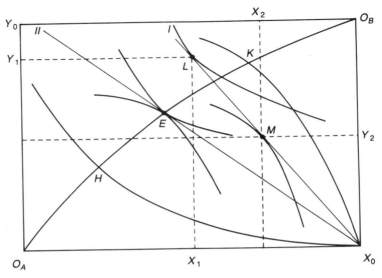

At the price ratio underlying *I*, there is an excess demand for *Y* and an excess supply of *X*. As the relative price of *Y* is increased the price ratio pivots towards *II*. If each agent faces the same relative price for *X* and *Y*, as they would in a competitive market, their demands for *X* and *Y* will just take up the economy's endowment of these goods at a point such as *E*.

for *X* in terms of *Y* in order to eliminate the excess demand for *Y* and the excess supply of *X*. The line characterising the price ratio facing our two agents would thus pivot to the left of *I*. Such a process of price adjustment could continue for some time, but would cease when the excess demand for each good was eliminated and the planned quantities demanded of each good by each agent just sum up to the economy's endowment of those goods. Such a competitive equilibrium would occur at a point such as *E*, at a price ratio given by the slope of *II*.

In Figure 24.3 *E* represents a distribution of the economy's endowment of goods between *A* and *B* that would be attained if they traded as price takers in a competitive market in equilibrium, and the first point to be noted is that it lies on the economy's contract curve, and indeed on that segment of it which we termed the economy's core. Hence our competitive equilibrium represents a state of affairs in which it would be impossible to make one of our agents better off, in the sense of moving that agent to a higher indifference curve, without simultaneously making the other worse off. We shall have much to say about this property of competitive equilibrium later when we discuss welfare economics. It should also be noted that there is no reason to believe that point *E* represents a unique equilibrium for the economy. There may well exist other price ratios at which our two agents' plans would also be mutually compatible and hence

on the contract curve. However, it is also true that the range of competitive equilibrium points is smaller than the range of points that lie within the economy's core. Readers may satisfy themselves of this by reproducing Figure 24.3 and drawing straight lines from X_0 to points H and K, the limiting points on the contract curve that lie in the economy's core. Clearly a competitive equilibrium at the price ratio implicit in either line would not be feasible. At the first of them there would exist an excess demand for X and an excess supply of Y and at the second an excess demand for Y and an excess supply of X.

Blocking Coalitions and the Core

The foregoing analysis offers a very specific description of how the economy achieves a general equilibrium. Individuals maximise utility subject to their initial endowments and prices are determined according to the balance of demand and supply. Another way of thinking about how resources are allocated in an exchange economy is based on the notion of coalitions — groups of individuals — which are formed to block particular allocations. Consider again Figure 24.3, where the initial endowment is at X_0. We can conceive of the economy having two types of individual, A and B; so that A and B are now groups or coalitions of agents. In Figure 24.3, coalition A starts the game with all of X and coalition B with all of Y. The coalitions then consider alternative allocations of resources. If the best they can do is to share out the new allocation in such a way that each member of the coalition is no better off, and some members of the coalition are worse off with the new allocation, the coalition in question can always refuse to trade and thereby *block* the new allocation.

We can now define the *core* more formally as follows. An allocation of resources is in the core if it represents a redistribution of resources from the initial endowment which cannot be blocked by any feasible coalition. In Figure 24.3, persons of type A will block any allocation below the indifference curve HX_0 and persons B will block any allocation above the indifference curve KX_0. Groups A and B will combine to block any allocation between HX_0 and KX_0 which is not on the contract curve. The core is therefore the segment of the contract curve between H and K in Figure 24.3.

*Competitive Equilibrium — a More Formal Treatment

A competitive equilibrium occurs when demand equals supply for every good simultaneously. The list, or *vector*, of prices at which all markets clear will be called the *equilibrium price vector*, and the resulting quantities of goods, the *equilibrium allocation of resources*. In this section, we provide

a simple formalisation of the price setting process, and discuss the concept of the core in yet more detail.

We can consider the *tâtonnement* process described earlier as a sequence of adjustments, or *iterations*, towards the equilibrium price vector. We can generalise the model to a large number of goods, so that g_i (for goods) represents the ith good where $i = 1, \ldots, n$, and j consumers are represented by the subscript $j = 1 \ldots n$. The demand and supply of goods are denoted by the superscripts d and s respectively. Then the price determining process can be described in the following way. The auctioneer selects one good relative to which the prices of all others are to be measured — the so-called *numeraire* of the system. This choice is quite arbitrary, because any good will serve the purpose equally well. Then the process of equilibrium price formation proceeds by steps.

Step 1.   The auctioneer calls out an initial list of prices, the price vector $\mathbf{p}^1$ which contains prices $p_1^1 \ldots p_n^1$, with the price of the numeraire good relative to itself being, of course, equal to one.

Step 2.   On the basis of these prices, consumers maximise utility given their initial endowment of goods, and derive their supplies and demands for each good g_{ij}^d and g_{ij}^s. At the level of each market, demand and supply for good i equals $\Sigma_j g_{ij}^d$ and $\Sigma_j g_{ij}^s$ respectively. Consumers inform the auctioneer of these *notional demands and supplies*, but no trade takes place as yet.

Step 3.   The auctioneer sums the demand and supplies for each good, and calculates the *excess demand*

$$ED_i = \sum_j g_{ij}^d - \sum_j g_{ij}^s \tag{24.1}$$

for each good, i. The auctioneer then alters the price vector according to the rule.

$$p_i^2 - p_i^1 = \alpha \, (ED_i) \tag{24.2}$$

for every i, where α is a positive constant. The auctioneer therefore raises the price of goods in excess demand, and reduces the price of goods in excess supply. An adjustment process of this kind is referred to as *Walrasian*.

Step 4.   The auctioneer calls out the new price vector, $\mathbf{p}^2$ and steps 1–4 are repeated again.

This process continues until the auctioneer changes no price, i.e. until $p^{k+1} = p^k$ where k is the number of iterations. This occurs of course where excess demands are zero for all goods. At that point, but not before, people are allowed to trade with one another.

The equilibrium price vector is therefore derived as the solution to n simultaneous equations; the excess demand functions for each good. However, in fact the equation system need only be solved for $(n-1)$ relative prices, because we can always, as we have seen, choose a single price, that of the numeraire, to be fixed at some predetermined level. This result arises from what is known as *Walras' Law*, which states that for each and every price vector, the *sum* of excess demands for all goods, valued in terms of the numeraire, must equal zero. Individuals always spend their entire budget on goods, so that at any price vector, the total value of each individual's excess demands for goods necessarily equals zero.

Consider the example of the two good model discussed earlier. Walras' Law tells us that

$$p_x(X^d - X^s) + p_y(Y^d - Y^s) = 0 \qquad (24.3)$$

Thus, if we have a certain value of excess demand in the market for good X, we must have excess supply to the same value in the market for good Y, and vice versa. Thus in the two good special case we actually only have a single equation to determine a single equilibrium relative price between the two goods. Because we know that if the market for X is in equilibrium, the market for Y must also be in equilibrium, we cannot solve two excess demand equations for two prices, but only for a single relative price, the price ratio, p_x/p_y.

More generally, in a system of excess demand equations, Walras' Law tells us that if $(n-1)$ markets are in equilibrium, then the nth market is also in equilibrium. We therefore only have $(n-1)$ prices for which to solve, and can fix the price of the nth good arbitrarily to any level. This nth good is, of course, the arbitrarily selected *numeraire* good, referred to earlier.

The Existence, Uniqueness and Stability of Equilibrium

The analysis of general equilibrium raises three important technical issues: whether the general equilibrium actually *exists*, whether it is *unique* and whether it is *stable*. We can introduce these issues only informally in this book, but interested readers with technical skills can follow up the analysis with more advanced texts listed at the end of this part.

The question of existence is fairly straightforward. In a general sense, we want to know whether the $(n-1)$ equation system of excess demand functions has a solution: the vector of $(n-1)$ equilibrium prices. In a two good economy, we know from Walras' Law that if demand equals supply in one market, excess demand will equal zero in the other. Therefore, we can think about the problem from the perspective of a single market, in which we will find an equilibrium if the demand curve is continuously downward sloping and the supply curve continuously upward sloping. (Strictly speaking, we also need to assume that the intercept of the supply

curve with the quantity axis lies to the left of the demand curve's intercept in order to ensure that equilibrium exists at a positive price and quantity.) If for some reason there are discontinuities or gaps in the demand and supply curves, they may not intersect at any well-defined price and quantity, and there will be no competitive equilibrium.

If demand curves monotonically slope down and supply curves monotonically slope up, excess demand is everywhere a diminishing function of price. The rule for the auctioneer — change price in proportion to excess demand — will then ensure that, if we start out of equilibrium, price will converge towards its equilibrium value, and excess demand go to zero. Moreoover that equilibrium will be unique.

However, consider a good which is a normal good at low levels of income, becomes inferior at higher levels of income and then reverts to being nomal. If the income effect outweighs the substitution effect of a price change in the relevant inferior range, the resulting demand curve could be downward sloping initially, then backward bending and finally downward sloping again. This case is depicted in Figure 24.4. We present it here as a logically conceivable case, which enables us to illustrate the possibility that there can exist multiple equilibria, and that not all of them need be stable. We do not mean to suggest in any way that it is empirically likely.

It will be remembered that the auctioneer's adjustment mechanism is to alter price according to equation (24.2), raising price when excess demand is positive and reducing price when it is negative. In Figure 24.4. the segments of the excess demand function lying to the left of A and the right of B are *stable* with this adjustment mechanism, but the segment lying between these points is *unstable*.. Consider first a disequilibrium

Figure 24.4

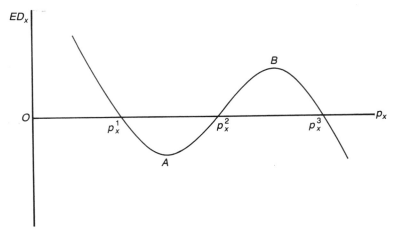

Excess demand for X as a function of p_x. As drawn, there are three equilibria in this market, at p_x^1, p_x^2 and p_x^3. The first and third of these are stable and the second unstable.

situation in the segment to the left of A, for example, a price below p_X^1. Excess demand is positive in that region and so the auctioneer lowers price back to the equilibrium, p_X^1. The same analysis applies in the segment of the excess demand curve that lies to the right of B except that price converges to p_X^3. However, in the segment AB the auctioneer's adjustment rule takes the market further away from equilibrium at px^2 rather than towards it. For example, between A and px^2, the market is in excess supply so the auctioneer lowers price, which takes us even further from the nearest equilibrium, px^2. Similarly between px^2 and B, the market is in excess demand so the auctioneer raises price, taking the system even further from the equilibrium. Market instability is therefore associated with a situation in which the demand or supply curves are perversely sloped, with the absolute value of the elasticity of demand greater than that of supply. It can be ruled out in an exchange economy if we assume that in general income effects do not outweigh substitution effects on the demand side of the economy.

Market Mechanisms and Planning

The *tâtonnement* process described informally earlier in this chapter, and more formally in the last but one section is often interpreted as the operation of a market economy in which the role of the auctioneer is played by 'market forces', namely, the general realisation by traders that the market is either tight or slack with prices being adjusted accordingly. It should be noted, however, that our formulation would also permit us to think of the job of the auctioneer being undertaken instead by planners. In principle, they could search for equilibrium prices in the manner outlined above, and then incorporate the equilibrium allocation of resources compatible with them in a national plan. A model of planning along these lines was discussed by Oskar Lange during the 1930s, and has since formed the basis for the analysis of so-called decentralised planning.

There are two important drawbacks to this method of price determination, however. The first concerns the motivation of economic agents. If, at the end of the day, the quantities to be bought and sold are set by planners, rather than freely chosen by individuals, there is no obvious reason for economic agents to act as if they are maximising their own utility functions at earlier stages of the iterative procedure. Motivating consumers, and particularly producers, to provide truthful information about how they would behave, therefore becomes a serious problem in a centrally planned economy. Secondly, the planners would face the problem of how to accumulate and process the huge quantity of information required to measure the demands and supplies for every good in the economy. In practice they are likely to be submerged by the sheer volume of information involved here. This assertion appears to borne out

by the operation of planning in Eastern Europe, where planners take numerous short cuts in the processing and accumulation of data about demands and supplies, with the consequence that the plans themselves are often internally inconsistent.

Concluding Comment

The properties of a state of general competitive equilibrium in an exchange economy sketched out earlier in the two person two good case are rather general, holding indeed for any economy made up of a finite number of agents, as a large body of advanced mathematical economic analysis has shown. If a competitive equilibrium exists for an exchange economy, it will lie within the economy's core, so called, and it will therefore involve a state of affairs in which no one agent can be made better off except at the expense of another. Readers who pursue further studies in microeconomics beyond the level of this book will in due course come across many extensions of the simple analysis dealt with here. We shall now extend the analysis in question in a particular direction and go on to discuss the nature of general competitive equilibrium in an economy in which production as well as trading takes place.

25

General Equilibrium with Production

Introduction

In this chapter we shall extend our discussion of general competitive equilibrium to an economy in which the goods which consumers buy are produced, rather than simply being delivered from the outside. Even so, we shall assume that the economy has fixed endowments of productive inputs, capital and labour services. We shall also confine our analysis to a two good economy in which the goods in question are produced using the two inputs. Moreover, in discussing the properties of competitive equilibrium in this production economy, we shall take it for granted that a *tâtonnement* process, such as we described in the last chapter, is at work to ensure that the equilibrium in question is in fact attained in that economy.

The Production Sector

Provided that we make the appropriate simplifying assumptions, we may analyse the production sector of the economy with the aid of a box diagram essentially similar to that deployed in the previous chapter.

Let us, therefore, assume that our two goods, X and Y, are produced by using the productive services of capital and labour. Let us also assume, as we did in our earlier analysis of the firm, that smooth production functions exist to translate input services into outputs of X and Y. Finally, let us assume that the quantities of factor services available to our economy are exogenously fixed.

In Figure 25.1 the quantity of labour service inputs (L) available to the

Figure 25.1

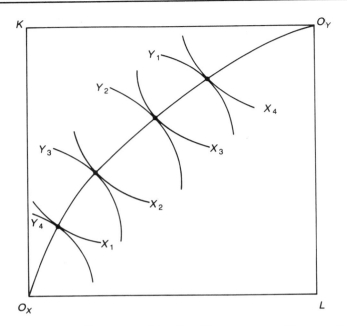

A production box diagram. The lengths of the *K* and *L* axes represent the amount of these two factor services available to the economy. Isoquants representing the output of *X* are drawn relative to the origin O_x and those representing the output of *Y* relative to the origin O_y. O_xO_y is a production contract curve and the economy will be in equilibrium somewhere along it if output takes place under competitive conditions. Figure 25.2 is directly derived from Figure 25.1.

economy is measured horizontally and that of capital services (*K*) vertically. If all available factor services are utilised and are fixed in overall quantity, we may measure inputs into the *X* industry from an origin at the bottom left-hand corner, and for the *Y* industry from the top right-hand corner. Any point within the box represents an allocation of factors between the two industries. We may draw the production functions for the two industries as isoquant maps — just as we drew the indifference maps of our individuals in Chapter 24 — so that any point within the box is also associated with particular levels of output of *X* and *Y*. Any point within the production box is, therefore, an allocation of productive resources in the economy, describing the shares of the two industries' outputs in total production, their respective capital–labour ratios and the amounts of labour and capital used in each.

The locus of tangencies between isoquants is directly analogous to the contract curve of our previous analysis. At any point on this locus, given the output of *X*, the output of *Y* is the maximum attainable, and vice versa. Thus, on this locus, 'technical efficiency', not just for each industry, but for the whole production side of the economy, is achieved.

Is there any reason to suppose that it would be a characteristic of competitive equilibrium in production that the two industries would be on the contract curve? There is indeed. Exactly as in the case of consumer exchange in the previous chapter, a *tâtonnement* process will ensure that the ratio of factor prices will adjust until the capital and labour markets clear simultaneously.

The argument can also be made in terms of the individual firm's optimisation process. A competitive factor market would have each unit of a particular factor of production being paid the same amount for its services regardless of the firm or industry employing it. Moreover, in an industry that is competitive *vis-à-vis* both output and factor markets, each factor receives a payment equal to the value of its marginal product, which is the marginal physical product of the factor multiplied by the price of the output to whose production it is contributing.

Now it will be remembered that the slope of an isoquant at any point measures the ratio of the marginal physical products of the two factors. It tells us by how much K must be increased in order to keep production constant in the face of the withdrawal of a small (in the limit, infinitesimal) quantity of L. If each factor of production gets the same payment in each industry, the ratio of the payments going to each factor must be the same in both industries, and this ratio must be equal to the ratio of their marginal physical products in both industries, if firms are competitive profit maximisers. At the same time we have assumed that all factors are fully employed. It is only at those points at which the isoquants of Figure 25.1 are tangent to each other that all these conditions are satisfied.

Again, note that we have said that a competitive equilibrium in production will involve an allocation of factors of production between industries that lies on the contract curve. We have said nothing about where it might lie, nor indeed is there anything which we can say about this on the basis of the information so far given.

Production Possibilities and the Transformation Curve

The ultimate aim of our analysis is to bring the consumption and production sectors together and to study the properties of their joint equilibrium. The next step towards this goal is the construction of the *transformation curve*. Consider Figure 25.1 once again. Each point in the box lies on both an X-isoquant and a Y-isoquant. Competitive equilibrium involves being on the contract curve and we may take the information implicit in that curve and display it in another way. In Figure 25.2 we measure quantities of X on the horizontal axis and Y on the vertical and draw the *transformation curve* which shows how the output of X and Y varies as we move along the production contract curve, i.e. how X is 'transformed' into Y. The point at which this transformation curve cuts the Y-axis on Figure 25.2 corresponds to the X-origin of the box diagram and the point at which

Figure 25.2

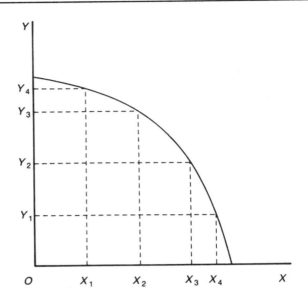

A competitive economy's transformation or production possibility curve. It shows, for given factor availability and technology, the maximum output of X attainable for a given output of Y. Its slope at any point measures the marginal cost of producing X in terms of units of Y. It is derived from Figure 25.1 by reading off the values of the X and Y isoquants as the output moves along the contract curve from O_x to O_y, and plotting pairs of these, e.g. X_1Y_4, as points on the transformation curve.

it cuts the X-axis corresponds to the Y-origin. Because this transformation curve for a competitive economy is derived from the contract curve, along which, for any output of Y, the output of X is maximised given the resources available in the economy, and vice versa, it may also be referred to as a *production possibility curve*, or *production frontier*.

In general, the shape that this competitive equilibrium transformation curve will take depends upon the nature of the production function. It has been drawn concave to the origin in Figure 25.2, but there is no general technical necessity for it to have this shape. Increasing returns to scale in one or both industries would lead to the curve being convex over some of its range, and if they were strong enough, over all of its range.

However, constant returns to scale will be assumed throughout the following analysis and it is easy to show that, given constant returns to scale, the production possibility curve is indeed concave to the origin. Figure 25.3 presents the relevant box diagram. Consider the straight line drawn between the origins in this case. It is technically feasible to vary the outputs of X and Y along this line, and since each industry is characterised by constant returns to scale, the rate at which output of X would have to be sacrificed for Y, i.e. the rate at which X would be

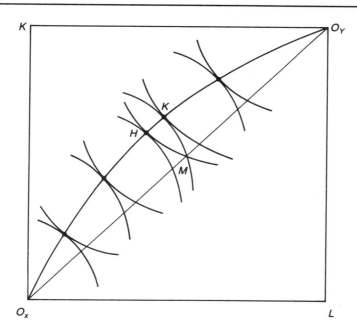

Figure 25.3

A production box diagram. With constant returns to scale, successive equidistant moves along the diagonal drawn between O_x and O_y involve equal changes in the output of X and equal changes in the output of Y. For any point on the diagonal such as M, except the two origins, a higher output of X or Y or both can be obtained by moving to the appropriate segment of the contract curve, HK in the case of point M. Figure 25.4 may be derived from Figure 25.3.

transformed into Y, would be the same at every point on it. Thus, a straight line transformation curve relating the output of X to that of Y, such as has been drawn in Figure 25.4, would correspond to moving along this diagonal.

Only two points on this diagonal are also on the contract curve — the two origins. For any other point on the diagonal it is possible to move to the contract curve and increase the output of at least one good without reducing the output of the other. Thus, relative to point M on the diagonal, anywhere between H and K on the contract curve involves higher output of X (at K) or Y (at H) or both. In terms of Figure 25.4, then, except at its intersection with the axes, the transformation curve derived from the contract curve lies outside the straight line derived from this diagonal, and hence must be generally concave in shape. This transformation curve is the production possibility curve, and is, as we have seen, the one that is relevant for a competitive economy. Only in the limiting case in which the contract curve itself was the diagonal would the production possibility curve be a straight line.

Figure 25.4

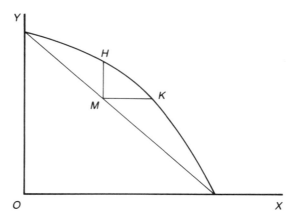

Movement along the diagonal in Figure 25.3 involves a constant ratio of changes in the outputs of *X* and *Y*. Hence the straight line on which *M* lies is constructed by reading off the values of the isoquants as we move up this diagonal. Because *M* represents a combination of output of *X* and *Y* that can be exceeded by moving to the contract curve, any point on this straight line, except those at which it meets the two axes, lies inside that implied by the contract curve. Hence, the production possibility curve, given constant returns to scale, will be generally concave to the origin except in the limiting case when the contract curve itself is a diagonal.

Such a state of affairs would arise if the production functions of the two industries were such that, at a given ratio of factor prices, each one used the two factors of production in the same proportion at any level of output. This would hold if all firms in each industry had identical homothetic constant return to scale production functions (see Chapter 10). If this rather stringent condition does not hold then, with constant returns to scale in each industry, the production frontier is concave to the origin.

Simultaneous Equilibrium in Consumption and Production

Production and consumption equilibria are brought together in Figure 25.5. Here we explicitly assume constant returns to scale, competitive equilibrium, and full employment of all resources, and draw the transformation curve concave. The key to understanding Figure 25.5 lies in grasping the fact that the slope of the transformation curve at any point measures the rate at which one good must be sacrificed in order to obtain more of the other. This slope then measures the *marginal* cost of *X* in terms of *Y* (and its inverse thus measures the marginal cost of *Y* in terms of *X*). But in perfectly competitive equilibrium the supply price of any good is equal to its long-run marginal cost of production. Therefore the slope

Figure 25.5

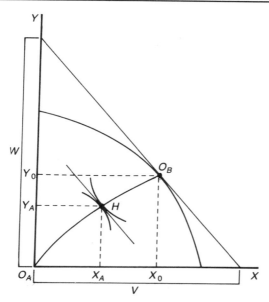

General equilibrium in the two-good/two-person/two-factor model. *W/V* measures the ratio of the marginal cost of and hence supply price of *X* to that of *Y*. The aggregate output mix is given at point O_B. Consumer *A* consumes X_A of *X* and Y_A of *Y*, while *B* consumes $X_0 - X_A$ of *X* and $Y_0 - Y_A$ of *Y*. Note that the slope of the indifference curves at *H*, which gives the ratio of the demand price of *X* to that of *Y*, must be equal to *W/V*.

of the transformation curve also measures the ratio of the prices at which the two goods will be supplied by competitive industries. Hence a simple competitive economy, such as the one which we are considering, will be in equilibrium when the outputs of the two goods are at levels at which the ratio of their prices, as given by the slope of the transformation curve, is such as to put our two consumers into equilibrium at a point on the consumption contract curve.

Such a situation is depicted in Figure 25.5. The equilibrium level of output is given at O_B with the ratio of the supply price of *X* to that of *Y* equal to *W/V*. We construct a consumption box diagram having one of its two origins at the equilibrium point on the transformation curve and the other at the origin relative to which the transformation curve is drawn. Within this box diagram the consumers' indifference curves cut the contract curve at *H*, their slopes at this point being equal to the slope of the transformation curve. Consumer *A* thus consumes X_A of *X* and Y_A of *Y* while *B* gets $X_O - X_A$ and $Y_O - Y_A$.

How does this distribution of consumption between the two consumers get settled? Consumers in this economy also own factor services and derive their incomes from selling them to firms. The point O_B of Figure 25.5 corresponds to a point such as *P* on Figure 25.6 where the slopes

Figure 25.6

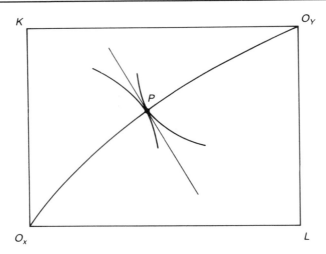

The production box diagram. Point P corresponds to O_B in Figure 25.5. The slope of the isoquants at this point gives the ratio of the price of labour services to that of capital services. Since the levels of output and the prices of output are both given by the analysis set out in Figure 25.5 and since factor payments exhaust output, the level of payments to factors of production is thus set. Given the ownership of factors, which is taken as exogenously determined in this analysis, the distribution of income is determined. This distribution must be such as to enable each consumer to be in equilibrium at point H in Figure 25.5, if the whole economy is to be in equilibrium.

of the isoproduct curves tell us what the relative payment rates for capital and labour will be. Values of the isoquant tell us the levels of output. Since factor payments exhaust output where there are constant returns to scale, factor payments are fully determined at this point. Hence, our situation of general equilibrium has the following property: the owner-ship of factor services, given exogenously, is distributed in such a way that the distribution of income corresponding to the output mix given by O_B is just such as to permit our two consumers willingly to achieve the consumption mix corresponding to point H. It is also, of course, implicit here that different distributions of resource ownership can result in different output mixes.

*The 'Robinson Crusoe' Economy

A simple illustration of some of the issues that arise in general equilibrium with production and consumption can be developed with reference to an even simpler economy than the one just discussed, namely a one person economy (or 'Robinson Crusoe') economy. Though such a set-up is severely oversimplified, not least because it has diverse activities on different sides of the market being undertaken by a single individual, the

logic of such an economy at many points carries over to one inhabited by many consumers and producers. It also enables us to consider a case in which the supply of inputs, in this case labour, is determined within the model, rather than being given exogenously, without unduly complicating the analysis.

On the supply side of his economy, we assume that Robinson Crusoe uses a single input, L, to produce output X. Hence, he may also be thought of as a consumer, who buys X and sells L. To bring out the relevance of his decisions to the general competitive case we make the artificial assumption that Robinson Crusoe is a price taker, making decisions on the basis of prices set by a Walrasian auctioneer who obeys an adjustment rule such as was described earlier by equation (24.4). The auctioneer initially chooses $(w_1 p_x^1)$. As a producer, Robinson Crusoe therefore seeks to maximise profits subject to a short-run production function which is assumed to display strictly diminishing returns. The maximisation problem is, therefore,

maximise with respect to X and L

$$\pi = p_x^1 X - w^1 L \tag{25.1}$$

subject to

$$X = f(L) \tag{25.2}$$

with first-order conditions,

$$p_x^1 \partial X / \partial L - w^1 = 0 \tag{25.3}$$

or

$$\partial X / \partial L = w^1 / p_x^1$$

Diagrammatically equation (25.1) can be rearranged in (X, L) space as an isoprofit map,

$$X = \frac{\pi}{p_x^1} + \frac{w^1}{p_x^1} L \tag{25.4}$$

which for a given wage and price can be plotted as a series of positively sloped parallel lines, with higher intercepts on the X axis being associated with higher levels of profit. In Figure 25.7a, we draw Robinson Crusoe's production decision for the given wage–price ratio, which is to choose the (X, L) combination which generates the largest volume of profit consistent with the available technology. Crusoe, therefore, chooses X and L at the tangency of the highest available isoprofit line with the short-run production function, which is at a point where equation (25.3) is satisfied. We denote this combination (X_1^s, L_1^d), with the profits earned being π_1. This economy yields positive profits despite the assumption of 'competition' (price-taking behaviour) because there are diminishing returns to labour (see Chapter 14) and, therefore in this one input case, to scale as well.

Figure 25.7

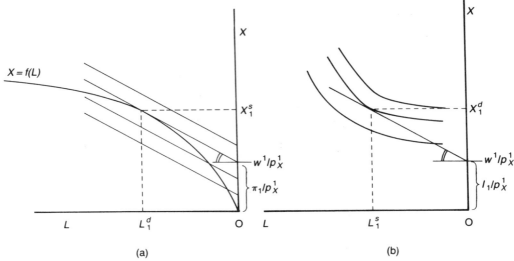

(a) Robinson Crusoe faces production function $X = f(L)$ with labour input measured in the negative quadrant. Given an isoprofit line with slope w^1/p_x^1, he chooses X_1^s and L_1^d to obtain the maximum available profits, π_1. (b) As consumer, Crusoe has unearned income I, and real wages w^1/p_x^1. He chooses (L_1^s, X_1^d).

Now consider Crusoe as a consumer. Given w^1 and p_x^1, he chooses X and L to maximise

$$U = U(L, X) \tag{25.5}$$

subject to

$$p_x^1 X = I + w^1 L \tag{25.6}$$

where I is some 'unearned' income endowment (see Chapter 5). The first-order condition here is

$$\frac{\partial U/\partial X}{\partial U/\partial L} = w^1/p_x^1 \tag{25.7}$$

Diagrammatically, we can represent utility function (25.5) by convex indifference curves, with the budget constraint (25.6) being rearranged to a budget line as follows:

$$X = \frac{I}{p_x^1} + \frac{w^1 L}{p_x^1} \tag{25.8}$$

For any given I, say I_1, Crusoe chooses (X_1^d, L_1^s) in Figure 25.7b, at the tangency between the budget line (25.8) and the highest available indifference curve which satisfies condition (25.7).

Let us now make the assumption that all the profits earned by Crusoe in production are spent in consumption. Hence, profits are fully paid out as 'unearned' income. Hence in the example above, $\pi_1 = I_1$. We can, therefore, bring the demand and supply sides of the Crusoe economy together in Figure 25.8 to illustrate price determination. At the initial prices (w^1, p_x^1), Robinson Crusoe finds that the demand for labour, L_1^d, exceeds the supply L_1^s. As we would expect from Walras' Law, he simultaneously discovers that his supply of goods exceeds demand.

The auctioneer will also have this information, and, acting on Walrasian principles, will raise the wage and lower the product price, calling out a new higher real wage (w^2/p_x^2). As we have drawn it, these are equilibrium prices, with demand equal to supply in both the goods and money market. However, one could equally imagine the case of over-shooting, in which the second price vector generates excess supply in the labour market, with excess demand in the goods market. The Walrasian price setting mechanism would still ultimately ensure that, provided the indifference curves were convex to the origin and the pro-duction function was strictly concave, a price vector would be found at which excess demands were zero in both markets.

This diagram allows us to investigate in more detail the role of technical assumptions in ensuring the uniqueness of competitive equilibrium. Con-sider for example the case where technology is characterised by constant returns, as illustrated in Figure 25.9(a). We can see that in the Robinson

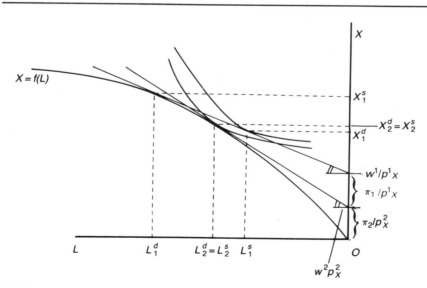

Figure 25.8

At initial price vector (w^1, p_x^1), we have excess demand in the labour market and excess supply in the goods market. The auctioneer therefore raises the real wage, for example to (w^2, p_x^2). With these prices, and the associated level of profits, demand equals supply in both markets simultaneously.

Crusoe economy, there is a point of competitive equilibrium, at (L^*, X^*). However, the Walrasian auctioneer will not be able to get the economy to that equilibrium point. Suppose that the auctioneer calls out a real wage such as w^1/p_x^1. Crusoe the producer will find that profits are maximised where output and employment are zero. If the auctioneer responds to the goods shortage and employment glut by reducing the real wage, for example to w^2/p_x^2, optimal output and, therefore, labour demand for Crusoe the producer the firm becomes infinite. If, by chance, the auctioneer isolates the equilibrium real wage w^3/p_x^3, Crusoe will find that the level of profit is independent of the level of output and employment, and is always zero. Crusoe's product supply and labour demand decision is therefore indeterminate in this case. Unless Crusoe the producer happens by chance to choose (L^*, X^*) when the auctioneer calls out (w^3, P_x^3), general equilibrium cannot be achieved.

A related problem arises in the case of increasing returns, illustrated in Figure 25.9(b). The production function in this case is strictly convex, so that at every conceivable real wage combination, tangency between the isoprofit line and the production function yields a loss. It appears to Robinson Crusoe, the producer, that he can in fact raise profits by increasing output and employment indefinitely, so that the first-order tangency conditions will never be satisfied. Though there is a competitive

Figure 25.9

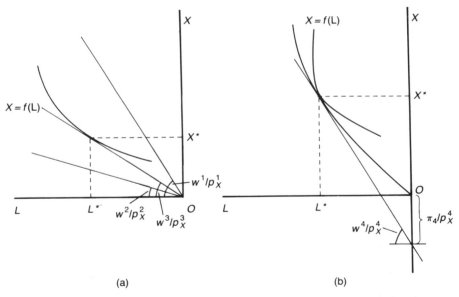

(a)   (b)

(a) With constant returns, the Walrasian adjustment procedure is unable to isolate the competitive equilibrium (X^*, L^*). Desired output supply and labour demand is always either infinite (with $w^2 p_x^2$), zero (with $w^1 p_x^1$) or indeterminate (with $w^3 p_x^3$). (b) With increasing returns, tangency between the isoprofit line and the production function occurs where profits are negative, for example at π_4 (in fact, at a profit minimum). Crusoe always chooses an infinite output supply and labour demand, whatever the real wage.

equilibrium at (L^*, X^*), the Walrasian price-setting mechanism once again is unable to lead Crusoe the producer to select that allocation.

In the case of constant returns, the excess demand functions for the two markets are therefore discontinuous, with small changes in relative prices at certain points leading to abrupt shifts from excess demand to excess supply and vice versa without necessarily reaching the point where excess demand equals zero. With increasing returns, the labour market is locked into a situation of excess demand and the goods market into one of excess supply, with no adjustment of price leading to sufficient changes in excess demands for them ever to reach zero. These non-convexities in production are, therefore, associated with non-existence of competitive equilibrium.

One can imagine similar arguments applying to the demand side. If employment and goods are perfect substitutes, so that the indifference curves are straight lines, we have an analogous argument to the case of constant returns. There will be discontinuities in the resulting excess demand functions and the competitive equilibrium may not be attainable by a *tâtonnement* process. If the indifference curves are not smoothly convex, we may have a case of multiple equilibria, as illustrated in the previous chapter, Figure 24.4. If, in addition, Crusoe has a backward-bending supply of labour curve for some relevant part of the range of the real wage, one or several of the equilibria must be unstable. Interested readers may wish to develop the appropriate diagrams for these cases themselves.

Concluding Comment

In this chapter we have concentrated on describing some of the attributes of competitive equilibrium in a simple two factor/two good/two person economy (though in the immediately preceding section we have dealt with aspects of the 'Robinson Crusoe' case in order to explore certain aspects of general equilibrium analysis a little more deeply). Needless to say, the attributes of so simple an economy would not be of much interest if they did not carry over to much more complex cases of many more goods, factors and persons. It would be far beyond the technical scope of this book to prove that they do so, but readers may accept that this can be, and has been, proved by others. The basic implication of the analysis of competitive equilibrium which we have carried out for a special simple case is this: if consumers maximise utility and if perfectly competitive firms maximise profits, then there usually exists a set of market prices that will render all their individual plans compatible with one another and with the overall constraint imposed on the economy by available resources and technology. In short, the price mechanism operating in a market economy can, at least in principle, provide a coherent solution to the social problem of scarcity.

The above mentioned solution is coherent in the sense that factors are allocated, income is distributed, and consumption goods are chosen in mutually consistent patterns, but whether such a solution is desirable is another question. The mere fact that it might exist tells us nothing about this matter. Nevertheless, questions about whether monopoly or competition does more to promote economic welfare, about the consequences of various tax and subsidy schemes for economic welfare, and so forth, are surely worth asking. Once the prior question of what constitutes economic welfare is settled, economic models of the type dealt with in this chapter may be used in many attempts to get to grips with these questions. We discuss these issues in the next chapter.

26

The Pareto Criterion and Competitive Equilibrium

Introduction

Up to now in this book we have dealt with questions about how consumers and firms will behave in various situations, and about the logic linking the predictions which we make about such behaviour to assumptions about the motives underlying it. These are *positive* questions, so-called. A prediction about behaviour is either right or wrong, and can be checked against data. A conclusion either follows from a set of assumptions or it does not, and the logic of an argument can be checked for its validity. This is not to say that such checks are always easy to perform. Real world data are often ambiguous and difficult to interpret, and long chains of logical argument are frequently hard to assess for rigour. However their outcome does not depend on any ethical stance that the economist carrying them out might bring to the task. Economist *A* might believe that self-interested utility-maximising behaviour is morally deplorable, while economist *B* might regard it with approval, but both would be able to agree on the assumptions necessary to derive from it the prediction that the quantity demanded of a commodity will increase as its price falls, and both, on consulting the same set of data, would be able to agree about whether or not this prediction was confirmed.

Positive economics is not the whole of the subject, however. We often wish to go beyond the description of a particular situation and pass judgement on it, to say that it is desirable or undesirable. We may also want to compare alternative situations and say something about their relative merits. Finally, and crucially, we may want to design economic policies intended to eliminate undesirable characteristics of an economy and replace them with desirable alternatives. In short, economics sometimes

deals with *normative* as well as positive questions, and these form the subject matter of *welfare economics*. This chapter, and the following one, are intended to provide an introduction to this body of analysis. In order to discuss normative questions, one must have norms. Our first task, therefore, is to describe an ethical principle widely used as a basis for welfare economics. This is the so-called *Pareto criterion*. When this has been described, we shall use it to assess the desirability of the state of general competitive equilibrium analysed in the last two chapters, and to compare such an equilibrium with one that might arise if some sector of the economy were to deviate from the competitive ideal.

In the course of this analysis it will become apparent that the Pareto criterion does not enable us to make comparisons between situations where questions about alternative income distributions are crucial. We shall defer detailed discussion of this issue until the next chapter where we shall also say something about situations in which markets seem to 'fail', in the sense that the operation of competitive mechanisms appears, in the light of the Pareto criterion, to need a little help from well-designed policies in order to achieve socially desirable ends.

The Pareto Criterion and Pareto Optimality

There can be no competely objective basis for selecting criteria upon which judgements about the superiority of one social situation over another may be made. Inevitably there is a normative element present in such a judgement and the discussion of normative criteria is more the business of moral philosophers than of economists. Welfare economics usually bypasses detailed normative debate by taking the *Pareto criterion* as its starting point. This criterion states that if, when the resources available to a society are reallocated among alternative uses, the *economic welfare* of at least one member of society is increased without that of any other member being reduced, then the economic welfare of that society has increased. An increase or decrease in an individual's economic welfare simply involves a movement from a lower to a higher indifference curve or vice versa. A *Pareto optimal* situation is then said to exist when it is no longer possible to reallocate resources so as to increase the economic welfare of one individual except at the expense of another.

This criterion is to some extent controversial. It identifies the welfare of society solely with the welfare of the individuals that make up the society. This is a defensible position but there are ethical systems which invest society itself, or groups within society (such as social classes) with a moral importance that is distinct from that attaching to individuals. In terms of such systems the Pareto criterion is at best inadequate and at worst meaningless.

Even granted the individualist ethic, the Pareto criterion is far from providing a complete guide to economic policy. It says nothing about the extent of the superiority of one situation over another, nor does it enable

us to distinguish between alternative situations, both of which may be Pareto superior to some starting situation, but which involve the welfare of different individuals being increased. A resource reallocation that makes a poor person better off by a pound a year and lowers the welfare of no other member of the community represents a movement to a Pareto superior situation, but so does a reallocation that makes a rich person better off by the same amount if no one else's welfare is altered. The Pareto criterion gives us no way of choosing between the two reallocations. Even though most of us would agree that questions about distribution are of central importance to the assessment of alternative situations, the criterion has nothing to say about the distribution of economic welfare between individuals. There are in general as many non-comparable Pareto optimal situations as there are distributions of income. In short, the Pareto criterion tries to distinguish between questions concerning what is usually termed the allocative efficiency of a particular economic situation from those dealing with the justness, or otherwise, of the income distribution ruling in that same situation. The distinction here is certainly one that can be made in principle, but, in practice, because payments to owners of factors of production are an integral part of the mechanism whereby a market economy allocates resources, questions about allocation and distribution tend to turn up together, as well shall see in due course.

Nevertheless, a standard that does not enable us to make all the judgements we might want to make may be useful for some purposes and it is worth looking at the implications of the Pareto criterion in more detail. In particular, it is worth showing that a situation of competitive equilibrium such as was described in the last chapter is Pareto optimal, a situation in which it is impossible to make one person better off without making someone else worse off.

The Pareto Criterion and Competitive Equilibrium in an Exchange Economy

Consider once again the simple exchange economy analysed in Chapter 24. It was described in terms of a simple box diagram such as we have drawn here as Figure 26.1. Let M represent any point not on the contract curve and hence an allocation of consumption goods between individuals that is inconsistent with competitive equilibrium. By moving from M to any point in the economy's core, that is any point on the contract curve between H and J, it is possible to make at least one or, in all but the limiting cases of H and J, both individuals better off. Hence any such move would take us to a Pareto superior situation. Note that this does not say that a move to *any* point on the contract curve from M involves an improvement of welfare. Points to the left of H and to the right of J involve one individual being made better off and the other worse off and hence are not comparable to M using the Pareto criterion.

However, it is the case that, for every point in our box diagram that

Figure 26.1

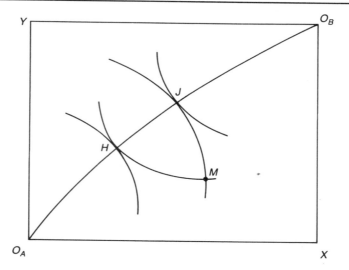

For any point, such as *M*, off the contract curve, there is a segment of the contract curve (*H J*) a movement to which would make at least one consumer better off without making the other worse off.

is *not* on the contract curve, there is at least one point *on* the contract curve that is Pareto superior to it. Moreover, any point on the contract curve is Pareto optimal. Consider point *H* in Figure 26.1, and let it represent any point on the contract curve. To move away from this point by leaving the contract curve will involve at least one and perhaps both individuals in a loss of economic welfare, while to move away from it up or down the contract curve involves the welfare of one individual being increased at the expense of the other.

Recall, however, that in Chapter 24, we showed that a situation of competitive equilibrium in this simple exchange economy would lie on the contract curve, and indeed within the economy's core. It must now be apparent to the reader that, according to the Pareto criterion, a competitive equilibrium is a desirable state of affairs; indeed, it is a Pareto optimal situation. In a simple exchange economy, the condition for Pareto optimality that the economy be on its contract curve implies that society's economic welfare is at a maximum (*not the unique maximum*) where the *marginal rates of substitution between goods are equalised among different consumers.*

The reader should note that this conclusion about the social desirability of being on the contract curve should not be extended by analogy to the cases of collusion between firms, or firms and unions, discussed in Chapters 17 and 22. In these cases, being on the contract curve maximises the welfare of those colluding, but emphatically not that of society as a whole.

Pareto Optimality in Production

The foregoing conclusion about the optimality of competitive equilibrium also holds for an economy with production. This is best shown by first considering the production sector of the economy in isolation, and then bringing it together with the consumption sector. Figure 26.2 reproduces the production box diagram analysed earlier. If it is possible to increase the output of one good without decreasing the output of another, it is possible to increase economic welfare. In this sense the Pareto criterion ensures that there is no waste in the allocation of inputs to alternative uses. The application to Figure 26.2 of arguments analogous to those made about the exchange economy described in Figure 26.1 should readily convince the reader that for any point not on the production contract curve there is at least one point on the curve at which the output of at least one of the goods is higher without that of the other being reduced. It should also be obvious that it is impossible to move along the contract curve without reducing the output of one good while that of the other is increased. Thus, as far as production is concerned, points on the contract curves (and of course all competitive equilibria lie on the contract curve) are required for Pareto optimality. The second condition for Pareto optimality is therefore that *marginal rates of technical substitution between inputs are equalised* between alternative uses. This argument, of course, amounts to a reaffirmation of a point made earlier: namely that the transformation curve for a competitive economy also represents its production frontier.

The foregoing argument reaffirms that the transformation curve between X and Y derived earlier (cf. Figure 25.1) specifies for any level

Figure 26.2

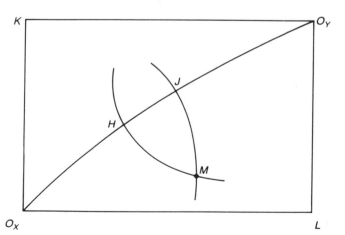

For any point off the contract curve such as *M*, there is a segment of the curve (*H J*) movement to which will permit the output of at least one good to be increased without reducing the output of the other.

of output of Y, what is the maximum output of X it is physically possible to produce, and vice versa. It divides the area of a figure such as 25.2 into a region below and on the curve, which contains bundles of X and Y whose production is feasible with available resources and technology, and a region which contains bundles whose production is not feasible. Thus, it represents the economy's production frontier, as we have already noted.

The Pareto Optimality of Competitive Equilibrium in a Production Economy

Now we saw earlier that a situation of competitive equilibrium would result in each good's market price being equal to long-run marginal cost. The economy's competitive equilibrium production pattern was thus at a point on the production frontier where the ratio of the goods' marginal production costs equalled the ratio of their market prices. It remains to show that such a situation is Pareto optimal.

In terms of our simple model, this is best done by considering a situation in which the market price of one of the two goods differs from its competitive level. There are many ways in which this could happen. The output of one good could be monopolised and a monopolist, other than a perfect price discriminator, would set price above marginal cost. Or a government could impose a per-unit sales tax (subsidy) on the output of a competitive industry thus raising (lowering) its price to consumers above (below) long-run marginal cost. In analysing such matters we must assume that the recipients of monopoly profits are also consumers; or that the proceeds of a tax (costs of a subsidy) are redistributed to (collected from) consumers as lump sum additions to (deductions from) their incomes. If we did not do so we would have to deal with the complexities that arise when the income accruing to members of an economy differs from the economy's output, and the analysis of such complexities would simply distract attention from the matter now to be dealt with.

We wish to show that an equilibrium situation in which the price of one good differs from its long-run marginal production cost is not Pareto optimal. We shall explicitly deal with a situation in which the price of Y is initially above marginal cost either because its production is monopolised or taxed, but readers should satisfy themselves that consideration of a subsidy to X would produce identical analysis. Figure 26.3 shows an equilibrium situation for an economy in such a situation. The key feature of Figure 26.3 as far as the current analysis is concerned is that the ratio of the market prices of X and Y differs from that which competitive equilibrium would produce. Monopoly pricing or a tax on Y raises its price above its competitive level so that the ratio of the prices of X and Y comes to fall short of the ratio of their marginal production costs. It should go without saying that when these ratios differ consumers will

Figure 26.3

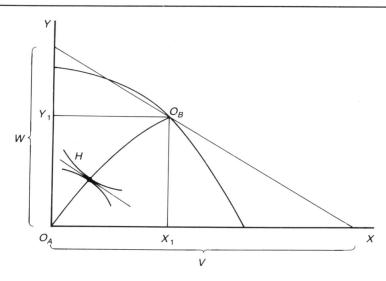

General equilibrium when the price of Y is above its competitive level, either as a result of monopoly pricing or the imposition of a tax. The ratio of the market price of X to that of Y is given by W/V and falls short of the ratio of their marginal production costs at (X_1, Y_1). The consumers' marginal rate of substitution between X and Y is given at H by the ratio of their market prices. More Y is in fact being sacrificed on the margin to obtain X than consumers are willing to sacrifice. The market price of X relative to that of Y is below its marginal cost of production in terms of Y and a Pareto gain in welfare is possible by substituting Y for X in production and consumption, given the distribution of income ruling at H.

allocate their expenditure between the two goods in accordance with relative market prices, and not in accordance with relative marginal costs of production.

Recall that the slope of an indifference curve measures the rate at which the consumer is just willing to trade one good for another to maintain satisfaction, or welfare, constant; the slope of the production frontier measures the rate at which it is physically possible to substitute one good for the other. If production of Y is monopolised or taxed, this leads both of our individuals to consume Y and X in quantities such that the amount of X that they are willing to give up for extra units of Y exceeds the amount that must in fact be given up as far as the technical conditions of production are concerned. Clearly then, a substitution of Y and X in production could lead to a Pareto superior situation as long as the consequences of such substitution for the distribution of income between the two consumers were offset in some way. Whenever the marginal rate of substitution between goods in consumption differs from that in production, a Pareto gain in welfare is possible. When the two rates of substitution are equal and the other conditions already discussed are satisfied, no such gain is possible. The final condition for Pareto optimality is therefore

equality between the marginal rate of transformation in production between goods and the (common) marginal rate of substitution at which individuals trade those goods.

Competitive Equilibrium and Pareto Optimality

We have derived the conditions for Pareto optimality — that outcomes occur on the relevant contract or production possibilities curves — and noted that those conditions are satisfied in competitive equilibrium. We can look at the relationship between competitive equilibrium and Pareto optimality in a slightly different way, by referring to the conditions which have to be satisfied for each to be achieved simultaneously.

The material developed in the previous sections of this chapter can be summarised as follows. Pareto optimality is attained for pure exchange when

$$mrs_{xy}^A = mrs_{xy}^B \tag{26.1}$$

Marginal rates of substitution between goods are equalised across all consumers (A and B in the two person case). In the production sector we additionally require that

$$mrts_{LK}^X = mrts_{LK}^Y \tag{26.2}$$

that marginal rates of technical substitution between inputs (labour and capital) are equalised across activities. Finally, the so-called *grand criterion* for simultaneous optimality in production and exchange is that

$$mrt_{XY} = mrs_{XY}^A = mrs_{XY}^B \tag{26.3}$$

The marginal rate of transformation of goods in production equals the (common to all consumers) marginal rates of substitution between the goods.

It is easy to see that these three conditions will always be satisfied in competitive equilibrium. Condition (26.1) will be satisfied because individuals face a common equilibrium price rate, Px/Py, to which utility maximisation leads each separately to equalise their marginal rate of substitution. Similarly, condition (26.2) is satisfied because firms face a common wage rate–capital cost ratio, w/r, at which profit maximisation leads them to equalise the marginal rate of technical substitution between inputs. Finally, condition (26.3) is satisfied because individuals face the *same* common equilibrium price ratio, Px/Py, as firms face in the two industries when choosing outputs so as to equalise price and marginal cost. The fact that both Pareto optimality and general competitive equilibrium imply conditions (26.1), (26.2), and (26.3) is highly suggestive that the allocations implied by each are identical. This important result is proved formally in more advanced texts listed at the end of the section.

Concluding Comment

In short, when a production and exchange economy is in competitive equilibrium, it is impossible to make anyone better off without making someone else worse off and a Pareto optimal situation therefore exists. This is a result of considerable importance, because it tells us the precise extent to which the coherent solution to the social problem of scarcity that a competitive economy generates is also desirable. A moment's reflection on the limitations of the Pareto criterion as a guide to the assessment of social welfare should convince the reader that, important though the result in question might be, it still leaves crucial aspects of this matter, notably those having to do with distributional questions, unresolved. The next chapter considers some of the issues involved here in more detail.

27

Pareto Optimality: Taxes, Externalities and Distribution

Introduction

The Pareto optimal properties of a perfectly competitive equilibrium lie at the root of a great deal of work on problems of economic policy. At one time the existence of this property was widely regarded as providing an argument in favour of competitive capitalism as a form of economic organisation. It would be hard nowadays to find a professional economist willing to defend such a position, at least when it is put so baldly, but it is worth looking more closely both at the nature of the competitive economy whose properties we have been studying, and at the nature of the optimum we have been considering. To do so will help us better understand the relevance of the Pareto criterion to real world economic problems, and crucially, the limits to that relevance; or the circumstances in which markets 'fail' to allocate resources in a Pareto efficient way.

In this chapter we shall consider in turn aspects of what the notion of Pareto optimality has to say about the design of taxation systems, and about the pervasive group of policy issues which, in everyday parlance are labelled *pollution problems*. Finally we shall discuss an issue of great social and political importance about which the Pareto criterion is self-consciously silent, namely the distribution of economic welfare among agents.

Taxation and Pareto Optimality

No form of economic organisation exists in a social vacuum. A competitive market economy needs, at the very least, a framework of law concerning

property rights and contracts, if it is to function smoothly, and laws need enforcing. This is the minimal necessity for its operating, but even the provision of this bare necessity would require the use of real resources: policemen and court officials must be fed, clothed and housed. Thus taxes must be levied in order to provide the necessary resources. Far from being some kind of interference with the operation of a competitive economy, the levying of taxes must, therefore, be a necessary condition for its existence.

As we have already seen in Chapter 26, to levy a tax on sales of one good leads the ratio of the market prices of goods to depart from the ratio of their marginal costs of production, and hence to a less than Pareto optimal allocation of resources. In terms of the analysis presented in the last chapter, the solution to the problem might appear to be simple: levy a sales tax at the same rate on each good, or, what apparently amounts to the same thing, levy an income tax.

There are two objections to this. First the impression of an income tax as a non-distorting tax arises from a rather special property of our model. The model assumes that the supply of productive resources to the economy is given. In general we would not expect this to be the case. We would expect the supply of labour to vary with the wage rate received; indeed we have analysed some of the factors underlying this phenomenon in Chapter 5, and have considered some of the general equilibrium implications in the case of the Robinson Crusoe economy analysed in Chapter 25.

Once we permit the owners of labour services to choose between work and leisure, we open up another area of choice where a tax can be distorting. An income tax ensures that workers will receive less for their marginal hour of work than those who purchase their output would be willing to pay for it. It is equivalent to levying a tax on every good in the economy except leisure, and hence leads to a misallocation of resources just like any other specific tax. The only tax that will not involve some such distortion is a tax which does not affect any choice about resource allocation. It must be independent of any consumption pattern or work pattern. The only such tax appears to be a poll tax, and even that is suspect if one takes the view that family size, and hence the future supply of labour, is partly the result of choices based on economic factors! Besides, it would be hard to find anyone willing seriously to defend using a poll tax as the sole source of government revenue from the point of view of distributional equity. In short, even in the most competitive economy conceivable, taxes have to be levied, and they are going to affect a great many other things than the allocation of resources.

Moreover, taxes are not the only potential source of distortion in the economy and, in addition to raising revenue, they may themselves be used to offset other distortions. For example, if the price of one particular good is already too high relative to its long-run marginal cost of production because the output of that good is monopolised, then to tax each

good equally will leave resources misallocated. In this case, it would be appropriate to levy taxes on other goods at a higher rate in order to off-set the effect of the initial monopoly. What is an appropriate pattern of taxes is dependent upon the initial pattern of resource allocation in an economy and there are no general rules to be laid down. There can be no general presumption in favour of an income tax over a sales tax on specific goods as a means of raising revenue or, indeed, in favour of any other particular pattern of taxation.

The Second-Best Principle

The implications of the foregoing arguments are easily summed up and are of considerable importance. An economy which was completely free of distortions, including those arising from taxes, would achieve Pareto optimality, but such an economy is a figment of the economist's imagina-tion, not a practical possibility. Governments are necessary, do exist, and do need to collect revenue. The problem, then, is not to design an economic policy regime that will deliver a Pareto optimal allocation of resources, a *first-best* allocation as it is called. Rather it is to design a system that will get the economy as close as possible to such an allocation, given the fact that taxes must be levied and do distort resource allocation. It is to achieve, in the terminology that economists have adopted, a *second-best* solution to the problem. Moreover, to the extent that economic policy has distributional goals and effects, these too must be weighed when policy is designed. We shall return to these distributional issues later in the chapter.

Externalities and Absence of Markets

Allocative (and distributive) problems also arise when so-called *externalities* are under analysis. Such effects can involve both costs and benefits and arise whenever an important, but nevertheless so far implicit, assump-tion of our analysis of competitive equilibrium is violated. In formally analysing the competitive equilibrium model we assumed that there were two, and only two, scarce resources; and in identifying its equilibrium properties with a Pareto optimal allocation of resources we took it for granted that there was a perfect market for every scarce resource available to the economy. Externalities arise whenever there is a scarce resource for which there is no such perfect market, and this is quite a common phenomenon in any actual economy. Indeed it lies at the heart of the so-called problem of pollution.

A simple example will illustrate the nature of the problem. Consider a river which is utilised by two groups of economic agents: fishermen for fishing and manufacturers for discharging waste materials. The river

is clearly a productive resource, but not necessarily scarce. It is a property of rivers that they can absorb a certain amount of waste material without their capacity to support life in their waters being affected, and as long as the amount of waste disposal undertaken is below this limit, the river, though productive, is nevertheless free. By free, we mean that there is enough of it to meet all demands being put upon it without any need to choose among alternative uses.

But now suppose that for some reason the manufacturers along the river expand their output and with it the volume of their waste disposal up to a level at which it affects fishing prospects. Part of the cost of the new higher level of manufactured output is clearly the fish lost to fishermen. However, this is not captured in the private costs of production facing manufacturers and, if they are profit maximisers (and are not fishermen), will be ignored by them. What has happened is that a resource that once was free has become scarce as the demand for its services has increased, but has not had a market price attached to it.

From the point of view of allocative efficiency, the marginal *private* cost facing manufacturers, upon which the pricing of their output is based, falls short of the marginal *social* cost upon which price ought to be based if an optimal allocation of resources in the Pareto sense is to be achieved. The output of manufacturers is thus too high, and the costs involved in lost fish are borne by fishermen instead of by the consumers and producers of manufactures. These costs are *external* to the market for the goods in whose production they are actually incurred.

Now one can have external benefits as well. Suppose the activities of manufacturers enhanced the fish-bearing capacity of our river in such a way that when manufacturing expanded so did the output of fish. In this case the private benefits of expanding manufactured output would fall short of the social benefits, since the greater yield in fish would not enter into the cost calculations of the manufacturers (unless they were fishermen). Their output would fall short of a Pareto optimal level. Indeed, everything in the foregoing analysis — and that which is to follow — is simply reversed in the case of external benefits and so there is no need to deal with the latter as a different case.

Property Rights and the Coase Theorem

How should an external dis-economy be dealt with? The answer obviously is to *internalise* the external cost so as to ensure that it has taken into account by the producers and consumers of manufactures. What may not be quite so obvious in the above example is that there is more than one way to accomplish this, each of which has different distributional implications. The most obvious solution would be to charge the manufacturers for discharging waste into the river in such a way that their outlay on waste disposal expenses reflected the costs imposed upon the fishermen

who could then be compensated for their losses. Alternatively, one could think of instituting a scheme whereby fishermen paid the manufacturer a certain sum for each fish taken from the river, thereby compensating the manufacturer for not polluting the water. The more waste disposal undertaken, the less revenue from fishermen and hence the costs of waste disposal would again come to be included in the manufacturers' cost and revenue calculations.

The second of these two solutions sounds unfair to fishermen, but that is because we have described our example in a particular way. We have had manufacturing expand to cause the externality problem; but suppose manufacturers had always maintained a given level of waste disposal and it was fishermen who found this level of disposal a hindrance to expanding their activities? In that case it would seem more reasonable for fishermen to pay the manufacturer to reduce its activities rather than to ask the manufacturer to compensate the fishermen.

The point here is that, as long as the cost of manufacturing operations, in terms of fish, or the cost of fish in terms of manufactured goods, are reflected in the cash revenues and outlays of firms involved in these activities, then correct (from a Pareto point of view) decisions about resource allocation will be made. It is the distributional consequences of the above two solutions that differ. In the first case we are essentially suggesting that the fishermen become owners of the river and rent out its waste disposal services to manufacturers, while in the second case that manufacturers become the owners of the river who may then sell fishing rights.

We have here an illustration of the so-called 'Coase Theorem' (named after its originator, Professor Ronald Coase of the University of Chicago) which says that, provided property rights in scarce resources are freely exchangeable in competitive markets, the distribution of their ownership among agents is irrelevant to ensuring their efficient use. However, it must be understood that this proposition relies on the assumption that transactions in competitive markets are essentially costless to implement.

In the foregoing example it is indeed feasible to think of solving the 'externality' problem by vesting in someone or other property rights in the resource that has become scarce, that is the river, and then allowing for market transactions among the parties involved, the manufacturers and the fishermen (and the owner of the river if not a member of one or the other groups), to solve the problem of allocating the resource.

Not all 'pollution' problems can, as a practical matter, be dealt with in this way. Consider for example the case of a group of householders who have been using the airspace around their homes to provide themselves with fresh air and peace and quiet, but who now find that an airport is to be set up in the vicinity. In this case, the airlines operating from the airport would use that same airspace for absorbing the kerosene fumes and the noise emitted by their aircraft, thus reducing its capacity to provide fresh air and peace and quiet. The problem here is formally

similar to the one considered earlier, but problems of allocating property rights in airspace, and of monitoring its use so that it can be charged for, are altogether more difficult. In this case, the problem as a practical matter might better be tackled by some direct form of government intervention, perhaps by levying taxes on aircraft movements, or by enforcing regulations concerning permissible noise levels and so on.

Achieving a Pareto Optimum and Changing the Income Distribution

The most obvious difficulty with the Pareto criterion, and one to which we have already referred, is its silence on the matter of the distribution of income. It is all very well to distinguish between allocative efficiency on the one hand and distributive justice on the other, and to have a criterion that deals only with the former, but payments made to factors of production are an integral part of the allocative mechanism. A competitive equilibrium may be optimal, but the movement to an optimal situation from a non-optimal situation is not the same thing as a movement to a socially superior, or preferred, situation. Such a movement may well involve making someone worse off. Consider again the example we used in the previous chapter, in which some such distortion as monopoly pricing or a tax leads to the price of Y exceeding its competitive value. The removal of such a distortion leads to an increase in the demand for Y and hence in the demand for the factor of production that is particularly heavily used in the production of Y. The factor's price will rise and the incomes of its owners increase, perhaps, though not necessarily, at the expense of reducing the incomes of the owners of the other factor. In Figure 27.1 the utility level of A, whose consumption is measured from the origin O_A, is lowered if the economy moves to the optimal situation.

Some Illustrations

A moment's reflection should convince the reader that the problem of making judgements about alternative situations in which the welfare of one group rises (or falls) at the same time as the welfare of others falls (or rises) commonly arises in the real world. Consider for example a country in which airline service was provided by a government regulated monopoly, which, as a condition of being allowed to maintain its monopoly power used some of the excess profits extracted from heavily travelled routes to subsidise the provision of loss-making services to more remote areas. Suppose it was proposed that the government take steps to end the airline monopoly and open up the industry to competition. If this step was taken, one might expect users of heavily travelled routes to benefit from the fact that fares there would fall. However, those living

Figure 27.1

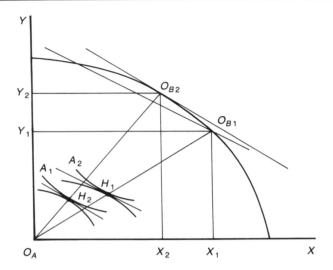

The change in the general equilibrium situation when the price of Y is restored to its competitive level. This figure depicts the *possible* outcome of such action, but not, in every detail, the *necessary* outcome. First, equality between the ratios of the goods' market prices and marginal production costs is restored in the move from X_1Y_1 to X_2Y_2. This must happen if the tax was the only source of discrepancy here. Figure 27.1 is drawn so that the structure of output shifts towards Y and the distribution of income changes in such a way as to reduce A's welfare. Point H_2 lies on a lower indifference curve for A than does point H_1. Note here that A's indifference map is drawn relative to O_A and hence does not shift between the two situations. This reduction in A's welfare is not a necessary outcome of the removal of the tax but it is a logically possible outcome. Hence, though the movement from the first situation to the second takes us from a non-Pareto optimal to a Pareto optimal situation, we cannot say that it represents a movement to a Pareto superior situation. Someone has been made worse off in the shift.

in more remote areas might face a sharp increase in travel costs, or even the loss of all airline service, and their welfare would fall. And what judgement would one make about the fall in the income of shareholders in the monopoly airline? How would one weight these issues in deciding whether or not to implement the proposal in question?

Or consider what might be involved in a plan to flood a mountain valley in order to enhance the water supply of some distant city. To carry through the plan would make the city dwellers better off, but the welfare of people living in the valley would be reduced. Can one make a decision about cases like these without assuming from the start that the welfare of one group is to be given greater weight in the decision-making process than that of another? Economists have developed the analysis of *compensation criteria* in an attempt to avoid the necessity of making judgements about whose welfare is to be given priority in just such instances. As we shall now see, this analysis can help, but it does not provide a complete solution to distributional problems, and it may raise questions in readers' minds about interpersonal comparisons of utility (see Chapter 4).

Compensation Criteria

Two compensation criteria have been proposed in order to enable us to judge the desirability of making changes that cause some people to gain and others to lose. The first suggests that a move from one situation to another would be desirable if those who gain from the move were able to compensate those who lose and still remain better off after the move. The second criterion suggests that the same move would be undesirable if the losers were able to compensate the gainers for remaining in the initial position and still themselves be better off than they would be if the move were to be made.

Unfortunately, these criteria do not cover all possible cases, for it is easy to construct examples in which it is simultaneously possible for the gainers to compensate the losers if a move is made (indicating the move is desirable) and for the potential losers to compensate the potential gainers if the move is. not made (indicating that the move is not desirable)! However, this does not always happen, and it will be convenient to discuss an unambiguous case first of all.

Consider once more the two person/two input/two output, general equilibrium model developed in previous chapters. In that model, just as the production box diagram yields a production frontier, so, once the outputs of X and Y are determined at a point such as O_B in Figure 26.3, does the consumption box diagram yield an analogous relationship that might be called a utility possibility curve. Such a relationship, derived in Figure 27.2, measures the maximum level of utility that A may obtain, given the level of utility made available to B and given a particular output mix of X and Y.

There exists one such utility possibility curve for every point on the production frontier. Since any reallocation of resources involves a change in the outputs of X and Y we may think of it as shifting the utility possibility curve.

Whether we can say anything about the desirability of any reallocation depends not only upon how the utility possibility curve is shifted by it, but also upon which point on the original curve we start from and upon which point on the new curve we arrive at. Let us look at some of the possibilities, dealing with the simple example of the restoration of the price of one good to a competitive level. One logically possible (but not logically necessary) consequence of the removal of monopoly or of a tax is a reallocation of resources which results in a pattern of output such that, for any given level of utility attained by A, B could attain a higher level.

Such an unambiguously outward shift of the utility frontier is shown in Figure 27.3. If, beginning at D, the removal of the tax results in the economy generating a consumption pattern that puts our two individuals at a point on the new frontier between E and F, then the new situation is unambiguously Pareto superior. But what if the new consumption

Figure 27.2

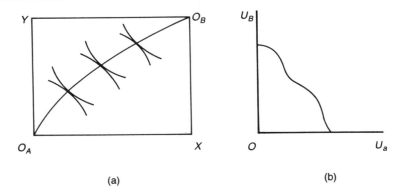

(a)   (b)

Panel (a) shows a consumption box diagram. Panel (b) shows the utility possibility curve
generated by moving along the contract curve. We can say that, as B's utility decreases,
A's increases as we move along the curve. However, if we are dealing with ordinal utility
functions we cannot say by how much. Thus the utility possibility curve slopes
downwards, but not at any defined rate, and is drawn as a wavy line in panel (b) to
remind the reader of this.

Figure 27.3

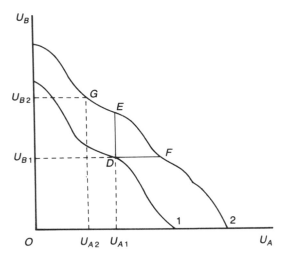

There is a different utility possibility curve for every composition of output, for every point
on a given production frontier. In terms of Figure 27.1, a movement from a structure of
output such as X_1Y_1 to X_2Y_2 produces a new utility possibility curve. It is possible (though
not necessarily the case) that the new curve lies everywhere outside the old one. If we
start at D and the change in output results in a shift to some point on the segment EF of
the second utility possibility curve, then the shift is unambiguously desirable from a Pareto
point of view. Both consumers are made better off. However, if we go, say, to point G, A
is made worse off and we cannot say that G is Pareto superior to D. However, B could
bribe A and make A better off than at D and still be left with a gain. Moreover, there is no
way that A could bribe B to move back to the first situation. Hence, according to the
compensation criteria, the move from utility possibility curve 1 to 2 is desirable.

pattern were to lie at G? Here A would be worse off than initially with U_{A2} rather than U_{A1}. But B could sacrifice utility by giving consumption goods to A until the latter was enjoying the same level of utility as initially while B was still better off. That is, the consumption pattern *could* move to E, and here we would have a situation in which one person (B) was better off without the other (A) being worse off. Equally, in order for A *to persuade B* to remain in the initial situation it would have to be possible to increase B's utility to at least U_{B2} in that starting situation while leaving A better off than at point G. This is clearly impossible. Thus, the new situation meets both compensation criteria and according to them would be judged superior to the original one.

Even in so clear-cut a case as this, though, one might have qualms about accepting that the move from D to G represented an unambiguously desirable step to take. It is *possible* to move from G to E, and hence it is *possible* to achieve a situation Pareto superior to that ruling at D. However, unless, after the move is made, the gainers are *actually* taxed and the losers *actually* compensated so as to move to E, the achievement of a Pareto superior situation is only a possibility, not an established fact. To accept the possibility of compensation as a sufficient criterion for regarding a change as desirable, rather than insisting that compensation be carried out, involves one in making stronger judgements than strict application of the Pareto criterion would permit.

In short, if a cost—benefit analysis of a particular economic project finds that the benefits outweigh the costs, but that these accrue to different people, the decision to proceed with the project without insisting that the losers be compensated by the gainers involves a comparison of the economic welfare of the two groups, the very thing that Pareto criterion seeks to avoid. To return to the example given earlier, if a valley is to be flooded to improve the water supply to a city, the inhabitants of the valley must actually be compensated to a level at which they willingly acquiesce in the flooding if the project is to be judged as constituting a Pareto improvement in society's economic welfare.

The Compensation Criteria in an Ambiguous Case

In any event, the two compensation criteria we have been discussing may well produce contradictory results. One example will suffice to demonstrate this point. It hinges on the perfectly straightforward proposition that there is no particular reason why the removal of a tax on one good should result in an unambiguously outward shift of the utility frontier. Hence, what we have here is not just an analytic curiosity, but an illustration of an extremely important limitation on the practical usefulness of compensation criteria. Suppose consumer A found Y a relatively unappealing good. Then to substitute Y for X in production could well result in A's maximum attainable level of utility falling. Such

Figure 27.4

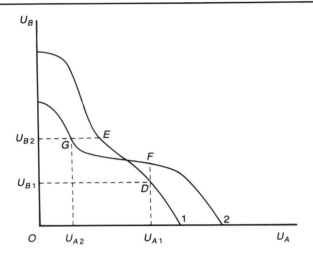

A change that involves a shift in composition of output can produce a new utility possibility curve that crosses the old one, and then the compensation criteria can prove contradictory and hence unhelpful. Suppose we start at *D* in the first situation and shift to *G* in the second. Consumer *B* can bribe *A* to accept the move by permitting a move to *F*, where *A* can enjoy U_{A1} just as at *D*, while *B* is left better off. However, once at *G*, *A* could bribe *B* to return to the original situation. In that situation point *E* is available and here U_{B2} is available to *B*, just as it is at *G*, while *A* is better off than at *G* where U_{A2} is obtained.

a situation is depicted in Figure 27.4. It is possible that the removal of monopoly or of a tax on *Y* could result in a reallocation of resources and redistribution of income between *A* and *B* such that there was a movement from *D* on utility frontier 1 to *G* on utility frontier 2. In this case *B* could certainly compensate *A* for making the change with a shift to point *F*. However, *A* could simultaneously compensate *B* for not making the change by a shift to point *E*.

The Utility Frontier

We may use the utility possibility curve construction to set out more clearly the nature of the distributional problem with which we have been dealing. For every point on the production frontier, there is a utility possibility curve derived from the relevant consumption contract curve. In principle, we can derive every such curve and plot them in a figure such as Figure 27.5. Some of these curves will lie entirely inside others, others will crisscross one another, and not necessarily only once. In just the same way as, in Chapter 10, we derived the isoquant as a boundary showing the *minimum* quantities of factors of production required to produce a given level of output, so in Figure 27.5 we derive an overall utility frontier from

Figure 27.5

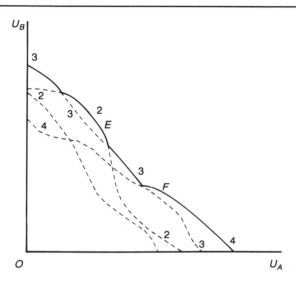

The derivation of the utility frontier. For every point on a given production possibility curve we have a different utility possibility curve. The potentially infinitely large number of such curves is reduced to four here only for the sake of geometric clarity. The utility frontier shows us the maximum amount of utility available to *A* given the utility available to *B*, and given, not a particular structure of output, but a particular set of productive resources. It is thus made up of those segments of the individual utility possibility curves that lie outside any other. This frontier is drawn here as a continuous curve and the segments of the utility possibility curves that lie inside the frontier as dotted curves.

all these utility possibility curves. It shows what is the maximum level of utility available for *A* given a certain level of utility for *B*, when fixed quantities of factors of production are available to be reallocated between the production of various goods. Thus, in terms of Figure 27.5 the movement from *E* to *F* not only represents a reallocation of utility in favour of individual *A*, it also represents a reallocation of resources such that the output mix changes from that underlying utility possibility curve 2 to that underlying utility possibility curve 4.

The Distribution of Welfare

The overall utility frontier of Figure 27.5 shows clearly why the Pareto criterion does not permit us to make all the judgements about the performance of an economic system that we might want to make. Every point on it is Pareto optimal and, without making explicit judgements about the distribution of economic welfare between our two individuals, we cannot choose between them. But can we at least say that, since every point on the frontier is Pareto optimal, we should nevertheless aim

economic policy at being somewhere on the frontier rather than inside it, and avoid discussing distribution in this way? Inspection of Figure 27.6 will readily confirm that we cannot do so. It would only be possible to say this if it were the case that every point on the frontier was Pareto superior to every point within it, and this is not true. For any point within the frontier, such as *D*, there is certainly a segment *EF* of the frontier that is made up of Pareto superior points, but a point such as *G* is not Pareto superior to *D*. To move there involves making someone worse off. Depending upon the judgements that one might make about the distribution of welfare between the two individuals whose situation is depicted in Figure 27.6, one might well regard point *D* as superior to *G* even though it is non-Pareto optimal. Thus, there can be no overall implication from the foregoing analysis that the achievement of Pareto optimality can always be regarded as desirable as an end in itself!

The story which we have been telling is abstract and complex, but it has a very clear-cut moral. It is, in general, impossible to make judgements about social welfare without also making judgements about the distribution of income. Allocative efficiency is not the only factor to be taken into account in judging a particular social situation or a particular form of social organisation. Its achievement puts one on the utility frontier, but the desirability of a particular distribution of utility between individuals must

Figure 27.6

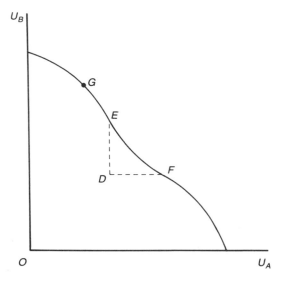

For any point inside the utility frontier, such as *D*, there is a segment of the frontier *EF*, any point on which is Pareto superior to *D*. However, a point such as *G* is not Pareto superior to *D* since *A* is worse off there. Despite the fact that *G*, like every point on the frontier, is a Pareto optimal point while no point within the frontier is, we cannot say that the achievement of Pareto optimality is always desirable in and of itself.

still be judged. Such judgements must involve the application of ethical criteria. That *does not* mean that they are arbitrary by any means, but it does mean that economics alone does not provide a sufficient basis for making them.

Concluding Comment

If there existed a market for every scarce resource; if all the costs and benefits of every aspect of productive activity were reflected in market transactions; and if there were no need to provide a background of enforceable legal arrangements, then one could talk about the Pareto optimal properties of competitive equilibrium without qualification. Even then, though, all the ethical problems concerning distribution that we have raised would remain to qualify one's judgements about the desirability of one such equilibrium relative to another. However, as soon as one considers the desirability, indeed, in some cases the necessity, of providing public goods, and as soon as one recognises the many ways in which the costs and benefits of various aspects of economic activity can escape the market and appear as 'externalities', then it becomes apparent that the solutions to such problems have both allocative and distributional consequences which require analysing together, and that the inter-connectedness of these problems is inherent in the operation of a market economy.

These matters are of fundamental importance. They mean that, as a practical matter, even if we ignore the question of distribution, we can still not rely on the operation of competitive markets to provide a *first-best* solution to the problem of allocating resources. Because externalities exist, and because some taxes have to be levied, the maximum feasible degree of competitiveness in the economy will in general provide an allocation of resources that is Pareto inferior to some *second-best* solution that could be achieved with some extra intervention on the part of government.

Thus the analysis that we have been pursuing in the last two chapters of this book in no way implies that a competitive economy free of any government intervention is in any sense the 'best' economy. Nor does that analysis provide any blanket justification for all the many different sorts of government intervention in economic life that one might encounter in practice. Rather it provides a set of analytic principles that enable coherent judgements to be made about the allocative, but *not the distributive*, aspects of such intervention, of absence thereof. It does not provide all the answers to all the questions one might raise about these issues, but that does not mean it is useless. The very fact that it helps us to think coherently about the type of issues we have discussed above surely means that it is a great deal better than nothing.

Questions for Study and Discussion for Part VIII

1. Consider a two person/two good exchange economy, illustrated by a box diagram as in Figure 24.2. Illustrate a three step process of Walrasian adjustment to equilibrium from an initial endowment in which there is excess demand for good X and excess supply of good Y in the first step and the converse in the second step.

2. Explain how, in a two input/two output economy, the allocation of resources might be improved if the (common) marginal rate of substitution for X and Y held by each of the two consumers were not equal to the marginal rate of transformation. By what mechanism is the condition ($mrs = mrt$) satisfied in a competitive equilibrium?

3. In a perfectly competitive economy, there are two individuals, A and B and two goods, X and Y, each in fixed supply. Before trading commences A has no X and B has no Y. Under what circumstances will they be at the same point after trading? Will the outcome be Pareto efficient?

4. Using a two person/two good exchange model, show with diagrams that:

   (a) the competitive equilibrium is Pareto optimal;
   (b) that every Pareto optimal allocation can be sustained as a competitive equilibrium if a suitable redistribution of endowments is made.

5. In a two good/two factor economy with a fixed quantity of factors, what happens to the transformation curve between the goods if a tax is imposed on the use of one factor in the production of one good (a) in a situation of perfectly competitive equilibrium in all markets in which there are no monopolies and no other taxes; (b) in a situation in which the use of the other factor in the production of the same good is already taxed?

6. (a) What assumptions must you make about the demand curve facing a monopolist in order to interpret the area under it as measuring the total gross benefit accruing to consumers from consuming its output?
   (b) What assumptions must you make in order to interpret the area under the long-run marginal cost curve as measuring the total cost to society of having the monopolist's output produced?
   (c) If the area under a monopolist's demand curve did measure the total benefit to society of consuming its output and the area under the long-run marginal cost curve did measure the total cost to society of producing the output, would the profit-maximising price and output decision result in the net benefit to society of the monopolist's activities being maximised? Would your answer change if the monopolist were able to indulge in perfect price discrimination?

7. In an otherwise distortion-free, perfectly competitive economy, the production of X is monopolised and the firm producing X makes positive profits for its owners. Consider the effects on the distribution of income and allocation of resources of the following suggested actions: (a) taxing the profits made in the production of X and distributing them to the rest of the community; (b) subsidising the production of X so that the firm produces the level of output that would be produced by a competitive industry; (c) a combination of (a) and (b). Which action would you prefer to see taken? Would your preference be influenced by the knowledge that the owners of the firm in question were the otherwise penniless inhabitants of an orphanage?

8. Should airline operators be surcharged on their landing and take-off fees at airports, the proceeds being redistributed to the inhabitants of nearby houses as compensation for their being disturbed by aircraft noise? If aircraft are forbidden to operate from a particular airport at night, should airline operators be compensated for the resulting losses by a tax levied on the inhabitants of nearby houses whose amenities are thereby improved?

9. Let the excess demand function for good X take the form in Figure Q9 below

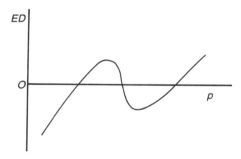

Figure Q9

(i)   Illustrate equilibrium price(s) in this market.
(ii) Which equilibria are stable and which unstable?
(iii) Discuss why the excess demand function may take this form.

*10. Suppose that Robinson Crusoe (see the section in Chapter 25) regards employment and goods as perfect substitutes on the demand side, and produces with a decreasing returns technology.

(i)   Does the Crusoe economy have a competitive equilibrium?
(ii) Illustrate the process whereby the Walrasian auctioneer adjusts real wages in order to find it.
(iii) Draw the excess demand functions for the goods and labour markets.

11. Discuss what might be the role for the government in an economy which is perfectly competitive.

12. Suppose that society is able to construct a social welfare function which allows us to rank distributions of welfare between individuals. In a two person world, this social welfare function can be represented by convex to the origin social indifference curves in utility space. Suppose that the utility frontier takes the form illustrated in Figure 27.6. Draw and explain the case when points such as G, E or F in Figure 27.6, which are on the utility frontier and Pareto optimal, are regarded as socially inferior to another point, call it H, which is not on the utility frontier and is therefore not Pareto optimal.

13. Discuss the view that the only tax which the government should use to raise revenue is a poll tax, because it has no effect on economic choices.

14. Discuss the relative merits of controlling negative external effects such as pollution by:

   (a) setting up markets to internalise the external cost;
   (b) taxes or subsidies to eradicate the gap between marginal private and marginal social cost;
   (c) direct regulation of the quantity of the externality produced.

Suggested Further Reading to Part VIII

Arrow, K.J. and Debreu, G. 1954. 'Existence of an Equilibrium for a Competitive Economy', *Econometrica*.

Arrow, K.J. and Hahn, F.H. 1971. *General Competitive Analysis*. Edinburgh: Oliver and Boyd.

Bailey, M.J. 1965. 'The Welfare Cost of Inflationary Finance', *Journal of Political Economy*, reprinted in Arrow and Scitovsky (eds) (*op. cit.*).

Bator, F. 1957. 'The Simple Analytics of Welfare Maximisation', *American Economic Review*, reprinted in Breit and Hochman (eds)(*op.cit.*).

Bator, F. 1958. 'The Anatomy of Market Failure', *Quarterly Journal of Economics*.

Coase, R. 1960. 'The Problem of Social Cost', *Journal of Law and Economics*. Reprinted in Breit and Hochman (eds)(*op.cit.*).

Henderson, A.M. 1947. 'The Pricing of Public Utility Undertakings', *The Manchester School*. Reprinted in Arrow and Scitovsky (eds)(*op.cit.*).

Johnson, H.G. 1971. *The Two Sector Model of General Equilibrium*, The Yrjö Jahnsson Lectures. London: Allen & Unwin, Chs 1 and 2.

Kaldor, N. 1939. 'Welfare Propositions of Economics and Inter-personal Comparisons', *Economic Journal*.

Koopmans, T. 1957. *Three Essays on the State of Economic Science*. New York: McGraw-Hill.

Lancaster, K. and Lipsey, R.G. 1956. 'The General Theory of the Second Best', *Review of Economic Studies*.

Little, I.M.D. 1957. *A Critique of Welfare Economics*. (2nd edn), Oxford: Oxford University Press.

Weintraub, R.E. 1974. *General Equilibrium Theory*. London: Macmillan.

Author Index

Subject Index

P.O. Box 1375
Barrhead
Glasgow
G78 1JJ

Tel: 0141 880 6839

Fax: 0870 124 9189

e-mail: teejaypublishers@btinternet.com

web page: www.teejaypublishers.co.ok

© TeeJay Publishers 2013
   First Edition published by TeeJay Publishers - June
2013

National 5 Textbook

Produced by members of the TeeJay Writing Group

T Strang, J Geddes and J Cairns.

PUPIL BOOK
N5

National 5 Textbook

This book, N5, covers the entire contents of the National 5 course in depth assuming pupils have completed CfE Level 4, and will also provide a firm foundation for those pupils who wish to continue into the Higher Mathematics Course.

- Pupils should have passed the equivalent of a CfE Level 4 qualification before beginning to use this book, and we recommend TeeJay's CfE Textbook 4⁺ for this.

- There are no A and B exercises. The N5 book covers the National 5 CfE course without the teacher having to pick and choose which questions to leave out and which exercises are important. They all are !

- Pupils who cope well with the contents of National 5 should be able to sit the SQA's external National 5 Exam at the end of the course.

- The book contains a 12 page "Chapter Zero", which primarily revises all those strands from CfE Level 4 that have been covered in TeeJay's Book 4⁺.

- Each chapter will have a "*Remember - Remember*" exercise as a summary.

- Every three chapters are covered by a Home Exercise and from Chapter 12 onwards, there is an additional Cumulative Exercise covering all work up to that point.

- There are 6 Non-Calculator exercises interspersed throughout the book.

- The book can be used as a free standing resource for pupils returning in S5 or S6 who intend to sit the National 5 examination, assuming they have covered the contents of the CfE Level 4 Course, by using TeeJay's Book CfE 4+, or equivalent.

- It includes a Specimen National 5 Exam, consisting of both a Calculator and a Non-Calculator Paper at the end of the book.

  We make no apologies for the multiplicity of colours used throughout the book, both for text and in diagrams - we feel it helps brighten up the pages !!

T Strang, J Geddes, J Cairns

(August 2013)

Contents

CfE National 5

Number Work   *Do not use a calculator in this chapter unless you see the* 🖩 *sign.*

1. Round each of the following to **two** significant figures :-

   (a) 3.765 (b) 1064

   (c) 8007 (d) 9.14987

   (e) 9.0909 (f) 19.97971.

2. Round each number to **one** significant figure and then **estimate** each of the following :-

   (a) 512×12 (b) 187×679

   (c) $648 \div 23$ (d) $1879 \div 44$

   (e) 8.07 million $\div 54879$.

3. Find :-

   (a) $6 + 7 \times 2$ (b) $5 - 4 \times 4$

   (c) $18 - 3 \times 4 + 1$ (d) $11 \times 3 - 18 \div 3$.

4. Insert brackets to make each statement correct.

   (a) $12 - 4 \times 3 = 24$

   (b) $12 + 2 \times 3 - 4 = -14$

   (c) $16 - 9 \div 5 \times - 1 + 1 = 0$.

Integers

5. Simplify :-

   (a) $(-6) + (-11)$ (b) $(-19) + (32)$

   (c) $20 - 55$ (d) $(-10) - 3$

   (e) $(-15) - 20 - 10$ (f) $(-10) + 10 + 7$

   (g) $8 - 10 - 3$ (h) $(-40) - 80 - 20$

   (i) $7 - (-4)$ (j) $(-3) - (-8)$.

6. Simplify these algebraic expressions :-

   (a) $5x + 10x$ (b) $a + (-5a)$

   (c) $9p - p$ (d) $(-y) + 6y$

   (e) $(-3t) - 7t$ (f) $(-5f) + 12f$

   (g) $(-2w) - 2w - 2w$ (h) $6a + 5b - a - 3b$.

7. If $x = 7$ and $y = -3$, write down the value of :-

   (a) $4 - x$ (b) $10 + y$

   (c) $x - 11$ (d) $y + 15$

   (e) $x - y$ (f) $y + x$.

8. Simplify :-

   (a) $5 - (-2)$ (b) $14 - (-4)$

   (c) $(-5) - (-7)$ (d) $(-9) - (-2)$

   (e) $(-6) - (-11)$ (f) $(-12) - (-12)$

   (g) $-(-3x) - (-x)$ (h) $(-8x^2) - (-8x^2)$.

9. If $p = -3$, $q = -2$ and $r = -4$, find :-

   (a) $p + q$ (b) $p - q$

   (c) $q - r$ (d) $q + r$

   (e) $p - r$ (f) $r + p$.

10. Work out the answers to the following :-

    (a) $4 \times (-5)$ (b) $(-8) \times 6$

    (c) $7 \times (-1)$ (d) $(-30) \times 0$

    (e) $3x \times (-4x)$ (f) $(-24) \div 6$

    (g) $(-20a) \div 5$ (h) $(-21t) \div 7$

    (i) $(-18t) \div 3t$ (j) $6 \times (-2) \times 3$

    (k) $(-6) \times (-8)$ (l) $(-30) \times (-4)$

    (m) $(-42) \div (-6)$ (n) $(-80) \div (-8)$

    (o) $(-3p) \times (-5p)$ (p) $(-7)^2$

    (q) $(-2)^6$ (r) $(-4)^2 - (-2)^3$.

11. Given $a = 6$, $b = 0$ and $c = -3$, calculate the values of :-

    (a) abc (b) $a + b - c$

    (c) $a^2 + b^2$ (d) $ab + bc + ca$

    (e) $a^2 - b + c$ (f) $2a^2 + 3c^2$

    (g) $a^3 + c^3$ (h) $a^2 - 2c^2$.

Angle Properties

12. **Copy** each figure and fill in the sizes of **all** the missing angles.

    (a)   (b)

    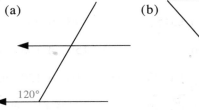

12. (c)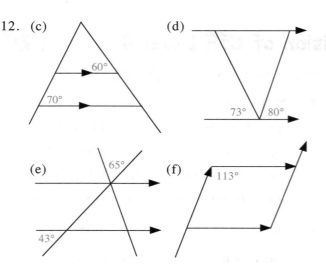
    (d)
    (e)
    (f)

13. **Copy** each figure and fill in the sizes of **all** the missing angles.

(a)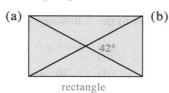

rectangle

(b)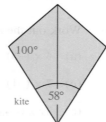

kite

(c)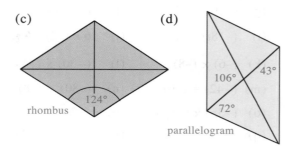

rhombus

(d)

parallelogram

14. Calculate the size of the **acute** angle between the two hands of a clock at :-

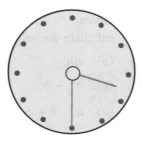

    (a) half past 3

    (b) quarter past one.

Percentages

15. Find the following **without** a calculator :-

    (a) 30% of £80   (b) 70% of £120

    (c) $66\frac{2}{3}$ % of £150   (d) 75% of £3000

    (e) 20% of £515   (f) 90% of 9 m

    (g) 2·5% of 50 kg   (h) 15% of 160 cm

    (i) 17·5% of £240   (j) 11% of 1200 ml

    (k) 49% of 800 mph   (l) 37·8% of 2 m.

16. Pearl Royal Bank's annual interest rate was 3·6%. Sandra deposited £1600 in Pearl Royal Bank.

Typical Savings Rate 3·6% p.a.

    (a) How much interest would she have received if she'd left it for 1 year ?

    (b) If Sandra withdrew her money after 5 months, how much interest should she have expected to receive ?

17. Davie scored 35 out of 40 in his French test paper.

    What was his percentage score ?

18. Write the following list in order, smallest first :-

    (a) $\frac{3}{4}$, 72%, 0·8, 0·77, (0·5 × 1·56)

    (b) (60% of 120), ($\frac{2}{3}$ of 105), (0·25 × 284).

Money Matters

19. (a) Baz's salary is £24 600 per annum.

        How much is his monthly pay ?

    (b) Jenny is paid £1650 per month.

        What is her annual salary ?

    (c) Jez earns £290·50 per week.

        How much does he earn in a year ?

    (d) Andy earns £12·40 per hour and works a 40 hour week.

        How much does he earn in a year ?

20. Alice works in telesales. She is paid £9·60 per hour.

    (a) How much will she earn in a week if she works for 48 hours ?

    Last week, Alice also worked 6 hours overtime, at **time and a half**.

    (b) How much did she earn for overtime ?

    (c) What was Alice's total pay for last week ?

21. (a) Baz earns a gross pay of £22 524 a year as a mechanic.

        His total deductions are £2376.

        What is his net pay ?

21. (b) Jerry ended up with a net income of £17450 per year as a window cleaner.

His gross income was £20140.

How much were his deductions ?

22. Kia has a gross income of £23500 per annum.

Her total deductions come to 15% of her gross pay.

(a) How much are Kia's deductions ?

(b) What is her net income ?

23. Hattie's payslip showed the following :-

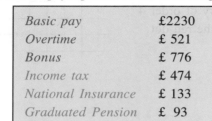

Basic pay	£2230
Overtime	£ 521
Bonus	£ 776
Income tax	£ 474
National Insurance	£ 133
Graduated Pension	£ 93

Calculate Hattie's final net pay.

24. Bill buys a £9500 motorbike.

He took a Hire Purchase agreement, paying a 20% deposit and 24 monthly payments of £423.

(a) How much would he have saved if he had paid cash ?

(b) Give a reason why he would take out H.P. rather than pay cash.

Use these exchange rates for questions 25 to 28.

British Pound (July 2013)	£1 =
Euro	1·22
American Dollar ($)	1·48

25. Change each of the following into euros :-

(a) £40   (b) £1245

(c) £876·40   (d) £122450.

26. Change :-

(a) £450 into $ (b) £1420 into $

(c) €1220 into £   (d) €427 into £

(e) $370 into £   (f) $1110 into £

(g) €610 into $ (h) $3552 into €.

27. Last year, Kev changed £1240 into 11780 Krone.

What was the exchange rate ?

28. Simon took £4600 on his two month tour.

He spent $3460 in America and €2440 in Italy.

How many £'s, to the nearest £, did he have left ?

Algebra

29. Simplify :-

(a) $13 \times x$ (b) $t \times t$

(c) $4a \times 5b$ (d) $2q^2 \times q$

(e) $15p \div p$ (f) $10x^2 y \div 5y$.

30. Multiply out the brackets :-

(a) $3(t + 2)$ (b) $5(2 - 4r)$

(c) $x(8 + x)$ (d) $-3a(5a - 3b)$.

31. Simplify :-

(a) $5(x + 2) + 6$ (b) $8(y + 3) - 7y$

(c) $12 - 4(t - 3)$ (d) $5(m + 1) + 4m$

(e) $6(1 - t) + 3(2 + t)$

(f) $6(3 - 2g) - 4(3 - 6g)$

(g) $15 - 4(a + 3)$ (h) $5m - 3(1 - 2m)$.

32. This shape consists of a rectangle measuring $(2x + 11)$ cm by 8 cm, surrounding a rectangle measuring $(4x - 1)$ cm by 4 cm.

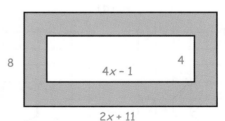

8   4

$4x - 1$

$2x + 11$

(a) Show that no matter what value x is, the grey area always remains the same.

(b) Explain why x cannot be greater than 6.

Symmetry

33. How many lines of symmetry are in each of the following shapes :-

(a) 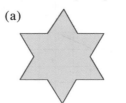   (b)

33. (c) 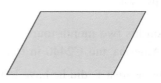 (d)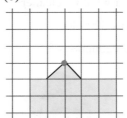

(e) (f)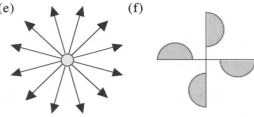

34. State the order of symmetry for each of the shapes in question 32.

35. Make a copy of each of the following shapes. Reflect each shape over the red dotted line of symmetry.

(a) (b)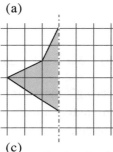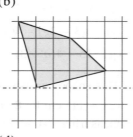

(c) (d)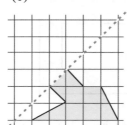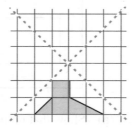

36. Make a copy of each of the following shapes. Create a shape which has half turn symmetry by rotating each shape by 180° around the red dot :-

(a) (b)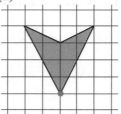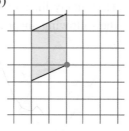

36. (c) 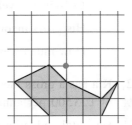 (d)

37. Copy this figure.

Complete the shape so that it has rotational symmetry of order 4 around the red dot.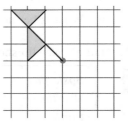

Tolerance

38. Describe in your own words the meaning of *mathematical* tolerance.

39. For each of the following tolerances, write down the minimum (min) and maximum (max) allowable sizes :-

(a) (10 ± 1) mm   (b) (15 ± 5) kg

(c) (20 ± 2) m   (d) $(1 \cdot 5 \pm 0 \cdot 3)$ kg

(e) (152 ± 3) mm   (f) $(7 \cdot 55 \pm 1 \cdot 2)$ mg.

40. Write each of these in tolerance form :-

(a) min = 12 cm   (b) min = 120 mm
     max = 16 cm   max = 140 mm

(c) min = 1·6 mg   (d) min = 2·5°
     max = 1·7 mg   max = 2·6°.

Linear Relationships

41. For each table below derive a formula in the form $y = mx$ or $y = mx + c$:-

(a)

x	1	2	3	4
y	3	6	9	12

(b)

x	0	1	2	3
y	1	4	7	10

41. (c)

x	2	3	4	5
y	4	7	10	13

(d)

x	−1	0	1	2
y	−7	−5	−3	−1

(e)

x	−1	0	1	2
y	16	17	18	19

(f)

x	−2	0	2	4
y	0	10	20	30

Careful with this one !

Equations and Inequalities

42. Copy each equation and find the value of x :-

(a) $16 + x = 11$
(b) $9x + 5 = 3x - 7$
(c) $11x - 2 = 6x + 18$
(d) $12x = 3x + 63$
(e) $3(2x - 4) = 4x + 14$
(f) $2(5x + 2) - 4(x - 3) = x + 36$.

43. Solve :-

(a) $\frac{1}{2}x - 1 = 5$
(b) $\frac{1}{4}x - \frac{1}{2} = \frac{4}{5}$
(c) $\frac{x + 2}{5} = 3$
(d) $1 + \frac{x - 2}{4} = 0$
(e) $\frac{5}{6}(2x + 2) = \frac{1}{4}x + 3$
(f) $\frac{x + 1}{3} + \frac{x + 4}{4} = 2$
(g) $\frac{7x - 1}{8} - \frac{x - 2}{4} = 3$.

44. Solve these inequalities :-

(a) $6c \le -30$
(b) $3d + 1 > 10$
(c) $3t - 4 < -10$
(d) $1 - x > -11$
(e) $6g + 1 \ge 15 - g$
(f) $15 - 2p \ge p + 3$
(g) $4(x + 1) \ge 24 - x$
(h) $3(1 - t) \le 2(3t + 6)$

Scientific Notation (Standard Form)

45. Write each of these in **scientific notation** :-

(a) 930 $(= 9 \cdot 3 \times 10 \cdots)$
(b) 8420
(c) 35 200
(d) 8 million
(e) 305 million
(f) $2\frac{3}{4}$ million
(g) 0·00085
(h) 0·07.

46. Write out each of the following numbers in "**normal**" number form :-

(a) $5 \cdot 9 \times 10^3$
(b) $8 \cdot 08 \times 10^5$
(c) $7 \cdot 1 \times 10^2$
(d) $2 \cdot 81 \times 10^4$
(e) $5 \cdot 8 \times 10^{-3}$
(f) $9 \cdot 9 \times 10^{-2}$
(g) $6 \cdot 2 \times 10^{-5}$
(h) 2×10^{-1}.

47. Use your EE or EXP buttons to find the following :-

(Give each answer in scientific notation)

(a) $150 \times (3 \cdot 8 \times 10^8)$
(b) $(2 \cdot 31 \times 10^6) \times (1 \cdot 35 \times 10^5)$
(c) $(5 \cdot 4 \times 10^{13}) \times (2 \cdot 5 \times 10^{-4})$
(d) $(5 \cdot 22 \times 10^8) \div (1 \cdot 8 \times 10^{-5})$
(e) $(3 \cdot 2 \times 10^{10})^2$
(f) $\dfrac{(4 \cdot 2 \times 10^8) \times (2 \cdot 5 \times 10^7)}{(3 \times 10^{-4})}$.

The Circle (Part 1)

48. Calculate the **circumference** of this circle.

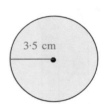

3·5 cm

49. Calculate the **perimeter** of these shapes :-

(a)

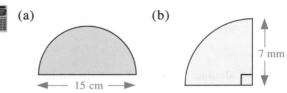

15 cm

(b)

7 mm

(c)

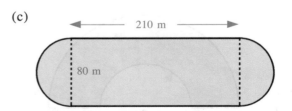

210 m

80 m

50. (a) Find the **diameter** of a circle with a circumference of 60 cm.

(b) Find the **radius** of a circle with circumference 250 mm

51. Calculate the **area** of each of these :-

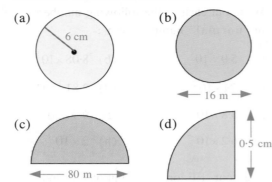

(a) 6 cm

(b) 16 m

(c) 80 m

(d) 0·5 cm

52. Calculate the **radius** of a circle with area $28\cdot26\,m^2$.

Area = 28·26 m²

53. Figure 1 shows a horseshoe magnet. The face of the arched part at the top consists of two semi-circles, with radii 2 centimetres and 4 centimetres.

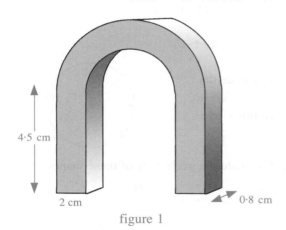

4·5 cm

2 cm

0·8 cm

figure 1

(a) Calculate the shaded area shown in figure 2 below.

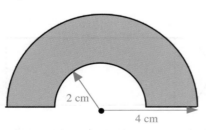

2 cm

4 cm

figure 2

(b) Use this to calculate the volume of metal required to make the magnet.
(*Answer correct to 1 decimal place*).

54. For each of the shapes below, calculate the **perimeters** :-

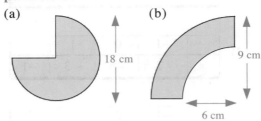

(a) 18 cm

(b) 9 cm

6 cm

Coordinates and Transformations

55. Plot each of the following on a Cartesian coordinate diagram.

A(4, 2), B(7, 0), C(4, –3), D(0, –2), E(–3, 5), F(–6, 0), and G(–2, –4).

56. Rectangle JKLM has vertices J(–1, –2), K(–2, –3), L(–4, –1) and M.

(a) State the coordinates of M.

(b) Reflect JKLM over the *y*-axis and state the vertices of the images J′K′L′M′.

(c) Reflect JKLM over the *x*-axis and state the images of J″K″L″M″.

57. For each point and their images, describe the reflection that has occurred :-

(a) A(5, 2) -> A′(5, –2)
(b) B(6, –2) -> B′(–6, –2)
(c) C(–4, –4) -> C′(4, 4)
(d) D′(7, 1) -> D″(–7, –1)
(e) E(–x, –y) -> E′(–x, y)
(f) F(–a, b) -> F′(b, a).

58. A triangle has vertices O(0, 0), T(4, 1), P(3, 4).

State the coordinates of the images of the vertices given that triangle OTP is rotated by 180° about the origin.

59. Triangle PQR has vertices P(1, 0), Q(4, 1) and R(2, –2).

PQR is rotated 180° about the origin and then reflected over the *x*-axis.

It is then given a translation of $\begin{pmatrix} -1 \\ 3 \end{pmatrix}$.

State the coordinates of the vertices of the triangle after these transformations are applied.

Pythagoras' Theorem

60. Calculate the lengths of the missing sides in the following right angled triangles :-

    (a)

    x cm

    9 cm

    9 cm

    (b)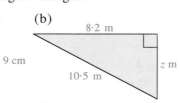

    8·2 m

    10·5 m

    z m

61. Shown is an isosceles triangle.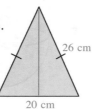

    (a) Calculate the height of the triangle.

    (b) Now calculate its **area**.

    26 cm

    20 cm

62.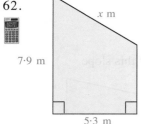

    x m

    7·9 m

    4·7 m

    5·3 m

    Calculate the value of x, which indicates the length of the sloping side of this shape.

    Answer to 2 significant figures.

63. For each of the following pairs of points :-
    (i) plot them on a coordinate diagram and
    (ii) find the length of the line joining them.

    (a) A(4, 3),   B(7, 7)

    (b) C(−1, 5),   D(4, 3)

    (c) E(−3, −2), F(5, −4).

64. A rectangle has a length of 10 cm.
    One of the diagonals is 14 cm long.

    Calculate the **perimeter** of the rectangle.

Time-Distance-Speed

65. Use the diagram shown to help choose the correct formula to answer these questions :-

    (a) James flew his plane at an average speed of 360 kilometres per hour for $3\frac{1}{2}$ hours.

        How far did James fly ?

    (b) Alice drove her bus for $2\frac{1}{2}$ hours and covered a distance of 125 miles.

        What was Alice's average speed ?

65. (c) Paula jogged 12 km at an average speed of 8 km/hr.

        How long did she take ?

    (d) Gio drove for two hours and 12 minutes at an average speed of 45 mph.

        How far did he travel ?

66. Use a calculator to change the following times to **decimal form** :-

    (a) 36 minutes   (b) 39 minutes

    (c) 2 hrs 20 mins   (d) 3 hrs 57 mins.

67. Neil's train travelled at an average speed of 56 km/hr.

    Alex's train travelled at an average speed of 60 km/hr.

    If Neil's journey is 70 km long and Alex's is 80 km, whose trip took longer, and by how many minutes ?

68. Brian walked to town, bought a bike, then cycled home.

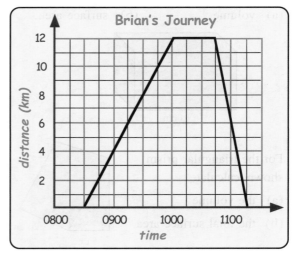

    (a) At what time did Brian leave his house ?

    (b) How far is it from Brian's house to the cycle shop ?

    (c) What was Brian's average walking speed ?

    (d) For how long was Brian in the shop ?

    (e) How long did it take Brian to get home ?

    (f) What was his average speed on the journey home ?

    (g) If Brian had jogged home at one and a half times his walking speed, at what time would he have arrived home ?

Proportion

69. Show all your working for each of these :-

    (a) Share £4500 between Ann and Tom in the ratio 2 : 3.

    (b) Share one million euros in a 7 : 3 ratio.

    (c) Share £8400 in a ratio of 4 : 3 : 1.

70. (a) Five cakes cost £4·50.

    How much would 6 cost ?

    (b) Nine biscuits cost £3·60.

    How much would 7 cost ?

71.  It takes 8 hours for 3 men to build a section of fence.

    How long would it take 4 men to build the same section ?

Volumes and Surface Areas

72. For the cuboid shown below, calculate its :-

    (a) volume   (b) surface area.

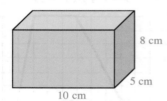

8 cm

5 cm

10 cm

73. For the triangular prism shown, calculate :-

    (a) the volume

    (b) the total surface area.

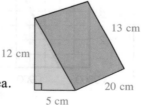

13 cm

12 cm

20 cm

5 cm

74.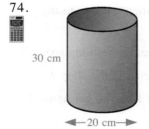

30 cm

←20 cm→

    (a) Calculate the **volume** of this tank, in cm³ and write down its **capacity** in litres.

    (b) Calculate the **curved surface area** of the cylinder.

    (c) Calculate its total surface area.

75. Calculate the volume of this cone.

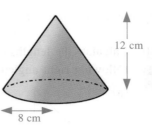

12 cm

8 cm

76.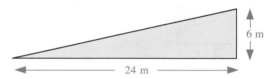

12 cm

8 cm

20 cm

    This shape consists of a cone on top of a cylinder on top of a hemisphere.

    Calculate the **total** volume of the shape.

Gradients and Lines

77. Calculate the **gradient** of this slope.

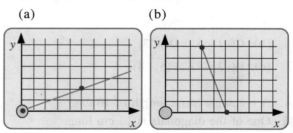

6 m

24 m

78. Calculate the gradient of each line below :-

    (a)   (b)

79. Write down the **gradients** and the **y-intercepts** of these lines :-

    (a) $y = 3x - 2$ (b) $y = 5 - 4x$.

80. Write down the **equation** of each of the following lines :-

    (a) $m = 4$, and its y-intercept is at –5.

    (b) gradient of –2, through the point (0, 3).

    (c) $m = -4$ and passing through the origin.

    (d) horizontal gradient through the point (5, 1).

    (e) vertical gradient through the origin.

81. Find the equation of each line below :-

(a)

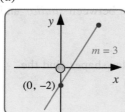

(b)

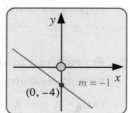

82. The graph below shows the temperature (T) of a kettle over a 5 minute period.

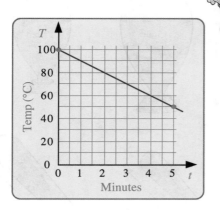

(a) Determine the gradient of the line.

(b) Write a formula to represent this line.

(c) Use your formula to estimate the temperature of the water after 7 minutes. (*Assume it continues to cool in this way*).

Factorising

83. Factorise fully :-

(a) $8a + 24$

(b) $4x + 10$

(c) $3b + bc$

(d) $7x - vx$

(e) $pt + pg$

(f) $a^2 + 2a$

(g) $15a - 10b + 5c$

(h) $2p^2 + 4pq - 6\,pr$

(i) $6t - t^2$

(j) $2c^2 - 6c$

(k) $5kh + 10hg$

(l) $15vw - 10vx$

(m) $11rs - 11s$

(n) $3y^2 + 9y$

(o) $3a^2c + ac^2$

(p) $18rs^2 - 30rs$

(q) $8x^2 - 12xa$

(r) $\frac{1}{5}ab + \frac{1}{5}bk$

(s) $15a^2bc^2 + 12b^2c$

(t) $15cde^2 + 12b^2ce$.

Angles in Circles

84. Calculate the value of a, b, c and d :-

(a)

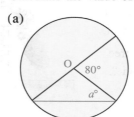

(b)

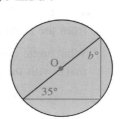

(c)

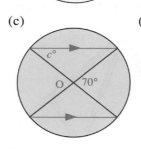

(d)

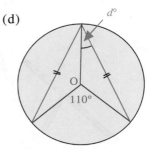

85. Calculate the value of x for each of these :-

(a)   (b)

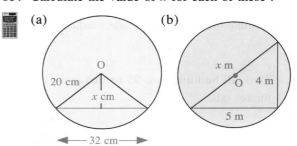

(c)

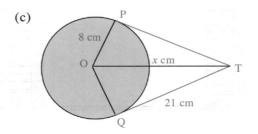

Right Angled Trigonometry

86. Calculate the value of x in each case (*to one decimal place*) :-

(a)   (b)

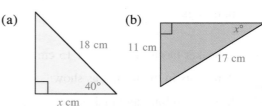

(c)

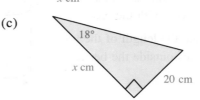

87. An 18 metre tree topples and comes to rest against a wall.

The base of the tree is 4·6 m from the foot of the wall.

What angle does the tree make with the ground ?

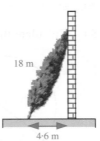

18 m

4·6 m

88. The diagram shows a roof beam structure.

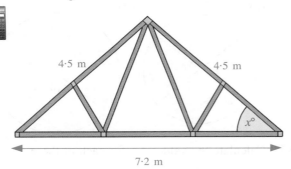

4·5 m   4·5 m

$x°$

7·2 m

Calculate the size of the angle marked $x°$.

89. Two tall buildings are 95 metres and 113 metres tall.

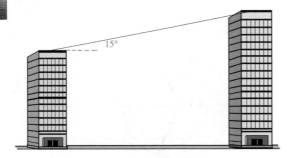

15°

A man standing on the top of the lower one looks up through an angle of elevation of 15° to see the top of the taller one.

Calculate the horizontal distance between the buildings.

90. A beaker has a **diameter** of 15 cm.

A rod sits in the beaker as shown.

It is 48 cm long and makes an angle of 68° with the base.

Calculate the length of the rod which lies outside the beaker.

? cm

68°

15 cm

Similar Figures

91. Explain the difference between *similar* and *congruent*.

92. For each pair of similar shapes find the missing measurement :-

(a)

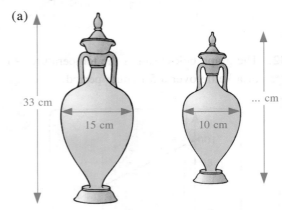

33 cm

15 cm

... cm

10 cm

(b)

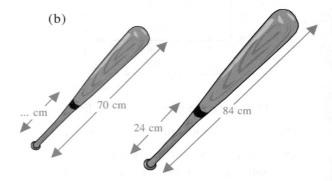

... cm

70 cm

24 cm

84 cm

93. Find the missing measurement :-

(a)   (b)

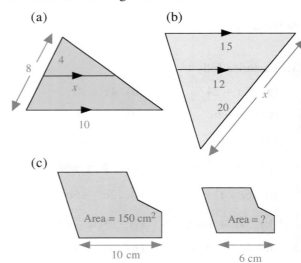

8   4

x

10

15

12

20

x

(c)

Area = 150 cm²

10 cm

Area = ?

6 cm

94. A bottle with a base diameter of 12 cm holds 1·6 litres of diluting orange juice.

A similar bottle has an 18 cm diameter base.

How many litres does the larger bottle hold ?

Fractions

95. Change to a mixed number :-

(a) $\frac{29}{5}$ (b) $\frac{46}{8}$.

96. Rewrite as a top-heavy fraction :-

(a) $5\frac{2}{3}$ (b) $6\frac{3}{5}$.

97. How many $\frac{1}{3}$ pizza slices can by sold from $4\frac{2}{3}$ pizzas ?

98. Find :-

(a) $\frac{5}{7} + \frac{1}{7}$ (b) $\frac{3}{4} - \frac{1}{2}$

(c) $\frac{5}{8} - \frac{1}{8}$ (d) $2\frac{2}{5} + 3\frac{4}{5}$

(e) $\frac{5}{6} - \frac{1}{4}$ (f) $4\frac{4}{5} + 1\frac{2}{3}$

(g) $5\frac{7}{8} - 2\frac{3}{5}$ (h) $3\frac{1}{2} - 1\frac{2}{3}$.

99. Find :-

(a) $\frac{1}{2} \times \frac{3}{5}$ (b) $\frac{7}{9} \times \frac{2}{3}$

(c) $3\frac{1}{2} \times 1\frac{1}{5}$ (d) $2\frac{3}{4} \times 2\frac{2}{3}$

(e) $\frac{1}{3}$ of $(\frac{4}{5} - \frac{1}{2})$ (f) $\frac{1}{3} \times \frac{3}{5} \times \frac{5}{7}$.

Statistical Analysis

100. Calculate the **mean**, **median**, **mode** and **range** :-
18, 21, 16, 17, 21, 18, 21, 20, 25, 28, 15.

101. The **mean** number of marks scored by three students in a test was 35.

When a 4th student's test was marked it was found that the mean of all four students had risen to 39.

What had the 4th student scored ?

102. The frequency table below shows the cost of a carton of milk in various shops in and around Dumfries.

Cost x	Freq f	$f \times x$
41p	4	
42p	7	
43p	10	
44p	6	
45p	3	

Total shops   Total cost

(a) What is the **modal** cost (the mode) ?

(b) What is the **median** cost ?

(c) State the **range**.

(d) **Copy** the table and complete the 3rd column to help determine the **mean** cost.

Graphs, Charts and Tables

103. Shown are the sales of two different companies selling garden chairs.

Red - *Garden Chairs*   **Green** - *Grass Chairs*

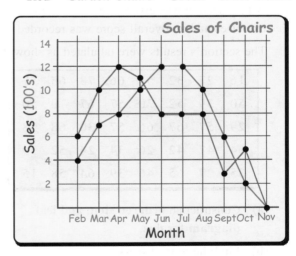

(a) Which company sold more chairs in :-

(i) March (ii) August

(iii) total over the 10 months ?

(b) Explain why you think sales are high from April to August and then drop.

104. (a) **Copy** and complete the table showing the favourite drink of a group of adults.

Drink	No.	Fraction	Angle
Tea	20	$\frac{20}{60}$	$\frac{20}{60} \times 360 = ...°$
Coffee	14		$\times 360 = ...°$
Milk	24		$\times 360 = ...°$
Chocolate	2		$\times 360 = ...°$
TOTAL	...		360°

(b) Construct a **pie chart** to represent the information shown.

105. Shown are the times (in minutes) it took a group of pupils to build a jigsaw puzzle.

Puzzle Times

0	7 8 8 8 8 9
1	0 3 5
2	3 3 3 4 6 9
3	5 5
4	0 0 0 2 5 5

(a) What was the :-

   (i) quickest   (ii) slowest time ?

(b) Find the **modal** time.

(c) Find the **median** time.

(d) How many pupils solved it in less than 22 minutes ?

106. A P.E. section was given a series of gym exercises and an overall score was recorded.

The section's results were tabulated as shown.

16	27	32	54	66	73	65	57
50	39	52	30	57	67	70	50
29	57	67	66	57	36	68	38
64	47	42	26	34	24	52	39
35	27	65	46	39	64	58	15

(a) Construct an **ordered stem and leaf diagram** for this.

(b) Find the **modal** mark.

(c) Find the **median** mark.

Pupils who score above 55 were given a commendation certificate.

(d) How many pupils received a certificate ?

Probability

107. A nine sided dice, numbered 1 to 9, is thrown.

Find :-

(a) P(4)

(b) P(even)

(c) P(10)

(d) P(prime).

108. It has been found that there is a three out of eight chance of an event happening.

What is the chance of the event NOT happening ?

109. Three sealed bags contain the following notes :-

Bag 1 - one £1, three £5, four £10, one £50

Bag 2 - nine £1, four £5, two £10, two £50.

Bag 3 - fifteen £1, five £5, three £10, three £50.

You can pick one note from one bag and keep it !

(a) Which bag will give you the best chance of picking a £50 note ?

(b) Which bag would you choose and why ?

(*Justify **both** answers with working*).

110. I toss three 1p coins in the air.

What is the probability that the three coins land all showing tails?

111. There are soft and hard centred chocolates in a box.

There is a 0·8 chance of picking a soft centre at random.

If there are 12 soft centres, how many chocolates in total are in the box ?

Logic Puzzle

112. What is the next line in the sequence below :–

   A
   1A
   111A
   311A
   13211A
   111312211A
   ???????????????

> **Removing Brackets and Simplifying - a Reminder**
>
> **Examples :-**   (Note the double negative = +*ve* in Examples 3, 6 & 7)
>
> 1. $7(3a - 2b)$ 2. $m^2(m + 6)$ 3. $-7v(x - 5)$ 4. $2(5g + 2h) - 3h$
>
> $= 21a - 14b$ $= m^3 + 6m^2$ $= -7vx + 35$ $= 10g + 4h - 3h$
>
> $= 10g + h$
>
> 5. $3(2x + 5) + 2(3x - 10)$ 6. $4(2a + 3) - 6(a - 2)$ 7. $10 - 9(x - 1)$
>
> $= 6x + 15 + 6x - 20$ $= 8a + 12 - 6a + 12$ $= 10 - 9x + 9$ [not $(x - 1)$!]
>
> $= 12x - 5$ $= 2a + 24$ $= 19 - 9x$

Exercise 1·1   Revision

1. Multiply out the brackets :-

    (a) $2(a + 9)$ (b) $6(x - 5)$ (c) $15(2 - h)$ (d) $3(m - n)$

    (e) $40(b - 3)$ (f) $3(8w + 1)$ (g) $4(7 - 3t)$ (h) $p(q + 2)$

    (i) $v(w - 13)$ (j) $a(8 + a)$ (k) $d(2k + 6e)$ (l) $9x(6x - y)$

    (m) $5(a + c - 3e)$ (n) $9(5 - 8v - 9y)$ (o) $c(c - g - 11k)$ (p) $-4(a + 3)$

    (q) $-x(7 + x)$ (r) $-v(2v - 7)$ (s) $-m(7m^2 - 10m)$ (t) $-x^2(2x^2 - 10x)$.

2. Multiply out the brackets and collect like terms :-

    (a) $2(y + 5) + 1$ (b) $6(p + 1) + 4$ (c) $9(a + 2) - 15$

    (d) $7(s + 2) - 16$ (e) $2(g + 5) + g$ (f) $5(a + 6) - 4a$

    (g) $20(2 + u) - 18u$ (h) $8d + 8(d + 3)$ (i) $7n + 2(4n + 5)$

    (j) $c + 4(2c - 1)$ (k) $5x + (x - 1)$ (l) $3p + 2(p + 2q)$

    (m) $40x + 2(x - 6y)$ (n) $4 + 2(a - 1)$ (o) $5 - 2(v - 5)$.

3. Simplify :-

    (a) $2(p + 1) + 5(p + 1)$ (b) $4(a - 1) + 2(a + 1)$ (c) $3(m - 6) + 8(m + 2)$

    (d) $7(1 - g) + 2(1 + g)$ (e) $2(3n - 2) - 5(2n - 4)$ (f) $9(x - 1) - 6(x + 2)$

    (g) $9(p - 1) - 6(p - 2)$ (h) $8(1 + 2a) - 8(1 - a)$ (i) $3(3 - t) - 5(1 - t)$

    (j) $x(x - 1) + 3(x - 1)$ (k) $x(x + 7) - 5x(x - 1)$ (l) $3x(2x + y) - 5x(3x - y)$.

4. Simplify :-

    (a) $6 - 5(x + 4)$ (b) $7 - 7(m - 1)$ (c) $9 - (y - 1)$

    (d) $10 - 3(1 - y)$ (e) $6(h - 2) + 12$ (f) $-2(d - 1) + 8d$

    (g) $a - (300 - a)$ (h) $20u - 20(u - 5)$ (i) $4x^2 - 2(x - 5x^2)$.

Multiplying Out "Double Brackets"

Look at this pair of brackets (double brackets) --- 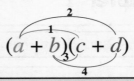 $(a + b)(c + d)$

To multiply out the double brackets, follow these steps :-

- multiply the two (F)irst terms in each bracket $a \times c$ (1)   *write the answer*
- multiply the two (O)utside terms in each bracket $a \times d$ (2)   *write the answer*
- multiply the two (I)nside terms in each bracket $b \times c$ (3)   *write the answer*
- multiply the two (L)ast terms in each bracket $b \times d$ (4)   *write the answer*

- Now write your four answers as an expression and **gather like terms** to finish.

$$(a + b)(c + d) = ac + ad + bc + bd$$

* **FOIL** :-   **F** - first × first,   **O** - outside terms,   **I** - inside terms,   **L** - last × last.

Example 1 :-

$(x+3)(x-4)$
$= x^2 - 4x + 3x - 12$
$= x^2 - x - 12$

Example 2 :-

$(x-2)(x-5)$
$= x^2 - 5x - 2x + 10$
$= x^2 - 7x + 10$

Example 3 :-

$(2x+1)(x-3)$
$= 2x^2 - 6x + x - 3$
$= 2x^2 - 5x - 3$

Example 4 :-

$(x+4)^2$
$= (x+4)(x+4)$
$= x^2 + 4x + 4x + 16$
$= x^2 + 8x + 16$

Exercise 1·2

1. Multiply out the brackets and simplify :-

   (a) $(x+3)(x+1)$ (b) $(x+5)(x+3)$ (c) $(x+2)(x+4)$ (d) $(x+3)(x+4)$

   (e) $(p+5)(p+5)$ (f) $(x+3)^2$ (g) $(p+2)(p+3)$ (h) $(m+5)^2$

   (i) $(x+2)(3x+1)$ (j) $(x+3)(2x+6)$ (k) $(2a+4)(2a+4)$ (l) $(3y+1)(3y+1)$

   (m) $(2m+1)(4m+3)$ (n) $(5m+2)(5m+1)$ (o) $(8g+2)(2g+3)$ (p) $(4+x)(x+5)$

   (q) $(3+2x)(6+3x)$ (r) $(10w+1)^2$ (s) $(3x+4)^2$ (t) $(2y+8)^2$.

2. Multiply out and simplify :-

   (a) $(x-3)(x-2)$ (b) $(x-2)(x-1)$ (c) $(x-3)(x-4)$ (d) $(p-4)(p-4)$

   (e) $(5-p)(p-5)$ (f) $(x-4)^2$ (g) $(x-10)^2$ (h) $(x-2)(4x-2)$

   (i) $(x-2)(5x-1)$ (j) $(x-3)(2x-3)$ (k) $(2a-3)(2a-3)$ (l) $(2a-3)(4a-1)$

   (m) $(2m-1)(2m-5)$ (n) $(2-3c)(6-2c)$ (o) $(5x-1)(5x-1)$ (p) $(2w-1)^2$.

3. Expand the brackets and simplify :-

(a) $(x+5)(x-2)$ (b) $(y-1)(y+4)$ (c) $(a-2)(a+3)$ (d) $(b+2)(b-1)$

(e) $(m-5)(m+3)$ (f) $(3+n)(1-n)$ (g) $(x+3)(2x-1)$ (h) $(a-4)(5a+1)$

(i) $(u-2)(3u+4)$ (j) $(3x+5)(3x-5)$ (k) $(7a+1)(2a-2)$ (l) $(4h-3)(5h+2)$

(m) $(x+y)(x+2y)$ (n) $(x+y)(x-2y)$ (o) $(x-y)(x+2y)$ (p) $(x-y)(x-2y)$

(q) $(a+b)(3a+4b)$ (r) $(2p+q)(p-2q)$ (s) $(5+2x)(2+x)$ (t) $(2-a)(1-a)$

(u) $(5-b)(3+2b)$ (v) $(p-q)(q+p)$ (w) $(1-y)(1+9y)$ (x) $(1-4k)(1-5k)$.

4. These are slightly harder :-

(a) $(x+2)(x^2+1)$ (b) $(x+3)(x^2+5)$ (c) $(x-2)(x^2+3)$ (d) $(x-4)(2x^2+3)$

(e) $(2x+1)(x^2-2)$ (f) $(5x-3)(2x^2+3)$ (g) $(x^2+3)(x^2+4)$ (h) $(x^2-2)(x^2+5)$

(i) $(x+y)(x^2+y^2)$ (j) $(2x-y)(x^2-y^2)$ (k) $(x^2-y^2)(3x+2y)$ (l) $(x^2-y^2)(x^2+y^2)$.

5. Calculate the area of each of these rectangles, in terms of the letters used :-

(a)

$(x+5)$

$(3x+1)$

(b)

$(2x-4)$

$(5x-3)$

(c)

$(x+y)$

$(3x+y)$

(d)

$(5a+2b)$

$(3a-2b)$

(e)

$(p+q)$

(p^2-q^2)

"Rainbows"

Further Example :-

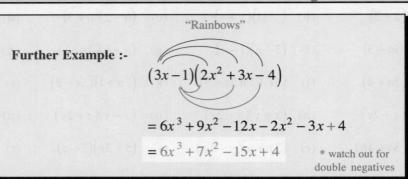

$$(3x - 1)(2x^2 + 3x - 4)$$

$$= 6x^3 + 9x^2 - 12x - 2x^2 - 3x + 4$$

$$= 6x^3 + 7x^2 - 15x + 4$$ * watch out for double negatives

6. Simplify :-

(a) $(x + 2)(x^2 + 4x + 1)$

(b) $(x + 1)(x^2 + 5x - 2)$

(c) $(x - 1)(x^2 + x - 3)$

(d) $(2a + 1)(3a^2 + 5a + 2)$

(e) $(3p - 2)(2p^2 - p - 4)$

(f) $(4y + 5)(2y^2 - 3y + 3)$.

Squaring Brackets - a Quick Method

Present	**Quick Method for Squaring**	**Further Example :-**
$(x+5)^2$	$(x+5)^2$ 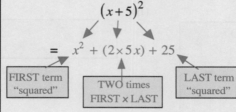	$(x-4)^2$ 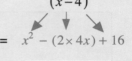
$= (x+5)(x+5)$		
$= x^2 + 5x + 5x + 25$	$= x^2 + (2 \times 5x) + 25$	$= x^2 - (2 \times 4x) + 16$
$= x^2 + 10x + 25$	FIRST term "squared" TWO times FIRST × LAST LAST term "squared"	$= x^2 - 8x + 16$
	$= x^2 + 10x + 25$	

7. Expand the following :-

(a) $(x + 3)^2$

(b) $(x + 7)^2$

(c) $(x + y)^2$

(d) $(y - 2)^2$

(e) $(y - 6)^2$

(f) $(x - y)^2$

(g) $(2x + 1)^2$

(h) $(3x + 4)^2$

(i) $(4a - 1)^2$

(j) $(2b - 10)^2$

(k) $(x + 3y)^2$

(l) $(a - 7b)^2$

(m) $(2x - 3h)^2$

(n) $(4v - 5w)^2$

(o) $(x^2 + 2)^2$

(p) $(y^2 - 4)^2$

(q) $\left(p + \dfrac{1}{p}\right)^2$

(r) $\left(q - \dfrac{1}{q}\right)^2$

(s) $\left(2x - \dfrac{1}{2x}\right)^2$

(t) $\left(5x - \dfrac{1}{5x}\right)^2$.

8. Calculate the area of each square in terms of x (and/or y) :-

(a)

$(3x + 2)$

(b)

$(5x - 1)$

(c)

$(3x + 6y)$

Multiplying Out Brackets, Tidying Up and "CUBING"

Example 1 :-

$$(x+2)^2 - x^2 - 12$$
$$= x^2 + 4x + 4 - x^2 - 12$$
$$= 4x - 8$$

Example 2 :-

Danger !

$$(2a+3)(3a-1) - (a+1)^2$$
$$= 6a^2 - 2a + 9a - 3 - [a^2 + 2a + 1] \quad \text{Careful}$$
$$= 6a^2 + 7a - 3 - a^2 - 2a - 1 \quad \text{careful with negative signs}$$
$$= 5a^2 + 5a - 4$$

Example 3 :- (Cubing)

$$(x+2)^3$$
$$= (x+2)(x+2)^2$$
$$= (x+2)(x^2 + 4x + 4) \quad \text{using quick method of squaring}$$
$$= x^3 + 4x^2 + 4x + 2x^2 + 8x + 8 \quad \text{using the now familiar "rainbow method"}$$
$$= x^3 + 6x^2 + 12x + 8$$

Exercise 1·3

1. Expand the brackets and simplify :-

(a) $(x-3)^2 - x^2 + 15$

(b) $(x+4)(x+3) - x^2 + 2$

(c) $(a-4)(a-3) - a^2 + 13$

(d) $(b+1)^2 - b^2 - 3$

(e) $(x+4)^2 - (x+1)(x+6)$

(f) $(x+1)(x+2) - (x-1)^2$

(g) $(2y+4)(3y+1) + (y+1)(2y-4)$

(h) $(5p-1)(2p+3) + (2p-2)(4p-1)$

(i) $(2x-3)(5x-1) + (3x-1)(x-1)$

(j) $(3x+5)(2x-4) + (2x-3)^2$

(k) $(2g+5)^2 + (4g-2)^2$

(l) $(2q+4)(3q+1) - (q+1)(4q+1)$

(m) $(5x+3)(2x-4) - (3x-1)(2x+1)$

(n) $(4x-1)(6x-3) - (3x-2)(4x-5)$

(o) $(6x-2)(2x+4) - (3x+3)^2$

(p) $(3x-6)^2 - (2x+4)^2$

(q) $a^2 - (a-5)^2 - 50$

(r) $24 - (3-w)^2 - 15 + w^2$

(s) $2(x+5)^2 - 3(x-4)^2$

(t) $5(2x-3)^2 - 6(x-2)^2$.

2. Expand :-

(a) $(x-2)^3$

(b) $(x+1)^3$

(c) $(a-1)^3$

(d) $(x+3)^3$

(e) $(k-3)^3$

(f) $(2x+1)^3$

(g) $(3x-2)^3$

(h) $3(x+2)^3$

(i) $2(x-5)^3$

(j) $(a+b)^3$

(k) $(p-q)^3$

(l) $(2x-2y)^3$.

Equations with Brackets

Example 1 :-

Solve :- $x(x + 7) = (x + 3)(x + 1)$

$\Rightarrow \quad x^2 + 7x = x^2 + 4x + 3$

$\Rightarrow \quad x^2 + 7x - x^2 - 4x = 3$

$\Rightarrow \qquad\qquad 3x = 3$

$\Rightarrow \qquad\qquad x = 1$

Example 2 :-

Solve :- $(x + 4)^2 = (x - 4)^2$

$\Rightarrow \quad x^2 + 8x + 16 = x^2 - 8x + 16$

$\Rightarrow \quad x^2 + 8x + 16 - x^2 + 8x - 16 = 0$

$\Rightarrow \qquad 16x = 0$

$\Rightarrow \qquad x = 0$

Example 3 :-

The rectangle and the square are equal in area.
Form an equation and solve it to find their dimensions.

x cm

$(x + 8)$ cm

$(x + 3)$ cm

$x(x + 8) = (x + 3)^2$

$\Rightarrow \quad x^2 + 8x = x^2 + 6x + 9$

$\Rightarrow \quad x^2 + 8x - x^2 - 6x = 9$

$\Rightarrow \qquad\qquad 2x = 9$

$\Rightarrow \qquad\qquad x = 4\cdot5$

Dimensions :- **Rectangle** .... 4·5 cm by 12·5 cm

Square .... 7·5 cm by 7·5 cm

Exercise 1·4

1. Multiply out the brackets and solve :-

(a) $x(x + 4) = x^2 + 20$

(b) $x(x + 5) = x^2 - 35$

(c) $x(3x + 6) = 3(x^2 - 10)$

(d) $(x + 5)(x - 3) = x(x - 1)$

(e) $x(x + 10) = (x + 4)(x - 2)$

(f) $(x + 4)^2 = x(x + 6)$

(g) $(x - 2)^2 = x(x + 4)$

(h) $(x + 1)^2 = x(x + 3)$

(i) $(x + 1)^2 = (x - 2)^2$

(j) $x^2 - x(x - 1) = 5$

(k) $x^2 - x(5 + x) + 20 = 5$

(l) $x^2 - (x - 4)^2 + 4 = 0$.

2. The pictures in each pair below have the same area. (*All sizes are in centimetres*).

(i) Make up an equation for each pair of pictures.

(ii) Solve the equation to find the dimensions of each picture.

(a)

x

$x + 8$

$x + 4$

$x + 3$

(b)

x

x

$x - 3$

$x + 6$

(c)

$x + 5$

x

$x + 8$

$x - 1$

(d)

$x - 4$

$x - 2$

$x - 8$

$x + 4$

1. Multiply out the brackets :-

   (a) $9(u + 7)$ (b) $3(2 - 4r)$ (c) $x(9 + 4x)$ (d) $-2m(5m - 20n)$.

2. Simplify :-

   (a) $6(x + 3) + 2x$ (b) $5 - 2(n - 2)$ (c) $10(2 - a) + 2(5 + 5a)$

   (d) $4(2 - 3w) - 3(2 - 5w)$ (e) $12 - 2(1 - h)$ (f) $10q - 2(1 - 5q)$.

3. Multiply out the brackets and simplify :-

   (a) $(a+7)(a+2)$ (b) $(b-3)(b-6)$ (c) $(c-2)(c+9)$ (d) $(2d+3)(6d+1)$

   (e) $(1-3e)(5-2e)$ (f) $(2y+3)(7y-1)$ (g) $(2k-5)^2$ (h) $\left(m+\dfrac{2}{m}\right)^2$

   (i) $(n+1)^3$ (j) $(2s-3)^3$ (k) $(x+2)(x+5)-x^2-10$

   (l) $(2x-1)(4x-2)-(3x+1)(x+1)$ (m) $(2y-1)(3y^2+4y-3)$.

4. Shown is a rectangle within a rectangle (*all measurements in cm*) :-

   - the larger has sides $(2k + 5)$ centimetres and $(k + 4)$ centimetres.
   - the smaller rectangle is separated from the larger by a **one centimetre** border all round.

   Write down an expression in x for :-

   (a) the length of the pink rectangle.

   (b) the breadth of the pink rectangle.

   (c) the area of the pink rectangle.

   (d) the area shown in yellow.

   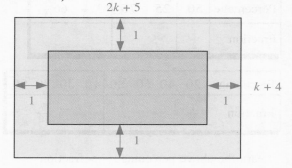

5. Multiply out the brackets and solve the equations :-

   (a) $x(x + 5) = x^2 - 45$ (b) $7x(x - 2) = 7x^2$ (c) $x(4x + 8) = 4(x^2 - 1)$

   (d) $(x + 3)(x - 1) = x(x - 6)$ (e) $x(x + 10) = (x + 8)(x - 3)$ (f) $(x + 7)^2 = (x + 1)^2$.

6. The photographs shown have the **same area**.

   Form an equation, and solve it to find the dimensions of each photograph (cm).

7. *Revision*. Factorise fully :-

   (a) $4a + 24$ (b) $21a - 28b$ (c) $cd + cg$ (d) $2b^2 - 10b$

   (e) $n^3 - n^2$ (f) $24k^2h + 36kh^2$ (g) $7a^3b - 21ab$ (h) $17st^2 - 17su^2$.

Mental Percentages

By now, you should be able to find a **percentage** of a quantity using a calculator :-

Example :-   Find $17\frac{1}{2}$% of £160   =>   • $(17\cdot5 \div 100) \times 160$ = £28·00

or   • $0\cdot175 \times 160$ = £28·00

But - you should also be able to do certain percentage calculations **MENTALLY**.

50% of 60p means
a half of 60p
(=> ÷ 2)

$33\frac{1}{3}$% of 120 g means
a third of 120 g
(=> ÷ 3)

75% of £20 means
three quarters of £20
(=> ÷ 4 then × 3)

80% of 350 means
four fifths of 350
(=> ÷ 5 then × 4)

Exercise 2·1

1. Make a COPY of these tables and complete :-

Percentage	50	25	75	$33\frac{1}{3}$	$66\frac{2}{3}$
Fraction	$\frac{1}{2}$				

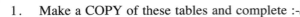

Percentage	20	40	60	80	10	30	70	90
Fraction	$\frac{1}{5}$						$\frac{7}{10}$	

Learn the above percentage —> fraction conversions. You will need them here :-

2. Find the following without a calculator :-

(a) 10% of £35   (b) 70% of £40

(c) 20% of £4·50   (d) 80% of 30p

(e) 25% of £1080   (f) $33\frac{1}{3}$% of £24

(g) 75% of £2·40   (h) 1% of £140

(i) 60% of £8000   (j) 50% of £30000

(k) 40% of £350   (l) 10% of 90p

(m) $66\frac{2}{3}$% of £12·60 (n) 90% of 20p

(o) 3% of £60   (p) 2·5% of £40.

3. 30% of the S4 pupils in Lochee Academy are left handed.

    If there are 160 pupils in S4 in the school, how many are **not** left handed ?

4. $33\frac{1}{3}$% of the trees in an orchard are apple trees, 25% are banana trees and the rest of them are lemon trees.

    If there are 480 trees in total in this orchard, how many are :-

(a) apple   (b) banana

(c) lemon   (d) not apple ?

Remember :-   17% means $\frac{17}{100}$ = 0·17

8% means $\frac{8}{100}$ = 0·08

5. Write each of the following as a fraction **AND** as a decimal :-

(a) 32%   (b) 45%

(c) 51%   (d) 31%

(e) 78%   (f) 8%

(g) 12·5%   (h) 2·5%.

6. Write these as fractions and **simplify** :-

(a) 35% = $\frac{35}{100}$ = $\frac{.....}{20}$

(b) 60% = $\frac{60}{100}$ = ...

(c) 55%   (d) 90%

(e) 15%   (f) 75%

(g) 4%   (h) 85%

(i) 5%   (j) 36%

(k) $2\frac{1}{2}$%   (l) 150%.

> **Remember** :- 17% of £420 means :-
> - $(17 \div 100) \times £420 = 71\cdot4 = £71\cdot40$
> - or $0\cdot17 \times £420 = 71\cdot4 = £71\cdot40$

7. Use your calculator to find the following :-

   (a) 8% of £40 = (8 ÷ 100) × 40 = £......

   (b) 15% of £80   (c) 32% of £60

   (d) 48% of £3500   (e) 36% of £7·50

   (f) 75% of £26·40   (g) 95% of £4

   (h) 7% of £80   (i) 3% of £15

   (j) $17\frac{1}{2}$% of £240   (k) 6·8% of £300.

8. During a storm, the level of rain which ran into a barrel outside my front door was 140 mm.

   During the night the water level rose by another 35%.

   What was the level of rain water in the barrel when I woke in the morning ?

9. Only 55% of young eels are expected to survive the first few weeks of their lives.

   In the River Lowis last year, 1·5 million eels were born.

   How many were expected to survive the early stages of their lives ?

10. Clackinshire Town Council decided to increase council tax by 6·5% this year.

    The Thomsons of Glenview paid council tax totalling £780 last year.

    What should they expect to be paying in total this year ?

11. Before training, it took me 55 seconds to run 400 metres.
    After a training schedule, I knocked 12% off my time.

    How long did it then take to run the 400 m ?

12. A coat is priced £180.

    In a sale, it was reduced by 15%.

    What will the coat then cost ?

13. A plane was flying at 35 000 feet when it hit a storm.

    The pilot lowered the plane's altitude by 45%.

    At what height was the plane then flying ?

14. A standard jar of coffee holds 240 grams.

    In a special offer, an extra 12% is offered at no extra cost.

    How much coffee does the new jar then contain ?

15. The Scotia Bank offers its customers an interest rate of 4·5% p.a. on their savings.

    Jemma deposits £1200 in a new Scotia bank account and leaves it there for 1 year.

Special Savings Rate
4·5% p.a.

    (a) What does the term "p.a." mean ?

    (b) How much interest will Jemma receive if she invests her £1200 in the account for 1 year ?

    (c) How much will her savings then be worth ?

16. Ted deposited £2500 with the Scotia Bank.

    (a) How much interest is Ted due if he leaves his savings there for 1 year ?

    (b) How much interest did Ted actually receive if he withdrew his savings after 6 months ?

17. Musa paid in £6000 to his building society special interest account where the annual interest rate was 4·2%.

    How much interest is Musa due if he removes all his money after a 9 month period ?

18. Who will get more interest :-

    Brian, who invests £4000 in the bank for 6 months if the annual rate is 5·2%

    or

    Nicole, who invests £3000 in her building society for 9 months where the annual interest rate is 4·6% ?

Expressing one Number as a Percentage of another Number

In many instances, you will be asked to express one number as a percentage of another one.

The process is quite simple and can be done using 3 steps as follows :-

Example :-   Davie scored **18 out of 25** in his Maths test.

=>   To find what 18 is, as a percentage of 25 :-

Davie
18 out
of 25
√

- write 18 as a fraction of 25 => $\frac{18}{25}$
- now do the "division" => $18 \div 25 = 0 \cdot 72$
- finally, multiply this decimal by 100 => $0 \cdot 72 \times 100 = \boxed{72\%}$

These 3 steps are used to show what one number is when expressed as a percentage of another.

Exercise 2·2

1. Copy the following and use your calculator to change each **fraction** to a **percentage** :-

    (a) $\frac{7}{50} = 7 \div 50$
    $= 0 \cdot ..... = (0 \cdot .... \times 100\%) = ... \%$

    (b) $\frac{1}{5} = 1 \div 5$
    $= 0 \cdot ..... = (0 \cdot .... \times 100\%) = ...\%$

    (c) $\frac{12}{50}$ (d) $\frac{20}{25}$ (e) $\frac{9}{20}$

    (f) $\frac{17}{20}$ (g) $\frac{23}{25}$ (h) $\frac{1}{8}$

    (i) $\frac{9}{25}$ (j) $\frac{7}{8}$ (k) $\frac{60}{80}$

    (l) $\frac{5}{8}$ (m) $\frac{13}{20}$ (n) $\frac{37}{74}$.

2. Change each of these marks to **percentages** :-

    (a) Julie scored 32 out of 40 $(\frac{32}{40})$
    $=> 32 \div 40 = 0 \cdot ..... \times 100\% = ... \%$.

    (b) Francis scored 27 out of 50.

    (c) Ricky scored 30 out of 80.

    (d) Chic scored 6 out of 20.

3. Of the 240 pupils in 4th year, 192 of them were following the National 5 Mathematics course.

    (a) What percentage were doing National 5 ?

    (b) What percentage were NOT ?

4. Jamie managed to get 14 out of 18 in his test.

    What was Jamie's percentage mark ?
    (*Answer correct to 1 decimal place*).

5. Determine the following marks as percentages, giving each correct to 1 decimal place :-

    (a) Jilly scored 65 out of 80 in Maths.

    (b) Rebecca scored 27 out of 35 in French.

    (c) Alistair scored 40 out of 41 in Physics.

6. Lucy recorded her monthly test scores :-

    Aug - $\frac{10}{20}$ Sep - $\frac{30}{50}$ Oct - $\frac{26}{40}$

    Nov - $\frac{48}{80}$ Dec - $\frac{7}{10}$ Jan - $\frac{75}{100}$

    Feb - $\frac{54}{60}$ Mar - $\frac{20}{25}$ Apr - $\frac{24}{24}$

    May - $\frac{34}{40}$.

    (a) Calculate Lucy's percentage scores over the 10 month period.

    (b) Draw a neat line graph to show Lucy's progress.

    (c) What was Lucy's average (**mean**) percentage mark ?

    (d) Describe the **trend** of her marks.

7. Nick sat a test out of a maximum of 60.

    His score was 82%,
    (*rounded to 1 decimal place*).

    What must his score have been ?

Percentage Profit and Loss

A shopkeeper buys an article for **£A** and sells it for **£B**. He will have made a :-

- **Profit** of   £(B − A) as long as **B** is greater than **A**.
- **Loss** of   £(A − B) as long as **A** is greater than **B**.

Generally, the shopkeeper is more interested in his **PERCENTAGE** profit.

—> He wants to know what his **profit** is, expressed as a **percentage** of what it **cost** him.

Example :-   Gerry the Grocer bought a barrel of 100 apples for £24·00.
He packed them into bags of 10 and sold them all for £3·20 per bag.

    (a)   Calculate his overall profit.

    (b)   Express this as a percentage of what it cost Gerry.

(a)

Actual Profit :-	
Cost Price	£24·00
Selling Price = 10 × £3·20	£32·00
Profit = £32·00 – £24·00 =	£8·00

(b)

Percentage Profit :-

$$= \frac{\text{actual profit}}{\text{cost price}} \times 100\%$$

$$= (8{\cdot}00 \div 24{\cdot}00) \times 100 = 33{\cdot}3\%$$

Exercise 2·3

1.   Susie bought a book for £15·00.
Five years later, she sold it for £18·00.

    Calculate her percentage profit.

    Copy and complete :-

Original value	£15·00
New value	£18·00
Profit = £(18 − 15) =	£...·...
% age profit = (3 ÷ 15) × 100% =	.... %

    (For the remainder of this exercise, set down all working using the 4 lines shown).

2.   Mr Jasimi bought bicycles
for £120 each. He sold them
for £138 each.

    Calculate Mr Jasimi's percentage profit.

3.   For each of the following, calculate the profit and the percentage profit :-

    (a)   cost price - 80p,   selling price - 90p.

    (b)   cost price - £1500, selling price - £1950.

3.   (c)   cost price - £16000, selling price - £16480.

    (d)   cost price - 40p, selling price - £1·00.

4.   My PacaDell computer cost me £500 new.
I sold it one year later for £350.

    Find how much I lost in the deal, and express this as a percentage of what it cost me.

5.   Calculate the loss and percentage loss each time.

    (a)   cost price - £160,   selling price - £112.

    (b)   cost price - £4000, selling price - £1260.

    (c)   cost price - 80p,   selling price - 10p.

6.   Davie's new Pickup
cost him £12000.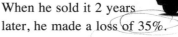

    When he sold it 2 years
later, he made a loss of 35%.

    How much must Davie have got for his Pickup ?

7.   Gerry the grocer wants to make a **40% profit**
on the vegetables he sells.
He bought a 50 kg sack of potatoes for £36
which he then repacked into 5 kg bags.

    For how much will Gerry need to sell each bag ?

Compound Interest

You should already know that if money is left in a bank for up to a year, it gains **interest**.

This is referred to as **Simple Interest** as is found by using percentages.

If you leave money in the bank for several years :-

- the interest is found **for the first year**
- this is then **added** to the **previous balance**
- the new interest for the next year is calculated on the **new balance**
- this is then added on again to the previous balance
- ... and so on until all the interest has been calculated.

This is referred to as **COMPOUND INTEREST**.

Example :-   Ailsa invests £800 in the Scotia Bank. Their **annual** rate is 4%.
Calculate the **compound interest** that builds up in the account.

Interest paid at 4% p.a.

First Year Balance		£800·00
1st Year Interest = 4% of £800·00	=	£32·00
Second Year Balance = £800·00 + £32·00	=	£832·00
2nd Year Interest = 4% of £832·00	=	£33·28
Third Year Balance = £832·00 + £33·28	=	£865·28
3rd Year Interest = 4% of £865·28	=	£34·61
=> Final Balance = £865·28 + £34·61	=	£899·89
=> **Total Interest** = £899·89 – £800·00	=	**£99·89**

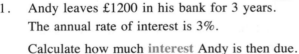

1. Andy leaves £1200 in his bank for 3 years.
    The annual rate of interest is 3%.

    Calculate how much **interest** Andy is then due.
    Copy and **complete** :-

1st Year Balance	£1200·00
1st Year Int = 3% of £1200·00	£........·....
2nd Year Balance = £1200 + ...	£........·....
2nd Year Int = 3% of £.....·...	£........·....
3rd Year Balance = £....... + ...	£........·....
3rd Year Int = 3% of £.....·...	£........·....
Final Balance =	£........·....
Total Interest =	£........·....

2. Nicki and Susan Dyer invested £480 in their
    building society account and left it there for
    two years. The annual interest rate was 3·5%.

    Calculate the **compound** interest that built up
    in their account over the 2 years.

3. Harry left his £25 000 Premium Bond winnings
    in a special savings account for 3 years.

    The annual rate of interest was 4·5%.

    How much were his savings then worth ?

4. Joan was told that if she left her savings of
    £2400 in the Scotia Bank for 5 years they
    would give her a special annual rate of 5·4%.

    How much would her £2400 be worth at the
    end of the 5 year period ?

5. Calculate the total compound interest due
    when the following investments are made :-

    (a) Colin deposited £360 in the bank for 3
         years with an annual interest rate of 2·5%.

    (b) Alex put by £5000 in the bank for 2
         years with an annual interest rate of 3·2%.

    (c) Tim paid in £600 to his bank and left it for
         2 years. The annual interest rate was $3\frac{1}{2}$%.

6. An internet bank offered a tremendous interest rate of 9% per year on savings.
    Jon and Ruth Williams invested their savings of £6000 in the internet bank.

    (a) How much were their savings worth after :-   (i) 1 year   (ii) 2 years ?

    (b) How many years would it take before their investment doubled in value ?

7.
    Rebecca was advised to invest her £12 000 life savings in a special High
    Interest Savings account, but she had to agree not to touch it for 4 years.

    The interest rates for the 4 year period were 4·5%, 5%, 5·3% and 4·9% respectively.

    (a) Calculate the value of her savings at the end of each year.

    (b) What was the total interest that had accrued on her account ?

    (c) Express this as a percentage of her original investment.

Depreciation and Appreciation

Most things you buy generally tend to **drop** or **DEPRECIATE** in value with time.

Example 1 :- A car, bought for £12 000, depreciated by :-

- 15% during its 1st year,
- 20% in its 2nd year.
- 25% during its 3rd year.

What was its actual value after 3 years ?

Initial Value		£12 000
1st Year depreciation = 15% of £12 000	=	£1800
Second Year Value = £12 000 – £1800	=	£10 200
2nd Year depreciation = 20% of £10 200	=	£2040
Third Year Value = £10 200 – £2040	=	£8160
3rd Year depreciation = 25% of £8160	=	£2040
=> **Final** Value = £8160 – £2040	=	**£6120**

Some valuables, like paintings, diamond rings and "special" types of cars **rise** or **APPRECIATE**.

Example 2 :- A Jack Vetriano painting, bought for £5000, appreciated by :-

- 60% during its 1st year.
- 80% during in its 2nd year.

What was the painting worth after 2 years ?

Initial Value		£5000
1st Year appreciation = 60% of £5000	=	£3000
Second Year Value = £5000 + £3000	=	£8000
2nd Year appreciation = 80% of £8000	=	£6400
=> **Final** Value = £8000 + £6400	=	**£14 400**

1. Jillian and Mike bought a dishwasher for £400.
   Its value **depreciated** by 20% every year.

   Calculate what it was worth after 3 years.

   Copy and complete :-

1st Year Value	£400
1st Year Dep. = 20% of £400 = £.......	
2nd Year Value = £400 – £80 = £.......	
2nd Year Dep. = 20% of £.... = £.......	
3rd Year Value = £.... – £.... = £.......	
3rd Year Dep. = 20% of £.... = £.......	
=> Final Value = £.... – £.... = £.......	

2. Zak bought his first
   motorbike at the start
   of 2010 for £6400.

   It **depreciated** in value by 25% every year
   he owned it.

   What was the bike worth by the end of :-

   (a) 2011   (b) 2012   (c) 2013 ?

3.  The Wallaces paid £90 000 for
   their house 3 years ago.

   Because of a new motorway
   passing 50 metres from their
   front door, they found that the
   house's value **dropped** by 5%
   the first year, 10% in the second and a further
   20% in the third year.

   How much was their house then worth ?

4. A hot air balloon was drifting along
   at a height of 16 000 feet, when it
   developed a leak.

   The balloon dropped by 8%
   every minute after that.

   What was the balloon's height after 3 minutes ?

5. Jules bought a Rolls Royce Silver Shadow and
   paid £48 000 for it.
   He discovered that the car **appreciated** in value
   by 6% during the first year he owned it and by
   8% in its 2nd year.

   What was the car then worth ?

6. The cost of buying an
   average weekly shopping
   for a family of 4 generally
   rises each year.

   Choice meats

   The James' family spent
   about £150 per week in Tesdas in 2010.

   If the cost of living rose by 4% per year, what
   would they have paid for their weekly shop in

   (a) 2011   (b) 2012   (c) 2013 ?

7. The graph below shows the "**cost of living**"
   annual rise between 2007 and 2012.

   (a) What was the cost of living rise in :-
       (i) 2008   (ii) 2010 ?

   (b) A new computer system cost £600 at the
       beginning of 2007. What would you
       expect to pay for it by the end of 2007 ?

   (c) A meal out for 4 costs on average £42 at
       the beginning of 2011. What would a
       similar meal cost by the end of 2011 ?

   (d) Greg and Sally paid £30 000 for their flat
       at the beginning of 2007.

       Estimate the flat's value at the end of :-

       (i) 2007   (ii) 2009   (iii) 2012 ?

8. The pressure in a boiler is 120 poundals.
   A faulty valve causes the pressure to rise in
   the boiler by 12% every hour.

   The situation will become dangerous when the
   pressure reaches 200 poundals.

   If it continues to rise this way, during which
   hour will the boiler's pressure reach danger
   level ?

Percentage Problems – Working Backwards

Consider the following problem - solving it is NOT as easy as you think !

> **Problem :-** A man receives a 10% pay rise.
>
> His **new** weekly pay becomes £440.
>
> **Question :-** What must his **original** pay have been ?

What **NOT** to do ! :- Do **not** simply find 10% of £440, (= £44), and subtract it => £396. ✗

Solution :- Note that, **after** a 10% rise, the man was then earning **110%** of his original pay !

New pay	= 110%	=	....	£440
=>	1%	=	£440 ÷ 110 =	£4
Original pay	= 100%	=	£4·00 × 100 =	**£400**

* study this example carefully

Note :- the 3 lines.

Always find 1% first.

It's really a **proportion** problem.

Exercise 2·6

1. After receiving a 20% rise, Jennifer's pay went up to £18 000 per year.

   What must Jennifer have been earning before her pay rise ?

   (*Hint* :- start with
=>	120%	= £18 000)
=>	1%	= £.........
=>	100%	= £.........

2. The painting I bought last year rose by 40% in value this year. It is **now** worth £560.

   How much must I have paid for the painting ?

3. Because of a fault in a thermostat, the temperature in an oven rises by 35% to 324°C.

   What was the temperature before the fault ?

4. 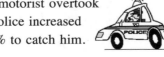 On his 14th birthday, Otis found he was 12% **taller** than he was on his previous birthday.

   He was 1·68 m tall on his 14th birthday.

   How tall was Otis on his 13th ?

5. When a speeding motorist overtook a police car, the police increased their speed by 60% to catch him.

   If the police car was then doing 80 mph, what was its speed before it accelerated ?

6. The bike I bought last year **dropped** in value by 20% this year.

   It is now only worth £160.

   How much must I have paid for the bike ?
   Copy and complete :-

New value =	80%	(100% − 20%) =	£160
=>	1%	=	£160 ÷ 80 =	£2
Old value =	100%	=	100 × £2	= £....

7. 15% of the maths students at Strathtay University dropped out of their course during their first year.
   That left 255 students remaining.

   How many students must there have been at the beginning of the year ?

8. When a window was left open for 10 minutes, the temperature dropped by 35% to 19·5°C.

   What was the temperature before the window was opened ?

9. When Donald sold his flat, he lost 3% of what he had originally paid for it.

   He only got £43 650 for his flat.

   What must Donald have paid for the flat when he bought it ?

1. Find the following **without** a calculator :-

    (a) 20% of £70   (b) 30% of £140

    (c) $33\frac{1}{3}$% of £120   (d) 5% of £8000

    (e) 60% of £3000   (f) $12\frac{1}{2}$% of £400.

2. Value Added Tax (**V.A.T.**) is added on to most goods bought, and is paid to the government. V.A.T. is charged at 20%.
    I bought a new cooker from Comco for £280 **plus** VAT.

    (a) Calculate the VAT due on the cooker.

    (b) How much did the cooker cost me ?

You may use a calculator for the rest of this page, but you must show all working clearly :-

3. Last December, I booked my holidays to the Canary Islands for £480. In May, I was told I had to pay a surcharge of 6%.

    How much did my holiday really cost me ?

4. A Bell PC I wanted to buy, was for sale in Agros priced £490.

    Cotem Stores was selling it for 12% less.

    How much were Cotems charging ?

5. Scotia Bank's annual interest rate was 4·8%.
    Bruce deposited £2400 in Scotia Bank.

    > Special Savings Rate
    > 4·8% p.a.

    (a) How much interest would he have received if he'd left it in the bank for 1 year ?

    (b) If Bruce withdrew his money after 7 months, how much interest should he have expected to receive ?

6. Change to a percentage :- (a) $\frac{17}{20}$ (b) $\frac{13}{16}$.

7. Georgie scored 27 out of 40 in her driving test written paper.

    She needs a score of 65% to pass. Did Georgie pass ? (*Justify*).

8. I bought an iPod for £200 and sold it for £145.

    (a) How much of a loss did I make ?

    (b) Express the loss as a percentage of what it cost.

9. Safe-Coe bought in a crate of 10 Christmas turkeys for £80·00.

    They manage to sell all of them for £11·50 each.

    Calculate the **total** profit and express it as a percentage of the cost price.

10. Julie invested £2000 in her bank for 3 years. The interest rate stayed fixed at 4·5% p.a.

    Calculate how much interest Julie was due at the end of the 3 year period.

11. Mr Fixit lends money at the very high interest rate of 15% **per month**, (*compound interest*).

    Tom borrows £500 from Mr Fixit and agrees to pay it back, with the interest, 3 months later.

    How much will Tom have to pay back ?

12. I bought a new car for £12500 in January 2010.

    Its value **depreciated** by 15% the first year, 20% the second and 25% during the third year.

    How much was it worth in January 2013 ?

13. When he reached 13, Donnie's dad increased his weekly pocket-money by 25%.

    Donnie's pocket money then went up to £15.

    How much did Donnie get per week when he was only 12 ?

14.  The shop's sale sign said

    "**20% off everything**".

    Jane bought a denim skirt in the sale for £24·00.

    What would it have cost Jane **before** the sale ?

Add, Subtract & Multiply Fractions Revision

You should already be aware of how to add, subtract and multiply fractions.
Here are a few reminders :-

Example 1 :-

$$\frac{3}{4} + \frac{5}{4}$$
$$= \frac{12}{20} + \frac{25}{20}$$
$$= \frac{37}{20}$$
$$= 1\frac{17}{20}$$

Example 2 :-

$$\frac{7}{8} - \frac{3}{5}$$
$$= \frac{35}{40} - \frac{24}{40}$$
$$= \frac{11}{40}$$

Example 3 :-

$$4\frac{3}{4} + 6\frac{2}{3}$$
$$= 10 \left(\frac{3}{4} + \frac{2}{3}\right)$$
$$= 10 \left(\frac{9}{12} + \frac{8}{12}\right)$$
$$= 10\frac{17}{12}$$
$$= 11\frac{5}{12}$$

Example 4 :-

$$7\frac{7}{9} - 2\frac{1}{3}$$
$$= 5 \left(\frac{7}{9} - \frac{1}{3}\right)$$
$$= 5 \left(\frac{7}{9} - \frac{3}{9}\right)$$
$$= 5\frac{4}{9}$$

Example 5 :-

$$9\frac{1}{4} - 3\frac{2}{3}$$
$$= 6 \left(\frac{1}{4} - \frac{2}{3}\right)$$
$$= 6 \left(\frac{3}{12} - \frac{8}{12}\right)$$
$$= 5 \left(\frac{12}{12} + \frac{3}{12} - \frac{8}{12}\right)$$
$$= 5\frac{7}{12}$$

Example 6 :-

$$3\frac{3}{4} \times 2\frac{1}{3}$$
$$= \frac{15}{4} \times \frac{7}{3}$$
$$= \frac{105}{12}$$
$$= 8\frac{9}{12}$$
$$= 8\frac{3}{4}$$

Exercise 3·1

1. Change each of the following into a top heavy fraction :-

   (a) $4\frac{1}{5}$ (b) $5\frac{5}{8}$ (c) $9\frac{3}{7}$ (d) $12\frac{9}{10}$.

2. Change each of the following into a mixed number :-

   (a) $\frac{15}{4}$ (b) $\frac{19}{3}$ (c) $\frac{42}{5}$ (d) $\frac{81}{11}$.

3. Work out and simplify where possible :-

   (a) $\frac{3}{8} + \frac{1}{8}$ (b) $\frac{5}{9} - \frac{2}{9}$ (c) $\frac{1}{5} + \frac{1}{4}$ (d) $\frac{1}{8} + \frac{1}{6}$

   (e) $\frac{1}{2} + \frac{1}{12}$ (f) $\frac{3}{4} - \frac{1}{8}$ (g) $\frac{3}{4} + \frac{1}{16}$ (h) $\frac{3}{5} - \frac{1}{2}$

   (i) $\frac{13}{16} - \frac{3}{8}$ (j) $\frac{9}{10} + \frac{3}{5}$ (k) $\frac{1}{2} - \frac{3}{11}$ (l) $\frac{17}{20} - \frac{3}{5}$

   (m) $\frac{1}{2} + \frac{1}{3} + \frac{1}{4}$ (n) $\frac{3}{4} + \frac{2}{3} - \frac{4}{5}$ (o) $\frac{9}{10} + \frac{1}{5} - \frac{19}{20}$ (p) $\frac{3}{4} + \frac{2}{3} - \frac{8}{12}$.

4. Calculate each of these, leaving your answer as a mixed number :-

   (a) $\frac{4}{3} + \frac{5}{4}$ (b) $5\frac{1}{5} + 8\frac{2}{5}$ (c) $7\frac{5}{6} - 3\frac{1}{6}$ (d) $5\frac{1}{5} + 4\frac{1}{4}$

   (e) $9\frac{1}{2} + 1\frac{3}{4}$ (f) $7\frac{7}{8} - 6\frac{3}{4}$ (g) $10\frac{7}{10} + 3\frac{1}{2}$ (h) $12\frac{2}{3} + 4\frac{4}{5}$

   (i) $8\frac{1}{4} - 5\frac{2}{3}$ (j) $20\frac{2}{7} - 15\frac{3}{4}$ (k) $10 - 7\frac{6}{13}$ (l) $100\frac{4}{5} - 99\frac{5}{6}$.

5. Multiply the following fractions and simplify where possible :-

   (a) $\frac{2}{3} \times \frac{1}{6}$ (b) $\frac{7}{10} \times \frac{5}{8}$ (c) $\frac{3}{16} \times \frac{2}{3}$ (d) $\frac{5}{8} \times \frac{8}{25}$

   (e) $\frac{5}{6} \times \frac{3}{4}$ (f) $\frac{8}{9} \times \frac{3}{32}$ (g) $\frac{4}{5} \times \frac{5}{8} \times \frac{1}{2}$ (h) $\frac{5}{6} \times \frac{12}{25} \times \frac{2}{5}$.

6. Calculate each of these, leaving your answer as a mixed number :-

   (a) $2\frac{1}{3} \times 3\frac{1}{2}$ (b) $2\frac{1}{5} \times 1\frac{1}{5}$ (c) $1\frac{1}{3} \times 4\frac{3}{4}$ (d) $3\frac{3}{7} \times 1\frac{2}{3}$

   (e) $2\frac{3}{5} \times 1\frac{1}{4}$ (f) $2\frac{5}{6} \times 4\frac{1}{2}$ (g) $2\frac{3}{10} \times 3\frac{1}{3}$ (h) $2\frac{1}{3} \times 2\frac{2}{5}$

   (i) $1\frac{1}{8} \times 2\frac{2}{9}$ (j) $7\frac{1}{2} \times 3\frac{3}{5}$ (k) $2\frac{1}{2} \times 2\frac{2}{15}$ (l) $9 \times 1\frac{7}{18}$.

7. A recipe for bread called for $\frac{2}{3}$ cups of white flour and $2\frac{1}{5}$ cups of whole meal flour.

   (a) How much flour was needed overall ?

   (b) How much more whole meal flour than white flour was required ?

8. Brian drank exactly $4\frac{1}{5}$ litres of water and $2\frac{3}{4}$ of milk yesterday.

   (a) How much fluid did he drink altogether ?

   (b) How much less milk than water ?

9. At Fabio's Restaurant 40 out of the 70 dishes on the menu are vegetarian.

Of the vegetarian dishes $\frac{5}{8}$ are pasta dishes.

What fraction of the dishes on the menu are vegetarian pasta ?

10. Jessie's mum found that she weighed $2\frac{1}{4}$ times as much as Jessie.

If Jessie weighs 28 kilograms, what did her mum weigh ?

11. On Monday, a team of window cleaners cleaned $\frac{5}{8}$ of the windows on a high rise building.

On Tuesday, as it was raining, they only managed to clean $\frac{2}{5}$ as many windows as Monday.

   (a) What fraction of the building's windows were cleaned on Tuesday ?

   (b) What fraction of the building's windows remained dirty ?

12. A cuboid has sides $2\frac{2}{5}$ m, $3\frac{3}{10}$ m and $2\frac{3}{11}$ m long.

Calculate the volume of the cuboid.

$2\frac{3}{11}$

$2\frac{2}{5}$

$3\frac{3}{10}$

 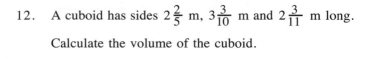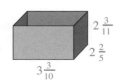

Division of Fractions

It is almost impossible to do fraction calculation like $(\frac{2}{3} \div \frac{3}{5})$ by actually **dividing**.

What we do instead, is change a "**division**" to a "**multiplication**" (*which is easier*) as follows :-

RULE* :-
- Leave the first fraction (*the left hand one*) as it is.
- Turn the second fraction (*the right hand one*) "**upside down**".
- Change the division sign ($\div$) to a multiplication ($\times$) and **multiply**.

$$\longrightarrow \quad \frac{2}{3} \div \frac{3}{5} \text{ becomes } \quad \frac{2}{3} \times \frac{5}{3} = \frac{10}{9} = 1\frac{1}{9}.$$

Example 1 :-
$$\frac{5}{6} \div \frac{2}{3}$$
$$\Rightarrow \frac{5}{6} \times \frac{3}{2}$$
$$\Rightarrow \frac{15}{12} = 1\frac{1}{4}$$

Example 2 :-
$$\frac{7}{8} \div \frac{3}{4}$$
$$\Rightarrow \frac{7}{8} \times \frac{4}{3}$$
$$\Rightarrow \frac{28}{24} = 1\frac{1}{6}$$

Example 3 :-
$$4\frac{4}{5} \div 1\frac{1}{3}$$
$$\Rightarrow \frac{24}{5} \div \frac{4}{3}$$
$$\Rightarrow \frac{24}{5} \times \frac{3}{4}$$
$$\Rightarrow \frac{72}{20} = 3\frac{3}{5}$$

* - Your teacher will explain the rule and how it works.

Exercise 3·2

1. Copy each of the following and complete :-

(a)
$$\frac{3}{4} \div \frac{3}{5}$$
$$= \frac{3}{4} \times \frac{5}{3}$$
$$= \frac{?}{12} = \frac{?}{4} = 1\frac{?}{4}$$

(b)
$$\frac{5}{6} \div \frac{1}{3}$$
$$= \frac{5}{6} \times \frac{3}{1}$$
$$= \frac{?}{6} = 2\frac{?}{6}$$

2. Divide the following and simplify :-

(a) $\frac{2}{5} \div \frac{2}{3}$ (b) $\frac{5}{6} \div \frac{7}{12}$

(c) $\frac{3}{7} \div \frac{6}{7}$ (d) $\frac{3}{10} \div \frac{4}{5}$

(e) $\frac{3}{8} \div \frac{5}{6}$ (f) $\frac{7}{12} \div \frac{7}{8}$

(g) $\frac{11}{16} \div \frac{5}{8}$ (h) $\frac{2}{9} \div \frac{1}{6}$

(i) $\frac{7}{10} \div \frac{3}{5}$ (j) $\frac{7}{16} \div \frac{3}{10}$

(k) $\frac{8}{9} \div \frac{3}{4}$ (l) $\frac{1}{5} \div \frac{1}{7}$.

3. How many $\frac{2}{5}$'s are there in $\frac{3}{10}$'s ?

4. How many pieces of cloth $\frac{1}{8}$ metre long, can I cut from a piece $\frac{2}{3}$ metre long ?

5. Copy and complete the following :-

(a)
$$2\frac{1}{4} \div 1\frac{1}{5}$$
$$= \frac{9}{4} \div \frac{6}{5}$$
$$= \frac{9}{4} \times \frac{5}{6}$$
$$= \ldots\ldots = \ldots\ldots$$

(b)
$$4\frac{2}{3} \div 1\frac{2}{5}$$
$$= \frac{14}{3} \div \frac{7}{5}$$
$$= \frac{14}{3} \times \frac{?}{?}$$
$$= \ldots\ldots = \ldots\ldots$$

6. Divide the following fractions in the same way (*simplify if possible*) :-

(a) $3\frac{1}{3} \div 1\frac{1}{2}$ (b) $2\frac{1}{5} \div 1\frac{1}{2}$

(c) $4\frac{2}{3} \div 1\frac{2}{5}$ (d) $2\frac{1}{4} \div 1\frac{2}{7}$

(e) $5\frac{1}{4} \div 1\frac{1}{6}$ (f) $6\frac{1}{2} \div 2\frac{1}{4}$

(g) $1\frac{3}{5} \div 4\frac{2}{3}$ (h) $7\frac{1}{2} \div 1\frac{3}{7}$

(i) $6 \div 1\frac{1}{2}$ (j) $8 \div 2\frac{2}{3}$.

7. $2\frac{1}{4}$ laps of the park took Tommy Muir, walking his dog, $12\frac{1}{2}$ minutes.

How long, on average did 1 lap take ?

1. Simplify these additions and subtractions as far as possible :-

    (a) $\frac{1}{2} + \frac{1}{3}$ 　　　　(b) $\frac{1}{2} + \frac{1}{8}$ 　　　　(c) $\frac{3}{4} + \frac{1}{3}$ 　　　　(d) $\frac{3}{4} + \frac{4}{5}$

    (e) $\frac{5}{8} - \frac{1}{2}$ 　　　　(f) $\frac{4}{5} - \frac{1}{2}$ 　　　　(g) $\frac{7}{8} - \frac{1}{4}$ 　　　　(h) $\frac{3}{4} - \frac{2}{3}$

    (i) $2\frac{2}{3} + 1\frac{1}{6}$ 　　　(j) $3\frac{3}{5} + 2\frac{3}{4}$ 　　　(k) $5\frac{1}{3} + 4\frac{3}{5}$ 　　　(l) $1\frac{1}{6} + 6\frac{3}{8}$

    (m) $2\frac{1}{2} - 1\frac{1}{5}$ 　　　(n) $3\frac{1}{8} - 1\frac{1}{4}$ 　　　(o) $10\frac{2}{5} - 4\frac{7}{10}$ 　　(p) $2\frac{1}{8} - \frac{3}{4}$.

2. Work out the multiplications :-

    (a) $\frac{1}{3} \times \frac{1}{2}$ 　　　　(b) $\frac{4}{5} \times \frac{1}{4}$ 　　　　(c) $\frac{3}{8} \times \frac{4}{3}$ 　　　　(d) $\frac{5}{8} \times \frac{4}{15}$

    (e) $\frac{8}{9} \times \frac{3}{4}$ 　　　　(f) $\frac{5}{12} \times \frac{24}{25}$ 　　　(g) $\frac{2}{3} \times \frac{21}{40}$ 　　　(h) $\frac{3}{7} \times \frac{7}{12}$

    (i) $1\frac{1}{2} \times 1\frac{1}{2}$ 　　　(j) $1\frac{1}{3} \times 2\frac{1}{4}$ 　　　(k) $1\frac{3}{5} \times 2\frac{1}{2}$ 　　　(l) $3\frac{1}{3} \times 2\frac{1}{4}$

    (m) $1\frac{1}{3} \times 1\frac{1}{8}$ 　　　(n) $2\frac{2}{5} \times 3\frac{3}{4}$ 　　　(o) $20 \times 1\frac{3}{4}$ 　　　(p) $1\frac{1}{3} \times 2\frac{1}{2}$.

3. Try these divisions :-

    (a) $4 \div \frac{1}{2}$ 　　　　(b) $5 \div \frac{1}{4}$ 　　　　(c) $8 \div \frac{2}{3}$ 　　　　(d) $6 \div 1\frac{1}{2}$

    (e) $15 \div 2\frac{1}{2}$ 　　　(f) $7 \div 2\frac{1}{3}$ 　　　(g) $\frac{9}{21} \div \frac{6}{7}$ 　　　(h) $5\frac{1}{2} \div 2\frac{1}{2}$

    (i) $\frac{1}{3} \div \frac{1}{6}$ 　　　　(j) $3\frac{1}{3} \div 1\frac{1}{3}$ 　　　(k) $5\frac{1}{2} \div 1\frac{2}{3}$ 　　　(l) $1\frac{1}{2} \div \frac{3}{4}$.

4. Work out :-

    (a) $\frac{1}{3}\left(\frac{1}{2} + \frac{1}{4}\right)$ 　　(b) $\frac{1}{5}\left(\frac{1}{9} + \frac{1}{6}\right)$ 　　(c) $\frac{1}{7}\left(\frac{1}{3} + \frac{3}{5}\right)$ 　　(d) $\frac{1}{7}\left(\frac{2}{3} + \frac{1}{2}\right)$

    (e) $2\frac{1}{3} + \frac{5}{6}$ *of* $1\frac{2}{5}$ 　　(f) $\frac{2}{5}$ *of* $3\frac{1}{2} + \frac{4}{5}$ 　　(g) $2\frac{2}{5} + \frac{4}{7}$ *of* $1\frac{2}{5} \div \frac{1}{2}$.

5. The Coffee Bean Shop can make lattes with either whole milk or skimmed milk.

    On Saturday, the shop went through $25\frac{3}{8}$ cartons of whole milk and $16\frac{5}{6}$ cartons of skimmed milk.

    How much more whole milk was used than skimmed milk ?

6.  On Friday, the farmers at Gricio's vineyard harvested $\frac{3}{5}$ of their crop of grapes.

    On Saturday, they picked only $\frac{3}{10}$ of Friday's takings.

    What fraction of the grapes had still to be harvested ?

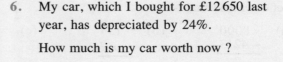

1. Multiply out the brackets and simplify fully :-

    (a) $3(x - 6)$ (b) $6(2x - 3) + 7$

    (c) $5(x - 3) + 2(x + 1) + 7(2x - 3) + 5$

    (d) $3(2x + 4) - 5(x - 6) + 3$

    (e) $11k - 6(2k + 1) + k + 6$.

2. Multiply out the brackets and simplify fully :-

    (a) $(y + 3)(y + 2)$ (b) $(k - 3)(k + 4)$

    (c) $(p - 3)(p - 5)$ (d) $(2y + 3)(y - 2)$

    (e) $(3w - 1)^3$ (f) $(4x + 2)^3$

    (g) $(x + 1)^2 - (x - 1)^2$

    (h) $(x + 2)^3 - (x - 2)^2$

    (i) $\left(x + \dfrac{1}{x}\right)^2$ (j) $\left(4x - \dfrac{1}{2x}\right)^2$.

3. A right angle triangle with base $3x + 1$ and height $2x - 4$ is removed from a yellow square of side $4x$.

    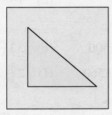

    Find the yellow area remaining, in terms of x.

4. I booked my £640 holiday in May.

    When I went to pay it in June I had to pay a 7·5% surcharge.

    How much did I have to pay in total ?

5. My bank only paid me 3·7% interest on my £2650 savings.

    They should have given me 4·2% interest.

    How much did they still owe me ?

6. My car, which I bought for £12 650 last year, has depreciated by 24%.

    How much is my car worth now ?

7. I bought a painting for £2760 two years ago.

    One art gallery said it had depreciated by 12%.

    Another said it had appreciated by 8%.

    How much of a difference is there between the two evaluations ?

8. How much was each item below **before** the sale discount ?

    (a) 10% discount   (b) 6% discount

    NOW only £45   NOW only £169·20

    (c) 40% off   (d) 24% off

    NOW only £72   NOW only £8056

9. Find :-

    (a) $\dfrac{1}{2} + \dfrac{3}{8}$ (b) $\dfrac{7}{8} + \dfrac{1}{5}$

    (c) $4\dfrac{4}{5} + 2\dfrac{1}{4}$ (d) $7\dfrac{1}{3} - 3\dfrac{3}{4}$

    (e) $4\dfrac{1}{2} + 3\dfrac{5}{7} - 1\dfrac{3}{8}$ (f) $\dfrac{1}{2} \times \dfrac{5}{7}$

    (g) $\dfrac{4}{9} \times \dfrac{3}{8}$ (h) $2\dfrac{1}{5} \times 3\dfrac{3}{4}$

    (i) $\dfrac{4}{5} \div \dfrac{2}{3}$ (j) $7\dfrac{1}{3} \div 2\dfrac{4}{9}$

    (k) $5\dfrac{2}{3} + 1\dfrac{3}{7} \times 2\dfrac{1}{3}$ (l) $2\dfrac{1}{2} \times 1\dfrac{3}{4} - 2\dfrac{1}{3}$

    (m) $\dfrac{1}{2} \times \dfrac{2}{3} \times \dfrac{3}{4} \times \dfrac{4}{5} \times \dfrac{5}{6} \times \dfrac{6}{7} \times \dfrac{7}{8} \times \dfrac{8}{9} \times \dfrac{9}{10}$.

1. Set down and find :-

(a) $8000 - 4213$

(b) 157×7

(c) 4526×500

(d) 67×19

(e) $8\overline{)3032}$

(f) 12^4

(g) $33\,500 \div 50$

(h) $40 - 8 \times 6$

(i) $7 \times (8 + 3) - 9$

(j) $99 - 66 \div 3$.

2. Set down and find :-

(a) $8 \cdot 345 - 6 \cdot 789$

(b) $5 - 3 \cdot 139$

(c) $7\overline{)43 \cdot 75}$

(d) $1 \cdot 903 \times 6$

(e) $3000 \times 0 \cdot 675$

(f) $476 \div 400$

(g) $\dfrac{7 \times 25 \cdot 4}{1000}$

(h) $34 \cdot 6 \div 10\,000$.

3. Change :-

(a) $80\,000$ cm to km

(b) $0 \cdot 006$ km to mm

(c) 54 ml to litres

(d) 36 g to kg.

4. Find :-

(a) $\frac{4}{5}$ of 775

(b) $\frac{7}{8}$ of 104

(c) $\frac{11}{19}$ of 3800.

5. Simplify :-

(a) $\frac{16}{64}$

(b) $\frac{42}{91}$

(c) $\frac{17}{680}$.

6. Find :-

(a) $\frac{3}{4} - \frac{3}{8}$

(b) $4\frac{3}{4} + 4\frac{1}{8}$

(c) $3 \times 5\frac{5}{6}$.

7. Express as a fraction :-
(in simplest form)

(a) 30%

(b) $12\frac{1}{2}\%$

(c) $133\frac{1}{3}\%$.

8. Find :-

(a) 25% of £1640

(b) 15% of £1500

(c) $33\frac{1}{3}\%$ of £$8 \cdot 40$

(d) $17 \cdot 5\%$ of £160

(e) $12\frac{1}{2}\%$ of £560

(f) $2\frac{1}{2}\%$ of £$4 \cdot 80$.

9. Find :-

(a) $29 + (-43)$

(b) $323 + (-37)$

(c) $(-47) + 55$

(d) $(-34) + (-44)$

(e) $16 - 124$

(f) $(-29) - 44$

(g) $32 - (-19)$

(h) $(-33) - (-44)$

(i) $(-6) \times 13$

(j) $(-x) - (-7x)$

(k) $(-2y) - 3y - 4y$

(l) $(-5) \times 18$

(m) $9 \times (-33)$

(n) $(-9) \times (-9)$

(o) $(-150) \div 15$

(p) $(-12x) \times (-3x)$

(q) $640y \div (-16y)$

(r) $(-117p) \div (-13p)$

(s) $\dfrac{(-4) \times (-12)}{(-6)}$.

10. (a) A rectangle has a perimeter of 24 cm. Given its length is $3x$ cm and its breadth is $2x$ cm, find x.

(b) A square has side 5 centimetres. Find, to the nearest whole number, the length of a diagonal.

11. (a) How far will a train travel in 48 minutes at an average speed of 150 km/hr ?

(b) A small plane covered the 640 km from Glasgow to London in 3 hours and 12 minutes.
Calculate its average speed.

Sketching Straight Lines

Earlier, we practiced **drawing** straight lines by constructing a table of values, plotting the corresponding coordinate points on a Cartesian Diagram and joining them up.

When **sketching** a straight line we really only need **two points** on the line.

> Substituting **three x-values** into the equation is usually the easiest if the line is of the form $y = mx + c$, but if the line is of the type $y - 2x + 2 = 0$, the easiest points to find are the **axes** points.
>
> i.e. (when $x = 0 \implies (0, ?)$ and when $y = 0 \implies (?, 0)$)

Example :-   Sketch the line $y - 2x + 4 = 0$.

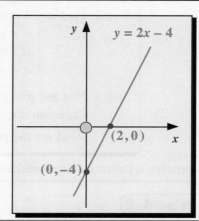

> **Step 1** Let $x = 0$ $y - 2 \times 0 + 4 = 0$
> $y = -4 \implies (0, -4)$
>
> **Step 2** Let $y = 0$ $0 - 2x + 4 = 0$
> $2x = 4$
> $x = 2 \implies (2, 0)$
>
> **Step 3** Plot the two points on a diagram
>   and draw a straight line through them.

Exercise 4·1

1. Find 3 points on the line $y = 2x - 2$ and sketch it.
   Copy and complete :-

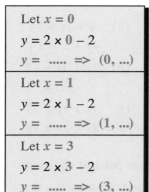

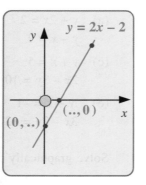

> Let $x = 0$
> $y = 2 \times 0 - 2$
> $y = \ldots\ldots \Rightarrow (0, \ldots)$
>
> Let $x = 1$
> $y = 2 \times 1 - 2$
> $y = \ldots\ldots \Rightarrow (1, \ldots)$
>
> Let $x = 3$
> $y = 2 \times 3 - 2$
> $y = \ldots\ldots \Rightarrow (3, \ldots)$

2. Find 3 points on each of these lines, plot them and sketch each line (*on a separate diagram*).

   (a) $y = 2x - 6$ (b) $y = 2x + 4$

   (c) $y = x + 2$ (d) $y = 4x - 4$

   (e) $y = 2x + 1$ (f) $y = 3x - 1$

   (g) $y = 5x + 20$ (h) $y = 4x - 16$

   (i) $y = 3 - x$ (j) $y = 5 - 4x$.

> **Remember - lines may be expressed differently.**

3. Sketch the line $2y - 2x - 4 = 0$.
   Copy and **complete** :-

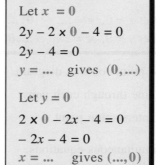

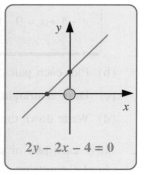

> Let $x = 0$
> $2y - 2 \times 0 - 4 = 0$
> $2y - 4 = 0$
> $y = \ldots$ gives $(0, \ldots)$
>
> Let $y = 0$
> $2 \times 0 - 2x - 4 = 0$
> $-2x - 4 = 0$
> $x = \ldots$ gives $(\ldots, 0)$

4. Sketch each line on a separate diagram.

   (a) $3y - 6x + 3 = 0$ (b) $2y - 2x + 2 = 0$

   (c) $4y + 8x - 8 = 0$ (d) $y - 4x + 4 = 0$

   (e) $2x - 4y = 12$ (f) $x + y = 3$

   (g) $2x + y = 5$ (h) $x + y = -1$

   (i) $3x + 4y = -12$ (j) $3x = 2y$.

Solving Simultaneous Equations - Graphically

If we are given the equations of two lines, for example $y = 2x - 4$ and $y = 5 - x$, we can find the point where they meet (**intersect**) by drawing both lines on the same diagram.

This is referred to as the "**simultaneous**" solution and the equations $y = 2x - 4$ and $y = 5 - x$ are called **simultaneous equations**.

Example :-   Find the coordinates of where the lines $y = 2x - 4$ and $y = 5 - x$ intersect.

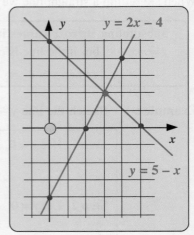

Step 1 Find any 3 points on the line $y = 2x - 4$.
  e.g.   Let $x = 0 \Rightarrow y = -4$ $(0, -4)$
       Let $x = 2 \Rightarrow y = 0$ $(2, 0)$
       Let $x = 4 \Rightarrow y = 4$ $(4, 4)$

Step 2 Find any 3 points on the line $y = 5 - x$.
  e.g.   Let $x = 0 \Rightarrow y = 5$ $(0, 5)$
       Let $x = 2 \Rightarrow y = 3$ $(2, 3)$
       Let $x = 4 \Rightarrow y = 1$ $(4, 1)$

Step 3 Plot and join each set of points on a Cartesian diagram.

Read off the point of intersection. $(3, 2)$

This process is called solving simultaneous equations **graphically**.

Exercise 4·2

1.   Find the coordinates of the point where the lines $y - x + 4 = 0$ and $y - 8 + x = 0$ intersect.

   (a) **Copy** and complete :-

$y - x + 4 = 0$	Let $x = 0$, $y = ...$	$(0, ...)$
	Let $y = 0$, $x = ...$	$(..., 0)$
$y - 8 + x = 0$	Let $x = 0$, $y = ...$	$(0, ...)$
	Let $y = 0$, $x = ...$	$(..., 0)$

   (b) Plot each pair of points on one diagram.

   (c) Draw a straight line through each pair.

   (d) Write down the intersection point.

2.   Solve each pair of simultaneous equations.
   (*Find 3 points on each line, plot the points, draw the lines and find the point of intersection*).

   (a) $y = 2x - 5$
      $y = x - 1$

   (b) $y = 3x - 1$
      $y = 2x - 3$

   (c) $y = x - 1$
      $y = 2 - 2x$

   (d) $y = 4x + 6$
      $y = 5 + 3x$

   (e) $y = 3x - 2$
      $y = 4x - 1$

   (f) $y = 6x - 4$
      $y = -2x$.

(*From now on, you decide which method you wish to use to help you draw the lines*).

3.   Solve each pair of simultaneous equations graphically.

   (a) $y + 2x = 2$
      $y - x = 2$

   (b) $y + 2x = 14$
      $4y + x = 14$

   (c) $y + x = 5$
      $2x - 3y = 10$

   (d) $2y + 3x = 12$
      $y - 2x = -8$

   (e) $y + x = -1$
      $3x - 2y = 12$

   (f) $3x + 2y = 12$
      $2x - 2y = 18$.

4.   Solve graphically these pairs of equations.

   (a) $y + 2x + 1 = 0$ and $2y - x - 8 = 0$

   (b) $3y - 2x - 6 = 0$ and $y + x - 2 = 0$

   (c) $y = 3x + 1$ and $y + 2x - 6 = 0$

   (d) $y = 4x - 1$ and $y - 2x = -3$.

5.   Explain why there are no solutions to the following pair of simultaneous equations.

   $$y = 3x + 4 \quad \text{and} \quad 2y - 6x + 8 = 0$$

   (*Hint : drawing the graph might help*).

Solving Simultaneous Equations - by Elimination

A pair of simultaneous equations can be solved graphically (as before) or **algebraically**.

If we start with 2 equations in 2 variables (letters), and manage to combine both equations to form one new equation and **eliminating** one of the variables - we can easily solve this single remaining equation.

Example 1 :- Solve this pair of equations.

$$x + y = 6 \quad .... \; 1$$
$$x - y = 4 \quad .... \; 2$$

Add equations 1 and 2.

$$\begin{array}{r} x + y = 6 \\ x - y = 4 \\ \hline 2x \quad\;\; = 10 \end{array} \quad \text{(the } y \text{ disappears)}$$

$$\Rightarrow \quad x = 5$$

Substitute this value into equation 1.

$$\Rightarrow \quad 5 + y = 6$$
$$\Rightarrow \quad y = 1$$

Solution is $y = 1$, $x = 5$ $(5, 1)$

Check by substituting the values for x and y into equation 2.

Example 2 :- Solve this pair of equations.

$$3x + 2y = 5 \quad .... \; 1$$
$$-3x + y = 1 \quad .... \; 2$$

Add equations 1 and 2.

$$\begin{array}{r} 3x + 2y = 5 \\ -3x + y = 1 \\ \hline 3y = 6 \end{array} \quad \text{(the } x \text{ disappears)}$$

$$\Rightarrow \quad y = 2$$

Substitute $y = 2$ into eqn 1

$$3x + 2 \times 2 = 5$$
$$\Rightarrow \quad 3x = 1$$
$$\Rightarrow \quad x = \tfrac{1}{3}$$

Solution is $x = \tfrac{1}{3}$, $y = 2$ $(\tfrac{1}{3}, 2)$

Check

This process of solving simultaneous equations is called **elimination**.

Exercise 4·3

1. Solve this pair of simultaneous equations.

$$2y + 3x = 16 \quad ..... \; 1$$
$$4y - 3x = 14 \quad ..... \; 2$$

Copy and complete :-

Add 1 and 2

$$\begin{array}{r} 2y + 3x = 16 \\ 4y - 3x = 14 \\ \hline 6y \quad\quad = ... \end{array} \quad \text{(the } x \text{ disappears)}$$

$$\Rightarrow \quad y = ...$$

Substitute $y = 5$ into equation 1.

$$2 \times 5 + 3x = 16$$
$$\Rightarrow \quad 3x = ...$$
$$\Rightarrow \quad x = ...$$

Solution is $x = ...$ and $y = ...$ $(..., ...)$

2. Solve this pair of simultaneous equations.

$$3y + 2x = 11 \quad ..... \; 1$$
$$y - 2x = 1 \quad ..... \; 2$$

3. Solve each pair of simultaneous equations.

    (a) $5y + 4x = 14$
          $3y - 4x = 2$

    (b) $5y + 4x = 13$
          $9y - 4x = 1$

    (c) $y + 7x = 24$
          $4y - 7x = -9$

    (d) $6y + 2x = 38$
          $4y - 2x = 12$

    (e) $7x - 3y = 2$
          $4x + 3y = 20$

    (f) $x - 8y = -16$
          $3x + 8y = 16$

    (g) $5y - 2x = 11$
          $2y + 2x = -4$

    (h) $3x + 4y = -21$
          $2y - 3x = 3.$

4. Re-arrange the second of these simultaneous equations so that x and y are on the left hand side, and then solve.

$$2x + 3y = 13$$
$$5x = 3y + 1.$$

5. Solve each pair of simultaneous equations.

    (a) $2x + y = 7$
          $4x = y + 11$

    (b) $5x - 2y = 1$
          $x = 2y - 7$

    (c) $4y = 8 - 2x$
          $8 = 2x - 3y$

    (d) $2y + 3x + 1 = 0$
          $y - 4 = 3x.$

Example :- Solve this pair of simultaneous equations

$$5y + 4x = 13 \quad .... \; 1$$
$$3y - x = 5 \quad .... \; 2$$

Can you see that if we try adding equations 1 and 2, the new equation we get is no simpler ?

We must "**work**" on one of the equations first.

> **Step 1** **Multiply** equation 2 **by 4** to form a new equation (call it equation 3).
>
> **Step 2** Notice we can now eliminate x by **adding** 1 and 3.
>
> **Step 3** Proceed as before.

$$5y + 4x = 13 \quad .... \; 1$$
$$3y - x = 1 \quad .... \; 2$$
$$4 \times 2 \Rightarrow 12y - 4x = 4 \quad .... \; 3$$

Now we can **add** 1 and 3.

$$5y + 4x = 13 \quad .... \; 1$$
$$12y - 4x = 4 \quad .... \; 3$$
$$1 + 3 \Rightarrow \quad 17y \quad = 17$$
$$\Rightarrow \quad y = 1$$

Substitute $y = 1$ into equation 1.

$$5 \times 1 + 4x = 13$$
$$\Rightarrow \quad 4x = 8$$
$$\Rightarrow \quad x = 2$$

Solution is $x = 2$, $y = 1$. $(2, 1)$

Check by substituting x and y into equation 2.

Exercise 4·4

1. Solve this pair of simultaneous equations.

$$2y + 3x = 12 \quad ..... \; 1$$
$$5y - x = 13 \quad ..... \; 2$$

Copy and complete :-

$$2y + 3x = 12 \quad ..... \; 1$$
$$5y - x = 13 \quad ..... \; 2$$
$$3 \times 2 \Rightarrow \quad 15y - 3x = ... \quad ..... \; 3$$

Add equation 1 and 3

$$2y + 3x = 12 \quad ..... \; 1$$
$$15y - 3x = ... \quad .... \; 3$$
$$\overline{17y \quad = ...}$$
$$\Rightarrow \quad y = ...$$

Substitute $y = ...$ in equation 1

$$2 \times ... + 3x = 12$$
$$\Rightarrow \quad 3x = ...$$
$$\Rightarrow \quad x = ...$$

Solution is $x = ...$, $y = ...$ $(..., ...)$

Check

2. Solve each pair of simultaneous equations.

$$4x + 2y = 14 \quad .... \; 1$$
$$2x - y = 5 \quad .... \; 2$$

(Hint : multiply equation 2 by 2).

3. For each pair of simultaneous equations :-
   - label each equation 1 and 2.
   - decide which equation to multiply.
   - decide what multiplier to use.
   - solve for x and y.

   (a) $2x + 6y = 36$ (b) $3x + 4y = 25$
        $3x - 2y = -1$ $x - 2y = 5$

   (c) $3x + 2y = 11$ (d) $3x + 4y = 22$
        $2x - y = -2$ $8x - 2y = 8$

   (e) $3x - 2y = 11$ (f) $x - y = 3$
        $7x + 8y = 51$ $3x + 5y = 1$

   (g) $4y + 9x = -27$ (h) $2y + 3x = -12$
        $8y - 3x = 9$ $y - x = -1$

   (i) $12y + 8x = -34$ (j) $4x + 3y = 14$
        $2y - 2x = 6$ $2x - y = -3$.

Example :-

Solve this pair of simultaneous equations.

$$5y + 2x = 12 \quad .... \; 1$$
$$3y - 3x = 5 \quad .... \; 2$$

This time **both** equations need to be multiplied.

$$5y + 2x = 12 \quad .... \; 1$$
$$4y - 3x = 5 \quad .... \; 2$$

$3 \times 1 \Rightarrow \qquad 15y + 6x = 36 \quad .... \; 3$

$2 \times 2 \Rightarrow \qquad \underline{8y - 6x = 10} \quad ...... \; 4$

$3 + 4 \Rightarrow \qquad 23y \qquad = 46$

$\qquad \Rightarrow \qquad \qquad y = 2$

Substitute $y = 2$ in equation 1

$$5 \times 2 + 2x = 12$$
$$\Rightarrow \qquad 2x = 2$$
$$\Rightarrow \qquad x = 1$$

Solution is $x = 1$, $y = 2$. $\qquad (1, 2)$

4. Solve this pair of simultaneous equations.

$$5y + 4x = 18 \quad ..... \; 1$$
$$4y - 3x = 2 \quad ..... \; 2$$

Copy and complete :–

$$5y + 4x = 18 \quad ..... \; 1$$
$$4y - 3x = 2 \quad ..... \; 2$$

$3 \times 1 \Rightarrow \; 15y + 12x = 54 \quad .... \; 3$

$4 \times 2 \Rightarrow \; 16y - 12x = ... \quad .... \; 4$

$3 + 4 \Rightarrow \; 31y \qquad = ...$

$\Rightarrow \qquad \qquad y = ...$

Substitute $y = ...$ in equation 1

$$5 \times ... + 4x = 18$$
$$\Rightarrow \qquad 4x = ...$$
$$\Rightarrow \qquad x = ...$$

Solution is $x = ...$, $y = ...$ $\quad (..., ...)$

(Check)

5. Solve this pair of simultaneous equations.

$$2y + 5x = 15 \quad .... \; 1$$
$$3y - 2x = 13 \quad .... \; 2$$

Hint • *multiply equation* 1×2

and • *multiply equation* 2×5.

6. Solve this pair of simultaneous equations.

$$4x + 3y = 22 \quad .... \; 1$$
$$2x - 2y = 4 \quad .... \; 2.$$

7. Label each equation and solve simultaneously.

(a) $3x + 4y = 10$ 　(b) $4x + 2y = 14$
　　$2x - 3y = 1$ 　　　　$7x - 3y = 5$

(c) $2x + 5y = 13$ 　(d) $6x + 7y = 27$
　　$3x - 2y = 10$ 　　　　$5x - 2y = -1$

(e) $5x - 6y = -11$ 　(f) $2x - 3y = -1$
　　$4x + 4y = 0$ 　　　　$5x + 4y = -14$

(g) $2x + 3y = 19$ 　(h) $4x + 8y = 2$
　　$6x - 2y = -9$ 　　　　$3x - 6y = -4 \cdot 5.$

8. Solve each pair of simultaneous equations.

(a) $2x + y = 5 \qquad .... \; 1$
　　$x + y = 3 \qquad .... \; 2$
　　(This time you must multiply eqn 2 by –1)

(b) $4x + 3y = 15 \qquad .... \; 1$
　　$x + y = 4 \qquad .... \; 2$
　　(This time you must multiply eqn 2 by –3)

(c) $7x + 3y = 22 \qquad .... \; 1$
　　$4x + 2y = 14 \qquad .... \; 2$
　　(This time you must multiply eqn 1 by –2)
　　　　　　and multiply eqn 2 by ...)

(d) $7x + 4y = 36 \quad .... \; (\times ...)$
　　$2x + 3y = 14 \quad .... \; (\times -4)$

(e) $6y + 3x = 9 \quad .... \; (\times 2)$
　　$5y + 2x = 8 \quad .... \; (\times -...)$

(f) $2x + 4y = -6$ 　(g) $4x + 7y = 10$
　　$3x + 3y = -3$ 　　　　$2x + 6y = 10$

(h) $5x + 2y = -19$ 　(i) $6x + 4y = -5$
　　$4x + 3y = -18$ 　　　　$8x + 3y = -2.$

9. Solve :-

(a) $3y + 2x = -10$ 　(b) $8x - 8y = -16$
　　$2y + 5x = -14$ 　　　　$5x - 3y = -28$

(c) $6y + 6x = 0$ 　(d) $8x + 6y = -8$
　　$7y + 5x = -1$ 　　　　$2x + 11y = -2$

(e) $3x = 2y - 5$ 　(f) $2y = 5x + 16$
　　$4x - 3y + 8 = 0$ 　　　$3y - 5x - 19 = 0$

(g) $2x - 3y - 13 = 0$ 　(h) $2x + y - 5 = 0$
　　$3x + 2y = 0$ 　　　　$3x - 4y - 13 = 0.$

Solving Problems using Simultaneous Equations

Many everyday problems can be solved using simultaneous equations.

Example :- **Bob** bought 5 balls and 2 teddies which cost him £11.

Jill paid £9 for 3 balls and 2 teddies.

Total Cost £11

Total Cost £9

How much does it cost for a ball and how much for a teddy ?

First we must set up two equations to represent **Bob** and **Jill's** purchases.

Let cost of one ball = £x,
and cost of one teddy = £y.

Bob : $5x + 2y = 11$ 1
Jill : $3x + 2y = 9$ 2

Now we solve these equations simultaneously.

$$5x + 2y = 11 \quad .... 1$$
$$3x + 2y = 9 \quad .... 2$$
$$-1 \times 2 \Rightarrow \quad -3x - 2y = -9 \quad .... 3$$
add 1 & 3 $\Rightarrow \quad 2x = 2$
$$\Rightarrow \quad x = 1$$

Substitute $x = 1$ in 2.
$$3 \times 1 + 2y = 9$$
$$\Rightarrow \quad 2y = 6$$
$$\Rightarrow \quad y = 3$$

One ball cost £1. One Teddy costs £3.

Check your answer by substitution.

Exercise 4·5

1. Reg paid 17 pence for four sweets and a lolly.

   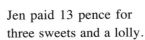

   Jen paid 13 pence for three sweets and a lolly.

   What is the cost of each sweet and each lolly ?

   Copy and complete :–

   Let cost of one sweet = x p
   and cost of one lolly = y p

   Reg : $4x + y = 17$ 1
   Jen : $3x + y = 13$ 2

   $-1 \times 2 \Rightarrow \quad -3x - y = -...$ 3

   $1 + 3 \Rightarrow \quad x = ...$

   Substitute $x = ...$ in equation 1

   $4 \times ... + y = 17$

   $\Rightarrow \quad y = ...$

   One sweet costs .... p. One lolly costs ...p.

2. Sally bought 4 hamburgers and 2 hotdogs at a cost of £14.

   Fred paid £20 for 7 hamburgers and 2 hotdogs.

   (a) Set up two equations to represent this information.

   (b) Find the cost of one hamburger.

   (c) Find the cost of one hotdog.

   (d) How much would Bill have to pay for three hamburgers and two hotdogs ?

3. Cheri pays £11 for 2 grow-bags and one plant.
   Ali pays £15 for 3 grow-bags and one plant.

   Find the cost of each grow-bag and each plant.

4. Shez buys 2 coffees and 2 donuts for £3.

   Jeri pays £4 for 3 coffees and 2 donuts.

   Baz bought one coffee **and** one donut.

   How much did Baz have to pay ?

5. Sara purchased three identical blouses and four
   skirts costing £60.

   May paid £33 for three blouses and one skirt.

   Find the cost of each blouse.

6. Mike and Fran went
   to the local pet shop.

   Mike bought three
   mice and a lizard
   for £16.

   Fran paid £27 for two
   mice and three lizards.

   Find the cost of each mouse and each lizard.

7. The weight of six DVD players and two Blu-Ray
   players is 22 kg.

   Four DVD's and a Blu-Ray player weighs 14 kg.

   Find the weight of a Blu-Ray player.

8. Three steak meals and two fish dishes cost £43.
   Five steak meals and five fish dishes cost £85.

   (a) How much would it cost for a steak meal ?

   (b) If I bought two fish dishes and a steak
       meal, how much change would I receive
       from £30 ?

9. Mr Forbes paid £60 for
   five adults and four
   children's puppet
   show tickets.

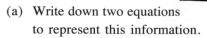

   Mrs Rae paid £21 for two
   adults and one child.

   (a) Write down two equations
       to represent this information.

   (b) Find the cost of :-
       (i) an adult ticket   (ii) a child's ticket.

   (c) Mr Allison bought four adult and five
       children's tickets.

       How much did he pay for the tickets ?

10. Miss Spencer bought 3 packs of white paper
    and 2 packs of coloured paper and found she
    had 1200 sheets of paper.

    Mr Lott had 2300 sheets from 4 packs of white
    and 5 coloured packs.

    How many sheets were in each pack ?

11. A group of teachers and
    pupils went on a school trip.

    The teachers hired three
    tandems (2-seater bikes)
    and four bicycles which cost £27.

    If they had hired four tandems and two bicycles
    it would have cost them £26.

    How much would the hire charge have been for
    five tandems ?

12. The *PHOTO-Shop* produce high quality
    photographic posters.

    Alex paid £255 for four A3 sized posters and
    three A2 sized posters, Sean paid £240
    for five A3 posters and two A2 posters and
    Tariq bought two A3 and one A2 poster.

    How much did Tariq have to pay ?

13. Tara spent £13·54 on 11 litres
    of petrol and 3 litres of
    oil for her car.

    It cost Jake £15·39 for
    15 litres of petrol and
    2 litres of oil.

    Find the cost of a litre of oil.

14. Four large jugs and three small cups can hold a maximum of 2250 millilitres of milk.

Six large jugs and two small cups can hold a maximum of 3·2 litres.

Can five large jugs hold two and a half litres ?

(*Explain your answer fully*).

15. Jason does circuit training every day.

On Monday he trains continuously for 20 minutes.

On a Tuesday, he does 30 minutes of continuous training.

His training on a Monday consists of 300 sit-ups and 200 squat jumps.

Tuesday consists of 150 sit-ups and 500 squat jumps.

On Wednesday, Jason does 100 sit-ups and 100 squat jumps.

How long, in minutes and seconds, does Jason's training last on a Wednesday ?

16. Jennifer uses identical circles and identical squares to make both patterns below.

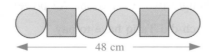

Calculate :-

(a) the **diameter** of one circle.

(b) the **area** of one square.

17. An advertising campaign uses two different size square posters to fit billboards.

Billboard 1

Billboard 2

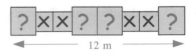

Billboard 3

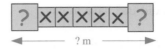

(a) Calculate the **total** length of the seven posters used in Billboard 3.

(b) Calculate the **total** area of all the posters used in Billboard 3.

18. Freda bought 4 oranges and 3 pears weighing 590g at a cost of £2·30 From Johnnie's Fruit and Veg Stall.

June paid £2·55 for 3 oranges and 5 pears weighing 690g from Johnnie's.

(a) Write down two equations involving the number of apples and pears and their **cost**.

(b) Solve these equations simultaneously.

(c) Write down two equations involving the weight of the fruit.

(d) Find also the weight of a single pear.

(e) Eddie bought ten oranges and a dozen pears.

What was the total cost and the total weight of his purchase ?

1. Sketch each line below on a separate diagram.

   (a) $y = 2x + 3$

   (b) $3x + 6y = 12$.

2. Solve **graphically** these simultaneous equations.

   $$y = 3x + 2 \quad .... 1$$
   $$y = 4 - x \quad .... 2$$

3. Solve each pair of simultaneous equations algebraically using **elimination**.

   (a) $3x + 4y = 13$
   $2x - 4y = 2$

   (b) $4x + 2y = 10$
   $7x - 2y = 12$

   (c) $3x + 5y = 13$
   $4x - y = 2$

   (d) $5x + 4y = 13$
   $x - 2y = -3$

   (e) $3y + 2x = 5$
   $2y + 5x = 7$

   (f) $8x - 8y = -8$
   $5x - 3y = 1$

   (g) $2y + 3x = 9$
   $5y + 2x = 17$

   (h) $2x - 7y = 24$
   $3x - 2y = 19$

   (i) $8y + 2x = 42$
   $3y + 7x = 47$

   (j) $8x - 8y = -56$
   $5x - 3y = -19$.

4. **Rearrange** this pair of simultaneous equations and then solve.

   $$2x + 3y - 10 = 0$$
   $$4x = 3y + 20.$$

5. 2 chairs and a table weigh 12 kg.

   5 chairs and a table weigh 22 kg.

   What is the weight of one chair ?

6. Percy bought eight fantas and three cokes costing £3·60.

   Marion spent £3·30 on seven fantas and three cokes.

   (a) Set up two equations to represent this information.

   (b) Solve these equations to find the cost of one coke.

   (c) How much would it cost for five fantas and two cokes ?

7. The Concert Hall staged "Swan Lake".

   Jake paid £76 for 3 stalls tickets and 2 circle tickets.

   Milo paid £122 for 5 stalls tickets and 3 circle tickets.

   Jeri bought 4 stalls tickets and 4 circle tickets.

   How much did Jeri pay for her tickets ?

8.  Two hamburgers and three fries cost £5.

   Five hamburgers and two fries cost £8·10.

   How much does a hamburger cost ?

9. Eight identical vans and four identical cars were parked bumper to bumper and the total length of all 12 vehicles was 58 metres.

   Six vans and five cars measured 50·5 metres.

   Calculate the length of two trucks and two cars.

10. Three towers, built from rectangular bricks, are shown below.

    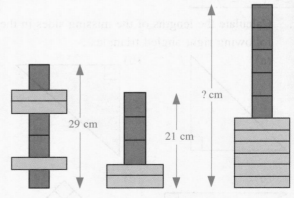

    Find the height of the tallest tower.

Revision of Pythagoras' Theorem
(You will have covered Pythagoras' Theorem at an earlier stage.)

Pythagoras was a famous Greek Mathematician who discovered an amazing connection between the three sides of **any right angled triangle**.

He discovered that the 3 sides of a right angled triangle were connected mathematically by the formula :-

$$c^2 = a^2 + b^2$$

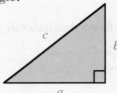

Calculating the length of the HYPOTENUSE of a right angled triangle

Example :-   Calculate the length of the **hypotenuse** of this right angled triangle.

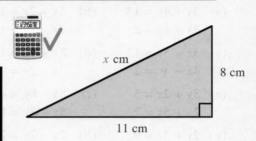

Solution :-   Begin with :-

$$x^2 = 11^2 + 8^2$$
$$\Rightarrow \quad x^2 = 121 + 64$$
$$\Rightarrow \quad x^2 = 185$$
$$\Rightarrow \quad x = \sqrt{185} = 13\cdot6.$$

x cm   8 cm   11 cm

Calculating the length of one of the SMALLER sides in a R.A.T.

Example :-   Calculate the length of the side marked *a* in this right angled triangle.

*note

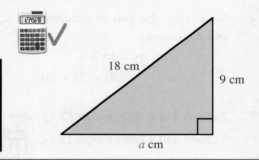

Solution :-   Begin with :-

$$a^2 = 18^2 - 9^2$$
$$\Rightarrow \quad a^2 = 324 - 81$$
$$\Rightarrow \quad a^2 = 243$$
$$\Rightarrow \quad a = \sqrt{243} = 15\cdot6.$$

18 cm   9 cm   *a* cm

Exercise 5·1

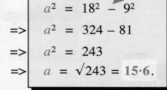

1. Calculate the lengths of the missing sides in the following right angled triangles :-

    (a)
    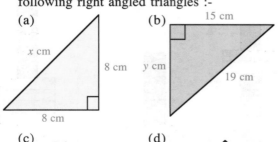
    x cm   8 cm   8 cm

    (b)
    15 cm   *y* cm   19 cm

    (c)
    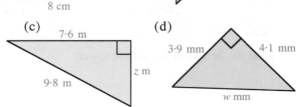
    7·6 m   *z* m   9·8 m

    (d)

    3·9 mm   4·1 mm   *w* mm

2. Shown is an isosceles triangle.

    (a) Calculate the height of the triangle.

    (b) Now calculate its **area**.

    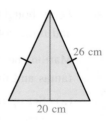
    26 cm   20 cm

3. Calculate the **area** of this rectangle :-

    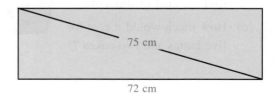
    75 cm   72 cm

4. Calculate the **perimeter** of this right angled triangle :-

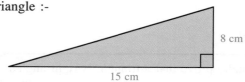

8 cm

15 cm

5.

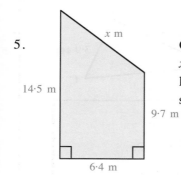

x m

14·5 m

9·7 m

6·4 m

Calculate the value of x, which indicates the length of the sloping side of this trapezium.

6. This shape consists of a rectangle with an isosceles triangle attached to its end.

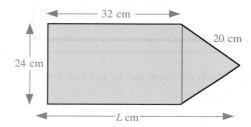

32 cm

20 cm

24 cm

L cm

(a) Calculate the total length (L) of the figure.

(b) Now calculate its area.

7. Shown are the points P(–3, –4) and G(6, 3).

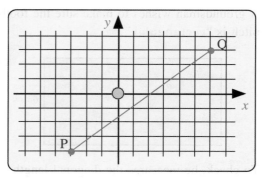

Draw a coordinate diagram, plot the two points and calculate the length of the line PQ.

8. Draw a new set of axes, plot the 2 points A(–1, 8) and B(6, –4) and calculate the length of the line AB.

9. Shown is an isosceles triangular prism.

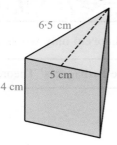

6·5 cm

5 cm

4 cm

(a) Calculate the **height** of the triangle, represented by the dotted line.

(b) Calculate the **volume** of the prism.

10. When a boy was asked to calculate the value of x, he proceeded as follows :-

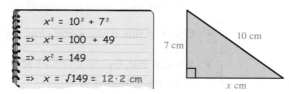

$$x^2 = 10^2 + 7^2$$
$$\Rightarrow x^2 = 100 + 49$$
$$\Rightarrow x^2 = 149$$
$$\Rightarrow x = \sqrt{149} = 12 \cdot 2 \text{ cm}$$

10 cm

7 cm

x cm

Explain in words, when the boy looked at his answer **and** at the triangle, why he should have known that his answer **had** to be **wrong**.

11. Shown is a trapezium with a line of symmetry.

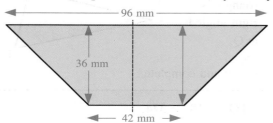

96 mm

36 mm

42 mm

Calculate the **perimeter** of the above trapezium.

12. A fortune teller has a "magic" glass globe. It rests embedded in a wooden plinth, as shown. The plinth measures 32 cm by 7 cm. The diameter of the globe is 30 cm.

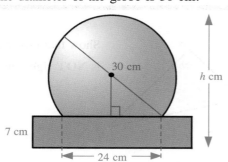

30 cm

h cm

7 cm

24 cm

Calculate the **overall height**, h of the figure.

The CONVERSE of Pythagoras' Theorem

Pythagoras' Theorem only works on a right angled triangle.

> We can use Pythagoras' Theorem **"in reverse"** to actually prove that a triangle **is** right angled.

Example :-

Look at triangle ABC opposite

We can prove it is right angled as follows :-

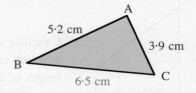

- Write down the 3 sides :- $AB = 5.2$, $AC = 3.9$, $BC = 6.5$.

- **Square** each side :- $AB^2 = 27.04$, $AC^2 = 15.21$, $BC^2 = 42.25$.

- **Add the two smaller** squares together :- $AB^2 + AC^2 = 27.04 + 15.21 = 42.25$.

- Check if this is the same value as the largest square :- $AB^2 + AC^2 = 42.25 = BC^2$.

- We say that, by the **CONVERSE of Pythagoras' Theorem**, the triangle is proven to be right angled at A.

Exercise 5·2

1. Check if this triangle is right angled at Q.

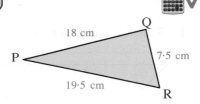

Copy and complete :-

> $PQ^2 = 18^2 = 324$,
>
> $QR^2 = 7.5^2 = ...$
>
> $PR^2 = ...^2 = ...$
>
> $PQ^2 + QR^2 = 324 + ... = ... = PR^2$
>
> by the Converse of Pythagoras' Theorem, triangle PQR must be r....... a...... at Q .

2.

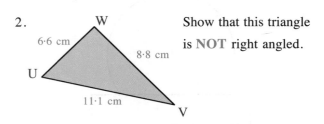

Show that this triangle is **NOT** right angled.

i.e. (*Show that* $UW^2 + VW^2 \neq UV^2$)

3. Decide which of these are or are not right angled triangles :-

(a)   (b)

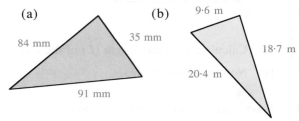

4. A groundsman wishes to make sure the football pitch is **"rectangular"**.

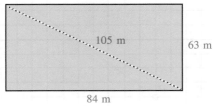

To check, he measures the diagonal length. Is the pitch rectangular ?

5. Has this flagpole been erected correctly, so that it is vertical ?

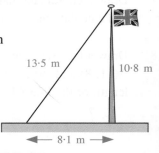

Pythagoras' Theorem applied to 3-Dimensional Problems

Pythagoras' Theorem only works on a right angled triangle, but right angled triangles appear in 3 Dimensional situations as well.

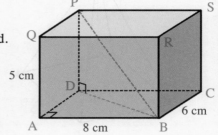

Example :- Calculate the length of the **space diagonal** of this cuboid.

Note :-
> A **face diagonal** is one joining the opposite vertices of any rectangular face of the cuboid (e.g. **BD**).
> A **space diagonal** is one joining one vertex of the cuboid to the furthest away vertex (e.g. **BP**).

Solution :- The answer is found by following 2 steps :-

Step 1 :- Space diagonal **BP** is the longest side in R.A.T. **BPD**. To find **BP**, we must first find **BD** in R.A.T. **BAD**.

Step 2 :- Now find **BP**, the longest side in R.A.T. **BPD**.

$$BD^2 = BA^2 + AD^2$$
$$BD^2 = 8^2 + 6^2 = 64 + 36 = 100$$
$$BD = \sqrt{100} = \textbf{10 cm}$$

$$BP^2 = BD^2 + DP^2$$
$$BP^2 = 10^2 + 5^2 = 100 + 25 = 125$$
$$BD = \sqrt{125} = \textbf{11·2 cm}$$

Exercise 5·3

1. (a) Calculate the length of the face diagonal **EG** (blue) of this cuboid.

   (b) Now calculate the length of the space diagonal **EX**, (yellow).

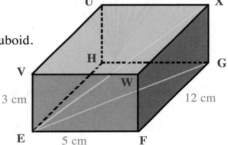

2. 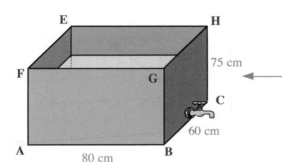 ← Calculate the length of the face diagonal **AC** of this water tank, and then calculate the length of the space diagonal **AH**.

3. Make a sketch of this shoe box and show, using two steps, how to calculate the length of its space diagonal. (*You may want to letter the vertices*).

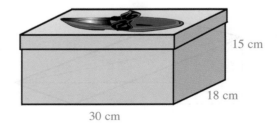

4. 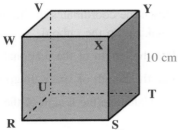 Calculate the length of the space diagonal **RY** of this cube.

5   Shown is a square based pyramid **ABCDV**.

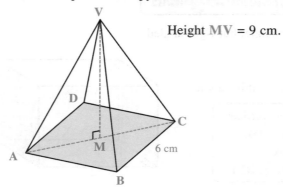

Height **MV** = 9 cm.

(a)   Calculate the length of the diagonal **AC**.

(b)   Write down the length of **AM**.

(c)   Calculate the length of the sloping edge **AV**.

6.   This Popcorn box is in the shape of a pyramid.

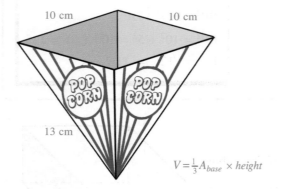

$$V = \tfrac{1}{3} A_{base} \times height$$

The square top has sides 10 cm, and the sloping edge is 13 cm long.

(a)   Calculate the length of the diagonal of the open top.

(b)   Calculate the **height** of the box.

(c)   Calculate the **volume** of the box, in cm^3.

7.   The side face of this wedge is in the shape of a right angled triangle.

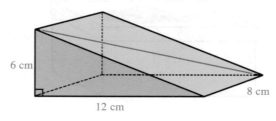

(a)   Calculate the length of the face diagonal of the **base** of the wedge.

(b)   Now calculate the length of the diagonal of the **sloping edge**. (*The red line*).

8.   A cone has a base diameter of 10 cm and its sloping edges are 13 cm long.

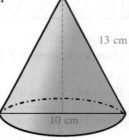

(a)   Calculate the **height** of the cone.

(b)   Now calculate the **volume** of the cone.

9.   This empty tin of McTivies biscuits measures 24 cm by 24 cm by 16 cm high.

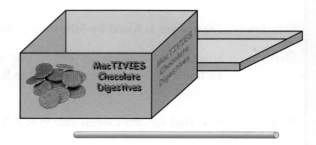

Would this wooden rod, 40 cm long, be able to fit in the box and still allow the tin to be fully closed with its lid on ?

10.   Just as you can plot a point in 2-dimensions using 2 coordinates **A(4, 3)**, you can plot points in 3-dimensions like **A(4, 3, 1)**. (*See below*).

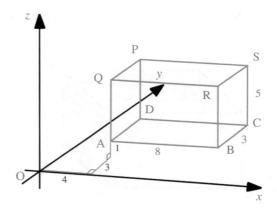

In the above figure, A is given by **A(4, 3, 1)**.
(*4 right, 3 back and 1 up*).
AB is parallel to the *x*-axis.

The cuboid measures 8 by 3 by 5 boxes.

(a)   Write down the coordinates of the other 7 points making up the cuboid.

(b)   Calculate the length of the diagonal **AC**.

(c)   Calculate the length of space diagonal **AS**.

(d)   *Harder*.   Calculate the length of the line **OS**.

Remember Remember.....?

1. Calculate the lengths of the sides marked x and y, correct to 3 significant figures.

    (a)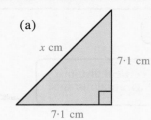

    (b)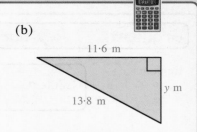

2. Plot the points **A**(–5, –7) and **B**(6, 1) on a coordinate diagram and calculate the length of the line **AB**.

3. Use the **Converse** of Pythagoras' Theorem to decide which, if any, of these triangles is right angled :-

    (a)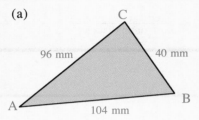

    (b)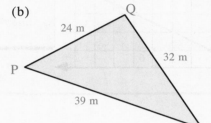

    (c)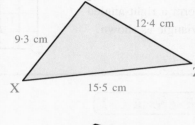

4. This figure looks like a kite, but is it really one ?
    Prove whether it is or is not a kite.

    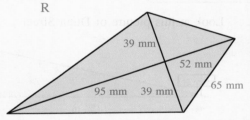

5.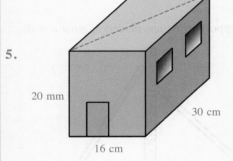

    A girl made a simple model house out of a cardboard box.

    (a) Calculate the length of the red dotted line.

    (b) Calculate the length of the **space diagonal** of the box.

6. Shown is a wedge - (*a right angled triangular prism*).

    Use Pythagoras' Theorem twice to calculate the
    length of the sloping dotted blue line.

    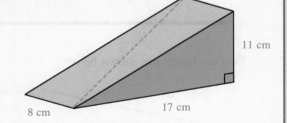

7. Shown is a square based pyramid and a cone.
    By calculating the height of both, decide which has the greater **volume** and by how much.

    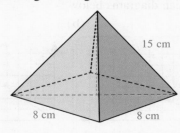

    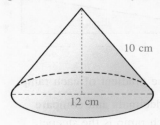

Gradients - Revision

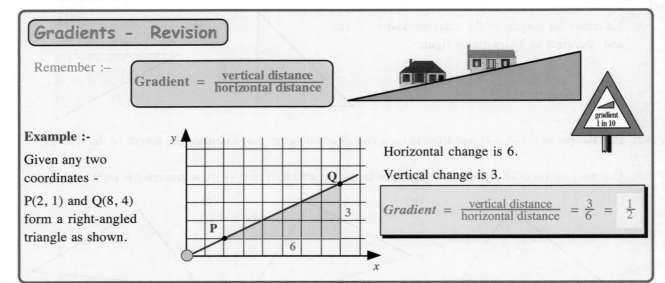

Remember :–

$$Gradient = \frac{vertical\ distance}{horizontal\ distance}$$

Example :-

Given any two coordinates -
P(2, 1) and Q(8, 4) form a right-angled triangle as shown.

Horizontal change is 6.

Vertical change is 3.

$$Gradient = \frac{vertical\ distance}{horizontal\ distance} = \frac{3}{6} = \frac{1}{2}$$

gradient 1 in 10

Exercise 6·1

1. Look at this picture of Dunn Street.

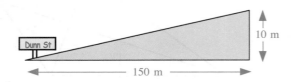

   Dunn St

   10 m

   150 m

   Copy and calculate its **gradient** like this :–

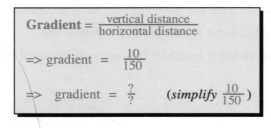

   $$Gradient = \frac{vertical\ distance}{horizontal\ distance}$$

   $$\Rightarrow gradient = \frac{10}{150}$$

   $$\Rightarrow gradient = \frac{?}{?} \quad (simplify\ \frac{10}{150})$$

2. Two car ramps are shown below.

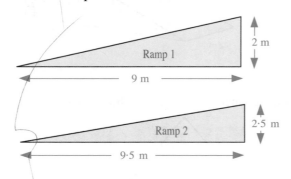

   Ramp 1   2 m

   9 m

   Ramp 2   2·5 m

   9·5 m

   (a) Calculate the gradient of each ramp.

   (b) Change to decimals and compare to find which ramp is the steeper.

3. Four hills have gradients,

   $$\frac{8}{25}, \quad 0\cdot26, \quad 25\% \quad and \quad 0\cdot3.$$

   Write the gradients in order, (steepest first).
   (Hint : change them all to decimals).

4. Two support struts are placed against a wall.

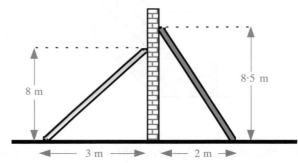

   8 m

   8·5 m

   3 m   2 m

   For safety reasons, the supports must have a gradient with a value between **4** and **5**.

   Which of the struts shown above is/are safe ?

5. Calculate the gradient of each line in the Cartesian diagrams below :-

   (a)   (b)

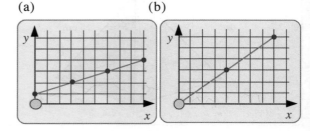

6. The diagram shows three coloured lines.

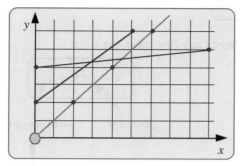

Find the gradient of each line.

> **Remember**
>
> - The gradient of a line AB can be written as m_{AB}.
> - Any line which slopes **upwards** from left to right has a **positive** gradient.
> - Any line which slopes **downwards** from left to right has a **negative** gradient.
> - Parallel lines have the same gradient
> - A horizontal line has $m = 0$.
> - A vertical line has an undefined gradient.

7. Copy and complete the calculation to find the gradient of the line shown.
   Vertical change is ....
   Horizontal change is ...

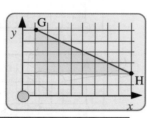

$$m_{GH} = \frac{\text{vertical distance}}{\text{horizontal distance}} = \frac{-?}{8} = -\frac{?}{?}$$

8. Calculate the gradient of each line in the Cartesian diagrams below :-

(a)   (b)

(c)   (d)

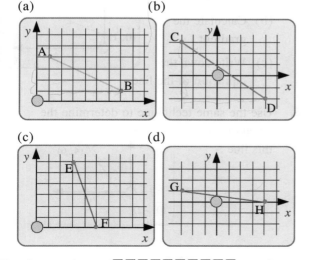

8. (e)   (f)

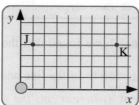   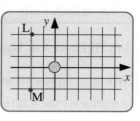

9. Find the gradient of the line passing through each set of points below :-

(a) P(0, 2), Q(4, 4)   (b) R(2, 0), S(4, 5)

(c) T(–1, 6), U(4, –2)   (d) V(8, –5), W(1, 2).

10. (a) Find :–   (i) m_{AB} (ii) m_{BC}

(iii) m_{CD} (iv) m_{AD}

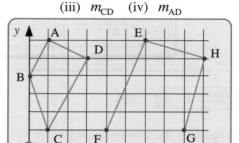

(b) Find the gradient of each side of EFGH.

(c) Which of the two shapes is a trapezium ?
     (*Justify your answer*).

11. A parallelogram, JKLM, has coordinates (1, 0), (4, 4), (6, 3) and (3, –1) respectively.

Find the gradients of both its **diagonals**.

12. Prove, **without** actually drawing a coordinate diagram, that the points A(–6, 1), B(–1, 0) and C(4, –1) all lie on the same straight line.

13. Show that the line through the pair of points (0, 1), (4, 7) and the line through (0, –3) and (4, 3) are **parallel** to each other
    (*Remember : parallel lines have equal gradients*).

14. Show that the line through the pair of points (1, –8) and (12, –3) and the line through (–5, –5), and (21, 6) are **NOT parallel** to each other.

15. Two lines AB and CD are parallel.
    State **two** possible coordinates for A given B(3, 2), C(–3, 6) and D(2, –4).

The Equation of a Straight Line - Revision

In CfE Level 4 or National 4, we found that the equation of (almost) any line takes the form :–

Where m represents the **gradient** of the line and

c represents the **y-intercept**. (*where it cuts the y-axis*).

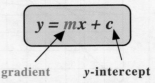

$$y = mx + c$$

gradient   y-intercept

Examples :-

(a) $y = 3x + 4$ has gradient 3 and y-intercept 4.

(b) A line with y-intercept –2 and gradient $\frac{3}{4}$ has equation $y = \frac{3}{4}x - 2$.

(c)
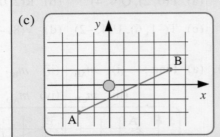

$m_{AB} = \frac{3}{6} = \frac{1}{2}$ y-intercept is –1

=> Equation of line AB is $y = \frac{1}{2}x - 1$

Exercise 6·2

1. Write down the **gradient** and **y-intercept** in each of these equations :-

(a) $y = 4x + 1$ (b) $y = 6x - 4$

(c) $y = -3x + 6$ (d) $y = \frac{1}{2}x + 5$

(e) $y = -\frac{1}{3}x - 7$ (f) $y = 10 - 2x$

(g) $y = -3 - x$ (h) $y = 4$.

2. Write down the **equation** of each of these lines :-

(a) $m = 2$, and the y-intercept is 1.

(b) $m = -3$, and the y-intercept is 5.

(c) gradient is $-\frac{1}{2}$, and it passes through (0, 4).

(d) $m = -6$ and line passes through the origin.

3. Line PQ cuts the y-axis at the point (0, 4) and is **parallel** to a line with equation $y = 3x - 5$.

(a) Write down the **gradient** of the line PQ.

(b) Write the equation of this line PQ.

4. For each of the lines shown at the top of the next column :-

(i)   calculate the gradient,

(ii)   write down the y-intercept,

(iii) write the equation of the line.

4. (a)
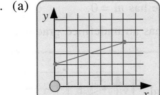
(b)
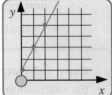

(c)
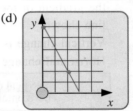
(d)

5. The line shown has equation $y = mx + c$.

(a) Write down the value of c.

(b) Calculate the gradient.

(c) Write down the equation of the line.

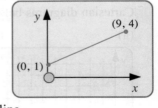

6. Use the same technique to determine the equation of this line :-

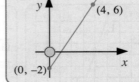

7. Write down the equation of each line below :-

(a)

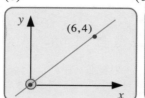

(b)

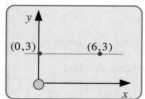

(c)

(d)

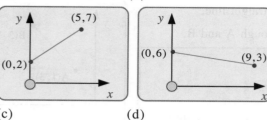

8. A line passes through R(0, −2) and S(3, 5).

(a) Show the line RS on a Cartesian diagram.

(b) Calculate the gradient of this line.

(c) Write down its y-intercept.

(d) Write down the equation of the line RS.

9. Find the **equation** of the line shown opposite.

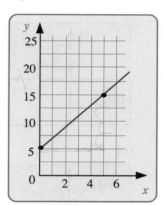

10. Write down the equations of these lines :-

(a)

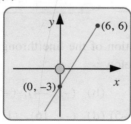

(b)

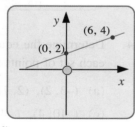

(c)

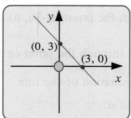

(d)

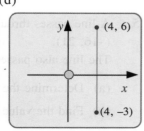

11. Match each of the following equations with their corresponding graphs shown below :-

(a) $y = 4x$

(b) $y = 3x - 2$

(c) $y = -3x$

(d) $y = -x - 4$

(e) $y = \frac{1}{2}x + 4$

(f) $y = -3$.

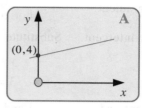

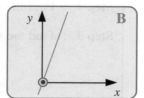

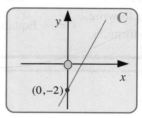

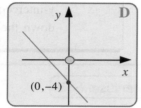

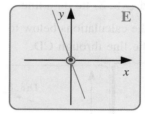

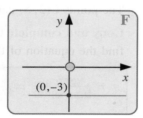

12. Find the equation of the line passing through each set of points below :-

(a) A(0, 3), B(2, 9)

(b) U(0, −1), V(4, 1)

(c) M(−2, 4), N(0, −4)

(d) Z(0, −10), W(3, 5).

13. Show that the line through the pair of points A(0, 2) and B(4, 8) and the line through C(0, −5) and D(4, 1) are **parallel** to each other.

(*Remember : parallel lines have equal gradients*).

14. Show that the line through the pair of points (2, −7) and (10, −3) and the line through (−3, −4), and (15, 2) are **NOT parallel** to each other.

15. Write down the equation of the line :-

(a) which goes through the point (0, 2) and is **parallel** to the line $y = 3x - 5$.

(b) **parallel** to the line $y = -x$ and passing through the point (0, −4).

(c) which passes through (2, −8) and (2, 47).

(d) which passes through (4, 5) and (6, 9).

Finding the Equation of a Line given any two points on it

Example :– The points A(1, 3) and B(3, 7) lie on a straight line.

Find the equation of the straight line through A and B.

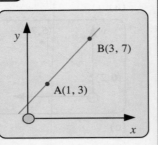

Step 1 : Sketch the line.

Step 2 : Find the gradient. $m = \dfrac{\text{vertical}}{\text{horizontal}} = \dfrac{4}{2} = 2$

Step 3 : Find the y-intercept.   Substitute A(1, 3) and $m = 2$ into

$$y = mx + c$$
$$\Rightarrow \quad 3 = 2 \times 1 + c \qquad \Rightarrow c = 1$$

Step 4 : Use gradient and y-intercept to write down the formula. $m = 2$ and the y-intercept is 1

$\Rightarrow$ Equation of line is $\boxed{y = 2x + 1}$

Exercise 6·3

1. The points C(2, 5) and D(8, 8) lie on a line.

    Copy and complete the calculations below to find the equation of the line through CD.

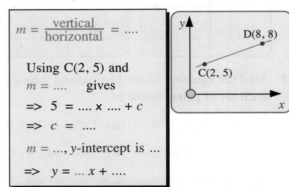

$$m = \frac{\text{vertical}}{\text{horizontal}} = ...$$

Using C(2, 5) and

$m = ...$ gives

$\Rightarrow \ 5 = ... \times .... + c$

$\Rightarrow \ c = ...$

$m = ..., \ y$-intercept is ...

$\Rightarrow \ y = ... x + ...$

2. Determine the equation of each line below :-

    (a)   (b)

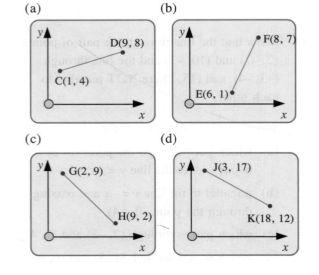

    (c)   (d)

3. Determine the equation of each line :-

    (a)   (b)

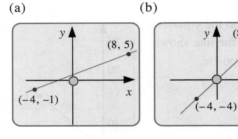

    (c)   (d)

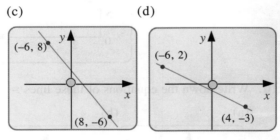

4. Determine the equation of the line through each set of points below :-

    (a) (–3, 2), (2, 7)   (b) (–1, –4), (–1, 9)

    (c) (–10, 4), (–4, –5) (d) (–1, 16), (1, –16).

5. A line passes through the points (–36, 6) and (–16, 21).
    The line also passes through the point (a, 24).

    (a) Determine the equation of the line.

    (b) Find the value of a.

Linear Equations in everyday use

A linear equation is usually written as $y = mx + c$, but other letters can be used to form a linear equation.

$y = ax + b$ and $P = mt + c$, could also represent straight lines.

Example :–

Bob earns £4 per hour.
A table can be drawn to show his earnings.

A graph can be plotted using h (hours) and P (pay) in place of x and y.

Other values can be found from the table or a formula can be made.

Gradient = 4 and the P-intercept is 0.

=> $\boxed{P = 4h}$

hours (h)	0	1	2	3	4
Pay (£P)	0	4	8	12	16

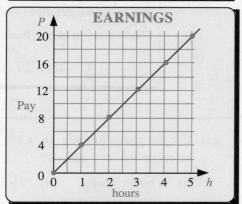

note :– $y = 2x^2 + 1$ and $y = -5x^3 + 4$ are **NOT** linear.
Can you see why not ?

Exercise 6·4

1. Write down which of these are linear equations.

   (a) $P = 7t + 2$ (b) $y = x^2 + 3$

   (c) $s = -3t$ (d) $3t + 4w + 2 = 0$

   (e) $2h - t^2 = 4$ (f) $x = 3y - 1$.

2. Maggie earns £6 an hour.

   (a) Copy and complete the table of values.

hours (h)	0	1	2	3	4
pay (£P)	0	6	...	...	...

   (b) From the table, plot 5 points on a Cartesian diagram.

   (c) Find the gradient m and P - intercept.

   (d) Write a formula representing the line.

   (e) Use your formula to find how much Maggie would earn in :-

   (i) 8 hours   (ii) $12\frac{1}{2}$ hours ?

   (f) How many hours would Maggie have to work to earn £72 ?

   (*Hint : set up an* **equation** *and solve it*).

3. Joe earns £9·50 an hour.

   (a) Use a table of values to construct a line graph involving P and h.

   (b) Write a formula representing the line.

   (c) Use your formula to find how much he would earn in 6 hours ?

   (d) How many hours would he need to work to earn £218·50 ?

4. A painter can paint a fence at a rate of 3 metres per hour.

   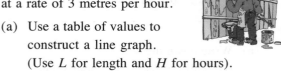

   (a) Use a table of values to construct a line graph.
   (Use L for length and H for hours).

   (b) Write a formula representing the line.

   (c) Use your formula to find how long it would take to paint a 45 metre fence.

5. Jennifer can make 7 paper roses every hour.

   (a) Construct a line graph to represent this information using t (time) and R (roses).

   (b) Write a formula and use it to find how long it would take to make 35 roses.

Example :-   Pete the plumber charges a call-out fee **plus** an hourly charge.

The line graph shows the relative costs where t is the time and C the cost.

The call-out fee is £20 (0 hours work).

=>   **The y-intercept is 20.**

The hourly charge is £10 per hour.

=>   **The gradient (m) = 10.**

The equation of the line is

$$C = 10t + 20$$

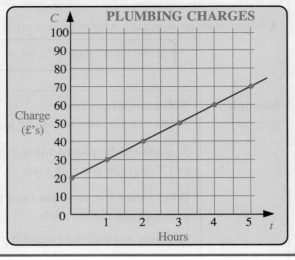

6. (a) Use the above formula $(C = 10t + 20)$ to calculate the total cost of :-

   (i)   4 hours work   (ii) $9\frac{1}{2}$ hours work.

   (b) If the charge is £80, form an equation (in t) and **solve** it to find the time taken.

7. Jack the joiner charges a call-out fee plus an hourly rate. Jack's charges are represented by the line graph below :-

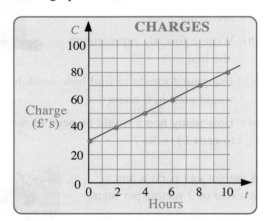

   (a) Write down the :-
       (i)   call-out fee   (ii)   hourly rate.
   (b) Calculate the :-
       (i)   gradient   (ii) y-intercept.
   (c) Make a formula to represent the line.
   (d) Use your formula to find the cost for :-

       (i)   7 hours   (ii) $9\frac{1}{2}$ hours work.

   (e) Use your formula to find how long would it take for a job costing £55.

8. Eric, an electrician, charges a call-out fee of £20 and charges £5 (C) for every hour (h).

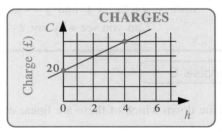

   (a) Write down a formula for the charge £C for h hours worked.

   (b) Calculate the cost for 5 hours worked.

9. The graph below shows a kite dropping from a height (H) of 100 metres to the ground at a steady rate (given in seconds s).

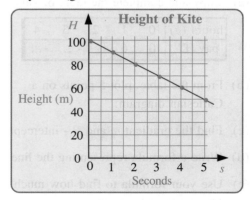

   (a) Determine the **gradient** of the line.

   (b) Write a formula to represent this line.

   (c) Use your formula to find the height of the kite after 6 seconds.

   (d) Use your formula to calculate how long it would take for the kite to land.

10. The "Bouncy Company" hire out bouncy castles.

They charge a £15 deposit and £10 per day.

(a) **Copy and complete** the table below to show the cost of their charges.

Days (d)	1	2	3	4
Cost (£C)	25	35	...	...

(b) **Copy and complete** the graph.

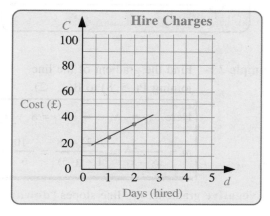

(c) Write a formula in terms of C and d.

(d) What will it cost to hire the bouncy castle for a week ?

11. A Carpet Cleaning firm hires out industrial cleaners. They charge a £5 deposit and a daily hire charge of £6.

(a) Construct a table of values from zero up to 5 days.

(b) **Copy and complete** the graph below.

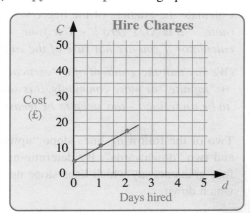

(c) Devise a formula and use it to find the length of hire for a £59 charge.

12. For each case below, develop a linear formula to represent the given information :-

(a)  Paul the plumber charges a call-out fee (F) of £60 plus a working rate of £20 per hour (h).

(b) The charge, (£C), for hiring a bicycle, consists of a £10 deposit plus £5 per day, (d), rental.

(c) A balloon filled with helium starts at a height (H) of 20 feet.

Every hour (t) the balloon loses 2 feet in height.

(d) The temperature, (T), in a living room begins at $-6°C$ and heats up at a steady rate of $4°C$ every hour (h).

13. Two "car-hire" companies advertise their charges as shown :-

Hire-A-Car :-
• £40 deposit
• and £10 per day.

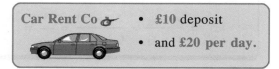

Car Rent Co
• £10 deposit
• and £20 per day.

(a) Construct a table of values for each of the companies.

(b) Draw two lines on the same diagram to represent each company's charges.

(c) After how many days is the cost the same for each company ?

(d) Write a formula for each company to represent their hire charges.

(e) Which company would you use for a :-

fortnight hire ?

...our answers

The Gradient of a Line – A New Formula

The formula $\boxed{\text{gradient} = \dfrac{\text{vertical}}{\text{horizontal}}}$ can always be used to measure of how **steep** the line is.

However, there is a more "mathematical" way of expressing this **gradient formula** :-

Given that $A(x_1, y_1)$ and $B(x_2, y_2)$ are any two points in a coordinate diagram, (as shown opposite),

$$\Rightarrow \quad m_{AB} = \frac{\text{vertical}}{\text{horizontal}} = \frac{BC}{AC}$$

$$\Rightarrow \quad \boxed{m_{AB} = \frac{y_2 - y_1}{x_2 - x_1}}$$

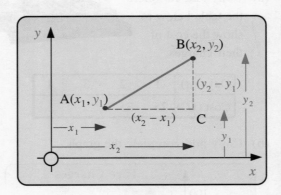

Example 1 :- Find the gradient of the line joining $A(-1, 3)$ to $B(7, 5)$.

> Here, $x_1 = -1, x_2 = 7, y_1 = 3, y_2 = 5$.
>
> $m = \dfrac{y_2 - y_1}{x_2 - x_1} = \dfrac{5 - 3}{7 - (-1)} = \dfrac{2}{8} = \dfrac{1}{4}$

Positive gradient => line slopes "**upwards**"

Example 2 :- Find the gradient of the line joining $P(-5, 8)$ to $B(1, -2)$.

> Here, $x_1 = -5, x_2 = 1, y_1 = 8, y_2 = -2$.
>
> $m = \dfrac{y_2 - y_1}{x_2 - x_1} = \dfrac{(-2) - 8}{1 - (-5)} = \dfrac{-10}{6} = -\dfrac{5}{3}$

Negative gradient => line slopes "**downwards**"

Exercise 6·5

1. Given that $C(3, 1)$ and $D(7, 4)$, copy and complete the following to find m_{CD}.

   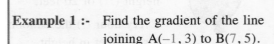

   > Here, $x_1 = 3, x_2 = \dots, y_1 = 1, y_2 = \dots$
   >
   > $\Rightarrow \quad m_{CD} = \dfrac{y_2 - y_1}{x_2 - x_1} = \dfrac{(\dots - 1)}{(\dots - 3)} = \dfrac{3}{\dots} = \dots$

2. Calculate the gradient of the line joining $R(-1, 2)$ to $S(1, 8)$. (i.e. find m_{RS}.)

3. Given $G(1, 9)$ and $H(7, 3)$, find m_{GH}. What does your answer tell you about the line GH ?

4. Use the gradient formula shown in Examples 1 and 2 above to determine the gradients of the lines joining the following pairs of points :-

   (a) $A(2, 1), B(8, 3)$ (b) $C(0, 3), D(10, 8)$

   (c) $E(1, -1), F(3, 5)$ (d) $G(-1, -3), H(2, 4)$

   (e) $I(4, 1), J(-1, 3)$ (f) $K(2, -3), L(-2, 5)$.

5. On a Cartesian diagram, plot the two points $R(2, 1)$ and $S(6, 1)$.

   (a) Calculate the gradient m_{RS}.

   (b) If the gradient of any line is **zero**, what can you say about the line ?

6. This time, draw a new diagram and plot the two points $U(4, -1)$ and $V(4, 3)$.

   Calculate the gradient of the line UV.
   (*note :- it is NOT zero ! - Use your calculator if you are not sure of the value*).

   (*We say that the gradient of a "vertical" line is "infinite" or more commonly, it is said to be **undefined** - too steep to be measured*).

7. Two of the following lines slope "upwards" and two "downwards". By determining the four gradients say which lines slope up and which down.

   (a) $F(-1, -2), G(3, 8)$ (b) $U(-3, 9), V(5, 5)$

   (c) $P(2, 12), Q(4, -2)$ (d) $S(10, 4), T(2, -4)$.

8. Find the gradients of the **two** lines joining A(–5, –2) to B(3, 2) and W(1, –5) to Z(5, –3).

   What do your two answers tell you about the line AB and the line WZ ?

9. Two points have coordinates P(2, 1) and Q(6, b). The gradient $m_{PQ} = 2$.

   Set up an equation and find the value of b.

10. For each of the following pairs of points, along with the given gradient, determine the values of p, q and r.

    (a) A(3, 1), B(5, p), $m_{AB} = 4$.

    (b) L(4, –1), M(0, q), $m_{LM} = -2$.

    (c) S(–1, –2), T(5, r), $m_{ST} = \frac{1}{2}$.

11. Draw a Cartesian diagram and plot the 4 points A(–2, –3), B(5, 0), C(6, 5) and D(–1, 2).

    (a) Show that $m_{BC} = m_{AD}$.

    (b) Show also that $m_{AB} = m_{DC}$.

    (c) What kind of quadrilateral does this prove ABCD is ?

12. In a similar way, show that PQRS is also a parallelogram, where P(0, –1), Q(5, 1), R(8, 6) and S(3, 4).

13. It is known that IJKL **is** a parallelogram, where I(1, 3), J(–1, 1) and K(–2, 5).

    Find the gradients of the two lines IL and KL. (*A sketch will help*).

14. R is the point (–6, 3), S(3, –6) and T(–2, –1).

    (a) Find the gradient m_{RT} and m_{TS}.

    (b) What does this prove about the 3 points R, T and S ?

    (c) Plot the three points on a coordinate diagram and check this out.

15. Without actually plotting the points, prove that each set of points lies on a straight line :-

    (a) A(0, 2), B(2, 4), C(4, 6)

    (b) D(–3, 5), E(–2, 4), F(–1, 3)

    (c) G(–5, 0), H(–1, –1), I(3, –2)

    (d) J(73, 14), K(64, 25), L(55, 36) M(46, 47).

The Equation of a Line - A more Mathematical Approach

Example :–   The points A(7, 5) and B(9, 15) lie on a straight line.

Find the equation of the straight line through A and B.

Step 1 : Sketch the line. ───────────►

Step 2 : Find the gradient. $m_{AB} = \dfrac{y_2 - y_1}{x_2 - x_1} = \dfrac{15 - 5}{9 - 7} = \dfrac{10}{2} = 5$

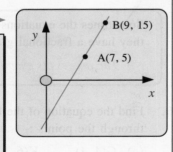

Step 3 : Find the y-intercept   Substitute A(7, 5) and $m = 5$ into

$$y = mx + c$$
$$\Rightarrow \quad 5 = 5 \times 7 + c \quad \Rightarrow c = -30$$

Step 4 : Use gradient and y-intercept to write down the formula. $m = 5$ and the y-intercept is –30

$\Rightarrow$ Equation of line is $y = 5x - 30$

Exercise 6·6

1. Given that C(3, 10) and D(7, 18), copy and complete the following to find m_{CD}.

   Here, $x_1 = 3, x_2 = ..., y_1 = 10, y_2 = ...$

   $\Rightarrow m = \dfrac{y_2 - y_1}{x_2 - x_1} = \dfrac{(.... - 10)}{(.... - 3)} = \dfrac{8}{...} = ...$

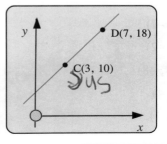

   $y = mx + c$
   $\Rightarrow \quad 10 = ... \times 3 + c$
   $\Rightarrow \quad c = ...$
   So $y = ... x + ...$

2. Find the equation of the lines which pass through each pair of points :-

   (a) E(2, 7),   F(6, 15)

   (b) G(1, 5),   H(3, 17)

   (c) I(1, 5),   J(21, 25)

   (d) K(4, 0),   L(−2, −12)

   (e) M(1, 0),   Q(−3, 4)

   (f) P(6, −1),   R(−8, −15)

   (g) T(1, 3),   V(−2, 9)

   (h) Z(1, 15),   A(−1, −13)

   (i) U(−3, 1),   K(17, 1)

   (j) G(0, −6),   P(2, 7).

3. A square has vertices at A(8, 6), B(12, 6), C(12, 2) and D(8, 2).

   (a) Find the equation of the line which passes through diagonal AC.

   (b) Find the equation of the line which passes through the other diagonal.

4. A circle has a diameter at P(−5, 0) and Q(−8, 3).

   Find the equation of this diameter.

5. A kite has vertices R(3, 2), S(3, 5), T(0, 5) and U(−4, −2).

   Find the equation of the kite's line of symmetry.

> Sometimes the equations are more difficult if they have a fractional gradient or y-intercept.
>
> *NB The process is exactly the same !*

6. Find the equation of the line which passes through the points :-

   (a) G(4, 4),   K(6, 5)

   (b) P(8, 3),   T(12, 4)

   (c) R(3, −1),   S(6, 1)

   (d) T(6, 0),   U(18, 4)

   (e) V(−5, 3),   W(5, 5)

   (f) K(10, 0),   L(−4, −7)

   (g) A(8, 7),   B(−4, −2)

   (h) C(5, 1),   D(−10, −8)

   (i) E(1, 0),   F(1·5, 4)

   (j) G(2·5, −1·5),   H(3·5, 1).

7. Find the equation of the line which passes through the points :-

   (a) E(1, $2\frac{1}{2}$),   F(−2, −$\frac{1}{2}$)

   (b) G(2·5, 7),   H(−0·5, −2)

   (c) J(1, $2\frac{1}{3}$),   K(−3, −$1\frac{2}{3}$)

   (d) L(6, $4\frac{1}{3}$),   M(−3, −$1\frac{2}{3}$)

   (e) P(4, $2\frac{1}{2}$),   Q(−2, −$\frac{1}{2}$)

   (f) R(5, 3·5),   S(−10, −8·5).

8. A rectangle ABCD has vertices at A(2, 1), B(4, −1), C(1, −4) and D.

   (a) Find the coordinates of D.

   (b) Find the equation of diagonal DB.

   (c) Find the equation of the line parallel to CA and passes through (0, $3\frac{1}{2}$).

9. (a) A line has a gradient of 2 and passes through the points (6, 16) and (1, k).

      Find the value of k.

   (b) A line passing through (h, −1) and (1, 8) has a gradient of −3.

      Find the value of h.

   (c) A line has a gradient of 1·5 and passes through (6, −3) and (4, t).

      Find the value of t.

10. Find the equation of each line from question 9.

11. Two points are defined as (p^2, p) and (p, p^2).
Find, in its simplest form, the gradient of the line through these two points.

12. A line passes through A(s, t) and B(t, s).
Prove that $m_{AB} = −1$.

13.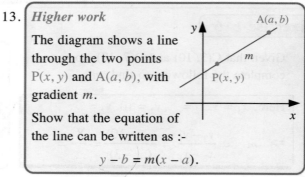

Higher work

The diagram shows a line through the two points P(x, y) and A(a, b), with gradient m.

Show that the equation of the line can be written as :-

$$y − b = m(x − a).$$

The General Equation of a Straight Line

The equation of any line can be written in the form $Ax + By + C = 0$.

This is called the **General Equation** of a line.

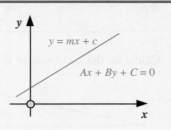

The General Equation can be **rearranged** so that the gradient and y-intercept are easier to obtain.

Example :- Find the gradient and y intercept of the line

$$5y - 2x + 1 = 0.$$

$5y - 2x + 1 = 0$

$=> \quad 5y = 2x - 1$

$=> \quad y = \frac{2}{5}x - \frac{1}{5}$

$=> \quad m = \frac{2}{5}$ and y-intercept is $(0, -\frac{1}{5})$

Exercise 6·7

1. The equation of a line is given by :-

$$2x + 3y - 1 = 0.$$

   Copy and complete the calculation below to find the **gradient** and the **y-intercept**.

   $2x + 3y - 1 = 0$
   $=> \quad 3y = -.... + ...$
   $=> \quad y = -....$
   $m = ...$ and the **y-intercept** is ....

2. Find the gradient and y-intercept of the equation :-

$$4y - 6x + 3 = 0.$$

   Copy and complete :

   $4y - 6x + 3 = 0$
   $=> \quad 4y = ... - ....$
   $=> \quad y = -....$
   $m = ...$ and the **y-intercept** is ....

3. Find the gradient and the y-intercept of each of the lines defined by the equations below :-

   (a) $2x + 4y + 6 = 0$ (b) $x + 2y - 1 = 0$

   (c) $3y - 3x + 1 = 0$ (d) $2y - 6x + 4 = 0$

   (e) $2x + y = 16$ (f) $3x + y + 1 = 0$

   (g) $3y + 3 = x$ (h) $2y + 8 = \frac{1}{2}x.$

4. The equation of a line is given by :-

$$4x + 2y - 8 = 0.$$

   (a) Rearrange the equation into the form

$$y = mx + c.$$

   (b) Draw this line on a Cartesian diagram. (*Hint - construct a table of values*).

5. Draw each of the lines with equations given below on Cartesian diagrams.

   (a) $2x + y + 1 = 0$ (b) $4x + 2y + 6 = 0$

   (c) $3x + 3y = 9$ (d) $2y - 4x - 2 = 0.$

6. Determine the gradient and the y-intercept of the line :-

$$x - y + 2 = 0.$$

   (Hint : *be careful with negative y-value*).

7. Find the gradient and y-intercept of each of these lines with equations :-

   (a) $3y = 9x + 15$ (b) $4y = 2x - 1$

   (c) $6x + 3y = 15$ (d) $4x + 2y - 8 = 0$

   (e) $2y + \frac{1}{2}x - 3 = 0$ (f) $5x - 4y + 1 = 0.$

8. Find the gradient and y-intercept of the line with equation $x - 2y = 4.$

1. Calculate the **gradient** of this ramp.

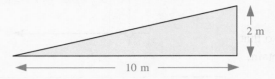

2. The gradient of four hills are given below :-

$$29\%, \quad 0{\cdot}28, \quad \tfrac{1}{3}, \quad 0{\cdot}3.$$

List the hills in order, **steepest** first.

3. Calculate the gradient of each line below :-

   (a)   (b)

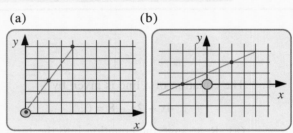

   (c)   (d)

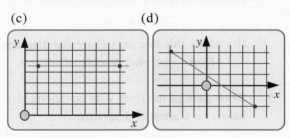

4. Calculate the gradient of :-

   (a) the line AB which passes through the points A(–3, –6) and B(1, 4).

   (b) the line CD which passes through the points C(–3, 2) and D(3, –6).

5. Write down the **gradients** and the **y-intercepts** of these lines :-

   (a) $y = 4x + 1$ (b) $y = 3 - x$.

6. Write down the **equation** of each of the following lines :-

   (a) $m = 2$, and its y-intercept is –3.

   (b) gradient of –1, through the point (0, –5).

   (c) $m = -5$ and passing through the origin

   (d) $m = 0$, through point (4, 5)

   (e) through point (–1, –4), parallel to *y-axis*.

7. Find the equation of each of these lines :-

   (a)   (b)

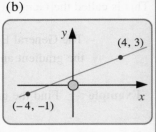

8. Write down the gradient and y-intercept of :-

   (a) $2y + 6x - 4 = 0$ (b) $4x + 5y = 0$.

9. Rearrange the line $2y + x - 4 = 0$ into the form

$$y = mx + c,$$

and show the line on a Cartesian diagram.

10. A Bike Hire company charges the following :-

BIKE HIRE
- **£10 deposit +**
- **£5 per day**

   (a) Construct a table of values for 1 to 5 days.

   (b) Plot the 5 points on a Cartesian diagram.

   (c) Devise a formula to represent the hire charges.

   (d) Use your formula to find the cost of hiring a bike for a week.

   (e) For how many days did I hire the bike if my bill came to £95 ?

11. Find the equation of the line which passes through the points :-

   (a) G(1, 4),   K(2, 6)

   (b) P(–1, 3),   T(2, 6)

   (c) R(4, –1),   S(6, 1)

   (d) T(–8, 0),   U(4, 4)

   (e) V(–6, 3),   W(3, 0)

   (f) K(18, 10), L(–14, 26)

   (g) M(–1, –3), N(–$\tfrac{1}{2}$, 4)

   (h) P(3·5, 2·5), Q(6·5, –3·5).

1. Sketch each line below on the same diagram :-

   (a) $y = 3x - 2$ (b) $2x + 4y + 8 = 0$.

2. Where do the two lines in question 1 intersect ?

3. Solve each of the following pairs of equations :-

   (a) $3x + y = 4$ (b) $5x + 2y = 10$
   $\quad\;\; x - y = 12$ $\quad\;\; 3x + 2y = 4$

   (c) $3x + y = 10$ (d) $4x + 3y = -7$
   $\quad\;\; 2x - 3y = 3$ $\quad\;\; 2x + y = -3$

   (e) $7x - 2y = 17$ (f) $3x + 5y = -33$
   $\quad\;\; 4x + 3y = -11$ $\quad\;\; 2y + 5x = -36$

   (g) $x = 6y - 2$ (h) $7y - 3x = -27$
   $\quad\;\; 2x + 5y = 13$ $\quad\;\; 4x - y - 11 = 0$.

4. Four steak pies and three cottage pies cost £19·50.

   A steak pie and two cottage pies cost £8.

   How much is it for a cottage pie ?

5. A 2·6 kg box has 6 tins of soup and 5 tins of vegetables.

   A 2·11 kg box has 5 tins of soup and 4 tins of vegetables.

   How heavy is a box with 2 tins of soup and 4 tins of vegetables ?

6. Find the value of x to 3 significant figures :-

   (a)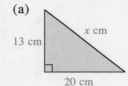

   13 cm x cm
   20 cm

   (b)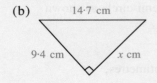

   14·7 cm
   9·4 cm x cm

   (c)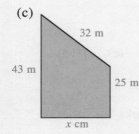

   32 m
   43 m   25 m
   x cm

   (d)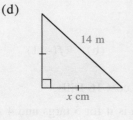

   14 m
   x cm

7. A cube has a side length of 10 cm.

   Find the length of a space diagonal, to one decimal place.

8. An architect plans to build a swimming pool with a rectangular base.

   He has dimensions as follows :-

   Length 20 metres

   Breadth 8 metres

   Diagonal distance 22·5 metres.

   Prove that the architect has made a mistake.

9. A square has a diagonal length of 30 cm.

   Find to three significant figures, the side length.

10. Which of the two slopes below is the steeper ?

    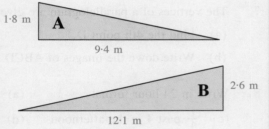

    1·8 m   **A**
    9·4 m

    B   2·6 m
    12·1 m

11. State the gradient and y-intercept of :-

    (a) $y = 6x - 1$ (b) $0·5x - y + 2 = 0$.

12. Write down the equation of the line that :-

    (a) has $m = 3$ and passes through $(4, 7)$

    (b) passes through $(4, 0)$ and the origin

    (c) has a vertical gradient through $(-4, 5)$.

13. Find the equation of each of the lines passing through the points :-

    (a) $(0, 2)$, $(6, 4)$ (b) $(-1, 4)$, $(0, 5)$

    (c) $(2, 2)$, $(7, 7)$ (d) $(6, 1)$, $(7, -1)$

    (e) $(5, -3)$, $(6, -6)$ (f) $(7, 16)$, $(11, -12)$.

1. Set down and find :-

    (a) $77·9 + 1·014$ (b) $30\overline{)9600}$ (c) $3765 ÷ 4$ (d) $\dfrac{4 \times 42·75}{2000}$.

2. A crate holds 5450 kg of potatoes. How many 8 kg bags can be **filled** from one crate ?

3. Change :-   (a) 4·7 m to mm   (b) 71 g to kg   (c) 5400 cubic cm to litres

    (d) 30 ml to litres   (e) $\frac{7}{8}$ km to cm   (f) 3·05 tonnes to g   (g) 9 hours to seconds.

4. Simplify :-   (a) $\dfrac{34}{51}$ (b) $\dfrac{36}{156}$ (c) $\dfrac{54}{360}$.

5. Find :-   (a) 30% of £5   (b) 75% of £3   (c) 90% of 9000

    (d) 7% of £3   (e) $12\frac{1}{2}$% of 6464   (f) $2\frac{1}{2}$% of 640   (g) 0·25% of £1 Million.

6. Find :-   (a) $(-26) - 17$ (b) $(-12) - (-42)$ (c) $(-55) + 67$

    (d) $(-3) \times 45$ (e) $(-30) \times (-15)$ (f) $(-20)^2$ (g) $(-40)^3$

    (h) $121 ÷ (-11)$ (i) $(-125) ÷ (-25)$ (j) $\dfrac{(-6) \times (-25)}{-15}$ (k) $-\frac{1}{3} \times (-81)$.

7. The vertices of a parallelogram are given as A(–1, 2), B(0, 6) and C(4, 5) and D.

    (a)   Find the 4th point D.

    (b)   Write down the images of ABCD if the parallelogram is reflected over the x-axis.

8. Write in 24 hour format :-   (a)   ten past midnight   (b)   10:10 a.m.

    (c) $\frac{1}{4}$ past 4 in the afternoon   (d)   7:10 p.m.   (e)   ten to ten at night.

9. How long is it from :-   (a)   7:23 p.m. to 2310   (b)   1019 to 10:20 p.m. ?

10. An army tank covers 70 kilometres in 3 hours and 30 minutes. Find the average speed of the tank.

11. A pane of glass is made from a rectangle and a semi-circle as shown.

    Calculate the area of the glass.

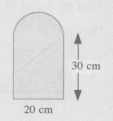

30 cm

20 cm

12. A right angled triangle has its longest side 13 centimetres, and one shorter side 12 centimetres long.

    Calculate the perimeter of the triangle.

13. If $f(x) = 3x^2 - 2x + 1$, find :-   (a) $f(-1)$ (b) $f(-11)$ (c) $f(1·5)$.

14. 3 zarks and a targ cost 17 Dills. 2 zarks and 3 targs cost 16 Dills.

    (a)   How much is it for a targ ?   (b)   How much is it for 5 targs and 4 zarks ?

> **Factorising - The Common Factor - Revision**
>
> **Remember :-**
>
> Factorise fully :-
>
> | 1. $5x + 10$ | 2. $12a - 16b$ | 3. $pq + pr$ | 4. $12x - 18x^2$ |
> |---|---|---|---|
> | $= 5(x + 2)$ | $= 4(3a - 4b)$ | $= p(q + r)$ | $= 6x(2 - 3x)$ |
>
> Check answers by removing the brackets
>
> 5 is *h.c.f.*
> *highest common factor*   4 is *h.c.f.*   *p* is *h.c.f.* $6x$ is *h.c.f.*

Exercise 7·1

1. COPY and complete :-

   (a) $3a + 12b = 3(\ldots\ldots)$
   (b) $2x + 6y = 2(\ldots\ldots)$
   (c) $8g + 6h = 2(\ldots\ldots)$

   (d) $ab + ac = a(\ldots\ldots)$
   (e) $pq + p = p(\ldots\ldots)$
   (f) $kj + k^2 = k(\ldots\ldots)$

   (g) $fg^2 + g = g(\ldots\ldots)$
   (h) $3mn + 3mp = 3m(\ldots\ldots)$
   (i) $6x + 9y = 3(\ldots\ldots)$

   (j) $24b - 16a = 8(\ldots\ldots)$
   (k) $12cd - 8d = 4d(\ldots\ldots)$
   (l) $9p + 21p^2 = 3p(\ldots\ldots)$.

2. Factorise the following, by considering the highest common factor in each case :-

   (a) $6a + 24$
   (b) $2x + 12$
   (c) $7p - 35$
   (d) $11a + 11b$

   (e) $7p - 7q$
   (f) $4c - 16h$
   (g) $8m - 24$
   (h) $13n + 39$

   (i) $4x + 10y$
   (j) $6u - 21v$
   (k) $30x - 55y$
   (l) $6r - 42u$

   (m) $12s + 30$
   (n) $44u - 33$
   (o) $27x - 45y$
   (p) $72a + 24c$

   (q) $121t - 11$
   (r) $42k + 28$
   (s) $17h - 51$
   (t) $96z - 128$.

3. Factorise fully :-

   (a) $2b + bc$
   (b) $8x - vx$
   (c) $cd + cg$
   (d) $a^2 + 3a$

   (e) $5t - t^2$
   (f) $2c^2 - 8c$
   (g) $4kh + 4hg$
   (h) $5vw - 10vx$

   (i) $17rs - 17s$
   (j) $3y^2 + 7y$
   (k) $12x^2 - 16xy$
   (l) $6q^2 + 9q$

   (m) $4d + 14d^2$
   (n) $52a - 13a^2$
   (o) $3y^2 - 21cy$
   (p) $18mn + 32n^2$

   (q) $a^2 + 4a^2b$
   (r) $ab^2 + 6ab$
   (s) $abc^2 + 7abc$
   (t) $a^2bc^2 + 7ab^2c$.

4. Completely factorise :-

   (a) $a^2 + 4ab - 7a$
   (b) $2xy - 4xz + x$
   (c) $p^3 + p^2$
   (d) $4n^3 - 16n$

   (e) $6a^2c + ac^2$
   (f) $18rs^2 - 30rs$
   (g) $8x^2 - 12ax$
   (h) $\frac{1}{5}gh + \frac{1}{5}hj$.

5. Factorise each of the following in simplest form :-

   (a) $15a^2bc^2 + 12b^2c$
   (b) $15cde^2 + 12b^2ce$

   (c) $21k^2gh^2 + 24k^2g^2h - 15kgh$
   (d) $21p^2ts^2 + 24pt^2s^2 - 15p^2s$.

Factorising Algebraic Expressions - "The Difference of Two Squares"

When expanding brackets, we discovered that .... $(a-b)(a+b) = a^2 + ab - ab - b^2 = a^2 - b^2$.

In reverse, when we factorise $a^2 - b^2$ we obtain the answer $(a+b)(a-b)$.

An algebraic expression of the form $a^2 - b^2$ is known as "a Difference of Two Squares" - obviously because both terms are squares and also the appearance of a minus sign.

Examples :-

Factorise :-   1. $x^2 - 9$
   $= (x-3)(x+3)$

2. $49 - x^2$
   $= (7-x)(7+x)$

3. $4x^2 - 25y^2$
   $= (2x)^2 - (5y)^2$
   $= (2x-5y)(2x+5y).$

Exercise 7·2

1.   Factorise, using the difference of two squares :-

(a) $x^2 - 4$ (b) $a^2 - 16$ (c) $b^2 - 25$ (d) $x^2 - 1$

(e) $1 - k^2$ (f) $81 - w^2$ (g) $64 - h^2$ (h) $100 - x^2$

(i) $x^2 - b^2$ (j) $w^2 - v^2$ (k) $4a^2 - 1$ (l) $x^2 - 25y^2$

(m) $36 - 49p^2$ (n) $81a^2 - 4b^2$ (o) $121v^2 - 100w^2$ (p) $64p^2 - 81q^2$

(q) $1 - 16a^2$ (r) $25 - 81x^2$ (s) $49 - 4k^2$ (t) $1 - 144y^2$.

Consider this example :- | Factorise $3x^2 - 48$ It is a "difference", but NOT of two squares !

$= 3(x^2 - 16)$ By removing the common factor,

$= 3(x-4)(x+4)$ we now have a difference of two squares.

---

2.   Factorise these fully :-

(a) $2x^2 - 18$
   $= 2(x^2 - 9)$
   $= \ldots\ldots\ldots$

(b) $3p^2 - 3$
   $= 3(p^2 - \ldots)$
   $= \ldots\ldots\ldots$

(c) $5a^2 - 80$
   $= 5(\ldots^2 - \ldots)$
   $= \ldots\ldots\ldots$

(d) $x^4 - 16$
   $= (x^2 - 4)(x^2 + 4)$
   $= (x-2)(x + \ldots)(x^2 + 4)$

(e) $4g^2 - 16$ (f) $7x^2 - 7y^2$ (g) $6v^2 - 150u^2$ (h) $10a^2 - 90b^2$

(i) $19x^2 - 19y^2$ (j) $aw^2 - av^2$ (k) $\pi m^2 - \pi n^2$ (l) $kp^2 - 36kq^2$

(m) $Ar^2 - 9As^2$ (n) $d^3 - 4d$ (o) $27x^3 - 48x$ (p) $a^4 - 1$

(q) $1 - k^4$ (r) $p^4 - q^4$ (s) $1 - 16y^4$ (t) $3d^4 - 48$.

3.   Shown is a square with side 5 centimetres cut out from a square of side k centimetres.

(a) Prove that the **pink** area can be expressed as :- $(k-5)(k+5)$ cm^2.

(b) Find the area when $k = 8{\cdot}5$.

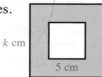

k cm

5 cm

Factorising Trinomials (or Quadratic Expressions)

Remember the "Rainbows" ? $(x+2)(x+3) = x^2 + 5x + 6$

Now we examine how to reverse the process and FACTORISE $x^2 + 5x + 6$ to obtain $(x+2)(x+3)$.

Example :-   Factorise $x^2 + 5x + 6$

• Draw up a small table

• In the front part of the table put the factors of the x^2.

x	
x	

• In the back part of the table put some* factors of the 6.

x	1	6	2	3
x	6	1	3	2

• Now, take it in turn to **multiply diagonally** with the x's and **add** looking for the middle term (in this case the $5x$).

x	1	6	2	3
x	6	1	3	2

$6 \times x + 1 \times x = 7x$ *no use.*

* ..... keep choosing factors until you find the ones which work - you may be lucky early !

x	1	6	2	3
x	6	1	3	2

$2 \times x + 3 \times x = 5x$ *Yes !*

$=> \quad x^2 + 5x + 6$ factorises to give $(x + 2)(x + 3)$

Examples :- Factorise ....

1. $x^2 + 3x - 10$

x	10	−10	2	−2
x	−1	1	−5	5

$= (x-2)(x+5)$

one must be ±ve and one must be −ve.

2. $x^2 - 9x + 20$

x	−10	−20	−4
x	−2	−1	−5

$= (x-5)(x-4)$

must use negatives because of the $-9x$!

Exercise 7·3

1.   Factorise these trinomials :-

(a) $x^2 + 2x + 1$ $= (x + ...)(x + ...)$

(b) $a^2 + 3a + 2$ $= (a + ...)(a + ...)$

(c) $k^2 + 7k + 10$ $= (k + ...)(k + ...)$

(d) $d^2 + 9d + 14$ $= (d + ...)(d + ...)$

(e) $x^2 - 2x + 1$

(f) $b^2 - 6b + 9$

(g) $c^2 - 9c + 18$

(h) $w^2 - 11w + 24$

(i) $x^2 + 3x - 4$

(j) $n^2 + n - 6$

(k) $p^2 + 2p - 15$

(l) $q^2 + 3q - 18$

(m) $x^2 - 3x - 4$

(n) $r^2 - 6r - 7$

(o) $y^2 - 4y - 12$

(p) $h^2 - 8h - 20$.

2.   Factorise the following quadratic expressions :-

(a) $x^2 - 5x - 6$

(b) $x^2 + 8x + 15$

(c) $x^2 - 4x - 5$

(d) $x^2 - 11x + 18$

(e) $y^2 - 2y - 15$

(f) $y^2 + 7y - 8$

(g) $y^2 - 9y + 14$

(h) $y^2 + 8y + 12$

(i) $a^2 - 14a + 49$

(j) $a^2 - 10a - 11$

(k) $a^2 + a - 30$

(l) $a^2 - 9a + 20$

(m) $c^2 - 8c + 15$

(n) $c^2 + 4c - 21$

(o) $c^2 - 6c - 27$

(p) $c^2 - 10c + 16$

(q) $k^2 + 9k - 10$

(r) $k^2 - 8k - 9$

(s) $k^2 - 2k - 35$

(t) $k^2 + 2k - 24$

(u) $v^2 + 2v - 8$

(v) $v^2 - 13v + 30$

(w) $v^2 - v - 12$

(x) $v^2 - 13v + 40$.

Harder Examples :-

Factorise :- 1. $3x^2 + 5x - 2$

$= (3x-1)(x+2)$

factors of $3x^2$ factors of -2

> Multiply **diagonally** and **add** to obtain **$5x$**

2. $6x^2 + 13x + 2$

$\Rightarrow$ try $3x$ and $2x$ doesn't work !!

$\Rightarrow$ try $6x$ and $1x$

$2 \times 6x + 1 \times x = 13x$ **Yes** !

factors are $(6x+1)(x+2)$

---

3.   Factorise the following and check each answer mentally.

(a) $2x^2 + 5x + 3$ (b) $2a^2 + 7a + 3$ (c) $6y^2 + 7y + 2$ (d) $3g^2 + 14g + 15$

(e) $12k^2 - 8k + 1$ (f) $2b^2 - 7b + 3$ (g) $8c^2 - 14c + 5$ (h) $3x^2 - 2x - 8$

(i) $3a^2 - 5a - 2$ (j) $5p^2 + 4p - 1$ (k) $2m^2 + m - 1$ (l) $3q^2 - 2q - 1$

(m) $8c^2 + 2c - 3$ (n) $8n^2 + 10n - 3$ (o) $12w^2 - 11w - 5$ (p) $4c^2 + 12c + 9$

(q) $24k^2 + 2k - 1$ (r) $1 + 3x - 18x^2$ (s) $15 - 7y - 2y^2$ (t) $x^2 + 8xy + 12y^2$

(u) $p^2 - 10pq + 24q^2$ (v) $b^2 + 3bc + 2c^2$ (w) $a^2 - 5ab - 14b^2$ (x) $2u^2 - 5uv - 3v^2$

(y) $9g^2 + 6gh - 8h^2$ (z) $9\sin^2\theta - 12\sin\theta + 4$.

More Difficult Examples :-

Factorise :- 1. $3x^2 - 75$

$= 3(x^2 - 25)$ *take out a common factor first*

$= 3(x+5)(x-5)$

2. $2x^2 - 8x - 24$

$= 2(x^2 - 4x - 12)$ *take out a common factor first*

$= 2(x-6)(x+2)$

---

4.   Factorise the following quadratic expressions :-

(a) $2x^2 - 200$ (b) $3x^2 - 27$ (c) $4x^2 - 16$ (d) $7x^2 - 63$

(e) $5x^2 - 5$ (f) $10x^2 - 40$ (g) $98 - 2x^2$ (h) $56 - 14x^2$

(i) $3x^2 - 3x - 60$ (j) $2x^2 - 8x - 64$ (k) $2x^2 - 46x - 48$ (l) $11x^2 - 11x - 66$

(m) $3x^2 + 18x - 21$ (n) $2x^2 - 36x + 64$ (o) $9x^2 + 18x + 9$ (p) $36x^2 + 39x + 3$.

Exercise 7·4   *Miscellaneous Exercise on Factorisation*

> ### ORDER OF FACTORISATION :-
> - *Look for a Common Factor and place it outside the bracket(s).*
> - *Watch for a Difference of Two Squares.*
> - *Complete the factorisation of any Trinomial which remains.*

Factorise fully :-

1. $6x + 36y$
2. $p^2 - 49$
3. $y^2 + 6y + 9$
4. $k^2 - k$

5. $v^2 - v - 6$
6. $1 - a^2$
7. $de + dh - dj$
8. $3c^2 - 12$

9. $m^2 - 8m$
10. $q^2 - 2q + 1$
11. $b^2 - 1$
12. $b^2 - b$

13. $b^2 - b - 2$
14. $2t^2 - 18$
15. $2x^2 - 32x$
16. $a^3 - a^2$

17. $2p^2 + 3p - 5$
18. $9n^2 + 6n + 1$
19. $81 - x^2$
20. $50 - 2c^2$

21. $18y - 6y^2$
22. $81 - 4b^2$
23. $2k^2 - k - 1$
24. $14x^2 + 42y^2$

25. $14m^2 - 56n^2$
26. $16x^2 - 8x + 1$
27. $3p^2q - 9pq^2$
28. $1 - 2u + u^2$

29. $3x^3 - 27x$
30. $6a^2 + 5a - 6$
31. $4x^2 + 4x - 8$
32. $10w - 40w^3$

33. $ak^2 - am^2$
34. $2x^2 - 7x - 15$
35. $p^7 - p^6 - p^5$
36. $x^4 - 81$

37. $2x^2 - 18$
38. $17x - 51$
39. $2x^2 - 12x + 36$
40. $9xy - 45x + 3y$

41. $5x^2 - 125$
42. $4x^2 - 24x + 36$
43. $3x^2 - 147$
44. $12x^2 + 14x - 6$

45. $3x^2 - 24x - 27$
46. $16x^2 - 16x + 4$
47. $24xy + 18y$
48. $a^2 + 4ab - 7a$.

Remember Remember..... ?

1. Factorise fully :-

   (a) $4a + 24$
   (b) $21a - 28b$
   (c) $cd + cg$
   (d) $2b^2 - 10b$

   (e) $n^3 - n^2$
   (f) $24k^2h + 36kh^2$
   (g) $r^2 - 100$
   (h) $5q^2 - 20$

   (i) $w^2 - 10w + 16$
   (j) $2m^2 + 7m + 6$
   (k) $5b^2 - 27b + 10$
   (l) $x^2 - xy - 2y^2$

   (m) $6x^2 + 7xy - 3y^2$
   (n) $x^2 - 14xy + 49y^2$
   (o) $1 - 25a^2$
   (p) $9n^2 - 9n - 18$

   (q) $3p^2 - 48p$
   (r) $7a^3b - 21ab$
   (s) $17st^2 - 17su^2$
   (t) $x^4 - 2x^2y^2 + y^4$

   (u) $3x^2 - 48$
   (v) $3x^2 - 3x - 60$
   (w) $8x^2 - 32$
   (x) $18x^4 - 12x^2 - 16$.

2. Shown is a picture of a rectangle containing a square hole and a rectangular hole. (*All sizes are in cm*).

   • the blue rectangle has sides $(3p + 1)$ cm
     and $(p + 1)$ cm.

   • the square has sides of length $(p - 2)$ cm.

   • the small rectangle measures 3 cm by 2·5 cm.

   (a) Write down an expression in x for :-

      (i) the area of the large rectangle

      (ii) the area of the square hole

      (iii) the area of the remaining blue shape.

   (b) Factorise your answer to (a), part (iii).

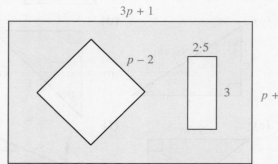

Chapter 8

Trigonometric Formulae

Scientific Calculator **required for all of this Chapter.**

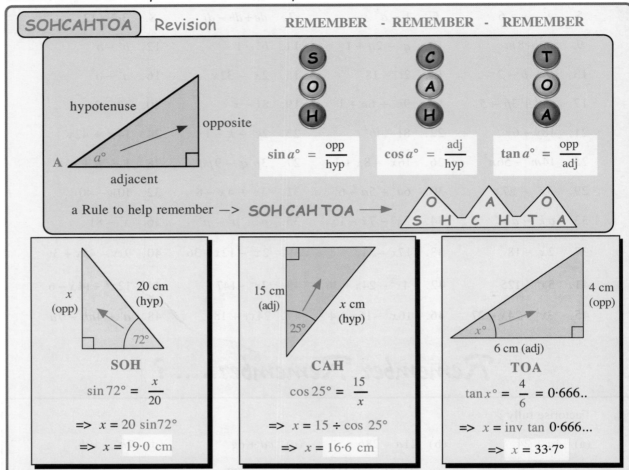

SOHCAHTOA Revision   REMEMBER - REMEMBER - REMEMBER

$$\sin a° = \frac{\text{opp}}{\text{hyp}} \qquad \cos a° = \frac{\text{adj}}{\text{hyp}} \qquad \tan a° = \frac{\text{opp}}{\text{adj}}$$

a Rule to help remember —> SOH CAH TOA

SOH

$$\sin 72° = \frac{x}{20}$$

$$\Rightarrow x = 20 \sin 72°$$

$$\Rightarrow x = 19·0 \text{ cm}$$

CAH

$$\cos 25° = \frac{15}{x}$$

$$\Rightarrow x = 15 \div \cos 25°$$

$$\Rightarrow x = 16·6 \text{ cm}$$

TOA

$$\tan x° = \frac{4}{6} = 0·666..$$

$$\Rightarrow x = \text{inv tan } 0·666...$$

$$\Rightarrow x = 33·7°$$

Exercise 8·1

1. Choose your ratio from **SOHCAHTOA** to find the value of *x* in each case, (*to 1 decimal place*).

(a) 8 cm, 30°, x

(b) 64°, x

(c) 71°, 60 cm, x

(d) 9 cm, 10 cm, 48°, x

(e) 8·5 cm, 65°, x

(f) x, 77°, 36 cm

2. Choose the correct ratio to find the size of angle *x*° in each case, (*to 1 decimal place*).

(a) 8 cm, x°, 15 cm

(b) x°, 65 cm, 45 cm

(c) 120 mm, 45 mm, x°

(d) 45 mm, 21 m, 31 m, x°

(e) x°, 6·7 cm, 7·7 cm

(f) 8·6 km, x°, 4·9 km

3. A flag pole is erected and held in place by a metal cable fixed to the ground 12 metres from the flags base.

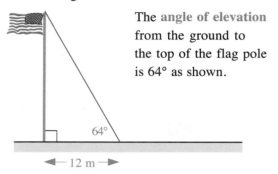

The **angle of elevation** from the ground to the top of the flag pole is 64° as shown.

Calculate the **height** of the flagpole.

4. A small boat is in distress and is observed by the coastguard on top of a cliff at an **angle of depression** of 25°.

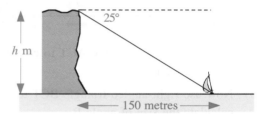

If the boat is 150 metres from the base of the cliff how many metres will the coastguard need to climb down to give assistance ?

5. A lean-to shed is 2·3 metres high at the front and 1·6 metres high at the back.

The width of the shed is 2·8 metres.

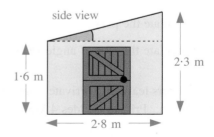

Find the angle of the slope of the roof.

6. A rectangle measures 20 cm by 8 cm.

    (a) Sketch the rectangle showing one diagonal.

    (b) Calculate the sizes of all the angles.

    (c) Calculate the size of the diagonal.

7. A submarine must dive to a depth of 40 metres. To do so, the submarine must travel 80 metres.

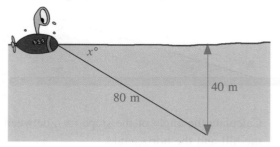

Calculate the angle the submarine must dive at.

8. A metal bracket is fixed to a wall to support a shelf.

The bracket has a horizontal length of 40 cm and an angled length of 50 cm.

Find to the nearest degree, the angle between the two arms of the bracket, (x),

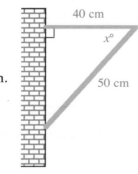

9. 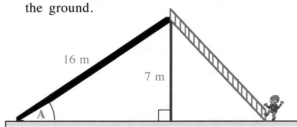 A balloon is tethered by a rope 20 metres above the ground. The rope is 30 metres long.

Find the angle, to the nearest degree, between the rope and the ground.

10. A slide 16 metres in length, is shown below. The top of the slide is 7 metres above the ground.

    (a) Calculate the angle that the slide makes with the ground.

    (b) The angle between the stair and the steps up to the slide is 46°.

         How far is it from the bottom of the steps to the bottom of the slide ?

11. A hill is 2 km long and slopes uniformly. Over its 2 km length, it rises by a total of 80 metres.

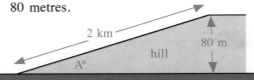

Calculate the angle of the slope (**A**), between the hill and the horizontal.

12. A flagpole is supported by two steel cables 18 m and 12·3 m in length.

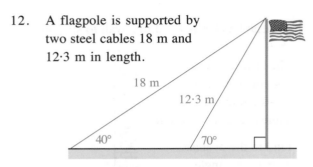

(a) Calculate the height of the flagpole.

(b) Calculate the ground distance between the foot of the 2 cables.

13. The figure shows a square PQRS with a right angled triangle APS attached.

AP = 12 centimetres,   ∠SAP = 60°.

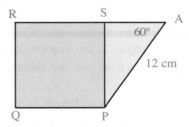

Calculate the **area** of square PQRS.

14. A rectangle is as shown.

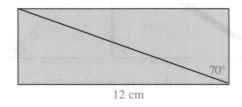

(a) Find the perimeter of this rectangle.

(b) Find the area of this rectangle.

(c) Find the length of the diagonal.

15. The diagram shows a sail from a yacht which is in the shape of a right angled triangle.

Calculate the size of angle *a*.

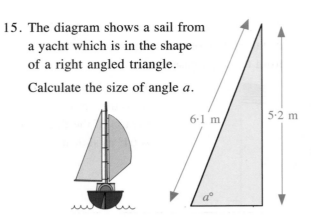

16. Triangle ABC has a line drawn from C at right angles to the line AB, meeting it at T.

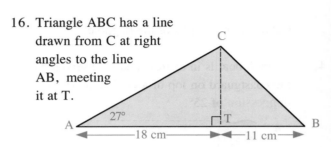

(a) Use right-angled triangle ACT to calculate the height CT.

(b) Now use right-angled triangle BCT to calculate the size of angle B.

17. ABCD is a quadrilateral with parallel sides AD and BC.

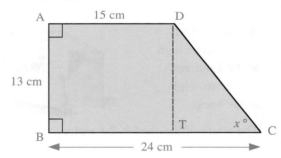

(a) Calculate the **perimeter** of ABCD.

(b) Calculate the size of angle DCT.

18. Two soldiers leave HQ. Private Cairns hikes 6 km North, Private Geddes 4 km East.

(a) From his position Private Cairns moves directly to Private Geddes.

What bearing did he take ?

(b) Both soldiers then moves 4 km South. They then hikes directly back to HQ.

What bearing should they take to go directly to HQ ?

What happens when you are **NOT** told the height of the triangle ?

In this case, you are given **two of the sides** and the **angle** between those sides.

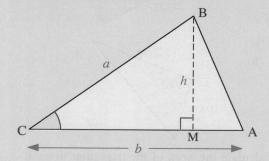

Reminder :-

You should already know a formula for finding the area of a triangle given the length of its **base** and its **height**.

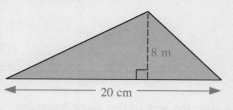

$$\text{Area} = \tfrac{1}{2} \times \text{base} \times \text{height}$$

$$= \tfrac{1}{2} \times 20 \times 8$$

$$= \mathbf{80 \text{ cm}^2}$$

Draw in height BM to make two RAT's.
Let BM = h units.

Using **SOHCAHTOA** in triangle BCM

$$\Rightarrow \quad \sin C = \frac{h}{a} \quad \Rightarrow \quad h = a\sin C$$

$$\Rightarrow \quad \text{AREA of triangle ABC} = \tfrac{1}{2} \times \text{base} \times \text{height}$$

$$\Rightarrow \quad \text{Area} = \tfrac{1}{2} ab \sin C.$$

Generally :- If given **2 sides** of a triangle and the **included angle**, whether acute or obtuse, then :-

$$\boxed{\text{Area of a Triangle} = \tfrac{1}{2} ab \sin C}$$

Example :-

Calculate the **area** of triangle PQR.

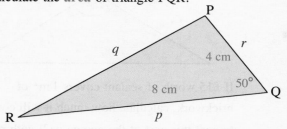

$$\begin{aligned} \text{Area} &= \tfrac{1}{2} pr \sin Q \\ &= \tfrac{1}{2} \times 4 \times 8 \times \sin 50° \\ &= \mathbf{12{\cdot}3 \text{ cm}^2} \quad \text{(to 3 sig. figs.)} \end{aligned}$$

1.   Calculate the area of each of these triangles, *(to 3 sig. figs.)* :-

(a)

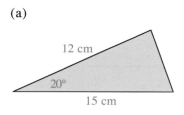

(b)

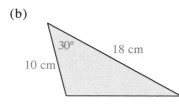

(c)

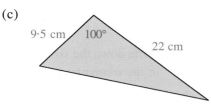

Answer to 3 significant figures unless stated :-

2. Calculate the **area** of each of these triangles :-

(a)

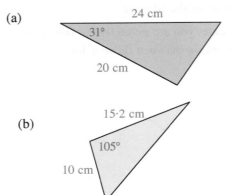

24 cm

31°

20 cm

(b)

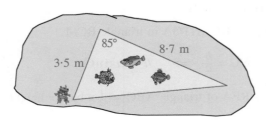

15·2 cm

105°

10 cm

3. Calculate the **area** of the triangular tropical fish pond in the garden.

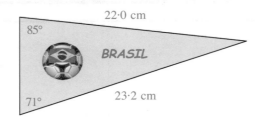

85°

8·7 m

3·5 m

4. A traffic island ABC is shown.

Find the **area** of the traffic island if :-

AB = 12·6 metres,
AC = 10 metres and
angle BAC = 58°.

B

C

A

5. This is a replica of Brazil's World Cup soccer pennant.

22·0 cm

85°

BRASIL

71°

23·2 cm

(a) Write down the size of the **third** angle in the triangular pennant.

(b) Calculate the **area** of the pennant.

6. Calculate the **area** of each of these triangles :-

(a)

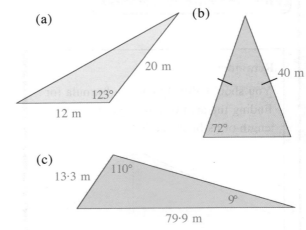

20 m

123°

12 m

(b)

40 m

72°

(c)

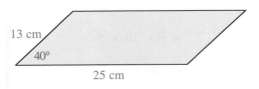

13·3 m

110°

9°

79·9 m

7. Calculate the area of this **parallelogram** :-

13 cm

40°

25 cm

8. After a very damp winter, the owner of this bungalow decided to protect the brickwork at the front of his garage by coating it with an orange all-weather waterproof sealant.

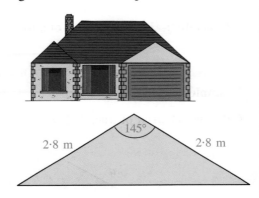

145°

2·8 m

2·8 m

If £15 worth of sealant covers 1 m² of brickwork, calculate how much it will cost him to coat this part of the garage wall with paint.

9. The **area** of this triangle ABC is **54 cm²**.

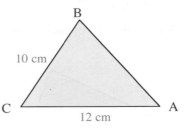

B

10 cm

C

A

12 cm

AC = 12 cm and BC = 10 cm.

Calculate the size of **acute** angle ACB.

10. An identification tag, made of plastic, is in the form of an isosceles triangle, with dimensions as shown.

The badge is 1·3 millimetres thick.

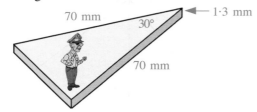

Calculate the **volume** of plastic required to make one tag.

11. Another traffic island, PQR, is shown.
The town council decide to lay red chip stones on the island.

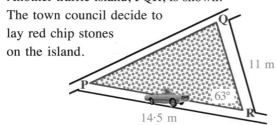

The price of the red chips is shown on this sign.

RED CHIPS
1 lorry-load - £15·00.
Covers 25 square metres

Will £45 be enough to cover the entire traffic island ?   *Explain fully with working*.

12. The side wall of a hut, with measurements shown, requires to be painted with green creosote.

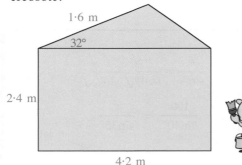

The wall consists of a rectangular base with a triangular top.

A litre of paint will cover (*on average*), 3 square metres.

A painter guesses that he will require 4 litres of paint.

Will he have enough paint ?

Justify your answer.

13. (a) Use your calculator to look up each of the following pairs of **sine** values :-

(i) sin 30° and sin 150°.

(ii) sin 50° and sin 130°

(iii) sin 10° and sin 170°

(iv) sin 105° and sin 75°

(v) sin 175° and sin 5°

(vi) sin 63° and sin 117°.

(b) What did you notice ?

Copy and complete :-

"for any acute angle *a*°,

=> sin *a*° = sin (180 − ...)°".

14. For each angle below, state its pair using 13(b).

(a) 60°   (b) 45°   (c) 110°

(d) 12°   (e) 177°   (f) 1°.

Check each of these on your calculator.

> Can you see that if you now know the value of the sine of an angle,
>
> then there are **two possible values** for the actual size of the angle ?
>
> (*This will be studied later in the course*).

15. The area of **both** triangles below is 78·6 cm².

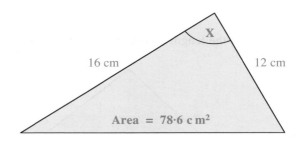

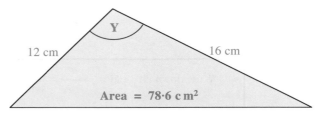

Calculate the sizes of acute angle **X** and obtuse angle **Y**.

Look at the (*non right angled*) triangle ABC.

We **cannot** use **SOHCAHTOA** in $\triangle$ABC since it is not a right angle triangle.

We can draw in altitude CM to create 2 right angled triangles.

Let CM = h units.

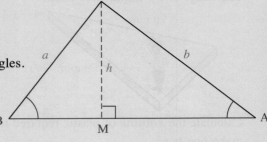

In $\triangle$ACM,

$$\sin A = \frac{h}{b}$$

$\Rightarrow \quad h = b\sin A$

In $\triangle$BCM,

$$\sin B = \frac{h}{a}$$

$\Rightarrow \quad h = a\sin B$

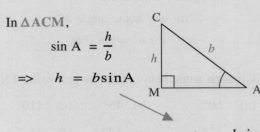

$\Rightarrow \quad b\sin A = a\sin B$

$\div$ both sides by sinAsinB $\quad \Rightarrow \quad \dfrac{b\sin A}{\sin A\sin B} = \dfrac{a\sin B}{\sin A\sin B}$

$\Rightarrow \quad \dfrac{a}{\sin A} = \dfrac{b}{\sin B}$

By symmetry, it can also be shown that :-

$$\frac{a}{\sin A} = \frac{c}{\sin C}$$

We now have a tremendously powerful formula that enables us to find missing sides and angles in non-right angled triangles - **the Sine Rule**.

The Sine Rule $\qquad$ in any $\triangle$ABC, $\quad \dfrac{a}{\sin A} = \dfrac{b}{\sin B} = \dfrac{c}{\sin C}$

Example :-

Calculate the length of side AB in triangle ABC.

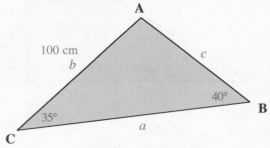

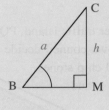

$$\frac{a}{\sin A} = \frac{b \checkmark}{\sin B \checkmark} = \frac{c \checkmark}{\sin C \checkmark}$$

$$\frac{100}{\sin 40°} = \frac{c}{\sin 35°}$$

$\Rightarrow \quad c = \dfrac{100\sin 35°}{\sin 40°}$

$\qquad\qquad = 89{\cdot}2$ cm

* note

- Write down all 3 ratios $\quad \dfrac{a}{\sin A} = \dfrac{b}{\sin B} = \dfrac{c}{\sin C}$
- tick the 2 angles and side you are given.
- tick the side you are asked to calculate.
- score out the 1 ratio not required.

Answer to 3 significant figures unless otherwise asked

1. Copy and complete the following to find the required length :-

   (a)

   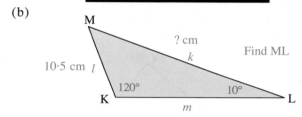

   Find RQ

$$\frac{p\checkmark}{\sin P\checkmark} = \frac{q}{\sin Q} = \frac{r\checkmark}{\sin R\checkmark}$$

$$\frac{p}{\sin 70°} = \frac{20}{\sin 80°}$$

$$p = \frac{20\sin ...°}{\sin ....°}$$

$$p = ... \text{ cm}$$

   (b)

   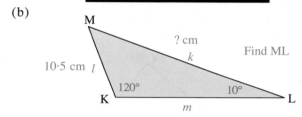

   ? cm

   Find ML

$$\frac{k\checkmark}{\sin K\checkmark} = \frac{l\checkmark}{\sin L\checkmark} = \frac{m}{\sin M}$$

$$\frac{k}{\sin 120°} = \frac{10·5}{\sin 10°}$$

$$k = \frac{.....\sin ...°}{\sin ....°}$$

$$k = ... \text{ cm}$$

2. Calculate the length of the marked side in each of the following triangles.

   (a)   (b)

   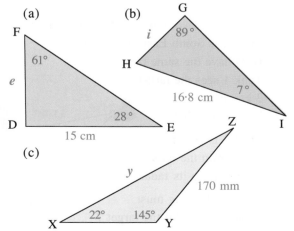

   (c)

3. In △ABC, calculate the size of :-

   (a) ∠ACB   (b) side AB.

   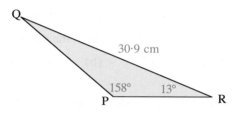

4. In △PQR, calculate the size of :-

   (a) ∠PQR   (b) side PR.

   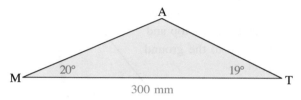

5. In △MAT, calculate the length of the **shortest** side.

   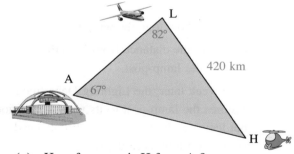

6. The diagram shows the positions of an airport (A), a light jet aircraft (L) and a helicopter (H).

   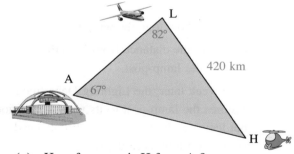

   (a) How far away is H from A ?

   (b) How far away is A from L ?

7. Shown is the wing of a passenger plane.

   Calculate the length of the leading edge of the wing.

   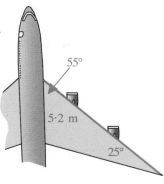

8. A yacht sets sail from a jetty, 40 metres from the lighthouse.

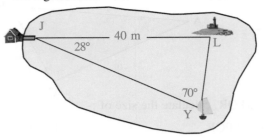

Its course makes an angle of 28° to the coast.

Find, (*to the nearest metre*), the distance :-

(a) from L to Y   (b) from J to Y.

9. A road traffic accident resulted in a 22 foot lamp-post ending up at an angle of 83° to the ground.

To secure the lamp-post, a strong wire has been attached to its top and tethered to the ground at G.

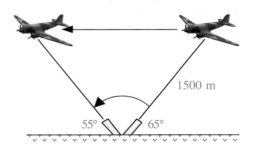

The wire makes an angle of 65° with the ground.

(a) Calculate how long the wire is.

(b) Calculate the distance from G to the foot of the lamp-post.

(c) One week later, the Lighting Department restores the lamp-post to its vertical position but leaves a shortened wire (still attached at G) for a few more days.

What is the length of the shortened wire ?

10. During a raid, a search-light follows a bomber as it flies at a constant height across the sky.

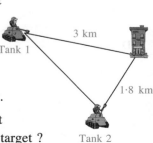

Calculate how far the bomber had flown.

11. A canopy is built over the front door of a house. To support it, two metal struts, MR and MS, are attached as shown.

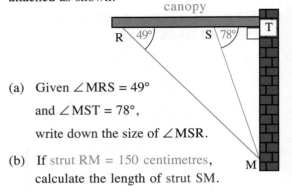

(a) Given ∠MRS = 49° and ∠MST = 78°, write down the size of ∠MSR.

(b) If strut RM = 150 centimetres, calculate the length of strut SM.

12. H.M.S. Tiger is positioned 100 kilometres west of H.M.S. Fearful when they both receive a distress signal from a yacht (at point Y).

The bearing of the yacht from H.M.S. Tiger is 045°.
The bearing of the yacht from H.M.S. Fearful is 310°.

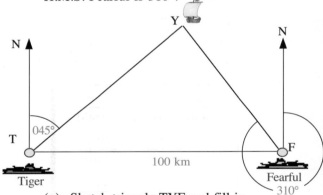

(a) Sketch triangle TYF and fill in the sizes of all three angles.

(b) Which ship will be closer to the yacht ?

(c) Calculate the distance from this ship to the yacht.

13. *Difficult.* Two tanks are on a firing range. Tank 2 is South East of Tank 1. Both have the same target. Tank 1 sees the target 3 km away on a bearing of 100°.

Tank 2 is 1·8 km away from the target according to its radar.

On what bearing must Tank 2 fire to hit the target ?

The Sine Rule - Finding an Angle

Example :-

In ΔABC, find the size of ∠ACB.

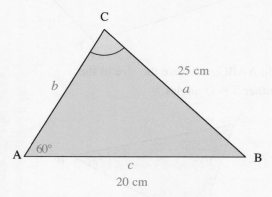

$$\frac{a\checkmark}{\sin A} = \frac{b}{\sin B} = \frac{c\checkmark}{\sin C}\checkmark$$

$$\Rightarrow \quad \frac{25}{\sin 60°} = \frac{20}{\sin C} \quad \text{Now Rearrange}$$

$$\Rightarrow \quad \sin C = \frac{20\sin 60°}{25}$$

$$\Rightarrow \quad \sin C = 0.6928 \qquad \text{INV sin}$$

$$\Rightarrow \quad \angle C = \boxed{43.9°} \quad \text{to 3 sig. figs.}$$

* You will find later in the course that ∠C could also, in theory, be (180 − 43.9) = 136.1°, (*The reason being that if sin C = 0.6928, there are* <u>2</u> *possible solutions*).

This is not the case here, since angle C is **acute**.

Exercise 8·4
Give your answer to 3 significant figures from now on.

1. Copy and complete the following to find the size of **obtuse** angle PQR.

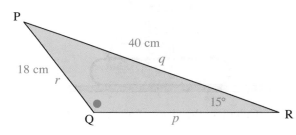

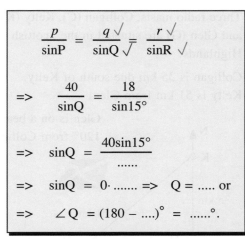

$$\frac{p}{\sin P} = \frac{q\checkmark}{\sin Q}\checkmark = \frac{r\checkmark}{\sin R}\checkmark$$

$$\Rightarrow \quad \frac{40}{\sin Q} = \frac{18}{\sin 15°}$$

$$\Rightarrow \quad \sin Q = \frac{40\sin 15°}{......}$$

$$\Rightarrow \quad \sin Q = 0.\text{.......} \Rightarrow Q = ... \text{ or}$$

$$\Rightarrow \quad \angle Q = (180 − ....)° = ...°.$$

CAREFUL - ANGLE Q IS OBTUSE

2. Copy and complete the following to find the marked angle in each case :-

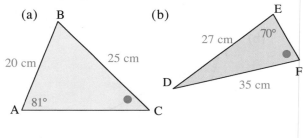

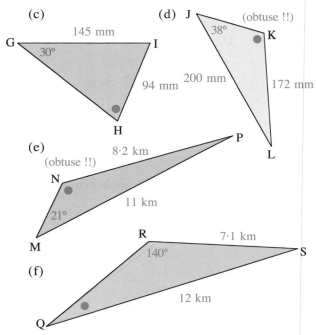

3. Find the size of obtuse ∠PTN in △PNT.

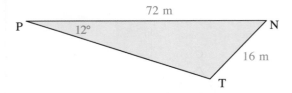

4. In △ABC, calculate the size of the other **TWO** angles.

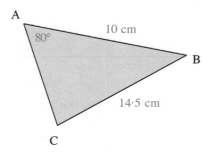

5. Calculate the sizes of :-
   (i) ∠APS   (ii) ∠FMR   (iii) ∠UDY.

   (a)

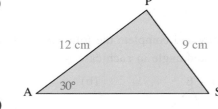

   (b)

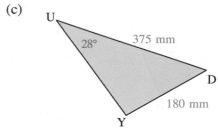

   (c)

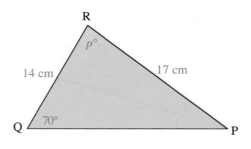

6. Calculate the size of the angle marked $p°$.

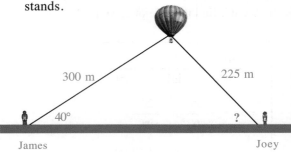

7. A hot air balloon is hovering above the ground. From James, the balloon is 300 metres away and its angle of elevation is 40°.
The balloon is 225 metres from where Joey stands.

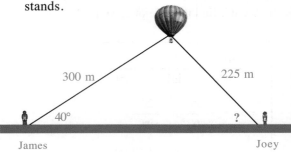

What is the angle of elevation of the balloon from Joey ?

8. The jib, GH, of a crane is 18 metres long. The wire, RH, is 25 metres long. Angle RGH = 142°.

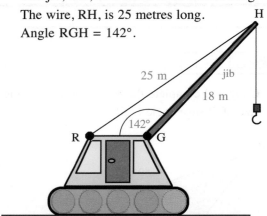

Calculate the sizes of angles GRH and RHG.

9. Three radio masts, Colligan (C), Kelty (K) and Glen (G) are situated in the Scottish Highlands.

Colligan is 35 km due south of Kelty.
Kelty is 51 km from Glen.

Glen is on a bearing of 120° from Colligan.

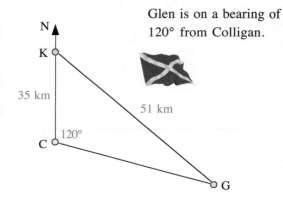

Calculate the bearing of Glen from Kelty.

The Cosine Rule - Missing Sides

Calculating the Length of a Side of a Triangle given Two Sides and the Included Angle.

Example :-

Calculate the length of AC.

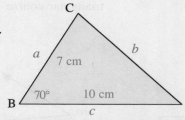

$$\frac{a\checkmark}{\sin A} = \frac{b\checkmark}{\sin B} = \frac{c\checkmark}{\sin C}$$

We **don't** have a group of **FOUR**.

=> We **cannot** use the **Sine Rule**.

We need a new rule to calculate a missing side in a triangle like this when the **Sine Rule** won't work.

Consider right angled $\triangle CAM$ formed in $\triangle ABC$ by drawing the perpendicular line from C to AB.

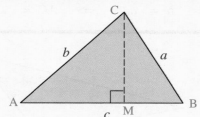

$$\sin A = \frac{CM}{b} \qquad\qquad \cos A = \frac{AM}{b}$$

$$=> \quad CM = b\sin A \qquad => \quad AM = b\cos A$$

Can you see :-
$$MB = c - AM$$
$$= c - b\cos A$$

By using **Pythagoras' Theorem** in $\triangle CMB$,

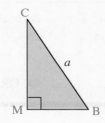

$$BC^2 = CM^2 + MB^2$$

$$=> \quad a^2 = (b\sin A)^2 + (c - b\cos A)^2$$

$$=> \quad a^2 = b^2\sin^2 A + c^2 - 2bc\cos A + b^2\cos^2 A$$

$$=> \quad a^2 = b^2(\sin^2 A + \cos^2 A)* + c^2 - 2bc\cos A$$

$$=> \quad a^2 = b^2 + c^2 - 2bc\cos A \quad ...... \text{ which is known as the Cosine Rule.}$$

Whenever two sides of a triangle and the angle between these two sides are given, the third side can be calculated using the **Cosine Rule** :-

$$a^2 = b^2 + c^2 - 2bc\cos A$$

* It is known that $\sin^2 A + \cos^2 A = 1$.

This proof shown above is probably beyond your understanding at this stage - it will be explained later on in the course, when you have more background knowledge.

Example :- Calculate the length of BC in $\triangle ABC$.

Two sides and included angle given => use **Cosine Rule**.

$$a^2 = b^2 + c^2 - 2bc\cos A$$

$$=> \quad a^2 = 23^2 + 15^2 - 2 \times 23 \times 15 \times \cos 25°$$

$$=> \quad a^2 = 128\cdot648$$

$$=> \quad a = 11\cdot3 \text{ to 3 sig. figs.}$$

Remember to press $\sqrt{}$

$$BC = \boxed{11\cdot3 \text{ cm}}$$

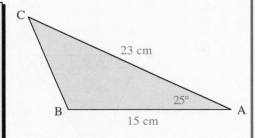

Answer to 3 significant figures.

1. **Copy and complete** the following to find the length of the third side :-

(a)

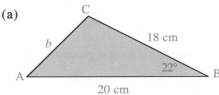

$$b^2 = a^2 + c^2 - 2ac\cos B$$
$$=> \quad b^2 = 18^2 + ...^2 - 2 \times ..... \times .....\cos 22°$$
$$=> \quad b^2 = ...$$
$$=> \quad b = ... \quad => \quad AC = ... \text{ cm}$$

(b)

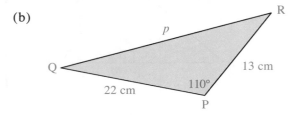

$$p^2 = q^2 + r^2 - 2qr\cos P$$
$$=> \quad p^2 = 13^2 + ...^2 - 2 \times ..... \times ....\cos....$$
$$=> \quad p^2 = ...$$
$$=> \quad p = ... \quad => \quad QR = ... \text{ cm}$$

2. Calculate the length of the unknown side in each of the following triangles :-

(a)

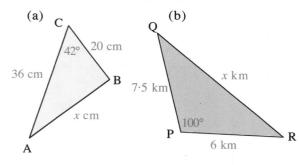

(b)

(c)

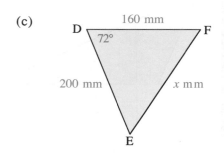

3. A yacht takes part in a race over a triangular course.

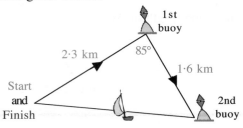

Calculate the length of the final stage of the race, from the 2nd buoy to the finishing line.

4. The pair of compasses shown opposite is used to draw a circle.

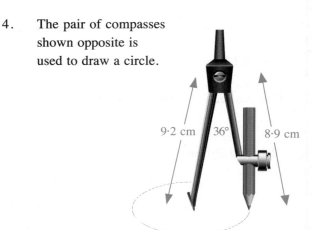

Calculate the **radius** of the circle.

5. The bonnet of a car is held open at an angle of 62°, by a metal rod.

PQ represents the bonnet, PR represents the metal rod and QR represents the distance from the base of the bonnet to the front of the car.

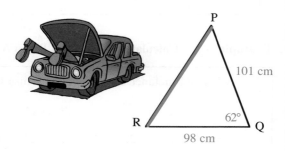

Calculate the length of the metal rod.

6. A triangular wall has been built round a compound of igloos.
It has sides measuring 18 metres and 22·5 metres.
The angle between these sides is 105°.

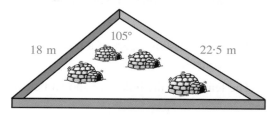

Calculate the total length of the **perimeter** wall.

7. A ship sailed south from a port (P) for a distance of 72 kilometres.
It then sailed on a bearing of 055° for 25 kilometres.

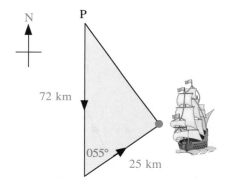

How far is the ship now from port ?

8. The town of Port Greenick is 20 miles north of Longbank and the town of Donburton lies 15 miles north-west of Longbank.

   (a) Make a (*rough*) sketch, showing the relative positions of the 3 towns.

   (b) Calculate how far it is from Donburton to Port Greenick.

9. The computer game "Dinosaur Islands" indicates the position of a helicopter base in relation to two islands, Juraso and Repto, inhabited by dinosaurs.

   From the helicopter base, the island of Juraso is 36 km away on a bearing of 050°.
   From the same base, the island of Repto is 22 km away on a bearing of 135°.

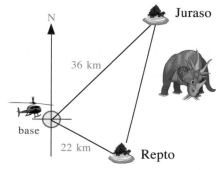

Calculate the distance between Juraso and Repto.

The Cosine Rule - Calculating an Angle

The **Cosine Rule** formula, used to calculate the length of a missing side, can be re-arranged to allow you to calculate the size of a missing angle.

(*As long as you know the lengths of all 3 sides*).

$$a^2 = b^2 + c^2 - 2bc\cos A$$
$$\Rightarrow \quad 2bc\cos A = b^2 + c^2 - a^2$$
$$\Rightarrow \quad \cos A = \frac{b^2 + c^2 - a^2}{2bc}$$

Example :-

Calculate the size of ∠BAC.

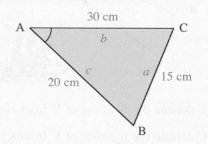

$$\cos A = \frac{b^2 + c^2 - a^2}{2bc}$$

$$\Rightarrow \quad \cos A = \frac{20^2 + 30^2 - 15^2}{2 \times 20 \times 30}$$

$$= 0·895833...$$

INV cos

$$\angle BAC = \mathbf{26·4°} \quad \text{to 3 sig. figs.}$$

Answer to 3 significant figures.

1. In a △ABC, to find ∠C, we can use the formula

$$\cos C = \frac{a^2 + b^2 - c^2}{2ab} .$$

This time we are dealing with △PQR.

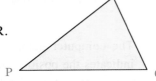

Using the Cosine Rule, write down a formula for calculating the size of each of the following angles :-

  (a)   ∠Q   (*cos Q = ...*)   (b)   ∠P

  (c)   ∠R.

2. Calculate the size of the marked angle in each of the following triangles :-

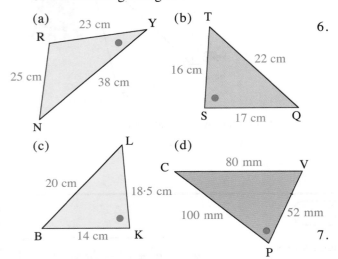

  (a)

  (b)

  (c)

  (d)

3. Calculate the size of the **largest** angle here.

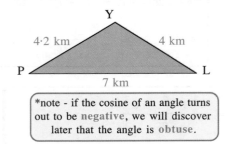

> *note - if the cosine of an angle turns out to be **negative**, we will discover later that the angle is **obtuse**.*

4. (a) Use the Cosine Rule to show that ∠RMF = 90°.

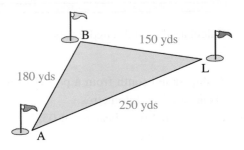

4. (b) Use the Converse of Pythagoras' Theorem to **confirm** that ∠RMF **is** a right angle.

5. The diagram shows part of a pitch & putt golf course.

The lengths of the holes are shown below.

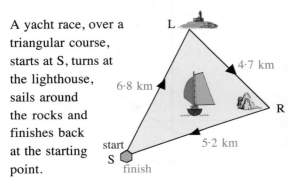

Calculate the size of obtuse angle ABL.

6. A yacht race, over a triangular course, starts at S, turns at the lighthouse, sails around the rocks and finishes back at the starting point.

Calculate the size of the angle LSR.

7. A steamboat leaves H and sails 40 km due north to K.

It then turns and sails 157 km to V.

It completes its journey by sailing 180 km back to H.

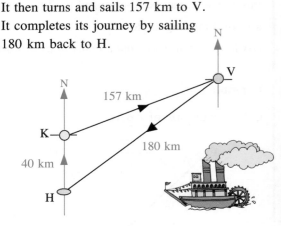

  (a)   Calculate the **bearing** of V from H.

  (b)   Calculate the **bearing** of V from K.

The Sine Rule, The Cosine Rule and SOHCAHTOA

Sometimes, a "**SOHCAHTOA**" question is disguised behind the Sine Rule or the Cosine Rule.
The following exercise gives you some practice at these types of questions.

Example :-

Two girls, who live 300 metres apart, are looking
up at what they believe to be a space rocket.

The angle of elevation of the rocket is 40° from
Gemma and 30° from Sammi.

Calculate :-

    (a) the distance from Sammi to the rocket.

    (b) the height the rocket is above the ground.

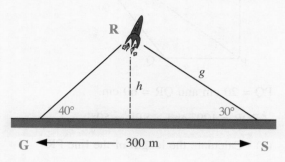

∠GRS is not given, but can be found easily.

(a) $\dfrac{g\checkmark}{\sin G\sqrt{}} = \dfrac{s}{\sin S\sqrt{}} = \dfrac{r\checkmark}{\sin R\sqrt{}}$

=> $\dfrac{g}{\sin 40°} = \dfrac{300}{\sin 110°}$

           R = 180 − 40 − 30

=> $g = \dfrac{300\sin 40°}{\sin 110°}$

       $g = \boxed{205\cdot2 \text{ m}}$

(b) $\sin 30° = \dfrac{h}{205\cdot2}$

        $h = 205\cdot2 \times \sin 30°$

          $= \boxed{102\cdot6 \text{ m}}$

The rocket is 102·6 m above the ground.

Exercise 8·7

1.   Inverness Caley Thistle advertise the return to
their football stadium on a helium balloon.

    The distance between the two points C and D
on the ground is 110 metres and the angle of
elevation from each point is shown on the
diagram below.

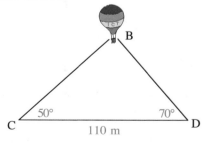

    From the base of the balloon (B), two holding
cables are attached to the ground at C and D.

    (a) Calculate length of the cable BC.

    (b) Calculate the height of the balloon.

2.   The path in the diagram below runs parallel
to the river.

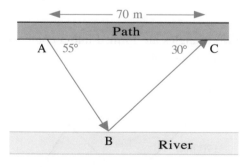

    Colin leaves the path at A, walks to the river
for a paddle (B) and rejoins the path further
on at C.

    (a) Calculate the distance from A to B.

    (b) Calculate the (*shortest*) distance between
the river and the path.

3. In the diagram shown, PQRS has been split into two triangles, one of which is right angled.

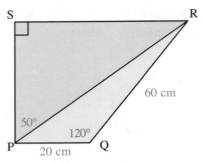

PQ = 20 cm and QR = 60 cm.

∠PQR = 120° and ∠SPR = 50°.

(a) Calculate the length of the line PR.

(b) Calculate the length of the line SP.

4. A TV signal is sent from a transmitter T, via a satellite S, to a village V.
The village is 400 miles from the transmitter.
The signal is sent out at an angle of 38° and is received in the village at an angle of 46°.

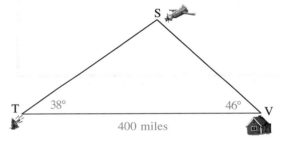

Calculate the height of the satellite above the ground.

5. Two triangles are formed into a composite shape, as shown.

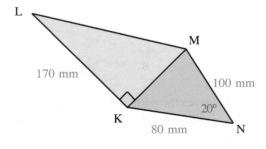

(a) Find the length of KM.

(b) Find the size of ∠KLM.

6. An aeroplane is flying parallel to the ground. Lights have been fitted at M and N as shown in the diagram below.

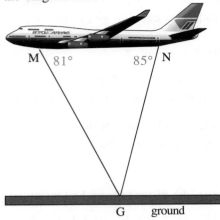

When the aeroplane is flying at a certain height, the beams from these lights meet exactly on the ground at G.

• The angle of depression of the beam of light from M to G is 81°.

• The angle of depression of the beam of light from N to G is 85°.

• The distance MN is 15 metres.

(a) Sketch triangle MGN and mark on all the sizes.

(b) Calculate the **height** of the aeroplane above G.

7. Two support cables, from the top (T) of a motorway light, are attached to the ground at A and B. A is 6 metres away from B.

The angles of elevation are 36° and 68°.

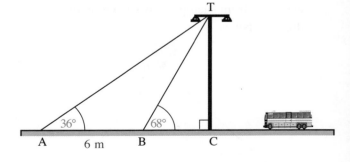

(a) Calculate the sizes of ∠ABT and ∠ATB.

(b) Calculate the length of wire BT.

(c) Calculate the height of pole TC.

Which Formula should I use ?

What you are given	What you should use
A side & the angle opposite this side	**the Sine Rule** $$\frac{a}{\sin A} = \frac{b}{\sin B} = \frac{c}{\sin C}$$
Two sides and the angle between the two sides	**the Cosine Rule** $$a^2 = b^2 + c^2 - 2bc\cos A$$
All three sides	**the Cosine Rule** $$\cos A = \frac{b^2 + c^2 - a^2}{2bc}$$
Two sides and the angle between the two sides (area required)	**Area of a Triangle** $$\text{Area} = \tfrac{1}{2}ab\sin C$$

Exercise 8·8

Answer to 3 significant figures each time here.

1. Calculate the **area** of these triangles :-

   (a)
   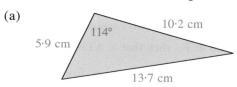

   (b)
   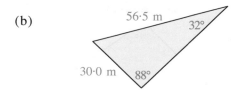

2. In $\triangle PQR$, find the length of the line **PQ**.

   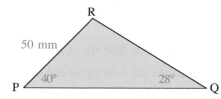

3. Calculate the size of $\angle BCA$.

   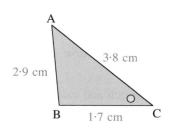

4. Calculate the length of the line **YZ**.

   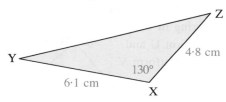

5. Calculate the size of $\angle DEF$.
   (*Think carefully about this one*).

   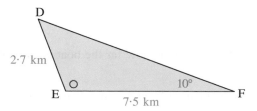

6. The area of a triangle GTD is 9130 cm².
   GT = 240 cm and TD = 80 cm.

   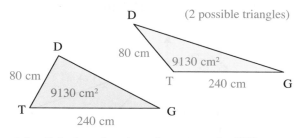

   (a) Calculate the size of **acute** angle GTD.

   (b) If angle GTD is **obtuse**, calculate its size.

7. A pulley system is used to raise objects up to the top of a high building.

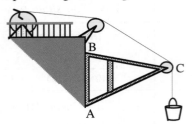

The triangular metal structure, ABC, is used to support the small pulley wheel.

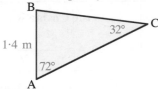

Calculate the length of the bar AC.

8. Two oil platforms in the North Sea are 70 miles apart. Platform U is on a bearing of 250° from platform V.

A rowing boat is spotted on a bearing of 025° from platform U and 320° from platform V.

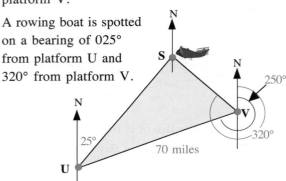

(a) Show that ∠USV = 65°.

(b) Now calculate how far the boat is from V.

9. A rescue boat, at R, picks up a distress call from a boat B, 35 km away, on a bearing of 120°.

At the same time, another distress call comes from a yacht Y, which is 17 km away from B and on a bearing of 220° from B.

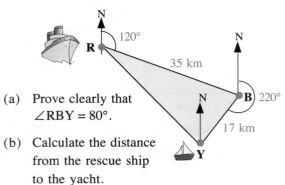

(a) Prove clearly that ∠RBY = 80°.

(b) Calculate the distance from the rescue ship to the yacht.

10. The diagram below shows the goalposts on an American Football field.
LP is perpendicular to the touchline, LN.

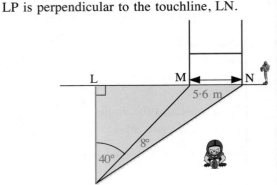

∠LPM = 40° and ∠MPN = 8°.
The distance MN between the goalposts is 5·6 metres.
To kick for goal, the kicker walks straight out from L to P.

Calculate the distance LP.

(Hint - find ∠PMN and the side PM first).

11. A coastguard at A is 19 kilometres due west of a coastguard at B.

In relation to the two coastguards, a tanker is spotted at T, such that ∠ATB = 78°.

The tanker is 13·7 km away from point A.

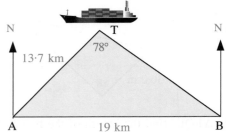

(a) Calculate the size of ∠TBA, then ∠TAB.

(b) Calculate the bearing of the tanker from A.

(c) Calculate the bearing of the tanker from B.

12. Two ships leave port together.

One sails on a course of 030° at 9 mph.

The other sails on a course of 090° at 12 mph.

Make a neat sketch and calculate how far apart they will be after 5 hours.

Remember Remember..... ?

Answer to 3 significant figures.

1. Calculate the **area** of these triangles :-

    (a)

    (b)

    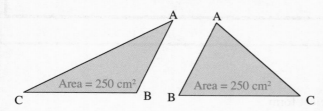

2. The area of a triangle ABC is 250 cm².

    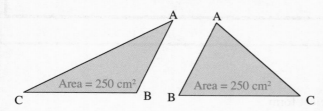

    AB = 20 cm and BC = 50 cm.

    Calculate **two** possible sizes for angle ABC.

3. Determine the size of obtuse ∠EFD.

    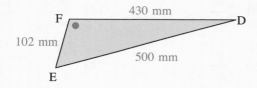

4. Find the length of the line **PR**.

    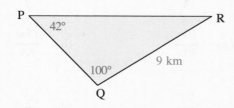

5. Calculate the length of the line **TU**.

    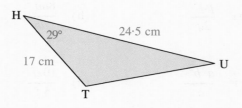

6. Determine the size of ∠GBC.

    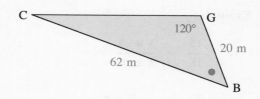

7. A statue lies directly East of a large palm tree. Treasure is buried **below ground** at an angle of 25° to the palm tree and at an angle of 34° to the statue as shown below.

    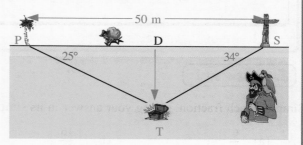

    The distance from the palm tree to the statue is 50 metres.

    (a) Calculate the distance from P to T.

    (b) Calculate how deep the pirate would have to go if he started at D and dug vertically down to the treasure at T.

8. A ship leaves N and sails to M on a course bearing 070°.

    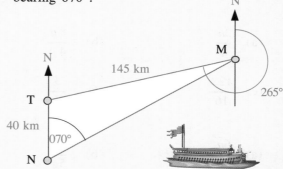

    At M, the ship changes course and sails on a bearing of 265° to T directly North of N.

    (a) Explain why ∠NTM = 95°.

    (b) If NT = 40 km and TM = 145 km, calculate the distance from M to N.

Simplifying Fractions - Reducing Fractions to their Simplest Form

Examples :-

1. $\dfrac{15}{18} = \dfrac{3 \times 5}{3 \times 6} = \dfrac{5}{6}$

2. $\dfrac{a^3}{a} = \dfrac{a \times a \times a}{a} = a^2$

3. $\dfrac{2p}{8p^2} = \dfrac{2 \times p}{8 \times p \times p} = \dfrac{1}{4p}$

4. $\dfrac{m^5}{m^2} = \dfrac{m \times m \times m \times m \times m}{m \times m} = m^3$

5. $\dfrac{(x-2)^2}{(x-2)^3} = \dfrac{(x-2)(x-2)}{(x-2)(x-2)(x-2)} = \dfrac{1}{(x-2)}$

Exercise 9·1

Simplify each fraction, giving your answer in its **simplest** form :-

1. (a) $\dfrac{6}{8}$ (b) $\dfrac{16}{20}$ (c) $\dfrac{25}{45}$ (d) $\dfrac{12}{30}$

    (e) $\dfrac{24}{72}$ (f) $\dfrac{21}{56}$ (g) $\dfrac{33}{110}$ (h) $\dfrac{3}{57}$.

2. (a) $\dfrac{y^2}{y}$ (b) $\dfrac{a^3}{a}$ (c) $\dfrac{b}{b^2}$ (d) $\dfrac{w^5}{w^5}$

    (e) $\dfrac{p}{p^4}$ (f) $\dfrac{q^2}{q^5}$ (g) $\dfrac{g}{g^7}$ (h) $\dfrac{t^8}{t^5}$.

3. (a) $\dfrac{3u}{u}$ (b) $\dfrac{8p}{4p}$ (c) $\dfrac{12x}{3}$ (d) $\dfrac{11d}{d}$

    (e) $\dfrac{12x}{16}$ (f) $\dfrac{3}{6k}$ (g) $\dfrac{10y}{50y}$ (h) $\dfrac{15m}{65}$.

4. (a) $\dfrac{6a^2}{a}$ (b) $\dfrac{g^2}{5g}$ (c) $\dfrac{9x}{6x^2}$ (d) $\dfrac{pq}{q}$

    (e) $\dfrac{xy^2}{y}$ (f) $\dfrac{xy^2}{x}$ (g) $\dfrac{pq^2}{2q}$ (h) $\dfrac{8ab^2}{ab}$.

5. (a) $\dfrac{p^2q}{p}$ (b) $\dfrac{p^2q}{q}$ (c) $\dfrac{a^3b^2}{a}$ (d) $\dfrac{10ef}{5f}$

5.   (e) $\dfrac{a^3 m}{ma^3}$ (f) $\dfrac{g^2 h^2}{gh}$ (g) $\dfrac{m^2 n^3}{n^2}$ (h) $\dfrac{12x^2 y}{18xy}$.

6.   (a) $\dfrac{(a + 3)^2}{(a + 3)}$ (b) $\dfrac{(b - 2)^2}{(b - 2)^3}$ (c) $\dfrac{(c - 4)^4}{(c - 4)}$ (d) $\dfrac{(d + 1)^3}{(d + 1)^2}$

    (e) $\dfrac{(e - 6)^4}{(e - 6)^2}$ (f) $\dfrac{(f + 7)^3}{(f + 7)^6}$ (g) $\dfrac{(2a - 1)^2}{(2a - 1)^3}$ (h) $\dfrac{(2 + 5x)^3}{(2 + 5x)^3}$

    (i) $\dfrac{(5 - w)^2}{(5 - w)}$ (j) $\dfrac{(3 - 4v)}{(3 - 4v)^3}$ (k) $\dfrac{(9 + t)^3}{(9 + t)}$ (l) $\dfrac{(a^2 + 1)^2}{(a^2 + 1)^3}$

    (m) $\dfrac{(4 - 3x^2)^3}{(4 - 3x^2)^5}$ (n) $\dfrac{(p^2 - 2p + 1)^3}{(p^2 - 2p + 1)^2}$ (o) $\dfrac{2(8 - q)}{q(8 - q)}$ (p) $\dfrac{h^2}{h^2(h + j)}$.

7.   (a) $\dfrac{(x + 1)(x + 2)}{(x + 1)}$ (b) $\dfrac{(p - 2)(p + 3)}{(p - 2)}$ (c) $\dfrac{(2a - 1)}{(a + 3)(2a - 1)}$

    (d) $\dfrac{(2q + 1)^2}{(2q + 1)(q - 5)}$ (e) $\dfrac{(m + 2)(m - 3)}{(m - 3)(m + 1)}$ (f) $\dfrac{(k - 7)(k + 7)}{(k + 7)(k - 7)}$

    (g) $\dfrac{(3x + 7)^2}{(3x + 6)(3x + 7)}$ (h) $\dfrac{(1 - 2p)(1 + 3p)^3}{(1 + 3p)^2(1 - 2p)^2}$ (i) $\dfrac{6(1 + x)(1 - x)^2}{9(1 + x)^2(1 - x)}$.

Factorising ...... and Simplifying Fractions

Revising Factorisation

Common Factor	Difference of 2 Squares	Trinomials
$pa + pb$	$x^2 - y^2$	$x^2 - 4x + 3$
$= p(a + b)$	$= (x - y)(x + y)$	$= (x - 1)(x - 3)$

Examples :-

1. $\dfrac{2p + 8}{10}$

    $= \dfrac{2(p + 4)}{10}$

    $= \dfrac{p + 4}{5}$

2. $\dfrac{a^2 - ab}{3a - 3b}$

    $= \dfrac{a(a - b)}{3(a - b)}$

    $= \dfrac{a}{3}$

3. $\dfrac{x^2 - 6x + 5}{x^2 - 1}$

    $= \dfrac{(x - 1)(x - 5)}{(x - 1)(x + 1)}$

    $= \dfrac{x - 5}{x + 1}$

1. Revision - Factorise fully :-

(a) $a^2 - 6a$

(b) $p^2 - 9$

(c) $y^2 + 9y + 8$

(d) $12q - 18$

(e) $x^2 - 8x + 16$

(f) $k^2 + k - 6$

(g) $2v^2 - 7v - 4$

(h) $4d^2 - 100$.

In the following questions, factorise fully, then simplify :-

2. (a) $\dfrac{3a - 6}{9}$

(b) $\dfrac{4}{4b - 20}$

(c) $\dfrac{8}{8p + 8}$

(d) $\dfrac{2q - 10}{2q + 10}$.

3. (a) $\dfrac{x + 2}{4x + 8}$

(b) $\dfrac{u - 2}{2u - 4}$

(c) $\dfrac{3 - 3m}{1 - m}$

(d) $\dfrac{a^2 - ab}{7a - 7b}$.

4. (a) $\dfrac{k - 2}{k^2 - 2k}$

(b) $\dfrac{c - 3}{c^2 - 9}$

(c) $\dfrac{3g + 15}{g^2 - 25}$

(d) $\dfrac{9x^2 + 9x}{9x}$.

5. (a) $\dfrac{x - 2}{x^2 - 3x + 2}$

(b) $\dfrac{x^2 + 6x + 9}{x + 3}$

(c) $\dfrac{x^2 + 5x}{x^2 + 4x - 5}$.

6. (a) $\dfrac{4x^2 - 9x + 2}{x - 2}$

(b) $\dfrac{x^2 - 1}{x^2 + 8x + 7}$

(c) $\dfrac{3x^2 - 3y^2}{x^2 - 2xy + y^2}$.

7. (a) $\dfrac{x^2 + 2x - 15}{5x + 25}$

(b) $\dfrac{3x^2 + 11x - 4}{2x + 8}$

(c) $\dfrac{10x - 5}{2x^2 - 3x + 1}$.

8. (a) $\dfrac{x^2 - 5x + 6}{x^2 - 2x - 3}$

(b) $\dfrac{4x^2 + 2x - 6}{2x^2 - 4x + 2}$

(c) $\dfrac{px + py}{x^2 - y^2}$.

9. (a) $\dfrac{m - m^2}{m^3 - m^2}$

(b) $\dfrac{p^2 - 4pq + 4q^2}{(p - 2q)^2}$

(c) $\dfrac{u^4 - 1}{u^2 - 1}$.

Algebraic Fractions - Addition and Subtraction

Examples :-

1. lcm of 3 & 4 is 12

$$\frac{3}{4} - \frac{1}{3} = \frac{9}{12} - \frac{4}{12} = \frac{5}{12}$$

2. lcm is x

$$\frac{4}{x} + \frac{5}{x} = \frac{4 + 5}{x} = \frac{9}{x}$$

3. lcm is $a \times b$

$$\frac{6}{a} - \frac{2}{b} = \frac{6 \times b}{a \times b} - \frac{2 \times a}{a \times b} = \frac{6b}{ab} - \frac{2a}{ab} = \frac{6b - 2a}{ab}$$

4. lcm is $p \times q$

$$\frac{p}{q} - \frac{q}{p} = \frac{p \times p}{p \times q} - \frac{q \times q}{p \times q} = \frac{p^2}{pq} - \frac{q^2}{pq} = \frac{p^2 - q^2}{pq}$$

5. lcm is $5x \times x$

$$\frac{4}{5x} + \frac{1}{x^2} = \frac{4 \times x}{5x \times x} + \frac{5 \times 1}{5x \times x} = \frac{4x}{5x^2} + \frac{5}{5x^2} = \frac{4x + 5}{5x^2}$$

Simplify these expressions :-

1. (a) $\dfrac{1}{7} + \dfrac{3}{7}$ (b) $\dfrac{2}{3} - \dfrac{1}{8}$ (c) $\dfrac{5}{6} - \dfrac{1}{4}$ (d) $\dfrac{7}{12} + \dfrac{3}{8}$.

2. (a) $\dfrac{3}{p} + \dfrac{5}{p}$ (b) $\dfrac{8}{m} - \dfrac{2}{m}$ (c) $\dfrac{6}{x} - \dfrac{1}{y}$ (d) $\dfrac{4}{v} + \dfrac{11}{w}$

   (e) $\dfrac{3}{m} + \dfrac{7}{n}$ (f) $\dfrac{9}{c} - \dfrac{8}{d}$ (g) $\dfrac{5}{d} - \dfrac{4}{3d}$ (h) $\dfrac{v}{3} - \dfrac{2w}{4}$.

3. (a) $\dfrac{3}{2m} - \dfrac{2}{5n}$ (b) $\dfrac{4}{5x} + \dfrac{1}{2y}$ (c) $\dfrac{5}{8a} - \dfrac{2}{3s}$ (d) $\dfrac{3}{4e} + \dfrac{7}{12h}$.

4. (a) $\dfrac{r}{s} + \dfrac{s}{r}$ (b) $\dfrac{b}{c} - \dfrac{c}{b}$ (c) $\dfrac{5x}{a} + \dfrac{3x}{b}$ (d) $\dfrac{p}{2a} - \dfrac{q}{4a}$.

5. (a) $\dfrac{2}{a^2} + \dfrac{3}{a}$ (b) $\dfrac{1}{g^2} - \dfrac{1}{g}$ (c) $\dfrac{7}{x} - \dfrac{2}{x^2}$ (d) $\dfrac{5}{t^2} - \dfrac{5}{t}$

   (e) $\dfrac{4}{m^2} - \dfrac{2}{5m}$ (f) $\dfrac{9}{4b} - \dfrac{6}{5b^2}$ (g) $\dfrac{2x}{3y} - \dfrac{5y}{4x}$ (h) $\dfrac{g}{6h} + \dfrac{5h}{9g}$.

More Complicated Examples :-

1. $\dfrac{2x+1}{2} - \dfrac{x-1}{3}$ lcm is 6

   $= \dfrac{3(2x+1)}{6} - \dfrac{2(x-1)}{6}$

   $= \dfrac{6x+3}{6} - \dfrac{2x-2}{6}$

   $= \dfrac{6x+3-(2x-2)}{6}$ Watch double $-ve$

   $= \dfrac{4x+5}{6}$

2. $\dfrac{3}{x+1} + \dfrac{1}{x-2}$ lcm is $(x+1)(x-2)$

   $= \dfrac{3(x-2)}{(x+1)(x-2)} + \dfrac{1(x+1)}{(x+1)(x-2)}$

   $= \dfrac{3(x-2)+1(x+1)}{(x+1)(x-2)}$

   $= \dfrac{3x-6+x+1}{(x+1)(x-2)}$

   $= \dfrac{4x-5}{(x+1)(x-2)}$

---

6. (a) $\dfrac{a+1}{3} + \dfrac{a-1}{2}$ (b) $\dfrac{p+3}{4} + \dfrac{p-2}{3}$ (c) $\dfrac{w+4}{8} + \dfrac{w+1}{4}$

   (d) $\dfrac{x-2}{4} + \dfrac{x+6}{5}$ (e) $\dfrac{g+1}{6} + \dfrac{g+2}{9}$ (f) $\dfrac{h-1}{2} + \dfrac{h-3}{4}$.

7. (a) $\dfrac{x+4}{2} - \dfrac{x+1}{3}$ (b) $\dfrac{w+5}{2} - \dfrac{w-3}{5}$ (c) $\dfrac{p-1}{3} - \dfrac{p+1}{4}$

   (d) $\dfrac{2a+1}{6} - \dfrac{a-1}{3}$ (e) $\dfrac{2v-1}{4} - \dfrac{3v-2}{6}$ (f) $\dfrac{4k+5}{9} - \dfrac{3k-4}{6}$.

8. (a) $\dfrac{4}{x+1} + \dfrac{1}{x+2}$ (b) $\dfrac{2}{x-2} + \dfrac{3}{x-3}$ (c) $\dfrac{5}{x-1} + \dfrac{2}{x+4}$

(d) $\dfrac{6}{x+2} - \dfrac{1}{x+1}$ (e) $\dfrac{5}{x-2} - \dfrac{3}{x+1}$ (f) $\dfrac{1}{x-7} - \dfrac{5}{x-1}$.

9. Try these :-

(a) $\dfrac{2}{x} + \dfrac{1}{x-1}$ (b) $\dfrac{5}{x} - \dfrac{1}{x-3}$ (c) $\dfrac{7}{x-2} + \dfrac{2}{x}$

(d) $\dfrac{8}{x} - \dfrac{6}{x^2}$ (e) $\dfrac{x-1}{x^2} + \dfrac{7}{x}$ (f) $\dfrac{4}{x} - \dfrac{x-2}{x^2}$

(g) $\dfrac{9}{x} - \dfrac{2-x}{x^2}$ (h) $\dfrac{a}{a-5} + \dfrac{a}{5-a}$ (i) $\dfrac{x}{2-x} - \dfrac{x}{x-2}$.

10. Solve these equations in **TWO** ways :-

(i) by adding or subtracting the fractions on the left hand side of the equation first,

(ii) by multiplying through the whole equation by the l.c.m. of the denominators.

(a) $\dfrac{x+2}{3} + \dfrac{x+3}{4} = 1$ (b) $\dfrac{2x-1}{5} + \dfrac{x+2}{10} = 3$

(c) $\dfrac{x-1}{2} - \dfrac{x-2}{5} = 1$ (d) $\dfrac{3x-5}{6} - \dfrac{x-7}{3} = 4$.

Which method did you find easier .... (i) or (ii) ?

Algebraic Fractions - Multiplication and Division

Examples :-

> Before dividing fractions, change to a multiplication first

1. $\dfrac{3}{4} \times \dfrac{2}{7}$

$= \dfrac{3 \times 2}{4 \times 7}$

$= \dfrac{6}{28}$

$= \dfrac{3}{14}$

2. $\dfrac{5x}{6} \times \dfrac{8}{x^2}$

$= \dfrac{5 \times \cancel{x} \times 8}{6 \times \cancel{x} \times x}$

$= \dfrac{40}{6x}$

$= \dfrac{20}{3x}$

3. $\dfrac{7}{10} \div \dfrac{14}{5}$

$= \dfrac{7}{10} \times \dfrac{5}{14}$

$= \dfrac{7 \times 5}{10 \times 14}$

$= \dfrac{35}{140}$

$= \dfrac{1}{4}$

4. $\dfrac{2pq}{3} \div \dfrac{6p}{q}$

$= \dfrac{2pq}{3} \times \dfrac{q}{6p}$

$= \dfrac{2 \times \cancel{p} \times q \times q}{3 \times 6 \times \cancel{p}}$

$= \dfrac{2q^2}{18}$

$= \dfrac{q^2}{9}$

Work out the following multiplications and divisions, giving each answer in its simplest form :-

1. (a) $\dfrac{2}{3} \times \dfrac{3}{7}$ (b) $\dfrac{3}{5} \times \dfrac{7}{9}$ (c) $\dfrac{5}{8} \times \dfrac{4}{5}$ (d) $\dfrac{5}{10} \times \dfrac{8}{25}$.

2. (a) $\dfrac{1}{2} \div \dfrac{5}{2}$ (b) $\dfrac{3}{4} \div \dfrac{5}{6}$ (c) $\dfrac{3}{5} \div \dfrac{9}{25}$ (d) $\dfrac{32}{7} \div \dfrac{12}{21}$.

3. (a) $\dfrac{p}{4} \times \dfrac{p}{2}$ (b) $\dfrac{5}{a} \times \dfrac{2}{a}$ (c) $\dfrac{x}{6} \times \dfrac{2}{x}$ (d) $\dfrac{3c}{7} \times \dfrac{14}{c}$

   (e) $\dfrac{3}{8k} \times \dfrac{2k}{21}$ (f) $\dfrac{5g}{3} \times \dfrac{4g}{10}$ (g) $\dfrac{4v}{5w} \times \dfrac{25}{6v}$ (h) $\dfrac{9t}{2s} \times \dfrac{8s}{6}$.

4. (a) $\dfrac{a}{4} \div \dfrac{a}{8}$ (b) $\dfrac{1}{x} \div \dfrac{3}{x}$ (c) $\dfrac{p}{5} \div \dfrac{2}{p}$ (d) $\dfrac{3m}{7} \div \dfrac{15m}{56}$

   (e) $\dfrac{7b}{3} \div \dfrac{7b}{9}$ (f) $\dfrac{4}{w} \div \dfrac{2}{9w}$ (g) $\dfrac{8k}{6} \div \dfrac{4}{3k}$ (h) $\dfrac{11}{9d} \div \dfrac{11d}{18d}$.

5. (a) $\dfrac{a^2}{3} \times \dfrac{1}{a}$ (b) $\dfrac{b}{7} \times \dfrac{7}{b^2}$ (c) $\dfrac{6g^2}{4} \times \dfrac{12}{3g}$ (d) $\dfrac{pq}{2} \times \dfrac{q}{p}$

   (e) $\dfrac{12v}{w} \times \dfrac{vw}{4}$ (f) $\dfrac{n^2}{m} \times \dfrac{m}{n}$ (g) $\dfrac{k^3}{9} \times \dfrac{54}{2k}$ (h) $\dfrac{2q^3}{r} \times \dfrac{5r}{2q^4}$.

6. (a) $\dfrac{m^3}{6} \div \dfrac{m^2}{3}$ (b) $\dfrac{p}{2q} \div \dfrac{p}{8q}$ (c) $\dfrac{k^2}{n} \div \dfrac{k}{n^2}$ (d) $\dfrac{1}{b^2} \div \dfrac{5}{b}$

   (e) $\dfrac{h^2}{t} \div \dfrac{9h}{3t}$ (f) $\dfrac{x^2}{y} \div \dfrac{5x^2}{y}$ (g) $\dfrac{18v^3}{w} \div \dfrac{9v}{w^2}$ (h) $\dfrac{4a^2q}{3} \div \dfrac{a}{12q}$.

7. (a) $\dfrac{7y}{24x^2} \times \dfrac{6x}{49y}$ (b) $\dfrac{2p^2}{5} \div \dfrac{p^3}{10}$ (c) $\dfrac{5mn^2}{2} \times \dfrac{6}{45mn}$

   (d) $\dfrac{(1+a)^4}{(1+b)^2} \times \dfrac{(1+b)}{(1+a)^3}$ (e) $\dfrac{(8-h)^2}{(8-4k)^4} \div \dfrac{(8-h)^3}{(8-4k)^3}$.

8. Calculate the **area** of the square and the rectangle.

   (a)   (b)

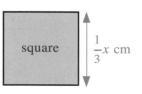

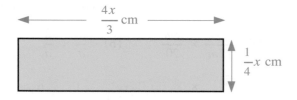

9. The area of this triangle is $\dfrac{(a+1)}{2}$ cm^2 .

   If the height of the triangle is $\dfrac{1}{a}$ cm , find its **breadth** in terms of a.

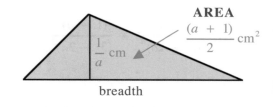

Remember Remember..... ?

1. **Simplify** each fraction, giving your answer in its **simplest form** :-

   (a) $\dfrac{a^2 b}{a}$

   (b) $\dfrac{5m^2 n}{15mn}$

   (c) $\dfrac{g^2}{g^2(g + h)}$

   (d) $\dfrac{(3q + 1)^2}{(3q + 1)(q - 7)}$.

2. **Factorise** these expressions **fully**, then simplify :-

   (a) $\dfrac{6x - 3}{3}$

   (b) $\dfrac{p + 7}{4p + 28}$

   (c) $\dfrac{5a + 35}{a^2 - 49}$

   (d) $\dfrac{m^2 - mn}{9m - 9n}$

   (e) $\dfrac{x - 2}{x^2 + x - 6}$

   (f) $\dfrac{y^2 - 1}{y^2 - 7y + 6}$

   (g) $\dfrac{x^2 + 3x - 10}{3x - 6}$

   (h) $\dfrac{5 - 6w + w^2}{25 - w^2}$

   (i) $\dfrac{a^2 - 3a - 4}{a^2 + 6a + 5}$

   (j) $\dfrac{6v^2 - v - 1}{2v^2 - 9v + 4}$

   (k) $\dfrac{p^2 - 2pq - 3q^2}{(p - 3q)^2}$.

3. **Simplify** :-

   (a) $\dfrac{6}{x} - \dfrac{1}{y}$

   (b) $\dfrac{1}{g^2} - \dfrac{1}{g}$

   (c) $\dfrac{7}{x} - \dfrac{2}{x^2}$

   (d) $\dfrac{x}{2y} - \dfrac{3y}{4x}$

   (e) $\dfrac{1}{2a} + \dfrac{1}{3a} - \dfrac{3}{4a}$

   (f) $\dfrac{1}{c^2} - \dfrac{1}{c} - 1$

   (g) $1 - \dfrac{1}{x}$

   (h) $\dfrac{x - 1}{4} + \dfrac{x + 2}{5}$

   (i) $\dfrac{2p + 1}{6} - \dfrac{p - 2}{3}$

   (j) $\dfrac{6}{x - 2} - \dfrac{2}{x + 1}$

   (k) $\dfrac{p}{p + q} - \dfrac{q}{p - q}$

   (l) $\dfrac{2}{x^2 - 1} + \dfrac{1}{x + 1}$

   (m) $\dfrac{3}{a^2 + 4a + 3} + \dfrac{1}{a + 3}$.

4. **Simplify fully** these multiplications and divisions :-

   (a) $\dfrac{5}{12m} \times \dfrac{3m}{20}$

   (b) $\dfrac{5}{a} \times \dfrac{2}{a}$

   (c) $\dfrac{2a^3}{c} \times \dfrac{3c^2}{6a^4}$

   (d) $\dfrac{3xy^2}{2} \times \dfrac{6}{27xy}$

   (e) $\dfrac{2}{x} \div \dfrac{8}{x}$

   (f) $\dfrac{1}{a^2} \div \dfrac{6}{a}$

   (g) $\dfrac{21p^3}{q} \div \dfrac{3p}{q^2}$

   (h) $\dfrac{5m^2 n}{2} \div \dfrac{m}{20n^2}$

   (i) $\dfrac{(1 - a)^2}{(3 + 2a)^4} \div \dfrac{(1 - a)^5}{(3 + 2a)^2}$

   (j) $\dfrac{(2 - x)^4}{(12 - 6x)^3} \div \dfrac{(2 - x)^3}{(12 - 6x)^2}$.

1. Factorise fully :–

(a) $3x - 9y$

(b) $42xy + 35y$

(c) $16x^2y - 12xy$

(d) $xyz - xy^2z + xz^2$

(e) $5y^2 - 10y^3$

(f) $x^2 + x - 12$

(g) $x^2 - 2x - 15$

(h) $x^2 + 9x + 14$

(i) $x^2 - 5x - 24$

(j) $x^2 - x - 110$

(k) $2x^2 + 7x + 3$

(l) $3x^2 + x - 10$

(m) $3x^2 - 12$

(n) $16x^4 - 81$.

2. Which of the three triangles below has the largest area ?

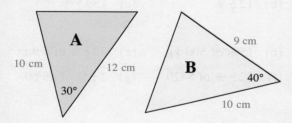

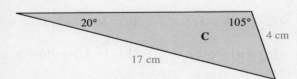

3. Find the size of the obtuse angle ABC.

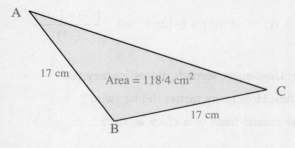

Area = 118·4 cm²

4. Find the value of x in each of the following :-

(a)

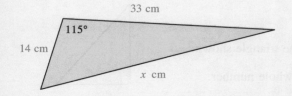

4. (b)

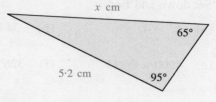

(c)

5. *Do not use a scale drawing for this question.*

During an army exercise, Platoon A left HQ and hiked 6 km due North. From HQ Platoon B hiked 5 km on a 070° bearing.

(a) *Sketch* the above information.

(b) How far are platoon A from B ?

(c) What is the bearing from :-

(i) A to B

(ii) B to A ?

6. Factorise fully :-

(a) $a^2 + 2a$

(b) $16t^2 - t$

(c) $25k^2 - 49$

(d) $300g^4 - 48g^2$

(e) $x^2 - x + 56$

(f) $x^2 - 3x - 18$

(g) $3x^2 - 5x - 2$

h $8x^2 + 2x - 6$.

7. Simplify each fraction in its simplest form :-

(a) $\dfrac{4x + 1}{2} + \dfrac{2x - 3}{3}$

(b) $\dfrac{6x + 3}{3} + \dfrac{x^2 - 4}{x + 2}$

(c) $\dfrac{x^2 + 3x - 28}{x + 7} + \dfrac{2x^2 - 32}{2x + 8}$

(d) $\dfrac{x^2 - x - 42}{x^2 + 7x + 6} \div \dfrac{x^2 - 10x + 21}{x^2 - 2x - 3}$.

1. Set down and find :-

   (a) $5^4 - 4^5$ 　　　 (b) $34\,400 \div 40$ 　　　 (c) $25 - 7 \times (6 - 4)$ 　　　 (d) $24 \div (3 + 5) + 17$

   (e) $4000 \times 0{\cdot}145$ 　 (f) $326 \div 200$ 　　　 (g) $\dfrac{6 \times 14{\cdot}4}{1000}$ 　　　 (h) $66{\cdot}6 \div 20\,000$.

2. Change :- 　　　 (a) $40\,000$ ml to litres 　 (b) $0{\cdot}006$ km to cm 　 (c) 54 g to kg

   (d) 36 mm to km 　　 (e) 1700 mm to km 　 (f) 130 hrs to seconds 　 (g) 36 km/hr to m/sec.

3. Find :- 　　　 (a) $\frac{2}{5}$ of 635 　　 (b) $\frac{5}{8}$ of 604 　　 (c) $\frac{11}{15}$ of 600.

4. Simplify :- 　　　 (a) $\frac{8}{96}$ 　　　 (b) $\frac{14}{96}$ 　　　 (c) $\frac{16}{640}$.

5. Find :- 　　　 (a) $\frac{3}{4} - \frac{2}{5}$ 　　 (b) $5\frac{1}{4} + 2\frac{3}{8}$ 　　 (c) $4 \times 5\frac{5}{6}$.

6. Express as a fraction :- 　 (a) 60% 　　 (b) $12\frac{1}{2}\%$ 　　 (c) $133\frac{1}{3}\%$.
   (*in its simplest form*)

7. Find :- 　　　 (a) 20% of £340 　 (b) 15% of 500 kg 　 (c) $33\frac{1}{3}\%$ of $6{\cdot}9$ m

   (d) $\frac{1}{2}\%$ of 3 kg 　 (e) $17{\cdot}5\%$ of 240 ml 　 (f) $12\frac{1}{2}\%$ of \$420 　 (g) $2\frac{1}{2}\%$ of £9·60.

8. Find :- 　　　 (a) $22 + (-33)$ 　 (b) $354 + (-46)$ 　 (c) $(-55) + 76$

   (d) $(-13) + (-34)$ 　 (e) $116 - 164$ 　 (f) $(-34) - 111$ 　 (g) $34 - (-27)$

   (h) $(-312) - (-144)$ 　 (i) $(-8) \times 17$ 　 (j) $(-x) - (-x)$ 　 (k) $(-3y) - 36y - y$

   (l) $(-7) \times 13$ 　 (m) $(-1)^{25}$ 　 (n) $(-6) \times (-6)$ 　 (o) $(-650) \div 5$

   (p) $(-24x) \times (-2x)$ 　 (q) $320y \div (-8y)$ 　 (r) $(-750p) \div (-15p)$ 　 (s) $\dfrac{(-3) \times (-15)}{(-5)}$.

9. (a) A tortoise travels 12 m at 10 metres per minute. How many seconds did its journey take ?

   (b) Alex swims at 1·4 metres per second for 2 minutes. How many metres did he swim ?

   (c) Find the acute angle between the hour hand and minute hand of a clock at 1315.

10. (a) State the gradient and y-intercept of :- 　　 (i) $y = 3 - x$ 　　 (ii) $3y + x + 1 = 0$.

    (b) Sketch each of the lines in part (a).

11. (a) Given that $\sin 30° = \frac{1}{2}$, find the value of x in the triangle shown.

    (b) Find the length of the other side to the nearest whole number.

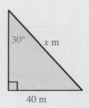

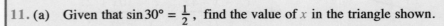

Chapter 10

Changing the Subject of a Formula ▢▢▢▢▢

Changing the Subject of a Formula (1)

Examples :- Change the subject of the formula to the letter shown in the bracket :-

1. $a + b = c$ (a)

    $a = c - b$ change side - change sign

2. $p = q + r$ (q)

    $q + r = p$ common sense line

    $q = p - r$ change side - change sign

3. $h = \dfrac{m}{n}$ (m)

    $\dfrac{h}{1} = \dfrac{m}{n}$ set up

    $m = hn$ cross multiply

4. $V = RS$ (S)

    $RS = V$ common sense line

    $S = \dfrac{V}{R}$ divide by R

5. $2y + u = w$ (y)

    $2y = w - u$ change side - change sign

    $y = \dfrac{w - u}{2}$ divide by 2

Exercise 10·1

In Questions 1 - 4, change the subject of the given formula to x :-

1. (a) $x - c = b$
    (b) $x + 5 = y$
    (c) $x + r = s$
    (d) $x - a = p$

    (e) $g = x + h$
    (f) $m = x - t$
    (g) $7 = c - x$
    (h) $k = l - x$.

2. (a) $\dfrac{x}{p} = q$
    (b) $\dfrac{x}{9} = m$
    (c) $\dfrac{x}{3} = 10$
    (d) $\dfrac{x}{n} = r$

    (e) $k = \dfrac{l}{x}$
    (f) $\dfrac{x}{g} = \dfrac{h}{4}$
    (g) $\dfrac{x}{a} = \dfrac{b}{c}$
    (h) $\dfrac{v}{w} = \dfrac{d}{4x}$.

3. (a) $2x + 5 = a$
    (b) $4x + p = q$
    (c) $5x - q = r$
    (d) $7x - y = m$

    (e) $ax + b = w$
    (f) $g = cx + 2$
    (g) $b = mx + q$
    (h) $e = v - wx$.

4. (a) $\dfrac{x + 1}{2} = 5$
    (b) $\dfrac{x + 1}{2} = y$
    (c) $\dfrac{x - 5}{2} = 3$
    (d) $\dfrac{x - 7}{4} = g$

    (e) $\dfrac{x + 2}{b} = c$
    (f) $\dfrac{x - 9}{r} = s$
    (g) $\dfrac{x - k}{d} = e$
    (h) $w = \dfrac{t + x}{v}$.

5. (a) The formula for the perimeter of this rectangle is $P = 2a + 2b$.

    Change the formula to b .

    (b) The formula for its area is $A = ab$

    Change the formula to b .

6. The formula for changing miles (M) into kilometres (K) is

$$M = \frac{5K}{8}$$

Change the subject of the formula to K.

7.

2w cm

The perimeter of this square of side $2w$ cm is given by the formula

$$P = 8w$$

(a) Change the subject to w.

(b) Calculate the length of a side of such a square with perimeter 480 cm.

8. The cost of hiring a chain saw is a one-off payment of £20, plus £7 per day.

The cost £C for n days is given by the formula $C = 20 + 7n$.

(a) Find the cost of hiring a chain saw for a fortnight.

(b) Change the subject to n and calculate n when $C = 230$.

HIRE
£20 + £7 per day

9. The cost of hiring a 4 x 4 vehicle is given by the formula

$$C = f + 6m$$

where £C is the total cost, f is a fixed amount and m is the miles travelled.

Change the subject of the formula to :-   (a) f (b) m.

10. The dimensions of a rectangle are as shown, (*in centimetres*), in the diagram below.

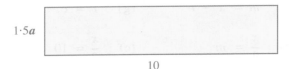

1·5a

10

(a) Write down a formula for the **perimeter**, (P cm) of the rectangle, in terms of a. $P = $ ....

(b) Change the subject of this formula to a.

11. The total cost (£T) of a party going to a football match is

$$T = 15A + 8U.$$

where A is the number of adults in the party and U is the number of children under 16 years old.

(a) Change the subject of the formula to

(i) A (ii) U.

(b) Calculate how many adults there were in a party at a match when the number of under 16's in the party was 3 and the total cost for the whole party was £144.

 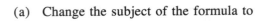

More complex examples :- Change the subject of the formula to the letter shown in the bracket :-

1. $p = a(x + n)$ (x)

   $p = ax + an$ expand bracket

   $ax + an = p$ common sense line

   $ax = p - an$ change side - change sign

   $x = \dfrac{p - an}{a}$ divide by a

2. $\dfrac{v + u}{w} = \dfrac{bw}{6}$ (v)

   $6(v + u) = bw^2$ multiply both sides by $6w$

   $6v + 6u = bw^2$ expand bracket

   $6v = bw^2 - 6u$ change side - change sign

   $v = \dfrac{bw^2 - 6u}{6}$ divide by 6

3. $p^2 = \dfrac{R}{Q}$ (p)

   $p = \sqrt{\dfrac{R}{Q}}$ square root both sides

4. $T = \frac{1}{5}k^2 h$ (k)

   $5T = k^2 h$ eliminate fraction $\times 5$

   $k^2 h = 5T$ common sense line

   $k^2 = \dfrac{5T}{h}$ divide by h

   $k = \sqrt{\dfrac{5T}{h}}$ square root both sides

5. $y = \frac{3}{4}(x + a)$ (x)

   $4y = 3(x + a)$ eliminate fraction $\times 4$

   $4y = 3x + 3a$ expand bracket

   $3x + 3a = 4y$ common sense line

   $3x = 4y - 3a$ change side - change sign

   $x = \dfrac{4y - 3a}{3}$ divide by 3

6. $m = \dfrac{5\sqrt{n}}{4}$ (n)

   $\dfrac{m}{1} = \dfrac{5\sqrt{n}}{4}$ set up

   $5\sqrt{n} = 4m$ multiply both sides by 4

   $\sqrt{n} = \dfrac{4m}{5}$ divide by 5

   $n = \dfrac{16m^2}{25}$ square both sides

Exercise 10·2

In Questions 1 - 4, change the subject of the given formula to the single letter shown in the bracket :-

1.   (a) $y = a(p + q)$ (p) (b) $k = b(c - d)$ (c) (c) $m = q(p - n)$ (n)

    (d) $k = b(c + d)$ (b) (e) $\dfrac{a - b}{c} = \dfrac{bc}{4}$ (a) (f) $\dfrac{x - y}{2} = \dfrac{p}{w}$ (y).

2.   (a) $m = kn^2$ (n) (b) $V = \pi r^2 h$ (r) (c) $p^2 + q^2 = r^2$ (p)

    (d) $a^2 = 2ab^2 + d$ (b) (e) $w = \frac{1}{2}uv^2$ (v) (f) $w = \frac{1}{4}h^3 p$ (h).

3.   (a) $b = \frac{2}{3}a$ (a) (b) $k = \frac{3}{5}l^2$ (l) (c) $V = \frac{1}{3}Ah$ (h)

    (d) $y = \frac{7}{8}x - u$ (x) (e) $g = \frac{1}{7}(k - 5)$ (k) (f) $W = \frac{3}{4}(2v + 1)$ (v).

4. (a) $g = \sqrt{f}$ (f) (b) $W = \frac{1}{4}\sqrt{v}$ (v)

    (c) $k = \frac{7\sqrt{m}}{n}$ (m) (d) $S = \sqrt{\frac{A}{\pi d}}$ (d)

    (e) $n = 2\pi\sqrt{\frac{L}{p}}$ (p) (f) $P = \frac{5}{2\sqrt{x}}$ (x) .

5. The volume of a cone with radius r cm and height h cm is given by the formula :-

    $$V = \frac{1}{3}\pi r^2 h$$

    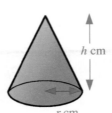

    Change the subject to r.

6. The volume of a sphere with radius r cm is given by the formula :-

    $$V = \frac{4}{3}\pi r^3$$

    Change the subject to r.

7. This tin of hot-dogs has a total surface area given by the formula :-

    $$A = 2\pi r(r + h)$$

    Change the formula to h.

More complex examples :-

When the variable you wish to make the subject appears more than once.

Example 1 :- Make x the subject :-

	$ax + b = cx + d$
(Move all the x's to left side).	$ax - cx = d - b$
(Take x out as a common factor).	$x(a - c) = d - b$
(Divide by the $(a - c)$).	$x = \dfrac{d - b}{a - c}$

Example 2 :- Make p the subject :-

	$Q = \dfrac{p + a}{p}$
(Multiply across by p).	$\Rightarrow pQ = p + a$
(Move all the p's to left side).	$\Rightarrow pQ - p = a$
(Take p out as a common factor).	$\Rightarrow p(Q - 1) = a$
(Divide through by the $Q - 1$).	$\Rightarrow p = \dfrac{a}{Q - 1}$

8. Try these harder examples. Change to x :-

    (a) $px + qx = r$ (b) $mx = nx + k$

    (c) $a(x - 2) = bx + m$ (d) $D = \dfrac{x - a}{3x}$

    (e) $g = \dfrac{h - x}{x}$ (f) $y = \dfrac{x + 1}{x - 1}$.

9. The **formula** for finding the circumference of a circle is $C = \pi d$.

    What happens to C if d :-

    (i)   **increases**   (ii)   **decreases**

    (iii) **is doubled**   (iv)   **is halved** ?

10. The **formula** for finding the area of a circle is $A = \pi r^2$.

    What happens to A if r :-

    (i)   **increases**   (ii)   **decreases**

    (iii) **is doubled**   (iv)   **is halved** ?

11. The **formula** for finding the time taken, given your speed and distance travelled is $T = \dfrac{D}{S}$.

    What happens to T if S :-

    (i)   **increases**   (ii)   **decreases**

    (iii) **is doubled**   (iv)   **is halved** ?

Remember Remember..... ?

1. Change the subject of each formula to x.

   (a) $x - g = h$ (b) $k = p - x$ (c) $y = \dfrac{v}{x}$ (d) $\dfrac{6}{w} = \dfrac{m}{3x}$

   (e) $gx + t = s$ (f) $a = b - cx$ (g) $\dfrac{x + 1}{5} = h$ (h) $m = \dfrac{p + x}{n}$

   (i) $b = a(x - c)$ (j) $V = 9x^2y$ (k) $p = \frac{1}{5}(2x + 5)$ (l) $a = \dfrac{5\sqrt{x}}{b}$.

2. (a) Write down the formula for finding the perimeter (P) of the shape shown.

   (b) Change the subject of the formula to a.

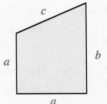

3. The equation of a straight line is $y = mx + c$.

   Change the subject of the formula to m.

4. The illumination from a light bulb is $I = \dfrac{C}{d^2}$. Change the subject to d.

5. The distance round this running track is $D = \pi x + 4x$.

   Change the subject to x.

6. The temperature in °F can be changed to °C using the formula $C = \dfrac{5}{9}(F - 32)$.

   Make F the subject of the formula.

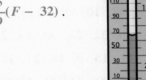

7. Change the subject of this formula to p :- $k = \dfrac{q - p}{p}$.

8. Change the formula $y = \dfrac{1 + x}{1 - x}$ so that x is the subject

9. A formula for calculating an electric current I is $I = \dfrac{nE}{R + nr}$.

   Make n the subject of this formula.

10. For the formula, $V = \dfrac{2}{w^2}$,

    (a) what happens to V if w is doubled ?

    (b) what happens to V if w is halved ?

Range, Mean, Median & Mode - a Reminder

Example :- Hazel buys 10 packets of rolos. The number of rolos in each packet is listed below.

9 7 8 6 9 7 9 10 6 9

Calculate the range, mean, median and mode.

RANGE - The **highest** number – the **lowest** number.

$$10 - 6 = 4$$

MEAN - "**Add**" all the data together and "**divide**" by the number of pieces of data.

$$\frac{9 + 7 + 8 + 6 + 9 + 7 + 9 + 10 + 6 + 9}{10} = 8$$

MEDIAN - The "**middle**" number, (*as long as the numbers are in "order"*).

6, 6, 7, 7, 8, 9, 9, 9, 9, 10

median = 8·5

MODE - The number that occurs "**most**".

6, 6, 7, 7, 8, 9, 9, 9, 9, 10

mode = 9

Exercise 11·1

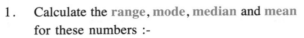

1. Calculate the **range**, **mode**, **median** and **mean** for these numbers :-

   (a) 2, 1, 3, 1, 5, 7, 16.

   (b) 4·6, 2·2, 5·3, 5·3, 4·0, 5·3, 2·7.

   (c) 107, 105, 93, 115, 105, 99.

   (d) 40, 32, 23, 30, 55, 25, 27, 40.

   (e) 11, 15, 9, 14, 21, 12, 21, 21.

   (f) 12 000, 15 000, 17 000, 15 000, 18 000.

2. Mr Davies buys 10 jars of jelly beans. He finds that they contain the following number of beans :-

   50, 52, 54, 52, 56, 50, 54, 49, 54, 54.

   (a) Calculate the **mean** number of jelly beans.

   (b) Look at the jar. Should he complain ?

   (c) Find the **median**.

   (d) What is the **mode** ?

Jelly Beans
average number
54 beans

3. The **mean** cost of 5 tyres is £48 . Four of the tyres cost £51, £44, £50 and £49. What was the cost of the fifth tyre ?

4. The table show the number of goals scored by a 3rd division football team each week.

No. of goals x	Freq f	$f \times x$
0	6	
1	12	
2	10	
3	8	
4	4	
...		...

   (a) Copy and complete the frequency table.

   (b) Find the total number of games.

   (c) Find the total number of goals scored.

   (d) Calculate the mean number of goals.

5. Here are the number of runs scored by a cricketer in his first four matches :-

   54   59   54   58

   (a) Find the mode and the median.

   (b) Which one - the mode or the median, gives the better picture of the cricketer's scoring performance ? (*Justify your answer*).

 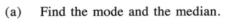

The Semi-Interquartile Range - A new Measure of Spread

Shown below are the ages of a group on a Sunday school trip.

$$2, \quad 6, \quad 6, \quad 7, \quad 7, \quad 7, \quad 7, \quad 8, \quad 8, \quad 8, \quad 10, \quad 10, \quad 11, \quad 13, \quad 25.$$

If we use the only measure of spread we have - the range - there is a slight problem.

$$\boxed{\text{Range} = \text{Highest} - \text{Lowest} = 25 - 2 = 23.}$$

- can you see that most of the children are aged 6 to 13 ?
- the Sunday school teacher is aged 25 and has her 2-year old son with her.
- the range of 23 gives a false impression of "how widely spread" the actual ages are.
- the range only concentrates on the two "end" ages and disregards all of the other ages.

We need a new measure of SPREAD which takes into account more of the numbers in the distribution.

Such a measure of spread exists - the semi-interquartile range, which we will study soon.

The Quartiles of a set of Numbers

The MEDIAN is the value that splits a distribution of ordered numbers into two equal bits.

$$2, \quad 6, \quad 6, \quad 7, \quad 7, \quad 7, \quad 7, \quad \boxed{8}, \quad 8, \quad 8, \quad 10, \quad 10, \quad 11, \quad 13, \quad 25.$$

$\longleftarrow$ 7 values $\longrightarrow$ median $\longleftarrow$ 7 values $\longrightarrow$

The QUARTILES are the 3 values that split a distribution of ordered numbers into four equal bits.

$$2, \quad 6, \quad 6, \quad \boxed{7}, \quad 7, \quad 7, \quad 7, \quad \boxed{8}, \quad 8, \quad 8, \quad 10, \quad \boxed{10}, \quad 11, \quad 13, \quad 25.$$

| $\longleftrightarrow$ | lower | $\longleftrightarrow$ | median | $\longleftrightarrow$ | upper | $\longleftrightarrow$ |
| 3 values | quartile Q_1 | 3 values | Q_2 | 3 values | quartile Q_3 | 3 values |

Can you see that, for the above group of ages,

the lower quartile $(Q_1) = 7$,   the middle quartile $(Q_2) = 8$,   the upper quartile $(Q_3) = 10$?

* the middle quartile (Q_2) is just another name for the median.

The quartiles must split up a distribution of ordered numbers in such a way that there is an equal number of values in each of the 4 "quarters" of the distribution.

Example :- Find the quartiles for the set :- 2, 3, 3, 4, 5, 5, 9, 10, 10, 10, 11, 12, 15, 17, 17, 19, 20.

Step 1 There are 17 values in the question.

This means that the **median** must be the 9th value.   => median = **10**.

2,   3,   3,   4,   5,   5,   9,   10, (10,) 10, 11, 12, 15, 17, 17, 19, 20.

Step 2 This now leaves 8 values in each half of the distribution.

The **middle** of the **LEFT** set is between the 4th and 5th value (up) => $Q_1 = \dfrac{4+5}{2} = 4.5$.

The **middle** of the **RIGHT** set is between the 4th and 5th value (down) => $Q_3 = \dfrac{15+17}{2} = 16$.

2,   3,   3,   4,   5,   5,   9,   10,   10,   10,   11,   12,   15,   17,   17,   19,   20.

4 values   4 values   4 values   4 values

$Q_1 = $ (4.5) $Q_2 = $ (10) $Q_3 = $ (16)

Exercise 11·2

1. (a) Copy the following 11 numbers. (*You should try to space them fairly widely and fairly evenly*).

8,   8,   9,   10,   10,   11,   11,   11,   12,   13,   14,

(b) Circle the **middle** value - the **median**.

(c) Forgetting this number, how many numbers are there in each of the left and the right halves ?

(d) Find the middle of the left set of numbers - the **lower quartile - Q_1**.

(e) Find the middle of the right set of numbers - the **upper quartile - Q_3**.

2. Find the **middle quartile** (the **median**), the **lower quartile** and the **upper quartile** for each of these :-

(a)   1,   3,   4,   7,   7,   9,   13.

(b)   13,   13,   15,   16,   21,   23,   24,   28,   29.

(c)   3·2,   3·5,   3·6,   3·8,   3·8,   4·0,   4·4,   4·4,   4·7,   5·3,   5·4,   5·9.

(d)   48,   51,   54,   54,   58,   64,   67,   71,   73,   78.

(e)   34,   31,   25,   35,   35,   23,   23,   40,   37,   27,   21,   29,   39.   (*order ?*)

3. Mrs Jones weighs the 65 children in Primary 7 and writes them all down in order.

Their weights, (in kilograms), are :-   34, 34, 35, 36, 36, 36, 37, ..., 50, 50, 51.

(a) Of the 65, which child's weight should be given as the **median** weight. (*the 30th, 31st, 32nd....*) ?

(b) Which of the 65 children's weights will give the **lower quartile** and which will give the **upper** ?

Quartiles - The "divide by 4" Rule

As you found in question 3, it is difficult at times, especially with a large group of numbers, to know which ones to look to for the median and quartiles. Here is a simple rule to help you :-

Step 1 Divide the **number** of values by 4. Note how many times 4 goes into it and the **remainder**.

Examples :- 17 values => $17 \div 4 = 4$ remainder **1**.

31 values => $31 \div 4 = 7$ remainder **3**.

Step 2 When you divide by 4, the answer tells you how many values are placed in each **quarter**.

Step 3 The **remainder** tells you how many extra values have to be considered $(0, 1, 2$ or $3)$

Example 1 :- **8 numbers** 2, 4, 5, 6, 8, 8, 9, 11.

$8 \div 4 = 2 \ r \ 0$ => **2** values in each quarter and **0** extra values to fit in.

2, 4, | 5, 6, | 8, 8, | 9, 11 => $Q_1 = 4 \cdot 5$, $Q_2 = 7$, $Q_3 = 8 \cdot 5$.

Example 2 :- **9 numbers** 3, 5, 6, 7, 9, 9, 10, 12, 15.

$9 \div 4 = 2 \ r \ 1$ => **2** values in each quarter and **1** extra value to fit in **symmetrically**.

3, 5, | 6, 7, 8, 8, 10, | 12, 15 => $Q_1 = 5 \cdot 5$, $Q_2 = 8$, $Q_3 = 11$.

Example 3 :- **10 numbers** 4, 6, 7, 8, 10, 10, 11, 13, 13, 16.

$10 \div 4 = 2 \ r \ 2$ => **2** values in each quarter and **2** extra values to fit in **symmetrically**.

4, 6, 7, 8, 10, | 10, 11, 13, 13, 16 => $Q_1 = 7$, $Q_2 = 10$, $Q_3 = 13$.

Example 4 :- **11 numbers** 1, 3, 4, 5, 7, 7, 8, 10, 10, 12, 14.

$11 \div 4 = 2 \ r \ 3$ => **2** values in each quarter and **3** extra values to fit in **symmetrically**.

1, 3, 4, 5, 7, 7, 8, 10, 10, 12, 14 => $Q_1 = 4$, $Q_2 = 7$, $Q_3 = 10$.

4. (a) Copy the following **18 numbers**. (*Try to space them fairly widely and fairly evenly*).

| 3, | 3, | 4, | 5, | 5, | 6, | 6, | 6, | 7, | 8, | 9, | 9, | 10, | 10, | 11, | 12, | 13, | 15. |

(b) Divide 18 by 4 => $18 \div 4 = ...$ remainder **2**.

(c) How many of the 18 values should be placed in each of the 4 quarters ?

(d) Decide where the remaining **2** values should be to maintain symmetry.

(e) Use this to determine the **lower quartile** (Q_1), **upper quartile** (Q_3) and **median** (Q_2).

5. Use the above method to find the **quartiles** and **median** for this set of 25 test marks :-

5, 5, 5, 6, 6, 7, 8, 10, 10, 11, 12, 12, 12, 12, 13, 15, 16, 17, 17, 18, 20, 20, 21, 24, 25.

The Semi-Interquartile Range

Let us look again at the example on the ages of the group on a Sunday school trip.

$$2, \; 6, \; 6, \; 7, \; 7, \; 7, \; 7, \; 8, \; 8, \; 8, \; 10, \; 10, \; 11, \; 13, \; 25.$$

We found the quartiles and these are shown below :-

$$2, \quad 6, \quad 6, \quad (7,) \quad 7, \quad 7, \quad 7, \quad (8,) \quad 8, \quad 8, \quad 10, \quad (10,) \quad 11, \quad 13, \quad 25.$$

lower quartile Q_1 median   upper quartile Q_3

RANGE :- You learned previously that the range was a simple measure of spread.

Range = highest − lowest = 25 − 2 = 23 (but this gave too "big" an answer).

If we now find the difference => upper quartile − lower quartile, and halve this answer,

we end up with a new measure of spread, called the semi-interquartile range. (S.I.Q.R.)*

$$*\text{Semi-Interquartile Range} \; = \; \frac{\text{Upper Quartile} - \text{Lower Quartile}}{2}$$

$$\text{S.I.Q.R} \; = \; \frac{Q_3 - Q_1}{2} \; = \; \frac{10 - 7}{2} \; = \; 1 \cdot 5$$

* In many instances, this measure of spread is preferable to the range. It does not simply rely on the two end values, the "highest" and "lowest" – rather, it takes into account more of the numbers in the distribution.

Exercise 11·3

1. Calculate the median and lower and upper quartiles for each of the following sets of values. Hence, calculate the semi-interquartile range of each.

    (a) 13, 13, 15, 19, 23, 23, 24, 26, 27.

    (b) 2·4, 2·6, 2·9, 2·9, 3·1, 3·1, 3·3, 3·6, 3·6, 3·8, 4·1, 4·1, 4·5, 4·7, 4·9, 5·0.

    (c) 101, 108, 109, 112, 112, 115, 120, 121, 125, 131, 131, 134, 135, 138, 140.

2. A group of 25 third year pupils was asked to say how many cousins they had.

    3, 1, 4, 2, 3, 4, 5, 2, 2, 4, 5, 1, 0, 6, 8, 2, 4, 4, 6, 2, 3, 1, 0, 9, 6.

    (a) Rearrange them in order starting with the lowest.

    (b) Calculate the mean, median and modal value.

    (c) Determine the lower and upper quartiles.

    (d) Calculate the range and the S.I.Q.R.

3. A shoe shop assistant took a note of the sizes of a popular make of trainers that were sold in her shop last week.

    $1, 4, 4, 4\frac{1}{2}, 5, 5, 5, 5\frac{1}{2}, 5\frac{1}{2}, 6, 6, 6, 6\frac{1}{2}, 6\frac{1}{2}, 10.$

    Calculate the range and the S.I.Q.R. and say why the S.I.Q.R. would be a better indicator of the true spread of the shoe sizes sold last week.

Box-Plots - 5 Point Diagrams

Let us look once more at the ages of the group on the Sunday school trip.

$$2, \ 6, \ 6, \ 7, \ 7, \ 7, \ 7, \ 8, \ 8, \ 8, \ 10, \ 10, \ 11, \ 13, \ 25.$$

We found that $Q_1 = 7$, $Q_3 = 10$, the **median** = 8, the **lowest** value is 2 and the **highest** is 25.

This can be represented on a **box-plot** (*or 5-point summary*) as shown below.

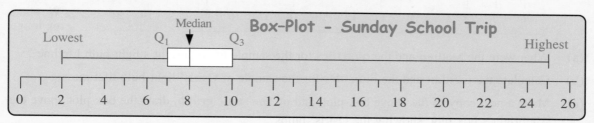

Box-Plots are very useful diagrams, particularly when you wish to compare 2 or more sets of values.

They are also sometimes referred to as **box-whisker** diagrams for obvious reasons.

Exercise 11·4

1.   James rolled two die, (*plural of dice*), twelve times, and noted the **total** score each time.

      $$3, \ 5, \ 6, \ 7, \ 7, \ 7, \ 8, \ 9, \ 9, \ 10, \ 10, \ 12.$$

(a)   Calculate the **median** as well as the **upper** and **lower quartiles**.

(b)   **Copy** this scale and draw a neat **box-plot** to represent the above scores.

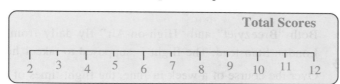

2.   A group of pupils took part in a sunflower growing competition and they all planted their sunflower seed at the same time.

Eight weeks later, the heights of the plants were measured (*to the nearest 5 cm*).

      $$35, \ 35, \ 40, \ 40, \ 40, \ 50, \ 50, \ 55, \ 60, \ 70, \ 85, \ 85, \ 95, \ 105.$$

(a)   Calculate the values of the three quartiles, Q_1, Q_2 and Q_3.

(b)   Draw a suitable scale and show the above heights on a neatly drawn labelled box-plot.

3.      The weights, (*in kilograms*), of the luggage of the 15 passengers boarding a plane bound for the Orkneys was recorded.

      15, 18, 14, 22, 19, 18, 14, 25, 24, 18, 10, 13, 21, 18, 24.

(a)   Rearrange the weights in order, smallest first and calculate the **median** and the **quartiles**.

(b)   Draw and label a box-plot showing these weights. (*Choose a suitable scale*).

4. Osiris claim that their light-bulbs last longer than Awlbright's bulbs.

   A sample of each was tested. **Osiris'** sample is shown below (*in months*).

   8, 9, 10, 10, 12, 14, 14, 14, 15, 15, 17, 17, 18.

   A box plot was created to represent **Awlbright's** sample and is shown below,

   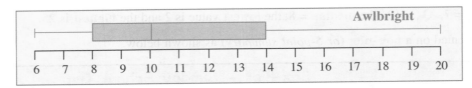

   Osiris

   We shine
   for longer

   (a) What were the **median** and the **quartiles** for the sample of Awlbright's light-bulb lifetime ?

   (b) Calculate the **median** and the **quartiles** for the sample of Osiris' light-bulb lifetime.

   (c) Make a neat copy of the above box-plot, and **on the same graph**, draw the box-plot above the Awlbright's box plot, showing the Osiris' bulbs.

   (d) Write a couple of sentences comparing the two samples.

5. A group of men and a group of women, in a local gym, decided to hold a competition.
   They counted how many pull-ups each person could do in a two minute period.

men	7	9	9	11	13	13	15	18	18	20	25	
women	5	5	6	7	7	10	12	12	14	14	15	17

   (a) Calculate the **medians** and **quartiles** for both the men and the women.

   (b) Draw a neat labelled **composite** box-plot diagram to show how the two groups fared.

   (c) Write a couple of sentences comparing the men competitors with the women.

6. Both "Breezyjet" and "High-on-Air" fly daily from Edinburgh to London Stanstead. The flight is supposed to take 1 hour.

   Over the course of a week in June, the flight-times of every Breezyjet and High-on-Air plane from Edinburgh to Stanstead was recorded in minutes.

Breezyjet -	55	57	61	63	66	66	67	70	70	72	72	75	75	77	80
High-on-Air -	61	61	61	62	63	65	65	65	66	66	68	68	68		

   (a) Draw a neat labelled composite box-plot diagram to show the above flight-times.

   (b) Make a statement comparing both company's flight-times from Edinburgh to London.

7. Three men hit 15 golf balls on a driving range, each using a number 6 iron.
   The box plot diagram shows the distances (in metres) they hit their golf balls.

   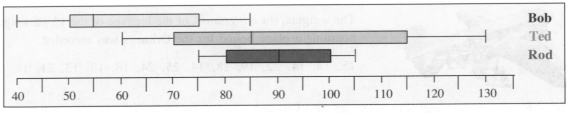

   Write a few sentences comparing the three men's driving skills, mentioning their **median** scores, the **spread** of their shots, who was likely to be the novice, who was most erratic and who was most consistent.

Standard Deviation - a better measure of Spread

Let us take a final look at the ages of the group on the Sunday School outing.

$$2,\ 6,\ 6,\ 7,\ 7,\ 7,\ 7,\ 8,\ 8,\ 8,\ 10,\ 10,\ 11,\ 13,\ 25.$$

The two measures of **SPREAD** we looked at were the **range** and the **semi-interquartile range**.

Neither of them is particularly satisfactory for the following reasons :-

- the **range** depends solely on the two end-values and totally ignores every other value.
- the **S.I.Q.R.** totally disregards the two end-values.

We require a new measure of spread that takes into account **ALL** the numbers in the distribution, not just the end-values or the quartiles.

This new measure is called the **STANDARD DEVIATION**.

Definition :- For a set of values (for example, the ages of the group above), the **standard deviation** is a measure of how "far away", on average, each of the values is, from the **mean**.

Let us explain exactly what we mean by following through a simpler example :-

Example :- Six pea-pods were opened and the number of peas in each was noted.

$$6,\ 7,\ 9,\ 9,\ 10,\ 13.$$

Calculate the **mean** and the **standard deviation**.

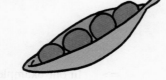

Step 1 Calculate the **mean** first.

A new notation :- If we think of any of the variables, (*the values*), as x's,

then the **mean** = (the sum of all the x's) ÷ (the number of values).

We have a **mathematical** way of expressing this, namely :-

$$\bar{x} = \frac{\sum x}{n}$$

where $\bar{x}$, (reads as "x bar"), is the **mean**.

and $\sum x$ means the "**sum of all the x's**".

and n is the **number** of values used.

In our example, $\bar{x} = \dfrac{\sum x}{n} = \dfrac{6+7+9+9+10+13}{6} = \dfrac{54}{6} = 9.$ the **mean**.

Step 2 We now draw up a table to show how "far" each of the six values, $(6, 7, 9, 9, 10, 13)$, is "away" from the mean ($\bar{x} = 9$).

x	$(x - \bar{x})$
6	$6 - 9 = -3$
7	$7 - 9 = -2$
9	$9 - 9 = 0$
9	$9 - 9 = 0$
10	$10 - 9 = 1$
13	$13 - 9 = 4$

cont'd ......

To find the "average" of these $(x - \bar{x})$'s, we should really add them together, then divide by 6.

A **problem** :- if we add $(-3) + (-2) + 0 + 0 + 1 + 4 \longrightarrow$ we get 0 !
       (*This is because they all "cancel" each other out*).

A **"neat"** trick :-   If we "square" these 6 values $((-3), (-2), 0, 0, 1, 4)$, all the negative signs disappear.

       => we add on an extra column showing $(x - \bar{x})^2$'s.

x	$(x - \bar{x})$	$(x - \bar{x})^2$
6	−3	$(-3)^2 = 9$
7	−2	$(-2)^2 = 4$
9	0	$(0)^2 = 0$
9	0	$(0)^2 = 0$
10	1	$(1)^2 = 1$
13	4	$(4)^2 = 16$

Step 3   We now find the "average" of the numbers in the last column. $(9 + 4 + 0 + 0 + 1 + 16) \div 6.$

We can use our new notation => $\text{average} = \dfrac{\sum(x - \bar{x})^2}{n} = \dfrac{30}{6} = 5.$ the average is 5

Step 4   But remember − these six numbers, $(9, 4, 0, 0, 1, 16)$, were the **squares** of the $(x - \bar{x})$'s.

       => As a final step, we find the **square root** of this "average", (the 5). => $\sqrt{5}$.

We call this measure of how far away the values are from the mean, the **standard deviation**. We have a special formula for it.

$$\text{standard deviation} = \sqrt{\dfrac{\sum(x - \bar{x})^2}{n}}$$

* this is not exactly the correct formula, but we'll explain this later.

=>   In our example, we have $s.d. = \sqrt{\dfrac{\sum(x - \bar{x})^2}{n}} = \sqrt{\dfrac{30}{6}} = \sqrt{5} = 2{\cdot}236.$

*   The important thing about this measure of **spread** is that it takes into account every one of the six numbers, and gives a "feel" for how far, on average, each value is from the middle of the distribution, (the **mean**).

The **lower** the standard deviation is, the more **tightly grouped** is the set of values.

Exercise 11·5

1.   Shown below are the number of touchdowns, made by the Cincinnati Crawlers in their last 5 matches.

       2,   3,   9,   6,   5.

Copy the following and calculate the **mean** and the **standard deviation**.

(a) $\text{mean} = \bar{x} = \dfrac{\sum x}{n} = \dfrac{2 + 3 + 9 + 6 + 5}{5} = ...$

(b)   **standard deviation** - see table $\longrightarrow$

$s.d. = \sqrt{\dfrac{\sum(x - \bar{x})^2}{n}} = \sqrt{\dfrac{.....}{5}} = \sqrt{....} = ...$

x	$(x - \bar{x})$	$(x - \bar{x})^2$
2	$2 - 5 = -3$	$(-3)^2 = 9$
3	$3 - 5 = -2$	....
9	......	....
6	......	....
5	......	....
	$\sum(x - \bar{x})^2 =$	

2. The first sentence James read in his new book had eight words in it.

The number of letters in each word was :- 1, 3, 4, 8, 5, 1, 7, 3.

Calculate the **mean** number of letters per word and the **standard deviation**.

Copy and complete the following :-

(a) mean $= \overline{x} = \dfrac{\sum x}{n} = \dfrac{1 + 3 + 4 + 8 + \ldots\ldots}{\ldots\ldots} = \ldots\ldots$

(b) **standard deviation** - see table ⟶

$$s.d. = \sqrt{\dfrac{\sum (x - \overline{x})^2}{n}} = \sqrt{\dfrac{\ldots\ldots}{\ldots\ldots}} = \sqrt{\ldots\ldots} = \ldots\ldots$$

You may use "*s.d.*", or "*s*" or "σ" to represent the term "standard deviation".

x	$(x - \overline{x})$	$(x - \overline{x})^2$
1	$1 - 4 = -3$	$(-3)^2 = 9$
3	......	....
4	......	....
8	......	....
5	......	....
1	......	....
7	......	....
3	......	....
	$\sum (x - \overline{x})^2 =$	......

Standard Deviation - the Real Formula

Statisticians discovered that they could get a better idea of the spread of a distribution of values by altering the formula for the standard deviation slightly.

They decided it worked better using $(n - 1)^*$ rather than just n.

The formula for the **standard deviation** became :-

$$s.d. = \sqrt{\dfrac{\sum (x - \overline{x})^2}{n - 1}}$$

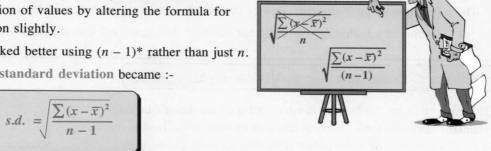

* the reason for this is too complicated to explain at this stage - wait till you go to University !!!!!

* From now on, use the new formula for standard deviation using (n – 1) rather than n.

3. The weights of the first four letters George weighed in his post office one morning, were :- 30 grams, 41 grams, 48 grams, 29 grams.

(a) Calculate the **mean** weight in grams.

(b) Draw up a table and use the formula, $s.d. = \sqrt{\dfrac{\sum (x - \overline{x})^2}{(n - 1)}}$,

to calculate the **standard deviation**.

4.

The school bus is supposed to arrive at Bromley Primary every day at 3.30 prompt.

The head teacher noted how many minutes late the driver was last week – 6 mins, 15 mins, 8 mins, 2 mins, 9 mins.

Calculate the **mean** number of minutes late and the **standard deviation** of the times.

5.   The Edinburgh Annual Paper Airplane Making contest was held in June.

The distances travelled by the planes of the last 8 competitors were :-

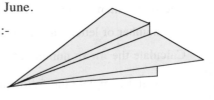

22 m, 35 m, 26 m, 28 m, 30 m, 24 m, 36 m, 23 m.

(a)   Calculate the **mean** distance travelled by the 8 planes.

(b)   Draw up a table and use it, along with the formula, to
calculate the **standard deviation** of the distances travelled.

6.      On a field trip, Susan collects 7 worms and measures their lengths.

6·5 cm, 4·7 cm, 10·2 cm, 9·1 cm, 8·8 cm, 12·0 cm, 7·5 cm.

Calculate the **standard deviation**.

7.   Two men were playing a "friendly" game of darts.

The scores, for each of their first six darts, are shown below.

Donald	18	22	17	20	15	16
Graeme	3	38	6	30	1	30

(a)   Show that both men scored the same **mean**.

(b)   By drawing up 2 separate tables, calculate the **standard deviation** of both men's scores.

(c)   Comment on what the two different standard deviations tell you about the men's scores.

Standard Deviation - an Alternative Formula

If the **mean** is an "awkward" decimal, all the calculations in your
standard deviation tables become difficult to work with. In this situation,
a **rearrangement** of the standard deviation formula can be used.

$$s = \sqrt{\frac{\sum x^2 - (\sum x)^2 / n}{(n-1)}}$$

Example :-   Calculate the mean and standard deviation for the numbers :- 3, 5, 2, 9, 1, 8.

mean :- $\bar{x} = \dfrac{\sum x}{n} = \dfrac{28}{6} = 4\cdot6666...$

s.d. :- $s = \sqrt{\dfrac{\sum x^2 - (\sum x)^2 / n}{(n-1)}}$

$s = \sqrt{\dfrac{184 - 28^2 / 6}{5}} = \sqrt{\dfrac{53\cdot33..}{5}} = \sqrt{10\cdot6....} = 3\cdot27$

x	x^2
3	9
5	25
2	4
9	81
1	1
8	64

$\sum x = 28 \qquad \sum x^2 = 184$

---

8.   Use the above formula to calculate the **mean** and the **standard deviation** of the following :-

(a)   4, 12, 9, 6.

(b)   45, 32, 37, 34, 40, 27.

(c)   6·2, 7·3, 9·1, 5·7, 11·4.

(d)   115, 130, 122, 129, 130, 133, 136.

9.   Re-calculate the **standard deviation** for the set of numbers :- 4, 12, 9, 6. (see question 8(a) above),
using your original formula given on page 113, and check it gives the same value.

1. Calculate the **mean**, **median**, **mode** and **range** :-

   15, 18, 13, 14, 18, 15, 18, 17, 22, 25, 12.

2. The mean age of five
   boys is 12 years old.

   Four of the boys' ages
   are 10, 9, 15 and 14.

   How old is the fifth boy ?

3. A Landscape Gardener orders turf from two
   suppliers. He recently kept a note of how many
   days it took for his last 10 orders from each
   supplier to be delivered.

Green Up	1	12	2	11	15	3	1	10	2	13
Turfers	6	6	8	7	5	6	7	7	5	8

   (a) For each supplier, calculate :-

       (i) the range
       (ii) the mean number of days.

   (b) As the gardener likes
       to plan his work in
       advance he prefers
       to order from the
       more consistent supplier.

       Which supplier is that, and why ?

   (c) Give one reason why he might order
       from his other supplier.

4. Suzie looked at her telephone bill and wrote
   down the duration of her last 15 calls (*to the
   nearest minute*).

   2, 3, 5, 5, 5, 7, 8, 12, 12, 13, 15, 15, 16, 17, 20.

   (a) Calculate the **median** and the **lower** and
       upper quartiles.

   (b) Calculate the **semi-interquartile** range.

5. Shown below are the hours worked by the part-
   timers at Q & B Super-Store :-

   12, 12, 14, 15, 17, 19, 19, 20, 20, 22, 24, 25, 27.

   (a) Calculate the **median** and the **quartiles**.

   (b) Draw a neatly labelled **box-plot** to show the
       distribution of the above hours.

6. 6 brand new Mini's were tested by pouring
   exactly 1 gallon of petrol into their tanks and
   carefully measuring how far they travelled
   before the cars came to a halt.

   The distances, in miles, were :-

   42, 43, 45, 49, 50, 53.

   (a) Calculate the **mean** number of miles.

   (b) Calculate the **standard deviation**.

7. Sid and Jock both
   hit 5 shots with their
   drivers off the tee.

   Shown below are
   the distances travelled
   by each ball, (in yards).

Sid :-	230, 275, 245, 220, 180.
Jock :-	225, 230, 240, 220, 235.

   (a) Show that both Sid's and Jock's **mean**
       driving distances were the same.

   (b) Calculate the **standard deviation** for both
       golfers and comment on who was the more
       consistent golfer.

8. Suzie checks out the price of a pint of semi-
   skimmed milk in six local garage shops.

   The cost in pence are :-

   54   49   46   57   52   48.

   Calculate :-
   (a) the mean price of a pint of milk.
   (b) the standard deviation of the prices.

   Suzie also checks out the price of a pint of milk
   in nearby supermarkets, finding the mean price
   there is 48p and the standard deviation is 2·2.

   (c) Make **two** valid comparisons between the
       two sets of prices.

Number Machines and Functions

Look at this example of a **Number Machine**.

This number machine feeds in any value (x), multiplies it by 3, and produces the answer $(3x)$.

We will refer to this "number machine" from now on as a **"function"**.

A **function** in mathematics is simply a **rule** for dealing with numbers, (or letters).

Notation :-

We tend to use certain letters (like f, g or h) to represent functions.

Example :- f is the function which takes any value, (x), **multiplies it by 3** and produces the value $3x$.

for short, we write :- $f : x \longrightarrow 3x$.   [this reads as "f takes x onto $3x$]

or even better as :- $\boxed{f(x) = 3x}$ [this reads as f of $x = 3x$].

Further Examples :-   Here are some examples of functions :-

$$f(x) = 5x - 1, \qquad f(x) = x^2 + 3, \qquad f(x) = x^2 - 2x + 1,$$

$$g(x) = 3\sin x°, \qquad f(x) = \sqrt{x}, \qquad h(x) = \frac{2}{x}.$$

A **function** in mathematics is simply a **rule** for handling numbers (or letters).

Example :-   Let us look at the function $f(x) = x^2 + 3$.

We will apply this function to the set of x-values $\{-2, -1, 0, 1, 2\}$.

$x = -2 \quad \Rightarrow \quad f(-2) = (-2)^2 + 3 = 4 + 3 = 7 \quad \Rightarrow$ we can think of 7 as the y-value.

$x = -1 \quad \Rightarrow \quad f(-1) = (-1)^2 + 3 = 1 + 3 = 4 \quad \Rightarrow$ we can think of 4 as the y-value.

$x = 0 \quad \Rightarrow \quad f(0) = (0)^2 + 3 = 0 + 3 = 3 \quad \Rightarrow$ we can think of 3 as the y-value.

$x = 1 \quad \Rightarrow \quad f(1) = (1)^2 + 3 = 1 + 3 = 4 \quad \Rightarrow$ we can think of 4 as the y-value.

$x = 2 \quad \Rightarrow \quad f(2) = (2)^2 + 3 = 4 + 3 = 7 \quad \Rightarrow$ we can think of 7 as the y-value.

We now have a series of coordinate points :-

$(-2, 7), (-1, 4), (0, 3), (1, 4), (2, 7),$

which we can plot on a Cartesian Diagram
and join up to form a smooth graph as shown.

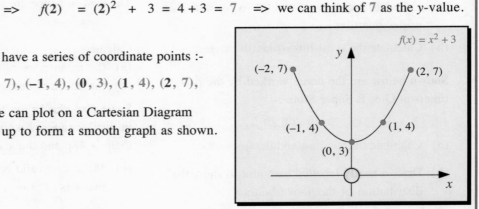

1. Consider the function $f(x) = 2x + 3$, and the set of x-values $\{-1, 0, 1, 2, 3\}$.

   (a) Find $f(3)$ = $\boxed{2 \times 3 + 3 \;=\; .... \;\Rightarrow\; (3, ...).}$

   (b) Similarly, find $f(-1), f(0), f(1)$ and $f(2)$.

   (c) Plot the 5 points on a coordinate diagram and join them up.

   (d) You should have obtained a straight line.

   $f(x) = 2x + 3$ [or $y = 2x + 3$] is referred to as a **linear** function. (*You have met this before*).

2. Consider a second linear function :-

   $$f(x) = \tfrac{1}{2}x - 2,$$

   and the set of x-values $\{-4, -2, 0, 2, 4\}$.

   (a) Evaluate $f(-4), f(-2), f(0), f(2)$, and $f(4)$, and list the coordinates of the five corresponding points.

   (b) Draw a coordinate diagram, plot the 5 points and join them up.

3. Consider the function $f(x) = 10 - x$, and the set of x-values $\{-1, 0, 1, 2, 3\}$.

   (a) Evaluate $f(-1), f(0), f(1), f(2)$ and $f(3)$.

   (b) Draw a coordinate diagram, plot the corresponding 5 points and join them up to show this 3rd **linear** function.

4. Consider the function $f(x) = 3x - 1$.

   (a) What is $f(4)$?

   (b) What is $f(25)$?

   (c) If $f(x) = 3x - 1$, write down an expression for $f(a)$ in terms of the letter a.

   (d) If in fact $f(a) = 20$, use part (c) to set up an equation in a and solve it to find the value of the letter a.   (i.e. solve $3a - 1 = 20$.)

5. A function is denoted by $f(x) = 6x - 2$.

   (a) Evaluate $f(3)$.

   (b) Write down an expression for $f(p)$.

   (c) If $f(p) = 40$, set up an equation in p, and solve it to find the value of p.

6. In this question, $f(x) = \tfrac{1}{2}x + 3$.

   (a) Evaluate $f(22)$.

   (b) Write down an expression for $f(z)$.

   (c) Given that $f(z) = 11$, form an equation in z and solve it to determine the value of z.

7. Consider the function $f(x) = x^2 - 1$ and the set of values $\{-2 \le x \le 2\}$.

   > Note :- $\{-2 \le x \le 2\}$ is simply a mathematical way of saying "consider all the numbers (the x-values), from -2 up to 2.

   (a) Find $f(2)$. $\boxed{(= 2^2 - 1 \;=\; 4 - 1 = ...).}$

   (b) Similarly, find $f(1), f(0), f(-1)$ *and* $f(-2)$.

   (c) Draw a coordinate diagram and plot the corresponding 5 points $(-2, 3), (-1, 0), ...$

   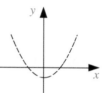

   (d) Join the 5 points up with a smooth curve.

   > This is called a **quadratic** function and will be studied in depth later on.
   >
   > (A **quadratic** function always has an x^2 term).

8. Consider the **quadratic** function $f(x) = 3x^2$, and the set of values $\{-2 \le x \le 2\}$.

   (a) Find $f(-2), f(-1), f(0), f(1)$ and $f(2)$.

   (b) Draw a coordinate diagram and plot the corresponding 5 points $(-2, 12), (-1, 3), ...$

   (c) Join the 5 points up with a smooth quadratic curve.

9. Consider the function $f(x) = x(x - 2)$ and the set of values $\{-1 \le x \le 3\}$.

   (a) Find $f(-1) = (-1) \times ((-1) - 2) \;=\; (-1) \times (-3)$

   (b) Find $f(0), f(1), f(2)$ and $f(3)$.

   (c) Draw a coordinate diagram and plot the corresponding 5 points $(-1, 3), (0, 0), ...$

   (d) Join the 5 points up to show yet again a smooth quadratic curve.

   > **Note** the U-shape you obtain from a quadratic function - this is always the case - a **parabola**.

10. Consider the function $f(x) = x^2$.

    (a) Evaluate $f(3)$.

    (b) Write down an expression for $f(a)$.

    (c) Given that $f(a) = 25$, set up an equation using a and solve it to determine the value(s) of a.   [**2 possible values !**]

11. Consider the function $f(x) = x^2 + 3$.

    (a) Evaluate $f(2)$.

    (b) Write down an expression for $f(p)$.

    (c) If $f(p) = 39$, set up an equation using a and solve it to determine the value(s) of p.   [**2 values again**]

12. Consider the function $f(x) = 5x - 3$.

    (a) Evaluate $f(10)$.

    (b) Write down an expression for $f(2a)$ in terms of a. (i.e. replace x by $2a$ in $f(x) = 5x - 3$).

    (c) Given that $f(2a) = 27$, set up an equation using a and solve it to find the value of a.

13. Find an expression in terms of the given letter for each of these :-

    (a) $f(x) = x + 3$.   Find $f(4a)$.

    (b) $g(x) = 2x - 3$.   Find $g(3p)$.

    (c) $h(x) = x - 5$.   Find $h(a^2)$.

    (d) $f(x) = 12 - x$.   Find $f(2q)$.

    (e) $f(x) = x^2$.   Find $f(3m)$.

    (f) $h(x) = 2x^2$.   Find $h(10t)$. (*careful !*)

14. For the function $f(x) = 4x - 1$, write down an expression for $f(t)$ and determine the value of t, given that $f(t) = 33$.

15. Consider the function $f(x) = 3x - 3$.

    Write down an expression for $f(n)$, and find the value of n, given that $f(n) = 37$.

16. A function is defined by $h(x) = x - 1$.

    Write down an expression for $h(r^2)$ and determine the values of r, given that $h(r^2) = 48$.

17. Consider the function $f(x) = 5x - 2$.
Another way of writing this is $y = 5x - 2$.

In function notation, $f(x)$ and y effectively represent the same thing.

On a coordinate diagram :-

- x measures the distance a point is measured **horizontally** from the **origin**.

- $f(x)$ (or y) measures the distance the point is **vertically** up (or down) from the **origin**,

    (a) Evaluate $f(10)$.

    (b) Write down an expression for $f(2p)$ in terms of p. (i.e. replace x by $2p$ in $f(x) = 5x - 2$).

    (c) Given that $f(2p) = 38$, set up an equation using p and solve it to find the value of p.

18. A new function is defined by $f(x) = \frac{1}{2}x + 3$.

    (a) Find $f(20)$.

    (b) Given that $f(c) = 9$, determine the value of c.

19. Look at the line shown opposite.

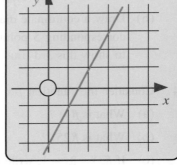

    (a) Where does it cut the y-axis ?

    (b) Calculate the gradient of the line.

    (c) Write down the equation of the line in the form $y = mx + c$.

    (d) Rewrite this in function notation, $f(x) = ...$

    (e) Find   (i) $f(20)$ (ii) $f(-6)$.

    (f) Given that $f(p) = 27$, determine the value of p.

    (g) Use this to write down the coordinates of the point (..., 27) which lies on the line.

Any function of the form :-

$$f(x) = ax^2 + bx + c \quad \text{(or } y = ax^2 + bx + c),$$

where a, b and c are numbers is called a **quadratic function**. (*b* and *c* can be 0 but *a* cannot be 0).

Examples :-

| $f(x) = x^2 + 2x + 3$ | $f(x) = 3x^2 - 2x - 5$ | $f(x) = 4x^2 + 6x$ |
| $f(x) = x^2 - 7$ | $f(x) = 10 - 2x - x^2$ | $f(x) = 5x^2$ |

are all examples of **quadratic functions**. (*You have already met quadratic expressions*).

Example :- Let us study the quadratic function $f(x) = x^2 - 2x - 3$, $\{-2 \le x \le 4\}$.

$f(-2) = (-2)^2 - 2(-2) - 3 = 4 + 4 - 3 = 5.$	
$f(-1) = (-1)^2 - 2(-1) - 3 = 1 + 2 - 3 = 0.$	
$f(0) = (0)^2 - 2(0) - 3 = 0 + 0 - 3 = -3.$	
$f(1) = (1)^2 - 2(1) - 3 = 1 - 2 - 3 = -4.$	
$f(2) = (2)^2 - 2(2) - 3 = 4 - 4 - 3 = -3.$	
$f(3) = (3)^2 - 2(3) - 3 = 9 - 6 - 3 = 0.$	
$f(4) = (4)^2 - 2(4) - 3 = 16 - 8 - 3 = 5.$	

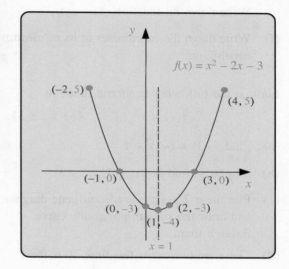

The above seven points have been plotted and can be seen opposite. The **quadratic** graph has been drawn as a smooth curve through these seven points. **Study the graph carefully**.

- This "**U**-shaped" curve is always produced from a **quadratic function**.

- This type of graph is referred to as a **parabola**.

- It always has a vertical line of symmetry (*shown dotted*). In this case it is the line $x = 1$.

- The two values of x where the graph cuts the x-axis are called the **zeros** or the **roots** of the quadratic function. In this case, the roots are at $x = -1$ and $x = 3$.

- There is always a **minimum turning point** in this type of graph. In this case at $(1, -4)$.

- The graph can look like an "inverted **U**" (*upside-down*), in some cases. (*See later*).

Note :- The **quadratic function** is one of the most important functions we will study in mathematics.

It occurs in lots of real-life situations and its graph, the **parabola**, can be seen in science, design, engineering and architecture.

1. Look at the most basic quadratic function

    $$f(x) = x^2, \qquad \{-3 \le x \le 3\}.$$

    (a) Find $f(-3) = (-3)^2 = \ldots$

    (b) Similarly, find $f(-2), f(-1), f(0), f(1), \ldots f(3)$.

    (c) Plot these 7 points on a coordinate diagram and draw the smooth **parabolic** curve through them.

    (d) There is only one **root** this time. (i.e. there is only 1 place where the graph cuts the x-axis). What is its value ?

    (e) Can you see the **line of symmetry** ? Write down its equation. $(x = \ldots)$.

    (f) Write down the coordinates of its **minimum turning point**.

2. Look at the following quadratic function

    $$f(x) = x^2 - 1, \qquad \{-3 \le x \le 3\}.$$

    (a) Find $f(-3) = (-3)^2 - 1 = \ldots$

    (b) Similarly, find $f(-2), f(-1), \ldots f(3)$.

    (c) Plot these 7 points on a coordinate diagram and draw the smooth **parabolic** curve through them.

    (d) There are two **roots** this time. (i.e. there are 2 places where the graph cuts the x-axis). What are the two values ?

    (e) Can you see the **line of symmetry** ? Write down its equation. $(x = \ldots)$.

    (f) Write down the coordinates of its **minimum turning point**.

    (g) Say how this graph ($f(x) = x^2 - 1$) differs from the basic graph ($f(x) = x^2$) in Qu 1.

3. Say what you think the graph of the function

    $$f(x) = x^2 + 3$$

    might look like in comparison to $f(x) = x^2$.

4. What do you think the graph of the function

    $$f(x) = x^2 - 5$$

    might look like in comparison to $f(x) = x^2$?

5. Look at the quadratic function

    $$f(x) = x^2 - 4x \qquad \{-1 \le x \le 5\}.$$

    (a) Find $f(-1) = \boxed{(-1)^2 - 4(-1) = 1 + 4 = \ldots}$

    (b) Similarly, find $f(0), f(1), \ldots, f(5)$.

    (c) Plot these 7 points on a coordinate diagram and draw the smooth **parabolic** curve through them.

    (d) There are two **roots**. What are the two values ?

    (e) Write down the equation of the **line of symmetry**.

    (f) Write down the coordinates of its **minimum turning point**.

6. A quadratic function is given by

    $$f(x) = x^2 + 3x \qquad \{-4 \le x \le 1\}.$$

    (a) Find $f(-4) = \boxed{(-4)^2 + 3(-4) = 16 - 12 = \ldots}$

    (b) Similarly, find $f(-3), f(-2), \ldots, f(1)$.

    (c) Plot these 6 points on a coordinate diagram and draw the smooth **parabolic** curve through them.

    (d) What are the two **roots** ?

    (e) Write down the equation of the **line of symmetry**.

    (f) Write down the coordinates of its **minimum turning point**.

7. This time, the quadratic function is given by

    $$f(x) = x^2 + 2x - 3 \qquad \{-4 \le x \le 2\}.$$

    (a) Find $f(-4) = \boxed{\begin{array}{l} (-4)^2 + 2(-4) - 3 \\ = 16 - 8 - 3 = \ldots \end{array}}$

    (b) Similarly, find $f(-3), f(-2), \ldots, f(2)$.

    (c) Plot these 7 points on a coordinate diagram and draw the smooth **parabolic** curve through them.

    (d) What are the two **roots** ?

    (e) Write down the equation of the **line of symmetry** .

    (f) Write down the coordinates of its **minimum turning point**.

8. Consider the quadratic function is given by

$$f(x) = x^2 - 2x - 8 \qquad \{-3 \le x \le 5\}.$$

(a) Find $f(-3) = $ ┃ $(-3)^2 - 2(-3) - 8$
    $= \quad 9 + 6 - 8 = ...$

(b) Similarly, find $f(-2), f(-1), ..., f(5)$.

(c) Plot these 9 points on a coordinate diagram and draw the smooth **parabolic** curve through them.

(d) What are the two **roots** ?

(e) Write down the equation of the **line of symmetry**.

(f) Write down the coordinates of its **minimum turning point**.

All of the quadratic functions you have studied so far have given the same "U-shaped" parabolic graph.

---

9. This time, the quadratic function is

$$f(x) = -x^2 \qquad \{-2 \le x \le 2\}.$$

(a) Find $f(-2) = $ ┃ $-(-2)^2 = ...$

(b) Similarly, find $f(-1), f(0), f(1)$ and $f(2)$.

(c) Plot these 5 points on a coordinate diagram and draw the smooth **parabolic** curve through them.

(d) What do you notice about the shape of the **parabola** this time ?

(e) What is different this time that caused the **parabola** to be "**upside-down**" ?

---

10. Consider the quadratic function

$$f(x) = 4x - x^2 \qquad \{-1 \le x \le 5\}.$$

(a) Find $f(-1) = $ ┃ $4(-1) - (-1)^2 = -4 - 1 = ...$

(b) Similarly, find $f(0), f(1), ... f(5)$.

(c) Plot these 7 points on a coordinate diagram and draw the smooth **parabolic** curve through them.

(d) What are the two **roots** ?

(e) Write down the equation of the **line of symmetry**.

(f) Write down the coordinates of its **maximum turning point**.

Quadratic functions always produce **parabolas**.
Some look like this :-   Others look like this :-

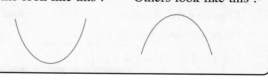

11. Write down, **in your own words**, how you could tell in advance, by just looking at the quadratic function, whether it will be a " $\cup$-shaped" graph (a **minimum**), or an "Inverted $\cup$-shaped ($\cap$)" graph, giving a **maximum**.

12. Without actually drawing these **parabolas**, state what shape of parabola will be produced from the following quadratic functions :-

(a) $f(x) = x^2 + 3x + 2$ (b) $f(x) = -x^2 + 6x$

(c) $f(x) = 9 - x^2$ (d) $f(x) = x^2 + 5x - 2$

(e) $f(x) = 12x - x^2$ (f) $f(x) = 3x^2 - 6x.$

13. (a) Draw the parabola corresponding to the quadratic function

$$f(x) = 9 - x^2 \qquad \{-3 \le x \le 3\}.$$

(b) What are the two **roots** ?

(c) Write down the equation of the **line of symmetry**.

(d) Write down the coordinates of its **maximum turning point**.

14. (a) Draw the parabola corresponding to the quadratic function

$$f(x) = 8 - 2x^2 \qquad \{-3 \le x \le 3\}.$$

(b) What are its two **roots** ?

(c) Write down the equation of the **line of symmetry** and the coordinates of its **maximum turning point**.

15. (a) Draw the parabola corresponding to the quadratic function

$$f(x) = x^2 - 4x + 4 \qquad \{0 \le x \le 4\}.$$

(b) How many **roots** does it have ?

(c) Write down the equation of the **line of symmetry** and the coordinates of its **minimum turning point**.

1. Consider the function $f(x) = 4x - 3$, and the set of x-values $\{-1, 0, 1, 2, 3\}$.

   (a) Find $f(-1)$ = $\boxed{4 \times (-1) - 3 = \ldots \Rightarrow (3, \ldots).}$

   (b) Similarly, find $f(0), f(1), f(2)$ and $f(3)$.

   (c) Plot the 5 points on a coordinate diagram and join them up to show the **linear** function :-
   $y = 4x - 3$.

2. Consider this time the function $f(x) = 5x - 2$.

   (a) What is $f(3)$?

   (b) What is $f(20)$?

   (c) If $f(x) = 5x - 2$, write down an expression for $f(t)$ in terms of the letter t.

   (d) If in fact $f(t) = 38$, use part (c) to set up an equation in t and solve it to find the value of the letter t.

3. Consider the function $f(x) = x^2 + 2$ and the set of values $\{-2 \le x \le 2\}$.

   (a) Find $f(2)$ = $\boxed{2^2 + 2 = 4 + 2 = \ldots.}$

   (b) Similarly, find $f(1), f(0), f(-1)$ and $f(-2)$.

   (c) Draw a coordinate diagram and plot the corresponding 5 points $(-2, 6), (-1, 3), \ldots$

   (d) Join the 5 points up with a smooth curve to represent the quadratic function :-
   $f(x) = x^2 + 2$.

4. Consider the quadratic function :-
   $$f(x) = 6x - x^2 \qquad \{-1 \le x \le 7\}.$$

   (a) Find $f(-1)$ = $\boxed{6(-1) - (-1)^2 = -6 - 1 = \ldots}$

   (b) Similarly, find $f(0), f(1), \ldots f(7)$.

   (c) Plot these 9 points on a coordinate diagram and draw the smooth **parabolic** curve through them.

   (d) What are the two **roots** ?

   (e) Write down the equation of the **line of symmetry**.

   (f) Write down the coordinates of its **maximum turning point**.

5. A function is defined by $f(x) = x + 5$.

   Write down an expression for $f(a^2)$ and determine the values of a, given that $f(a^2) = 41$.

6. A function is defined by $f(x) = 4\sqrt{x} + 5$.

   (a) Find the value of $f(36)$.

   (b) Calculate the value of w, given that
   $$f(w) = 45.$$

7. Without actually drawing these curves, state what shape of parabola will be produced from the following quadratic functions :-

   (a) $f(x) = x^2 + 4x - 5$ (b) $f(x) = -x^2 + 9x$

   (c) $f(x) = 16 - 2x^2$ (d) $f(x) = x^2 - 2$

   (e) $f(x) = 8x - x^2$ (f) $f(x) = 2x^2 - 6x$.

8. (a) Draw the parabola corresponding to the quadratic function
   $$f(x) = 4 - x^2 \qquad \{-3 \le x \le 3\}.$$

   (b) What are the two **roots** ?

   (c) Write down the equation of the **line of symmetry** .

   (d) Write down the coordinates of its **maximum turning point**.

9. Consider the function $f(x) = x(x + 4)$, and the set of values $\{-5 \le x \le 1\}$.

   (a) Find $f(-5), f(-4), \ldots, f(1)$.

   (b) Draw a coordinate diagram and plot the corresponding 7 points $(-5, 5), (-4, 0), \ldots$

   (c) Join the 7 points up to show yet again a smooth quadratic curve.

   (d) Write down the equation of the **line of symmetry** .

   (e) Write down the coordinates of its **minimum turning point**.

1. Change the subject of each formula to x :-

(a) $x - y = k$

(b) $3x + w = g$

(c) $2xy + 1 = h$

(d) $0.5x - fg = 0$

(e) $V = 2x$

(f) $y = mx + c$

(g) $ax - b = cx$

(h) $P = \dfrac{(x^2 + t^2)}{2}$.

2. The formula for displacement is defined as

$$s = ut + \tfrac{1}{2}at^2 .$$

Change the subject of this formula to :-

(a) u

(b) a.

3. Find the mean, median, mode and range for :-

(a) 4, 4, 6, 7, 8, 11, 15

(b) 8·6, 9·4, 11, 6·7, 8, 9·4, 10·6, 9·6

(c) 112, 212, 121, 212, 222, 111, 122.

4. The mean age of a 5-a-side football team is 22. When the substitute is added the mean is 25. How old is the substitute ?

5. Ross looked at his last 20 calls on his mobile.

14 12 10 8 11 18 19 22 28 3

11 18 14 1 15 21 20 27 36 9

Each number has been rounded up to the nearest minute.

(a) Calculate the semi–interquartile range.

(b) Use the above information to construct a box plot.

Last month, Ross had constructed the box plot below from his calls.

(c) Write a couple of sentences to compare last month's box plot with his last 20 calls this month.

6. (a) A function is defined as $f(x) = 3x - 7$.

Find the values for each number in the set
$\{-2, -1, 0, 1, 2, 3\}$.

(b) Use the same set from part (a) to find the values for the function $f(x) = 2x^2 - 1$.

7. Find $f(-2)$, $f(-1)$, $f(0)$ and $f(1)$, given

$$f(x) = x^2 + 2x - 1.$$

8. Given $f(x) = 4x - 6$, find k given $f(2k) = 10$.

9. For both the parabola below, state :-

• the roots

• the maximum or minimum turning point

• the equation of the line of symmetry.

(a)

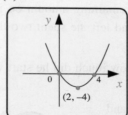

(b)

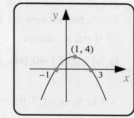

10. Sketch each of these parabolas, indicating :-

• the roots,

• the y-intercept and

• the line of symmetry.

(a) $f(x) = x^2 - x + 6$, $\{-3 \le x \le 4\}$

(b) $y = x^2 - 2x$, $\{-2 \le x \le 4\}$

(c) $f(x) = x^2 + 2x - 8$, $\{-5 \le x \le 3\}$

(d) $y = x^2 - 4$, $\{-3 \le x \le 3\}$

(e) $f(x) = 2 - x - x^2$, $\{-3 \le x \le 2\}$.

11. A function is defined as $f(x) = ax^2 + bx + c$, where $a < 0$ and $c > 0$.

Sketch the graph of this function.

12. Simplify fully $(x + 3)(2x - 3) - (x - 4)^2$.

13. A painting, bought two years ago for £8000, depreciated in value by 8% in its first year.

This year, the painting appreciated and is now valued at £8450.

By what percentage, to one decimal place, must the painting have appreciated this year ?

14. Find :–

(a) $\frac{21}{4} + 4\frac{1}{3}$ (b) $11\frac{1}{3} \times 2\frac{1}{5}$

(c) $8\frac{1}{4} \div 3\frac{1}{6}$ (d) $\frac{11}{7} \div 1\frac{1}{2}$.

15. George has some money.
He spent one quarter of it on sweets.
He spent half of the remaining amount on juice.
From the money he had left, he spent two thirds of it on a comic.

If he had £1·40 left, how much did he start with ?

16. Vikki bought 3 mice and 2 hamsters, costing her a total of £30·60.

Mellisa spent £61·10 on 4 mice and 5 hamsters.

How much does it cost for a hamster ?

17. Find the perimeter of the shape below giving your answer to 3 significant figures :–

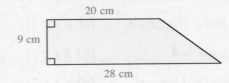

18. State the gradient and y-intercept of :–

(a) $y = 3x - 1$ (b) $2y + 3x - 7 = 0$.

19. Find the equation of the lines passing through :–

(a) $(0, -3)$, $(6, 1)$ (b) $(-2, -3)$, $(1, 3)$.

20. Factorise fully :–

(a) $x^2 - 7x + 30$ (b) $2x^2 - 3x - 9$.

21. Simplify fully $(x^2 + x - 6) \div (x^2 - 4)$.

22. Find the value of x in each of the following :–

(a)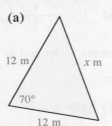

(b)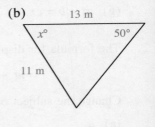

23. Change the subject of each formula to x :–

(a) $x^2 - y^2 = r^2$ (b) $\frac{4}{x - 1} = \frac{x + 1}{y}$.

24. Draw an appropriate statistical diagram to illustrate the following information :–

Max	– 24
Range	– 11
Median	– 16
1st Quartile	– 15
3rd Quartile	– 20.

25. Find the standard deviation of :–

10, 13, 13, 14, 15, 19, 23, 23.

26. Sketch each of the following functions :–

(a) $y = 4x - 3$, $\{-2 \le x \le 2\}$

(b) $f(x) = x^2 + 2x - 8$, $\{-5 \le x \le 3\}$.

27. The volume of a cone with radius r cm and height h cm is given by :–

$$V = \tfrac{1}{3}\pi r^2 h .$$

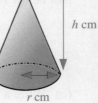

What happens to V when :–

(a) r is **doubled**

(b) r is **halved** ?

 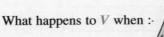

1. Change :-
   (a) 8·6 km to mm
   (b) 670 g to tonnes
   (c) $\frac{7}{8}$ kg to g
   (d) 0·125 km to cm
   (e) 8·5 hours to seconds
   (f) 4 ml to litres
   (g) 0·001 m to mm.

2. Find :-
   (a) 90% of £2
   (b) 15% of 3 cm
   (c) 95% of 2000
   (d) $1\frac{1}{2}$% of 4 m
   (e) 3% of 3 kg
   (f) $2\frac{1}{2}$% of 64 km
   (g) $22\frac{1}{2}$% of 320.

3. Find :-
   (a) $(-12) - (-42)$
   (b) $(-55) + 67$
   (c) $(-30) \times (-15)$
   (d) $(-30)^3$
   (e) $144 \div (-6)$
   (f) $(-25) \div (-125)$
   (g) $\dfrac{(-9) \times (-10)}{(-6)}$.

4. (a) A bowl holds 24·50 litres of punch. How many 80 ml cups can be **filled** from one bowl ?
   (b) A truck can carry 3·2 tonnes of rubble. How many trips will it make to carry 128 tonnes ?
   (c) 200 sweets in a bag. 150 bags in a box. 400 boxes in a crate. How many sweets in a crate ?

5. Draw a neat set of coordinate axes and plot :- A(−1, 2), B(4, 2) and C(7, −2).
   (a) Find the 4th point (D) such that ABCD is a **rhombus**.
   (b) The rhombus is given a 180° rotation about the origin. Write the images of the vertices.

6. Write in 24 hour format :-
   (a) five to five in the morning
   (b) noon
   (c) ten to midnight
   (d) 8:40 p.m.
   (e) $\frac{1}{4}$ to 8 in the evening.

7. How long is it from :-
   (a) 2127 to 2212
   (b) 1134 to 9:20 p.m. ?

8. (a) A car covers 125 kilometres in 1 hour and 15 minutes. Find the average speed of the car.
   (b) A truck travelling at 60 m.p.h. travels 45 miles. How many minutes did the journey take ?

9. A flower bed is made from a rectangle and a quarter circle as shown.
   Calculate the perimeter of the flower bed.

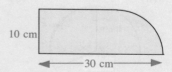

10. Prove that if a triangle has shorter sides $3x$ and $4x$ and has hypotenuse $5x$, then it must be right angled, for every value of x

11. If $f(x) = 2x^2 - 3x + 4$, find :-
    (a) $f(0)$
    (b) $f(-1)$
    (c) $f(0·5)$.

12. Ellie invested £8400 in a stock fund. She left it for 3 years and earned 10% interest per annum. How much was her investment worth after 3 years ?

13. Simplify the expression :- $(2x + 1)^2 + (5x - 1)(x + 2) - (3x - 1)^2$.

Finding an Arc Length

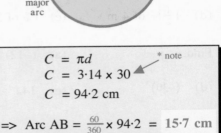

An **ARC** is a part, (or fraction), of the circumference of a circle.

Arc AB, (the **red** part), is called the **minor** arc.

Arc AB, (the **blue** part), is called the **major** arc.

Example :-   Find the length of the **minor** arc AB.

| Step 1 | Calculate the full circumference $C = \pi d$. |
| Step 2 | Find the required fraction of the circumference. |

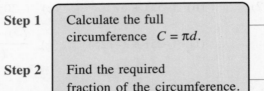

$$C = \pi d$$
$$C = 3\cdot14 \times 30 \quad \text{* note}$$
$$C = 94\cdot2 \text{ cm}$$

$$\Rightarrow \text{ Arc AB} = \tfrac{60}{360} \times 94\cdot2 = \boxed{15\cdot7 \text{ cm}}$$

* note

The **major arc** AB is found in the same way by multiplying the circumference by the fraction $\frac{300}{360}$.

Exercise 13·1

1.   Copy and complete the calculation to find the length of the **minor arc** of the circle shown :-

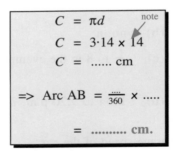

$$C = \pi d \quad \text{note}$$
$$C = 3\cdot14 \times 14$$
$$C = \ldots\ldots \text{ cm}$$

$$\Rightarrow \text{ Arc AB} = \tfrac{\ldots}{360} \times \ldots\ldots$$

$$= \ldots\ldots\ldots \text{ cm.}$$

2.   Find the length of each **minor** arc :-

(a)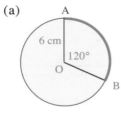

(b)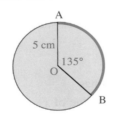

(c)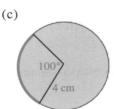

(d)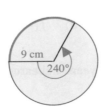

3.   Find the length of the **major** arc in question 2(a).

Sometimes the words **minor** or **major** are not used.

4.   Calculate the **arc length** in each of these :-

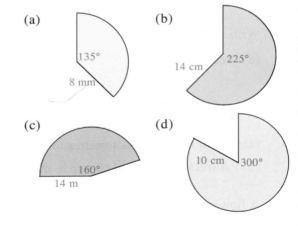

(a)   135° 8 mm

(b)   225° 14 cm

(c)   160° 14 m

(d)   10 cm 300°

5.   Calculate the **perimeter** of each shape :-

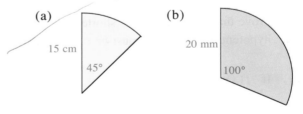

(a)   15 cm 45°

(b)   20 mm 100°

6.   The shape trapped between two radii and an arc is called a **sector** of a circle.

Calculate the **perimeter** of a sector which is a fifth of a circle with diameter 5 centimetres. (*A sketch would help*).

Finding the Area of a Sector

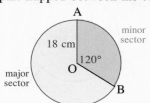

Shown is sector AOB

A **sector** is a part, (or a fraction) of the **area** of a circle.
The **sector** is the part trapped between the two radii and the arc.

Sector AOB, (the **pink** part), is called the **minor** sector.

Sector AOB, (the **blue** part), is called the **major** sector.

Example :- Find the area of the **minor** sector.

Step 1	Calculate the area of the whole circle :- $A = \pi r^2$
Step 2	Calculate the required fraction.

$A = \pi r^2$

$A = 3 \cdot 14 \times 18 \times 18$

$A = 1017 \cdot 36$ cm^2

$\Rightarrow$ Minor sector AOB $= \frac{120}{360} \times 1017 \cdot 36$

$= \textbf{339} \cdot \textbf{12 cm}^2$

The area of the **major sector** AOB is found in the
same way, by multiplying by the fraction $\frac{240}{360}$.

Exercise 13·2

1. Copy and complete the calculation to find the
    area of the minor sector of this circle :-

    $A = \pi r^2$

    $A = 3 \cdot 14 \times 10 \times 10$

    $A = \ldots\ldots$ cm^2

    Minor sector AOB

    $= \frac{\ldots}{360} \times \ldots\ldots$

    $= \ldots\ldots\ldots$ cm^2.

2. Find the area of each **minor** sector :-

    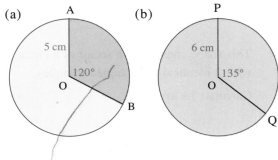

    (a)

    (b)

3. (a) Find the area of the **major** sector in
        question 1.

    (b) Find the area of the **major** sector in
        question 2(a).

4. Calculate the **area** of each sector :-

    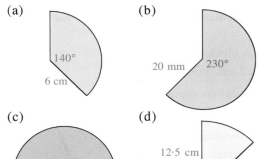

    (a)

    (b)

    (c)

    (d)

    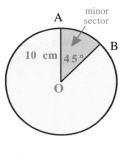

    (e)

    (f)

5. Calculate the area of the
    small sector which has
    been "removed" from
    the circle shown.

    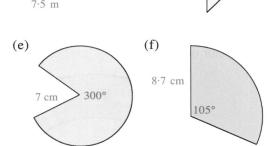

Mixed Exercise

(Answer to 2 decimal places where necessary).

1. For each shape below, find :-

   (i) the arc length (ii) the sector area.

   (a)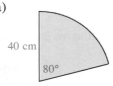

   40 cm
   80°

   (b)

   135°
   5·5 mm

2. The **net** of a wizard's hat is shown.

   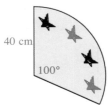

   40 cm
   100°

   Calculate the area of material needed to make the hat.

3. An **eighth** of a circular pizza, with diameter 40 cm, is heated in a microwave.

   Calculate the area of the top of the pizza piece.

4. A clock pendulum is 35 centimetres long.

   It swings though an angle of 40° as shown.

   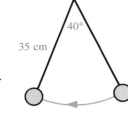

   40°
   35 cm

   Calculate the distance through which the end of the pendulum swings.

5. Part of a hairpin bend on a racetrack forms the sector of a circle.

   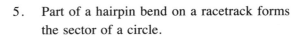
   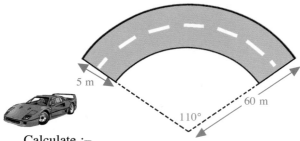

   5 m
   110°
   60 m

   Calculate :–

   (a) the outside length of this part of the track.

   (b) the inside length of this part of the track.

6. Find the perimeter of the shape below. (Shown in red).

   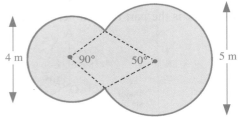

   4 m
   90°   50°
   5 m

7. A logo is made from three different shapes.

   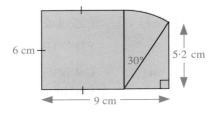

   6 cm
   30°
   5·2 cm
   9 cm

   • a square of side 6 centimetres,
   • a right angled triangle,
   • a sector of a circle .

   Calculate :-

   (a) the **perimeter** of the logo.

   (b) the **area** of the logo.

8. The **red** shaded area shown is called a **segment** of the circle.

   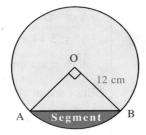

   O
   12 cm
   A   Segment   B

   (a) Calculate the **area** of the sector OAB.

   (b) Now calculate the area of the right angled triangle OAB.

   (c) Finally, find the area of the **red** segment.

9. This shape consists of a sector of a circle with 2 identical right angled triangles.

   Calculate its **area**.

   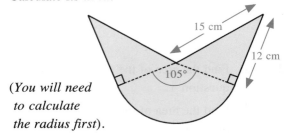

   15 cm
   12 cm
   105°

   (You will need to calculate the radius first).

Finding the Angle at the Centre, given the Arc Length

You can rearrange the formula, $\boxed{\text{Arc length} = \frac{\text{angle}}{360} \times \pi d}$ to help you find the **angle** at the centre.

Example :- If the arc length AB of a circle, radius 12 cm, is 12·56 cm, find the angle at the centre.

$$C = \pi d$$
$$C = 3\cdot14 \times 24 \quad \text{note}$$
$$C = 75\cdot36 \text{ cm}$$

=> Angle at centre ($x°$) is given by :-

$$x = \frac{12\cdot56}{75\cdot36} \times 360°$$

note $\quad x = \boxed{60°}$

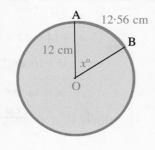

If you are given the arc length, then the formula needed to calculate the **centre angle** is :–

$$\text{Angle } (x°) = \frac{\text{arc length}}{\text{circumference}} \times 360°$$

Exercise 13·4

1. The minor arc length AB is 6·28 centimetres.
   Calculate the size of the angle at the centre.

   Copy and complete :-

   $$C = \pi d \quad \text{note}$$
   $$C = 3\cdot14 \times 16$$
   $$C = 50\cdot24 \text{ cm}$$

   $$\text{Angle } (x) = \frac{\cdots}{50\cdot24} \times 360°$$
   $$= \ldots°$$

2. For each of the 2 sectors shown below,
   calculate the size of the angle at the centre :-

   (a)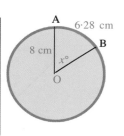

   (b)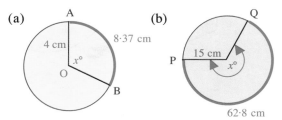

3. A sector of a circle, with a **diameter** of 25 cm,
   has an arc length of 39·25 cm.

   Calculate the size of the angle at the centre.

4. Find the angle at the centre of each sector :-

   (a) 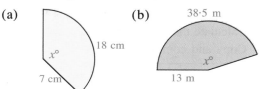 (b)

   (c) 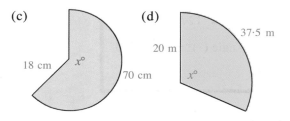 (d)

5. This sector has an arc length of 241·78 mm.

   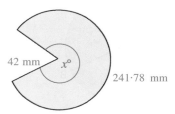

   (a) Find the size of the angle at the centre.

   (b) Calculate the area of the blue sector.

Finding the Angle at the Centre, given the Area

You can rearrange the formula $\boxed{\text{Area of Sector} = (\frac{\text{angle}}{360}) \times \pi r^2}$ to help find the **angle** at the centre.

Example :- Find the angle at the centre, given that the area of the minor sector AOB is 75·36 cm^2.

$$A = \pi r^2$$
$$A = 3 \cdot 14 \times 12 \times 12$$
$$A = 452 \cdot 16 \text{ cm}^2$$

Angle at centre is found as follows :-

$$\Rightarrow \quad \text{angle } (x°) = \frac{75 \cdot 36}{452 \cdot 16} \times 360$$

$$x = \boxed{60°}$$

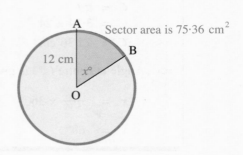

Sector area is 75·36 cm^2

The formula needed to calculate the **angle at the centre**, given the sector area is :-

$$\text{Angle} = \frac{\text{area of sector}}{\text{area of circle}} \times 360°$$

Give each angle correct to one decimal place.

1. The area of the minor sector POQ is 1·57 cm^2
   Calculate the size of angle x.
   Copy and complete :-

   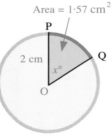
   Area = 1·57 cm^2

   $$A = \pi r^2$$
   $$A = 3 \cdot 14 \times 2 \times 2$$
   $$A = 12 \cdot 56 \text{ cm}^2$$
   $$\text{Angle } (x) = \frac{1 \cdot 57}{\text{......}} \times 360°$$
   $$= \text{.....}°$$

2. Find the size of angle x and angle y :-

   (a) 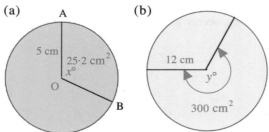   (b)

3. The sector of a circle, with a radius of 5 cm, has an area of 65·5 cm^2.

   Calculate the angle at the centre of the sector.

4. Find the angle at the centre of each sector :-

   (a)   (b)

   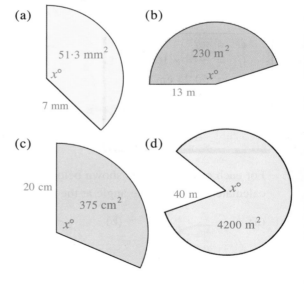

   (c)   (d)

5. The sector shown has an area of 572·22 cm^2.

   (a) Find the size of the angle at the centre.

   (b) Find the length of the **major** arc.

   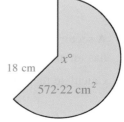

(Answer to 3 significant figures where necessary).

1. Calculate the arc length in each of these :-

   (a)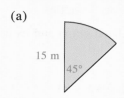
   15 m
   45°

   (b)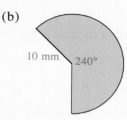
   10 mm
   240°

2. Calculate the area of each sector in question 1.

3. Find the angle at the centre of each sector :-

   (a)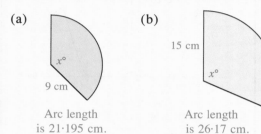
   x°
   9 cm

   Arc length
   is 21·195 cm.

   (b)
   15 cm
   x°

   Arc length
   is 26·17 cm.

   (c)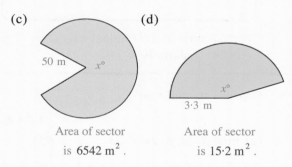
   50 m
   x°

   Area of sector
   is 6542 m².

   (d)
   x°
   3·3 m

   Area of sector
   is 15·2 m².

4. When a Chinese style straw hat is cut open, it forms the sector of a circle.

   cut here

   The sector of the circle has a radius of 26 centimetres.

   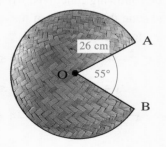
   26 cm
   A
   O
   55°
   B

   Calculate the area of straw needed to make the hat.

5. A cheese triangle is one of eight in a circular pack of cheese.

   The label is an isosceles triangle of side 3 cm, with an angle of 40°, and the whole pack has a radius of 5 cm.

   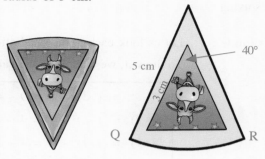
   P
   40°
   5 cm
   3 cm
   Q
   R

   (a) Write down the size of ∠QPR.

   (b) Calculate the **silver** area in the diagram, which indicates the difference between the area of the cheese sector and the triangular label.

6. A company logo consists of a **circle** with a **right angled triangle** removed from it as shown below.

   (a) Calculate the total **green** area.

   A gold trim is fitted around the edges of the triangle and the circle.

   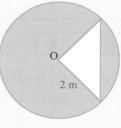
   O
   2 m

   (b) Calculate, **to the nearest centimetre**, the length of gold trim needed.

7. A path runs around part of a circular lawn. which has a diameter of 15 metres.

   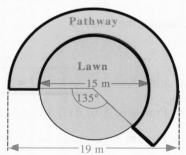
   Pathway
   Lawn
   15 m
   135°
   19 m

   Calculate :–

   (a) the total perimeter of the path.

   (b) the area covered by the path.

The Quadratic Function

Earlier in the book, you met **functions**, and in particular, you looked at the **Quadratic Function**.

In this Chapter, we are going to study the Quadratic Function in great depth, its related graph and its use in solving **Quadratic Equations**.

Example :-   Let us look back at the quadratic function $f(x) = x^2 - 4$, $\{-3 \le x \le 3\}$.

To draw it, we determine the value of $f(x)$ for various values of x.

$$f(-3) = (-3)^2 - 4 = 9 - 4 = 5$$
$$f(-2) = (-2)^2 - 4 = 4 - 4 = 0$$
$$f(-1) = (-1)^2 - 4 = 1 - 4 = -3$$
$$f(0) = (0)^2 - 4 = 0 - 4 = -4$$
$$f(1) = (1)^2 - 4 = 1 - 4 = -3$$
$$f(2) = (2)^2 - 4 = 4 - 4 = 0$$
$$f(3) = (3)^2 - 4 = 9 - 4 = 5$$

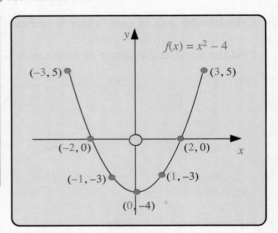

Now plot the points $(-3, 5)$, $(-2, 0)$ etc.

The **quadratic** graph is called a :-

PARABOLA.

The equation of the (dotted) **axis of symmetry** above is $x = 0$.

Exercise 14·1

1. Consider the function

    $f(x) = x^2 + 3$ $\{-2 \le x \le 2\}$.

    (a) Find $f(-2) = $ $(-2)^2 + 3 = 4 + 3 = ...$

    (b) Find also $f(-1)$, $f(0)$, $f(1)$ and $f(2)$.

    (c) Plot the 5 points on an x-y diagram and draw
        the **parabola** representing the function $f(x)$.

2. Consider the function

    $f(x) = x^2 - 3x$ $\{-1 \le x \le 4\}$.

    (a) Find $f(-1) = $ $(-1)^2 - 3 \times (-1) = ...$

    (b) Find also $f(0)$, $f(1)$, $f(2)$, $f(3)$ and $f(4)$.

    (c) Plot the 6 points on an x-y diagram and draw
        the **parabola** representing the function $f(x)$.

    (d) What are the **zeros**, or **roots** of the function ?
        (*i.e. where does it cut the x-axis ?*).

3. Consider the function

    $$f(x) = x^2 - 2x - 8 \qquad \{-3 \le x \le 5\}.$$

    (a) Find $f(-3)$, $f(-2)$, $f(-1)$ .... $f(5)$.

    (b) Plot the 9 points on an x-y diagram and draw
        the **parabola** representing the function $f(x)$.

    (c) What are the **roots** of the function ?

    (d) What is the equation of the axis of symmetry ?
        (*It is of the form :-* $x = ...$).

4. Sketch the following functions, write down their
    roots and state the equation of the **axis of
    symmetry** for each :-

    (a) $f(x) = x^2 - 4x$ $-1 \le x \le 5$

    (b) $y = x^2 - 2x - 3$ $-2 \le x \le 4$

    (c) $f(x) = x^2 + x - 6$ $-4 \le x \le 3$

    (d) $y = 4 - x^2$ $-3 \le x \le 3$

    (e) $f(x) = x^2 - x - 2$ $-2 \le x \le 3$.

    (*Retain these graphs - you will need them later*).

Quadratic Equations

You have seen how to solve **linear** equations of the following type :-

$$3x - 1 = 14$$
$$3x = 14 + 1$$
$$3x = 15$$
$$x = 5$$

$$4(x - 1) = 18$$
$$4x - 4 = 18$$
$$4x = 18 + 4$$
$$4x = 22$$
$$x = 5\tfrac{1}{2}$$

$$7x - 2 = 4x + 19$$
$$7x - 4x = 19 + 2$$
$$3x = 21$$
$$x = 7$$

In this chapter, we are going to solve **quadratic** equations like :-

$$x^2 - 4 = 0, \qquad x^2 - 3x = 0, \qquad x^2 - 2x - 8 = 0, \qquad 9 - x^2 = 0$$

Quadratic Equations – a graphical solution

Example :- Solve :- $x^2 - 3x = 0$.

In the previous exercise, we drew the graph of :-
$$y = x^2 - 3x.$$

If we replace the y with 0,

i.e. we find where the y-coordinate is zero,

i.e. we find where the graph cuts the x-axis,

then we end up solving :- $x^2 - 3x = 0$.

From the graph, the solutions to :-
$$x^2 - 3x = 0.$$
are at $x = 0$ and $x = 3$.

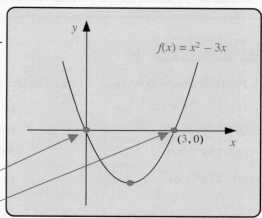

$f(x) = x^2 - 3x$

$(3, 0)$

Exercise 14·2

1. Shown is the graph of :-
   $$y = x^2 + 2x.$$
   From the graph, write
   down the solution to :-
   $$x^2 + 2x = 0.$$

2.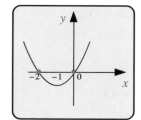

   This is the parabola
   associated with :-
   $$y = x^2 - 9.$$
   From the graph, write
   down the solution to :-
   $$x^2 - 9 = 0$$

3. This is the graph of :-
   $$y = x^2 + 2x - 3.$$
   Use the graph to write
   down the solution to
   the quadratic equation :-
   $$x^2 + 2x - 3 = 0.$$

   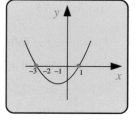

4. Look back at the parabolas you drew in
   question 4 of **Exercise 14·1**.

   Use the graphs you drew to solve these
   quadratic equations :-

   (a) $x^2 - 4x = 0$ (b) $x^2 - 2x - 3 = 0$

   (c) $x^2 + x - 6 = 0$ (d) $4 - x^2 = 0$

   (e) $x^2 - x - 2 = 0$.

Quadratic Equations (an Algebraic approach - without using a graph)

It takes an awfully long time to draw the graph of the function $y = x^2 - 2x - 8$

just so we can solve the equation :- $\boxed{x^2 - 2x - 8 = 0.}$

There is a **much much** quicker way than this using the art of **factorisation** learned in Chapter 7.

Revision of Factorising

Examples :-

Type 1 - Common Factor	Type 2 - Difference of 2 squares	Type 3 - Trinomials
$x^2 - 4x = x(x - 4)$	$x^2 - 9 = (x - 3)(x + 3)$	$x^2 + 6x + 8 = (x + 2)(x + 6)$
$3x^2 - 9x = 3x(x - 3)$	$x^2 - 25 = (x - 5)(x + 5)$	$x^2 - 2x - 15 = (x - 5)(x + 3)$
$6x^2 + 4x = 2x(3x + 2)$	$16x^2 - 9 = (4x - 3)(4x + 3)$	$x^2 + x - 72 = (x + 9)(x - 8)$

Exercise 14·3 (*Revision*)

1. **Factorise** the following :- **(take out the common factor)**.
   (a) $x^2 - 3x = x(x - ...)$
   (b) $x^2 + 6x = x(.........)$
   (c) $x^2 - 10x$
   (d) $6x^2 - 12x$
   (e) $8x^2 + 10x$
   (f) $18x^2 + 24x$
   (g) $15x - 5x^2$
   (h) $12xy - 16x^2$
   (i) $20ab^2 + 24a^2b$
   (j) $12x^3 + 8x^2$
   (k) $\frac{1}{2}x^2 + \frac{1}{2}x$
   (l) $8x - 12x^2 + 16x^3$.

2. **Factorise** the following :- **(difference of two squares)**.
   (a) $x^2 - 16 = (x + ...)(x - ...)$
   (b) $x^2 - 49 = (x + ...)(.........)$
   (c) $x^2 - 81$
   (d) $4x^2 - 9$
   (e) $x^2 - 100$
   (f) $49x^2 - 64y^2$
   (g) $81x^2 - 100z^2y^2$
   (h) $10x^2 - 40$ (common factor first)
   (i) $32x^2 - 50y^2$
   (j) $3x^2 - 75$
   (k) $36 - a^2$
   (l) $20 - 45a^2b^2$.

3. **Factorise** the following :- **(trinomials expressions)**.
   (a) $x^2 + 5x + 6 = (x + ...)(x + ...)$
   (b) $x^2 - 6x + 8$
   (c) $24 + 10x + x^2$
   (d) $x^2 - 2x - 35$
   (e) $x^2 - 11x + 18$
   (f) $28 - 3x - x^2$
   (g) $x^2 + 19x + 18$
   (h) $42 + x - x^2$
   (i) $x^2 - xy - 90y^2$
   (j) $x^2 + 10xy + 25y^2$
   (k) $36 - 12x + x^2$
   (l) $x^2 - 15x + 56$.

4. **Factorise** the following :- **(a mixture)**.
   (a) $x^2 - 9x$
   (b) $x^2 - 144$
   (c) $x^2 - 9x + 18$
   (d) $9x^2 - 49$
   (e) $121 - 100x^2$
   (f) $35 + 2x - x^2$
   (g) $x^2 + x - 90$
   (h) $x^2 + 16x + 39$
   (i) $x^2 + 2xy - 8y^2$
   (j) $30 - x - x^2$
   (k) $20 - 9x + x^2$
   (l) $5x^2 - 45$.

Quadratic Equations   (Solving using Factorisation)

To solve the quadratic equation, $x^2 - 2x - 8 = 0,$ without a graph, is almost impossible if you leave the quadratic expression in its present format.

"What number, if you square it, take 2 times the number away then take a further 8 away gives 0"?

Consider the equation :-

=> in its **factorised** form, it becomes :-

$$x^2 - 2x - 8 = 0$$
$$(x - 4)(x + 2) = 0$$

How does this help us solve the equation ?

Look at this problem :-   " I'm thinking of two numbers, (A and B) which
when multiplied, give 0. What could they be ?".

=>   0 and 5,   6 and 0,   0 and 23,   115 and 0 are possibilities.

Look again at the same problem, but with the added complication that neither A
nor B is allowed to be 0 !

=>   Now there is **NO** solution.

Very Important :-   If two numbers are multiplied to give 0, then **at least one of them must be 0.**

Let us look again at our quadratic equation.

By **factorising** it, we have :-

but, as shown above, this means that either =>

=>   which solves, fairly easily to give =>

$$x^2 - 2x - 8 = 0,$$
$$(x - 4) \times (x + 2) = 0.$$
$$(x - 4) = 0 \text{ or else } (x + 2) = 0$$
$$x = 4 \quad \text{or} \quad x = -2$$

This is your first **quadratic equation** solved by using **factorisation**.

Examples :-

Type 1 - Common Factor	Type 2 - Difference of 2 squares	Type 3 - Trinomials
$x^2 - 4x = 0$	$x^2 - 9 = 0$	$x^2 + 6x + 8 = 0$
$x(x - 4) = 0$	$(x - 3)(x + 3) = 0$	$(x + 2)(x + 4) = 0$
$x = 0 \text{ or } x - 4 = 0$	$x - 3 = 0 \text{ or } x + 3 = 0$	$x + 2 = 0 \text{ or } x + 4 = 0$
=> $x = 0$ or 4	=> $x = 3$ or -3	=> $x = -2$ or -4

Exercise 14·4

1.   These quadratic expressions have already been factorised. **Copy** and complete to find the solutions :-

(a)
$$x(x - 3) = 0$$
$$x = 0 \text{ or } x - 3 = 0$$
$$x = 0 \text{ or } .....$$

(b)
$$x(x + 7) = 0$$
$$x = 0 \text{ or } x + 7 = 0$$
$$x = ... \text{ or } ...$$

(c)
$$3x(2x - 6) = 0$$
$$3x = 0 \text{ or } 2x - 6 = 0$$
$$x = ... \text{ or } ...$$

2. Copy and find the solutions :-

(a) $x(x + 5) = 0$ (b) $x(x - 10) = 0$ (c) $3x(x + 8) = 0$

(d) $5x(2x - 3) = 0$ (e) $4x(3x + 6) = 0$ (f) $\frac{1}{2}x(x - 3) = 0$.

3. These quadratic expressions have also been factorised. Copy and complete to find the solutions :-

(a)
$$(x - 3)(x + 3) = 0$$
$$x - 3 = 0 \text{ or } x + 3 = 0$$
$$x = 3 \text{ or } .....$$

(b)
$$(x + 2)(x - 2) = 0$$
$$x + 2 = 0 \text{ or } x - 2 = 0$$
$$x = ... \text{ or } ...$$

(c)
$$(2x - 7)(2x + 7) = 0$$
$$2x - 7 = 0 \text{ or } 2x + 7 = 0$$
$$x = ... \text{ or } ...$$

4. Copy and find the solutions :-

(a) $(x + 5)(x - 5) = 0$ (b) $(x - 4)(x + 4) = 0$ (c) $(x - 11)(x + 11) = 0$

(d) $(x + 8)(x - 8) = 0$ (e) $(2x + 10)(2x - 10) = 0$ (f) $(5x - 5)(5x + 5) = 0$.

5. These quadratic expressions have also been factorised. Copy and complete to find the solutions :-

(a)
$$(x - 3)(x - 4) = 0$$
$$x - 3 = 0 \text{ or } x - 4 = 0$$
$$x = 3 \text{ or } .....$$

(b)
$$(x + 2)(x - 5) = 0$$
$$x + 2 = 0 \text{ or } x - 5 = 0$$
$$x = ... \text{ or } ...$$

(c)
$$(2x + 1)(3x - 7) = 0$$
$$2x + 1 = 0 \text{ or } 3x - 7 = 0$$
$$x = ... \text{ or } ...$$

6. Copy and find the solutions :-

(a) $(x + 3)(x + 6) = 0$ (b) $(x - 2)(x - 8) = 0$ (c) $(x - 4)(x + 9) = 0$

(d) $(x + 8)(x - 3) = 0$ (e) $(2x + 10)(3x - 6) = 0$ (f) $(5x - 5)(2x + 3) = 0$.

7. Factorise these quadratic expressions and find the solutions :-

(a)
$$x^2 - 8x = 0$$
$$x(x - ...) = 0$$
$$x = 0 \text{ or } x - ... = 0$$
$$x = ... \text{ or } .....$$

(b)
$$x^2 + 12x = 0$$
$$x(x + ...) = 0$$
$$x = 0 \text{ or } x + ... = 0$$
$$x = ... \text{ or } ...$$

(c)
$$3x^2 - 12x = 0$$
$$3x(x - ...) = 0$$
$$3x = 0 \text{ or } x - ... = 0$$
$$x = ... \text{ or } ...$$

8. Copy and find the solutions :-

(a) $x^2 - 6x = 0$ (b) $x^2 + 19x = 0$ (c) $2x^2 - 8x = 0$

(d) $4x^2 + 20x = 0$ (e) $5x^2 - 100x = 0$ (f) $10x^2 - 15x = 0$.

9. Factorise these quadratic expressions and find the solutions :-

(a)
$$x^2 - 16 = 0$$
$$(x + 4)(x - ...) = 0$$
$$x + 4 = 0 \text{ or } x - ... = 0$$
$$x = ... \text{ or } .....$$

(b)
$$x^2 - 49 = 0$$
$$(x - ...)(x + ...) = 0$$
$$x - ... = 0 \text{ or } x + ... = 0$$
$$x = ... \text{ or } ...$$

(c)
$$4x^2 - 25 = 0$$
$$(2x + 5)(2x - ...) = 0$$
$$2x + 5 = 0 \text{ or } 2x - ... = 0$$
$$x = ... \text{ or } ...$$

10. Copy and find the solutions :-

(a) $x^2 - 9 = 0$ (b) $x^2 - 36 = 0$ (c) $x^2 - 81 = 0$

(d) $9x^2 - 16 = 0$ (e) $49x^2 - 1 = 0$ (f) $100 - x^2 = 0$.

11. **Factorise** these quadratic expressions and find the solutions :-

(a)
$x^2 + 8x + 12 = 0$
$(x + 2)(x + ...) = 0$
$x + 2 = 0$ or $x + ... = 0$
$x = ...$ or .....

(b)
$x^2 - 12x + 20 = 0$
$(x - 2)(x - ...) = 0$
$x - 2 = 0$ or $x - ... = 0$
$x = ...$ or ...

(c)
$x^2 - 2x - 15 = 0$
$(x + 3)(x - ...) = 0$
$x + 3 = 0$ or $x - ... = 0$
$x = ...$ or ...

12. **Copy** and find the solutions :-

(a) $x^2 + 5x + 4 = 0$

(b) $x^2 + 19x + 90 = 0$

(c) $x^2 + 11x + 30 = 0$

(d) $x^2 - 12x + 20 = 0$

(e) $x^2 - 10x + 24 = 0$

(f) $x^2 - 15x + 50 = 0$

(g) $x^2 + 2x - 15 = 0$

(h) $x^2 - 3x - 18 = 0$

(i) $x^2 - 7x - 30 = 0$

(j) $42 - x - x^2 = 0$

(k) $24 + 10x - x^2 = 0$

(l) $72 + x - x^2 = 0$.

Harder Quadratic Equations   (Trinomials)

To solve quadratic equations like :- $3x^2 + 5x - 2 = 0$ or $6x^2 + 13x + 2 = 0$ requires the
Saint Andrew's Cross method of factorising, learned earlier.

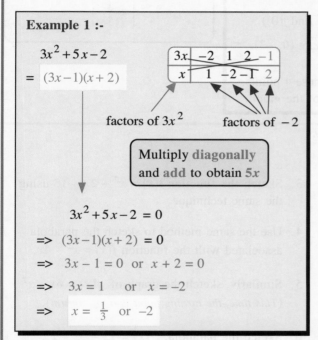

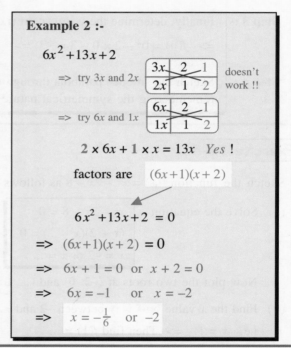

13. **Copy** and find the solutions :-

(a) $3x^2 - 8x - 3 = 0$

(b) $2x^2 + 11x + 15 = 0$

(c) $5x^2 + 23x - 10 = 0$

(d) $4x^2 - 9x + 2 = 0$

(e) $3x^2 + 10x - 8 = 0$

(f) $2x^2 + 5x + 3 = 0$

(g) $6x^2 - 11x + 3 = 0$

(h) $4x^2 + 16x + 15 = 0$

(i) $10x^2 - 4x - 6 = 0$

(j) $6x^2 - 17x - 3 = 0$

(k) $9x^2 - 6x - 8 = 0$

(l) $15x^2 - 13x - 6 = 0$.

14. **Copy** and find the solutions to this **mixture** of quadratic equations :-

(a) $2x^2 + 14x = 0$

(b) $10x^2 - 15x = 0$

(c) $x^2 - 121 = 0$

(d) $36x^2 - 25 = 0$

(e) $x^2 + 10x + 21 = 0$

(f) $x^2 - 13x + 30 = 0$

(g) $x^2 + 2x - 35 = 0$

(h) $x^2 - 3x - 4 = 0$

(i) $x^2 - x - 90 = 0$

(j) $2x^2 - 13x + 15 = 0$

(k) $6x^2 + 17x - 14 = 0$

(l) $4x^2 - 20x + 9 = 0$.

We can make a quick sketch of a parabola, given its equation, using **factorisation** to determine the roots. Along with two other points, the **y-intercept** and the **turning point**, we can complete the graph easily.

Example :- Make a quick sketch of the parabola associated with $f(x) = x^2 - 2x - 3$.

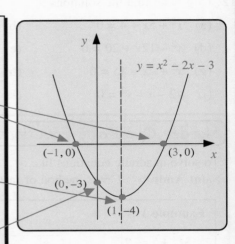

Step 1 :- Solve the equation $\quad x^2 - 2x - 3 = 0$

$$(x + 1)(x - 3) = 0$$

$$x = -1 \text{ or } x = 3.$$

Now plot the two **roots** at $(-1, 0)$ and $(3, 0)$.

Step 2 :- Find the x-value **half way** between the roots -1 & 3.

$\Rightarrow \quad x = 1. \quad \Rightarrow \quad$ Then find $f(1) = 1^2 - 2 \times 1 - 3 = -4$.

Now plot the **minimum turning point** at $(1, -4)$.

Step 3 :- Finally, determine the y-intercept (i.e. find $f(0)$).

$\Rightarrow \quad f(0) = 0^2 - 2 \times 0 - 3 = -3 \quad \Rightarrow \quad$ Plot $(0, -3)$.

Step 4 :- Sketch the **smooth** parabola through these 4 points, remembering the symmetrical nature of the graph.

Exercise 14·5

1. Sketch the function $f(x) = x^2 - 2x - 8$ as follows

   (a) Solve the equation

   | $x^2 - 2x - 8 = 0$ |
   | $(x + 2)(x - ...) = 0$ |
   | $x = -2$ or $x = ...$. |

   Now plot the two roots at $(-2, 0)$ and $(..., 0)$.

   (b) Find the x-value **half way** between -2 and ... .
   i.e. $x = 1$. $\Rightarrow$ Then find $f(1) = ...$.
   Now plot the **turning point** at $(1, ...)$.

   (c) Determine the **y-intercept** (i.e. find $f(0)$).
   $\Rightarrow \quad f(0) = 0^2 - 2 \times 0 - 8 = ...$ Plot $(0, -...)$.

   (d) Sketch the parabola through these 4 points.

2. In a similar way, sketch the parabola
   $$f(x) = x^2 - 4x - 5.$$

   (a) Find the two roots.

   (b) Find the minimum turning point.

   (c) Find the y-intercept and sketch the graph.

3. Sketch the function $f(x) = x^2 + 2x - 15$ using the same technique.

4. Use the same method to sketch the parabola associated with the function $f(x) = x^2 - 4x$.

5. Similarly, sketch the graph of $f(x) = 6x - x^2$.
   (*This time, the turning point is a maximum*).

6. Sketch the parabola, $f(x) = 12 - 4x - x^2$.
   (*Remember* $12 - 4x - x^2 = (6 + x)(2 - x)$).

7. Make quick sketches of the following functions, in each case indicating the **roots**, the **turning point** and the **y-intercept** :-

   (a) $f(x) = x^2 - 6x - 7$

   (b) $f(x) = x^2 - 8x + 15$

   (c) $f(x) = x^2 - 8x$

   (d) $f(x) = 3x^2 - 3$

   (e) $f(x) = 3 - 2x - x^2$.

Intersection of a Line and a Parabola

We can also use factorisation to discover the coordinates of the points where a line and a parabola meet, without the need to draw a graph showing the line and the parabola.

Example :- Find the coordinates of the two points, P and Q, where the parabola $y = x^2 - 4x + 5$ and the line $y = -x + 3$ * meet. (*The sketch shows P and Q*).

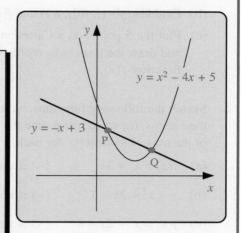

Solution :- At the 2 points P and Q, the y-coordinate of the line and the y-coordinate of the parabola are identical.

=> Set the two functions equal to each other.

$$=> \quad x^2 - 4x + 5 = -x + 3$$

rearrange $=> \quad x^2 - 4x + 5 + x - 3 = 0$

$$=> \quad x^2 - 3x + 2 = 0$$

factorise $=> \quad (x - 1)(x - 2) = 0$

$$=> \quad x = 1 \text{ or } x = 2$$

To find the y-coordinates, replace x with 1 and 2 in *

=> when $x = 1$, $y = -1 + 3 = 2$ => P(1, 2)

=> when $x = 2$, $y = -2 + 3 = 1$ => Q(2, 1)

Exercise 14·6

1. Find the coordinates of the two points where the parabola $y = x^2 - 2x + 5$ and the line $y = 2x + 2$ meet as follows :-

   (a) Set $x^2 - 2x + 5 = 2x + 2$ and rearrange the expression by moving all terms to the left side.

   (b) This means solving $x^2 - 4x + 3 = 0$.

   (c) Substitute your two x-values back into the equation $y = 2x + 2$ to find the y-values.

   (d) Write down the coordinates of the two points of intersection.

2. Use the above method to find where the parabola $y = x^2 - x - 5$ and the line $y = 3x + 7$ meet.

3. Find where the parabola $y = x^2 + 3x - 5$ and the line $y = 2x + 1$ meet.

4. Determine where the parabola $y = x^2 - 2x$ and the line $y = 3x - 4$ meet.

5. Find where the parabola $y = 7 - 2x - x^2$ and the line $y = 3x + 1$ intersect.

6. The diagram below shows the two parabolas, $y = x^2 - 6x + 13$ and $y = x^2 - 2x + 5$ meeting at P.

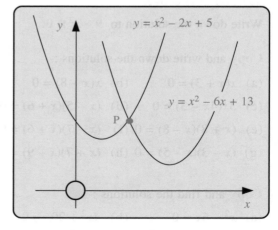

   By setting $x^2 - 2x + 5 = x^2 - 6x + 13$ and solving, find the coordinates of point P.

7. Use the above method to find where the parabolas $y = x^2 - x - 5$ and $y = x^2 - 3x + 7$ meet.

Remember Remember..... ?

1. Consider the function
$$f(x) = x^2 - 2, \qquad \{-2 \leq x \leq 2\}.$$

   (a) Find $f(-2) = (-2)^2 - 2 = 4 - 2 = ...$

   (b) Find also $f(-1), f(0), f(1)$ and $f(2)$.

   (c) Plot the 5 points on a Cartesian diagram and draw the **parabola** representing the function $f(x)$.

2. Sketch the following functions, write down their **zeros**, (or **roots**), and state the equation of the **axis of symmetry** for each :-

   (a) $f(x) = x^2 + 3x$ $\{-4 \leq x \leq 1\}$

   (b) $y = x^2 + 2x - 3$ $\{-4 \leq x \leq 2\}$

   (c) $f(x) = x^2 - 2x - 8$ $\{-3 \leq x \leq 5\}$

   (d) $y = 9 - x^2$ $\{-4 \leq x \leq 4\}$

   (e) $f(x) = x^2 - x - 6$ $\{-3 \leq x \leq 4\}$.

3. Shown is the graph of :-
$$y = x^2 - 2x.$$
   From the graph, write down the solution to :-
$$x^2 - 2x = 0.$$

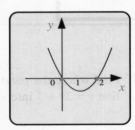

4. Look at the graph of $y = 9 - x^2$ you drew in question 2(d) above.

   Write down the solution to $9 - x^2 = 0$.

5. **Copy** and write down the solutions :-

   (a) $x(x + 3) = 0$ (b) $x(x - 8) = 0$

   (c) $3x(4x - 3) = 0$ (d) $(x - 5)(x + 6) = 0$

   (e) $(x + 8)(x - 8) = 0$ (f) $(x - 7)(x + 6) = 0$

   (g) $(x - 3)(x - 5) = 0$ (h) $(x + 7)(x - 9) = 0$.

6. **Copy** and find the solutions :-

   (a) $x^2 - 6x = 0$ (b) $4x^2 + 20x = 0$

   (c) $5x^2 - 100x = 0$ (d) $10x^2 - 15x = 0$

   (e) $x^2 - 64 = 0$ (f) $16x^2 - 9 = 0$

   (g) $25x^2 - 1 = 0$ (h) $49 - x^2 = 0$.

7. **Copy** and find the solutions :-

   (a) $x^2 + 6x + 8 = 0$ (b) $x^2 + 14x + 40 = 0$

   (c) $x^2 - 11x + 18 = 0$ (d) $x^2 - 2x - 48 = 0$

   (e) $x^2 + 3x - 28 = 0$ (f) $20 - x - x^2 = 0$

   (g) $14 + 5x - x^2 = 0$ (h) $x^2 - 15x + 56 = 0$.

8. **Copy** and find the solutions :-

   (a) $2x^2 + 9x - 5 = 0$ (b) $3x^2 - 11x + 6 = 0$

   (c) $5x^2 + 14x - 3 = 0$ (d) $4x^2 - 4x - 3 = 0$

   (e) $3x^2 - 2x - 8 = 0$ (f) $2x^2 - 7x + 5 = 0$

   (g) $6x^2 - 7x - 3 = 0$ (h) $4x^2 + 23x - 6 = 0$.

9. Sketch the function $f(x) = x^2 + 2x - 3$ as follows :-

   (a) Solve the equation
$$x^2 + 2x - 3 = 0$$
$$(x + 3)(x - ...) = 0$$
$$x = -3 \text{ or } x = ...$$
   Now plot the two roots at $(-3, 0)$ and $(..., 0)$.

   (b) Find the x-value **half way** between -3 and $...$.
   i.e. $x = -1$. $\Rightarrow$ Then find $f(-1) = ...$.
   Now plot the **turning point** at $(-1, ...)$.

   (c) Determine the y-intercept (i.e. find $f(0)$).
   $\Rightarrow$ $f(0) = 0^2 + 2 \times 0 - 3 = ...$ Plot $(0, -...)$.

   (d) Sketch the parabola through these 4 points.

10. Sketch the function $f(x) = x^2 + 4x - 12$, using the same technique.

11. Use the same method to sketch the parabola associated with the function $f(x) = x^2 - 9$.

12. Find the coordinates of the two points where the parabola $y = x^2 - x + 1$ and the line $y = 3x + 6$ meet. (*Hint* :- set $x^2 - x + 1 = 3x + 6$ *and solve*).

13. Use the same method to find where the parabola $y = x^2 - 2x - 5$ and the line $y = -4x + 10$ meet.

What is a Vector ?

There are two types of measurable quantities in this world :-

SCALARS and VECTORS.

Definition :- A **scalar** quantity is one that only requires **size** (or **magnitude**) to define it fully.
It does **not** require a sense of "**direction**" to be assigned to it.

Examples :-

Time	-	3 seconds, 5 minutes, 4 days, a year.
Length	-	8 cm, 25 metres, 2·7 kilometres, half a mile.
Area	-	35 mm^2, 17 cm^2, 250 m^2, 3 acres.
Speed	-	160 km/hr, 3500 mph, 25 cm per sec.

Definition :- A **vector** quantity is one that requires, not just **magnitude** (or **size**) to define it, but needs an indication of its **direction**.

Examples :-

Displacement - (movement) : If you want to describe a walk you have just done, it is not good enough to just tell how far you have gone.
You have to tell where you went or in other words, what **direction** you took.

Velocity - A pilot would be in trouble if all he gave to air traffic control was what speed he was doing. He would have to tell them his speed **and** in what **direction** he was travelling.

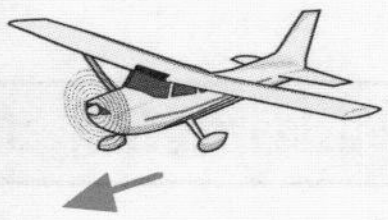

Force - When a force is applied to slide a box of matches, just knowing the "strength" of the force is not enough. You won't be able to tell where the box ends up without being told in what **direction** the force was being applied.

Representing a Vector

We can represent a vector by what is called a **directed line segment**.

The diagram shows a **journey** from A to B, written as $\overrightarrow{AB}$ or $\underline{u}$.

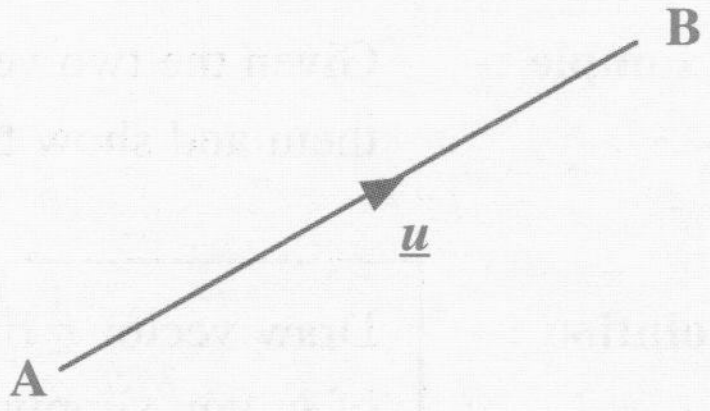

(Some books use bold italics $\boldsymbol{u}$, but this is difficult for you to show).

Instead, in this chapter, we will emphasise it is a vector by underlining it, thus representing it as the vector $\underline{u}$.

Note that :- The **magnitude** of the vector, or displacement, is represented by the length of the line.
The **direction** of the vector is shown by the arrow.

Equivalent Vectors

A vector journey simply tells you where you end up at, in relation to where you began your journey. For this reason, if two or more directed line segments have the **same length and the same direction**, then they represent the same **vector** (journey). These four vectors are all equivalent.

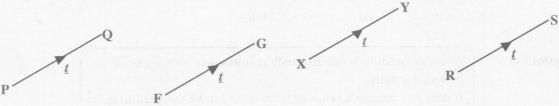

In other words :- $\overrightarrow{PQ} = \overrightarrow{FG} = \overrightarrow{XY} = \overrightarrow{RS} = \underline{t}$.

Can you also see why vector $\overrightarrow{DE} = -\underline{t}$? (*the opposite direction*).

Adding Vectors

Shown are two vectors $\underline{u}$ and $\underline{v}$.

Imagine you took a journey along in the direction of vector $\underline{u}$, then turned and took a second journey in the direction $\underline{v}$.

To find the single equivalent vector journey, as far as your starting point and finishing point is concerned, you simply redraw the vectors and add them **nose** to **tail**.

This new **single** journey, equivalent to both combined journeys, is the vector :-

$$\underline{u} + \underline{v}.$$

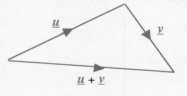

Multiplying a Vector by a Scalar (a number)

Shown this time is the vector $\underline{a}$.

Imagine you took a journey in the same direction as vector $\underline{a}$, but travelled twice (or three times) as far.

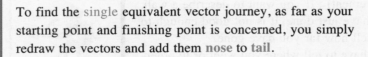

This time, the new vector can be represented by a directed line segment, parallel to the vector, but twice (or three times) as long.

i.e. $2\underline{a}$ (or $3\underline{a}$).

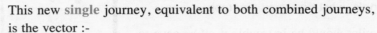

Example :- Given the two vectors $\underline{b}$ and $\underline{d}$, sketch them and show the vector $\underline{b} + 2\underline{d}$.

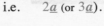

Solution :-

Draw vector $\underline{b}$ first. Then, onto the end of $\underline{b}$, you simply add on a vector equivalent to, but twice the length of $\underline{d}$.

The **blue arrowed line** represents the vector $\underline{b} + 2\underline{d}$.

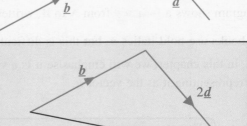

1. This vector is given as :- $\overrightarrow{AB}$ = $\underline{u}$.

Name each of these vectors in **two** ways :-

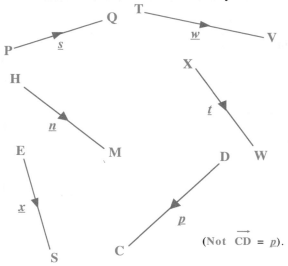

(Not $\overrightarrow{CD}$ = $\underline{p}$).

2. Sketch this vector $\underline{u}$.

(a) Now sketch the vector $2\underline{u}$.

(b) Sketch the vector $3\underline{u}$.

(c) Sketch the vector $-\underline{u}$.

(d) Sketch the vector $-4\underline{u}$.

3. Sketch these two vectors $\underline{a}$ and $\underline{b}$.

3. (a) Now sketch the vector $2\underline{b}$.

(b) Sketch the vector showing $\underline{a} + \underline{b}$ and mark $\underline{a} + \underline{b}$ on your diagram.

(c) This time, sketch the vector $\underline{b} + \underline{a}$.
(*i.e. start drawing $\underline{b}$ first, then $\underline{a}$*).

(d) Do the vectors you have drawn in parts (b) and (c) look the same ?

(e) What does this tell you about how you draw vectors $\underline{a} + \underline{b}$ or $\underline{b} + \underline{a}$?

(f) Similarly, sketch the vector $\underline{a} + 2\underline{b}$.

(g) Sketch the vector $2\underline{a} + \underline{b}$.

(h) Do the vectors $\underline{a} + 2\underline{b}$ and $2\underline{a} + \underline{b}$ look the same in your sketches ?

4. Sketch the vectors $\underline{p}$ and $\underline{q}$.

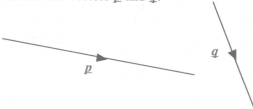

(a) Sketch the vector $\underline{p} + \underline{q}$.

(b) Now sketch an label vectors $-\underline{p}$ and $-\underline{q}$.

(c) Sketch the vector $-(\underline{p} + \underline{q})$.
(*This is the same as $\underline{p} + \underline{q}$ but in the opposite direction*).

(d) From your sketches in part (b), show the vector $-\underline{p} + -\underline{q}$. Is it the same as $-(\underline{p} + \underline{q})$?

Subtracting Vectors

If you wish to **subtract** vectors such as $\underline{a} - \underline{b}$, it is easier to draw the vectors $\underline{a}$ and $-\underline{b}$, then **add**.

=> $\boxed{\underline{a} - \underline{b} = \underline{a} + -\underline{b}.}$

Example :- Draw $-\underline{b}$ first. =>

Then add $\underline{a} + -\underline{b}$ => $\underline{a} - \underline{b} = \underline{a} + -\underline{b}$ =>

5. Sketch the vectors r and s.

(a) Sketch the vector $r + s$.

(b) Now sketch and label vector $r - s$.

(c) Sketch the vector $s - r$. (*Draw s first*).

(d) Sketch the vector $-2s$.

(e) Now sketch $r - 2s$.

(f) Sketch $3s - 2r$.

6. Shown is the vector n.

(a) Sketch n.

(b) Sketch $-n$.

(c) Try to sketch the vector $n + -n$.

When you add a vector to its negative, you end up where you started. (*They cancel each other*).

> This is referred to as the zero vector.
> $u + -u$ is the same as $u - u = 0$. (*Note how its written*).

Representing Vectors in 2 Dimensions

We can introduce numerical values for vectors by representing them on a 2 dimensional grid as shown.

Vector $\overrightarrow{AB} = n$ represents a journey, (a translation), from point A to point B, and this can be achieved by starting at A, moving 6 boxes right, then 4 boxes up, and arriving finally at point B.
We can represent this as follows :-

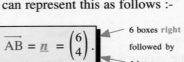

$\overrightarrow{AB} = n = \begin{pmatrix} 6 \\ 4 \end{pmatrix}$.

6 boxes right
followed by
4 boxes up

> The 6 is referred to as the horizontal component of the vector.
> The 4 is referred to as the vertical component.

In the diagram, two other vectors are shown, $\overrightarrow{RS}$ and $\overrightarrow{PQ}$.

To travel from point R to point S, you move 4 right and 5 down. => 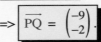 $\overrightarrow{RS} = \begin{pmatrix} 4 \\ -5 \end{pmatrix}$. * note the negative component.

To travel from point P back to point Q, you move 9 left and 2 down. => $\overrightarrow{PQ} = \begin{pmatrix} -9 \\ -2 \end{pmatrix}$. * note both the components are negative.

Adding Vectors in 2 Dimensions

We have already seen that to add two vectors, you simply draw the first, then join the tail of the second onto the head of the first.

This is easily seen in two dimensions.

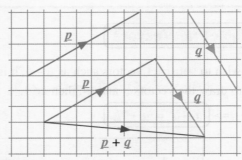

Shown are 2 vectors, $p = \begin{pmatrix} 7 \\ 4 \end{pmatrix}$ and $q = \begin{pmatrix} 3 \\ -5 \end{pmatrix}$.
To find what vector $p + q$ looks like, we add.

Note that :- $p + q = \begin{pmatrix} 7 \\ 4 \end{pmatrix} + \begin{pmatrix} 3 \\ -5 \end{pmatrix} = \begin{pmatrix} 7 + 3 \\ 4 + (-5) \end{pmatrix} = \begin{pmatrix} 10 \\ -1 \end{pmatrix}$.

> To add two vectors whose components are known, you simply add the corresponding components.

1. Use brackets to write down the 2 dimensional components of the following vectors :-

Example :- $\overrightarrow{AB} = \underline{p} = \begin{pmatrix} 4 \\ 2 \end{pmatrix}$.

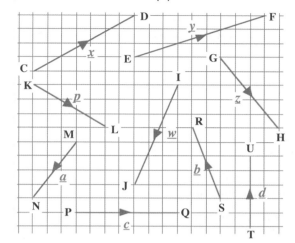

2. On squared paper, draw and label representatives of the following vectors :-

(a) $\underline{p} = \begin{pmatrix} 4 \\ 2 \end{pmatrix}$ (b) $\underline{q} = \begin{pmatrix} 5 \\ 3 \end{pmatrix}$

(c) $\underline{r} = \begin{pmatrix} 4 \\ -2 \end{pmatrix}$ (d) $\underline{s} = \begin{pmatrix} 1 \\ -5 \end{pmatrix}$

(e) $\overrightarrow{AB} = \begin{pmatrix} -2 \\ 3 \end{pmatrix}$ (f) $\overrightarrow{HK} = \begin{pmatrix} -5 \\ 0 \end{pmatrix}$

(g) $\overrightarrow{UV} = \begin{pmatrix} -8 \\ -3 \end{pmatrix}$ (h) $\overrightarrow{ST} = \begin{pmatrix} 0 \\ -6 \end{pmatrix}$.

3. (a) On squared paper, draw the vector $\underline{a} = \begin{pmatrix} 3 \\ 2 \end{pmatrix}$.

   (b) Beside it, draw the vector $2\underline{a}$.

3. (c) Write down the components of vector $2\underline{a}$.

   Can you see that $2\underline{a} = \begin{pmatrix} 6 \\ 4 \end{pmatrix} = 2 \times \begin{pmatrix} 3 \\ 2 \end{pmatrix} = 2 \times \underline{a}$?

> If you multiply a vector $\underline{a}$ by a number (a scalar), you simply multiply each component of the vector by that number.

In question 4, you are not required to draw the vectors. However, if you feel it would help, please feel free to do so.

4. Given $\underline{r} = \begin{pmatrix} 6 \\ 2 \end{pmatrix}$ and $\underline{s} = \begin{pmatrix} 4 \\ -3 \end{pmatrix}$, find :-

   (a) $\underline{r} + \underline{s}$ (b) $\underline{r} - \underline{s}$

   (c) $2\underline{r}$ (d) $3\underline{s}$

   (e) $2\underline{r} + 3\underline{s}$ (f) $3\underline{s} - 2\underline{r}$

   (g) $4\underline{r} - \underline{s}$ (h) $-\underline{r}$

   (i) $\underline{r} + -\underline{r}$ (j) $\underline{s} - \underline{s}$.

5. Draw vectors $\underline{a} = \begin{pmatrix} 5 \\ 2 \end{pmatrix}$, $\underline{b} = \begin{pmatrix} -1 \\ -4 \end{pmatrix}$ and $\underline{c} = \begin{pmatrix} -4 \\ 2 \end{pmatrix}$.

   (a) On your grid show how to add $\underline{a} + \underline{b}$.

   (b) Check from your drawing :- $\underline{a} + \underline{b} = \begin{pmatrix} 4 \\ -2 \end{pmatrix}$.

   (c) Without the aid of a drawing, find $\underline{a} + \underline{b} + \underline{c}$.

   (d) Explain your answer.

6. Solve these vector equations for vector $\underline{x}$.

   (a) $\underline{x} + \begin{pmatrix} 2 \\ 4 \end{pmatrix} = \begin{pmatrix} 7 \\ 9 \end{pmatrix}$ (b) $\underline{x} - \begin{pmatrix} 2 \\ 8 \end{pmatrix} = \begin{pmatrix} 5 \\ -3 \end{pmatrix}$

   (c) $2\underline{x} = \begin{pmatrix} 10 \\ -6 \end{pmatrix}$ (d) $5\underline{x} = \begin{pmatrix} 200 \\ -80 \end{pmatrix}$

   (e) $3\underline{x} - \begin{pmatrix} 4 \\ -1 \end{pmatrix} = \begin{pmatrix} 11 \\ 7 \end{pmatrix}$ (f) $6\underline{x} - \begin{pmatrix} 2 \\ 5 \end{pmatrix} = 2\underline{x} + \begin{pmatrix} 10 \\ -1 \end{pmatrix}$.

Vectors represented in a Coordinate Diagram

An obvious place to represent vectors is in a Cartesian Diagram, with the positions of points being given in terms of a fixed point O, the **origin**.

Shown are 3 points A(2, 4), B(8, 3) and C(5, -1).

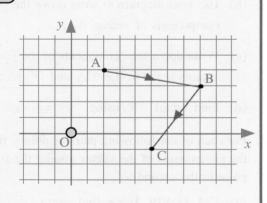

• Check that vector $\overrightarrow{AB} = \begin{pmatrix} 6 \\ -1 \end{pmatrix}$ and vector $\overrightarrow{BC} = \begin{pmatrix} -3 \\ -4 \end{pmatrix}$.

• Check both diagrammatically, and using components that, by adding the two vectors, we get $\overrightarrow{AB} + \overrightarrow{BC} = \begin{pmatrix} 3 \\ -5 \end{pmatrix} = \overrightarrow{AC}$.

• Check both diagrammatically, and using components that, by adding the vectors, we get $\overrightarrow{AB} + \overrightarrow{BC} + \overrightarrow{CA} = \begin{pmatrix} 0 \\ 0 \end{pmatrix}$, where $\overrightarrow{CA} = \begin{pmatrix} -3 \\ 5 \end{pmatrix}$.

It is often handy to record the position of a point
in relation to the origin by using **components**.

Here, the points P and Q are given by P(2, 5) and Q(8, 2).

Can you see that vector $\overrightarrow{OP} = \begin{pmatrix} 2 \\ 5 \end{pmatrix}$ and vector $\overrightarrow{OQ} = \begin{pmatrix} 8 \\ 2 \end{pmatrix}$?

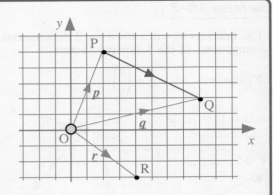

Vectors like $\overrightarrow{OP}$, that define the **position** of a point in
relation to the **origin** are defined by the vector $\underline{p}$.

Similarly, **position vector** $\overrightarrow{OQ} = \underline{q} = \begin{pmatrix} 8 \\ 2 \end{pmatrix}$ and **position vector** $\overrightarrow{OR} = \underline{r} = \begin{pmatrix} 4 \\ -3 \end{pmatrix}$.

If you know the coordinates of two points P and Q, it is easy to determine the
components of the vector joining them, without having to draw up a diagram.

In the above diagram, can you see that, in vector terms, the journey from P to Q
can be completed by leaving P, going to the origin O, then going from O to Q ?

In vector terms, this means :- $\overrightarrow{PQ} = \overrightarrow{PO} + \overrightarrow{OQ} = -\underline{p} + \underline{q}$ or by reversing these, $= \underline{q} - \underline{p}$.

=> $\boxed{\overrightarrow{PQ} = \underline{q} - \underline{p}.}$ *This is a very important technique for determining
vector components and should be learned.*

i.e. to find the vector $\overrightarrow{PQ}$, joining two points P and Q, you simply subtract the position
vector $\underline{p}$ of the first point from the position vector $\underline{q}$ of the second point.

Example :- Determine the components of the vector $\overrightarrow{QR}$ in the above diagram.

Solution :- Vector $\overrightarrow{QR} = \underline{r} - \underline{q} = \begin{pmatrix} 4 \\ -3 \end{pmatrix} - \begin{pmatrix} 8 \\ 2 \end{pmatrix} = \begin{pmatrix} -4 \\ -5 \end{pmatrix}.$ *(Check this out from the figure above).*

Exercise 15·3

1. (a) Plot the 2 points A(4, 1) and B(6, 8).

    (b) Use your diagram to write down the
         components of vector $\overrightarrow{AB}$.

    (c) Write down the components of the position
         vectors $\underline{a}$ and $\underline{b}$. (i.e. $\overrightarrow{OA}$ and $\overrightarrow{OB}$).

    (d) Find vector $\overrightarrow{AB}$, using $\overrightarrow{AB} = \underline{b} - \underline{a}$.

2. For each of the following pairs of points, find
    the components of the vector joining the first
    point to the second :-

    (a) U(4, 1), V(9, 3) i.e. find vector $\overrightarrow{UV}$.

    (b) S(0, 5), T(7, 2)   (c) J(2, -3), K(5, 6)

    (d) P(-3, -4), Q(6, 0)   (e) C(6, 2), D(1, -4)

    (f) G(2, -5), H(-1, 3)   (g) A(-2, 7), B(-4, -5).

3. The coordinates of 6 points are P(1, 1), Q(5, 4),
    A(3, -2), B(7, 1), U(-4, 2) and V(0, 5).

    (a) Find the vector $\overrightarrow{PQ}$. $(\underline{q} - \underline{p})$.

    (b) Find the vectors $\overrightarrow{AB}$ and $\overrightarrow{UV}$.

    (c) What does this tell you about the three
         lines, PQ, AB and UV ?

4. M(1, -3), N(2, 1), R(4, -3) and S(6, 5).

    (a) Find the vectors $\overrightarrow{MN}$ and $\overrightarrow{RS}$.

    (b) Describe clearly the connection(s)
         between the lines MN and RS.

5. A(-1, -2), B(2, 4), C(7, 6) and D(4, 0).

    (a) Without plotting the points, find the
         components of the vectors $\overrightarrow{AB}$ and $\overrightarrow{DC}$.

    (b) What can you say about lines AB and DC ?

    (c) What type of quadrilateral does this fact
         tell you ABCD must be ?

The Magnitude of a Vector

A vector, (like displacement, velocity or force), requires direction as well as a sense of "size" to define it fully.

Sometimes we are only interested in the **size** of a vector, e.g. the **length** of the line, the **strength** of the force, or just the **speed** of an object. These are **scalar** quantities.

This is referred to as the **magnitude** of the vector, and when we are given a vector in component form, it is easy to calculate this, using **Pythagoras' Theorem**.

Given vector $\overrightarrow{AB}$ or $\underline{u}$, the **magnitude** is denoted by :-

$$\boxed{|\overrightarrow{AB}| \text{ or } |\underline{u}|.}$$

(The "bars" either side, (the modulus sign), denotes the magnitude or "size" of the vector).

Example :- The diagram shows two points A(1, 5) and B(9, -1). Find the length of the line AB.

Solution 1 :- One way of tackling the problem would be to draw a horizontal line from A and a vertical line from B to form a right angle triangle, count the horizontal and vertical number of boxes, then use **Pythagoras' Theorem** to determine the length of the sloping line AB.

A second, and more mathematical approach, is to use **vectors**.

The benefit of this is that you do not require a diagram to work with.

Solution 2 :- Step 1 :- Use A(1, 5) and B(9, -1) to find $\overrightarrow{AB} = \underline{b} - \underline{a} = \begin{pmatrix} 9 \\ -1 \end{pmatrix} - \begin{pmatrix} 1 \\ 5 \end{pmatrix} = \begin{pmatrix} 8 \\ -6 \end{pmatrix}$.

The 8 and (–)6 are the lengths of the sides of the right angled triangle.

Step 2 :- Now use Pythagoras' as follows :- For **length**, think of **magnitude** instead.

$$|\overrightarrow{AB}| = \sqrt{8^2 + (-6)^2} = \sqrt{64 + 36} = \sqrt{100} = 10.$$

In general, if vector $\overrightarrow{AB} = \underline{u} = \begin{pmatrix} p \\ q \end{pmatrix}$, => Magnitude $\boxed{|\overrightarrow{AB}| = |\underline{u}| = \sqrt{p^2 + q^2}.}$

Exercise 15·4

1. Calculate the distance from A(3, 1) to B(7, 4).
   Copy and **complete** :-

   $$\overrightarrow{AB} = \underline{b} - \underline{a} = \begin{pmatrix} 7 \\ 4 \end{pmatrix} - \begin{pmatrix} 3 \\ 1 \end{pmatrix} = \begin{pmatrix} \cdots \\ \cdots \end{pmatrix}.$$
   $$|\overrightarrow{AB}| = \sqrt{\cdots^2 + \cdots^2} = \sqrt{\cdots} = \cdots.$$

2. In a similar way, calculate the **magnitude**, (distance), between each pair of points here :-

   (a) U(4, 1), V(7, 5)   (b) S(0, 5), T(12, 0)

   (c) J(2, –3), K(10, 3)   (d) P(–3, –4), Q(6, 8)

   (e) C(6, 2), D(10, 2)   (f) O(0, 0), H(15,8).

3. Not all square roots are **exact** of course. Calculate the distance from the two points P(5, 2) and Q(8, 5). *(See next column)*.

3. **Copy** and **complete** :-

   $$\overrightarrow{PQ} = \underline{q} - \underline{p} = \begin{pmatrix} 8 \\ 5 \end{pmatrix} - \begin{pmatrix} \cdots \\ \cdots \end{pmatrix} = \begin{pmatrix} \cdots \\ \cdots \end{pmatrix}.$$
   $$|\overrightarrow{PQ}| = \sqrt{\cdots^2 + \cdots^2} = \sqrt{18} = \cdots$$

4. Calculate the **magnitude** of the vector joining these pairs of points :-

   (a) I(5, 1), J(7, 5)   (b) E(0, 5), F(8, 9)

   (c) M(1, –3), N(7, 3)   (d) X(–3,–4), Y(5, 0)

   (e) S(5, 6), T(10, –4)   (f) B(3, –1), C(6, 8).

5. S(2, –1), T(4, 3) and R(–2, 1) are 3 points.

   (a) Use the above method to calculate the lengths of the 3 sides of triangle STR.

   (b) Use your answer to part (a) to explain clearly what kind of triangle STR is.

1. Calculate the **magnitude** of the following vectors :-

    (a) $\underline{u} = \begin{pmatrix} 5 \\ 5 \end{pmatrix}$, $|\underline{u}| = ...$ (b) $\underline{s} = \begin{pmatrix} -3 \\ 6 \end{pmatrix}$, $|\underline{s}| = ...$

    (c) $\underline{a} = \begin{pmatrix} -9 \\ 3 \end{pmatrix}$, $|\underline{a}| = ...$ (d) $\underline{v} = \begin{pmatrix} -4 \\ -8 \end{pmatrix}$, $|\underline{v}| = ...$

2. Given C(2, 3), P(8, 11), Q(10, -3) and R(-6, 9), show that P, Q and R could be points which lie on the circumference of a circle having its centre at point C.

    (*Hint : calculate the lengths of CP, CQ, ...*).

3. The coordinate diagram shows the position of two ships, the **Platypus** and the **Queensway**, in relation to **Oriskay** harbour, (*distances in km*).

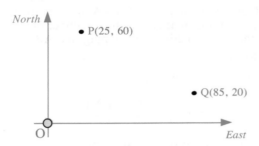

    (a) Describe, using components, the vector journey that the Platypus would have to travel to reach the Queensway.

    (b) Use this to determine how far apart the two ships are at present, (*the magnitude*).

4. A force is applied to a large box in order to slide it from point A to point B.

    This force is represented by the vector $\overrightarrow{AB}$.

    A second force is then applied to move the box from point B to a new point C.

    This force is represented by the vector $\overrightarrow{BC}$.

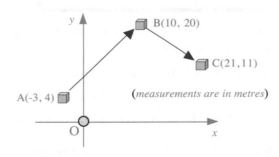

(*measurements are in metres*)

    (a) Find the components of forces $\overrightarrow{AB}$ & $\overrightarrow{BC}$.

    (b) Find the component of the **resultant** force (*i.e. the single force*), which if applied, would have moved the box directly from point A to point C.

4. (c) Find the **magnitude** of this resultant force.

5. A boy attempts to swim across a river from point F to point G.

    Unfortunately, the current is forcing him downstream and he ends up at point H instead.

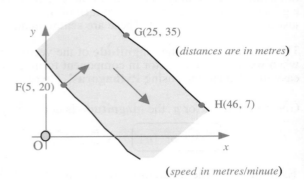

(*distances are in metres*)

(*speed in metres/minute*)

    Vector $\overrightarrow{FG}$ represents the velocity of the journey he hoped to take him from F to G.

    Vector $\overrightarrow{GH}$ represents the velocity of the flowing stream that forces the swimmer to end up at H.

    (a) Find the components of $\overrightarrow{FG}$ and $\overrightarrow{GH}$.

    (b) Find $\overrightarrow{FH}$. This represents his actual journey.

    (c) Calculate the **speed** he was swimming at, the speed of the river and the **resultant** speed in his actual swim from F to H.

6. Three ropes are tied to a box and three boys pull the ropes in various directions as shown below.

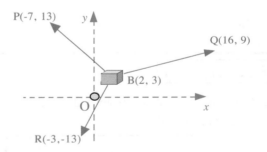

    The coordinates of the box are (2, 3).

    The coordinates of the three points indicate, in relation to the box, the **strength** and **direction** of the force applied by each boy.

    (a) Determine the component values of the three forces, $\overrightarrow{BP}$, $\overrightarrow{BQ}$ and $\overrightarrow{BR}$.

    (b) Find the **magnitude** of each force.

    (c) Add the 3 forces together, $\overrightarrow{BP} + \overrightarrow{BQ} + \overrightarrow{BR}$.

    (d) Explain your answer in terms of how, and in which direction, the box actually moves.

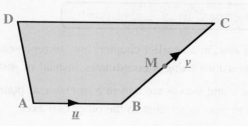

Alternative Vector Journeys

As we said earlier, a displacement, (or vector), represents a journey from point A to point B.

As far as the vector is concerned, only the **finishing** point, **in relation to the starting** point, is important.

What **route** you take is **irrelevant**.

Examples :- This diagram above represents a **trapezium** with side DC equal to 2 × side AB in length.

Vector $\overrightarrow{AB} = \underline{u}$ and vector $\overrightarrow{BC} = \underline{v}$.

Find, in terms of $\underline{u}$ and $\underline{v}$, the following vectors :-

(a) $\overrightarrow{DC}$ (b) $\overrightarrow{AC}$ (c) $\overrightarrow{AD}$ (d) $\overrightarrow{BM}$ (*where M is the mid-point of BC*) (e) $\overrightarrow{DM}$.

Solutions :- (a) $\overrightarrow{DC} = 2 \times \overrightarrow{AB}$ (since it is **parallel** to <u>and</u> **double** the length of AB) $= 2\underline{u}$.

(b) $\overrightarrow{AC} = \overrightarrow{AB} + \overrightarrow{BC} = \underline{u} + \underline{v}$.

* note the "–" sign

(c) $\overrightarrow{AD} = \overrightarrow{AB} + \overrightarrow{BC} + \overrightarrow{CD} = \underline{u} + \underline{v} + -2\underline{u} = \underline{v} - \underline{u}$.

(d) $\overrightarrow{BM} = \frac{1}{2}$ of $\overrightarrow{BC} = \frac{1}{2}\underline{v}$.

(e) $\overrightarrow{DM} = \overrightarrow{DA} + \overrightarrow{AB} + \overrightarrow{BM}$ or $\overrightarrow{DC} + \overrightarrow{CM} = 2\underline{u} - \frac{1}{2}\underline{v}$.

Exercise 15·6

1. Shown is parallelogram PQRS, with vector $\overrightarrow{PQ} = \underline{u}$ and vector $\overrightarrow{PS} = \underline{v}$.

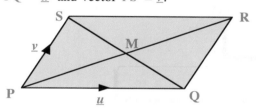

Find the following vectors in terms of $\underline{u}$ and $\underline{v}$:-

(a) $\overrightarrow{QR}$ (b) $\overrightarrow{SR}$ (c) $\overrightarrow{PR}$

(d) $\overrightarrow{QS}$ (e) $\overrightarrow{PM}$ (f) $\overrightarrow{SM}$.

2. The trapezium below has EF parallel to HG and HG = 4 × EF in length.

Vector $\overrightarrow{EF} = \underline{a}$ and vector $\overrightarrow{EH} = \underline{b}$.

M and N are the **mid-points** of FG and HG.

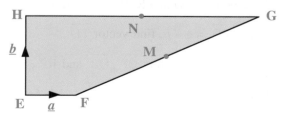

Find the following vectors in terms of $\underline{a}$ and $\underline{b}$:-

(a) $\overrightarrow{HG}$ (b) $\overrightarrow{EG}$ (c) $\overrightarrow{EN}$

(d) $\overrightarrow{FG}$ (e) $\overrightarrow{GN}$ (f) $\overrightarrow{MN}$.

3. This time, ABCDEF is a hexagon with centre P.

Vector $\overrightarrow{AB} = \underline{r}$.

Vector $\overrightarrow{FE} = \underline{s}$.

Find the following in terms of $\underline{r}$ and $\underline{s}$:-

(a) $\overrightarrow{ED}$ (b) $\overrightarrow{BC}$

(c) $\overrightarrow{FC}$ (d) $\overrightarrow{AF}$

(e) $\overrightarrow{BE}$ (f) $\overrightarrow{AE}$.

4. Trapezium UVWX has UV parallel to WX and XW = 2 × UV in length. $\overrightarrow{UV} = \underline{h}$ and $\overrightarrow{VW} = \underline{k}$.

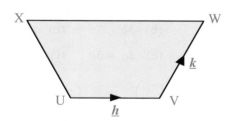

(a) Find these vectors in terms of $\underline{h}$ and $\underline{k}$:-

(i) $\overrightarrow{XW}$ (ii) $\overrightarrow{UW}$

(iii) $\overrightarrow{VX}$ (iv) $\overrightarrow{UX}$.

In fact, $\underline{h} = \begin{pmatrix} 4 \\ 0 \end{pmatrix}$ and $\underline{k} = \begin{pmatrix} 2 \\ 4 \end{pmatrix}$.

(b) Find the components of $\overrightarrow{XW}$, $\overrightarrow{UW}$ & $\overrightarrow{UX}$.

(c) Find $|\overrightarrow{VW}|$, $|\overrightarrow{UW}|$ & $|\overrightarrow{VX}|$.

Vectors in 3 Dimensions

We saw, in an earlier chapter, how to represent a point in 3 dimensions using 3 coordinates instead of just 2.

The x and y-axes are lain in a **horizontal** plain and the z axis is **vertical** in relation to the other two axes.

Can you see that the 2 points are **P(2, 3, 6)** and **Q(7, –2, 4)**?

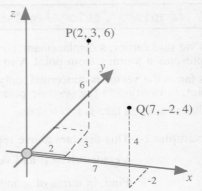

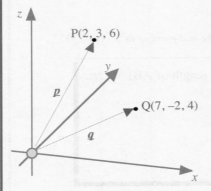

The **blue** arrow shows a 3-dimensional vector indicating the position of the point **P(2, 3, 6)**, from the origin.

The **brown** arrow shows a 3-dimensional vector giving the position of the point **Q(7, –2, 4)**, from the origin.

These two **position vectors** can be represented by :-

$$\Rightarrow \quad \underline{p} = \begin{pmatrix} 2 \\ 3 \\ 6 \end{pmatrix} \text{ and } \underline{q} = \begin{pmatrix} 7 \\ -2 \\ 4 \end{pmatrix}.$$
← the x component
← the y component
← the z component

As with in 2 dimensions, we can find the vector :- $\overrightarrow{PQ} = \underline{q} - \underline{p} = \begin{pmatrix} 7 \\ -2 \\ 4 \end{pmatrix} - \begin{pmatrix} 2 \\ 3 \\ 6 \end{pmatrix} = \begin{pmatrix} 5 \\ -5 \\ -2 \end{pmatrix}.$

Also, the **magnitude** can be found using **Pythagoras' Theorem**, (*applied in 3 dimensions*).

$$|\overrightarrow{OP}| = \sqrt{2^2 + 3^2 + 6^2} = \sqrt{4 + 9 + 36} = \sqrt{49} = 7.$$

$$|\overrightarrow{PQ}| = |\underline{q} - \underline{p}| = \sqrt{5^2 + (-5)^2 + (-2)^2} = \sqrt{25 + 25 + 4} = \sqrt{54} = 7\cdot 35.$$

Exercise 15·7

1. Given that $\underline{a} = \begin{pmatrix} 4 \\ 3 \\ -2 \end{pmatrix}$ and $\underline{b} = \begin{pmatrix} 3 \\ -2 \\ 5 \end{pmatrix}$, find :-

   (a) $2\underline{a}$ (b) $3\underline{b}$ (c) $\underline{a} + \underline{b}$

   (d) $\underline{a} - \underline{b}$ (e) $2\underline{a} + 3\underline{b}$ (f) $-2(\underline{a} + \underline{b})$.

2. Given that $\underline{p} = \begin{pmatrix} 1 \\ -2 \\ 2 \end{pmatrix}$ and $\underline{q} = \begin{pmatrix} -3 \\ 4 \\ 12 \end{pmatrix}$, find :-

   (a) $\underline{p} + \underline{q}$ (b) $\underline{p} - \underline{q}$ (c) $-3\underline{p}$

   (d) $|\underline{p}|$ (e) $|\underline{q}|$ (f) $|\underline{p} + \underline{q}|$

   (g) Is it true that $|\underline{p}| + |\underline{q}| = |\underline{p} + \underline{q}|$?

3. Solve these **vector equations** for vector $\underline{x}$:-

   (a) $\underline{x} + \begin{pmatrix} 1 \\ 2 \\ 4 \end{pmatrix} = \begin{pmatrix} 7 \\ 2 \\ 1 \end{pmatrix}$ (b) $\underline{x} - \begin{pmatrix} 2 \\ -1 \\ 5 \end{pmatrix} = \begin{pmatrix} -2 \\ 1 \\ -5 \end{pmatrix}$

3. (c) $2\underline{x} = \begin{pmatrix} 4 \\ -6 \\ 8 \end{pmatrix}$ (d) $-3\underline{x} = \begin{pmatrix} -9 \\ 12 \\ 0 \end{pmatrix}$

   (e) $4\underline{x} - \begin{pmatrix} 2 \\ 5 \\ 12 \end{pmatrix} = \begin{pmatrix} -2 \\ 3 \\ -4 \end{pmatrix}$ (f) $5\underline{x} + \begin{pmatrix} 1 \\ 3 \\ 2 \end{pmatrix} = 3\underline{x} + \begin{pmatrix} 9 \\ 1 \\ 6 \end{pmatrix}$.

4. P(1, 5, 8), Q(4, –1, 2) and R(6, 3, –4) are 3 points.

   (a) Write down the position vectors, $\underline{p}$, $\underline{q}$ and $\underline{r}$ of the 3 points P, Q and R. (i.e. $\overrightarrow{OP}$ etc.)

   (b) Using $\overrightarrow{PQ} = \underline{q} - \underline{p}$, find vector $\overrightarrow{PQ}$.

   (c) Similarly, find vectors $\overrightarrow{QP}$, $\overrightarrow{QR}$ and $\overrightarrow{RP}$.

   (d) Find $\overrightarrow{PQ} + \overrightarrow{QP}$.

   (e) Explain your answer.

   (f) Now find $\overrightarrow{PQ} + \overrightarrow{QR} + \overrightarrow{RP}$.

   (g) Explain this answer.

5. Shown is the cuboid ABCDEFGH. Sketch it.

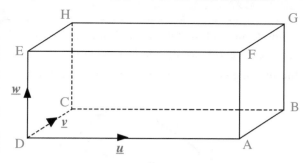

$\overrightarrow{DA}$ = $\underline{u}$, $\overrightarrow{DC}$ = $\underline{v}$ and $\overrightarrow{DE}$ = $\underline{w}$.

Find, in terms of $\underline{u}$, $\underline{v}$ and $\underline{w}$, the vector :-

(a) $\overrightarrow{EF}$ (b) $\overrightarrow{AB}$ (c) $\overrightarrow{DF}$

(d) $\overrightarrow{DH}$ (e) $\overrightarrow{AG}$ (f) $\overrightarrow{DG}$

On your sketch, show the point R, the mid-point of AB, the point S, the middle of face ABGF and X at the very centre of the cuboid.

(g) $\overrightarrow{AR}$ (h) $\overrightarrow{DR}$ (i) $\overrightarrow{AS}$

(j) $\overrightarrow{DS}$ (k) $\overrightarrow{DX}$ (l) $\overrightarrow{HX}$.

6. In the above, $\underline{u} = \begin{pmatrix} 12 \\ 0 \\ 0 \end{pmatrix}$, $\underline{v} = \begin{pmatrix} 0 \\ 3 \\ 0 \end{pmatrix}$, and $\underline{w} = \begin{pmatrix} 0 \\ 0 \\ 4 \end{pmatrix}$.

Find the following :-

(a) $\overrightarrow{DH}$ (b) $\overrightarrow{DF}$ (c) $\overrightarrow{DG}$

(d) $|\overrightarrow{DH}|$ (e) $|\overrightarrow{DF}|$ (f) $|\overrightarrow{DX}|$.

7. Shown is a rectangular based pyramid with lengths 8 boxes and 6 boxes and with point P directly above the centre of rectangle ABCD.

AB is parallel to the x-axis.

The height of the pyramid is 12 boxes and the coordinates of point A are A(5, 3, 1).

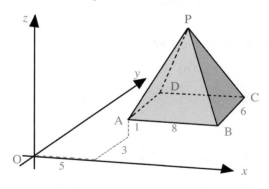

(a) Write down the position vector, $\underline{a}$, of A.

(b) Write down the position vectors of the other 4 points, B, C, D and P.

(c) Find vectors, $\overrightarrow{AB}$, $\overrightarrow{BC}$ and $\overrightarrow{AP}$.

7. (d) Calculate the **magnitude** of the face diagonal vector $\overrightarrow{AC}$, (i.e. $|\overrightarrow{AC}|$).

(e) Calculate the **length** of AP. (i.e. $|\overrightarrow{AP}|$).

8. From the control tower (O) at an airport, the flight path of a small plane is being tracked. (*Distances are in kilometres*).

       P shows where the plane is at 1500.

       Q shows where the plane is at 1530.

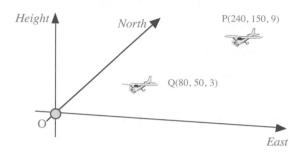

(a) Write down the position vectors $\underline{p}$ and $\underline{q}$ of P and Q in relation to the control tower.

(b) Calculate how far away the plane is from the control tower at 1500 and 1530 (**magnitude**). (*Give each answer to the nearest kilometre*).

(c) Determine the components of the flight from P to Q. (i.e. $\overrightarrow{PQ}$).

(d) By calculating $|\overrightarrow{PQ}|$, find the speed of the plane from P to Q.

(e) Explain why, if the plane keeps to its present flight path, it will arrive at the control tower.

9. The basket, B, of a hot air balloon is tethered to 3 points P, Q and R on the ground.

The coordinates of B, P, Q and R are given in relation to another point O.

The coordinates of all the points are given below.

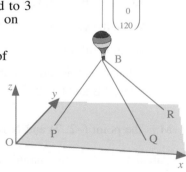

P(8, 10, 0), Q(20, 5, 0), R(17, 30, 0), B(15, 15, 40).

The vectors $\overrightarrow{BP}$, $\overrightarrow{BQ}$ and $\overrightarrow{BR}$ represent the forces acting on the ropes holding the balloon.

The upwards arrow shows the vertical force acting on the balloon caused by the hot air.

(a) Find the vectors $\overrightarrow{BP}$, $\overrightarrow{BQ}$ and $\overrightarrow{BR}$.

(b) By adding all 4 (force) vectors together, explain why the balloon remains in its fixed position.

1. Sketch the vectors $\underline{a}$ and $\underline{b}$.

   (a) Sketch the vector $\underline{a} + \underline{b}$.

   (b) Now sketch and label vector $\underline{a} - \underline{b}$.

   (c) Sketch the vector $\underline{b} - \underline{a}$.

   (d) Sketch the vector $-2\underline{a}$.

   (e) Sketch $3\underline{b} - 2\underline{a}$.

2. Given $\underline{p} = \begin{pmatrix} 5 \\ -1 \end{pmatrix}$ and $\underline{q} = \begin{pmatrix} -3 \\ -2 \end{pmatrix}$, find :-

   (a) $\underline{p} + \underline{q}$ (b) $\underline{q} - \underline{p}$

   (c) $3\underline{p}$ (d) $-2\underline{q}$

   (e) $2\underline{p} + 3\underline{q}$ (f) $4\underline{q} - 2\underline{p}$.

3. Solve these **vector equations** for vector $\underline{x}$:-

   (a) $\underline{x} + \begin{pmatrix} 3 \\ 5 \end{pmatrix} = \begin{pmatrix} 4 \\ -2 \end{pmatrix}$ (b) $\underline{x} - \begin{pmatrix} 1 \\ 6 \end{pmatrix} = \begin{pmatrix} 5 \\ -2 \end{pmatrix}$

   (c) $2\underline{x} = \begin{pmatrix} 12 \\ -4 \end{pmatrix}$ (d) $7\underline{x} = \begin{pmatrix} -14 \\ 35 \end{pmatrix}$

   (e) $4\underline{x} - \begin{pmatrix} 2 \\ -3 \end{pmatrix} = \begin{pmatrix} 6 \\ 11 \end{pmatrix}$ (f) $5\underline{x} - \begin{pmatrix} 1 \\ 4 \end{pmatrix} = 2\underline{x} + \begin{pmatrix} -7 \\ -1 \end{pmatrix}$.

4. The coordinates of 4 points are :-

     A(2, –3), B(8, 1), C(12, 1) and D(0, –7).

   (a) Write the vectors $\overrightarrow{AB}$ and $\overrightarrow{CD}$ in component form.

   (b) What does this tell you about the two lines lines, AB and CD ?

5. M is the point (–2, 7) and N is (3, –5).

   Calculate $|\overrightarrow{MN}|$, the magnitude of MN.

6. Given that $\underline{v} = \begin{pmatrix} 2 \\ -4 \\ 4 \end{pmatrix}$ and $\underline{w} = \begin{pmatrix} -4 \\ 3 \\ 12 \end{pmatrix}$, find :-

   (a) $\underline{v} + \underline{w}$ (b) $\underline{v} - \underline{w}$ (c) $-2\underline{v}$

   (d) $|\underline{v}|$ (e) $|\underline{w}|$

   (f) Does $|\underline{v}| + |\underline{w}| = |\underline{v} + \underline{w}|$? Explain.

7. In the figure below, the directed line segments represent vectors as shown. For example .....
the line segment $\overrightarrow{PR}$ is represented by vector $\underline{b}$.

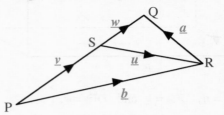

What line segment is represented by vector :-

   (a) $\underline{b} - \underline{u}$ (b) $\underline{w} - \underline{a}$

   (c) $\underline{v} + \underline{u} - \underline{b}$ (d) $\underline{b} + \underline{a} - \underline{v} - \underline{w}$?

8. Solve these **vector equations** for vector $\underline{x}$:-

   (a) $\underline{x} + \begin{pmatrix} 1 \\ -2 \\ -1 \end{pmatrix} = \begin{pmatrix} 5 \\ 3 \\ -1 \end{pmatrix}$ (b) $2\underline{x} - \begin{pmatrix} -3 \\ 7 \\ -5 \end{pmatrix} = \begin{pmatrix} 11 \\ -9 \\ 17 \end{pmatrix}$.

9.   ABCDHEFG is a cuboid.
K lies **two thirds** of the way along HG.
L lies **one quarter** of the way along FG.

   $\overrightarrow{AD} = \underline{u}$,

   $\overrightarrow{AB} = \underline{v}$,

   $\overrightarrow{AE} = \underline{w}$.

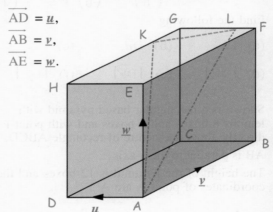

Find, in terms of $\underline{u}, \underline{v}$ and $\underline{w}$, the vector :-

   (a) $\overrightarrow{FG}$ (b) $\overrightarrow{HG}$ (c) $\overrightarrow{LG}$

   (d) $\overrightarrow{GK}$ (e) $\overrightarrow{AL}$ (f) $\overrightarrow{AK}$.

10.

An aircraft flying at a constant speed on a straight flight path takes 2 minutes to fly from A to B and one minute from B to C. Relative to a suitable set of axes, A is the point (–1, 3, 4) and B is (3, 1, –2).

Find the coordinates of point C.

1. Calculate the following arc lengths :-

(a)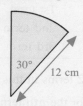

(b)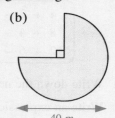

2. Calculate the area of each sector in question 1.

3. Find the angle, x, in each sector.

(a)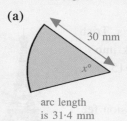

arc length is 31·4 mm

(b)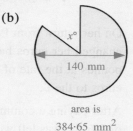

area is 384·65 mm²

4. A part circular blue stage is built for a rock concert as shown.

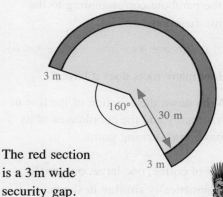

The red section is a 3 m wide security gap.

Calculate the :-

(a) area of the blue stage

(b) area of the security gap

(c) perimeter of the security gap.

5. Sketch each of the following functions stating their roots, line of symmetry and turning point :-

(a) $y = x^2 - 4$ (b) $f(x) = x^2 + 5$

(c) $f(x) = x^2 + x - 6$ (d) $y = x^2 - 2x - 15$

(e) $y = 4 - x^2$ (f) $f(x) = 3 - 2x - x^2$.

6. Solve for x :-

(a) $(x - 3)(x + 1) = 0$ (b) $x^2 - 4x = 0$

(c) $x^2 - 5x + 6 = 0$ (d) $x^2 - 14x = 51$

(e) $2x^2 - 5x - 3 = 0$ (f) $6x^2 - 2x - 4 = 0$.

7. Find the minimum value of $x^2 - 4x - 60$.

8. Find the intersection of the parabola and the line shown below.

$$y = x^2 + x - 12$$
$$y = 2x - 6.$$

9. Given $\underline{a} = \begin{pmatrix} 4 \\ -1 \\ 0 \end{pmatrix}$ and $\underline{b} = \begin{pmatrix} 1 \\ -3 \\ 4 \end{pmatrix}$, find :-

(a) $\underline{a} + 2\underline{b}$ (b) $3\underline{a} - \underline{b}$

(c) $2\underline{a} + 3\underline{b}$ (d) $-2\underline{a} - 3\underline{b}$.

10. Solve these **vector equations** for vector $\underline{x}$.

(a) $\underline{x} + \begin{pmatrix} 1 \\ 7 \end{pmatrix} = \begin{pmatrix} 8 \\ 3 \end{pmatrix}$

(b) $\underline{x} - \begin{pmatrix} -3 \\ 3 \end{pmatrix} = \begin{pmatrix} -4 \\ -1 \end{pmatrix}$

(c) $4\underline{x} - \begin{pmatrix} 2 \\ 5 \end{pmatrix} = \underline{x} + \begin{pmatrix} 10 \\ -2 \end{pmatrix}$.

11. Four of the vertices of cuboid ABCDEFGH are given.

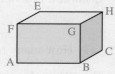

A(1, 2, 3), B(6, 2, 3), C(6, 5, 3) and H(6, 5, 7).

(a) Find the components of the vectors :-

(i) $\overrightarrow{AB}$ (ii) $\overrightarrow{AD}$

(iii) $\overrightarrow{DE}$ (iv) $\overrightarrow{EC}$.

(b) Find the components of the space diagonal vector starting at point C.

(c) What single vector journey would be equivalent to the journeys made from A to B, then to C, then to D and then to A ?

12. Derive a **formula** from the table below.

Q	2	6	10	14
P	2	22	42	62

(a) Find P, when $Q = 50$.

(b) Find Q, when $P = 152$.

13. Simplify these expressions :-

(a) $\dfrac{5}{x} - \dfrac{x}{x + 2}$ (b) $\dfrac{1}{x} - \dfrac{x - 5}{x^2}$

(c) $\dfrac{1}{x - 1} - \dfrac{1}{x + 1}$ (d) $\dfrac{2}{(x + 1)} - \dfrac{1}{2(x + 1)^2}$.

14. Joe earns £12·50 an hour as a painter.

He gets paid **time and a third** on a Saturday and **double time** on a Sunday.

Last week Joe worked :-

- 9 am to 4.30 pm (Mon - Thurs),
- 6 hours on Saturday and
- $2\frac{1}{2}$ hours on Sunday.

Calculate his **total** weekly wage.

15. Draw the parabola corresponding to the quadratic function :-

$$f(x) = x(x - 4) \qquad \{-1 \le x \le 5\}.$$

(a) How many roots does it have ?

(b) Write down the equation of the **line of symmetry** and the coordinates of its **minimum** turning point.

16. Sketch the following lines, indicating both the y-intercept and gradient :-

(a) $y = 2x - 4$ (b) $y = 1 - x$

(c) $2x + 4y = 0$ (d) $0·25x = 2y + 1$

(e) $y + px - k = 0$, where $p < 0$ and $k > 0$.

17. A pattern of numbers is found as follows :-

$4 + 2 - 1$	1st term
$8 + 4 - 3$	2nd term
$12 + 6 - 5$	3rd term

(a) Write down the next 2 terms in this pattern.

(b) Write an expression for the **nth** term in this pattern and express it in its simplest form.

18. Change the subject of the formula

$$W = 3 - \frac{2}{M} \qquad \text{to } M.$$

19. On her return from Paris, Trish changed her euros back into pounds at the rate of 1·15 euros to the £.

After paying a commission fee of 2% she was left with £196.

How many **euros** had Trish brought home ?

20. Draw the parabola corresponding to the quadratic function :-

$$f(x) = 5 + 4x - x^2 \qquad \{-2 \le x \le 6\}.$$

(a) How many roots does it have ?

(b) Write down the equation of the **line of symmetry** and the coordinates of its **maximum turning point**.

21. Two tins of coffee, one large, one small, are mathematically **similar** in shape.

The height of a small tin is 12 cm, and the large one's height of 18 cm.

The cost of a tin of coffee depends only on the volume of coffee in the tin.

If a small tin costs £1·76, what should a large tin of coffee cost ?

22. The equation of a parabola is :-

$$y = x^2 - 6x + 8.$$

(a) Determine the coordinates of the points of intersection with the x and y-axes.

(b) Find the equation of the **axis of symmetry**.

(c) Find the coordinates of the **minimum turning point**.

1. Set down and find :-

   (a) $3^5 - 2^7$ (b) $25\,500 \div 25$ (c) $10 - 3 \times 5$ (d) $6 \times (8 + 6) \div 7 - 1$

   (e) $8000 \times 3\cdot45$ (f) $78 \div 300$ (g) $\dfrac{(-3) \times 11}{(-60)}$ (h) $32\cdot8 \div 8000.$

2. Change :-   (a) 100 000 g to tonnes   (b) 0·04 km to mm   (c) 72 kg to mg

   (d) 187 m to km   (e) 170 mm to km   (f) 17 hrs to seconds   (g) 720 km/hr to m/sec.

3. Find :-   (a) $\frac{4}{5}$ of 640   (b) $\frac{8}{11}$ of 7777   (c) $\frac{12}{19}$ of 1938.

4. Simplify :-   (a) $\dfrac{11}{888888}$ (b) $\dfrac{71}{284}$ (c) $\dfrac{128}{4096}.$

5. Find :-   (a) $\frac{4}{7} - \frac{3}{8}$ (b) $5\frac{1}{4} + 2\frac{3}{8}$ (c) $4\frac{2}{7} \div 1\frac{1}{5}.$

6. Express as a fraction :–   (a) 95%   (b) $112\frac{1}{2}$%   (c) 0·5%.
   (*in its simplest form*).

7. Find :-   (a) 10% of 34 cm   (b) 15% of 5 kg   (c) $33\frac{1}{3}$% of 1·08 m

   (d) $1\frac{1}{2}$% of 40 km   (e) 17·5% of £248   (f) $12\frac{1}{2}$% of $120   (g) 22% of 9 km.

8. Find :-   (a) $72 + (-15)$ (b) $(-33) + (-44)$ (c) $234 - 456$

   (d) $53 - (-53)$ (e) $(-9) \times 126$ (f) $(-5x) - (-4x)$ (g) $(-8) \times (-14)$

   (h) $(-13x) \times (-6x)$ (i) $1280y \div (-32y)$ (j) $(-180p) \div (-12p)$ (k) $\dfrac{(-5) \times (-40)}{(-500)}.$

9. (a) Jo spent half her money on cakes and a third of what remained of her money on juice.
       If she has £2·40 left, how much money did she start with ?

   (b) A box of twelve cakes cost £24·96. How much would you expect to pay for a box of 5 cakes ?

   (c) Find the acute angle between the hands of a clock at 1415.

10. (a) State the gradient and y-intercept of :-   (i) $y = 7 - 2x$ (ii) $y + 3x - 1 = 0.$

    (b) Sketch each of the lines in part (a).

11. Shown is an eighth of a circle with a radius of 4 cm.

    (a) Calculate the area of this shape.

    (b) Calculate the perimeter of this shape.

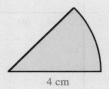

4 cm

12. (a) Calculate, to the nearest whole number, the standard deviation of :- 3, 5, 5, 7, 10, 12.

    (b) Construct a box plot for the data in part (a).

Introduction

Shown are the graphs of 3 functions :- Linear, Quadratic and the lesser known, Hyperbolic.

A **Linear** function

$f(x) = 2x - 3$

$y = 2x - 3$

A **Quadratic** function

$f(x) = x^2 - 2x - 3$

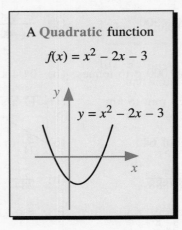

$y = x^2 - 2x - 3$

A **Hyperbolic** function

$f(x) = \frac{12}{x}$

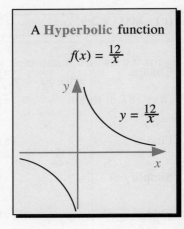

$y = \frac{12}{x}$

We will now begin to study the graphs of the trig functions, $y = \sin x°$, $y = \cos x°$ and $y = \tan x°$.

The Sine Function ($y = \sin x°$)

There are **computer** or **graphics packages** that could assist here.

You are going to look up the sine of various angles from 0° to 360° and plot them on a graph

(a) Copy this table and use your calculator to complete it (*to 2 decimal places each time*).

x	0	30	60	90	120	150	180	210	240	270	300	330	360
$\sin x°$	0	0·50	0·87	1·00	0·87	...	...	−0·50	...	...	...	...	...

(b) Now take a sheet of A4 two millimetre graph paper and use it in the landscape position.
Plot your 13 points from the table and join them up with a smooth curve.

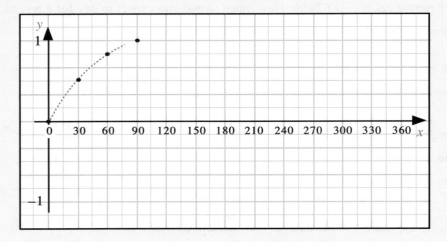

Your graph should have ended up looking like this :-

$y = \sin x°$

Study it carefully.

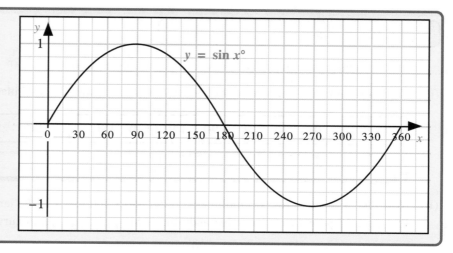

1. (a) Practice sketching the graph **several** times on a smaller scale like this :-

   Note the smooth "wavy" shape.

   (b) What is the **highest** value the graph attains ?

   (c) What is its **lowest** value ?

   (d) For what values of "x" does the curve cut the x-axis ?

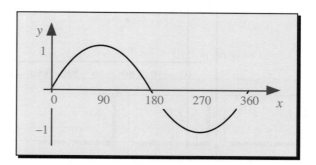

2. (a) Make a new neat small sketch of $y = \sin x°$, but this time extend the x-axis to go from $-360°$ to $+720°$. (*see below*).

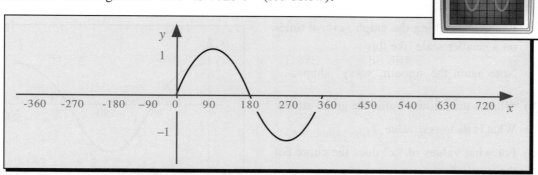

   (b) Use your calculator to find $\sin 450°$, $\sin 540°$, $\sin 630°$ and $\sin 720°$, plot these points on your diagram and sketch the next "bit" of the sine graph.

   (c) Repeat for $\sin(-90°)$, $\sin(-180°)$, $\sin(-270°)$ and $\sin(-360°)$ and draw this "bit" of the sine graph.

   (d) For the graph of $y = \sin x°$, state the **maximum** and **minimum** values. (*How high and low it goes*).

   (e) If you **halve** the "vertical distance" between the **maximum** and **minimum** values, this is referred to as the **amplitude** of the graph. What is the **amplitude** of the sine graph ?

   (f) The "horizontal distance" between points on the graph where the pattern repeats itself is called the **period** of the graph. What is the **period** of the sine graph ?

The Cosine Function ($y = \cos x°$)

You are going to look up the cosine of various angles from 0° to 360° and plot them on a graph.

(a) Copy this table and use your calculator to complete it (to 2 decimal places each time).

x	0	30	60	90	120	150	180	210	240	270	300	330	360
$\cos x°$	1	0·87	0·50	0	–0·50	...	...	...	...	...	...	...	...

(b) Now take a sheet of A4 two millimetre graph paper and use it in the landscape position.
Plot your 13 points from the table and join them up with a smooth curve.

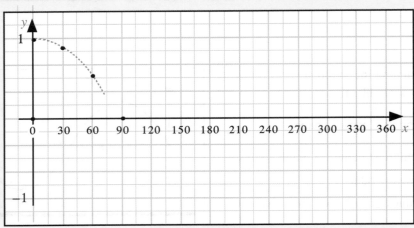

Show your finished smooth cosine graph to your teacher.

Exercise 16·2

1. (a) Practice sketching the graph **several** times on a smaller scale like this :-

    Note again the smooth "wavy" shape.

    (b) What is the **highest** value the graph attains ?

    (c) What is its **lowest** value ?

    (d) For what values of "x" does the curve cut the x-axis ?

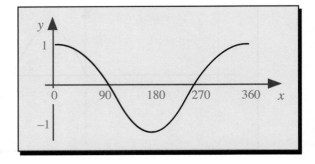

2. (a) Make a new neat sketch of $y = \cos x°$, and extend the x-axis to go from –360° to +720°.

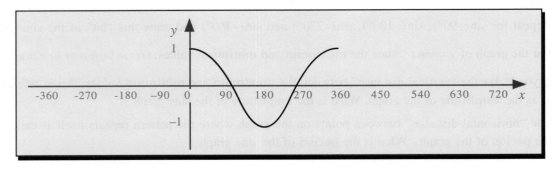

2. (b) Use your calculator to find $\cos 450°$, $\cos 540°$, $\cos 630°$ and $\cos 720°$, plot these points on your diagram and sketch the next "bit" of the cosine graph.

(c) Repeat for $\cos(-90°)$, $\cos(-180°)$, $\cos(-270°)$ and $\cos(-360°)$ and draw this "bit" of the cosine graph.

(d) For the graph of $y = \cos x°$, state the **maximum** and **minimum** values. (*how high and low it goes*).

(e) What is the **amplitude** of the cosine graph ?

(f) The "horizontal distance" between points on the graph where the pattern repeats itself is called the **period** of the graph. What is the **period** of the cosine graph ?

3. (a) Without looking at the last few pages, make a quick sketch of $y = \sin x°$ and $y = \cos x°$, marking in the important values on both the x and the y-axes.

(b) Write a couple of sentences describing both graphs - in what ways are they similar and in what ways are they different ? (*Shape, maximum/minimum values, amplitudes, periods*) ?

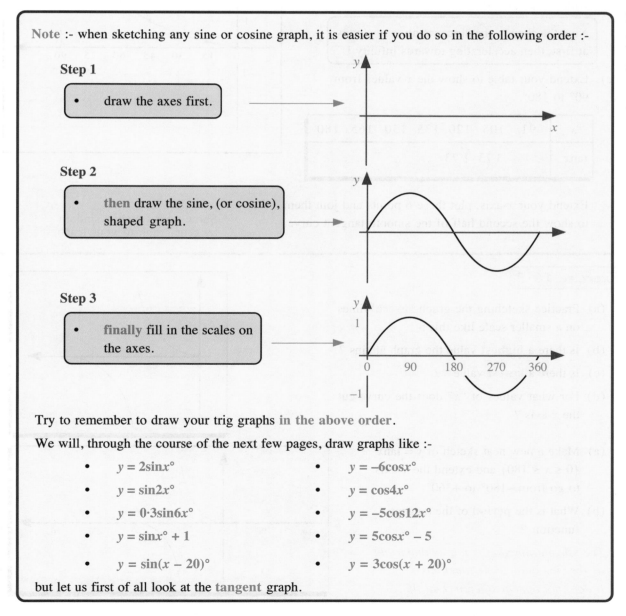

Note :- when sketching any sine or cosine graph, it is easier if you do so in the following order :-

Step 1
- draw the axes first.

Step 2
- **then** draw the sine, (or cosine), shaped graph.

Step 3
- **finally** fill in the scales on the axes.

Try to remember to draw your trig graphs **in the above order**.

We will, through the course of the next few pages, draw graphs like :-

- $y = 2\sin x°$
- $y = \sin 2x°$
- $y = 0·3\sin 6x°$
- $y = \sin x° + 1$
- $y = \sin(x - 20)°$

- $y = -6\cos x°$
- $y = \cos 4x°$
- $y = -5\cos 12x°$
- $y = 5\cos x° - 5$
- $y = 3\cos(x + 20)°$

but let us first of all look at the **tangent** graph.

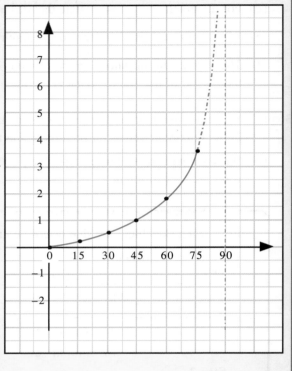

The Tangent Function ($y = \tan x°$)

The tangent graph looks totally different from the sine and cosine graphs.

(a) Copy this table and use your calculator to complete it (*to 2 decimal places each time*).

x	0	15	30	45	60	75	89	90
$\tan x°$	0	0·27	0·58	1·00	1·73	3·73	57·3	?

At 90°, we say the tangent is **undefined** (it is too large a number to find - **infinity** !)

(b) Now take a sheet of A4 two millimetre graph paper (or half-cm paper) and use it in the portrait position.

Plot the 7 points from the table and join them up with a smooth curve.

Note the shape - the slope rising very slowly at first, then accelerating towards infinity !

(c) Extend your table to show the x-values from 90° to 180°.

x	91	105	120	135	150	165	180
$\tan x°$	-57·3	-3·73	-1·73	...	...	...	...

Extend your x-axis, plot these 6 points and join them to show the second half of the smooth tangent curve.

Show your finished smooth tangent graph to your teacher.

Exercise 16·3

1. (a) Practice sketching the graph **several** times on a smaller scale like this :-

   (b) Is there a **highest** value the graph attains ?

   (c) Is there a **lowest** value   ?

   (d) For what values of "x" does the curve cut the x-axis ?

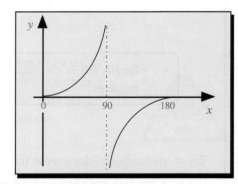

2. (a) Make a new neat sketch of $y = \tan x°$ $\{0 \le x \le 180\}$ and extend the x-axis to go from −180° to +360°.

   (b) What is the **period** of the tangent function ?

The tangent function is not as important as the sine and cosine functions.
It does not appear often in real life.

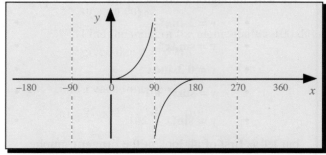

Other Sine and Cosine Functions ($y = a\sin x°$ and $y = a\cos x°$)

$y = 2\sin x°$

You are going to draw the graph of $y = 2\sin x°$ by looking up various values of x.

For example, | when $x = 30$ => $\sin x° = 0.5$ => $2\sin x° = 2 \times 0.5 = 1$ |

(a) Copy this table and use your calculator to complete it (*to 2 decimal places each time*).

x	0	30	60	90	120	150	180	210	240	270	300	330	360
$2\sin x°$	0	1·00	1·73	2·00	1·73	...	...	−1·00	...	...	...	...	...

(b) Draw a set of axes on squared paper, plot the above 13 points and join them up with a smooth curve.

Show your graph of :-

$$y = 2\sin x°$$

to your teacher.

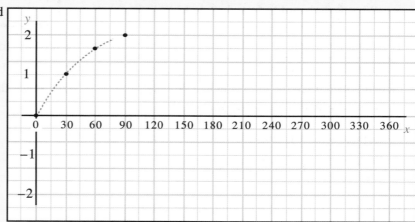

Exercise 16·4

1. (a) This time, just sketch the graph $y = 2\sin x°$ on a smaller scale like this :-

   (b) What is the **highest** value the graph attains ?

   (c) What is its **lowest** value ?

   (d) What is the **period** of $y = 2\sin x°$?

   (e) For what values of "x" does the curve cut the x-axis ?

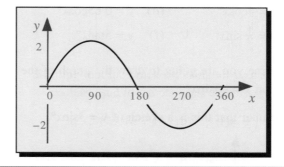

You should have noticed the following :-

* the graph is **identical** in shape to that of $y = \sin x°$.

* its **maximum** and **minimum** values are now +2 and −2, so its **amplitude** is **2**.

* its period is still 360° – it is not altered by the $2\sin x°$.

You will find :- the maximum/minimum value of $y = 3\sin x°$ is +3 and −3. Its period is still 360°

the maximum/minimum value of $y = -5\sin x°$ is +5 and −5. Its period is still 360°

the maximum/minimum value of $y = 10\cos x°$ is +10 and −10. Its period is still 360°

the maximum/minimum value of $y = \frac{1}{2}\sin x°$ is $+\frac{1}{2}$ and $-\frac{1}{2}$. Its period is still 360°

2. (a) This time, you are going to **sketch** the graph of $y = 5\sin x°$.

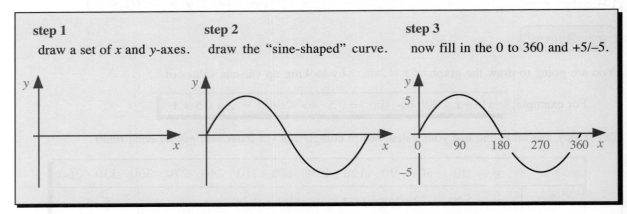

| step 1 | step 2 | step 3 |
| draw a set of x and y-axes. | draw the "sine-shaped" curve. | now fill in the 0 to 360 and +5/–5. |

(b) What is the **maximum** value and what is the **minimum** value the graph attains ?

(c) What is the **amplitude** and **period** of $y = 5\sin x°$?

3. (a) Sketch the graph of $y = 10\cos x°$, $\{0 \leq x \leq 360\}$.

remember - axes first,
then cosine-shaped
graph and **lastly** the scales.

(b) What are the **maximum-minimum** values ?

(c) What is the amplitude and the period of
$y = 10\cos x°$?

4. Make neat sketches of the following trig. graphs,
using the x–values - $\{0 \leq x \leq 360\}$:-

(a) $y = 8\sin x°$ (b) $y = 60\sin x°$

(c) $y = 4\cos x°$ (d) $y = 0{\cdot}65\cos x°$

(e) $y = \frac{1}{2}\sin x°$ (f) $y = 5\tan x°$.

5. This time you are going to draw the graph of the
function $y = -3\sin x°$.

Remember that this is a sketch of $y = 3\sin x°$.

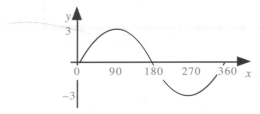

(a) How do you think $y = -3\sin x°$ will differ ?

(b) What are the **maximum-minimum** values ?

(c) What is the amplitude and the period of
$y = -3\sin x°$?

6. Make a neat labelled sketch of :-

(a) $y = -2\cos x°$ (b) $y = -0{\cdot}5\sin x°$

7. Each of the following trig graphs represents a
function of the form $y = a\sin x°$ or $y = a\cos x°$.

Write down the equation of each function.

(a)

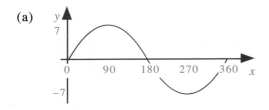

(b)

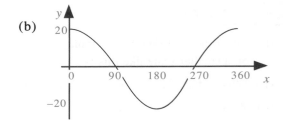

(c)

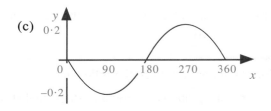

(d)

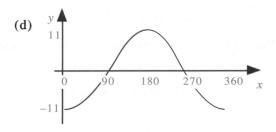

More Sine and Cosine Functions ($y = \sin ax°$ and $y = \cos ax°$)

$y = \sin 2x°$

We are going to study the $y = \sin 2x°$ for various values of x.

For example,   when $x = 30$ => $2x = 60$ => $\sin 2x° = \sin 60° = 0.87$

(a) Copy this table and use your calculator to complete it (to 2 decimal places each time).

x	0	30	45	60	90	120	135	150	180
$\sin 2x°$	0	0.87	1.00	0.87	0	−0.87	...	...	...

(b) Draw a set of axes on squared paper, plot the above nine points and join them up with a smooth curve.

Show your graph of $y = \sin 2x°$ to your teacher.

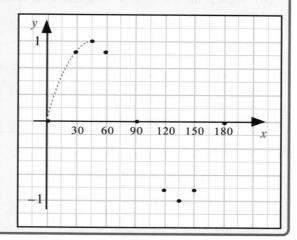

Exercise 16·5

1. (a) This time, just sketch the graph $y = \sin 2x°$ on a smaller scale like this :-

   (b) What is the **highest** value the graph attains ?

   (c) What is its **lowest** value ?

   (d) What is the **amplitude** and the **period** of $y = \sin 2x°$?

   (e) For what values of "x" does the curve cut the x-axis ?

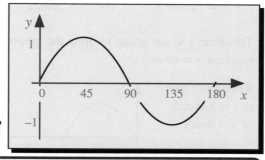

You should have noticed the following :-

- the graph is **identical** in shape to that of $y = \sin x°$.
- its **maximum** and **minimum** values are still +1 and −1, and its **amplitude** is still 1.
- its period is no longer 360° – its period is now 360° ÷ 2 = 180°.

You will find that :-   the period of $y = \sin 3x°$ has a period of $360 ÷ 3 = 120°$

the period of $y = \sin 10x°$ has a period of $360 ÷ 10 = 36°$

the period of $y = \cos 4x°$ has a period of $360 ÷ 4 = 90°$

the period of $y = \tan 2x°$ has a period of $180 ÷ 2 = 90°$.

2. (a) This time, you are going to **sketch** the graph of $y = 3\sin4x°$.

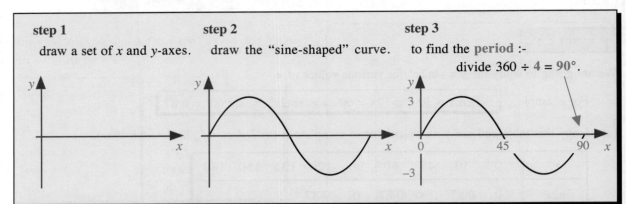

step 1
draw a set of x and y-axes.

step 2
draw the "sine-shaped" curve.

step 3
to find the **period** :-
divide $360 \div 4 = 90°$.

(b) What is the **maximum** value and what is the **minimum** value of the function ?

(c) What is the **period** of $y = 3\sin4x°$?

3. (a) Sketch the graph of $y = \cos3x°$.

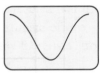

remember - axes first,
then cosine-shaped
graph and **lastly** the scales.

(b) What are the **maximum-minimum** values ?

(c) What is the period of $y = \cos3x°$?

4. Make neat sketches of the following trig. graphs :-

(a) $y = 6\sin3x°$ (b) $y = 50\sin6x°$

(c) $y = 5\cos2x°$ (d) $y = 0\cdot7\cos4x°$

(e) $y = 12\sin\frac{1}{2}x°$ (f) $y = 5\tan2x°$. (*careful*)

5. This time you are going to draw the graph of the
function $y = -9\sin3x°$.

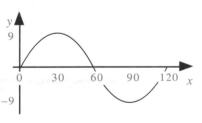

Remember that
this is a sketch
of $y = 9\sin3x°$.

(a) How do you think $y = -9\sin3x°$ will differ ?

(b) What are the **maximum-minimum** values ?

(c) What is the period and amplitude of
$y = -9\sin3x°$?

6. Make a neat labelled sketch of **1 cycle** of :-

(a) $y = -12\cos5x°$ (b) $y = -0\cdot2\sin6x°$

(c) $y = -0\cdot1\sin\frac{1}{2}x°$ (d) $y = -\frac{1}{8}\cos30x°$.

7. Each of the following trig graphs represents a
function of the form $y = a\sin bx°$ or $y = a\cos bx°$.

Write down the equation of each function.

(a)
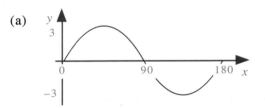

(b)
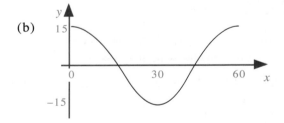

(c)
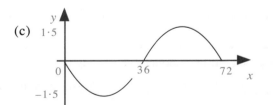

(d)
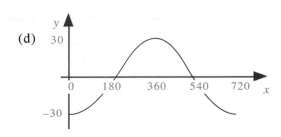

When the sine or cosine function has a number added on (or subtracted), the simple effect is to "slide" the basic sine or cosine function upwards (or downwards) by that amount.

Example 1 :- $y = \sin x° + 1$

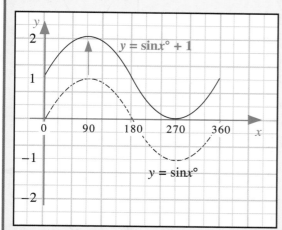

Example 2 :- $y = 6\cos x° - 3$

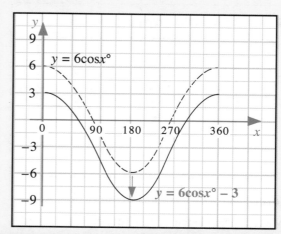

Note :-
- The **period** of the new function with the added (or subtracted) term remains **the same**.
- The **amplitude** stays the same. (*Half the difference between the highest and lowest points*).
- But the **maximum** and the **minimum** values change.

    In **example 1**, the maximum and minimum changes from 1 and –1 —> to 2 and 0.

    In **example 2**, the maximum and minimum changes from 6 and –6 —> to 3 and –9.

- To draw $y = \sin x + 2$, simply sketch the graph of $y = \sin x$ and **move each point up by 2**.

Exercise 16·6

1. Shown below is a sketch of the function
   $$y = \sin x°.$$

   (a) Make a neat copy of the graph, showing the graph dotted as in the sketch.

   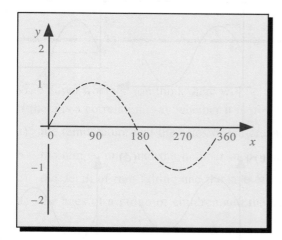

   (b) On your drawing, show also the graph of the function :- $y = \sin x° - 1$.

2. (a) Make a neat (dotted) sketch of the function
   $$y = \cos x°,$$
   showing all the main features and values.

   (b) On the same graph, show the function :-
   $$y = \cos x + 2.$$

3. (a) This time, make a sketch showing $y = 4\sin x°$.

   (b) On the same graph, show the function :-
   $$y = 4\sin x - 2,$$
   showing all its main features.

4. (a) Now, sketch the graph of the function :-
   $$y = 6\cos x°,$$

   (b) On the same graph, show $y = 6\cos x + 3$,
   indicating all the main features and values.

5. Make neat sketches of each of the following, showing all the main features and values.

(*hint :- sketch the "basic" trig function first*).

(a) $y = 2\sin x° + 2$ (b) $y = \cos x° - 3$

(c) $y = 40\sin x° - 40$ (d) $y = 12\cos x° - 6$.

6. Shown below is the graph of $y = -4\sin 5x°$.

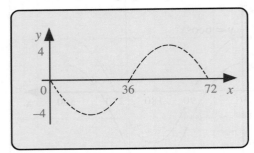

(*Remember why it is "upside-down"*).

Make a neat sketch of this (dotted) curve, and show on it the graph of $y = -4\sin 5x° + 4$.

7. Sketch the graph of $y = -6\cos x°$, (*dotted*), and show also the graph of $y = -6\cos x° - 3$, indicating all of its main features and values.

8. Make neat sketches of each of the following, showing all the main features and values.

(a) $y = -3\sin x° + 3$ (b) $y = -\cos x° - 2$

(c) $y = 10 - 10\sin x°$ (d) $y = -1 - 2\cos x°$.

9. Work out the equation of the following trig function from its graph :-

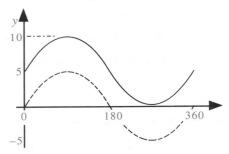

10. Determine the equation of this trig graph :-

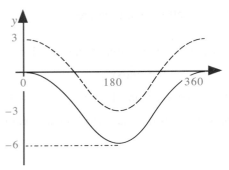

11. Determine the equation of each of the following trig functions from their graphs :-

(a)   (b)

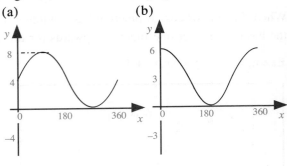

(c)   (d)

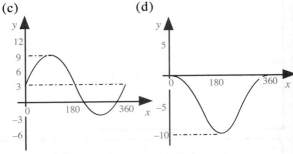

(e)   (f)

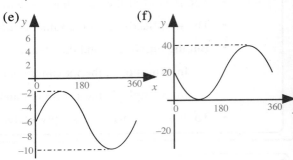

12. **Harder** - Each of these functions is of the form :-

$$y = a\sin\underline{b}x + c.$$

Determine the equation of each.

(a)   (b)

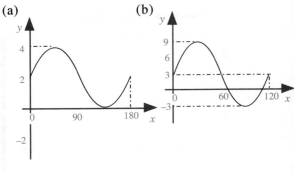

(c)   (d)

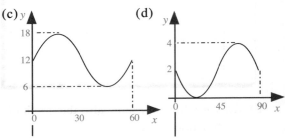

13. The pedal on this bicycle crank is rotated.

Its height above (and below) the centre of the shank is noted as the pedal rotates.

This is shown on the graph below.

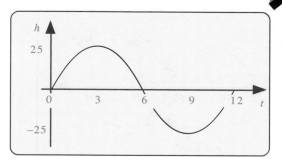

- t represents the time (in seconds)
- h represents the height (in centimetres).

(a) What is the **period** of the graph ?
(*This is the time taken for 1 rotation*).

(b) Write down the equation of the graph :-

$$h = \dots \sin \dots t°.$$

14. The water level rises and falls every 12 hours in a harbour as the tide comes in and out.

A graph, showing the depth (d m) of water measured from point **P**, is shown below. The time (t) is measured in hours.

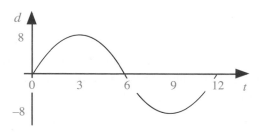

(a) How high above P is the water at high tide ?

(b) Write down the equation of the graph :-

$$d = \dots \sin \dots t°.$$

15. A chalk-mark is made on the tyre of a bicycle wheel.

As the wheel rotates along the ground, its height in centimetres is recorded and shown on the graph below.

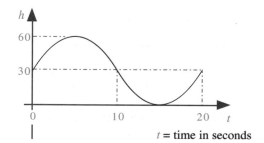

t = time in seconds

(a) From the graph, say what the diameter of the wheel must be.

(b) What is the period of the graph ?

(c) Write down the equation of the graph :-

$$h = \dots \sin \dots t° + \dots .$$

16. The graph below shows the average number of hours of daylight, (*each day*), there is throughout the year starting from the month of June.

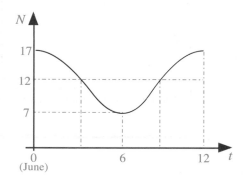

- N is the number of hours sunshine daily
- t is the number of months after June.

(a) What is the maximum number of hours of sunshine each day, and in which month ?

(b) What is the minimum number, and when ?

(c) The **equinoxes** (*Spring and Autumn*) are when there is an equal number of hours of light and dark. Which months ?

(d) Find the equation of the graph in the form :-

$$N = \dots \cos \dots t° + \dots .$$

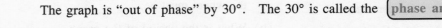

Phase Angles

So far we have
- "*stretched*" the sine graph vertically — e.g. $y = 10\sin x°$.
- "*stretched/squashed*" the sine graph horizontally — e.g. $y = \sin 4x°$.
- "*moved*" the sine graph up or down — e.g. $y = \sin x° + 2$.

What we have NOT done yet, is to slide the sine graph right or left. We are going to consider that now.

Look at this sine graph :-

The dotted graph is $y = \sin x°$.

The **blue** graph is the sine graph <u>after</u> it has been "slid" 30° to the **right**.

We represent this using the function :-

$$y = \sin(x - 30)°.$$

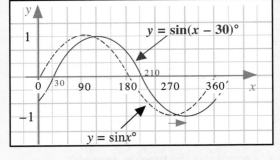

The graph is "out of phase" by 30°. The 30° is called the phase angle.

Example 1 :- Write down the equation of this **blue** trig graph :-

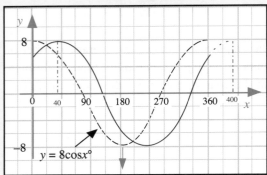

Solution 1 :- It is the cosine graph, moved 40° right.
=> $y = 8(\cos x - 40)°$

Example 2 :- Sketch the graph of :-
$$y = 3\sin(x + 25)°.$$

Solution 2 :- Start with the graph of $y = 3\sin x°$, then "slide" it 25° **LEFT**.

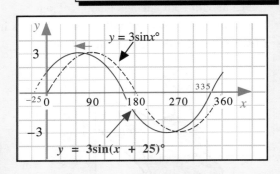

Exercise 16·7

1. Write down the equations of these trig graphs :-

(a)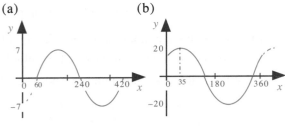

(b)

(c)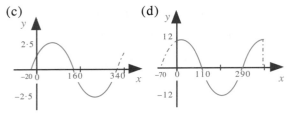

(d)

(e)

(f)

2. Sketch the graphs of the following trig functions, $(0 \le x \le 360)$, showing the maximum and minimum values and where the curves cut the x-axis :-

(a) $y = \sin(x - 15)°$ (b) $y = \cos(x - 35)°$
(c) $y = 5\sin(x - 10)°$ (d) $y = 7\cos(x - 75)°$
(e) $y = 2\sin(x + 30)°$ (f) $y = 10\cos(x + 25)°$
(g) $y = -\sin(x - 50)°$ (h) $y = -2\cos(x - 40)°$
(i) $y = 0·3\sin(x + 70)°$ (j) $y = 55\cos(x - 20)°$.

N5 - Chapter 16   this is page 168   Trig Graphs

Remember Remember..... ?

1. Sketch the sine graph, the cosine graph and the tangent graph, $\{0 \le x \le 360\}$, on different diagrams, indicating the shape of each and all the important points through which they pass.

2. Write down the equations of the following graphs :-

(a)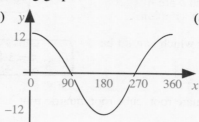

(b)

(c)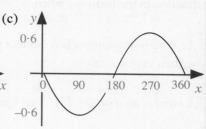

3. Write down the equations of the following graphs :-

(a)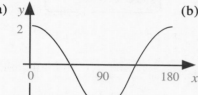

(b)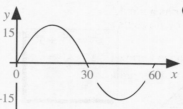

(c)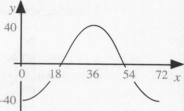

4. Write down the equations of the following graphs :-

(a)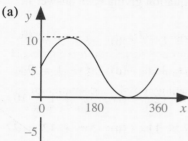

(b)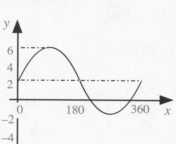

(c)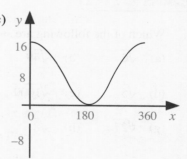

5. Write down the equations of the following graphs :-

(a)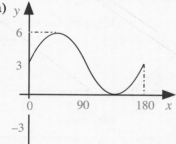

(b)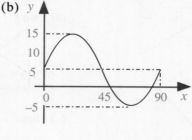

(c)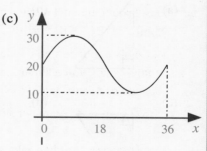

6. Make a neat sketch of each function, showing the shape, scale and important points on your graphs.

(a) $y = 25\sin x°$

(b) $y = 10\cos x°$

(c) $y = \sin 3x°$

(d) $y = 8\cos 4x°$

(e) $y = \sin x° + 1$

(f) $y = 2\sin x° - 2$

(g) $y = 20\cos x° + 10$

(h) $y = -2\sin 6x°$

(i) $y = 4\cos 2x° - 4.$

(j) $y = \frac{5}{2}\cos x°$

(k) $y = -\frac{1}{2}\sin 6x°$

(l) $y = 2\cdot4\cos x° - 2.$

Surds

A **rational** number is one which can be written as a fraction in the form $\dfrac{a}{b}$, where a and b are **integers**.

(e.g. $\dfrac{7}{1}$, $\dfrac{3}{4}$, $-\dfrac{1}{2}$, $4\ (=\dfrac{4}{1})$, $0.5\ (=\dfrac{1}{2})$...)

An **irrational** number is a number which **cannot** be written in this form.

(e.g. $\pi = 3.1412....$ **cannot** be expressed as $\dfrac{a}{b}$)

A **surd** is an *irrational root*, (a square root, cube root, quartic root, ...).

$\sqrt{2}$, $\sqrt{3}$ are surds.

$\sqrt{16}$ is **not** a surd since $\sqrt{16} = 4$ ← (*rational*)

Example :-   Calculate the length of the hypotenuse of the right angled triangle shown below, leaving your answer as a **surd**.

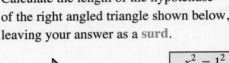

$$x^2 = 1^2 + 1^2$$
$$x^2 = 2$$
$$x = \sqrt{2}$$

N.B. If you use a calculator and write 1·41421, this is a rounded decimal and **not exact**. ($\sqrt{2}$ is exact).

Exercise 17·1

1.   Which of the following are **surds** :-

(a) $\sqrt{2}$ (b) $\sqrt{49}$ (c) $\sqrt{121}$

(d) $\sqrt{5}$ (e) $\sqrt[3]{1000}$ (f) $\sqrt{3}$

(g) $\sqrt[3]{27}$ (h) $\sqrt{8}$ (i) $\sqrt[3]{8}$.

2.   Express x as a **surd** each time here :-

(a)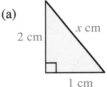

(b)

(c)

(d)

(e)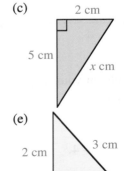

(f)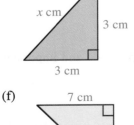

3.   Solve each equation giving each answer in **surd** form :-

(a) $x^2 - 1 = 1$ (b) $x^2 - 3 = 2$

(c) $x^2 + 1 = 3$ (d) $x^2 + 1 = 9$

(e) $x^2 + 1 = 12$ (f) $3x^2 + 1 = 10$

(g) $2x^2 + 7 = 11$ (h) $5x^2 + 12 = 27$.

4.   Write the **exact** value of each trigonometric ratio in **surd** form :-

(a) $\sin x°$ (b) $\cos x°$

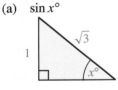   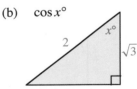

(c) $\tan x°$ (d) $\tan x°$.

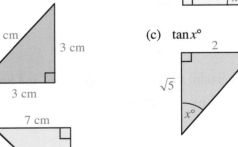

5.   A rectangle has dimensions 8 cm by 5 cm. Calculate the **exact** length of a diagonal.

Simplifying Surds

Surds can be **simplified** using the normal rules of algebra.

Can you see that $\sqrt{2} \times \sqrt{3} = 2 \cdot 449 = \sqrt{6}$?

Generally, we can state that $\sqrt{a} \times \sqrt{b} = \sqrt{ab}$

Example 1:- Simplify $3\sqrt{2} + 4\sqrt{2}$

$$3\sqrt{2} + 4\sqrt{2} = 7\sqrt{2}$$

(Since $3x + 4x = 7x$)

Example 2 :- Simplify $\sqrt{32}$

$$\sqrt{32} = \sqrt{(16 \times 2)}$$
$$= \sqrt{16} \times \sqrt{2} = 4\sqrt{2}$$

(Since $\sqrt{a} \times \sqrt{b} = \sqrt{ab}$)

To simplify a surd, try to express it as a **product** of two numbers, one of which is a **perfect square**.

Exercise 17·2

1. Add or subtract these surds :-

(a) $4\sqrt{2} + 5\sqrt{2}$ (b) $7\sqrt{2} - 4\sqrt{2}$

(c) $6\sqrt{3} + 7\sqrt{3}$ (d) $13\sqrt{7} - 7\sqrt{7}$

(e) $5\sqrt{5} + \sqrt{5}$ (f) $\sqrt{3} + 2\sqrt{3} - 3\sqrt{3}$

(g) $12\sqrt{2} - 11\sqrt{2}$ (h) $3\sqrt{7} + 2\sqrt{7} - 5\sqrt{7}$

(i) $7\sqrt{13} - 8\sqrt{13}$ (j) $3\sqrt{3} - 2\sqrt{3} - 4\sqrt{3}$

(k) $\sqrt{2} + \sqrt{2}$ (l) $\sqrt{11} + \sqrt{11} + \sqrt{11}$

(m) $5\sqrt{5} + 3\sqrt{5} + 4\sqrt{5} - 6\sqrt{5}$

(n) $11\sqrt{2} + \sqrt{2} + 6\sqrt{2} + 2\sqrt{2} - 19\sqrt{2}$.

2. Simplify :-

(a) $\sqrt{12}$ (b) $\sqrt{20}$ (c) $\sqrt{44}$

(d) $\sqrt{8}$ (e) $\sqrt{50}$ (f) $\sqrt{300}$

(g) $\sqrt{45}$ (h) $\sqrt{18}$ (i) $\sqrt{125}$

(j) $\sqrt{72}$ (k) $\sqrt{450}$ (l) $\sqrt{225}$.

3. Find the **exact** value of y as a **surd** in its simplest form :-

(a)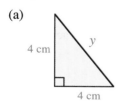

(b)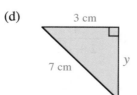

(c)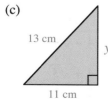

(d)

4. A cube has side 20 cm. Calculate, in **simplest form**, the **exact** length of the :-

(a) **face** diagonal **BR**.

(b) **space** diagonal **AR**.

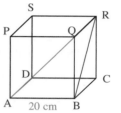

5. 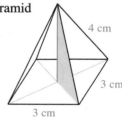 A cuboid has dimensions 3 cm by 4 cm by 5 cm.

Find the **exact** value of the length of one of its **space diagonals**.

6. (Difficult) A square based pyramid has dimensions as shown.
(*Sloping sides are 4 cm.*)

Calculate the exact value of the pyramid's **height**.

(*Hint : start with Pythagoras*)

Remember $\sqrt{a} \times \sqrt{b} = \sqrt{ab}$

$$\sqrt{2} \times \sqrt{10} = \sqrt{2 \times 10} = \sqrt{20}$$
$$\sqrt{20} = \sqrt{4} \times \sqrt{5} = 2\sqrt{5}$$

7. **Simplify** as far as possible :-

(a) $\sqrt{3} \times \sqrt{8}$ (b) $\sqrt{5} \times \sqrt{8}$

(c) $\sqrt{6} \times \sqrt{12}$ (d) $\sqrt{7} \times \sqrt{8}$

(e) $\sqrt{15} \times \sqrt{16}$ (f) $\sqrt{2} \times \sqrt{3} \times \sqrt{5}$

(g) $\sqrt{2} \times \sqrt{3} \times \sqrt{2}$ (h) $\sqrt{8} \times \sqrt{2} \times \sqrt{5}$

(i) $\sqrt{3} \times \sqrt{3} \times \sqrt{3}$ (j) $\sqrt{3} \times \sqrt{5} \times \sqrt{15}$.

8. Find as a **surd**, in its simplest form, the value of x each time.

(a)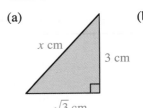

(b)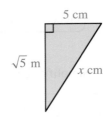

(c)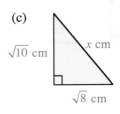

(d)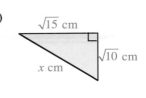

The usual algebra rules apply for brackets.

$$(2 + \sqrt{2})(3 + \sqrt{2}) \quad \text{(FOIL)}$$

$$= 2 \times 3 + 2 \times \sqrt{2} + \sqrt{2} \times 3 + \sqrt{2} \times \sqrt{2}$$

$$= 6 + 2\sqrt{2} + 3\sqrt{2} + 2$$

$$= 8 + 5\sqrt{2} \quad \text{(This is in simplest form)}$$

9. Multiply out the brackets and simplify :-

(a) $(2 + \sqrt{2})(4 + \sqrt{2})$

(b) $(4 + \sqrt{2})(3 + \sqrt{2})$

(c) $(4 + \sqrt{2})(3 - \sqrt{2})$

(d) $(2 + \sqrt{3})(3 + \sqrt{3})$

(e) $(1 + \sqrt{5})(2 - \sqrt{5})$

(f) $(2 - \sqrt{7})(5 - \sqrt{7})$

(g) $(\sqrt{2} + \sqrt{8})(1 + \sqrt{8})$

(h) $(\sqrt{3} + \sqrt{12})(3 + \sqrt{12})$

(i) $(\sqrt{5} + \sqrt{6})(\sqrt{5} + \sqrt{6})$

(j) $(\sqrt{8} + \sqrt{2})(\sqrt{2} + \sqrt{8})$

(k) $(2 + \sqrt{2})^2$ (l) $(1 + \sqrt{3})^2$

(m) $(2 - \sqrt{2})^2$ (n) $(1 - \sqrt{3})^2$

(o) $(3 - \sqrt{5})^2$ (p) $(1 + \sqrt{3})^3$.

The fraction $\dfrac{2}{\sqrt{3}}$ can be simplified -

(change the surd denominator by multiplication).

multiply top and bottom by √3 $\dfrac{2}{\sqrt{3}} \times \dfrac{\sqrt{3}}{\sqrt{3}} = \dfrac{2\sqrt{3}}{3}$ it now has a rational denominator

This is called (**rationalising the denominator.**)

10. **Rationalise the denominator** in each fraction and simplify as far as possible.

(a) $\dfrac{4}{\sqrt{3}} \times \dfrac{\sqrt{3}}{\sqrt{3}}$ (b) $\dfrac{5}{\sqrt{2}}$ (c) $\dfrac{4}{3\sqrt{5}}$

(d) $\dfrac{15}{\sqrt{5}}$ (e) $\dfrac{7}{2\sqrt{14}}$ (f) $\dfrac{20}{\sqrt{8}}$

(g) $\dfrac{16}{5\sqrt{8}}$ (h) $\dfrac{\sqrt{5}}{\sqrt{10}}$ (i) $\dfrac{10}{\sqrt{20}}$.

Extension - used at Higher Level.

Given $2 + \sqrt{3}$ we say that $2 - \sqrt{3}$ is the **conjugate**.

Also $-1 - \sqrt{3}$ has **conjugate** $-1 + \sqrt{3}$.

11. Write down the **conjugate** of each expression :-

(a) $2 + \sqrt{5}$ (b) $3 + \sqrt{3}$

(c) $2 - \sqrt{7}$ (d) $6 - \sqrt{2}$

(e) $-1 + \sqrt{2}$ (f) $-5 + \sqrt{3}$.

The **conjugate** can be used to **rationalise the denominator** of more complicated expressions.

$$\dfrac{3}{4 + \sqrt{2}} \times \dfrac{4 - \sqrt{2}}{4 - \sqrt{2}} = \dfrac{12 - 3\sqrt{2}}{16 + 4\sqrt{2} - 4\sqrt{2} - 2} = \dfrac{12 - 3\sqrt{2}}{14}$$

N.B. rational number

12. Use the **conjugate** to **rationalise** each denominator :-

(a) $\dfrac{2}{1 + \sqrt{3}} \times \dfrac{1 - \sqrt{3}}{1 - \sqrt{3}}$

(b) $\dfrac{4}{2 + \sqrt{2}}$ (c) $\dfrac{32}{4 - \sqrt{8}}$

(d) $\dfrac{10}{5 - \sqrt{12}}$ (e) $\dfrac{4 + \sqrt{3}}{2 - \sqrt{3}} \times \dfrac{2 + \sqrt{3}}{2 + \sqrt{3}}$.

Powers or **indices** are used as a means of writing repeated calculations in a shorter way.

Examples :-

2^4 is read as "2 to the power of 4"

$2^4 = 2 \times 2 \times 2 \times 2 = 16$ (The 4 is called the **power**, the **index** or **exponent**).

$y \times y \times y \times y \times y = y^5$ (The **power**, **index** or **exponent** is 5).

Exercise 17·3

1. Write down the **index**, **(exponent)** of each term.

   (a) 2^3 (b) 3^3 (c) 5^4

   (d) 6^2 (e) 2^8 (f) 3^5

   (g) 10^9 (h) x^{21} (i) x^{-2}

   (j) $y^{8·5}$ (k) $x^{\frac{2}{3}}$ (l) x^y .

2. Write down each of these as products :-

   (a) $2^6 = 2 \times 2 \times 2 \times 2 \times ... \times ... = ...$

   (b) 2^3 (c) 6^2 (d) 5^4

   (e) 2^8 (f) 3^3 (g) 10^9

   (h) 2^{10} (i) 3^5 (j) k^3

   (k) $(-2)^4$ (l) $(-2)^3$ (m) $(-2)^5$

   (n) $(-3)^4$ (o) $(-1)^6$ (p) $(-1)^{51}$

   (q) x^4 (r) t^5 (s) y^7 .

3. Write down each expression using indices :-
   (Example :- $2 \times 2 \times 2 = 2^3$)

   (a) $3 \times 3 \times 3 \times 3 \times 3 \times 3 \times 3$

   (b) $2 \times 2 \times 2 \times 2 \times 2 \times 2 \times 2$

   (c) $4 \times 4 \times 4$

   (d) $7 \times 7 \times 7 \times 7 \times 7$

   (e) $(-3) \times (-3) \times (-3)$

   (f) $(-2) \times (-2)$

   (g) $k \times k \times k \times k \times k \times k$

   (h) $p \times p \times p \times p$

   (i) $z \times z \times z \times z \times z$

   (j) $(-t) \times (-t) \times (-t)$

   (k) $(-y) \times (-y) \times (-y) \times (-y) \times (-y)$

   (l) $3 \times 3 \times 3 \times 3 \times 3 \times 3 \times 3 \times 3 \times 3 \times 3$.

4. Find the value of the **index** each time :-

   (a) $2^x = 64$ (b) $5^x = 625$

   (c) $3^x = 243$ (d) $10^x = 1\,000\,000$

   (e) $17^x = 289$ (f) $12^x = 12$.

5. Use the x^y *or* y^x *or* $\wedge$ button on your calculator.

$3^4 = 3\ x^y\,4$ $= 81$	$3^4 = 3\ y^x\,4$ $= 81$	$3^4 = 3 \wedge 4$ $= 81$

   Use your calculator to find :-

   (a) 5^3 (b) 2^{15} (c) 17^5

   (d) 3^{15} (e) $(2·5)^4$ (f) $(0·4)^4$

   (g) $(-3)^7$ (h) $(-1·1)^5$ (i) 2^{-1} .

6. Darren says to his dad,
   "Stop giving me £10 per week
   pocket money. Instead, give me
   1 pence this week, 2p next,
   4p the next and keep doubling
   it for a year".

   How much would his dad have to give him
   on week 52 ?

7. Note :- $2^2 \times 2^3 = (2 \times 2) \times (2 \times 2 \times 2) = 2^5$.
   Express each of these as a power :-

   (a) $2^3 \times 2^4$ (b) $2^2 \times 2^7$

   (c) $3^2 \times 3^3$ (d) $5^2 \times 5^2$

   (e) $3^2 \times 3^2$ (f) $10^2 \times 10^4$.

8. What do you notice about your answers to
   question 7 ?

Rules of Indices

Rule 1 $\boxed{a^m \times a^n = a^{m+n}}$

To multiply powers of a number, **add** the indices.

Rule 2 $\boxed{\dfrac{a^m}{a^n} = a^{m-n}}$

To divide powers of a number, **subtract** the indices.

Rule 3 $\boxed{\left(a^m\right)^n = a^{mn}}$

To take "*powers*" of "*powers*" of a number, **multiply** the indices.

Example 1 :-
$$x^2 \times x^3$$
$$= x \times x \times x \times x \times x$$
$$= x^5$$

Example 2 :-
$$\frac{x^5}{x^3}$$
$$= \frac{x \times x \times x \times x \times x}{x \times x \times x}$$
$$= x^2$$

Example 3 :-
$$\left(x^2\right)^3$$
$$= x^2 \times x^2 \times x^2$$
$$= x^6$$

Exercise 17·4

1. Use **Rule 1** above to simplify :-

   (a) $x^2 \times x^3$ (not x^6) (b) $x^3 \times x^4$

   (c) $k^5 \times k^4$ (d) $w^2 \times w^2$

   (e) $q^7 \times q^6$ (f) $x^3 \times x^{-1}$

   (g) $x^5 \times x^{-2}$ (h) $p^7 \times p^{-4}$

   (i) $k^7 \times k^{-8}$ (j) $s^{-4} \times s^2$

   (k) $q^{-1} \times q^{-2}$ (l) $r^{-5} \times r^{-9}$

   (m) $x^2 \times x^3 \times x^4$ (n) $q^3 \times q^5 \times q^2$

   (o) $y^6 \times y^1 \times y^3$ (p) $y^{-2} \times y^{-1} \times y^{-3}$

   (q) $y^{-3} \times y^2 \times y^2$

   (r) $b^7 \times b^9 \times b^{-2} \times b^{-11}$

   (s) $a^{-3} \times a^4 \times a^2 \times a^{-5} \times a^3$.

2. Copy and complete :-

   $$a^2 \times b^5 \times a^4 \times b^{-1} = a^{....} \times b^{....} = a^{..}b^{..}$$

3. Simplify as far as possible :-

   (a) $a^5 \times b^3 \times a^{-2} \times b^4$

   (b) $k^4 \times p^6 \times p^{-4} \times k^{-1}$

   (c) $c^7 \times t^5 \times c^{-6} \times t^{-3}$

   (d) $a^5 \times b^3 \times c^2 \times a^{-3} \times c$.

Example :- Simplify $3x^5 \times 2x^3$

Deal with the **3** and the **2** first
(i.e. 3×2) then the indices.

$$3x^5 \times 2x^3 = 6x^8$$

4. Simplify as far as possible :-

   (a) $2x^3 \times 4x^2$ (b) $5x^4 \times 3x^3$

   (c) $4k^4 \times 4k^5$ (d) $7k^6 \times 2k^3$

   (e) $11p^2 \times 5p^4$ (f) $4p^7 \times 5p^{-2}$

   (g) $6y^7 \times y^{-5}$ (h) $9z^{12} \times z^{-8}$

   (i) $3 \times 4q^2 \times 2q^3$ (j) $3t^8 \times t^{-3} \times 2t^{-4}$.

5. Use **Rule 2** above to simplify :-

   (a) $\dfrac{x^5}{x^3}$ (b) $\dfrac{x^4}{x^2}$ (c) $x^7 \div x^4$

   (d) $\dfrac{y^8}{y^3}$ (e) $y^{10} \div y^6$ (f) $\dfrac{y^9}{y^8}$

   (g) $\dfrac{a^{11}}{a^7}$ (h) $\dfrac{b^{15}}{b^{11}}$ (i) $c^{18} \div c^{10}$

   (j) $\dfrac{z^{1\cdot5}}{z^{1\cdot2}}$ (k) $\dfrac{p^{6\cdot6}}{p^{4\cdot8}}$ (l) $\dfrac{t^7}{t^2}$

   (m) $t^5 \div t^{-3}$ (n) $x^{-7} \div x^3$ (o) $y^{-5} \div y^{-2}$.

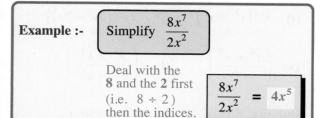

Example :- Simplify $\dfrac{8x^7}{2x^2}$

Deal with the **8** and the **2** first (i.e. $8 \div 2$) then the indices.

$$\dfrac{8x^7}{2x^2} = 4x^5$$

6. Simplify as far as possible :-

(a) $\dfrac{9x^5}{3x^3}$ (b) $\dfrac{16y^8}{4y^5}$ (c) $\dfrac{8y^6}{6y^2}$

(d) $\dfrac{20k^{12}}{16k}$ (e) $\dfrac{36p^7}{24p^6}$ (f) $14x^7 \div 7x^4$

(g) $\dfrac{12p^4}{4p^{-2}}$ (h) $\dfrac{21q^3}{14q^{-2}}$ (i) $\dfrac{18w^{-3}}{16w^2}$

(j) $\dfrac{4w^5x^3}{2w^2x^2}$ (k) $\dfrac{27x^2z^3}{21x\,z^{-2}}$ (l) $48x^2 \div 12x^{-1}$.

7. Use **Rule 3** to simplify :-

(a) $\left(x^3\right)^2$ (b) $\left(x^4\right)^2$ (c) $\left(x^3\right)^3$

(d) $\left(y^4\right)^3$ (e) $\left(y^3\right)^4$ (f) $\left(y^6\right)^5$

(g) $\left(a^7\right)^4$ (h) $\left(a^9\right)^6$ (i) $\left(a^{11}\right)^8$

(j) $\left(a^{-3}\right)^2$ (k) $\left(b^{-5}\right)^4$ (l) $\left(b^5\right)^{-4}$

(m) $\left(c^{-2}\right)^{-3}$ (n) $\left(c^{-4}\right)^{-6}$ (o) $\left(a^x\right)^y$.

Example :- Simplify $\left(2x^3\right)^4$

Deal with the power of **2** first (i.e. 2^4) then the indices.

$$\left(2x^3\right)^4 = 16x^{12}$$

8. Simplify as far as possible :-

(a) $\left(3x^4\right)^2$ (b) $\left(5x^2\right)^3$ (c) $\left(4x^5\right)^3$

(d) $\left(10x^3\right)^3$ (e) $\left(3x^4\right)^5$ (f) $\left(-2x^4\right)^6$

(g) $\left(15x^{2.5}\right)^2$ (h) $\left(3x^{0.5}\right)^6$ (i) $\left(-3x^{-4}\right)^5$.

9. Simplify as far as possible :-

(a) $\left(\dfrac{1}{2}x^3\right)^2$ (b) $\left(\dfrac{2}{3}x^4\right)^3$ (c) $\left(0{\cdot}25x^6\right)^3$.

10. Simplify as far as possible :-

(a) $\dfrac{x^5 \times x^4}{x^3} = \dfrac{x^{\cdots}}{x^{\cdots}} = x^{\cdots}$

(b) $\dfrac{y^9 \times y^{-3}}{y^3 \times y^2} = \dfrac{y^{\cdots}}{y^{\cdots}} = y^{\cdots}$

(c) $\left(\dfrac{x^3 \times x^5}{x^4}\right)^4 = \left(\dfrac{x^{\cdots}}{x^{\cdots}}\right)^4 = \left(x^{\cdots}\right)^4 = x^{\cdots}$

11. Simplify as far as possible :-

(a) $\dfrac{x^3 \times x^4}{x^5}$ (b) $\dfrac{y^7 \times y^{-2}}{y^3 \times y}$

(c) $\dfrac{z^{11} \times z^{-7}}{z^{-8} \times z^6}$ (d) $\dfrac{b^9 \times b^2 \times b^4}{b^4 \times b^3 \times b^2}$

(e) $\dfrac{k^7 \times k^{-2} \times k^{-6}}{k^9 \times k^{-5} \times k^{-3}}$ (f) $\left(\dfrac{z^4 \times z^2}{z^3}\right)^2$

(g) $\left(\dfrac{h^3 \times h^4 \times h^5}{\left(h^3\right)^2}\right)^2$ (h) $\left(x^3 \times x^5 \times x^2\right)^{1.5}$

(i) $\left(2x^3 \times 4x^{-1} \times x^2\right)^3 \times \left(5x^3 \times 2x^{-1}\right)^4$

(j) $\left(t \times t^4 \times t^{-2}\right)^x$.

Rule 4 $a^0 = 1$

since $a^m \times a^0 = a^{m+0} = a^m$

then $a^0 = 1$ *check on your calculator*

Examples :- $x^0 = 1$ $5^0 = 1$

12. Simplify :-

(a) y^0 (b) p^0 (c) t^0

(d) 3^0 (e) 8^0 (f) 71^0

(g) $4x^0$ (h) $16a^0$ (i) $8{\cdot}2t^0$

(j) $5{\cdot}3^0$ (k) $\left(2^5\right)^0$ (l) $\left(c^8 \times c^{-8}\right)^4$.

13. **Simplify** as far as possible :-

(a) $\left(\dfrac{z^3 \times z^4}{z \times z^6}\right)^0$ (b) $\left(\dfrac{p^7 \times p^5 \times p^2}{\left(p^3\right)^3}\right)^0$.

(i) $x^{-3}\left(x^5 + x^2\right)$ (j) $2y^{-1}\left(3y^2 - 2y^3\right)$

(k) $\left(\dfrac{x^4 \times x^5}{x^{-6}}\right)^2$ (l) $\left(\dfrac{k^2 \times k^3}{k^{-1} \times k^{-2}}\right)^3$

(m) $(2x^2 \times 3y^3)^4$ (n) $(3a^{-2} \times 4b^5)^2$.

Rule 5 $a^{-m} = \dfrac{1}{a^m}$

since $a^m \times a^{-m} = a^{m+(-m)} = a^0 = 1$

then $a^{-m} = \dfrac{1}{a^m}$

Example :- $x^{-3} = \dfrac{1}{x^3}$ $4^{-2} = \dfrac{1}{4^2} = \dfrac{1}{16}$

14. Rewrite each of these expressing each with a **positive power (exponent)** :-

(a) x^{-k} (b) p^{-h} (c) c^{-2}

(d) k^{-1} (e) w^{-12} (f) 5^{-2}

(g) 1^{-5} (h) $\left(x^{-5}\right)^2$ (i) $\left(x^3\right)^{-2}$

(j) $\dfrac{1}{x^{-3}}$ (k) $\dfrac{5}{x^{-2}}$ (l) $\dfrac{8}{2x^{-1}}$

(m) $\left(\dfrac{1}{x^4}\right)^{-2}$ (n) $\left(\dfrac{h^6}{h^{10}}\right)^{-2}$ (o) $\left(\dfrac{x^6}{x^4}\right)^{-2}$

15. Given $f(x) = x^{-2}$, calculate :-

(a) $f(2)$ (b) $f(-4)$ (c) $f\left(\dfrac{1}{3}\right)$.

16. Given $f(x) = 5x^{-3}$, calculate :-

(a) $f(3)$ (b) $f(0\cdot5)$ (c) $f\left(\dfrac{3}{y^2}\right)$.

17. **Simplify** (give your answer with **positive** indices)

(a) $p^5 \times p^4 \times p^3$ (b) $y^{-5} \times y^4 \times y^3$

(c) $\dfrac{y^5}{y^2}$ (d) $\dfrac{z^6}{z^{11}}$

(e) $\left(x^5\right)^4$ (f) $\left(x^3\right)^{-2}$

(g) $\dfrac{10t^8}{2t^2}$ (h) $\dfrac{6m^3}{3m^6}$

18. (a) A large **rectangular** piece of land has length $6\cdot2 \times 10^5$ m and 5×10^3 m breadth.

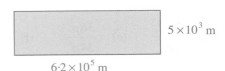

5×10^3 m

$6\cdot2 \times 10^5$ m

Calculate the **area** of the land.

(b) A rectangular garden has length x^5 metres and breadth x^3 metres.

Calculate the value of x if the area of the garden is 256 m².

x^5 m

x^3 m

(c) A cube has side 3^5 millimetres.

Find the **volume** of the cube expressed as a power of 3.

3^5 mm

(d) Brad thinks of $3^2 \times 3^4 \times 3^{-1}$. Erin thinks of $2^5 \times 2^8 \times 2^{-4}$.

How much bigger is Erin's number ?

(e) The mass of a decaying radioactive element can be found using the formula :-

$$m = e^{-0\cdot02t},$$

where m is the mass (in grams) and t is the time in days.

Find the mass of the element after 100 days given that $e = 2\cdot718$.

19. Find x each time here :-

(a) $2^x \times 2^x = 64$ (b) $3^{x+1} = 243$

(c) $4^{2x-3} = 64$ (d) $5^{x^2} = 625$.

Fractional Indices

From **Rule 1** ($a^m \times a^n = a^{m+n}$) and $\left(a^{\frac{1}{2}}\right)^2 = a^{\frac{1}{2}} \times a^{\frac{1}{2}} = a^1 = a$ => therefore $\boxed{a^{\frac{1}{2}} = \sqrt{a}}$

From this we can also deduce the following :-

$$\left(a^{\frac{1}{3}}\right)^3 = a^{\frac{1}{3}} \times a^{\frac{1}{3}} \times a^{\frac{1}{3}} = a$$
$$\Rightarrow \quad a^{\frac{1}{3}} = \sqrt[3]{a}$$

$$\left(a^{\frac{2}{3}}\right)^3 = a^{\frac{2}{3}} \times a^{\frac{2}{3}} \times a^{\frac{2}{3}} = a^2$$
$$\Rightarrow \quad a^{\frac{2}{3}} = (\sqrt[3]{a})^2$$

Therefore **Rule 6** $\boxed{a^{\frac{m}{n}} = (\sqrt[n]{a})^m}$ where m is the **power** and n is the **root**.

Example 1 :- $\boxed{a^{\frac{4}{3}} = (\sqrt[3]{a})^4}$ **Example 2 :-** $\boxed{8^{\frac{2}{3}} = (\sqrt[3]{8})^2 = 2^2 = 4}$

Exercise 17·5

1. Use **Rule 6** to express these as **roots**.

   (a) $x^{\frac{1}{2}}$ (b) $x^{\frac{1}{3}}$ (c) $y^{\frac{1}{5}}$

   (d) $y^{\frac{2}{3}}$ (e) $2z^{\frac{3}{4}}$ (f) $c^{\frac{3}{2}}$

   (g) $k^{\frac{7}{3}}$ (h) $p^{\frac{8}{5}}$ (i) $5t^{\frac{5}{2}}$

   (j) $a^{-\frac{1}{2}}$ (k) $3p^{-\frac{1}{3}}$ (l) $4g^{-\frac{4}{5}}$.

2. Evaluate :-

   (a) $9^{\frac{1}{2}}$ (b) $36^{\frac{1}{2}}$ (c) $100^{\frac{1}{2}}$

   (d) $27^{\frac{1}{3}}$ (e) $64^{\frac{1}{3}}$ (f) $125^{\frac{1}{3}}$

   (g) $8^{\frac{2}{3}}$ (h) $125^{\frac{2}{3}}$ (i) $1000^{\frac{4}{3}}$

   (j) $1^{\frac{4}{5}}$ (k) $16^{\frac{3}{4}}$ (l) $32^{\frac{3}{5}}$

   (m) $(-8)^{\frac{1}{3}}$ (n) $(-27)^{\frac{2}{3}}$ (o) $4^{-\frac{1}{2}}$

   (p) $16^{-\frac{3}{4}}$ (q) $1000^{-\frac{1}{3}}$ (r) $(-8)^{-\frac{1}{3}}$.

3. Write each of these with a **fractional index**.

   (a) $\sqrt[3]{x^2}$ (b) $\sqrt[3]{y^5}$ (c) $\sqrt[3]{y^4}$

   (d) $\sqrt{x^3}$ (e) $\sqrt[3]{y}$ (f) $\sqrt[5]{z^2}$

   (g) $\sqrt[8]{a^5}$ (h) $\sqrt[3]{a^8}$ (i) $\sqrt{k^5}$

   (j) $\sqrt[8]{p^2}$ (k) $\sqrt[4]{k^2}$ (l) $\sqrt{k^4}$.

4. Simplify and give each answer with a **positive index** (use your rules of indices) :-

   (a) $\left(c^2 \times c^4\right)^{\frac{1}{2}}$ (b) $\left(x^4 \times x^5\right)^{\frac{1}{3}}$

   (c) $\left(2x^5 \times 8x^3\right)^{\frac{1}{2}}$ (d) $\left(y^3 \times y\right)^{\frac{1}{4}}$

   (e) $\left(w^{\frac{1}{2}}\right)^2$ (f) $\left(4t^{\frac{1}{2}}\right)^2$

   (g) $\left[\dfrac{1}{x^2}\right]^{\frac{1}{2}}$ (h) $\left[\dfrac{1}{x^6}\right]^{\frac{1}{3}}$

   (i) $\left[\dfrac{x^8}{x^5}\right]^{\frac{1}{3}}$ (j) $\left[\dfrac{x^{-4}}{x^2}\right]^{\frac{1}{2}}$.

5. Multiply out the brackets, using all your **rules of indices** used in the previous exercises.

   (a) $3a^2(5a^3 + 4a^{-2})$ (b) $p^{\frac{1}{2}}(p^{\frac{1}{2}} + p^{-\frac{1}{2}})$

   (c) $6d^{\frac{1}{3}}(2d^{\frac{2}{3}} - 5d^{-\frac{1}{3}})$ (d) $2m^{-\frac{3}{4}}(3m^{\frac{7}{4}} + 4m^{\frac{3}{4}})$

   (e) $(k^{\frac{1}{2}} + 1)(k^{\frac{1}{2}} - 1)$ (f) $(t^{\frac{1}{2}} + t^{-\frac{1}{2}})(t^{\frac{1}{2}} - t^{-\frac{1}{2}})$

   (g) $\left[x + \dfrac{1}{x}\right]\left[x - \dfrac{1}{x}\right]$ (h) $\left[2y + \dfrac{3}{y}\right]\left[3y - \dfrac{1}{y}\right]$

   (i) $(x + x^{-1})^2$ (j) $(m^{\frac{1}{2}} + 1)^2$

   (k) $(2a^{\frac{1}{2}} - 3)^2$ (l) $\left[x + \dfrac{1}{x}\right]^2$

   (m) $\left[2d - \dfrac{3}{d}\right]^2$ (n) $\left[d^{\frac{1}{2}} + \dfrac{1}{d^{\frac{1}{2}}}\right]^2$.

1. Which of the following are **surds** :-

(a) $\sqrt{16}$ (b) $\sqrt{7}$ (c) $\sqrt{27}$

(d) $\sqrt[3]{27}$ (e) $\sqrt[4]{10000}$ (f) $\sqrt{0\cdot25}$.

2. Solve each equation leaving an your answer as a **surd** :-

(a) $x^2 + 1 = 8$ (b) $2x^2 - 1 = 5$.

3. Simplify :-

(a) $4\sqrt{2} + 3\sqrt{2}$ (b) $8\sqrt{7} + \sqrt{7}$

(c) $8\sqrt{3} - 4\sqrt{3}$ (d) $5\sqrt{5} - \sqrt{5}$

(e) $7\sqrt{11} - 6\sqrt{11}$ (f) $4\sqrt{3} + 2\sqrt{3} - 3\sqrt{3}$

(g) $4\sqrt{5} - 7\sqrt{5}$ (h) $5\sqrt{2} + \sqrt{2} - 3\sqrt{2}$

(i) $\sqrt{8}$ (j) $\sqrt{200}$

(k) $\sqrt{800}$ (l) $\sqrt{9000}$

(m) $\sqrt{2} \times \sqrt{3}$ (n) $\sqrt{6} \times \sqrt{8}$

(o) $\sqrt{32} \times \sqrt{2}$ (p) $\sqrt{2} \times \sqrt{2} \times \sqrt{5}$

(q) $\sqrt{1\cdot5} \times \sqrt{6}$ (r) $\sqrt{15} \times \sqrt{3} \times \sqrt{5}$.

4. Multiply out the brackets and **simplify** :-

(a) $\left(1 + 2\sqrt{3}\right)\left(2 + \sqrt{3}\right)$

(b) $\left(-3 + 2\sqrt{5}\right)\left(2 - 3\sqrt{5}\right)$

(c) $\left(3 + \sqrt{2}\right)^2$

(d) $\left(2 - 3\sqrt{5}\right)^2$

(e) $\left(1 + \sqrt{2}\right)\left(2 - 2\sqrt{2}\right)\left(3 + 3\sqrt{2}\right)$.

5. **Rationalise the denominator** in each fraction :-

(a) $\dfrac{1}{\sqrt{2}}$ (b) $\dfrac{2}{\sqrt{3}}$ (c) $\dfrac{12}{\sqrt{5}}$

(d) $\dfrac{2\sqrt{5}}{3\sqrt{6}}$ (e) $\dfrac{2}{\sqrt{8}}$ (f) $\dfrac{2}{1 + \sqrt{3}}$ * .

6. Find x each time (*as a surd in its simplest form*) :-

(a)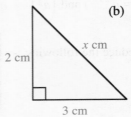

(b)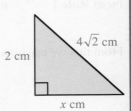

(c)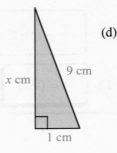

(d)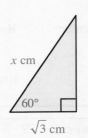

7. Simplify :-

(a) $x^5 \times x^2$ (b) $z^6 \times z^{-2}$

(c) $3m^5 \times 4m^{-3}$ (d) $p^7 \times p^{-4} \times p$

(e) $\left(4x^3\right)^2$ (f) $\left(3x^5\right)^2$

(g) $\dfrac{10x^5}{5x^2}$ (h) $\dfrac{12y^4x}{3x^2y^{-5}}$

(i) $\dfrac{8x^7}{2x^{-1}}$ (j) $\left(3z^2w^{-1}\right)^3$

(k) $p^7 \times \left(p^{-1}\right)^3$ (l) $\dfrac{y^5 \times y^3}{y^{-2}}$

(m) $g^3(g^{-2} - 2)$ (n) $\dfrac{24x^3y}{18x^2y^3}$.

8. Simplify :-

(a) $16^{\frac{1}{2}}$ (b) $64^{\frac{1}{3}}$ (c) $8^{\frac{2}{3}}$

(d) $\left(\sqrt{100}\right)^3$ (e) $\left(\sqrt[3]{8}\right)^5$ (f) $81^{\frac{3}{4}}$.

9. Simplify, (answer with a **positive indices**) :-

(a) $(x^{\frac{1}{2}} + 2)(x^{-\frac{1}{2}} - 3)$ (b) $3t^{\frac{1}{2}}\left(2t^{\frac{1}{2}} - 5t^{-\frac{1}{2}}\right)$

(c) $p^{-\frac{1}{3}}\left(p^6 + p^{-3} - p\right)$ (d) $\left(k + \dfrac{1}{k}\right)^2$

(e) $\left(m + \dfrac{1}{m}\right)\left(m - \dfrac{1}{m}\right)$ (f) $\left(d^2 + \dfrac{2}{d}\right)\left(d^2 - \dfrac{3}{d}\right)$.

Scattergraphs

A **Scattergraph** is a statistical graph which makes comparisons of two sets of data.

Example :-   This scattergraph displays the *heights* and *weights* of the players in a Basketball team.

- Sam weighs 40 kg.
- Lou is 130 cm tall. He weighs 25 kg.

Basketball Team

(Scattergraph with players: Tim, Nick, Joe, Don, Sam, Alex, Lou — Height (cm) vs Weight (kg))

Exercise 18·1

1. For the scattergraph above, write down the **height** and **weight** of each player.

2. The scattergraph below shows the **ages** and **weights** of several children.

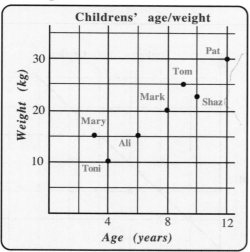

Childrens' age/weight

(Scattergraph: Weight (kg) vs Age (years), children: Pat, Tom, Mark, Shaz, Mary, Ali, Toni)

(a) Who is the :- (i) youngest
              (ii) lightest
              (iii) oldest
              (iv) heaviest child ?

(b) Write down the **age** and **weight** of each child.

(c) Child "*x*" is older than Ali, younger than Pat and is lighter than Shaz.

    What is child "*x*" called ?

3. Draw a scattergraph to show the **weights** (*in kg*) and the **shoe sizes** of a group of pupils.

	Mat	Bill	Fred	Jan	Tam
Weight	20	15	30	25	35
Shoe size	4	3	6	6	10

4. For both (a) and (b) below, construct a scattergraph to represent each set of data.

(a)	May	Zak	Jack	Tippi	Guy
Height (cm)	120	115	130	145	135
Weight (kg)	40	30	60	75	80

(b)	Jan	Feb	Mar	Apr	May
Car Sales	25	20	30	55	45
Profit (£1000)	25	30	35	60	50

5. Construct a scattergraph from the **Maths** and **English** grades of the ten pupils below.

Name	Eng	Maths
Tom	1	2
Dick	1	3
Bill	2	4
Jerry	3	4
Nick	6	7

Name	Eng	Maths
Neil	3	3
Iain	2	3
Jack	2	2
Ewan	6	6
Bob	4	5

In this example, we again show the Maths and English Grades for 10 pupils.

Name	Eng	Maths
Tom	1	2
Dick	1	3
Bill	2	4
Jerry	3	4
Nick	6	7

Name	Eng	Maths
Neil	3	3
Iain	2	3
Jack	2	2
Ewan	6	6
Bob	4	5

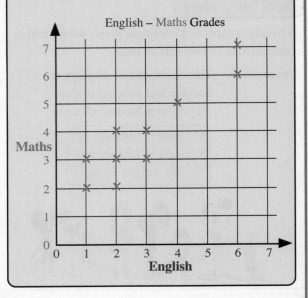

Each pair of grades is plotted on a **Scattergraph**.

Can you see there is a **fairly strong connection** between the two sets of grades ?

If two sets of values are so strongly connected that it is possible to make a fairly accurate estimate of one of the values, knowing the other, we say there is a strong **correlation** between the two sets of values.

Can you see that this is the case - there is indeed a fairly strong **positive correlation** between the Maths and the English Grades ?

(*Positive because the grouping of pairs of values is "sloping upwards" from left to right*).

Line of Best Fit

The correlation in this example is good enough to allow us to draw a **"best-fitting line"** through the group.

Though the line is only an "estimate", it should :-

- go through as many points as possible
- split the group up so there are roughly as many points above the line as there are below it.

Shown is a good estimate of the **line of best fit**.

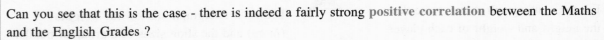

Equation of the Line of Best Fit

Earlier, you learned that almost every line drawn on an **Cartesian** diagram has its equation :-

$$y = mx + c,$$

where $(0, c)$ gives the y-intercept and m is the gradient.

In our example, the y-intercept is at $(c =)$ 1 and by drawing a small triangle we find the gradient (m) is 1.

=> the equation of the above line of best fit is :- $\boxed{y = x + 1.}$

We can also use the line (or its equation) to make further **estimates**.

If an eleventh boy, Harry, is known to have scored 5 in English, the equation of the line tells us that a fair estimate for his Maths Grade would be $y = (5) + 1 = 6$. i.e. he got a **6** for Maths.

1. This scattergraph shows the ages and the shoe sizes of several children.

   (a) Who :-

      (i)   is the **youngest**

      (ii) has the **smallest** shoe size

      (iii) is the **oldest**

      (iv) takes the **largest** shoe size ?

   (b) Is there a **strong** correlation, a **weak** correlation or **no** correlation at all ?

   (c) **Copy** the scattergraph and draw in, by eye, the **line of best fit**.

   (d) Determine the **equation** of this line.

   (e) Use the line of best fit to estimate the shoe size for Stephen who is aged 6.

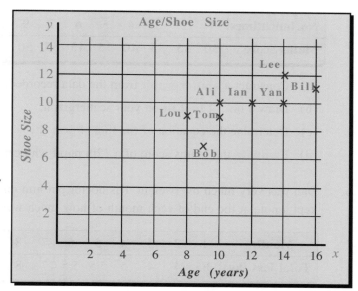

2.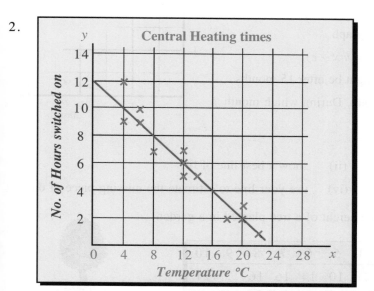

   This scattergraph shows the number of hours a lady had her central heating on each day, plotted against the average daily temperature on each of those days.

   This graph shows a **strong negative correlation** since all the points lie roughly on a straight line going **downwards** from left to right.

   The **line of best fit** is also shown.

   (a) Determine the equation of the line.

   (b) Use your line to estimate how many hours she would expect to run her central heating for, if the average temperature one day was 16°C.

3. Write down whether you think there will be a **correlation** between :- (If there is a correlation, say whether it is **positive** or **negative**).

   (a) the temperature and the sales of ice-cream in June.

   (b) the temperature and the number of people on a beach each day.

   (c) the depth of rain falling and the sale of umbrellas.

   (d) the ages of a group of children and the number of coins in their pockets.

4. Write down two of your own examples of pairs of measurements where there would be a :-

   (a) a **positive** correlation   (b) **negative** correlation   (c) **no** correlation between the pairs.

5. Mr Jones recorded the number of times 11 pupils came up for lunchtime help in the run-up to their Maths exam. He also listed the pupils' actual exam scores.

The results are shown in the table below.

No. lunchtimes	1	2	3	4	5	6	7	9	10	11	12
Maths Score	30	35	35	40	35	45	55	50	50	55	55

(a) Construct a **scattergraph** from the data recorded.

(b) Draw a **line of best fit** on your scattergraph.

(c) Determine the equation of **the line of best fit**.

(d) **Estimate** the Maths score of a 12th pupil who came up 8 times for lunchtime tutorials.

6. Dan was very much overweight. His doctor put him on a strict diet in January and Dan kept a note at the end of each month of how much weight he had lost (in total).

Month	1	2	3	4	5	6	7	8	9	10	11	12
Total loss (kg)	3·5	4	4	5	5·5	5·5	7	8	6·5	8	9	9

(a) Draw up a set of axes as shown and plot the 12 pairs of pieces of data from the table above.

(b) Draw a line of best fit on your scattergraph.

(c) Determine its equation (in the form $y = mx + c$).

(d) Estimate what his total weight loss might be after 15 months.

(e) Dan actually gained weight at one point. During which month ?

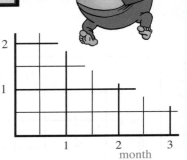

7. For each set of data below :-

(i) construct a scattergraph.   (ii) show a best line of fit.

(iii) determine the equation of the line.   (iv) use your line to estimate the missing piece of data.

(a) The data below shows the age and the height of a tree planted in a garden.

age (years)	1	2	3	4	5	6	7	8	9	10
height (m)	4	5	6	10	10	14	16	16	?	21

(b) The data shows the number of rats still alive in a warehouse, after poison was put down.

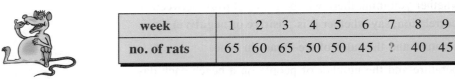

week	1	2	3	4	5	6	7	8	9	10	11	12
no. of rats	65	60	65	50	50	45	?	40	45	30	25	25

(c) A group of eight pupils compared their French and English marks in two tests.

French	10	35	60	24	56	17	42	49
English	23	57	88	40	85	33	62	?

A Mixture of Statistical Graphs

1. Use this table to construct a **Comparative Line Graph** to show the sales (in £10 000) of items in two toy shops.

	Feb	Mar	Apr	May	Jun	Jul
Harrots	3	4	6	5	8	6·5
Manleys	2	2	4	6	7·5	10

2. (a) **Copy** and complete the table showing the various makes of 600 cars sold in a showroom in one year.

    (b) Construct a **pie chart** to represent the information shown.

Make	No.	Fraction	Angle
Ford	200	$\frac{200}{600}$	$\frac{200}{600} \times 360 = ...°$
Vauxhall	150		$\times 360 = ...°$
Seat	175		$\times 360 = ...°$
Fiat	75		$\times 360 = ...°$
TOTAL	...		**360°**

3. A researcher noted the **diameter** and **weight** of the eggs laid by a hen in a fortnight.

    (a) Is there a correlation between the weights and the diameters of the eggs ?

    (b) One of the eggs had a diameter of 50 mm.

    How heavy was this egg ?

    (c) The next egg the hen laid had a diameter of 42 mm. Estimate its weight in grams.

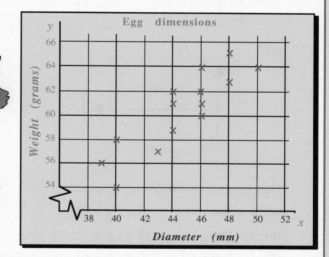

4. The ages and weights of a group of young people are recorded in the table.

Age	10	10	11	12	13	14	15	16	16	17	18	19
Weight (kg)	30	20	30	35	45	35	45	60	50	75	65	?

    (a) Construct a **scattergraph** to represent this information.

    (b) Write a sentence to explain the **correlation** in this example.

    (c) Draw a **Line of Best Fit** on your scattergraph.

    (d) Estimate, using your line, the weight of the 19 year old.

5. A platoon of soldiers was given a series of training exercises and graded out of a possible 70 marks.

    The platoon's results were tabulated as shown.

    (a) Construct an ordered **Stem and Leaf Diagram** for this.

    (b) Find the **modal** mark.

    (c) Find the **median** mark.

    (d) Soldiers who score above 50 are given a two day pass.

    How many soldiers receive a pass ?

11	22	27	49	61	68	60	52
45	34	47	25	52	62	65	45
24	52	62	61	52	31	63	33
59	42	37	21	29	19	47	34
30	22	60	41	34	59	53	10

1. Write down the equations of the following :-

   (a)

   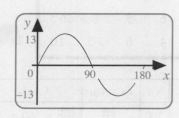

   (b)

   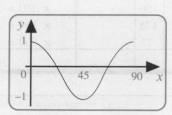

   (c)

   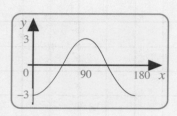

2. Sketch each of the following graphs :-

   (a) $y = 3\sin x$ $\{0 \leq x \leq 360\}$

   (b) $y = 4\cos x$ $\{0 \leq x \leq 360\}$

   (c) $y = 2\sin x + 1$ $\{0 \leq x \leq 360\}$

   (d) $y = 4\cos x - 3$ $\{0 \leq x \leq 180\}$

   (e) $y = 6\sin x + 7$ $\{0 \leq x \leq 180\}$

   (f) $y = 2\cos x - 3$ $\{0 \leq x \leq 720\}$

   (g) $y = \tan x + 2$ $\{90 \leq x \leq 180\}$.

3. Simplify fully :-

   (a) $2\sqrt{5} + 3\sqrt{5}$ (b) $7\sqrt{2} + 3\sqrt{2} - \sqrt{2}$

   (c) $\sqrt{1600}$ (d) $\sqrt{72}$

   (e) $\sqrt{1800}$ (f) $\sqrt{5} \times \sqrt{5}$

   (g) $\sqrt{3} \times \sqrt{5} \times \sqrt{6}$ (h) $(\sqrt{2} + 1)(\sqrt{2} - 3)$

   (i) $(\sqrt{3} - 2)^3$ (j) 2^6

   (k) $(-3)^5$ (l) $3x^3 \times 4x^4$

   (m) $2x^6 \times 3x^{-3} \times 5x$ (n) $6y^4 \div 3y^{-2}$.

4. Simplify fully :-

   (a) $64^{0.5} - 2^3$ (b) $\sqrt[3]{64^2}$

   (c) $k^3 \times (k^{-2})^3$ (d) $p^6(\sqrt{p} + p^2)$.

5. Rationalise the denominator :-

   (a) $\dfrac{2}{\sqrt{2}}$ (b) $\dfrac{\sqrt{8}}{\sqrt{3}}$.

6. The ages of people who visited a post office one afternoon is as follows :-

   26 34 33 17 45 67 65 54 37 71

   44 11 54 43 36 65 44 52 29 34

   19 34 65 43 23 17 65 81 65 80

   (a) Construct an ordered stem and leaf graph to show the information above.

   (b) Use your graph to determine the median age, the modal age and the range in ages.

7. The table shows the number of T-shirts sold in a shop one day.

   Construct a pie chart to show this information.

Type	Sold
X-Large	5
Large	20
Medium	50
Small	15

8. The heights (in cm) and the weights (in kg) of people at a class are shown.

   (a) Construct a scattergraph of this information.

   (b) Describe any correlation indicated by this graph.

   (c) Show on your graph a best fitting line.

   (d) Find the equation of your line and use it to estimate the weight of someone 170 cm tall.

Weight kg	Height cm
30	150
45	160
40	150
45	155
20	140
25	130
50	155
35	165
35	155

9. The sequence of multiples of 4 is

$$4, \ 8, \ 12, \ 16, \ 20, \ ....$$

Consecutive numbers from this sequence can be added using the following pattern :-

$$
\begin{aligned}
4 + 8 + 12 + 16 &= \mathbf{2 \times 4 \times 5} \\
4 + 8 + 12 + 16 + 20 &= \mathbf{2 \times 5 \times 6} \\
4 + 8 + 12 + 16 + 20 + 24 &= \mathbf{2 \times 6 \times 7}
\end{aligned}
$$

(a) Express :- $4 + 8 + 12 + \ ..... \ + 48$
   in the same way.

(b) The 1st n numbers in this pattern
   are added.

   Find a **formula** for the total in terms of n.

10. Simplify fully :-

$$\frac{x^2 + 2xy - 3y^2}{x^2 + 3xy}.$$

11. Change the subject to h :- $\ g = \dfrac{9\sqrt{h}}{k}$.

12. Gilbert had £1320 to take on holiday to Pisa.
   He changed it into euros at a rate of 1·20€ to
   the £, spent 1285€ in Italy and changed
   the remainder back into pounds when
   he came home.
   The rate of exchange was then 1·15€ to the £.

   How much UK money did he receive ?

13. A function is defined by $h(x) = 5x^2 - 3$.

   Write down an expression for $h(a)$ and calculate
   the value(s) of a, given that $h(a) = 42$.

14. (a) For the figure below, explain why the
   triangles CED and CAB are **similar**.

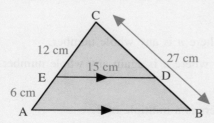

(b) Calculate the length of :-

   (i) AB   (ii) DB.

15. Solve :-

   (a) $2x^2 = 12x$ (b) $x^2 - 10x + 24 = 0$.

16. Write down the equation of the graph below :-

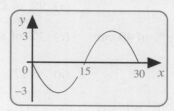

17. Make a neat sketch of the function $y = 5\cos 3x°$,
   showing the shape, scale and the important
   values on your graph.

18. Express each of the following as a surd in its
   simplest form :-

   (a) $\sqrt{96}$ (b) $\sqrt{98} + \sqrt{2}$

   (c) $3\sqrt{50}$ (d) $\dfrac{5}{\sqrt{k}}$.

19. Remove the brackets and simplify :-

   (a) $p^{\frac{1}{2}}\left(p + \dfrac{2}{p}\right)$.   (b) $(2x^{\frac{1}{2}} + x^{-\frac{1}{2}})^2$.

20. At a point in time three planets
   are *collinear* (*in a straight line*).

   Travelling from Planet A to B
   would take twice as long as
   travelling from B to C.

(a) Given, on some relative universal scale, that
   A(12, 24, 20) and B(20, 36, 16), find C.

(b) Given that one unit on this scale is *one
   light year*, calculate how many light years
   it would take to get from A to C.

(c) Explain the meaning of "*a light year*".

21. A bag of six apples and five oranges
   weighs 3·8 kg and costs £2·80.

   A bag of four apples and three oranges
   weighs 2·4 kg and costs £1·80.

   How much would you expect
   one apple and one orange :-

(a) to weigh   (b) to cost ?

1. Change :-
   (a) 0·0005 km to mm
   (b) 5000 mg to tonnes
   (c) $\frac{7}{8}$ litres to ml
   (d) 0·0125 tonnes to g
   (e) 9·2 hours to seconds
   (f) 0·4 ml to litres
   (g) 0·02 m to mm.

2. Find :-
   (a) 9% of £5
   (b) 11% of 3 cm
   (c) 85% of 1500
   (d) $2\frac{1}{2}$% of 40 cm
   (e) 3% of 8 km
   (f) $1\frac{1}{2}$% of £64
   (g) $22\frac{1}{2}$% of 680.

3. Find :-
   (a) $(-17) - (-33)$
   (b) $(-111) + 234$
   (c) $(-40) \times (-34)$
   (d) $(-20)^3 - (-10)^4$
   (e) $243 \div (-6)$
   (f) $(-15) \div 300$
   (g) $\dfrac{(-40) \times (-300)}{(-1200)}$.

4. (a) Four boys have a mean age of 17. When another boy is added, the mean drops to 15. What is the age of the new boy ?

   (b) 40 binks in a tiddi. Fifty tiddis in a splinki. 140 splinkiis in a toppi. How many binks in a toppi ?

5. The vertices of a parallelogram are A(−2, 3), B(1, 4), C(7, 0) and D(a, −b).
   (a) Find the values of a and b.
   (b) Write down the images of the vertices if given a 90° clockwise rotation about the point (−2, −3).

6. Write in 24 hour clock :- (a) five to ten at night   (b) quarter to noon.   (c) 9:10 p.m.

7. How long is it from :-   (a) 8:36 pm to 2116   (b) 2317 to 1006 the next day ?

8. (a) A plane travels 525 kilometres in 1 hours and 45 minutes. Find the average speed of the plane.
   (b) A truck travelling at 45 m.p.h. travels 25 miles. How many *minutes* did the journey take ?

9. An estimate for π as a fraction is :- $\pi = \frac{22}{7}$.

   Use this value for π to calculate the perimeter of the shape shown which consists of a semi-circle and an isosceles triangle.

   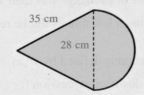

10. Find in simplest form :- (a) $\sqrt{40}$
    (b) $5\sqrt{2} - \sqrt{2}$
    (c) $\sqrt{8} + 3\sqrt{32} - \sqrt{72}$
    (d) $16^{\frac{5}{4}} \times 8^0$
    (e) $4^{\frac{3}{2}}$
    (f) $64^{\frac{5}{6}}$
    (g) $(4^3 \times 4^{-1}) \div 4^{-3}$.

11. **Difficult - Extension**
    - Any *even number* can be expressed in the form $2n$, where n is any whole number.
    - Any *odd number* can be expressed in the form $2n + 1$, where n is again any whole number.
    (a) **Prove** that every even number squared is also even.
    (b) **Prove** that the sum of any three consecutive numbers is a multiple of 3.
    (c) **Prove** that the sum of any three consecutive even numbers is a multiple of 6.
    (d) **Prove** that the difference between the squares of two consecutive whole numbers is odd.

Completed Square Form 1

Consider this **special** set of numbers - the **square** numbers or the set of **perfect squares**.

$4 = 2^2 =$ $9 = 3^2 =$ $16 = 4^2 =$ $25 = 5^2 =$

Numbers like 5, 11, 15 are not **perfect squares**, but can be written as a **perfect square**, ± a number.

$5 = 2^2 + 1 =$ $11 = 3^2 + 2 =$ $15 = 4^2 - 1 =$

The same situation occurs in **algebra**. Consider the following **special** quadratics :-

$x^2 + 2x + 1,\quad x^2 + 4x + 4,\quad x^2 - 8x + 16,\quad 4x^2 + 4x + 1$ -   they are also "**perfect squares**".

$x^2 + 2x + 1 = (x + 1)^2,\ x^2 + 4x + 4 = (x + 2)^2,\ x^2 - 8x + 16 = (x - 4)^2,\ 4x^2 + 4x + 1 = (2x + 1)^2,$ etc.

An algebraic expression like $x^2 + 2x + 3$ is **not** a **perfect square** but we can write it as **almost** one.

Example 1 :-
$x^2 + 2x + 3$
$= x^2 + 2x + 1\ (+2)$
$= (x + 1)^2 + 2$

Example 2 :-
$x^2 + 4x + 9$
$= x^2 + 4x + 4\ (+5)$
$= (x + 2)^2 + 5$

Example 3 :-
$x^2 - 8x + 11$
$= x^2 - 8x + 16\ (-5)$
$= (x - 4)^2 - 5$

Rule :- this way of rewriting a quadratic expression is called expressing it in **completed square form**.

Step 1 :-   Separate the first 2 terms from the last   => $x^2 + 10x + 27 = (x^2 + 10x)\ \ \ + 27$

Step 2 :-   Add on (*half of the x term*)^2 inside the brackets   => $(x^2 + 10x + 25)\ \ \ + 27$

Step 3 :-   Subtract this same number outside the brackets   => $(x^2 + 10x + 25)\ - 25\ + 27$

Step 4 :-   Write the expression in **completed square form** => $(x + 5)^2 + 2.$

Exercise 19·1

1. Write $y = x^2 - 6x + 10$ in completed square form.

    (a) **Copy** and **complete** :-

    $y = x^2 - 6x + 10$
    => $y = (x^2 - 6x)\ \ \ + 10$
    => $y = (x^2 - 6x + 9)\ - 9\ + 10$
    => $y = (x - ...)^2 + ...$

    (b) **Copy** and **complete** :-

    $y = x^2 - 12x + 30$
    => $y = (x^2 - 12x)\ \ \ + 30$
    => $y = (x^2 - 12x + ...)\ - ...\ + 30$
    => $y = (x - ...)^2 - ....$

2. Write $y = x^2 + 2x + 5$ in **completed square form**.

3. Write each of the following in **completed square form**, showing each stage of your working :-

    (a) $y = x^2 - 4x + 7$

    (b) $y = x^2 + 20x + 90$

    (c) $y = x^2 - 8x - 5$

    (d) $y = x^2 + 14x.$

4. Do the same here. (*Fractions required*).

    (a) $y = x^2 + 3x + 4$

    (b) $y = x^2 + 5x + 9$

    (c) $y = x^2 - x - 2$

    (d) $y = 4x^2 + 4x + 5.$ (*Extension work - Hard*).

Graph of a Quadratic in Completed Square Form

In an earlier chapter, you learned how to sketch **quadratic functions** of the form $y = x^2 - 2x - 8$ quickly by using **factorisation** techniques. The graph formed is called a **parabola**.

Reminder :-   Sketch the graph of $y = x^2 - 2x - 8$.

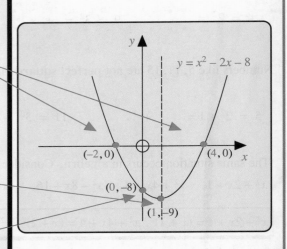

step 1 :-   set $y = 0$ => $x^2 - 2x - 8 = 0$
                       => $(x - 4)(x + 2) = 0$
                       => $x = 4$ or $x = -2$

         cuts x axis at the points $(4, 0)$ and $(-2, 0)$.

step 2 :-   find the **minimum turning point**.

         take "half way" between the roots 4 and –2.

         i.e. at $x = 1$ => Now find y when $x = 1$.

            => $y = 1^2 - 2 \times 1 - 8 = -9$

            => minimum turning point at $(1, -9)$.

step 3 :-   find the y-intercept by replacing x by 0.

            => $y = 0^2 - 2 \times 0 - 8 = -8$

            => y-intercept is at $(0, -8)$.

step 4 :-   sketch the graph through these 4 points.

If a **quadratic function** has been expressed in **completed square form** :-

$$y = (x - 2)^2 + 3 \quad - \text{ it is much easier to draw its graph.}$$

Check it really is a quadratic function :- $[(x - 2)^2 + 3 = x^2 - 4x + 4 + 3 = x^2 - 4x + 7]$ √

Example :-   Sketch the graph of $y = (x - 2)^2 + 3$.

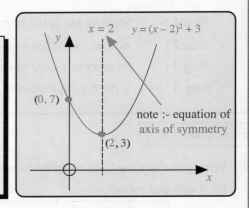

Think !   The **square** of anything can **never** be negative.

       The smallest value of $(x - 2)^2$ is **zero** at $x = 2$.

       =>   The MINIMUM value of $(x - 2)^2 + 3$
            is $0 + 3 = 3$ and this occurs at $x = 2$.

       =>   The **minimum turning point** is $(2, 3)$.

       =>   Set $x = 0$ to find the y-intercept - $(0, 7)$.
       Now sketch the parabola through these points.

note :- equation of axis of symmetry

Rule :-   Any quadratic function of the form $y = (x - a)^2 + b$ will have a **minimum** at (a, b).

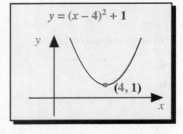

$y = (x - 4)^2 + 1$

$(4, 1)$

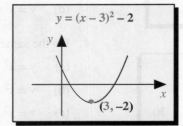

$y = (x - 3)^2 - 2$

$(3, -2)$

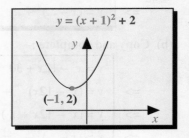

$y = (x + 1)^2 + 2$

$(-1, 2)$

1. Consider the quadratic :- $y = (x - 3)^2 + 2$.

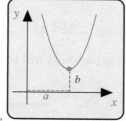

(a) What must you replace x with in $(x - 3)^2 + 2$ to make $(x - 3) = 0$?

(b) When x is replaced with this value, what will the value of y be ?

(c) What are the coordinates of the **minimum** turning point (a, b) ?

(d) Sketch the parabola showing this minimum turning point, write down the **equation** of the **axis of symmetry**.

2. Consider the quadratic :- $y = (x - 2)^2 - 1$.

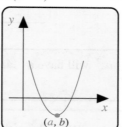

(a) What must you replace x with in $(x - 2)^2 - 1$ to make $(x - 2) = 0$?

(b) When x is replaced with this value, what will the value of y be ?

(c) What are the coordinates of the **minimum** turning point (a, b) ?

(d) Sketch the parabola showing this minimum turning point, write down the **equation** of the **axis of symmetry**.

3. We can improve our sketch of :- $y = (x + 4)^2 - 3$.

(a) Write down the coordinates of the **minimum** turning point P(a, b).   (*note* :- $x \neq 4$)

(b) Replace x with 0 in $y = (x + 4)^2 - 3$ to determine where the graph cuts the y-axis.

(c) Plot this point also and sketch the parabola.

4. Use this **two-step** approach to sketch the following parabolas showing both the **minimum** turning point and the y-intercept for each.

(a) $y = (x - 2)^2 + 5$ (b) $y = (x - 1)^2 + 3$

(c) $y = (x + 3)^2 + 1$ (d) $y = (x - 2)^2 - 6$

(e) $y = (x + 1)^2 - 1$ (f) $y = (x - 5)^2 - 8$

(g) $y = (x + 2)^2 - 1$ (h) $y = (x - 3)^2$.

5. (a) Write down the coordinates of the **minimum** turning point of this parabola.

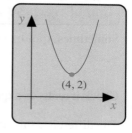

(b) Assuming the parabola is of the form :-

$$y = (x - a)^2 + b,$$

write down the equation of the parabola.

6. All of the following parabolas are of the form :-

$$y = (x - a)^2 + b.$$

Write down the equation of each parabola and the **equation** of the **axis of symmetry**.

(a)
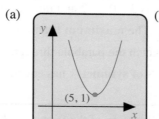

(b)
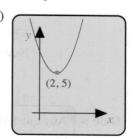

(c)
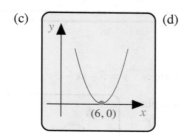

(d)
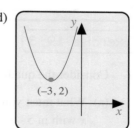

(e)
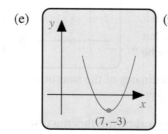

(f)
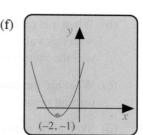

7. The diagram shows the "basic" parabola :-

$$y = x^2.$$

The parabola is then "slid" 12 boxes **right** and 5 boxes **down** and is shown dotted.

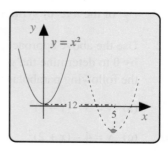

(a) Write down the equation of the dotted parabola.

(b) Determine the coordinates of its y-intercept.

Completed Square Form (2)   Maximum Turning Points

Sometimes, quadratic functions come in completed square form a bit differently :-

$$y = 3 - (x - 2)^2.$$

Check it really is a quadratic function :- $[3 - (x - 2)^2 = 3 - (x^2 - 4x + 4) = -x^2 + 4x - 1]$ √

The difference this time is that the "$-x^2$" term shows that the parabola will be upside-down.

note :- equation of
axis of symmetry

Example :-   Sketch the graph of $y = 3 - (x - 2)^2$.

     Think !   The square of anything can never be negative.

         The smallest value of $(x - 2)^2$ is zero at $x = 2$.

         =>   The MAXIMUM value of $3 - (x - 2)^2$

             is $3 - 0 = 3$ and this occurs at $x = 2$.

         =>   The maximum turning point is $(2, 3)$.

         Now sketch the parabola through this point.

         The axis of symmetry has equation $x = 2$.

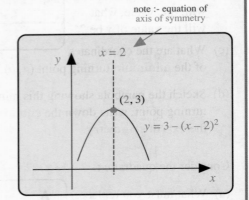

Rule :-   Any quadratic function of the form $y = b - (x - a)^2$ will have a **maximum** at (a, b).
The equation of the **axis of symmetry** is $x = a$.

Exercise 19·3

1.   Consider the quadratic :- $y = 5 - (x - 3)^2$.

     (a) What must you replace
         x with in $5 - (x - 3)^2$
         to make $(x - 3) = 0$?

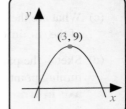

     (b) When x is replaced
         with this value, what
         will the value of y be ?

     (c) What are the coordinates of the **maximum**
         turning point (a, b)?

     (d) Sketch the parabola showing this **maximum**
         turning point and write down the equation
         of the **axis of symmetry**.

2.   Use the above approach, along with **replacing x
     by 0** to determine the **y-intercept**, to help sketch
     the following parabolas :-

     (a) $y = 3 - (x - 1)^2$ (b) $y = 8 - (x - 3)^2$

     (c) $y = 4 - (x + 2)^2$ (d) $y = 1 - (x + 1)^2$

     (e) $y = -2 - (x - 3)^2$ (f) $y = -1 - (x - 4)^2$

     (g) $y = -5 - (x + 3)^2$ (h) $y = -(x - 5)^2$.

3.   (a) Write down the
         coordinates of the
         maximum turning point
         of this parabola.

     (b) Assuming the parabola
         is of the form :-

$$y = b - (x - a)^2,$$

         write down the equation of the parabola and
         the equation of the **axis of symmetry**.

4.   Write down the equation of each parabola,
     the coordinates of the **y-intercept** and the
     equation of the **axis of symmetry**.

(a)

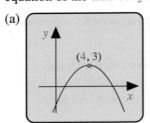

(b)

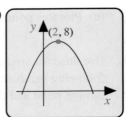

(c)

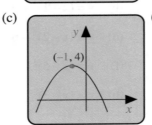

(d)

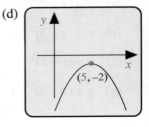

Quadratics of the form $y = kx^2$

You should know by now what the "basic" parabola $y = x^2$ looks like.

It has a **minimum** turning point at $O(0, 0)$.

Any parabola, of the form $y = kx^2$, has a similar shape.

$y = 2x^2, \quad y = 5x^2, \quad y = -3x^2, \quad y = -x^2, \quad y = \frac{1}{2}x^2$

All have a **minimum** (or **maximum**) turning point at $O(0, 0)$.

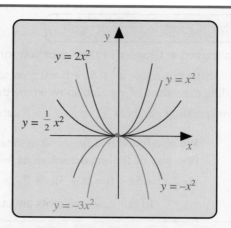

Example :- The parabola $y = kx^2$ passes through the point $P(2, 12)$. Determine the value of k.

Solution :- Since the parabola $y = kx^2$ passes through the point $P(2, 12)$, then we should be able to replace x with 2 and y with 12 in $y = kx^2$.

$\Rightarrow \quad y = kx^2$
$\Rightarrow \quad 12 = k \times 2^2$
$\Rightarrow \quad 12 = 4k$
$\Rightarrow \quad k = 3 \qquad \Rightarrow \boxed{y = 3x^2}$

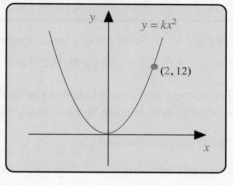

Exercise 19·4

1. The parabola $y = kx^2$ passes through the point $(3, 18)$.

   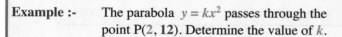

   (a) Replace $x = 3$ and $y = 18$ in $y = kx^2$ to determine the value of k.

   (b) Write down the **equation** of the parabola.

4. The parabola $y = kx^2$ passes through the point $(2, -8)$.

   (a) Replace $x = 2$ and $y = -8$ in $y = kx^2$ to determine the value of k. (*negative*)

   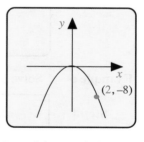

   (b) Write down the **equation** of the parabola.

2.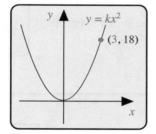

   The parabola $y = kx^2$ passes through the point $(4, 80)$.

   (a) Replace $x = 4$ and $y = 80$ in $y = kx^2$ to determine the value of k.

   (b) Write down the **equation** of the parabola.

5.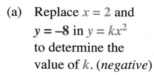

   The parabola $y = kx^2$ passes through the point $(5, -75)$.

   (a) Replace $x = 5$ and $y = -75$ in $y = kx^2$ to determine the value of k.

   (b) Write down the **equation** of the parabola.

3. Determine the equation of the parabola with the **origin** as **minimum turning** point through :-

   (a) $(5, 50)$ (b) $(2, 16)$ (c) $(5, 100)$

   (d) $(-2, 12)$ (e) $(-1, 7)$ (f) $(4, 8)$.

6. Determine the equation of the parabola with the **origin** as **maximum turning** point through :-

   (a) $(2, -12)$ (b) $(3, -36)$ (c) $(1, -11)$

   (d) $(-4, -32)$ (e) $(-1, -6)$ (f) $(-6, -12)$.

The Quadratic Formula

We learned in Chapter 14 that when you solve the
quadratic equation $x^2 + 5x + 6 = 0$, you are really
finding the values of x which show where the
corresponding parabola $y = x^2 + 5x + 6$ cuts the x-axis.

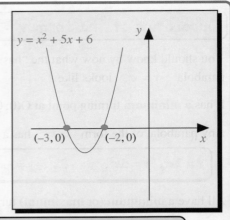

We also found that **factorising** the expression was the
best way of finding the solutions (*the roots*).

=> $\quad x^2 + 5x + 6 = (x + 3)(x + 2) = 0$

=> $\qquad$ In this case, the roots are at $x = -3$ and -2.

Quadratic Equations that do NOT Factorise - The Quadratic Formula

Example :- $\quad$ Solve the quadratic equation $x^2 + 5x + 3 = 0$.

=> $\quad$ You can try and try if you like, but you won't be able to factorise $x^2 + 5x + 3$!!!

To solve quadratic equations that you cannot factorise (*or even those which you can*), we have a
special formula that can be used, along with a calculator, to solve them instead.

The Quadratic Formula :-

Every quadratic equation can be rearranged into the form :-

$$ax^2 + bx + c = 0.$$

We can find the solution to this by using the following formula :-

$$x = \frac{-b \pm \sqrt{b^2 - 4ac}}{2a}$$

called the **quadratic formula**.

> The **PROOF** of this
> may be given to you by
> your class teacher.

Example :- $\quad$ Solve the quadratic equation $x^2 + 5x + 3 = 0$.

Step 1 $\quad$ • $\quad$ compare the two :- $x^2 + 5x + 3 = 0$

$$ax^2 + bx + c = 0 \qquad \Rightarrow \boxed{a = 1, \ b = 5 \text{ and } c = 3.}$$

Step 2 $\quad$ • $\quad$ use the formula :- $\quad x = \frac{-b \pm \sqrt{b^2 - 4ac}}{2a}$

$$\Rightarrow \quad x = \frac{-5 \pm \sqrt{5^2 - 4 \times 1 \times 3}}{2 \times 1}$$

$$\Rightarrow \quad x = \frac{-5 \pm \sqrt{25 - 12}}{2}$$

$$\Rightarrow \quad x = \frac{-5 + \sqrt{13}}{2} \text{ or } x = \frac{-5 - \sqrt{13}}{2}$$

$$\Rightarrow \quad x = \frac{-5 + 3 \cdot 606}{2} \text{ or } \frac{-5 - 3 \cdot 606}{2}$$

$$\Rightarrow \quad x = (-1 \cdot 394 \div 2) \text{ or } (-8 \cdot 606 \div 2) \quad \Rightarrow \quad x = -0 \cdot 697 \text{ or } -4 \cdot 303$$

(Answer to 2 decimal places each time).

1. Look at the quadratic equation :- $x^2 + 6x + 4 = 0$.

   (a) Compare this with $ax^2 + bx + c = 0$ and hence write down the values of a, b and c.

   (b) Copy and complete the following :-

   $$x = \frac{-b \pm \sqrt{b^2 - 4ac}}{2a}$$

   $$\Rightarrow \quad x = \frac{-6 \pm \sqrt{6^2 - 4 \times 1 \times 4}}{2 \times 1}$$

   $$\Rightarrow \quad x = \frac{-6 \pm \sqrt{36 - 16}}{2} = \frac{-6 \pm \sqrt{20}}{2}$$

   $$\Rightarrow \quad x = (-6 - 4.4..) \div 2 \text{ or } (-6 + 4·4..) \div 2$$

   $$\Rightarrow \quad x = \text{........ or ....}$$

2. Solve the quadratic equation :- $x^2 + 8x + 2 = 0$, using the method shown above.

3. Solve each of these quadratic equations :-

   (a) $x^2 + 7x + 4 = 0$ (b) $x^2 + 10x + 7 = 0$

   (c) $x^2 + 6x + 8 = 0$ (d) $x^2 + 7x + 10 = 0$.

4. Look at your answer to questions 3(c) and 3(d).

   Though you used the quadratic formula, the **whole number answers** should have alerted you to the fact the quadratic equation could have been solved much easier - by **factorising** !!

   (a) Solve $x^2 + 6x + 8 = 0$ by **factorising**.

   (b) Solve $x^2 + 7x + 10 = 0$ by **factorising**.

5. This one is a little trickier. Solve $x^2 - 4x + 2 = 0$.

   Copy down the two equations :-

   $$x^2 - 4x + 2 = 0$$
   $$ax^2 + bx + c = 0$$

   Copy :- $a = 1$, $b = -...$ and $c = ...$.

   Use the formula (*carefully*) :-

   $$x = \frac{-b \pm \sqrt{b^2 - 4ac}}{2a} \quad \text{note}$$

   note

   $$\Rightarrow \quad x = \frac{-(-4) \pm \sqrt{(-4)^2 - 4 \times 1 \times 2}}{2 \times 1}$$

   $$\Rightarrow \quad \text{Now complete the question.}$$

6. Solve these **quadratic equations** :-

   (a) $x^2 - 6x + 3 = 0$ (b) $x^2 - 8x + 5 = 0$

   (c) $x^2 - 7x + 1 = 0$ (d) $x^2 - 8x + 15 = 0$.

7. Another thing to be careful of !

   Solve :- $x^2 + 3x - 5 = 0$.

   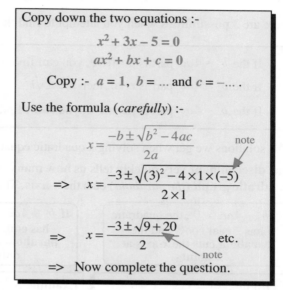

   Copy down the two equations :-

   $$x^2 + 3x - 5 = 0$$
   $$ax^2 + bx + c = 0$$

   Copy :- $a = 1$, $b = ...$ and $c = -...$.

   Use the formula (*carefully*) :-

   $$x = \frac{-b \pm \sqrt{b^2 - 4ac}}{2a} \quad \text{note}$$

   $$\Rightarrow \quad x = \frac{-3 \pm \sqrt{(3)^2 - 4 \times 1 \times (-5)}}{2 \times 1}$$

   $$\Rightarrow \quad x = \frac{-3 \pm \sqrt{9 + 20}}{2} \quad \text{etc.}$$

   note

   $$\Rightarrow \quad \text{Now complete the question.}$$

8. Solve these **quadratic equations** :-

   (a) $x^2 + 4x - 6 = 0$ (b) $x^2 + 6x - 2 = 0$

   (c) $x^2 - 3x - 5 = 0$ (d) $x^2 - x - 4 = 0$.

9. ... and a does not always have to be **1**.

   Solve :- $3x^2 + 4x - 5 = 0$.

   Copy down the two equations :-

   $$3x^2 + 4x - 5 = 0$$
   $$ax^2 + bx + c = 0$$

   Copy :- $a = 3$, $b = ...$ and $c = -...$.

   Use the formula (*carefully*) :-

   $$x = \frac{-b \pm \sqrt{b^2 - 4ac}}{2a}$$

   $$\Rightarrow \quad x = \frac{-4 \pm \sqrt{(4)^2 - 4 \times 3 \times (-5)}}{2 \times 3} \quad \text{note}$$

   $$\Rightarrow \quad \text{Now complete the question.}$$

10. Solve these **quadratic equations** :-

    (a) $2x^2 + 5x + 3 = 0$ (b) $3x^2 + 10x + 2 = 0$

    (c) $2x^2 - 3x - 4 = 0$ (d) $4x^2 - 3x - 2 = 0$.

11. Try to solve this **quadratic equation** :-

    $$x^2 + 3x + 4 = 0.$$

    What goes wrong ? Try to find out why.

The Discriminant

Let us look a bit more carefully at the quadratic formula :- $x = \dfrac{-b \pm \sqrt{b^2 - 4ac}}{2a}$.

In particular, we are going to consider just the $b^2 - 4ac$ part. This is referred to as the **discriminant.**

The **quadratic formula** requires that you find the **square root** of the **discriminant**.

There are **3 possibilities** when you attempt to find the square root of a number :-

- If the $b^2 - 4ac$ part is **positive**, you **can** find it and the $\pm\sqrt{b^2 - 4ac}$ means you get **2** answers.
- If the $b^2 - 4ac$ part is **zero**, then the $\pm\sqrt{b^2 - 4ac} = \pm 0$ and this means you only get **1** answer.
- If the $b^2 - 4ac$ part is **negative**, you **can't** find the square root of a negative number => **0** answers.

The solutions we get when solving a quadratic equation are referred to as the **roots** of the equation.

The **discriminant** very quickly tells us **how many roots** there are, and it also tells us how many times the quadratic graph (*the parabola*) cuts the x-axis. This helps us quickly see what the **parabola** looks like.

| If $b^2 - 4ac > 0$, the quadratic has **2 real roots** and the parabola cuts the x-axis at **2 points**. | If $b^2 - 4ac = 0$, the quadratic has **equal roots** and the parabola cuts the x-axis at only **1 point**. | If $b^2 - 4ac < 0$, the quadratic has **0 real roots**. The **parabola** does **not** cross the x-axis at all. |

Example :- $y = x^2 + 5x + 6$

$\Rightarrow b^2 - 4ac = 25 - 4 \times 1 \times 6 = 1$

$\Rightarrow$ Since $b^2 - 4ac > 0$

$\Rightarrow$ There are **2 real roots.**

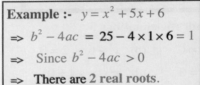
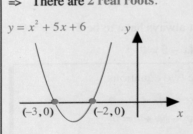

Example :- $y = x^2 + 6x + 9$

$\Rightarrow b^2 - 4ac = 36 - 4 \times 1 \times 9 = 0$

$\Rightarrow$ Since $b^2 - 4ac = 0$

$\Rightarrow$ There is only **1 real root.**

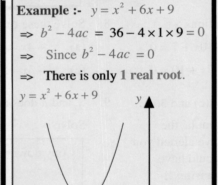

Example :- $y = -x^2 - 4x - 5$

$b^2 - 4ac = 16 - 4 \times -1 \times -5 = -4$

$\Rightarrow$ Since $b^2 - 4ac < 0$

$\Rightarrow$ There are **0 real roots.**

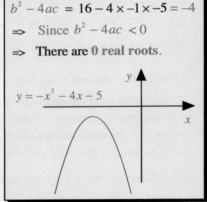

Exercise 19·6

1. Find the **discriminant** for each equation :-

   (a) $x^2 + 7x + 3 = 0$ (b) $x^2 + 8x + 16 = 0$

   (c) $x^2 + 3x + 4 = 0$ (d) $2x^2 + 7x + 6 = 0$.

2. Find the **discriminant** for each of these and use it to determine the **nature** of the roots :-

   (a) $x^2 + 4x + 1 = 0$ (b) $x^2 + x + 4 = 0$
   (c) $x^2 + 3x - 2 = 0$ (d) $x^2 + 10x + 25 = 0$
   (e) $x^2 - 2x + 5 = 0$ (f) $3x^2 + 7x + 4 = 0$
   (g) $2x^2 + 3x - 2 = 0$ (h) $4x^2 + 9x + 6 = 0$
   (i) $2x^2 + 2x + \frac{1}{2} = 0$ (j) $-x^2 + 5x - 7 = 0$
   (k) $x^2 = 3x + 3$ (l) $3x^2 = 3 - 5x$.

3. Assume $px^2 + 6x + 1 = 0$ has **1 root**. Find p.

   Copy and **complete** :-

   If there is only 1 root, then $\begin{array}{l} b^2 - 4ac = 0 \\ \Rightarrow \quad 6^2 - 4p = 0 \\ \Rightarrow \quad p = \ldots \end{array}$

4. $ax^2 + 4x - 2 = 0$ has **equal roots**. Find a.

5. $x^2 + bx + 25 = 0$ has **1 root**. Find **2 values** for b.

6. $px^2 + 8x - 2 = 0$ has **2 real roots**. Set up an inequality in p, and solve for p.

7. $mx^2 + 6x + m = 0$ has **equal roots**. Find m.

8. $x^2 + 6x - t = 0$ has **no real roots**. Solve for t.

1. Express in **completed square form** :-

   (a) $y = x^2 + 6x + 12$ (b) $y = x^2 + 5x - 2$.

2. Consider the quadratic :- $y = (x - 5)^2 + 3$.

   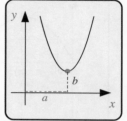

   (a) What must you replace x with in $(x - 5)^2 + 3$ to make $(x - 5) = 0$?

   (b) When x is replaced with this value, what will the value of y be ?

   (c) Find the **minimum** turning point at (a, b).

   (d) Sketch the parabola showing this minimum turning point.

3. By finding both the **minimum** turning point and the **y-intercept**, make neat sketches of the following **parabolas** :-

   (a) $y = (x - 1)^2 + 4$ (b) $y = (x + 2)^2 + 5$

   (c) $y = (x - 4)^2 - 2$ (d) $y = (x - 3)^2$.

4. Use the above approach, along with replacing x by **zero** to determine the **y-intercept**, to help sketch the following parabolas :-

   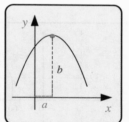

   (*All have a maximum turning point*).

   (a) $y = 6 - (x - 2)^2$ (b) $y = 4 - (x - 1)^2$

   (c) $y = 5 - (x + 3)^2$ (d) $y = -1 - (x + 2)^2$.

5.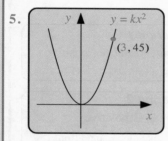

   The parabola $y = kx^2$ passes through the point $(3, 45)$.

   (a) Replace $x = 3$ and $y = 45$ in $y = kx^2$ to find k.

   (b) Write down the **equation** of the parabola.

6. Determine the equation of the parabola with the **origin** as the **minimum turning** point through :-

   (a) $(5, 50)$ (b) $(2, 16)$ (c) $(5, 100)$.

7. Determine the equation of the parabola with the **origin** as the **maximum turning** point through :-

   (a) $(4, -80)$ (b) $(1, -10)$ (c) $(-2, 36)$.

8. All of the following parabolas are of the form :-

   $$y = (x - a)^2 + b \quad \text{or} \quad y = b - (x - a)^2.$$

   Write down the equation of each parabola and the equation of the **axis of symmetry** each time.

   (a)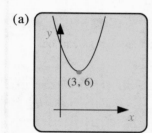

   (b)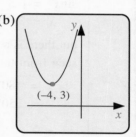

   (c)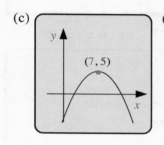

   (d)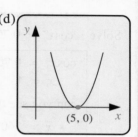

   (e)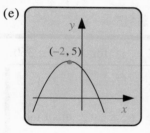

   (f)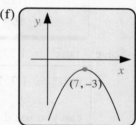

9. Use the **discriminant** to determine the **nature** of the roots of these **quadratic equations** :-

   (a) $2x^2 + 12x + 18 = 0$ (b) $x^2 + 5x + 7 = 0$.

10. Solve the following **quadratic equations** by using the **quadratic formula** :-

    (a) $x^2 + 5x + 3 = 0$ (b) $x^2 - 6x + 4 = 0$

    (c) $2x^2 + 7x + 4 = 0$ (d) $5x^2 - 6x - 4 = 0$.

11. Shown is the **parabola** :-

    $$y = x^2 - 5x + 3.$$

    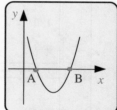

    Use the **quadratic formula** to determine the coordinates of the two points **A** and **B**.

12. (a) It is known that the quadratic equation $nx^2 + 8x + 2 = 0$ has only **1 root**. Find n.

    (b) If $x^2 - 6x + 3d = 0$ has **no real roots**, find the range of values for d.

Solving Trig. Equations (with the aid of a Graph)

Solve $\sin x° = 0.5$ for $0 \leq x \leq 360$.

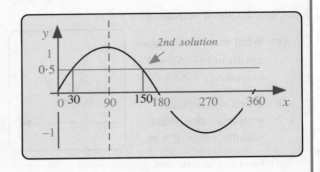

$\sin x° = 0.5$ *(Find $\sin^{-1}(0.5)$)*

$\quad x = 30°$

but there is a 2nd answer as can be
seen from the graph

$=> x = 180° - 30°$ *by symmetry*

$\quad\quad = 150°$ *of sine graph*

$\quad x = 30°$ or $150°$

Solve $\cos x° = 0.707$ for $0 \leq x \leq 360$.

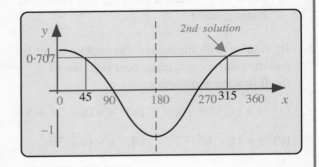

$\cos x° = 0.707$ *(Find $\cos^{-1}(0.707)$)*

$\quad x = 45°$

can you see the 2nd answer ?

$=> x = 360° - 45°$ *by symmetry*

$\quad\quad = 315°$ *of cosine graph*

$\quad x = 45°$ or $315°$

Solve $\tan x° = 1.732$ for $0 \leq x \leq 360$.

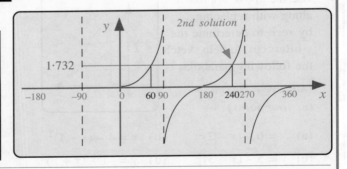

$\tan x° = 1.732$ *(Find $\tan^{-1}(1.732)$)*

$\quad x = 60°$

can you see the 2nd answer this time ?

$=> x = 180° + 60°$ *by periodicity*

$\quad\quad = 240°$ *of tan graph*

$\quad x = 60°$ or $240°$

Solving Trig. Equations using "the Four Quadrants"

Your teacher will explain this section to you fully

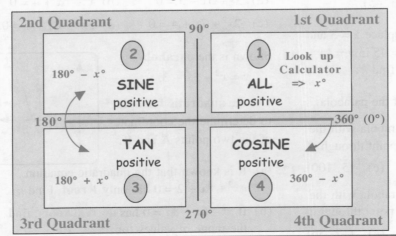

Quadrant 1
All sin, cos, & tan positive
Use Calculator

Quadrant 2
Only sin is positive
Take Quadrant 1 angle from 180°

Quadrant 3
Only tan is positive
Add Quadrant 1 angle on to 180°

Quadrant 4
Only cos is positive
Take Quadrant 1 angle from 360°

Example 1 :- Solve $\cos x° = 0·707$ $0 \le x \le 360$.

S	A
T	C

$\cos x° = 0·707$ (cos $+ve$ => use quadrants 1 & 4)

Quadrant 1   Quadrant 4

$x = 30°$ or $x = 360° - 30°$

(Find $\cos^{-1}(0·707)$) $= 330°$

taking Q1 angle from 360°

$x = 30°$ or $x = 330°$

Example 2 :- Solve $\sin x° = -0·342$ $0 \le x \le 360$.

$\sin x° = -0·342$ (sin $-ve$ => use quadrants 3 & 4) Use the $-ve$ sign to determine Quadrants but DO NOT feed $-ve$ into your calculator.

Q1 angle is 20° ($Sin^{-1}(0·342)$)

Quadrant 3   Quadrant 4

$x = 180° + 20°$ or $x = 360° - 20°$

$x = 200°$ or $x = 340°$

Use Inv Sin 0·342 to find the 1st quadrant angle and place it in the chosen quadrants.

Example 3 :- Solve $3\tan x° + 5 = 0$ $0 \le x \le 360$.

$3\tan x° + 5 = 0$

$3\tan x° = -5$

$\tan x° = -\frac{5}{3} = -1·666...$ (tan $-ve$, => use quadrants 2 & 4)

Q1 angle is 59° ($Tan^{-1}(1·666..)$)

Quadrant 2   Quadrant 4

$x = 180° - 59°$ or $x = 360° - 59°$

$x = 121°$ or $x = 301°$

Use Inv Tan 1·66666 to find the 1st quadrant angle and place it in Q2 & Q4

In this exercise, answer correct to 3 significant figures.

1. With the help of the graphs and using your calculator, solve the following equations for $0 \le x \le 360$.

(a) $\sin x° = 0·259$ (b) $\sin x° = -0·5$

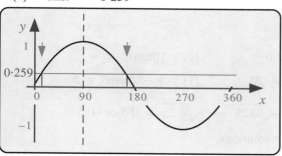

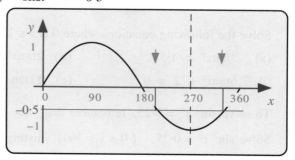

1. (c) $\cos x° = 0.087$

(d) $\cos x° = -0.766$

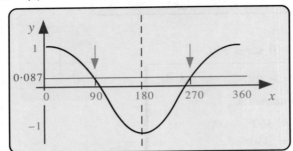

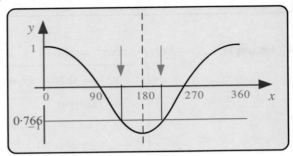

(e) $\tan x° = 2.75$.

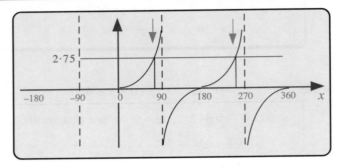

2. Solve the following trigonometric equations where $0 \le x \le 360$.

(a) $\sin x° = 0.707$ (b) $\sin x° = 0.375$ (c) $\sin x° = 0.999$

(d) $\sin x° = 0.729$ (e) $\sin x° = 0.139$ (f) $\sin x° = 0.839$

(g) $\cos x° = 0.707$ (h) $\cos x° = 0.927$ (i) $\cos x° = 0.208$

(j) $\tan x° = 1$ (k) $\tan x° = 0.158$ (l) $\tan x° = 4.915$.

3. Solve the following equations for $0 \le x \le 360$.

(a) $\sin x° = -0.342$ (b) $\sin x° = -0.866$ (c) $\sin x° = -0.105$

(d) $\sin x° = -0.216$ (e) $\sin x° = -0.592$ (f) $\sin x° = -0.843$

(g) $\cos x° = -0.174$ (h) $\cos x° = -0.937$ (i) $\cos x° = -0.122$

(j) $\tan x° = -1$ (k) $\tan x° = -3.708$ (l) $\tan x° = -5.671$

(m) $\tan x° = -1.387$ (n) $\tan x° = -16.35$ (o) $\tan x° = -0.173$.

4. Solve the following equations where $0 \le x \le 360$.

(a) $2\sin x° = 1$ (b) $5\sin x° - 4 = 0$ (c) $5\sin x° = -3$

(d) $6\sin x° + 1 = 0$ (e) $4\sin x° + 1 = 1.5$ (f) $12 + 9\sin x° = 8$.

5. Solve the following equations where $0 \le x \le 360$.

(a) $6\cos x° = 3$ (b) $10\cos x° - 2 = 0$ (c) $3\cos x° = -2$

(d) $7\cos x° + 4 = 0$ (e) $9\cos x° + 7 = 2$ (f) $18 + 4\cos x° = 15$.

6. Solve the following equations where $0 \le x \le 180$.

(a) $3\tan x° = 1.5$ (b) $2\tan x° - 7 = 0$ (c) $10\tan x° = -1$

(d) $6\tan x° + 2 = 0$ (e) $11\tan x° + 7 = 20$ (f) $3 - 5\tan x° = 5$.

7. To solve $\sin^2 x° = 0.25$, remember that $=> \sin x° = +\sqrt{0.25}$ or $-\sqrt{0.25} = 0.5$ or -0.5.

Solve $\sin^2 x° = 0.25$, $\{0 \le x \le 360\}$, listing all **four** solutions.

8. **Solve**, when in each case $\{0 \leq x \leq 360\}$.

    (a) $\cos^2 x° = 0{\cdot}75$ (b) $\tan^2 x° = 1$ (c) $5\cos^2 x° - 4 = 0$.

9. A **mixture** - solve these equations for $0 \leq x \leq 360$.

    (a) $3\tan x° - 8 = 0$ (b) $9\sin x° + 6 = 2$ (c) $3\cos x° + 6 = 8$

    (d) $2\tan x° + 3 = 8$ (e) $7\cos x° + 5 = 0$ (f) $2 + 2\sin x° = 1$

    (g) $4 - 6\cos x° = 9$ (h) $7\tan x° + 2 = 0{\cdot}45$ (i) $4 - 2\sin x° = 6$

    (j) $\sin^2 x° = 0{\cdot}16$ (k) $\cos^2 x° = 0{\cdot}25$ (l) $\tan^2 x° = 36$

    (m) $5\sin x° - 2 = \sin x°$ (n) $7\cos x° + 4 = \cos x°$ (o) $3\tan x° - 5 = 2\tan x°$.

10. The curve with equation $y = 2\cos x° + 6$, $0 \leq x \leq 360$, meets the line with equation $y = 5$ at the points P and Q where Q is to the right of P.

    Calculate the coordinates of P and Q.

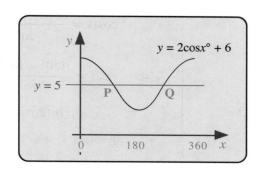

11. The curve with equation $y = 3 - 8\sin x°$, $0 \leq x \leq 360$, meets the line with equation $y = -2$ at the points A and B where A is to the left of B.

    Calculate the coordinates of A and B.

What if the limit is not $0 \leq x \leq 360$?

Solve $\sin x° = 0{\cdot}5$, $0 \leq x \leq 720$.

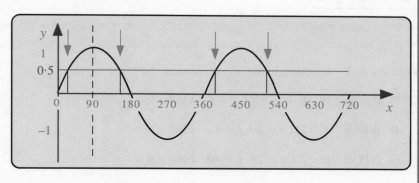

    4 Answers for x this time :-

•	$x =$	**30°**	(from calculator)	**Quadrant 1**	
•	$x = 180° - 30°$	$= \mathbf{150°}$	(symmetry of sine curve)	**Quadrant 2**	
•	$x = 360° + 30°$	$= \mathbf{390°}$	(periodicity of sine wave)	**Quadrant 5**	Quadrant 1 - 2nd time round
•	$x = 360° + 150°$	$= \mathbf{510°}$	(periodicity of sine wave)	**Quadrant 6**	Quadrant 2 - 2nd time round

12. Solve these trigonometric equations, this time for $0 \leq x \leq 720$.

    (a) $\sin x° = 0{\cdot}866$ (b) $\sin x° = -0{\cdot}866$ (c) $\cos x° = 0{\cdot}940$

    (d) $\cos x° = -0{\cdot}940$ (e) $2\sin x° - 1 = 0$ (f) $5\cos x° + 1 = -1{\cdot}5$.

The Cosine Rule with Negatives

In an earlier Trig. chapter, one example which required the use of the cosine rule was about finding angle B on a pitch & putt golf course. The example told us that angle B was obtuse and the drawing made that clear - but if we had not been given that information we may have thought that the angle was 81·9°, whereas the answer was actually 98·1°.

We now examine why that was the case.

$$\cos B = \frac{a^2 + l^2 - b^2}{2al}$$

$$\Rightarrow \quad \cos B = \frac{150^2 + 180^2 - 250^2}{2 \times 150 \times 180}$$

$$= -0.140740... \qquad (\cos -ve, \text{ use quadrants 2 \& 3})$$

quadrant 1 angle is 81·9° from calculator

Quadrant 2   **Quadrant 3**

$\angle B = 180° - 89·9°$ disregard here due to property of Δ.

$\angle B = 98·1°$ obtuse

Use the Cosine Rule to find the required angle in each of the following examples.
Not ALL angles asked for are obtuse. Answer correct to 3 significant figures.

In questions **1 - 4**, calculate the angles named :-

1. In $\triangle$ ABC, $a = 8, b = 10, c = 15$. Find $\angle C$.

2. In $\triangle$ DEF, $d = 12, e = 10, f = 8$. Find $\angle F$.

3. In $\triangle$ PQR, $p = 20, q = 25, r = 40$. Find $\angle R$.

4. In $\triangle$ KLM, $k = 3·4, l = 3, m = 1·6$. Find $\angle K$.

5. Calculate the size of the largest angle in the triangle with sides of lengths 4·5 cm, 3·3 cm and 2·9 cm.

6. In $\triangle$ XYZ, XY = 2 cm, YZ = 2 cm and XZ = 3 cm. Calculate the size of $\angle$XYZ.

7. A tall ship leaves port P and sails 50 km due north to T.

    It then turns and sails 134 km to M.

    It completes its journey by sailing 175 km back to P.

    (a) Calculate the size of angle PTM.

    (b) Write down the **bearing** of M from T.

    (c) Work out the **bearing** of T from M.

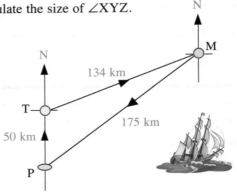

Some useful Trigonometrical Formulae / Trigonometrical Identities

$$\sin^2 A + \cos^2 A$$
$$= \left(\frac{y}{r}\right)^2 + \left(\frac{x}{r}\right)^2$$
$$= \frac{y^2}{r^2} + \frac{x^2}{r^2}$$
$$= \frac{y^2 + x^2}{r^2}$$
$$= \frac{r^2}{r^2} \quad \text{since } x^2 + y^2 = r^2$$
$$= 1$$

Look at the following diagram.

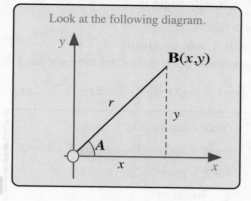

$$\frac{\sin A}{\cos A} = \frac{y}{r} \div \frac{x}{r}$$
$$= \frac{y}{r} \times \frac{r}{x}$$
$$= \frac{y}{x}$$
$$= \tan A$$

$$\sin^2 A + \cos^2 A = 1$$
rearranged => $\sin^2 A = 1 - \cos^2 A$
rearranged => $\cos^2 A = 1 - \sin^2 A$

$$\tan A = \frac{\sin A}{\cos A}$$

These are referred to as **Trigonometric Identities**.   (The left side is **IDENTICAL** to the **right** side).

Example 1 :-

Calculate $\cos x°$, $0 \le x \le 90$ when $\sin x° = 0.8$.
without using a trig calculator

$$\cos^2 x° = 1 - \sin^2 x°$$
$$= 1 - (0.8)^2$$
$$= 1 - 0.64$$
$$= 0.36$$
$$\cos x° = \sqrt{0.36}$$
$$= 0.6$$

Example 2 :-

Prove that :- $(\cos P + \sin P)^2 - 2\cos P \sin P = 1$.

Left Hand Side (L.H.S.) :-

$(\cos P + \sin P)^2 - 2\cos P \sin P$

$= \cos^2 P + 2\cos P \sin P + \sin^2 P - 2\cos P \sin P$

$= \cos^2 P + \sin^2 P$

$= 1$

$=$ Right Hand Side (R.H.S.)

Exercise 20·3

1. Calculate, *to 1 decimal place* :-

    (a) $\cos x°$, $0 \le x \le 90$ when $\sin x° = 0.5$.

    (b) $\cos x°$, $0 \le x \le 90$ when $\sin x° = 0.6$.

    (c) $\sin x°$, $0 \le x \le 90$ when $\cos x° = 0.4$.

    (d) $\sin x°$, $0 \le x \le 90$ when $\cos x° = 0.7$.

2. $\sin x° = \frac{3}{5}$ and angle x is **acute**.

    (a) Find the value of $\cos x°$

    (b) Now find the value of $\tan x°$.

3. If $\sin y° = \frac{4}{5}$, and angle y is **obtuse**, find :-

    (a) $\cos y°$ (b) $\tan y°$.

4. If $\cos z° = \frac{5}{13}$, and angle z is **acute**, find :-

    (a) $\sin z°$ (b) $\tan z°$.

5. Given $\cos A = \frac{5}{13}$ and $\sin B = \frac{3}{5}$, where both A and B are **acute**, find the value of :-

    (a) $\sin A$ (b) $\tan A$

    (c) $\cos B$ (d) $\tan B$

    (e) $\dfrac{\tan A - \tan B}{1 + \tan A \tan B}$.

Remember :- An **identity** involving "*x*" is simply a rule that can be proven to be **true** for **all** values of *x*.

To **prove** an **identity**, you generally begin by :-

- stating the left hand side (**L.H.S.**)
- "playing" about with it, and eventually
- showing that it is the same as (**identical to**) the right hand side (**R.H.S.**).

Example 3 :- Prove that :- $(\sin X - \cos X)(\sin X - \cos X) = 1 - 2\sin X \cos X$

> L.H.S :- $(\sin X - \cos X)(\sin X - \cos X)$
>
> $=$ $\sin^2 X - \sin X \cos X - \sin X \cos X + \cos^2 X.$
>
> $=$ $\sin^2 X + \cos^2 X - 2\sin X \cos X$
>
> $=$ $1 - 2\sin X \cos X$
>
> $=$ R.H.S. $\Rightarrow$ hence – proven !

6.   Prove the following trigonometric **identities** :-

(a) $5\cos^2 A + 5\sin^2 A = 5$

(b) $4\cos^2 A = 4 - 4\sin^2 A$

(c) $2\cos^2 A - 1 = 1 - 2\sin^2 A$

(d) $6\cos^2 A - 5 = 1 - 6\sin^2 A$

(e) $(\cos X + \sin X)^2 = 1 + 2\sin X \cos X$

(f) $(\cos P - \sin P)^2 + 2\sin P \cos P = 1$

(g) $(\cos X + \sin X)(\cos X - \sin X) = 2\cos^2 X - 1$

(h) $(\cos X - \sin X)(\cos X + \sin X) = 1 - 2\sin^2 X$

(i) $\tan P \cos P = \sin P$

(j) $\dfrac{1 - \cos^2 \alpha}{\cos^2 \alpha} = \tan^2 \alpha$

(k) $\dfrac{1 - \sin^2 \alpha}{\sin^2 \alpha} = \dfrac{1}{\tan^2 \alpha}$

(l) $\dfrac{\sin \beta}{\cos \beta} + \dfrac{\cos \beta}{\sin \beta} = \dfrac{1}{\cos \beta \sin \beta}$.

7.   Prove that these **identities** are true :-

(a) $5\sin^2 A + 3\cos^2 A = 2\sin^2 A + 3$

(b) $4\cos^2 \alpha - 2\sin^2 \alpha = 6\cos^2 \alpha - 2$

(c) $(2\cos P + 3\sin P)^2 + (3\cos P - 2\sin P)^2 = 13$

(d) $\tan Q + \dfrac{1}{\tan Q} = \dfrac{1}{\sin Q \cos Q}$

(e) $(\sin \beta + \cos \beta)^2 - (\sin \beta - \cos \beta)^2 = 4\sin \beta \cos \beta$.

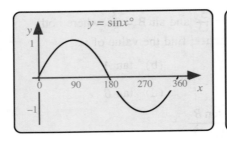

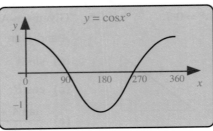

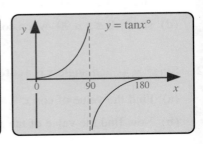

Remember Remember..... ?

1. With the help of the graphs and using your calculator, solve the following equations.

    (a) $\sin x° = 0·766$ $0 \le x \le 360$

    (b) $\cos x° = -0·643$ $0 \le x \le 360$.

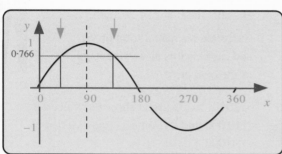 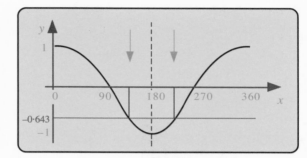

2. Solve the following trigonometric equations where $0 \le x \le 360$, answering to 3 significant figures :-

    (a) $\sin x° = 0·469$

    (b) $\cos x° = 0·438$

    (c) $\tan x° = 0·532$

    (d) $\sin x° = -0·616$

    (e) $\cos x° = -0·985$

    (f) $\tan x° = -1·192$.

3. Solve the following trigonometric equations for $0 \le x \le 360$, answering to 3 significant figures :-

    (a) $10\sin x° - 5 = 0$

    (b) $7\cos x° + 5 = 2$

    (c) $2 - 8\tan x° = 4$

    (d) $\sin^2 x° = 0·49$

    (e) $7\cos x° + 1 = 3\cos x°$

    (f) $11\tan x° + 2 = 5·28$.

4. The curve with equation $y = 3\sin x° + 6$,
   $0 \le x \le 360$, meets the line with equation
   $y = 5$ at the points D and E.

   Form an equation and solve it to find the
   coordinates of D and E.

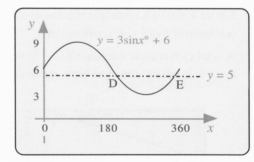

5. Solve these trigonometric equations, where $0 \le x \le 720$,
   answering to 3 sig. figs. :-

    (a) $\sin x° = 0·707$

    (b) $\cos x° = -0·906$.

6. A yacht takes part in a race over a triangular course.

   What angle must the yacht have turned through at
   the 1st buoy in order to head directly for the 2nd buoy ?

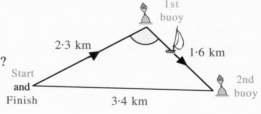

7. $\cos P = -\dfrac{12}{13}$, and angle P is **obtuse**.

   Find the **exact** value of both $\sin P$ and $\tan P$. (*No calculator*).

8. Prove the following trigonometric identities :-

    (a) $8\cos^2 A = 8 - 8\sin^2 A$?

    (b) $\dfrac{1 - \cos^2 \alpha}{\cos^2 \alpha} \times \dfrac{1 - \sin^2 \alpha}{\sin^2 \alpha} V = 1$

    (c) $(1 - \sin^2 \alpha)\tan^2 \alpha = \sin^2 \alpha$

    (d) $\cos^4 \beta - \sin^4 \beta = \cos^2 \beta - \sin^2 \beta$.

1. Expand and simplify :-

   (a) $(2a + 3b)(a - 5b)$ (b) $(3x - 5)^2$

   (c) $(x - 2)^3$ (d) $(x + 3)^2 - (x + 2)^2$

   (e) $(4x - 3)^2 - (2x + 3)(4x - 1)$

   (f) $4(2t - 2)^2 - (4t - 1)^2$.

2. The side of this cube is $3x$ centimetres.

   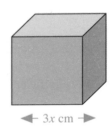

   ← $3x$ cm →

   The expression for the volume in cubic centimetres is equal to the expression for the surface area in square centimetres.

   Calculate the length of a side of the cube.

3. Figure 1 shows a rectangle measuring $(2x + 3)$ centimetres by $(x + 4)$ centimetres.

   A smaller rectangle measuring $(x + 6)$ centimetres by $(x + 2)$ centimetres has been removed.

   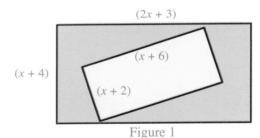

   $(2x + 3)$

   $(x + 4)$

   $(x + 6)$

   $(x + 2)$

   Figure 1

   Figure 2 shows a single rectangle $(x + 3)$ centimetres long and x centimetres wide.

   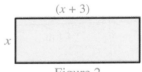

   $(x + 3)$

   x

   Figure 2

   Prove that the green area is equal to the blue area.

4. A jar of coffee had its weight reduced by 25% to a new weight of 360 g.

   What was the weight of the jar before the reduction ?

5. A shopkeeper buys 80 pairs of jeans for £680 altogether.

   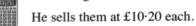

   He sells them at £10·20 each.

   Calculate his actual total profit and express this as a percentage of the cost price.

6. In 2010, an electrical shop was valued at £210 000 and its contents were valued at £150 000.

   The value of the shop appreciated by 5% each year, whereas the value of the contents depreciated by 12% each year.

   What was the total value of the shop and its contents in 2013 ?

7. 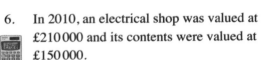 After VAT (at 20%) was added on, a garage bill came to £342.

   What was the bill without the VAT ?

8. Find :-

   (a) $1\frac{1}{2} + 2\frac{3}{4}$ (b) $4\frac{2}{3} - \frac{1}{6}$

   (c) $\frac{8}{9} - \frac{2}{5}$ (d) $7\frac{1}{2} + 3\frac{5}{8}$

   (e) $6\frac{3}{5} + 5\frac{2}{3}$ (f) $3\frac{5}{6} - 3\frac{1}{2}$

   (g) $6\frac{1}{3} - 2\frac{3}{4}$ (h) $8 - 4\frac{7}{11}$.

9. Find :-

   (a) $\frac{12}{15} \times \frac{5}{8}$ (b) $\frac{2}{9} \times \frac{7}{8}$

   (c) $4\frac{1}{2} \times 2\frac{1}{6}$ (d) $2\frac{1}{4} \times 3\frac{1}{9}$

   (e) $\frac{1}{5} \div \frac{1}{2}$ (f) $\frac{6}{7} \div \frac{3}{5}$

   (g) $5\frac{1}{4} \div 1\frac{2}{5}$ (h) $\frac{3}{5}$ of $(2\frac{2}{5} + \frac{6}{25})$.

10. A triangular traffic island has measurements as shown.

     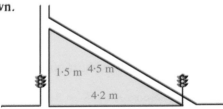

    1·5 m   4·5 m

    4·2 m

    Is the island in the shape of a right angled triangle ? Explain with working.

11. A golfer uses this part-cylinder plastic shape to practice putting on the carpet at home. It is 14 cm wide and 5 cm high.

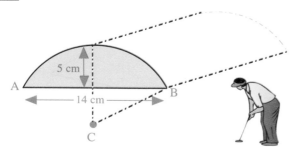

The cross section of the shape is a segment of a circle with centre C, as shown.

CB is the radius of the circle.

Calculate the length of CB.

12. RM, a vertical pole 2 metres high, is situated at the corner of a rectangular garden, PQRS.

PQ is 12 metres long and QR is 8 metres long.

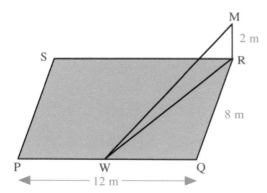

The pole casts a shadow over the garden.

It reaches W, the midpoint of PQ.

Calculate the length of the line MW, giving your answer as a surd in its simplest form.

13. Write down the gradients of these lines and state the coordinates of the y-intercept each time :-

(a) $y = 3x - 2$ (b) $y = -\frac{1}{2}x + 2$

(c) $2y - 3x + 6 = 0$ (d) $4x - y = 0$.

14. A straight line has the form $y = mx + c$.

Sketch a possible graph of a line where $0 < m < 1$ and $c < 0$.

15. The graph below shows part of the journey made by a delivery van, leaving the depot, travelling to Torbert and returning.

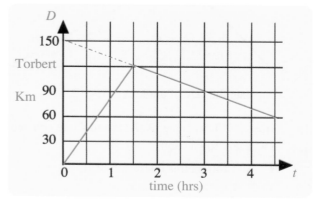

(a) Find the equation of the line representing the journey from the depot to Torbert.

($D = ...$)

(b) Determine the equation of that part of the journey representing the return to the depot.

(c) If the driver maintains the speed on the return journey, how long will the return journey take to the depot ?

16. (a) Find the equation of the line passing through the points $(-1, -2)$ and $(2, 10)$.

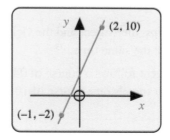

(b) State the coordinates of the point where the line crosses the y-axis.

17. Calculate the area of this triangle :-

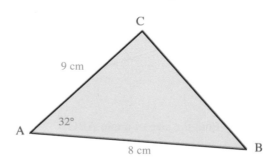

18. The area of the triangle below is $54 \cdot 1$ cm^2.

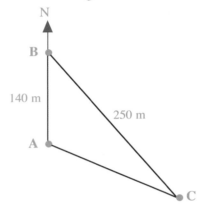

8 cm

A

14 cm

Area = $54 \cdot 1$ cm^2

Calculate the size of angle A.

19. Three C.C.T.V. cameras, A, B and C are situated in Kilmary town centre.

- A is 140 metres due south of B.
- B is 250 metres from C.
- C is on a bearing of 120° from A.

N

B

140 m

250 m

A

C

Calculate the bearing of C from B.

20. Two ships, the Argent and the Gelt leave port Banco at the same time.

The Argent follows a course of 045° for 20 km.
The Gelt travels on a course of 108° for 30 km.

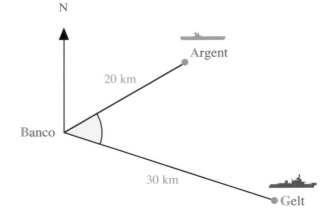

N

Argent

20 km

Banco

30 km

Gelt

(a) Find the size of angle ABG.

(b) Calculate the distance between the Argent and the Gelt.

21. The diagram shows part of a pitch and putt golf course.

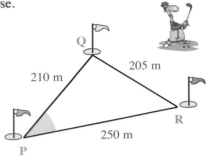

Q

205 m

210 m

R

P

250 m

The length of PQ is 210 metres, QR is 205 metres and PR is 250 metres.

Calculate the size of angle QPR (shaded), correct to the *nearest whole degree*.

Do **not** use a scale drawing.

22. A rescue boat, at R, picks up a distress call from a boat B, 350 km away, on a bearing of 120°.

At the same time, another distress call comes from a yacht Y, which is 170 km away from B and on a bearing of 220° from B.

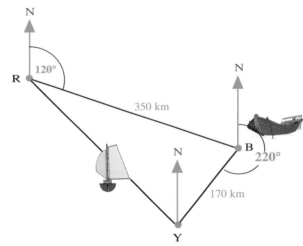

N

120°

R

350 km

N

B

220°

N

170 km

Y

(a) Show clearly why angle RBY = 80°.

(b) The rescue boat is obliged to respond to the **nearest** distress call first.

Will the people on the boat or those on the yacht be rescued first ?

(*You must support your answer by showing working*).

23. Factorise fully :-

(a) $4x^2 - 6x$ (b) $\pi r^2 h - 2\pi r h$

(c) $x^2 + 2x - 35$ (d) $x^2 - 12x + 36$

(e) $x^2 - 21x - 72$ (f) $x^2 + xy - 72y^2$

23. contd.

(g) $5x^2 - 45$ (h) $27x^2 - 12$

(i) $3x^2 - 20x + 12$ (j) $8x^2 + 16x - 10$

(k) $6y^2 - 13y + 6$ (l) $15 - 2x - x^2$.

24. Simplify :-

(a) $\dfrac{1}{x} + \dfrac{1}{y}$ (b) $\dfrac{2}{x} + \dfrac{3}{2x}$

(c) $\dfrac{1}{x} + \dfrac{2}{x+1}$ (d) $\dfrac{5}{x+3} - \dfrac{4}{x-3}$

(e) $\dfrac{3}{x^2} + \dfrac{2}{x}$

(f) $\dfrac{3}{x(x-4)} + \dfrac{4}{x(x-2)}$

(g) $\dfrac{1}{(x+1)(x+2)} + \dfrac{2}{(x+1)(x+3)}$

(h) $\dfrac{5}{x(x-2)} - \dfrac{3}{x(x+4)}$

(i) $\dfrac{1}{x^2-4} + \dfrac{1}{x^2-2x}$.

25. Simplify :-

(a) $\dfrac{(x-4)}{x(x-4)}$ (b) $\dfrac{(x+3)(x-3)}{x(x+3)}$

(c) $\dfrac{(x-6)}{x^2-6x}$ (d) $\dfrac{x^2-9}{x^2-3x}$

(e) $\dfrac{x^2+6x+8}{x^2+5x+6}$ (f) $\dfrac{x^2-16}{x^2+9x+20}$.

26. Change the subject each time to the variable shown in red.

(a) $y = ax + b$ (b) $P = 2(m + n)$

(c) $V = \frac{4}{3}\pi r^3$ (d) $3h = \dfrac{1}{2V}$

(e) $ax + b = cx + d$ (f) $T = \dfrac{1}{2\pi}\sqrt{\dfrac{L}{g}}$

(g) $p(x - c) = q(x + d)$ (h) $D = \sqrt{\dfrac{E+1}{E-1}}$.

27. Solve the following pairs of simultaneous equations :-

(a) $3x - 4y = 23$ (b) $7x + 5y = 1$
    $5x + 2y = 21$ $4x + 3y = 0$

(c) $3{\cdot}5x - 2y = 23$
    $5x + 1{\cdot}5y = 28{\cdot}5$.

28. George bought 5 fish suppers and 2 pie suppers from Aldo's for £31.

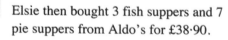

Elsie then bought 3 fish suppers and 7 pie suppers from Aldo's for £38·90.

How much would it cost in Aldo's for 4 fish suppers and 3 pie suppers ?

29. The cost of hiring a car depends on the number of days for which the car is hired and the number of litres of petrol used.

(a) Alasdair hired a Beetle for 3 days and used 50 litres of petrol. The total cost was £160.
Let x pounds be the cost per day of hiring the car, and y pounds be the cost of one litre of petrol.

Write an equation involving x and y which satisfies the above condition.

(b) Sandra hired a Beetle for 4 days and used 60 litres of petrol. Her total bill came to £204.
Write down a second equation in x and y which satisfies this condition.

(c) Find the cost per day of hiring a Beetle and the cost of 1 litre of petrol.

30. Simplify :-

(a) $\sqrt{80}$ (b) $\sqrt{2000}$

(c) $5\sqrt{5} + 20\sqrt{5}$ (d) $\sqrt{80} + \sqrt{20}$

(e) $3\sqrt{2} \times 5$ (f) $2\sqrt{3} \times 3\sqrt{2}$

(g) $\sqrt{3} + 4\sqrt{12} - \sqrt{27}$

(h) $5\sqrt{6} \times 4\sqrt{2}$ (i) $2\sqrt{2} \times 3\sqrt{5}$

(j) $3\sqrt{2}(2\sqrt{2} - 1)$ (k) $5\sqrt{8}(2\sqrt{8} - 3\sqrt{2})$

(l) $(2\sqrt{3} - 1)(3\sqrt{3} - 2)$

(m) $(5\sqrt{5} + \sqrt{3})^2$.

31. Simplify :-

(a) $3x^4 \times 2x^3$

(b) $\dfrac{12a^6}{2a^{-1}}$

(c) $(3p^3)^2$

(d) $(2a^2b^3)^0$

(e) $(2x + \frac{1}{x})^2$

(f) $3a^{\frac{1}{2}}(3a^{\frac{3}{2}} + 4a^{-\frac{1}{2}})$

(g) $(x^{\frac{1}{2}} + x^{-\frac{1}{2}})^2$

(h) $(\sqrt{x} + \dfrac{1}{\sqrt{x}})^2$

(i) $x^2 \times (x^3)^{-3}$

(j) $\dfrac{1}{x^4} \times (x^2)^{-4}$

(k) $\dfrac{2m^2 \times 3m^{-3}}{12m}$

(l) $(y^{-2} \div y^{-1})^{-1}$

(m) $\dfrac{6(y^{-3} \times y^2)^{-1}}{2y^{-1}}$.

32. Evaluate :-

(a) $25^{\frac{1}{2}}$

(b) $8^{-\frac{2}{3}}$

(c) $5^0 + 2^{-1}$

(d) $4^{-1} + 2^{-1}$

(e) $81^{\frac{1}{4}}$

(f) $27^{-\frac{1}{3}}$

(g) $64^{-\frac{2}{3}}$

(h) $16^{\frac{1}{2}} \div 8^{\frac{1}{3}}$.

33. Express with a rational denominator, (*in its simplest form*) :-

(a) $\dfrac{2}{\sqrt{6}}$

(b) $\dfrac{\sqrt{15}}{\sqrt{3}}$

(c) $\dfrac{3\sqrt{2}}{2\sqrt{3}}$

(d) $\sqrt{2} + \dfrac{4}{\sqrt{2}}$.

34. (a) PQRS is a square of side 2 cm.

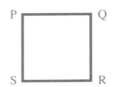

Write down the ratio of the length of PQ to the length of PR.

(b) Show that in every square the ratio of the length of a side to the length of a diagonal is $1 : \sqrt{2}$.

35. (a) Given $f(a) = a^2 - 5a - 12$, find $f(-1)$.

(b) Evaluate $f(-2)$, given $f(p) = p^3 + p^2 - p$.

(c) Given $g(t) = 2t^2 - 3t$, find $g(-3)$.

(d) Evaluate $t(-1)$, given $t(q) = 3q^3 - 2q^2 + 4$.

(e) Given $f(x) = x^3 - 2x + 1$, find $f(-2a)$.

(f) If $f(x) = 2 - 3x$, find a given $f(a) = \dfrac{1}{2}$.

(g) If a function is defined as $f(t) = 3 - 5t$, find x given $f(x) = 18$.

(h) A function is defined as $f(p) = 2p - \dfrac{1}{2}$. Find y given $f(y) = \dfrac{7}{2}$.

(i) Given $f(x) = 5x - 7$ and $g(x) = 1 - 3x$, find p for $f(p) = -g(p)$.

(j) A set of values can be found using the formula $f(x) = x^3 - x^2 - 2x$, $x = 0, 1, 2, 3...$ Find the first three numbers in the set.

36. Sketch the cubic function :- $f(x) = x^3 - x$, with x having values $-3 \le x \le 3$.

37. Given $\underline{v} = \begin{pmatrix} 3 \\ -4 \end{pmatrix}$ and $\underline{w} = \begin{pmatrix} -6 \\ -2 \end{pmatrix}$, find :-

(a) $\underline{v} + \underline{w}$

(b) $\underline{w} - \underline{v}$

(c) $3\underline{v}$

(d) $-3\underline{w}$

(e) $2\underline{v} - 2\underline{w}$

(f) $|\underline{v}|$.

38. Given that $\underline{a} = \begin{pmatrix} 6 \\ -5 \\ -2 \end{pmatrix}$ and $\underline{b} = \begin{pmatrix} -3 \\ 4 \\ -12 \end{pmatrix}$, find :-

(a) $\underline{a} + \underline{b}$

(b) $\underline{b} - \underline{a}$

(c) $-2\underline{a}$

(d) $|\underline{b}|$.

39. Solve for vector $\underline{x}$:-

(a) $6\underline{x} - \begin{pmatrix} 2 \\ -3 \end{pmatrix} = 4\underline{x} + \begin{pmatrix} -4 \\ -1 \end{pmatrix}$

(b) $3\underline{x} - \begin{pmatrix} 3 \\ -7 \\ -5 \end{pmatrix} = -2\underline{x} + \begin{pmatrix} 12 \\ -8 \\ 10 \end{pmatrix}$.

40. PABCD is a pyramid with a rectangular base ABCD.

Relative to an appropriate axis,

$$\overrightarrow{PA} = \begin{pmatrix} -7 \\ -13 \\ -11 \end{pmatrix}, \ \overrightarrow{AB} = \begin{pmatrix} 6 \\ 6 \\ -6 \end{pmatrix} \text{ and } \overrightarrow{AD} = \begin{pmatrix} 8 \\ -4 \\ 4 \end{pmatrix}.$$

$\overrightarrow{BT} = \frac{1}{4} \overrightarrow{BC}$.

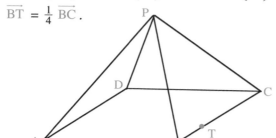

Find $\overrightarrow{PT}$ in component form.

41. The line KN is divided into 3 equal parts by the points L and M, as shown.

K has coordinates $(3, -1, 2)$ and N is $(9, 2, -4)$.

(a) Find the components of $\overrightarrow{KN}$ and $\overrightarrow{KL}$.

(b) Determine the coordinates of L and M.

42. Solve these quadratic equations by factorising :-

(a) $x^2 - 4x = 0$ (b) $3x^2 + 6x = 0$

(c) $12x^2 - 8x = 0$ (d) $x^2 - 9 = 0$

(e) $x^2 - 25 = 0$ (f) $16 - 9x^2 = 0$

(g) $x^2 + 6x + 8 = 0$ (h) $x^2 - 3x - 10 = 0$

(i) $21 - 4x - x^2 = 0$ (j) $2x(3x - 5) = 24$

(k) $4x^2 + 8x - 5 = 0$ (l) $(x - 2)^2 = 9$.

43. Find the coordinates of points P, Q, R, S, T, U, V and W on these parabolas :-

(a)

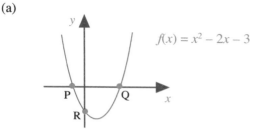

43. (b)

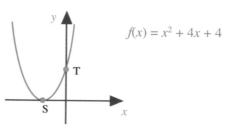

(c)

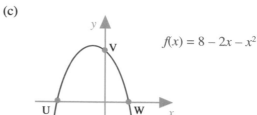

44. A flea jumps from point A and lands at point B.

Its path is that of a parabola with equation $y = 36 + 9x - x^2$ where x is the horizontal distance travelled and y is its height.

(All measurements are in centimetres).

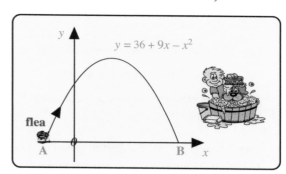

(a) Calculate how far the flea has travelled horizontally from A to B.

(b) Calculate the maximum height reached by the flea during its jump.

45. Elsie wrote down the duration of her last 15 mobile phone calls (to the nearest minute).

1   12   15,   5   16   6   25   3
12   13   4   15   5   17   8.

(a) Calculate the median and the lower and upper quartiles.

(b) Calculate the semi-interquartile range.

(c) Draw an appropriate statistical diagram to show the distribution of the above times.

46. Find the mean, median, mode and range of the numbers :-

$$7, \ 4, \ 3, \ 1, \ 3, \ 5, \ 8, \ 5, \ 3, \ 9.$$

47. Three of the four Bone Brothers are quite sporty. The average age of the 4 boys is 14 years.

Ivan is 12   Mel is 10   Bob is 15   Craig

How old is Craig, the eldest brother ?

48. A vending machine offers delicious hot soup. Each cup it fills should hold 230 ml of soup. During normal operation, the mean volume dispensed per cup should be within 4 ml of the 230 ml and the standard deviation of any sample should be less than 7 ml.

Sample cups are found to hold (in ml) :-

225   230   240   220   225   232   224

(a) Calculate the mean volume of soup per cup.

(b) Calculate the standard deviation.

(c) Is the machine functioning correctly ? Explain.

49. The following stem-and-leaf diagram shows the scores of 50 boys in a golf tournament.

Golf Scores

6	3 4
6	5 5 5 6 6 6 6 7 7 8 9 9 9
7	0 0 0 0 0 1 1 2 3 3
7	5 6 6 6 7 8
8	0 0 1 1 2 2 3
8	5 6 6 6 7 8 9
9	2 3 4
9	7 8

8 | 0 represents a score of 80

(a) Write down the median golf score.

(b) Calculate the semi-interquartile range for these scores.

49. (c) Sketch the boxplot below and fill in the correct values to illustrate the golf scores in this sample.

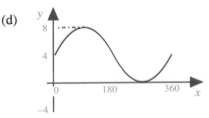

50. State the **maximum** and **minimum** values of these trigonometric functions and their **periods**.

(a) $y = 5\sin x°$

(b) $y = 8\cos 2x°$

(c) $y = -3\sin 4x°$

(d) $y = \frac{1}{2}\cos 3x°$

(e) $y = \tan 2x°$

(f) $y = 2\sin x° + 1$

(g) $y = 10\cos x° - 10$

(h) $y = 1 - \sin x°$

(i) $y = 5\cos(2x - 30)°$

(j) $y = 75\sin(6x - 24)°$

(k) $y = 6 - 3\sin 4x°$

(l) $y = -3\cos \frac{1}{2}x°$.

51. Sketch the following graphs showing all the main points :-

(a) $y = 3\sin 2x°$

(b) $y = 2\cos 3x° + 1$.

52. Write down the **equations** of these trig curves :-

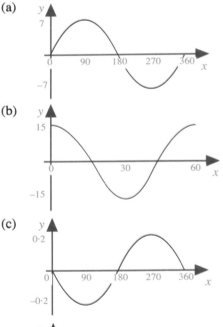

53. The diagram below shows the graph of the trig function

$$f(x) = k \sin bx°, \quad 0 \le x \le 180°.$$

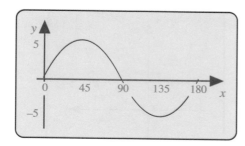

Find the value of k and the value of b.

54. On a certain day the depth, D metres, of water in a shallow harbour, h hours after midnight, is given by the formula :-

$$D = 4·5 + 2·5 \sin(30h)°.$$

(a) Find the depth of water in the harbour at 3 pm.

(b) The depth of water in the harbour is recorded each hour.

What is the maximum difference in the depths of water in the harbour over the 24 hour period ?

55. (a) Calculate the length of the minor arc AB.

(b) Calculate the area of the major sector AOB.

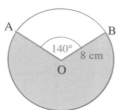

56.

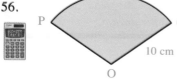

Given that the area of sector POQ is 78·5 cm², calculate the size of $\angle POQ$.

57. AC is the arc of a circle centre O and radius 20 cm.

Calculate :-

(a) the area of sector AOC.

(b) the area of triangle AOC.

(c) the green shaded area.

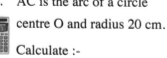

58. The diagram shows the rear wiper on a car's back window.

The rear glass is in the shape of a trapezium with sizes given.

The wiper blade is 40 centimetres long and it sweeps through an angle of 105°.

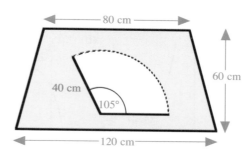

Calculate the area of glass not cleaned by the wiper blade.

59.

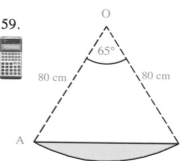

The base for a rocking horse is made from the arc of a circular piece of wood, with a triangular section ABO cut off.

The radius of the circle is 80 centimetres and $\angle AOB = 65°$.

(a) Calculate the area of the sector AOB.

(b) Calculate the area of the segment.

(c) Calculate the volume of wood used to make the base (15 cm wide) of the rocking horse.

60. Write each of the following in completed square form, showing each stage of your working :-

(a) $y = x^2 - 6x + 3$ (b) $y = x^2 + 5x + 8$.

61. Solve these quadratic equations by using the quadratic formula :-

(a) $x^2 + 7x + 5 = 0$ (b) $2x^2 - 9x + 6 = 0$

(c) $3x^2 = 5 - x$ (d) $(x - 4)^2 - 10 = 0$.

62. Each of these parabolas are of the form

$y = (x - a)^2 + b$ or $y = b - (x - a)^2$.

Write down :-

(i) the values of a and b in each case.

(ii) the equation of each **axis of symmetry**.

(iii) the coordinates of the point where each parabola crosses the y-axis.

(a)   (b)

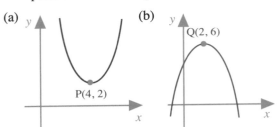

(c)   (d)

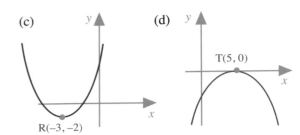

63. Both of these parabolas are of the form $y = kx^2$, where k can be positive or negative.

Write down the equation of each parabola.

(a)   (b)

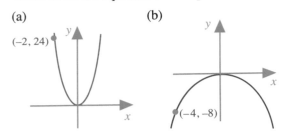

64. Find the **discriminant** for each of these and use it to determine the **nature** of the roots :-

(a) $x^2 + 5x + 2 = 0$ (b) $x^2 + 3x + 3 = 0$

(c) $2x^2 + 3x - 2 = 0$ (d) $3x^2 + 6x + 3 = 0$.

65. $x^2 + px + 16 = 0$ has 1 root. Find 2 values for p.

66. $ax^2 + 6x - 1 = 0$ has 2 real roots.

Set up an inequality in a, and solve for a.

67. Shown is the graph of the function

$$y = 3x^2 - 2x - 2.$$

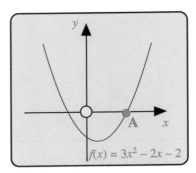

Determine the coordinates of the point A where the graph cuts the positive part of the x-axis.

Give your answer to 2 decimal places.

68. This **scattergraph** shows the sales of cups of hot bovril at a football ground.

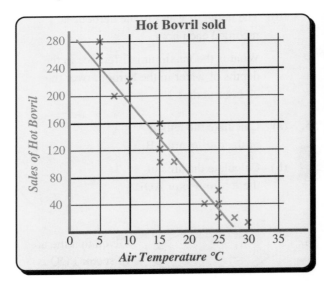

This would be called a strong negative correlation since all the points lie roughly on a straight line going downwards from left to right.

The line is called a line of best fit.

Use the line of best fit to estimate :-

(a) the sales at 20°C.

(b) the temperature when the sales were approximately 240 cups.

69. This table shows the cost of various taxi fares and the distances travelled.

(a) Copy the graph.

(b) Use the table below to plot the points on the graph.

Distance (km)	Cost (£)
2	2·00
3	2·50
2	1·75
5	3·25
5	3·50
6	4·00

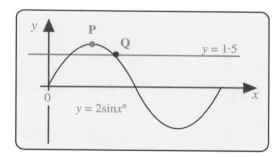

Taxi Fares

Cost of ride

Distance Travelled (km)

(c) Does this graph show a strong negative or positive correlation ?

(d) Draw a line of best fit on your graph.

(e) Determine the equation of this line. ($y = $ ....)

(f) Estimate how much a 4 kilometre journey would cost.

70. Solve these trigonometric equations, $0 \leq x \leq 360$:-

(a) $\sqrt{3}\cos x° - 1 = 0$

(b) $2\sin x° + 0·6 = \tan 40°$

(c) $6\sin x° + 8 = 2\sin x° + 7$

(d) $10\cos x° - 3 = 6\cos x°.$

71. The diagram shows the graph of $y = 2\sin x°$.

(a) Write down the coordinates of the point marked P.

(b) The line $y = 1·5$ is also shown on the diagram.

Determine the coordinates of the point Q, where the line and the curve intersect.

72. The diagram shows the graph of $y = \cos x°$, $0 \leq x \leq 360$.

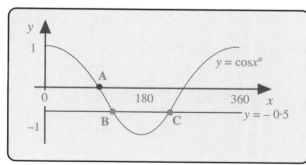

(a) Write down the coordinates of point A.

The straight line $y = -0·5$ cuts the graph at B and C.

(b) Find the coordinates of B and C.

National 5 Specimen Paper 1

Time 1 Hour

Marks

1. Evaluate :- $\frac{2}{3}$ of $3\frac{1}{2} - 1\frac{3}{5}$.

   3

2. A line passes through two points A(0, $-t$) and B(2, 5t).

   (a) Find the gradient of the line in terms of t.

   2

   (b) Find the equation of the line in terms of x, y and t.

   2

3. Shown is an inverted rectangular based pyramid with lengths 8 boxes and 2 boxes and with point T directly below the centre of rectangle PQRS.

   PQ is parallel to the x-axis.

   The height of the pyramid is 9 boxes and the coordinates of points S are S(6, 3, 10).

   (a) Write down the coordinates of the other 4 points P, Q, R and T.

   2

   (b) Find $|\overrightarrow{RT}|$, the magnitude of vector $\overrightarrow{RT}$, expressing your answer as a surd in its simplest form.

   3

4. Solve the equation :-

   $$2x^2 - x - 6 = 0$$

   3

5. The times taken, in minutes, for an athlete practising for the half marathon was recorded, and a summary of these times are listed below.

Maximum time	:	95
Range	:	35
Lower quartile	:	70
Semi-Interquartile Range	:	7
Median	:	75

   Draw an appropriate statistical diagram to illustrate the athlete's times.

   3

Marks

6. (a) Multiply out the brackets and simplify :-

$$x^{\frac{1}{3}}\left(x^{-1} + 4x^{-\frac{1}{3}}\right).$$

2

(b) Find the exact value of this expression when $x = 27$.

1

7. (a) Express $\dfrac{2}{\sqrt{8}}$ as a fraction with a **rational** denominator.

(Give your answer as a surd in its **simplest** form).

2

(b) Change the subject of the formula below to "r":-

$$p + 4 = \frac{qr^2}{2}.$$

3

8. *Napier's* shop sign uses a parabola for the n.

The equation of the parabola is :-

$$y = 9 - (x - 2)^2.$$

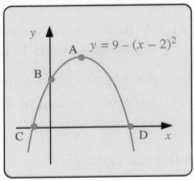

(a) State the coordinates of the turning point A.

2

(b) Write down the coordinates of point B, on the y-axis.

2

(c) Work out the coordinates of the point D which lies on the x-axis.

2

(d) Determine the length of the line CD.

1

9. Express $\dfrac{7}{x - 4} - \dfrac{5}{x - 1}$, $x \neq 4$, $x \neq 1$

as a single fraction in its simplest form.

3

10. Angus and Noreen are out purchasing PC games and Gamestation games.

    They go to a store where all PC games are one price and all Gamestation games are one price.

    (a) Angus buys 3 PC games and 2 Gamestation games.

         His bill comes to £135.

         Write down an algebraic equation to illustrate this.

    1

    (b) Noreen buys 5 PC games and 3 Gamestation games.

         Her bill is £215.

         Write down an algebraic equation to illustrate this.

    1

    (c) Calculate the cost of one Gamestation game.

    3

11. A tunnel entrance has centre C and a circular arc of diameter 20 metres.

    Water surface PQ is 16 metres wide.

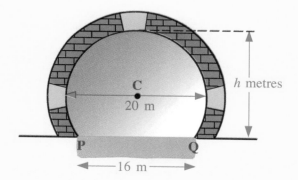

    Calculate the height (h metres) of the tunnel entrance.

    4

[END OF QUESTION PAPER]

National 5 Specimen Paper 2

Time 1 Hour 30 minutes

Marks

1. A comet travels at a speed of $1 \cdot 6 \times 10^8$ km/hr.

   What distance would the comet have travelled after $4 \cdot 2 \times 10^3$ hours ?

   (*Give your answer in scientific notation*).

   3

2. A car is found to lose 28% of its value each year, (*based on the value at the start of each year*).

   What would be the value of a £25 000 sports car after 3 years ?

   3

3. The trapezium below has PQ parallel to SR and SR = 3 × PQ in length.
   Vector $\overrightarrow{PQ} = \underline{a}$ and vector $\overrightarrow{PS} = \underline{b}$.
   T and U are the **mid-points** of QR and SR.

   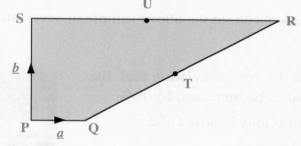

   Find the following vectors in terms of $\underline{a}$ and $\underline{b}$:-

   (a) $\overrightarrow{PR}$ (b) $\overrightarrow{QU}$ (c) $\overrightarrow{QT}$.

   4

4. The diagram shows two parabolas with equations $y = x^2 + 4x - 5$ and $y = kx^2$.

   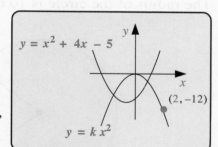

   (a) For the parabola $y = x^2 + 4x - 5$, write its equation in the form $y = (x - a)^2 + b$, where a and b are integers.

   2

   (b) For the parabola $y = kx^2$ which passes through the point $(2, -12)$, calculate the value of k and write down the equation of this parabola.

   3

5. Find the range of values of h such that $hx^2 + 6x - 3 = 0$, $h \neq 0$, has 2 real roots.

6. Solve the equation :–

$$x^2 = x + 5.$$

(*Give your answers correct to one decimal place*).

7. The weights, in kilograms, of seven college students are shown below.

> 53,   42,   57,   64,   48,   49,   72.

(a) Calculate the mean of these weights.

(b) Calculate the standard deviation of these weights.

(c) The mean and standard deviation of **all** of the college students were found to be 60 and 5·6 respectively.

Make **two** statements about the above sample of seven students.

2

8. Due to an increase in the cost of aviation fuel, the price of a holiday had to be increased by 10%.

The new price of the holiday is now £682.

What was its original price ?

9. A circle has a segment removed as shown below.

The radius of the circle is 10 centimetres and angle AOB = 60°.

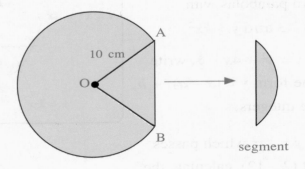

Calculate the area of the segment.

10. A plasticene ball is made in the shape of a sphere with radius 10 centimetres.

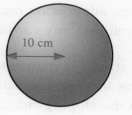

10 cm

(a) Calculate the volume of the sphere.

Some of the plasticene from the sphere is remoulded to make a cone as shown.

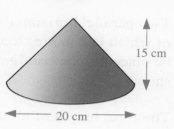

15 cm

(b) How much plasticene is left over
after making the cone ?

20 cm

The remaining plasticene is made into a cuboid with height 25 cm, and with a square base of length y cm.

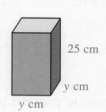

25 cm

y cm

y cm

(c) Calculate the value of y, to 3 significant figures.

11. (a) Solve algebraically the equation :-

$$2\cos x° - 1 = 0, \qquad 0 \le x \le 360 .$$

(b) Hence, or otherwise, find the solution of the equation :-

$$2\cos\tfrac{1}{2}x° - 1 = 0, \qquad 0 \le x \le 360 .$$

12. A woman in an orienteering competition covers the following course.

From the starting point A, she walks to point B, 8 kilometres away and on a bearing of 080°.

From B, the woman then travels on a bearing of 210° for 7 kilometres to get to point C.

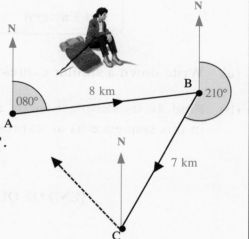

N

N

080°

A

8 km

B

210°

N

7 km

C

(a) Explain clearly why angle ABC = 50°.

From C, she then returns directly to the starting point A.

(b) How far did she have to walk to get from C to A ?

13. A large advertising mural is to be secured to the side of a multi-storey car-park using 8 metal struts.

Two struts, $4x$ metres long, two struts $2x$ metres long and two struts, x metres long form the sloping sides.

Two parallel horizontal struts, one of which is 8 metres long, must be placed in the configuration shown.

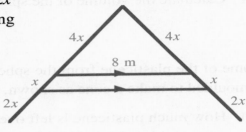

The **total** length of all the 8 struts needed measures 60 metres.

Find the value of x.

4

14. A mosaic pattern is arranged as shown using coloured balls.

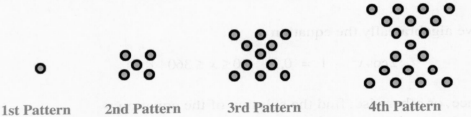

| 1st Pattern | 2nd Pattern | 3rd Pattern | 4th Pattern |

Any number in this sequence can be found as follows :-

1st Pattern	$(1 \times 2) - 1 = 1$
2nd Pattern	$(2 \times 3) - 1 = 5$
3rd Pattern	$(3 \times 4) - 1 = 11$

(a) Write down a similar expression for the 4th pattern.

1

(b) Find, **in its simplest form**, an expression for the nth pattern in this sequence as an expression in terms of n.

2

[END OF QUESTION PAPER]

Answers to National 5

1. a 3·8   b 1100   c 8000
   d 9·1   e 9·1   f 20
2. a 5000 b 140000 c 30
   d 50   e 160
3. a 20   b –11   c 7   d 27
4. a $(12 – 4) \times 3$ b $(12 + 2) \times (3 – 4)$
   c $(16 – 9) \div 5 \times (-1 + 1)$ is 1 possibility
5. a –17   b 13   c –35   d –13
   e –45   f 7   g –5   h –140
   i 11   j 5
6. a $15x$ b $-4a$ c $8p$ d $5y$
   e $-10t$ f $7f$ g $-6w$ h $5a + 2b$
7. a –3   b 7   c –4
   d 12   e 10   f 4
8. a 7   b 18   c 2   d –7
   e 5   f 0   g $4x$ h 0
9. a –5   b –1   c 2
   d –6   e 1   f –7
10. a –20   b –48   c –7   d 0
    e $-12x^2$ f –4   g $-4a$ h $-3t$
    i –6   j –36   k 48   l 120
    m 7   n 10   o $15p^2$ p 49
    q 64   r 24
11. a 0   b 9   c 36   d –18
    e 33   f 99   g 189   h 18
12. a   b

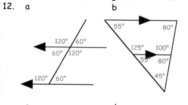

   c   d

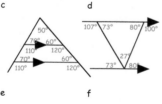

   e   f

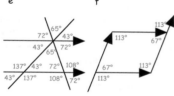

13. a   b

   e   f

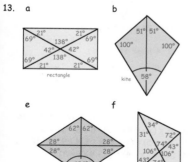

14. a 75°   b 52·5°
15. a £24   b £84   c £100   d £2250
    e £103   f 8·1 m   g 1·25 kg   h 24 cm
    i £42   j 132 ml   k 392mph   l 0·756 m
16. a £57·60   b £24
17. 87·5%
18. a 72%, ³/₄, 0·77, (0·5 × 1·56), 0·8
    b (²/₃ of 105), (0·25 × 284), (60% of 120)
19. a £2050   b £19800
    c £15106   d £25792
20. a £460·80   b £86·40
    c £547·20
21. a £20148   b £2690
22. a £3525   b £19975
23. £2827
24. a £2552   b various
25. a €48·80   b   €1518·90
    c €1069·21   d €149389
26. a $666   b $2101·60
    c £1000   d £350
    e £250   f £750
    g $740   h €2928
27. 9·5 Krone to the £
28. £262
29. a $13x$ b t^2 c $20ab$
    d $2q^3$ e 15   f $2x^2$
30. a $3t + 6$ b $10 – 20r$
    c $8x + x^2$ d $-15a^2 + 9ab$
31. a $5x + 16$ b $y + 24$
    c $24 – 4t$ d $9m + 5$
    e $12 – 3t$ f $6 + 12g$
    g $3 – 4a$ h $11m – 3$
32. a $8(2x + 11) – 4(4x – 1) = 92$ (constant)
    b $4x – 1$ must be $< 2x + 11 \Rightarrow x < 6$
33. a 6,   b 5,   c 0,
    d 2,   e 12,   f 0,
34. a 6   b 5   c 0
    d 2   e 12   f 0
35. a   b

   c   d

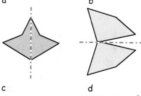

36. a   b

   c   d

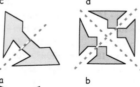
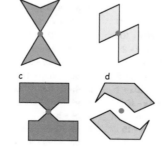

37.

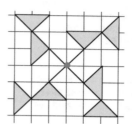

38. Tolerance is a the amount, either way,
    a measurement is allowed to be out by
    to still be acceptible.
39. a 9 to 11 mm   b 10 to 20 kg
    c 18 to 22 m   d 1·2 to 1·8 kg
    e 149 to 155 mm   f 6·35 to 8·75 mg
40. a (14 ± 2) cm   b (130 ± 10) mm
    c $(1·65 \pm 0·05)$ mg   d $(2·55 \pm 0·05)°$
41. a $y = 3x$ b $y = 3x + 1$
    c $y = 3x – 2$ d $y = 2x – 5$
    e $y = x + 17$ f $y = 5x + 10$
42. a 5   b –2   c 4
    d 7   e 13   f 4
43. a 12   b 5¹/₅   c 13   d –2
    e ¹⁶/₁₉   f 1¹/₇   g 4¹/₅
44. a $c \leq -5$ b $d > 3$ c $t < -2$ d $x < 12$
    e $g \geq 2$ f $p \leq 4$ g $x \geq 4$ h $t \geq -1$
45. a $9·3 \times 10^2$ b $8·42 \times 10^3$
    c $3·52 \times 10^4$ d 8×10^6
    e $3·05 \times 10^8$ f $2·75 \times 10^6$
    g $8·5 \times 10^{-4}$ h 7×10^{-2}
46. a 5900   b 808000
    c 710   d 28100
    e 0·0058   f   0·099
    g 0·000062   h 0·2
47. a $5·7 \times 10^{10}$ b $3·1185 \times 10^{11}$
    c $1·35 \times 10^{10}$ d $2·9 \times 10^{13}$
    e $1·024 \times 10^{21}$ f $3·5 \times 10^{19}$
48. 22·0 cm
49. a 38·6 cm   b 25·0 cm
    c 671 m
50. a 19·1 cm   b 39·8 mm
51. a 113 cm²   b 201 m²
    c 2512 m²   d 0·196 cm²
52. 3 cm
53. a 18·8 cm²   b 29·5 cm³
54. a 60·4 cm   b 29·6 cm
55. see plotted points
56. a M(–3, 0)
    b J'(1, –2), K'(2, –3), L'(4, –1), M'(3, 0)
    c J"(–1, 2), K"(–2, 3)< L"(–4, 1), M"(–3, 0)
57. a reflect over x-axis
    b reflect over y-axis
    c reflect over x-axis then the y-axis
        or reflect through origin
    d reflect over x-axis then the y-axis
        or reflect through origin
    e reflect over x-axis
    f rotation of 90° clockwise around origin
58. O(0, 0), T(–4, –1), P'(–3, –4)
59. P'(–2, 3), Q'(–5, 4), R'(–3, 1)
60. a 12·7 cm   b 6·56 m
61. a 24 cm   b 240 cm²
62. 6·2 m
63. a 5   b 5·39   c 8·25 units

64. 39.6 cm
65. a 1260 km   b 50 mph
    c 1 hr 30 min   d 99 miles
66. a 0.6 hr   b 0.65 hr   c 2.33 hr   d 3.95 hr
67. Neil 1 hr 15 mins, Alex - 1 hr 20 mins
    Alex took 5 mins longer
68. a 0830 b 12 km   c 8 km/hr
    d 45 min   e 30 min   f 24 km/hr
    g 1145
69. a Anne - £1800, Tom - £2700
    b €700000, €300000
    c £4200, £3150, £1050
70. a £5.40 b £2.80
71. 6 hours
72. a 400 cm^3 b 340 cm^2
73. a 600 cm^3 b 660 cm^2
74. a 9420 cm^3 - 9.42 litres
    b 1884 cm^2 c 2512 cm^2
75. 804 cm^3
76. 5861 cm^3
77. 0.25 or 1 in 4
78. a $^2/_5$ b -3
79. a grad = 3, y-intercept = $(0, -2)$
    b grad = -4, y-intercept = $(0, 5)$
80. a $y = 4x - 5$ b $y = -2x + 3$
    c $y = -4x$ d $y = 1$ e $x = 0$
81. a $y = 3x - 2$ b $y = -x - 4$
82. a grad = -10,   b $T = -10t + 100$
    c $30°C$
83. a $8(a + 3)$ b $2(2x + 5)$
    c $b(3 + c)$ d $x(7 - v)$
    e $p(t + g)$ f $a(a + 2)$
    g $5(3a - 2b + c)$ h $2p(p + 2q - 3r)$
    i $t(6 - t)$ j $2c(c - 3)$
    k $5h(k + 2g)$ l $5v(3w - 2x)$
    m $11s(r - 1)$ n $3y(y + 3)$
    o $ac(3a + c)p$ $6rs(3s - 5)$
    q $4x(2x - 3a)$ r $^1/_5b(a + k)$
    s $3bc(5a^2c + 4b)$ t $3ce(5de + 4b^2)$
84. a 40 b 55 c 35 d 27.5
85. a 12 b 6.40 c 19.4
86. a 13.8 cm   b 40.3 c 61.6 cm
87. $75.2°$
88. $36.9°$
89. 67.2 m
90. 8 cm approx
91. Similar means the shapes look the same
    though one is smaller than the other. Their
    angles match up and their sides are in the
    same ratio.
    Congruent means the two shapes are
    identical, both in the sizes of the angles
    and in the lengths of their sides.
92. a 22 cm   b 20 cm
93. a 5 b 25 c 54 cm^2
94. 5.4 litres
95. a $5^4/_5$ b $5^3/_4$
96. a $^{17}/_3$ b $^{33}/_5$
97. 14
98. a $^6/_7$ b $^1/_4$ c $^1/_2$ d $6^1/_5$
    e $^7/_{12}$ f $6^7/_{15}$ g $3^{11}/_{40}$ h $1^5/_6$
99. a $^3/_{10}$ b $^{14}/_{27}$ c $4^1/_5$
    d $7^1/_3$ e $^1/_{10}$ f $^1/_7$
100. mean = 20, med = 20, mode = 21, range = 13
101. 51
102. a 43p   b 43p   c 4p   d 42.9p
103. a (i) Grass Chairs   (ii) Garden Chairs
      (iii) same   b Summer weather
104. a Angles are $120°$, $84°$, $144°$, $12°$
    b See pie-chart with the above angles
      shown in the sectors.
105 a (i) 7 mins   (ii) 45 mins   d 9
    b 23 mins   c 23 mins

106. a

1	5 6
2	4 6 7 7 9
3	0 2 4 5 6 8 9 9 9
4	2 6 7
5	0 0 2 2 4 7 7 7 7 8
6	4 4 5 5 6 6 7 7 8
7	0 3

    b 57 c 50 d 16
107. a $^1/_9$ b $^4/_9$ c 0 d $^4/_9$
108. five out of eight or 0.625
109. a Bag 2 b Bag 1
    more £20, £10, and £5 notes than £1 notes
110. $^1/_8$
111. 15
112. Try it yourself

Answers to Chapter 1 Page 13

Exercise 1·1 page 13

1.   a $2a + 18$ b $6x - 30$ c $30 - 15h$
    d $3m - 3n$ e $40b - 120$ f $24w + 3$
    g $28 - 12t$ h $pq + 2p$ i $vw - 13v$
    j $8a + a^2$ k $2dk + 6de$ l $54x^2 - 9xy$
    m $5a + 5c - 15e$ n $45 - 72v - 81y$
    o $c^2 - cg - 11ck$ p $-4a - 12$
    q $-7x + x^2$ r $-2v^2 + 7v$
    s $-7m^3 + 10m^2$ t $-2x^4 + 10x^3$
2.   a $2y + 11$ b $6p + 10$
    c $9a + 3$ d $7s - 2$
    e $3g + 10$ f $a + 30$
    g $40 + 2u$ h $16d + 24$
    i $15m + 10$ j $9c - 4$
    k $6x - 1$ l $5p + 4q$
    m $42x - 12y$ n $2a + 2$
    o $10 - 2v$
3.   a $7p + 7$ b $6a - 2$
    c $11m - 2$ d $9 - 5g$
    e $-4n + 16$ f $3x - 21$
    g $3p + 3$ h $8a$
    i $2t + 4$ j $x^2 + 2x + 3$
    k $-9x^2 + 8xy$
4.   a $2 - 5x$ b $14 - 7m$
    c $10 - y$ d $7 + 3x$
    e $6h$ f $6d + 2$
    g $2a - 300$ h 100
    i $14x^2 - 2x$

Exercise 1·2 page 14

1.   a $x^2 + 4x + 3$ b $x^2 + 8x + 15$
    c $x^2 + 6x + 8$ d $x^2 + 7x + 12$
    e $p^2 + 10p + 25$ f $x^2 + 6x + 9$
    g $p^2 + 5p + 6$ h $m^2 + 10m + 25$
    i $3x^2 + 7x + 2$ j $2x^2 + 12x + 18$
    k $4a^2 + 16a + 16$ l $9y^2 + 6y + 1$
    m $8m^2 + 10m + 3$ n $25m^2 + 15m + 2$
    o $16g^2 + 28g + 6$ p $x^2 + 9x + 20$
    q $6x^2 + 21x + 18$ r $100w^2 + 20w + 1$
    s $9x^2 + 24x + 16$ t $4y^2 + 32y + 64$
2.   a $x^2 - 5x + 6$ b $x^2 - 3x + 2$
    c $x^2 - 7x + 12$ d $p^2 - 8p + 16$
    e $-p^2 + 10p - 25$ f $x^2 - 8x + 16$
    g $x^2 - 20x + 100$ h $4x^2 - 10x + 4$
    i $5x^2 - 11x + 2$ j $2x^2 - 9x + 9$
    k $4a^2 - 12a + 9$ l $8a^2 - 14a + 3$
    m $4m^2 - 12m + 5$ n $6c^2 - 22m + 12$
    o $25x^2 - 10x + 1$ p $4w^2 - 4w + 1$
3.   a $x^2 + 3x - 10$ b $y^2 + 3y - 4$
    c $a^2 + a - 6$ d $b^2 + b - 2$
    e $m^2 - 2m - 15$ f $-n^2 - 2n + 3$
    g $2x^2 + 5x - 3$ h $5a^2 - 19a - 4$

    i $3u^2 - 2u - 8$ j $9x^2 - 25$
    k $14a^2 - 12a - 2$ l $20h^2 - 7h - 6$
    m $x^2 + 3xy + 2y^2$ n $x^2 - xy - 2y^2$
    o $x^2 + xy - 2y^2$ p $x^2 - 3xy + 2y^2$
    q $3a^2 + 7ab + 4b^2$ r $2p^2 - 3pq - 2q^2$
    s $2x^2 + 9x + 10$ t $a^2 - 3a + 2$
    u $-2b^2 + 7b + 15$ v $p^2 - q^2$
    w $-9y^2 + 8y + 1$ x $20k^2 - 9k + 1$
4.   a $x^3 + 2x^2 + x + 2$ b $x^3 + 3x^2 + 5x + 15$
    c $x^3 - 2x^2 + 3x - 6$ d $2x^3 - 8x^2 + 3x - 12$
    e $2x^3 + x^2 - 4x - 2$ f $10x^3 - 6x^2 + 15x - 9$
    g $x^4 + 7x^2 + 12$ h $x^4 + 3x^2 - 10$
    i $x^3 + x^2y + xy^2 + y^3$ j $2x^3 - x^2y + 2xy^2 - y^3$
    k $3x^3 + 2x^2y - 3xy^2 - 2y^3$
    l $x^4 - y^4$
5.   a $(x + 5)(3x + 1) = 3x^2 + 16x + 5$
    b $(5x - 3)(2x - 4) = 10x^2 - 26x + 12$
    c $(x + y)(3x + y) = 3x^2 + 4xy + y^2$
    d $(5a + 2b)(3a - 2b) = 15a^2 - 4ab - 4b^2$
    e $(p^2 - q^2)(p + q) = p^3 + p^2q - q^2p - q^3$
6.   a $x^3 + 6x^2 + 9x + 2$ b $x^3 + 6x^2 + 3x - 2$
    c $x^3 - 4x + 3$ d $6a^3 + 13a^2 + 9a + 2$
    e $6p^3 - 7p^2 - 10p + 8$ f $8y^3 - 2y^2 - 3y + 15$
7.   a $x^2 + 6x + 9$ b $x^2 + 14x + 49$
    c $x^2 + 2xy + y^2$ d $y^2 - 4y + 4$
    e $y^2 - 12y + 36$ f $x^2 - 2xy + y^2$
    g $4x^2 + 4x + 1$ h $9x^2 + 24x + 16$
    i $16a^2 - 8a + 1$ j $4b^2 - 40b + 100$
    k $x^2 + 6xy + 9y^2$ l $a^2 - 14ab + 49b^2$
    m $4x^2 - 12hx + 9h^2$ n $16v^2 - 40vw + 25w^2$
    o $x^4 + 4x^2 + 4$ p $y^4 - 8y^2 + 16$
    q $p^2 + 2 + 1/p^2$ r $q^2 - 2 + 1/q^2$
    s $4x^2 - 2 + 1/4x^2$ t $25x^2 - 2 + 1/25x^2$
8.   a $(3x + 2)^2 = 9x^2 + 12x + 4$
    b $(5x - 1)^2 = 25x^2 - 10x + 1$
    c $(3x + 6y)^2 = 9x^2 + 36xy + 36y^2$

Exercise 1·3 page 17

1.   a $-6x + 24$ b $7x + 14$
    c $-7a + 25$ d $2b - 2$
    e $x + 10$ f $5x + 1$
    g $8y^2 + 12y$ h $18p^2 + 3p - 1$
    i $13x^2 - 21x + 4$ j $10x^2 - 14x - 11$
    k $20g^2 + 4g + 29$ l $2q^2 + 9q + 3$
    m $4x^2 - 15x - 11$ n $12x^2 + 5x - 7$
    o $3x^2 + 2x - 17$ p $5x^2 - 52x + 20$
    q $10a - 75$ r $6w$
    s $-x^2 + 44x + 2$ t $14x^2 - 36x + 21$
2.   a $x^3 - 6x^2 + 12x - 8$ b $x^3 + 3x^2 + 3x + 1$
    c $a^3 - 3a^2 + 3a - 1$ d $x^3 + 9x^2 + 27x + 27$
    e $k^3 - 9k^2 + 27k - 27$ f $8x^3 + 12x^2 + 6x + 1$
    g $27x^3 - 54x^2 + 36x - 8$
    h $3x^3 + 18x^2 + 36x + 24$
    i $2x^3 - 30x^2 + 150x - 250$
    j $a^3 + 3a^2b + 3ab^2 + b^3$
    k $p^3 - 3p^2q + 3pq^2 - q^3$
    l $8x^3 - 24x^2y + 24xy^2 - 8y^3$

Exercise 1·4 page 18

1.   a $x = 5$ b $x = -7$ c $x = -5$
    d $x = 5$ e $x = -1$ f $x = -8$
    g $x = 0.5$ h $x = 1$ i $x = 0.5$
    j $x = 5$ k $x = 3$ l $x = 1.5$
2.   a $x(x + 8) = (x + 3)(x + 4)$, 12×20 15×16
    b $x^2 = (x + 6)(x - 3)$, 6×6, 12×3
    c $x(x + 5) = (x + 8)(x - 1$, 4×9, 3×12
    d $(x - 2)(x - 4) = (x + 4)(x - 8)$,
       18×16 and 24×12

Remember Remember Ch 1 page 19

1. a $9u + 63$ b $6 - 12r$
   c $9x + 4x^2$ d $-10m^2 + 40mn$
2. a $8x + 18$ b $9 - 2n$
   c 30 d $2 + 3w$
   e $10 + 2h$ f $20q - 2$
3. a $a^2 + 9a + 14$ b $b^2 - 9b + 18$
   c $c^2 + 7c - 18$ d $12d^2 + 20d + 3$
   e $6e^2 - 17e + 5$ f $14y^2 + 19y - 3$
   g $4k^2 - 20k + 25$ h $m^2 + 4 + 4/m^2$
   i $n^3 + 3n^2 + 3n + 1$ j $8s^3 - 36s^2 + 54s - 27$
   k $7x$ l $5x^2 - 12x + 1$
   m $6y^3 + 5y^2 - 10y + 3$
4. a $2k + 3$ b $k + 2$
   c $2k^2 + 7k + 6$ d $6k + 14$
5. a $x = -9$ b $x = 0$ c $x = -0{\cdot}5$
   d $x = {}^3/_8$ e $x = -4^4/_5$ f $x = -4$
6. $x^2 = x^2 + 4x - 32$, $x = 8$, 8×8, 16×4
7. a $4(a + 6)$ b $7(3a - 4b)$
   c $c(d + g)$ d $2b(b - 5)$
   e $n^2(n - 1)$ f $12kh(2k + 3h)$
   g $7ab(a^2 - 3)$ h $17s(t^2 - u^2)$

Answers to Chapter 2 Page 20

Exercise 2·1 page 20

1. 50 25 75 $33^1/_3$ $66^2/_3$
   $^1/_2$ $^1/_4$ $^3/_4$ $^1/_3$ $^2/_3$
   20 40 60 80 10 30 70 90
   $^1/_5$ $^2/_5$ $^3/_5$ $^4/_5$ $^1/_{10}$ $^3/_{10}$ $^7/_{10}$ $^9/_{10}$
2. a £3·50 b £28 c 90p d 24p
   e £270 f £8 g £1·80 h £1·40
   i £4800 j £15000 k £140 l 9p
   m £8·40 n 18p o £1·80 p £1
3. 112 pupils
4. a 160 b 120 c 200 d 320
5. a $^{32}/_{100} = {}^8/_{25} = 0{\cdot}32$
   b $^{45}/_{100} = {}^9/_{20} = 0{\cdot}45$
   c $^{51}/_{100} = 0{\cdot}51$
   d $^{31}/_{100} = 0{\cdot}31$
   e $^{78}/_{100} = {}^{39}/_{50} = 0{\cdot}78$
   f $^8/_{100} = {}^2/_{25} = 0{\cdot}08$
   g $^1/_8 = 0{\cdot}125$
   h $^1/_{40} = 0{\cdot}025$
6. a $35\% = {}^{35}/_{100} = {}^7/_{20}$
   b $60\% = {}^{60}/_{100} = {}^3/_5$
   c $55\% = {}^{55}/_{100} = {}^{11}/_{20}$
   d $90\% = {}^{90}/_{100} = {}^9/_{10}$
   e $15\% = {}^{15}/_{100} = {}^3/_{20}$
   f $75\% = {}^{75}/_{100} = {}^3/_4$
   g $4\% = {}^4/_{100} = {}^1/_{25}$
   h $85\% = {}^{85}/_{100} = {}^{17}/_{20}$
   i $5\% = {}^5/_{100} = {}^1/_{20}$
   j $36\% = {}^{36}/_{100} = {}^9/_{25}$
   k $2^1/_2\% = {}^1/_{40}$
   l $150\% = {}^{150}/_{100} = {}^3/_2$
7. a £3·20 b £12 c £19·20 d £1680
   e £2·70 f £19·80 g £3·80 h £5·60
   i 45p j £42 k £20·40
8. 189 mm
9. 825 000 eels
10. £830·70
11. 48·4 sec
12. £153
13. 19250 feet
14. 268·8g
15. a per annum/yearly b £54 c £1254
16. a £112·50 b £56·25
17. £189
18. Brian £104
    Nicole £103·50 so Brian will get 50p more.

Exercise 2·2 page 22

1. a 14% b 20% c 24% d 80%
   e 45% f 85% g 92% h 12·5%
   i 36% j 87·5% k 75% l 62·5%
   m 65% n 50%
2. a 80% b 54% c 37·5% d 30%
3. a 80% b 20%
4. 77·8%
5. a 81·3% b 77·1% c 97·6%
6. a Aug 50% Sep 60% Oct 65%
   Nov 60% Dec 70% Jan 75%
   Feb 90% Mar 80% Apr 100%
   May 85%
   b see diagram c 73·5%
   d Generally, her test marks improve as the year goes on.
7. 49

Exercise 2·3 page 23

1. Profit £3 - % profit 20%
2. 15%
3. a 10p, 12·5% b £450, 30%
   c £480, 3% d 60p, 150%
4. £150, 30%
5. a £48, 30% b £2740, 68·5%
   c 70p, 87·5%
6. £7800
7. £5·04

Exercise 2·4 page 24

1. Final balance = £1311·72
   Total interest = £111·72
2. £34·19
3. £28529·15
4. £3121·87
5. a £27·68 b £325·12 c £42·74
6. a (i) £6540 (ii) £7128.60 b after 9 yrs
7. a 1st year £12540 2nd year £13167
   3rd year £13864.85 4th year £14544.23
   b £2544·23 c 21·2%

Exercise 2·5 page 25

1. Final value £204.80
2. a £4800 b £3600 c £2700
3. £61560
4. 12459 feet
5. £54950·40
6. a £156 b £162·24 c £168·73
7. a (i) 3% (ii) 4·8%
   b £624 c £43.26
   d (i) £31200 (ii) £33293
   (iii) £36728
8. During the 5th hour.

Exercise 2·6 page 27

1. £15000 2. £400 3. 240°C
4. 150 cm 5. 50 mph 6. £200
7. 300 8. 30°C 9. £45000

Remember Remember Ch 2 page 28

1. a £14 b £42 c £40
   d £400 e £1800 f £50
2. a £56 b £326
3. £508·80
4. £431·20
5. a £115·20 b £67·20
6. a 85% b 81·25%
7. 67·5% (yes)
8. a £55 b 27·5%
9. profit = £35 % profit = 43·75%
10. £282·33
11. £760·44
12. £6375
13. £12
14. £30

Answers to Chapter 3 Page 29

Exercise 3·1 page 29

1. a $^{21}/_5$ b $^{45}/_8$ c $^{66}/_7$ d $^{129}/_{10}$
2. a $3^3/_4$ b $6^1/_3$ c $8^2/_5$ d $7^4/_{11}$
3. a $^1/_2$ b $^1/_3$ c $^9/_{20}$ d $^7/_{24}$
   e $^7/_{12}$ f $^5/_8$ g $^{13}/_{16}$ h $^1/_{10}$
   i $^7/_{16}$ j $1^1/_2$ k $^5/_{22}$ l $^1/_4$
   m $1^1/_{12}$ n $^{37}/_{60}$ o $^3/_{20}$ p $^3/_4$
4. a $2^7/_{12}$ b $13^3/_5$ c $4^2/_3$ d $9^9/_{20}$
   e $11^1/_4$ f $1^1/_8$ g $14^1/_5$ h $17^7/_{15}$
   i $2^7/_{12}$ j $4^{15}/_{28}$ k $2^7/_{13}$ l $^{29}/_{30}$
5. a $^1/_9$ b $^7/_{16}$ c $^1/_8$ d $^1/_5$
   e $^5/_8$ f $^1/_{12}$ g $^1/_4$ h $^4/_{25}$
6. a $8^1/_6$ b $2^{16}/_{25}$ c $6^1/_3$ d $5^5/_7$
   e $3^1/_4$ f $12^3/_4$ g $7^2/_3$ h $5^3/_5$
   i $2^1/_2$ j 27 k $5^1/_3$ l $12^1/_2$
7. a $2^{13}/_{15}$ b $1^8/_{15}$
8. a $6^{19}/_{20}$ b $1^9/_{20}$
9. $^5/_{14}$
10. 63 kg
11. a $^1/_4$ b $^1/_8$
12. 18 m^3

Exercise 3·2 page 31

1. a $1^1/_4$ b $2^1/_2$
2. a $^3/_5$ b $1^3/_7$ c $^1/_2$ d $^3/_8$
   e $^9/_{20}$ f $^2/_3$ g $1^1/_{10}$ h $1^1/_3$
   i $1^1/_6$ j $1^{11}/_{24}$ k $1^5/_{27}$ l $1^2/_5$
3. $^3/_4$
4. $5^1/_3$
5. a $1^7/_8$ b $3^1/_3$
6. a $2^2/_9$ b $1^7/_{15}$ c $3^1/_3$ d $1^3/_4$
   e $4^1/_2$ f $2^8/_9$ g $^{12}/_{35}$ h $5^1/_4$
   i 4 j 3
7. $5^5/_9$ mins.

Remember Remember Ch 3 page 32

1. a $^5/_6$ b $^5/_8$ c $1^1/_{12}$ d $1^{11}/_{20}$
   e $^1/_8$ f $^3/_{10}$ g $^5/_8$ h $^1/_{12}$
   i $3^5/_6$ j $6^7/_{20}$ k $9^{14}/_{15}$ l $7^{13}/_{24}$
   m $1^3/_{10}$ n $1^7/_8$ o $5^7/_{10}$ p $1^3/_8$
2. a $^1/_6$ b $^1/_5$ c $^1/_2$ d $^1/_6$
   e $^2/_3$ f $^2/_5$ g $^7/_{20}$ h $^1/_4$

2.   i $2^1/_4$ j 3 k 4 l $7^1/_2$
     m $1^1/_2$ n 9 o 35 p $3^1/_3$

3.   a 8 b 20 c 12 d 4
     e 6 f 3 g $1/_2$ h $2^1/_5$
     i 2 j $2^1/_2$ k $3^3/_{10}$ l 2

4.   a $1/_4$ b $1/_{18}$ c $2/_{15}$ d $1/_6$
     e $3^1/_2$ f $2^1/_5$ g 4

5. $8^{13}/_{24}$

6. $11/_{50}$

Turn off that Calculator 1 page 34

1.   a 3787 b 1099 c 2263000 d 1273
     e 379 f 20736 g 670 h -8
     i 68 j 77

2.   a 1.556 b 1.861 c 6.25 d 11.418
     e 2025 f 1.19 g 0.1778 h 0.00346

3.   a 0.8 km b 6000 mm c 0.054 l   θ.0

4.   a 620 b 91 c 2200

5.   a $1/_4$ b $6/_{13}$ c $1/_{40}$

6.   a $3/_8$ b $8^7/_8$ c $17^1/_2$

7.   a $3/_{10}$ b $1/_8$ c $1^1/_3$

8.   a £410 b £225 c £2.80
     d £28 e £70 f £0.12

9.   a -14 b 286 c 8
     d -78 e -108 f -73 g 51
     h 11 i -78 j $6x$ k $-9y$
     l -90 m -297 n 81 o -10
     p $36x^2$ q -40 r 9 s -8

10. a 2.4 b 7 cm

11. a 120 km b 200 km/hr

Answers to Chapter 4 Page 35

Exercise 4·1 page 35

1.   2. (a)   (b)

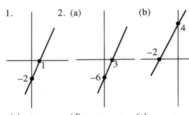

(c)   (d)   (e)

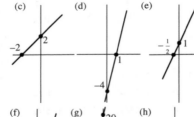

(f)   (g)   (h)

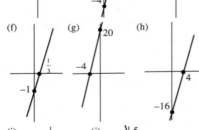

(i)   (j)

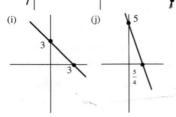

3.   4. (a)

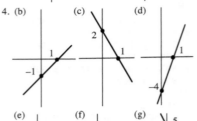

4. (b)   (c)   (d)

(e)   (f)   (g)

(h)   (i)   (j)

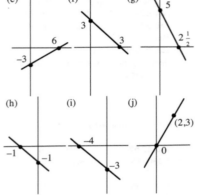

Exercise 4·2 page 36

1. $(6, 2)$
2. a $(4, 3)$ b $(-2, -7)$ c $(1, 0)$
     d $(-1, 2)$ e $(-1, -5)$ f $(0.5, -1)$
3. a $(0, 2)$ b $(6, 2)$ c $(5, 0)$
     d $(4, 0)$ e $(2, -3)$ f $(6, -3)$
4. a $(-2, 3)$ b $(0, 2)$
     c $(1, 4)$ d $(-1, -5)$
5. Lines are parallel.

Exercise 4·3 page 37

1. $(2, 5)$
2. $(1, 3)$
3. a $(1, 2)$ b $(2, 1)$ c $(3, 3)$ d $(4, 5)$
     e $(2, 4)$ f $(0, 2)$ g $(-3, 1)$ h $(-3, -3)$
4. $(2, 3)$
5. a $(3, 1)$ b $(2, 4.5)$ c $(4, 0)$ d $(-1, 1)$

Exercise 4·4 page 38

1. $(2, 3)$ 2. $(3, 1)$
3. a $(3, 5)$ b $(7, 1)$ c $(1, 4)$ d $(2, 4)$
     e $(5, 2)$ f $(2, -1)$ g $(-3, 0)$ h $(-2, -3)$
     i $(-3.5, -0.5)$ j $(0.5, 4)$
4. $(2, 2)$
5. $(1, 5)$
6. $(4, 2)$
7. a $(2, 1)$ b $(2, 3)$ c $(4, 1)$ d $(1, 3)$
     e $(-1, 1)$ f $(-2, -1)$ g $(0.5, 6)$ h $(-0.5, 0.5)$
8. a $(2, 1)$ b $(3, 1)$ c $(1, 5)$
     d $(4, 2)$ e $(-1, 2)$ f $(1, -2)$
     g $(-1, 2)$ h $(-3, -2)$ i $(0.5, -2)$
9. a $(-2, -2)$ b $(-11, -9)$ c $(0.5, -0.5)$ d $(-1, 0)$
     e $(1, 4)$ f $(-2, 3)$ g $(2, -3)$ h $(3, -1)$

Exercise 4·5 page 40

1. Sweet 4p. Lolly 1p
2. a $4x + 2y = 14$, $7x + 2y = 20$
     b £2 c £3 d £12
3. Grow-bag £4. Plant £3

4. £1.50
5. £8
6. Mouse £3. Lizard £7
7. 2 kg
8. a £9 b £5
9. a $5a + 4c = 60$, $2a + c = 21$
     b (i) £8 (ii) £5 c £57
10. White 200 sheets. Coloured 300 sheets.
11. £25
12. £105
13. £1.47
14. No. 5 jugs needs 2·55 litres.
15. 500 secs. (8 mins 20 secs)
16. a 8 cm   b 64 cm²
17. a 9 m   b 13 m²
18. a $4x + 3y = 2.30$, $3x + 5y = 2.55$
     b Orange 35p. Pear 30p.
     c 90g   d 1880g. £7.10.

Remember Remember Ch 4 page 43

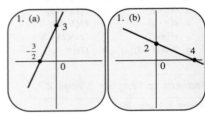

1. (a)   1. (b)

2. $(\frac{1}{2}, 3\frac{1}{2})$
3. a $(3, 1)$ b $(2, 1)$ c $(1, 2)$ d $(1, 2)$
     e $(1, 1)$ f $(2, 3)$ g $(1, 3)$ h $(5, -2)$
     i $(5, 4)$ j $(1, 8)$
4. $(5, 0)$
5. $3^1/_3$ kg
6. a $8x + 3y = 3.60$, $7x + 3y = 3.30$
     b 40p   c £2.30
7. £120
8. £1.30
9. 18 m
10. 43 cm.

Answers to Chapter 5 Page 44

Exercise 5·1 page 44

1. a 11.3 cm   b 11.7 cm
     c 6.19 m   d 5.66 mm
2. a 24 cm   b 240 cm²
3. 1512 cm²
4. 40 cm
5. $x = 8$
6. a 48 cm   b 960 cm²
7. 11.4 boxes
8. 13.9 boxes
9. a 6 cm   b 60 cm³
10. x, being smaller side, should end up < 10
11. 228 mm   12. 31 cm.

Exercise 5·2 page 46

1. $PQ^2 + QR^2 = 324 + 56.25 = 380.5 = PR^2$
     By the Converse of Pythagoras' Theorem,
     it IS a RAT.
2. $6.6^2 + 8.8^2 = 43.56 + 77.44 = 121$
     $\neq 123.21 = 11.1^2$
     Therefore, it IS NOT a RAT
3. a yes   b no

4. $84^2 + 63^2 = 7056 + 3939 = 11025 = 105^2$
By the Converse of Pythagoras' Theorem, it IS a RAT

5. $8 \cdot 1^2 + 10 \cdot 8^2 = 65 \cdot 61 + 116 \cdot 64$
$= 182 \cdot 25 = 13 \cdot 5^2$
By Converse of Pythagoras' Theorem, it IS a RAT and the flagpole could be vertical.

Exercise 5·3 page 47
1. a 13 cm   b 13·3 cm
2. AC = 100 cm => AH = 125 cm
3. 38·1 cm
4. 17·3 cm
5. a 8·49 cm   b 4·24 cm   c 9·95 cm
6. a 14·1 cm   b 10·9 cm   c 364cm²
7. a 14·4 cm   b 15·6 cm
8. a 12 cm   b 314 cm³
9. Space diagonal = 37·5 cm.
   40 cm rod is too long to fit in.
10. a B(12, 3, 1), C(12, 6, 1), D(4, 6, 1), P(4, 6, 6)
    Q(4, 3, 6), R(12, 3, 6), S(12, 6, 6)
    b 8·54 units   c 9·90 units   d 14·7

Remember Remember Ch 5   page 49
1. a 10·0 cm   b 7·48 m
2. 13·6 boxes
3. a $96^2 + 40^2 = 9216 + 1600 = 10816 = 104^2$
   By the Converse of Pythagoras' Theorem, it is a RAT
   b $24^2 + 32^2 = 576 + 1024 = 1600$
   $\neq 1521 = 39^2$
   Therefore, it IS NOT a RAT
   c $9 \cdot 3^2 + 12 \cdot 4^2 = 86 \cdot 49 + 153 \cdot 76$
   $= 240 \cdot 25 = 15 \cdot 5^2$
   By Converse of Pythagoras' Theorem, it is a RAT
4. $39^2 + 52^2 = 1521 + 2704 = 4225 = 65^2$
   This means angle between diagonals = 90°
   Because the 2 smaller parts of one diagonal are equal, the longer diagonal is a line of symmetry, - which means it IS a kite.
5. a 34 cm   b 39·4 cm
6. 21·8 cm
7. Height of pyramid = 13·9 cm,
   Height of cone = 8 cm
   Volume of pyramid = 296·4 cm³,
   Volume of cone = 301·4 cm³
   Cone has bigger volume by 5 cm³approx.

Answers to Chapter 6 Page 50

Exercise 6·1 page 50
1. $1/15$
2. Ramp 1 $2/9$ (0·2222)
   Ramp 2 $5/19$ (0·263)   Ramp 2 is steeper
3. $8/25$ 0·3 0·26 25%
4. Ladder on left NOT safe (2·66666 < 4)
   Ladder on right Safe (4 < 4·25 < 5)
5. a $1/3$ b $3/4$
6. red - 1, blue - $4/45$, green - $1/10$
7. $-1/2$
8. a $-1/2$ b $-5/7$ c -3 d $-1/7$
   e 0   f undefined
9. a $1/2$ b $5/2$ c $-8/5$ d -1
10. a (i) 2 (ii) -3 (iii) 2 (iv) $-1/2$
    b (i) $5/2$ (ii) 0 (iii) 4 (iv) $-1/3$
    c ABCD (since $m_{AB} = m_{CD}$)

11. $m_{JL} = 3/5$ $m_{MK} = 5$
12. Proof
13. $m = 3/2$
14. $m_1 = 5/11$ $\neq m_2 = 11/26$
15. (2, 4), (4, 0), (5, -2) etc

Exercise 6·2 page 52
1. a m = 4, (0, 1)   b m = 6, (0, -4)
   c m = -3, (0, 6)   d m = 1/2, (0, 5)
   e m = $-1/3$, (0, -7) f m = -2, (0, 10)
   g m = -1, (0, -3)   m = 0, (0, 4)
2. a y = 2x + 1
   b y = -3x + 5
   c y = $-1/2$x + 4
   d y = -6x
3. a m = 3   b y = 3x + 4
4. a m = 1/3, (0, 2),   y = $1/3$x + 2
   b m = 2, (0, 1),   y = 2x + 1
   c m = 2/3, (0, 2),   y = $2/3$x + 2
   d m = -2, (0, 6),   y = -2x + 6
5. a c = 1   b m = 1/3
   c y = $1/3$x + 1
6. y = 2x - 2
7. a y = x + 2   b y = $-1/3$x + 6
   c y = $2/3$x   d y = 3
8. a see drawing   b m = 7/3
   c (0, -2)   d y = 7/3x - 2
9. y = 2x + 5
10. a y = $3/2$x - 3   b y = $1/3$x + 2
    c y = -x + 3   d x = 4
11. a B b C c E
    d D   e A   f F
12. a y = 3x + 3   b y = $1/2$x - 1
    c y = -4x - 4   d y = 5x - 10
13. both have gradients = $3/2$
14. $m_1 = 1/2$, $m_2 = 1/3$
15. a y = 3x + 2   b y = -x - 4
    c x = 2   d y = 2x - 3

Exercise 6·3 page 54
1. y = $1/2$x + 4
2. a y = $1/2$x + 3·5   b y = 3x - 17
   c y = -x + 11   d y = $-1/3$x + 18
3. a y = $1/2$x + 1   b y = x
   c y = -x + 2   d   y = $-1/3$x - 1
4. a y = x + 5   b x = -1
   c y = $-3/2$x - 11   d y = -16x
5. a y = $3/4$x + 33   b a = -12

Exercise 6·4 page 55
1. a,c,d and f
2. a hours(h) 0 1 2 3 4
   pay(£p) 0 6 12 18 24
   b see diagram   c m = 6 (0, 0)
   d P = 6h   e (i) £48 (ii) £75
   f 12 hours
3. a hours(h) 0 1   2   3   4
   pay(£p) 0 9·50 19 28·50 38
   see diagram   b p=9·5h
   c £57   d 23 hours
4. a Length(Lm) 0 1 2 3 4
   Hours(H) 0 3 6 9 12
   see diagram   b H=3L c 15 hours
5. a Time(t) 0 1 2 3 4
   Roses(R) 0 7 14 21 28

see diagram   b R = 7t   t = 5 hours
6. a (i) £60 (ii) £115   b 6 hours
7. a (i) £30 (ii) £5 an hour
   b (i) m = 5 (ii) (0,30)
   c C = 5t + 30 d (i) £65   (ii) £77·50
   e 5 hours
8. a C = 5h + 20   b £45
9. a m = -10   b H = -10s + 100
   c 50m   d 10 sec
10. a Days(d)   1   2   3   4
    Cost(£C) 25 35 45 55
    b see diagram   c C = 10d + 15
    d £85
11. a Days(d)   0 1 2 3 4
    Cost(£C) 5 11 17 23 29
    b see diagram   c C = 6 D + 5, 9 days
12. a F = 20h + 60   b C = 5d + 10
    c H = -2t + 20   d T = 4h - 6
13. a Hire-a-car
    Days(d)   0 1 2 3 4
    Cost(£C) 40 50 60 70 80
    Car Rent Co.
    Days(d)   0 1 2 3 4
    Cost(£C) 10 30 50 70 90
    b see diagram   c 3 day
    d Hire-a-car   H = 10d + 40
    Car Rent Co.   C = 20d + 10
    e (i) either   (ii) Hire-a-car

Exercise 6·5 page 58
1. $3/4$
2. 3
3. -1 - sloped downwards
4. a $1/3$ b $1/2$ c 3
   d $7/3$ e $-2/5$ f -2
5. a 0   b horizontal (parallel to x-axis)
6. not possible - error
7. a $5/2$ - up   b $-1/2$ - down
   c -7 - down   d 1 - up
8. $1/2$ and $1/2$ - parallel
9. b = 9
10. a p = 9 b q = 7 c r = 1
11. a both = 5   b both = $3/7$
    c parallelogram
12. show $m_{PQ} = m_{RS} = 2/5$
    show $m_{PS} = m_{QR} = 5/3$
13. $m_{IL} = -4$, $m_{KL} = 1$
14. a $m_{RT} = -1$, $m_{TS} = -1$
    b must lie on the same line
    c see sketch
15. Check gradients are the same

Exercise 6·6 page 59
1. y = 2x + 4
2. a y = 2x + 3   b y = 6x - 1
   c y = x + 4   d y = 2x - 8
   e y = -x + 1   f y = -x + 5
   g y = -2x + 5   h y = 14x + 1
   i y = 1   j y = 6·5x + 6
3. a y = -x + 14   b y = x - 6
4. y = -x - 5
5. y = x + 2
6. a y = $1/2$x + 2   b y = $1/4$x + 1
   c y= $2/3$x - 3   d y = $1/3$x - 2
   e y = $1/5$x + 4   f y = $1/2$x - 5
   g y = $3/4$x + 1   h y = $3/5$x - 2
   i y = 8x - 8   j y = 2·5x - 7·75
7. a y = x + 1½   b y = 3x - ½
   c y = x + $4/3$ d y = $2/3$x + $1/3$

7. e $y = \tfrac{1}{2}x + \tfrac{1}{2}$ f $y = \tfrac{4}{5}x - \tfrac{1}{2}$
8. a D(1, 2)   b $y = \tfrac{1}{5}x - \tfrac{9}{5}$
   c $y = 5x + 3{\cdot}5$
9. a $k = 6$ b $h = 4$
   c $t = -6$
10. a $y = 2x + 4$ b $y = 3x + 5$
    c $y = \tfrac{3}{2}x - 12$
11. $m = {}^{(p-1)}/_{(1-p)} = -1$
12. Proof

Exercise 6·7 page 61

1. $m = {}^{-2}/_3$ $(0, \tfrac{1}{3})$
2. $m = \tfrac{3}{2}$ $(0, {}^{-3}/_4)$
3. a $m = -\tfrac{1}{2}$ $(0, {}^{-3}/_2)$ b $m = -\tfrac{1}{2}$ $(0, \tfrac{1}{2})$
   c $m = 1$ $(0, {}^{-1}/_3)$ d $m = 3$ $(0, -2)$
   e $m = -2$ $(0, 16)$ f $m = -3$ $(0, -1)$
   g $m = -\tfrac{1}{3}$ $(0, -1)$ h $m = \tfrac{1}{4}$ $(0, -4)$
4. a $y = -2x + 4$ b see diagram
5. see diagrams
6. $m = 1$ $(0, 2)$
7. a $m = 3$ $(0, 5)$ b $m = \tfrac{1}{2}$ $(0, {}^{-1}/_4)$
   c $m = -2$ $(0, 5)$ d $m = -2$ $(0, 4)$
   e $m = -\tfrac{1}{4}$ $(0, {}^{3}/_2)$ f $m = {}^{5}/_4$ $(0, \tfrac{1}{4})$
8. $m = \tfrac{1}{2}$ $(0, -2)$

Remember Remember 6 page 62

1. $m = \tfrac{1}{5}$
2. $\tfrac{1}{3}$ $0{\cdot}3$ 29% $0{\cdot}28$
3. a $\tfrac{3}{2}$ b $\tfrac{1}{2}$ c 0 d $-\tfrac{5}{7}$
4. a $\tfrac{5}{2}$ b $-\tfrac{4}{3}$
5. a $m = 4$ $(0, 1)$ b $m = -1$ $(0, 3)$
6. a $y = 2x - 3$ b $y = -x - 5$
   c $y = -5x$ d $y = 5$
   e $x = -1$
7. a $y = 2x - 7$ b $y = \tfrac{1}{2}x + 1$
8. a $m = -3$ $(0, 2)$ b $m = -\tfrac{4}{5}$ $(0, 0)$
9. $y = -\tfrac{1}{2}x + 2$
10. a 1   2   3   4   5
      15   20   25   30   35
    b sketch
    c $C = 5d + 10$ d £45
    e 17 days
11. a $y = 2x + 2$ b $y = x + 4$
    c $y = x - 5$ d $y = \tfrac{1}{3}x + 2\tfrac{2}{3}$
    e $y = -\tfrac{1}{3}x + 1$ f $y = -\tfrac{1}{2}x + 19$
    g $y = 14x + 11$ h $y = -2x + 4\tfrac{1}{2}$

Turn off that Calculator 2 page 6

1. a $78{\cdot}914$ b 320 c $941{\cdot}25$ d $0{\cdot}0855$
2. 681
3. a 4700 mm   b 0·071 kg
   c 5·4 l   d 0·03 l
   e 87500 cm   f 3050000 g
   g 32400 secs
4. a $\tfrac{2}{3}$ b $\tfrac{3}{13}$ c $\tfrac{3}{20}$
5. a £1·50 b £2·25 c 8100
   d £0·21 e 808 f 16   g £2500
6. a -43   b 30   c 12
   d -135 e 450 f 400   g -64000
   h -11 i 5 j -10 k 27
7. a (3, 1) b (-1, -2), (0, -6), (4, -5), (3, -1)
8. a 0010 b 1010
   c 1615 d 1910 e 2150
9. a 3 hr 47 mins   b 12 hr 1 min
10. 20 km/hr
11. 757 cm²
12. 30 cm

---

13. a 6   b 386   c 4·75
14. a 2 dills b 30 dills

Answers to Chapter 7 Page 65

Exercise 7·1 page 65

1. a $3(a + 4)$ b $2(x + 3y)$ c $2(4g + 3h)$
   d $a(b + c)$ e $p(q + 1)$ f $k(j + k)$
   g $g(fg + 1)$ h $3m(n + p)$ i $3(2x + 3y)$
   j $8(3b - 2a)$ k $4d(3c - 2)$ l $3p(3 + 7p)$
2. a $6(a + 4)$ b $2(x + 6)$ c $7(p - 5)$
   d $11(a + b)$ e $7(p - q)$ f $4(c - 4h)$
   g $8(m - 3)$ h $13(n + 3)$ i $2(2x + 5y)$
   j $3(2u - 7v)$ k $5(6x - 11y)$ l $6(r - 7u)$
   m $6(2s + 5)$ n $11(4u - 3)$ o $9(3x - 5y)$
   p $24(3a + c)$ q $11(11t - 1)$ r $14(3k + 2)$
   s $17(h - 3)$ t $32(3z - 4)$
3. a $b(2 + c)$ b $x(8 - v)$ c $c(d + g)$
   d $a(a + 3)$ e $t(5 - t)$ f $2c(c - 4)$
   g $4h(k + g)$ h $5v(w - 2x)$ i $17s(r - 1)$
   j $y(3y + 7)$ k $4x(3x - 4y)$ l $3g(2g + 3)$
   m $2d(2 + 7d)$ n $13a(4 - a)$ o $3y(y - 7c)$
   p $2n(9m + 16n)$ q $a^2(1 + 4b)$ r $ab(b + 6)$
   s $abc(c + 7)$ t $abc(ac + 7b)$
4. a $a(a + 4b - 7)$ b $x(2y - 4z + 1)$
   c $p^2(p + 1)$ d $4n(n^2 - 4)$
   e $ac(6a + c)$ f $6rs(3s - 5)$
   g $4x(2x - 3a)$ h $\tfrac{1}{5}h(g + j)$
5. a $3bc(5a^2c + 4b)$ b $3ce(5de + 4b^2)$
   c $3kgh(7kh + 8kg - 5)$
   d $3ps(7pts + 8t^2s - 5p)$

Exercise 7·2 page 66

1. a $(x - 2)(x + 2)$ b $(a - 4)(a + 4)$
   c $(b - 5)(b + 5)$ d $(x - 1)(x + 1)$
   e $(1 - k)(1 + k)$ f $(9 - w)(9 + w)$
   g $(8 - h)(8 + h)$ h $(10 - x)(10 + x)$
   i $(x - b)(x + b)$ j $(w - v)(w + v)$
   k $(2a - 1)(2a + 1)$ l $(x - 5y)(x + 5y)$
   m $(6 - 7p)(6 + 7p)$ n $(9a - 2b)(9a + 2b)$
   o $(11v - 10w)(11v + 10w)$
   p $(8p - 9q)(8p + 9q)$ q $(1 - 4a)(1 + 4a)$
   r $(5 - 9x)(5 + 9x)$ s $(7 - 2k)(7 + 2k)$
   t $(1 - 12y)(1 + 12y)$
2. a $2(x - 3)(x + 3)$ b $3(p - 1)(p + 1)$
   c $5(a + 4)(a - 4)$
   d $6(x - 2)(x + 2)(x^2 + 4)$
   e $4(g - 2)(g + 2)$ f $7(x - y)(x + y)$
   g $6(v + 5u)(v - 5u)$ h $10(a - 3b)(a + 3b)$
   i $19(x - y)(x + y)$ j $a(w - v)(w + v)$
   k $\pi(m - n)(m + n)$ l $k(p - 6q)(p + 6q)$
   m $A(r - 3s)(r + 3s)$ n $d(d + 2)(d - 2)$
   o $3x(3x - 4)(3x + 4)$
   p $(a - 1)(a + 1)(a^2 + 1)$
   q $(1 - k)(1 + k)(1 + k^2)$
   r $(p - q)(p + q)(p^2 + q^2)$
   s $(1 - 2y)(1 + 2y)(1 + 4y^2)$
   t $3(d - 2)(d + 2)(d^2 + 4)$
3. a Pink area $= k^2 - 5^2 = (k - 5)(k + 5)$
   b 47·25cm²

Exercise 7·3 page 67

1. a $(x + 1)(x + 1)$ b $(a + 2)(a + 1)$
   c $(k + 5)(k + 2)$ d $(d + 7)(d + 2)$
   e $(x - 1)(x - 1)$ f $(b - 3)b - 3)$
   g $(c - 6)(c - 3)$ h $(w - 3)(w - 8)$
   i $(x + 4)(x - 1)$ j $(n - 3)(n - 2)$
   k $(p + 5)(p - 3)$ l $(q + 6)(q - 3)$
   m $(x - 4)(x + 1)$ n $(r - 7)(r + 1)$
   o $(y - 6)(y + 2)$ p $(h - 10)(h + 2)$
2. a $(x - 6)(x + 1)$ b $(x + 3)(x + 5)$
   c $(x - 5)(x + 1)$ d $(x - 9)(x - 2)$

---

   e $(y - 5)(y + 3)$ f $(y + 8)(y - 1)$
   g $(y - 7)(y - 2)$ h $(y + 6)(y + 2)$
   i $(a - 7)(a - 7)$ j $(a - 11)(a + 1)$
   k $(a + 6)(a - 5)$ l $(a - 4)(a - 5)$
   m $(c - 5)(c - 3)$ n $(c + 7)(c - 3)$
   o $(c - 9)(c + 3)$ p $(c - 8)(c - 2)$
   q $(k + 10)(k - 1)$ r $(k - 9)(k + 1)$
   s $(k - 7)(k + 5)$ t $(k + 6)(k - 4)$
   u $(v + 4)(v - 2)$ v $(v - 3)(v - 10)$
   w $(v - 4)(v + 3)$ x $(v - 8)(v - 5)$
3. a $(2x + 3)(x + 1)$ b $(2a + 1)(a + 3)$
   c $(3y + 2)(2y + 1)$ d $(3g + 5)(g + 3)$
   e $(6k - 1)(2k - 1)$ f $(2b - 1)(b - 3)$
   g $(4c - 5)(2c - 1)$ h $(3x + 4)(x - 2)$
   i $(3a + 1)(a - 2)$ j $(5p - 1)(p + 1)$
   k $(2m - 1)(m + 1)$ l $(3q + 1)(q - 1)$
   m $(4c + 3)(2c - 1)$ n $(4n - 1)(2n + 3)$
   o $(4w - 5)(3w + 1)$ p $(2c + 3)(2c + 3)$
   q $(4k + 1)(6k - 1)$ r $(1 + 6x)(1 - 3x)$
   s $(5 + y)(3 - 2y)$ t $(x + 6y)(x + 2y)$
   u $(p - 12q)(p + 2q)$ v $(b + 2c)(b + c)$
   w $(a - 7b)(a + 2b)$ x $(2u + v)(u - 3v)$
   y $(3g + 4h)(3g - 2h)$
   z $(3\sin\theta - 2)(3\sin\theta - 2)$
4. a $2(x - 10)(x + 10)$ b $3(x - 3)x + 3)$
   c $4(x - 2)(x + 2)$ d $7(x - 3)(x + 3)$
   e $5(x - 1)(x + 1)$ f $10(x - 2)(x + 2)$
   g $2(7 - x)(7 + x)$ h $14(2 - x)(2 + x)$
   i $3(x + 4)(x - 5)$ j $2(x + 4)(x - 8)$
   k $2(x + 1)(x - 24)$ l $11(x + 2)(x - 3)$
   m $3(x - 1)(x + 7)$ n $2(x - 2)(x - 16)$
   o $9(x + 1)(x + 1)$ p $3(12x + 1)(x + 1)$

Exercise 7·4 page 68

1. $6(x + 6y)$ 2. $(p + 7)(p - 7)$
3. $(y + 3)(y + 3)$ 4. $k(k - 1)$
5. $(v - 3)(v + 2)$ 6. $(1 - a)(1 + a)$
7. $d(e + h - j)$ 8. $3(c - 2)(c + 2)$
9. $m(m - 8)$ 10. $(q - 1)(q - 1)$
11. $(b - 1)(b + 1)$ 12. $b(b - 1)$
13. $(b - 2)(b + 1)$ 14. $2(t - 3)(t + 3)$
15. $2x(x - 16)$ 16. $a^2(a - 1)$
17. $(2p + 5)(p - 1)$ 18. $(3n + 1)(3n + 1)$
19. $(9 - x)(9 + x)$ 20. $2(5 - c)(5 + c)$
21. $6y(3 - y)$ 22. $(9 - 2b)(9 + 2b)$
23. $(2k + 1)(k - 1)$ 24. $14(x^2 + 3y^2)$
25. $14(m - 2n)(m + 2n)$ 26. $(4x - 1)(4x - 1)$
27. $3pq(p - 3q)$ 28. $(1 - u)(1 - u)$
29. $3x(x - 3)(x + 3)$ 30. $(3a - 2)(2a + 3)$
31. $4(x + 2)(x - 1)$ 32. $10w(1 - 2w)(1 + 2w)$
33. $a(k - m)(k + m)$ 34. $(2x + 3)(x - 5)$
35. $p^5(p^2 - p - 1)$ 36. $(x + 3)(x - 3)(x^2 + 9)$
37. $2(x + 3)(x - 3)$ 38. $17(x - 3)$
39. $2(x^2 - 6x + 18)$ 40. $3(3xy - 15x + y)$
41. $5(x - 5)(x + 5)$ 42. $4(x - 3)(x - 3)$
43. $3(x - 7)(x + 7)$ 44. $2(3x - 1)(2x + 3)$
45. $3(x - 1)(x - 8)$ 46. $4(2x - 1)(2x - 1)$
47. $6y(4x + 3)$ 48. $a(a + 4b - 7)$

Remember Remember 7 page 69

1. a $4(a + 6)$ b $7(3a - 4b)$
   c $c(d + g)$ d $2b(b - 5)$
   e $n^2(n - 1)$ f $12kh(2k + 3h)$
   g $(r - 10)(r + 10)$ h $5(q - 2)(q + 2)$
   i $(w - 8)(w - 2)$ j $(2m + 3)(m + 2)$
   k $(5b - 2)(b - 5)$ l $(x - 2y)(x + y)$
   m $(3x - y)(2x + 3y)$ n $(x - 7y)(x - 7y)$
   o $(1 - 5a)(1 + 5a)$ p $9(n + 1)(n - 2)$
   q $3p(p - 16)$ r $7ab(a^2 - 3)$
   s $17s(t - u)(t + u)$
   t $(x - y)(x - y)(x + y)(x + y)$
2. a (i) $3p^2 + 4p + 1$ (ii) $p^2 - 4p + 4$
      (iii) $2p^2 + 8p - 10$
   b $2(p + 5)(p - 1)$

Exercise 8·1 page 70

1. a 4 cm   b 18·5 cm   c 19·5 cm
   d 14·9 cm   e 4·0 cm   f 36·9 cm
2. a 61·9°   b 46·2°   c 22·0°
   d 47·4°   e 49·0°   f 34·7°
3. 24·6 m
4. 69·9 m
5. 14·0°
6. a sketch of rectangle 20 cm by 8 cm
   b 21·8°, 90° and 68·2°   c 21·5 cm
7. 30°
8. 36·9°
9. 41·8°
10. a 25·9°   b 21·1 m
11. 2·29°
12. a 11·6 m   b 9·58 m
13. 108 cm^2
14. a 32·7 cm   b 52·4 cm^2 c 12·8 cm
15. 58·5°
16. a 9·17 cm   b 39·8°
17. a 67·8 cm   b 55·3°
18. a 146·3°   b 315°

Exercise 8·2 page 73

1. a 30·8 cm^2 b 45 cm^2 c 102·9 cm^2
2. a 124 cm^2 b 73·4 cm^2
3. 15·2 m^2
4. 53·4 m^2
5. a 24°   b 104 cm^2
6. a 101 m^2 b 470 m^2 c 465 m^2
7. 209 cm^2
8. £33·73
9. 64·2°
10. 1590 mm^2
11. Yes - area = 71 m^2 and £45 buys 75 m^2
12. Yes - Area = 11·9 m^2
13. a (i) 0·5   (ii) 0·766   (iii) 0·174
   (iv) 0·966   (v) 0·087   (vi) 0·891
   b Sin a = sin (180 - a)
14. a 120°   b 135°   c 70°
   d 168°   e 3°   f 179°
15. X = 55°   Y = 125°

Exercise 8·3 page 76

1. a 19·1 cm   b 52·4 cm
2. a 8·05 cm   b 2·05 cm   c 260 mm
3. a 80°   b 25·2 cm
4. a 9°   b 12·9 cm
5. AM = 155 mm
6. a 452 km   b 235 km
7. 12·1 m
8. a 20·0 m   b 42·2 m
9. a 24·1 ft   b 7·50 ft   c 23·2 ft
10. 1586 m
11. a 102°   b 116 cm
12. a
   b Tiger   c 64·5 km
13. 028°

Exercise 8·4 page 79

1. 145°
2. a 52·2°   b 46·5°   c 50·5°
   d 134°   e 151°   f 22·4°
3. 111°
4. ∠ACB = 42·8°,   ∠CBA = 57·2°
5. a 108°   b 127·7°   c 74°
6. 59°   7. 59°
8. 11·7° and 26·3°
9. 156°

Exercise 8·5 page 81

1. a 7·51 cm   b 29·1 cm
2. a 25·0 cm   b 10·4 km   c 214 mm
3. 2·68 km
4. 5·60 cm
5. 103 cm
6. 72·7 m
7. 61·2 km
8. a see sketch   b 14·2 miles
9. 40·5 km

Exercise 8·6 page 83

1. a $CosQ = \dfrac{p^2 + r^2 - q^2}{2pr}$ b $CosP = \dfrac{q^2 + r^2 - p^2}{2qr}$
   c $CosR = \dfrac{p^2 + q^2 - r^2}{2pq}$
2. a 39·5°   b 83·6°   c 74·5°   d 52·7°
3. 117°
4. a Proof   b Proof
5. 98·1°
6. 43·6°
7. a 049·5°   b 60·6°

Exercise 8·7 page 85

1. a 119 m   b 91·4 m
2. a 35·1 m   b 28·8 m
3. a 72·1 km   b 46·4 cm
4. 178 miles
5. a 36·9 mm   b 12·3°
6. a see sketch   b 61·5 m
7. a 112° & 32°   b 6·66 m   c 6·18 m

Exercise 8·8 page 87

1. a 27·5 m^2 b 734 m^2
2. 98·7 mm
3. 46·3°
4. 9·89 cm
5. 141°
6. a 72°   b 108°
7. 2·56 m
8. a Proof   b 54·6 m
9. a Proof   b 36·2 km
10. 20·6 m
11. a ∠TBA = 44·9°,   ∠TAB = 57·1°
   b 032·9°   c 314·9°
12. 54·1 miles

Remember Remember 8 page 89

1. a 74·4 cm^2 b 16 700 mm^2
2. 30° or 150°
3. 129°
4. 13·2 km
5. 12·7 km
6. 43·8°
7. a 32·6 m   b 13·8 m
8. a Proof   b 154 km

Exercise 9·1 page 90

1. a $^3/_4$ b $^4/_5$ c $^5/_9$ d $^2/_5$
   e $^1/_3$ f $^3/_8$ g $^3/_{10}$ h $^1/_{19}$
2. a y b a^2 c $^1/_b$ d 1
   e $^1/_{p^3}$ f $^1/_{q^3}$ g $^1/_{g^6}$ h t^3
3. a 3   b 2   c $4x$ d 11
   e $^{3x}/_4$ f $^1/_{2k}$ g $^1/_5$ h $^{3m}/_{13}$
4. a $6a$ b $^9/_5$ c $^3/_{2x}$ d p
   e xy f y^2 g $^{pq}/_2$ h $8b$

5. a pq b p^2 c a^2b^2 d $2e$
   e 1   f gh g m^2n h $^{2x}/_3$
6. a $(a + 3)$ b $^1/_{(b-2)}$
   c $(c - 4)^3$ d $d + 1$
   e $(e - 6)^2$ f $^1/_{(f+7)^3}$
   g $^1/_{(2a-1)}$ h 1
   i $(5 - w)$ j $^1/_{(3-4v)^2}$
   k $(9 + t)^2$ l $^1/_{(a^2+1)}$
   m $^1/_{(4-3x^2)^2}$ n $p^2 - 2p + 1$
   o $^2/_q$ p $^1/_{(h+j)}$
7. a $(x + 2)$ b $(p + 3)$
   c $^1/_{(a+3)}$ d $^{(2q+1)}/_{(q-5)}$
   e $^{(m+2)}/_{(m+1)}$ f 1
   g $^{(3x+7)}/_{(3x+6)}$ h $^{(1+3p)}/_{(1-2p)}$
   i $^{2(1-x)}/_{3(1+x)}$

Exercise 9·2 page 92

1. a $a(a - 6)$ b $(p + 3)(p - 3)$
   c $(y + 1)(y + 8)$ d $6(2q - 3)$
   e $(x - 4)(x - 4)$ f $(k - 2)(k + 3)$
   g $(2v + 1)(v - 4)$ h $4(d + 5)(d - 5)$
2. a $^{(a-2)}/_3$ b $^1/_{(b-5)}$
   c $^1/_{(p+1)}$ d $^{(q-5)}/_{(q+5)}$
3. a $^1/_4$ b $^1/_2$ c 3   d $^a/_7$
4. a $^1/_k$ b $^1/_{(c+3)}$ c $^3/_{(g-5)}$ d $x + 1$
5. a $^1/_{(x-1)}$ b $x + 3$ c $^x/_{(x-1)}$
6. a $4x - 1$ b $^{(x-1)}/_{(x+7)}$
   c $^{3(x+y)}/_{(x-y)}$
7. a $^{(x-3)}/_5$ b $^{(3x-1)}/_2$ c $^5/_{(x-1)}$
8. a $^{(x-2)}/_{(x+1)}$ b $^{(2x+3)}/_{(x-1)}$
   c $^p/_{(x-y)}$
9. a $^{-1}/_m$ b 1   c $u^2 + 1$

Exercise 9·3 page 93

1. a $^4/_7$ b $^{13}/_{24}$ c $^7/_{12}$ d $^{23}/_{24}$
2. a $^8/_p$ b $^6/_m$
   c $^{(6y-x)}/_{xy}$ d $^{(4w+11v)}/_{vw}$
   e $^{(3n+7m)}/_{mn}$ f $^{(9d-8c)}/_{cd}$
   g $^{11}/_{3d}$ h $^{(4v-6w)}/_{12}$
3. a $^{(15n-4m)}/_{10mn}$ b $^{(8y+5x)}/_{10xy}$
   c $^{(15s-16a)}/_{24as}$ d $^{(9h+7e)}/_{12eh}$
4. a $^{(r^2+s^2)}/_{rs}$ b $^{(b^2-c^2)}/_{bc}$
   c $^{(5bx+3ax)}/_{ab}$ d $^{(2p-q)}/_{4a}$
5. a $^{(2+3a)}/_{a^2}$ b $^{(1-g)}/_{g^2}$
   c $^{(7x-2)}/_{x^2}$ d $^{(5-5t)}/_{t^2}$
   e $^{(20-2m)}/_{5m^2}$ f $^{(45b-24)}/_{20b^2}$
   g $^{(8x^2-15y^2)}/_{12xy}$ h $^{(3g^2+10h^2)}/_{18gh}$
6. a $^{(5a-1)}/_6$ b $^{(7p+1)}/_{12}$
   c $^{(3w+6)}/_8$ d $^{(9x+14)}/_{20}$
   e $^{(5g+7)}/_{18}$ f $^{(3h-5)}/_4$
7. a $^{(x+10)}/_6$ b $^{(3w+31)}/_{10}$
   c $^{(p-7)}/_{12}$ d $^1/_2$
   e $^1/_{12}$ f $^{(22-k)}/_{18}$

8.   a $(5x+9)/(x+1)(x+2)$ b $(5x-12)/(x-2)(x-3)$
    c $(7x+18)/(x-1)(x+4)$ d $(5x+4)/(x+1)(x+2)$
    e $(2x+11)/(x+1)(x-2)$ f $(34-4x)/(x-1)(x-7)$

9.   a $(3x-2)/x(x-1)$ b $(4x-15)/x(x-3)$
    c $(9x-4)/x(x-2)$ d $(8x-6)/x^2$
    e $(8x-1)/x^2$ f $(3x+2)/x^2$
    g $(10x-2)/x^2$ h 0
    i $2x/(2-x)$

10. a $-5/7$ b 6
    c $11/3$ d 15

Exercise 9·4 page 95
1.   a $2/7$ b $7/15$ c $1/2$ d $4/25$
2.   a $1/5$ b $9/10$ c $5/3$ d 8
3.   a $p^2/8$ b $10/a^2$ c $1/3$ d 6
    e $1/28$ f $2g^2/3$ g $10/3w$ h $6t$
4.   a 2 b $1/3$ c $p^2/10$ d $8/5$
    e 3 f 18 g k^2 h $2/d$
5.   a $a/3$ b $1/b$ c $6g$ d $q^2/2$
    e $3v^2$ f n g $3k^2$ h $5/q$
6.   a $m/2$ b 4 c kn d $1/5b$
    e $h/3$ f $1/5$ g $2v^2w$ h $16aq^2$
7.   a $1/28x$ b $4/p$ c $n/3$
    d $(1+a)/(1+b)$ e $1/(8-4k)(8-h)$
8.   square : $x^2/9$ rectangle : $x^2/3$
9.   breadth = $a(a+1)$

Remember Remember Ch 9 page 96
1.   a ab b $m/3$
    c $1/(g+h)$ d $(3q+1)/(q-7)$
2.   a $2x-1$ b $1/4$
    c $5/(a-7)$ d $m/9$
    e $1/(x+3)$ f $(y+1)/(y-6)$
    g $(x+5)/3$ h $(1-w)/(5+w)$
    i $(a-4)/(a+5)$ j $(3v+1)/(v-4)$
    k $(p+q)/(p-3q)$
3.   a $(6y-x)/xy$ b $(1-g)/g^2$
    c $(7x-2)/x^2$ d $(2x^2-3y^2)/4xy$
    e $1/12a$ f $(1-c-c^2)/c^2$
    g $(x-1)/x$ h $(9x+3)/20$
    i $5/6$ j $(4x+10)/(x-2)(x+1)$
    k $(p^2-2pq-q^2)/(p+q)(p-q)$
    l $1/(x-1)$ m $(a+4)/(a^2+4a+3)$
4.   a $1/16$ b $10/a^2$
    c c/a d $y/3$
    e $1/4$ f $1/6a$
    g $7p^2q$ h $50mn^3$
    i $1/(3+2a)^2(1-a)^3$ j $(2-x)/(12-6x) = 1/6$

Turn off that Calculator 3 page 98
1.   a -399 b 860 c 11 d 20
    e 580 f 1·63 g 0·0864 h 0·00333
2.   a 40   b 600
    c 0·054   d 0·000036

---

    e 0·0017   f 468000
    g 10m/sec
3.   a 254 b 377·5 c 440
4.   a $1/12$ b $7/48$ c $1/40$
5.   a $7/20$ b $75/8$ c $231/3$
6.   a $3/5$ b $1/8$ c $11/3$
7.   a £68 b 75 kg c 2·3 m
    d 15 g e 42 ml f \$52·50 g 24p
8.   a -11 b 308 c 21
    d -47 e -48 f -145 g 61
    h -168 i -136 j 0   k $-40y$
    l -91 m -1 n 36 o -130
    p $48x^2$ q -40 r 50 s -9
9.   a 72 s b 168 m c 22·5°
10. a (i) -1, (0, 3)   (ii) $-1/3$, $(0, -1/3)$
    b See sketches
11. a 80 m b 69

Answers to Chapter 10 Page 99

Exercise 10·1 page 99
1.   a $x = b + c$ b $x = y - 5$
    c $x = s - r$ d $x = p + a$
    e $x = g - h$ f $x = m + t$
    g $x = c - 7$ h $x = l - k$
2.   a $x = pq$ b $x = 9m$
    c $x = 30$ d $x = nr$
    e $x = l/k$ f $x = gh/4$
    g $x = ab/c$ h $x = dw/4v$
3.   a $x = (a-5)/2$ b $x = (q-p)/4$
    c $x = (r+q)/5$ d $x = (m+y)/7$
    e $x = (w-b)/a$ f $x = (g-2)/c$
    g $x = (b-q)/m$ h $x = (v-e)/w$
4.   a $x = 9$ b $x = 2y - 1$
    c $x = 11$ d $x = 4g + 7$
    e $x = bc - 2$ f $x = rs + 9$
    g $x = de + k$ h $x = wv - t$
5.   a $b = (P-2a)/2$ b $y = A/a$
6. $K = 8M/5$
7.   a $w = P/8$ b 120 cm
8.   a £118
    b $n = (c-20)/7$, 30 days
9.   a $f = c - 6m$ b $m = (C-f)/6$
10. a $P = 3a + 20$ b $a = (P-20)/3$
11. a (i) $A = (T-8U)/15$ (ii) $U = (T-15A)/8$
    b 8 adults

Exercise 10·2 page 101
1.   a $p = y/a - qb$ $C = k/b + d$
    c $n = p - m/q$ d $b = k/(c+d)$
    e $a = (bc^2+4b)/4$ f $y = x - 2p/w$
2.   a $n = \sqrt{\dfrac{m}{k}}$ b $r = \sqrt{\dfrac{V}{\pi h}}$
    c $p = \sqrt{r^2 - q^2}$ d $b = \sqrt{\dfrac{a^2-d}{2a}}$
    e $v = \sqrt{\dfrac{2w}{u}}$ f $h = \sqrt[3]{\dfrac{4w}{P}}$
3.   a $a = 3b/2$ b $l = \sqrt{\dfrac{5k}{3}}$
    c $h = 3V/A$ d $x = 8/7(y+u)$
    e $k = 7g + 5$ f $V = (4w-3)/6$

---

4.   a $f = g^2$ b $v = 16w^2$
    c $m = (kn/7)^2$ d $d = A/\pi s^2$
    e $p = 4\pi^2 L/n^2$ f $x = 25/4P^2$
5. $r = \sqrt{\dfrac{3V}{\pi h}}$ 6. $r = \sqrt[3]{\dfrac{3V}{4\pi}}$
7. $h = A/2\pi r - r$ or $(A - \pi r^2)/2\pi r$
8.   a $x = r/(p+q)$ b $x = k/(m-n)$
    c $x = (m+2a)/(a-b)$ d $x = a/(1-3D)$
    e $x = h/(g+1)$ f $x = (y+1)/(y-1)$
9.   (i) C increases   (ii) C decreases
    (iii) C doubles   (iv) C is halved
10. (i) A increases   (ii) A decreases
    (iii) A is quadrupled (iv) A is quartered
11. (i) T decreases   (ii) T increases
    (iii) T is halved   (iv) T is doubled

Remember Remember Ch 10 page 103
1.   a $x = h + g$ b $x = p - k$
    c $x = v/y$ d $x = wm/18$
    e $x = (s-t)/g$ f $x = (b-a)/c$
    g $x = 5h - 1$ h $x = mn - p$
    i $x = b/a + c$ j $x = \sqrt{\dfrac{V}{9y}}$
    k $x = (5p-5)/2$ l $x = (ab/5)^2$
2.   a $P = 2a + b + c$ b $a = (P-b-c)/2$
3. $m = (y-c)/x$
4. $d = \sqrt{\dfrac{C}{I}}$
5. $x = D/(\pi+4)$
6. $F = (9C+160)/5$ or $F = 9C/5 + 32$
7. $p = q/(k+1)$
8. $x = (y-1)/(y+1)$
9. $n = IR/(E-IR)$
10. a V is quartered   b V is multiplied by 4.

Answers to Chapter 11 Page 104

Exercise 11·1 page 104
1.   a R 15 Mo 1   Mean 5   Med 3
    b R 3·1 Mo 5·3 Mean 4·2 Med 4·6
    c R 22 Mo 105 Mean 104 Med 105
    d R 32 Mo 40 Mean 34   Med 31
    e R 12 Mo 21 Mean 15·5 Med 14·5
    f R 6000 Mo 15000 Mean 15400 Med 15000
2.   a 52·5 b Yes c 53 d 54
3.   £46
4.   a Total $f = 40$ $fx = 0$ 12 20 24 16 Tot = 72
    b 40 c 72 c 1·8
5.   a Mo 54 Med 56 b Median

Exercise 11·2 page 105
1.   b 11 c 5   d 9   e 12
2.   a Q1 : 3   Q2 : 7   Q3 : 9
    b Q1 : 14   Q2 : 21   Q3 : 26
    c Q1 : 3·7 Q2 : 4·2 Q3 : 5
    d Q1 : 54   Q2 : 61   Q3 : 71
    e Q1 : 24   Q2 : 31   Q3 : 36
3.   a 33rd
    b Q1 - between 16th & 17th
      Q3 - between 49th and 50th.
4.   b 4   c 4   d 5th & 14th
    e Q1 : 5   Q2 : 7·5   Q3 : 10
5.   Q1 : 7·5   Q2 : 12   Q3 : 17·5

Exercise 11·3 page 108

1. a Med 23, Q1 = 14, Q3 = 25, SIQR = 5·5
   b Med 3·6, Q1 = 3,   Q3 = 4·3, SIQR = 0·65
   c Med 121, Q1 = 112, Q3 = 134, SIQR = 11
2. a 0,0,1,1,2,2,2,2,2,3,3,3,4,4,4,4,4,5,5,6,6,6,8,9
   b Median 3 Mean 3·5 Mode 2 or 4
   c Q1 2 Q3 5   d Range 9   SIQR 1·5
3. Range 9, SIQR 0·75.

Exercise 11·4 page 109

1. a Median 7·5   Q1 : 6·5   Q3 : 9·5
   b
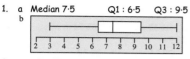
2. a Q1 : 40   Q2 : 52·5 Q3 : 85
   b
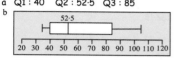
3. a Q1 : 14   Q2 : 18   Q3 : 22
   b
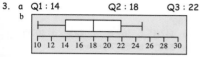
4. a Awlbright Q1 : 8   Q2 : 10 Q3 : 14
   b Osiris   Q1 : 10 Q2 : 14 Q3 : 16
   c
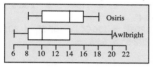
   d Osiris has a higher mean- will last longer.
5. a Men   Q1 : 9   Q2 : 13 Q3 : 18
      Women Q1 : 6·5 Q2 : 11 Q3 : 14
   b
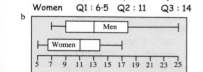
   c The men have a higher median, therefore
      on average can do more pull-ups.
6. a
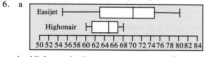
   b High-on-air times are more grouped
      therefore more consistant.
      They have a shorter mean time therefore
      shorter average flight time.
7. Rod's hits are more grouped so more
   consistant. He also has a higher mean
   therefore on average his hits go further.
   Ted can hit further but is very inconsistant
   and has a lower mean than Rod.
   Bob with his lowest mean is the novice.

Exercise 11·5 page 112

1. a 5   b 2·45   2. a 4   b 2·398
3. a 37   b 9·13   4. a 8   b 4·74
5. a 28   b 5·318
6. 2·41
7. a Both means are 18
   b Donald : 2·61   Graeme : 16·41
   c Donald's s.d. is lower => more consistant.
8. a Mean - 7·75,   s.d. : 3·5
   b Mean - 35·8   s.d. : 6·31
   c Mean - 7·94   s.d. : 2·33
   d Mean - 127·857 s.d. : 7·11
9. 3·5

Remember Remember Ch 11 page 115

1. Mean 17   Median 17
    Mode 18   Range 13

---

2. 12
3. a i 14 & 3   ii 7 & 6·5
    b Turfers - numbers not so spread out
    c May receive his order quicker
4. a Med = 12,   Q1 = 5, Q3 = 15 b SIQR = 5
5. a Med = 19   Q1 = 14·5   Q3 = 23
    b

6. a 47   b 4·34
7. a mean = 230, b Sid = 34·8, Jock = 7·9
8. a 51p   b 4·1
    c On average, supermarket is cheaper but
       prices vary more in supermarkets

Answers to Chapter 12 Page 116

Exercise 12·1 page 112

1. a (3, 9)
    b (-1, 1), (0, 3), (1, 5), (2, 7)
    c Straight line graph
2. a (-4, -4), (-2, -3), (0, -2), (2, -1), (4, 0)
    b Straight line graph
3. a (-1, 11), (0, 10), (1, 9), (2, 8), (3, 7)
    b Straight line graph
4. a 11   b 74
    c $f(a) = 3a - 1$ d $a = 7$
5. a 16   b $f(p) = 6p - 2$
    c $p = 7$
6. a 14   b $f(z) = 0.5z + 3$
    c $z = 16$
7. a (2, 3)
    b (1, 0), (0, -1), (-1, 0), (-2, 3)
    c d

8. a (-2, 12), (-1, 3), (0, 0), (1, 3), (2, 12)
    b

9. a (-1, 3),
    b (0, 0), (1, -1), (2, 0), (3, 3)
    c

10. a (3, 9)   b $f(a) = a^2$
    c +5, -5
11. a (2, 7)   b $f(p) = p^2 + 3$
    c +6, -6
12. a 47   b $f(2a) = 10a - 3$
    c $a = 3$
13. a $f(4a) = 4a + 3$ b $g(3p) = 6p - 3$
    c $h(a^2) = a^2 - 5$ d $f(2q) = 12 - 2q$
    e $f(3m) = 9m^2$ f $f(10t) = 200t^2$
14. $f(t) = 4t - 1$, $t = {}^{17}/_2$
15. $f(n) = 3n - 3$, $n = {}^{40}/_3$
16. $h(r^2) = r^2 - 1$, $r = \pm 7$
17. a 48   b $f(2p) = 10p - 2$
    c $p = 4$

---

18. a 13   b $c = 12$
19. a (0, -3)   b $m = 2$
    c $y = 2x - 3$ d $f(x) = 2x - 3$
    e (i) 37   (ii) -15
    f $p = 15$ g (15, 27)

Exercise 12·2 page 1120

1. a (-3, 9)
    b (-2, 4),(-1, 1),(0, 0),(1, 1),(2, 4),(3, 9)
    c

    d 0   e $x = 0$ f (0, 0)
2. a (-3, 8)
    b (-2, 3),(-1, 0),(0, -1),(1, 0),(2, 3),(3, 8)
    c

    d (-1, 0), (1, 0)   e $x = 0$
    f (0, -1)   g move down 1 place.
3. Moved up 3 places.
4. Moved down 5 places.
5. a (-1, 5)
    b (0, 0),(1, -3),(2, -4),(3, -3),(4, 0),(5, 5)
    c

    d 0, 4   e $x = 2$ f (2, -4)
6. a (-4, 4)
    b (-3, 0), (-2, -2), (-1, -2), (0, 0), (1, 4)
    c

    d (-3, 0), (0, 0)   e $x = -1.5$
    f (-1.5, -2.25)
7. a (-4, 5)
    b (-3, 0), (-2, -3), (-1, -4), (0, -3),
       (1, 0), (2, 5)
    c

    d (-3, 0), (1, 0)   e $x = -1$ f (-1, -4)
8. a (-3, 7)
    b (-2, 0), (-1, -5), (0, -8), (1, -9), (2, -8),
       (3, -5), (4, 0), (5, 7)
    c

    d (-2, 0), (4, 0)   e $x = 1$ f (1, -9)

9. a (−2, 4)
    b (−1, −1), (0, 0), (1, −1), (2, −4)

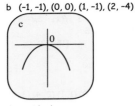

    d upside down
    e negative
10. a (−1, −5)
    b (0, 0), (1, 3), (2, 4), (3, 3), (4, 0), (5, −5)

    d (0, 0), (4, 0)   e x = 2
    f (2, 4)
11. positive x² ⌣   negative x² ⌢
12. a ⌣ b   c ⌢ d ⌢
    e ⌣ f ⌢
13.

    b (−3, 0), (3, 0)   c x = 0   d (0, 9)
14.

    b (−2, 0), (2, 0)   c x = 0   max (0, 8)
15.

    b 1   c x = 2   min (2, 0)

Remember Remember Ch 12 page 122

1. a (−1, −7)
    b (0, −3), (1, 1), (2, 5), (3, 9)
    c straight line graph
2. a (3, 13)   b (20, 98)
    c f(t) = 5t − 2   d t = 8
3. a (2, 6)
    b (1, 3), (0, 2), (−1, 3), (−2, 6)

4. a (−1, −7)
    b (0, 0), (1, 5), (2, 8), (3, 9), (4, 8), (5, 5),
       (6, 0), (7, −7),

    d (0, 0), (6, 0)
    e x = 3   f (3, 9)
5. f(a²) = a² + 5,   a = ± 6
6. a 29   b w = 100
7. a ⌣ b   c ⌢ d ⌣
    e ⌣ f ⌢
8.

    b (−2, 0), (2, 0)   c x = 0   d (0, 4)
9. a (−5, 5), (−4, 0), (−3, −3), (−2, −4),
       (−1, −3), (0, 0), (1, 5)

(graph labelled b c)

    d x = −2   e (−2, −4)

Turn off that Calculator 4 page 125

1. a 8600000 mm   b 0·00067 tonne
    c 875 g   d 12500 cm
    e 30600 secs   f 0·004 l
    g 1 mm
2. a £1·80 b 0·45 cm c 1900
    d 0·06 m e 0·09 kg f 1·6 km g 72
3. a 30   b 12   c 450
    d −27000 e −24   f 0·2   g −15
4. a 306   b 40   c 12000000
5. a (2, −2) b (1, −2), (−4, −2), (−7, 2), (−2, 2)
6. a 0455 b 1200
    c 2350 d 2040 e 1945
7. a 45 min b 9 hr 46 min
8. a 100 km/hr   b 45 min
9. 75·7 cm
10. Converse of Pythagoras
11. a 4   b 9   c 3
12. £11180·40
13. a 19x − 2

Answers to Chapter 13 Page 126

Exercise 13·1 page 126

1. 5·5 cm
2. a 12·56 cm b 11·78 cm
    c 6·98 cm   d 18·84 cm
3. a 25·12 cm b 19·63
    c 18·14   d 37·68 cm
4. a 18·84 mm b 54·95 cm
    c 39·08 m   d 52·33 cm
5. a 41·8 cm   b 74·89 mm
6. 13·14 cm

Exercise 13·2 page 127

1. 39·25 cm²
2. a 26·17 cm² b 42·39 cm²
3. a 274·75 cm² b 52·33 cm²

---

4. a 43·96 cm²   b 802·44 cm²
    c 83·41 cm²   d 54·51 cm²
    e 128·22 cm²   f 69·32 cm²
5. 163·54 cm²

Exercise 13·3 page 128

1. a (i) 55·8 cm   (ii) 1116·44 cm²
    b (i) 12·95 mm   (ii) 35·62 mm²
2. 1395·56 cm²
3. 157 cm²
4. 24·42 cm
5. a 115·13 m   b 105·54 m
6. 22·9 m
7. a 29·34 cm   b 53·22 cm²
8. a 113·04 cm² b 72 cm²   c 41·04 cm²
9. 182·18

Exercise 13·4 page 129

1. 45°
2. a 120°   b 240°
3. 180°
4. a 147·4° b 169·8° c 223° d 107·5°
5. a 330°   b 5077·38 mm²

Exercise 13·5 page 130

1. 45°   2. a 115·6°   b 238·9°
3. 300·4°
4. a 120·0° b 156·0° c 107·5° d 301·0°
5. a 202·5° b 63·6 cm

Remember Remember Ch 13 page 131

1. a 11·8 m   b 41·9 mm
2. a 88·3 m²   b 209 mm²
3. a 135° b 100° c 300° d 160°
4. 1800 cm²
5. a 360° ÷ 8 = 45°   b 6·92 cm²
6. a 10·6 m²   b 19·4 m
7. 70·7 m   b 66·7 m²

Answers to Chapter 14 Page 132

Exercise 14·1 page 132

1. a (−2, 7) b (−1, 4), (0, 3), (1, 4), (2, 7)

2. a (−1, 4)
    b (0, 0), (1, −2), (2, −2), (3, 0), (4, 4)

    d (0, 0), (3, 0)
3. a (−3, 7), (−2, 0), (−1, −5), (0, −8), (1, −9),
       (2, −8), (3, −5), (4, 0), (5, 7)

    c (−2, 0), (4, 0)   d x = 1

4.

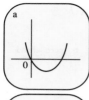
a

(0, 0), (4, 0) $x = 2$

b

(-1, 0), (3, 0) $x = 1$

c

(-3, 0), (2, 0) $x = -0.5$

d

(-2, 0), (2, 0) $x = 0$

e

(-1, 0), (2, 0) $x = 0.5$

Exercise 14·2 page 133

1. -2, 0
2. -3, 3
3. -3, 1
4. a 0, 4 b -1, 3 c -3, 2
    d -2, 2 e -1, 2

Exercise 14·3 page 134

1. a $x(x - 3)$ b $x(x + 6)$
    c $x(x - 10)$ d $6x(x - 2)$
    e $2x(4x + 5)$ f $6x(3x + 4)$
    g $5x(3 - x)$ h $4x(3y - 4x)$
    i $4ab(5b + 6a)$ j $4x^2(3x + 2)$
    k $\frac{1}{2}x(x + 1)$ l $4x(2 - 3x + 4x^2)$

2. a $(x + 4)(x - 4)$ b $(x + 7)(x - 7)$
    c $(x + 9)(x - 9)$ d $(2x + 3)(2x - 3)$
    e $(x + 10)(x - 10)$ f $(7x + 8y)(7x - 8y)$
    g $(9x + 10zy)(9x - 10zy)$
    h $10(x + 2)(x - 2)$
    i $2(4x + 5y)(4x - 5y)$
    j $3(x + 5)(x - 5)$
    k $(6 + a)(6 - a)$
    l $5(2 + 3ab)(2 - 3ab)$

3. a $(x + 2)(x + 3)$ b $(x - 2)(x - 4)$
    c $(x + 6)(x + 4)$ d $(x + 5)(x - 7)$
    e $(x - 2)(x - 9)$ f $(7 + x)(4 - x)$
    g $(x + 1)(x + 18)$ h $(7 - x)(6 + x)$
    i $(x + 9y)(x - 10y)$ j $(x + 5y)(x + 5y)$
    k $(6 - x)(6 - x)$ l $(x - 7)(x - 8)$

4. a $x(x - 9)$ b $(x + 12)(x - 12)$
    c $(x - 3)(x - 6)$ d $(3x + 7)(3x - 7)$
    e $(11 - 10x)(11 + 10x)$
    f $(7 - x)(5 + x)$ g $(x + 10)(x - 9)$
    h $(x + 3)(x + 13)$ i $(x + 4y)(x - 2y)$
    j $(6 + x)(5 - x)$ k $(x - 4)(x - 5)$
    l $5(x + 3)(x - 3)$

Exercise 14·4 page 135

1. a 0, 3   b 0, -7   c 0, 3
2. a 0, -5   b 0, 10   c 0, -8
    d 0, $^3/_2$ e 0, -2   f 0, 3
3. a 3, -3   b -2, 2   c $^7/_2$, $^7/_2$
4. a -5, 5   b 4, -4   c 11, -11
    d -8, 8   e -5, 5   f 1, -1
5. a 3, 4   b -2, 5   c $-^1/_2$, $^7/_3$
6. a -3, -6   b 2, 8   c 4, -9
    d -8, 3   e -5, 2   f 1, $-^3/_2$
7. a 0, 8   b 0, -12   c 0, 4
8. a 0, 6   b 0, -19   c 0, 4
    d 0, -5   e 0, 20   f 0, $^3/_2$
9. a -4, 4   b 7, -7   c $-^5/_2$, $^5/_2$
10. a 3, -3   b 6, -6   c 9, -9
    d $^4/_3$, $-^4/_3$ e $^1/_7$, $-^1/_7$ f 10, -10
11. a -2, -6   b 2, 10   c -3, 5
12. a -1, -4   b -9, -10   c -5, -6
    d 2, 10   e 4, 6   f 5, 10
    g -5, 3   h 6, -3   i 10, -3
    j 6, -7   k 12, -2   l 9, -8
13. a $-^1/_3$, 3 b $-^5/_2$, -3 c $^2/_5$, -5
    d $^1/_4$, 2   e $^2/_3$, -4 f $-^3/_2$, -1
    g $^1/_3$, $^3/_2$ h $-^3/_2$, $-^5/_2$ i $-^3/_5$, 1
    j $-^1/_6$, 3 k $-^2/_3$, $^4/_3$ l $^6/_5$, $-^1/_3$
14. a 0, -7   b 0, $^3/_2$ c 11, -11
    d $-^5/_6$, $^5/_6$ e -7, -3 f 10, 3
    g -7, 5   h -1, 4   i 10, -9
    j $^3/_2$, 5   k $^2/_3$, $-^7/_2$ l $^1/_2$, $^9/_2$

Exercise 14·5 page 138

1. a -2, 4 b (1, -9)(0, -8)

d

2. a -1, 5 b (2, -9) c (0, -5)

3. Roots : -5, 3 min : (-1, -16) y-int : (0, -15)

4. Roots : 0, 4 min : (2, -4) y-int : (0, 0)

5. Roots : 0, 6 max : (3, 9) y-int : (0, 0)

6. Roots : -6, 2 max : (-2, 16) y-int : (0, 12)

7. a Roots:7, -1 min:(3, -16) y-int:(0, -7)

b Roots: 3, 5 min:(4, -1) y-int:(0, 15)

c Roots:0, 8 min:(4, -16) y-int:(0, 0)

d Roots: -1, 1 min: (0, -3) y-int: (0, -3)

e Roots:-3, 1 min:(-1, 4) y-int:(0, 3)

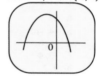

Exercise 14·6 page 139

1. a $x^2 - 4x + 3 = 0$ b $x = 1$, $x = 3$
    c $y = 4$, $y = 8$ d (1, 4) (3, 8)
2. (-2, 1) (6, 25)
3. (-3, -5) (2, 5)
4. (4, 8) (1, -1)
5. (-6, -17) (1, 4)
6. (2, 5)
7. (6, 25)

Remember Remember Ch 14 page 140

1. a (-2, 2) b (-1, -1), (0,-2), (1, -1), (2, 2)

c

2. a 0, -3 $x = -1.5$

b 1, -3 $x = -1$

c 4, -2 $x = 1$

d -3, 3 $x = 0$

e 3, -2 $x = 0.5$

3. 0, 2
4. ± 3
5. a 0, -3   b 0, 8
    c $0, \frac{3}{4}$ d 5, -6
    e -8, 8   f 7, -6
    g 3, 5   h -7, 9
6. a 0, 6   b 0, -5
    c 0, 20   d $0, \frac{3}{2}$
    e ± 8 f $\pm \frac{3}{4}$
    g $\pm \frac{1}{5}$ h ± 7
7. a -2, -4   b -4, -10
    c 2, 9   d -6, 8
    e -7, 4   f -5, 4
    g 7, -2   h 8, 7
8. a $\frac{1}{2}, -5$ b $\frac{2}{3}, 3$
    c $\frac{1}{5}, -3$ d $-\frac{1}{2}, \frac{3}{2}$
    e $-\frac{4}{3}, 2$ f $\frac{5}{2}, 1$
    g $-\frac{1}{3}, \frac{3}{2}$ h $\frac{1}{4}, -6$
9. Roots : (-3, 0), (1, 0) min : ((-1, -4)
    y-int : (0, -3)

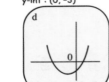

10. Roots : (-6, 0), (2, 0) min : (-2, -16)
     y-int : (0, -12)

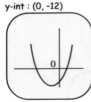

11. Roots : (-3, 0), (3, 0) min : (0, -9)
     y-int : (0, -9)

12. (-1, 3), (5, 21)
13. (-5, 30), (3, -2)

Answers to Chapter 15 Page 141

Exercise 15·1 page 141

1. a $\overrightarrow{PQ} = \underline{s}$ b $\overrightarrow{TV} = \underline{w}$
    c $\overrightarrow{HM} = \underline{n}$ d $\overrightarrow{XW} = \underline{t}$
    e $\overrightarrow{ES} = \underline{x}$ f $\overrightarrow{DC} = \underline{p}$
2. see sketches
3. a - c see sketches   d yes
    e   you can add vectors in any order
    f - g see sketches   h no
4. a - d see sketches
5. a - f see sketches
6. a - b see sketches   c you get back to the
    start => total displacement = zero.

Exercise 15·2 page 145

1. a $\overrightarrow{CD} = \underline{x} = \begin{pmatrix} 7 \\ 4 \end{pmatrix}$ b $\overrightarrow{EF} = \underline{y} = \begin{pmatrix} 9 \\ 3 \end{pmatrix}$
    c $\overrightarrow{GH} = \underline{z} = \begin{pmatrix} 4 \\ -5 \end{pmatrix}$ d $\overrightarrow{KL} = \underline{p} = \begin{pmatrix} 5 \\ -3 \end{pmatrix}$
    e $\overrightarrow{IJ} = \underline{w} = \begin{pmatrix} -3 \\ -7 \end{pmatrix}$ f $\overrightarrow{MN} = \underline{a} = \begin{pmatrix} -3 \\ -4 \end{pmatrix}$
    g $\overrightarrow{SR} = \underline{b} = \begin{pmatrix} -3 \\ 5 \end{pmatrix}$ h $\overrightarrow{TU} = \underline{d} = \begin{pmatrix} 0 \\ 5 \end{pmatrix}$
    i $\overrightarrow{PQ} = \underline{c} = \begin{pmatrix} 7 \\ 0 \end{pmatrix}$
2. see sketches
3. a - b see sketches   c $\begin{pmatrix} 6 \\ 4 \end{pmatrix}$ - yes
4. a $\begin{pmatrix} 10 \\ -1 \end{pmatrix}$ b $\begin{pmatrix} 2 \\ 5 \end{pmatrix}$ c $\begin{pmatrix} 12 \\ 4 \end{pmatrix}$ d $\begin{pmatrix} 12 \\ -9 \end{pmatrix}$
    e $\begin{pmatrix} 24 \\ -5 \end{pmatrix}$ f $\begin{pmatrix} 0 \\ -13 \end{pmatrix}$ g $\begin{pmatrix} 20 \\ 11 \end{pmatrix}$ h $\begin{pmatrix} -6 \\ -2 \end{pmatrix}$
    i $\begin{pmatrix} 0 \\ 0 \end{pmatrix}$ j $\begin{pmatrix} 0 \\ 0 \end{pmatrix}$
5. a see sketch   b it does
    c $\begin{pmatrix} 0 \\ 0 \end{pmatrix}$ d you end back
    at the beginning again
6. a $\begin{pmatrix} 5 \\ 5 \end{pmatrix}$ b $\begin{pmatrix} 7 \\ 5 \end{pmatrix}$ c $\begin{pmatrix} 5 \\ -3 \end{pmatrix}$
    d $\begin{pmatrix} 40 \\ -16 \end{pmatrix}$ e $\begin{pmatrix} 5 \\ 2 \end{pmatrix}$ f $\begin{pmatrix} 3 \\ 1 \end{pmatrix}$

Exercise 15·3 page 146

1. a see sketch   b $\begin{pmatrix} 2 \\ 7 \end{pmatrix}$
    c $\begin{pmatrix} 4 \\ 1 \end{pmatrix}$ and $\begin{pmatrix} 6 \\ 8 \end{pmatrix}$ d $\begin{pmatrix} 2 \\ 7 \end{pmatrix}$
2. a $\begin{pmatrix} 5 \\ 2 \end{pmatrix}$ b $\begin{pmatrix} 7 \\ -3 \end{pmatrix}$ c $\begin{pmatrix} 3 \\ 9 \end{pmatrix}$ d $\begin{pmatrix} 9 \\ 4 \end{pmatrix}$
    e $\begin{pmatrix} -5 \\ -6 \end{pmatrix}$ f $\begin{pmatrix} -3 \\ 8 \end{pmatrix}$ g $\begin{pmatrix} -2 \\ -12 \end{pmatrix}$

3. a $\begin{pmatrix} 4 \\ 3 \end{pmatrix}$ b $\begin{pmatrix} 4 \\ 3 \end{pmatrix}, \begin{pmatrix} 4 \\ 3 \end{pmatrix}$
    c parallel
4. a $\begin{pmatrix} 1 \\ 4 \end{pmatrix}, \begin{pmatrix} 2 \\ 8 \end{pmatrix}$ b parallel and
    twice the length
5. a $\begin{pmatrix} 3 \\ 6 \end{pmatrix}, \begin{pmatrix} 3 \\ 6 \end{pmatrix}$ b parallel & equal
    c parallelogram

Exercise 15·4 page 147

1. 5
2. a 5   b 13   c 10
    d 15   e 4   f 17
3. 4·24
4. a 4·47 b 8·94 c 8·49
    d 8·94 e 11·18 f 9·49
5. a 4·47 and 4·47 and 6·32
    b Isosceles

Exercise 15·5 page 148

1. a   7·07   b   6·71
    c   9·49   d   8·94
2. Radius = 10 units
3. a $\begin{pmatrix} 60 \\ -40 \end{pmatrix}$ b   72·1 km
4. a $\overrightarrow{AB} = \begin{pmatrix} 13 \\ 16 \end{pmatrix}$, $\overrightarrow{BC} = \begin{pmatrix} 11 \\ -9 \end{pmatrix}$
    b $\begin{pmatrix} 24 \\ 7 \end{pmatrix}$ c 25 m
5. a $\begin{pmatrix} 20 \\ 15 \end{pmatrix}, \begin{pmatrix} 21 \\ -28 \end{pmatrix}$ b $\begin{pmatrix} 41 \\ -13 \end{pmatrix}$
    c 25 m/min, 35 m/min, 43 m/min
6. a $\begin{pmatrix} -9 \\ 10 \end{pmatrix}, \begin{pmatrix} 14 \\ 6 \end{pmatrix}$ and $\begin{pmatrix} -5 \\ -16 \end{pmatrix}$
    b 13·45, 15·23 and 16·76
    c $\begin{pmatrix} 0 \\ 0 \end{pmatrix}$
d   resultant force is zero - no movement

Exercise 15·6 page 149

1. a $\underline{v}$ b $\underline{u}$ c $\underline{u} + \underline{v}$ d $\underline{v} - \underline{u}$
    e $\frac{1}{2}\underline{u} + \frac{1}{2}\underline{v}$ f $\frac{1}{2}\underline{u} - \frac{1}{2}\underline{v}$
2. a $4\underline{a}$ b $\underline{b} + 4\underline{a}$ c $\underline{b} + 2\underline{a}$
    d $\underline{b} + 3\underline{a}$ e $-2\underline{a}$
    f $\frac{1}{2}\underline{b} - \frac{1}{2}\underline{a}$
3. a $\underline{r}$ b $\underline{s}$ c $2\underline{r}$ d $\underline{s} - \underline{r}$
    e $2\underline{s} - 2\underline{r}$ f $2\underline{s} - \underline{r}$
4. a i $2\underline{h}$ ii $\underline{h} + \underline{k}$ iii $\underline{k} - 2\underline{h}$
    iv $\underline{k} - \underline{h}$
    b $\begin{pmatrix} 8 \\ 0 \end{pmatrix}, \begin{pmatrix} 6 \\ 4 \end{pmatrix}$ and $\begin{pmatrix} -2 \\ 4 \end{pmatrix}$
    c 4·47, 7·21 and 7·21

Exercise 15·7 page 150

1. a $\begin{pmatrix} 8 \\ 6 \\ -4 \end{pmatrix}$ b $\begin{pmatrix} 9 \\ -6 \\ 15 \end{pmatrix}$ c $\begin{pmatrix} 7 \\ 1 \\ 3 \end{pmatrix}$
    d $\begin{pmatrix} 1 \\ 5 \\ -7 \end{pmatrix}$ e $\begin{pmatrix} 17 \\ 0 \\ 11 \end{pmatrix}$ f $\begin{pmatrix} -14 \\ -2 \\ -6 \end{pmatrix}$
2. a $\begin{pmatrix} -2 \\ 2 \\ 14 \end{pmatrix}$ b $\begin{pmatrix} 4 \\ -6 \\ -10 \end{pmatrix}$ c $\begin{pmatrix} -3 \\ 6 \\ -6 \end{pmatrix}$
    d 3   e 13   f 14·3   g no

3. a $\begin{pmatrix} 6 \\ 9 \\ -3 \end{pmatrix}$ b $\begin{pmatrix} 0 \\ 0 \\ 0 \end{pmatrix}$ c $\begin{pmatrix} 2 \\ -3 \\ 4 \end{pmatrix}$

d $\begin{pmatrix} 3 \\ -4 \\ 0 \end{pmatrix}$ e $\begin{pmatrix} 0 \\ 2 \\ 2 \end{pmatrix}$ f $\begin{pmatrix} 4 \\ -1 \\ 2 \end{pmatrix}$

4. a $\underline{p} = \begin{pmatrix} 1 \\ 5 \\ 8 \end{pmatrix}$, $\underline{q} = \begin{pmatrix} 4 \\ -1 \\ 2 \end{pmatrix}$ and $\underline{r} = \begin{pmatrix} 6 \\ 3 \\ -4 \end{pmatrix}$

b $\begin{pmatrix} 3 \\ -6 \\ -6 \end{pmatrix}$ c $\begin{pmatrix} -3 \\ 6 \\ 6 \end{pmatrix}$, $\begin{pmatrix} 2 \\ 4 \\ -6 \end{pmatrix}$ and $\begin{pmatrix} -5 \\ 2 \\ 12 \end{pmatrix}$

d $\begin{pmatrix} 0 \\ 0 \\ 0 \end{pmatrix}$

e A vector + its negative gives zero

f $\begin{pmatrix} 0 \\ 0 \\ 0 \end{pmatrix}$

g Go round 3 sides of a triangle and you return to your starting point i.e. the zero vector.

5. a $\underline{u}$ b $\underline{v}$ c $\underline{u} + \underline{w}$ d $\underline{v} + \underline{w}$

e $\underline{v} + \underline{w}$ f $\underline{u} + \underline{v} + \underline{w}$ g $\frac{1}{2}\underline{v}$

h $\underline{u} + \frac{1}{2}\underline{v}$ i $\frac{1}{2}\underline{v} + \frac{1}{2}\underline{w}$

j $\underline{u} + \frac{1}{2}\underline{v} + \frac{1}{2}\underline{w}$ k $\frac{1}{2}\underline{u} + \frac{1}{2}\underline{v} + \frac{1}{2}\underline{w}$

l $-\frac{1}{2}\underline{v} - \frac{1}{2}\underline{w} + \frac{1}{2}\underline{u}$

6. a $\begin{pmatrix} 0 \\ 3 \\ 4 \end{pmatrix}$ b $\begin{pmatrix} 12 \\ 0 \\ 4 \end{pmatrix}$ c $\begin{pmatrix} 12 \\ 3 \\ 4 \end{pmatrix}$

d 5 e 12·65 f $6\frac{1}{2}$

7. a $\begin{pmatrix} 5 \\ 3 \\ 1 \end{pmatrix}$ b $\begin{pmatrix} 13 \\ 3 \\ 1 \end{pmatrix}$, $\begin{pmatrix} 13 \\ 9 \\ 1 \end{pmatrix}$, $\begin{pmatrix} 5 \\ 9 \\ 1 \end{pmatrix}$ & $\begin{pmatrix} 9 \\ 6 \\ 13 \end{pmatrix}$

c $\begin{pmatrix} 8 \\ 0 \\ 0 \end{pmatrix}$, $\begin{pmatrix} 0 \\ 6 \\ 0 \end{pmatrix}$ & $\begin{pmatrix} 4 \\ 3 \\ 12 \end{pmatrix}$ d 10 e 13

8. a $\begin{pmatrix} 240 \\ 150 \\ 9 \end{pmatrix}$ and $\begin{pmatrix} 80 \\ 50 \\ 3 \end{pmatrix}$

b 283 km and 94 km

c $\begin{pmatrix} -160 \\ -100 \\ -6 \end{pmatrix}$

d dist = 189 km, speed = 378 km/hr

e $\overrightarrow{OQ} = \frac{1}{3}\overrightarrow{OP}$ means their paths are parallel and heading for the point O.
Also, OQ + QP = OP means Q lies on the line of OP.

9. a $\begin{pmatrix} -7 \\ -5 \\ -40 \end{pmatrix}$, $\begin{pmatrix} 5 \\ -10 \\ -40 \end{pmatrix}$ and $\begin{pmatrix} 2 \\ 15 \\ -40 \end{pmatrix}$ b $\begin{pmatrix} 0 \\ 0 \\ 0 \end{pmatrix}$

All forces cancel out meaning balloon is stationary.

Remember Remember Ch 15 page 152

1. see sketches

2. a $\begin{pmatrix} 2 \\ -3 \end{pmatrix}$ b $\begin{pmatrix} -8 \\ -1 \end{pmatrix}$ c $\begin{pmatrix} 15 \\ -3 \end{pmatrix}$

d $\begin{pmatrix} 6 \\ 4 \end{pmatrix}$ e $\begin{pmatrix} 1 \\ -8 \end{pmatrix}$ f $\begin{pmatrix} -22 \\ -6 \end{pmatrix}$

3. a $\begin{pmatrix} 1 \\ -7 \end{pmatrix}$ b $\begin{pmatrix} 6 \\ 4 \end{pmatrix}$ c $\begin{pmatrix} 6 \\ -2 \end{pmatrix}$

d $\begin{pmatrix} -2 \\ 5 \end{pmatrix}$ e $\begin{pmatrix} 2 \\ 2 \end{pmatrix}$ f $\begin{pmatrix} -2 \\ 1 \end{pmatrix}$

4. a $\begin{pmatrix} 6 \\ 4 \end{pmatrix}$ and $\begin{pmatrix} -12 \\ -8 \end{pmatrix}$

b $\overrightarrow{CD} = -2\overrightarrow{AB}$ means parallel and twice the length.

5. 13

6. a $\begin{pmatrix} -2 \\ -1 \\ 16 \end{pmatrix}$ b $\begin{pmatrix} 6 \\ -7 \\ -8 \end{pmatrix}$ c $\begin{pmatrix} -4 \\ 8 \\ -8 \end{pmatrix}$

d 6 e 13 f no
The sum of the lengths of any 2 sides of a triangle is always greater than the length of the 3rd side.

7. a $\overrightarrow{PS}$ (= $\underline{v}$) b $\overrightarrow{SR}$ (= $\underline{u}$)
c $\overrightarrow{PP} = \underline{O}$ d $\overrightarrow{PP} = \underline{O}$

8. a $\begin{pmatrix} 4 \\ 5 \\ 0 \end{pmatrix}$ b $\begin{pmatrix} 4 \\ -1 \\ 6 \end{pmatrix}$

9. a $\underline{u}$ b $\underline{v}$ c $\frac{3}{4}\underline{u}$ d $-\frac{1}{3}\underline{v}$
e $\underline{v} + \underline{w} + \frac{1}{4}\underline{u}$ f $\underline{u} + \underline{w} + \frac{2}{3}\underline{v}$

10. C(5, 0, -5).

Turn off that Calculator 5 page 155

1. a 115 b 1020 c -5 d 11
e 27600 f 0·26 g 0·55 h 0·0042
2. a 0·1 tonne b 40000 mm
c 72000000 mg d 0·187 km
e 0·00017 km f 61200 seconds
g 200 m/sec
3. a 512 b 5656 c 1224
4. a $^1/_{80000}$ b $^1/_4$ c $^1/_{32}$
5. a $^{11}/_{56}$ b $7^5/_8$ c $3^4/_7$
6. a $^{19}/_{20}$ b $1^1/_8$ c $^1/_{200}$
7. a 3·4 cm b 0·75 kg c 0·36 m
d 0·6 km e £43·40 f $15 g 1·98 km
8. a 57 b -77 c -222
d 106 e -1134 f -x g 112
h $78x^2$ i -40 j 15 k $^{-2}/_5$
9. a £7·20 b £10·40 c 22·5°
10. a (i) -2, (0, 7) (ii) -3, (0, 1)
b see sketches
11. a 6·28 cm² b 11·14 cm
12. a 3 b see sketch

Answers to Chapter 16 Page 156

Exercise 16·1 page 156

1. a Sketch sine graph from 0° to 360°
b 1 c -1 d 0, 180, 360
2. a Sketch sine graph from -360° to 720°
bc Graph with 3 sine waves, start (-360,0) rising to (-270,1), then (-180,0), (-90,-1), (0,0), (90,1) and so on.....
d max 1 min -1 e amp = 1 f 360°

Exercise 16·2 page 158

1. a Sketch cosine graph from 0° to 360°
b 1 c -1 d 90, 270
2. a Sketch cosine graph from -360° to 720°
bc Graph with 3 cos waves, starting (-360,1) rising to (-270,0), then (-180,-1), (-90,0), (0,1), (90,0) and so on.....
d max 1 min -1 e amp = 1 f 360°

3. a Sketches of sin & cos graphs
b Sin graph start at (0,0) Cos start at (0,1) Both have max value 1 and min value -1, amplitude = 1 and period 360°.

Exercise 16·3 page 160

1. a Sketch tan graph from 0° to 180°
b no c no d 0°, 180°
2. a Sketch tan graph from -180° to 360° starting (-180,0) rising to line at $x = -90$, then from below at $x = 90$ to (0,0), then rising to line at $x = 90$, then from below at $x = 90$ to (180,0) and so on.....
b 180°

Exercise 16·4 page 161

1. a Sketch graph of $2\sin x$ from 0° to 360°
b 2 c -2 d 360
e 0, 180, 360.
2. a Sketch graph of $5\sin x$ from 0° to 360° starting at (0,0) rising to (90,5), then to (180,0), (270,-5) and (360,0)
b max = 5 min = -5 c amp =5 per = 360°
3. a Sketch graph of $10\cos x$ from 0° to 360° starting at (0,10) falling to (90,0), then to (180,-10), (270,0) and (360,10)
b max = 10 min = -10
c amp = 10 per = 360°
4. a Sin curve thro' (0,0), (90,8), (180,0), (270,-8), (360,0).
b Sin curve thro' (0,0), (90,60), (180,0), (270,-60), (360,0)
c Cos curve thro' (0,4), (90,0), (180,-4), (270,0), (360,4)
d Cos curve thro' (0,0·65), (90,0), (180,-0·65), (270,0), (360,0·65)
e Sin curve thro' (0,0), (90,0·5), (180,0), (270,-0·5), (360,0)
f Tan curve, similar to tan$x$, but steeper.
5. a Reflect $3\sin x$ in x-axis.
b max = 3 min = -3
c amp = 3 per = 360°.
6. a Cos curve thro' (0,-2), (90,0), (180,2), (270,0), (360,-2)
b Sin curve thro' (0,0), (90,-0·5), (180,0), (270,0·5), (360,0).
7. a $y = 7\sin x°$ b $y = 20\cos x°$
c $y = -0·2\sin x°$ d $y = -11\cos x°$

Exercise 16·5 page 163

1. a Sketch graph of $\sin 2x$ from 0° to 180°
b 1 c -1 d amp = 1, P = 180°
e 0, 90, 180.
2. a Sketch graph of $3\sin 4x$ from 0° to 90°
b max = 3 min = -3 c per = 90°
3. a Sketch graph of $\cos 3x$ from 0° to 120°
b max = 1 min = -1 c per = 120°
4. a Sin curve thro' (0,0), (30,6), (60,0), (90,-6), (120,0).
b Sin curve thro' (0,0), (15,50), (30,0), (45,-50), (60,0)
c Cos curve thro' (0,5), (45,0), (90,-5), (135,0), (180,5)
d Cos curve thro' (0,0·7), (22·5,0), (45,-0·7), (67·5,0), (90,0·7)
e Sin curve thro' (0,0), (180,12), (360,0), (540,-12), (720,0)
f Tan graph from 0° to 90° starting (0,0) rising to line at $x = 45$, then from below at $x = 45$ to (0,0), rising to line at $x = 90$.
5. a Reflect $9\sin 3x$ in x-axis.
b max = 9 min = -9
c amp = 9 per = 120°.
6. a Cos curve thro' (0,-12), (18,0), (36,12), (54,0), (72,-12)

b Sin curve thro' (0,0), (15,-0·2), (30,0), (45,0·2), (60,0)

c Sin curve thro' (0,0), (180,-0·1), (360,0), (540,0·1), (720,0)

d Cosine graph passing through :-
(0,$-\frac{1}{8}$), (3,0), (6,$\frac{1}{8}$), (9,0), (12,$-\frac{1}{8}$)

7. a $y = 3\sin2x°$ b $y = 15\cos6x°$
   c $y = -1·5\sin5x°$ d $y = -30\cos\frac{1}{2}x°$

Exercise 16·6 page 165

1. a Sketch sin$x$ graph from 0° to 360°
   b Sketch sin$x$ graph but moved 1 unit down the y-axis.

2. a Sketch cos$x$ graph from 0° to 360°
   b Sketch cos$x$ graph but moved 2 units up the y-axis.

3. a Sketch 4sin$x$ graph from 0° to 360°
   b Sketch 4sin$x$ graph but 2 units down the y-axis. Passes thro' (0,-2), (90,2), (180,-2), (270,-6), (360,-2)

4. a Sketch 6cos$x$ graph from 0° to 360°
   b Sketch 6cos$x$ graph but move 3 units up the y-axis. Passes thro' (0,9), (90,3), (180,-3), (270,3), (360,9)

5. a Sin wave passing thro' (0,2), (90,4), (180,2), (270,0), (360,2)
   b Cos wave passing thro' (0,-2), (90,-3), (180,-4), (270,-3), (360,-2)
   c Sin wave passing thro' (0,-40), (90,0), (180,-40), (270,-80), (360,-40)
   d Cos wave passing thro' (0,6), (90,-6), (180,-18), (270,-6), (360,6)

6. Sin wave passing thro' (0,4), (18,0), (36,4), (54,8), (72,4)

7. Cos wave passing thro' (0,-9), (90,-3), (180,3), (270,-3), (360,-9)

8. a Sin wave passing thro' (0,3), (90,0), (180,3), (270,6), (360,3)
   b Cos wave passing thro' (0,-3), (90,-2), (180,-1), (270,-2), (360,-3)
   c Sin wave passing thro' (0,10), (90,0), (180,10), (270,20), (360,10)
   d Cos wave passing thro' (0,-3), (90,-1), (180,1), (270,-1), (360,-3)

9. a $y = 5\sin x° + 5$
10. a $y = 3\cos x° - 3$
11. a $y = 4\sin x° + 4$ b $y = 3\cos x° + 3$
    c $y = 6\sin x° + 3$ d $y = 5\cos x° - 5$
    e $y = 4\sin x° - 6$ f $y = -20\sin x° + 20$
12. a $y = 2\sin2x° + 2$ b $y = 6\sin3x° + 3$
    c $y = 6\sin6x° + 12$ d $y = -2\sin4x° + 2$
13. a 12 secs   b $h = 25\sin30t°$
14. a 8 metres   b $d = 8\sin30t°$
15. a 30 cm   b 20 secs
    c $h = 30\sin18t° + 30$
16. a 17 in June   b 7 in Dec.
    c March & Sept   d $N = 5\cos30t° + 12$

Exercise 16·7 page 168

1. a $y = 7\sin(x - 60)°$ b $20\cos(x - 35)°$
   c $2·5\sin(x + 20)°$ d $12\sin(x + 70)°$
   e $-6\sin(x - 15)°$ f $0·2\cos(x - 55)°$
2. See Diagrams

Remember Remember Ch 16 page 169

1. Sketch sin, cos, tan graphs from 0° to 360°
2. a $y = 5\sin x°$ b $y = 12\cos x°$
   c $y = -0·6\sin x°$
3. a $y = 2\cos2x°$ b $y = 15\sin6x°$
   c $y = -40\cos5x°$
4. a $y = 5\sin x° + 5$ b $y = 4\sin x° + 2$
   c $y = 8\cos x° + 8$
5. a $y = 3\sin2x° + 3$ b $y = 10\sin4x° + 5$
   c $y = 10\sin10x° + 20$

6. a Sin curve thro' (0,0), (90,25), (180,0), (270,-25), (360,0).
   b Cos curve thro' (0,10), (90,0), (180,-10), (270,0), (360,10)
   c Sin curve thro' (0,0), (30,1), (60,0), (90,-1), (120,0).
   d Cos curve thro' (0,8), (22·5,0), (45,-8), (67·5,0), (90,8)
   e Sin curve thro' (0,1), (90,2), (180,1), (270,0), (360,1)
   f Sin curve thro' (0,-2), (90,0), (180,-2), (270,-4), (360,-2)
   g Cos curve thro' (0,30), (90,10), (180,-10), (270,10), (360,30)
   h Sin curve thro' (0,0), (15,-2), (30,0), (45,2), (60,0) etc
   i Cos curve thro' (0,0), (45,-4), (90,-8), (135,-4), (180,0).
   j Cos curve thro' (0,^{5}/₂), (90,0), (180, $^{-5}$/₂), (270,0), (360,^{5}/₂).
   k Sin curve thro' (0,0), (15,-¹/₂), (30,0), (45,-¹/₂), (60,0) etc
   l Cos curve thro' (0,0·4), (90,-2), (180,-4·4), (270,-2), (360,0·4).

Answers to Chapter 17 Page 170

Exercise 17·1 page 170

1. a, d, f, h are surds
2. a $\sqrt{5}$ b $\sqrt{10}$ c $\sqrt{29}$
   d $\sqrt{18}$ e $\sqrt{5}$ f $\sqrt{51}$
3. a $\sqrt{2}$ b $\sqrt{5}$ c $\sqrt{2}$ d $\sqrt{8}$
   e $\sqrt{11}$ f $\sqrt{3}$ g $\sqrt{2}$ h $\sqrt{3}$
4. a $^1/_{\sqrt{3}}$ b $^{\sqrt{3}}/_2$ c $^2/_{\sqrt{5}}$ d $^3/_{\sqrt{6}}$
5. $\sqrt{89}$ cm

Exercise 17·2 page 171

1. a $9\sqrt{2}$ b $3\sqrt{2}$ c $13\sqrt{3}$ d $6\sqrt{7}$
   e $6\sqrt{5}$ f 0   g $\sqrt{2}$ h 0
   i $-\sqrt{13}$ j $-3\sqrt{3}$ k $2\sqrt{2}$ l $3\sqrt{11}$
   m $6\sqrt{5}$ n $\sqrt{2}$
2. a $2\sqrt{3}$ b $2\sqrt{5}$ c $2\sqrt{11}$ d $2\sqrt{2}$
   e $5\sqrt{2}$ f $10\sqrt{3}$ g $3\sqrt{5}$ h $3\sqrt{2}$
   i $5\sqrt{5}$ j $6\sqrt{2}$ k $15\sqrt{2}$ l 15
3. a $4\sqrt{2}$ b $4\sqrt{5}$ c $4\sqrt{3}$ d $2\sqrt{10}$
4. a $20\sqrt{2}$ b $20\sqrt{3}$
5. $5\sqrt{2}$ cm   6. $^{\sqrt{23}}/_{\sqrt{2}}$
7. a $2\sqrt{6}$ b $2\sqrt{10}$ c $6\sqrt{2}$ d $2\sqrt{14}$
   e $4\sqrt{15}$ f $\sqrt{30}$ g $2\sqrt{3}$ h $4\sqrt{5}$
   i $3\sqrt{3}$ j 15
8. a $2\sqrt{3}$ b $\sqrt{30}$ c $3\sqrt{2}$ d 5
9. a $10 + 6\sqrt{2}$ b $14 + 7\sqrt{2}$
   c $10 - \sqrt{2}$ d $9 + 5\sqrt{3}$
   e $-3 + \sqrt{5}$ f $17 - 7\sqrt{7}$
   g $12 + 3\sqrt{2}$ h $18 + 9\sqrt{3}$
   i $11 + 2\sqrt{30}$ j 18
   k $6 + 4\sqrt{2}$ l $4 + 2\sqrt{3}$
   m $6 - 4\sqrt{2}$ n $4 - 2\sqrt{3}$
   o $14 - 6\sqrt{5}$ p $6\sqrt{3} + 10$
10. a $^{4\sqrt{3}}/_3$ b $^{5\sqrt{2}}/_2$
    c $^{4\sqrt{5}}/_{15}$ d $3\sqrt{5}$
    e $^{\sqrt{14}}/_4$ f $5\sqrt{2}$
    g $^{4\sqrt{2}}/_5$ h $^{\sqrt{2}}/_2$
    i $\sqrt{5}$
11. a $2 - \sqrt{5}$ b $3 - \sqrt{3}$
    c $2 + \sqrt{7}$ d $6 + \sqrt{2}$
    e $-1 - \sqrt{2}$ f $-5 - \sqrt{3}$
12. a $\sqrt{3} - 1$ b $4 - 2\sqrt{2}$
    c $16 + 8\sqrt{2}$ d $^{(50 + 20\sqrt{3})}/_{13}$
    e $11 + 6\sqrt{3}$

Exercise 17·3 page 173

1. a 3   b 3   c 4   d 2
   e 8   f 5   g 9   h 21
   i -2   j 8·5   k $^2/_3$ l y
2. a 64   b 8   c 36   d 625
   e 256   f 27   g 1000000000
   h 1024   i 243   j $k \times k \times k$
   k 16   l -8   m -32   n 81
   o 1   p -1   q $x \times x \times x \times x$
   r $t \times t \times t \times t \times t \times t$
   s $y \times y \times y \times y \times y \times y \times y$
3. a 3^7 b 2^7 c 4^3 d 7^5
   e $(-3)^3$ f $(-2)^2$ g k^6 h p^4
   i z^5 j $(-t)^3$ k $(-y)^5$ l 3^{10}
4. a 6   b 4   c 5
   d 6   e 2   f 1
5. a 125   b 32768
   c 1419857   d 14348907
   e 39·0625   f 0·0256
   g -2187   h -1·61051
   i 0·5
6. 2^{51} pence
7. a 2^7 b 2^9 c 3^5
   d 5^4 e 3^4 f 10^6
8. When multiplying - add indices.

Exercise 17·4 page 174

1. a x^5 b x^7 c k^9 d w^4
   e q^{13} f x^2 g x^3 h p^3
   i k^{-1} j s^{-2} k q^{-3} l r^{-14}
   m x^9 n q^{10} o y^{10} p y^{-6}
   q y r b^3 s a
2. a^6b^4
3. a a^3b^7 b k^3p^2 c ct^2 d $a^2b^3c^3$
4. a $8x^5$ b $15x^7$ c $16k^9$ d $14k^9$
   e $55p^6$ f $20p^5$ g $6y^2$ h $9z^4$
4. i $24q^5$ j $6t$
5. a x^2 b x^2 c x^3 d y^5
   e y^4 f y g a^4 h b^4
   i c^8 j $z^{0·3}$ k $p^{1·8}$ l t^5
   m t^8 n x^{-10} o y^{-3}
6. a $3x^2$ b $4y^3$ c $\frac{4}{3}y^4$ d $\frac{5}{4}k^{11}$
   e $\frac{3}{2}p$ f $2x^3$ g $3p^6$ h $\frac{3}{2}q^5$
   i $\frac{9}{8}w^{-5}$ j $2w^3x$ k $\frac{9}{7}xz^5$ l $4x^3$
7. a x^6 b x^8 c x^9 d y^{12}
   e y^{12} f y^{30} g a^{28} h a^{54}
   i a^{88} j a^{-6} k b^{-20} l b^{-20}
   m c^6 n c^{24} o a^{xy}
8. a $9x^8$ b $125x^6$ c $64x^{15}$ d $1000x^9$
   e $243x^{20}$ f $64x^{24}$ g $225x^5$ h $729x^3$
   i $-243x^{-20}$
9. a $\frac{1}{4}x^6$ b $\frac{8}{27}x^{12}$ c $0·015625x^{18}$
10. a x^6 b y c x^{16}
11. a x^2 b y c z^6 d b^6

11. e k^{-2} f z^6 g h^{12} h x^{15}
   i $5120000x^{20}$ j t^{3x}

12. a 1 b 1 c 1 d 1
   e 1 f 1 g 4 h 16
   i 8·2 j 1 k 1 l 1

13. a 1 b 1

14. a $\dfrac{1}{x^k}$ b $\dfrac{1}{p^h}$ c $\dfrac{1}{c^2}$ d $\dfrac{1}{k}$

   e $\dfrac{1}{w^{12}}$ f $\dfrac{1}{5^2}$ g $\dfrac{1}{1^5}$ h $\dfrac{1}{x^{10}}$

   i $\dfrac{1}{x^6}$ j x^3 k $5x^2$ l $4x$

   m x^8 n h^8 o $\dfrac{1}{x^4}$

15. a $\dfrac{1}{4}$ b $\dfrac{1}{16}$ c 9

16. a $\dfrac{5}{27}$ b 40 c $\dfrac{5}{27}y^6$

17. a p^{12} b y^2 c y^3 d $\dfrac{1}{z^5}$

   e x^{20} f $\dfrac{1}{x^6}$ g $5t^6$ h $\dfrac{2}{m^3}$

   i $x^2 + \dfrac{1}{x}$ j $6y - 4y^2$

   k x^{30} l k^{24}

   m $1296x^8 y^{12}$ n $\dfrac{144b^{10}}{a^4}$

18. a $3 \cdot 1 \times 10^9 \ cm^2$ b 2
   c 3^{15} d 269 e 0·135 grams

19. a 3 b 4 c 3 d 2

Exercise 17·5 page 177

1. a $\sqrt{x}$ b $\sqrt[3]{x}$ c $\sqrt[5]{y}$ d $\sqrt[3]{y^2}$
   e $2\sqrt[4]{z^3}$ f $\sqrt{c^3}$ g $\sqrt[3]{k^7}$ h $\sqrt[5]{p^8}$
   i $5\sqrt[5]{t^5}$ j $^1/\sqrt{a}$ k $^3/3\sqrt{p}$ l $^4/5\sqrt{g^4}$

2. a 3 b 6 c 10 d 3
   e 4 f 5 g 4 h 25
   i 10000 j 1 k 8 l 8
   m -2 n 9 o 0·5 p $\dfrac{1}{8}$

   q $\dfrac{1}{10}$ r $-\dfrac{1}{2}$

3. a $x^{\frac{2}{3}}$ b $y^{\frac{5}{3}}$ c $y^{\frac{4}{3}}$ d $x^{\frac{3}{2}}$

   e $y^{\frac{1}{3}}$ f $z^{\frac{2}{5}}$ g $a^{\frac{5}{8}}$ h $a^{\frac{8}{3}}$

   i $k^{\frac{5}{2}}$ j $p^{\frac{1}{4}}$ k $k^{\frac{1}{2}}$ l k^2

4. a c^3 b x^3 c $4x^4$ d y

   e w f $16t$ g $\dfrac{1}{x}$ h $\dfrac{1}{x^2}$

   i x j $\dfrac{1}{x^3}$

5. a $15a^5 + 12$ b $p + 1$
   c $12d - 30$ d $6m + 8$
   e $k - 1$ f $t - \dfrac{1}{t}$
   g $x^2 - \dfrac{1}{x^2}$ h $6y^2 + 7 - \dfrac{3}{y^2}$

i $x^2 + 2 + \dfrac{1}{x^2}$ j $m + 2m^{1/2} + 1$

k $4a - 12a^{1/2} + 9$ l $x^2 + 2 + \dfrac{1}{x^2}$

m $4d^2 - 12 - \dfrac{9}{d^2}$ n $d + 2 + \dfrac{1}{d}$

Remember Remember Ch 17 page 178

1. b and c are surds
2. a $\sqrt{7}$ b $\sqrt{3}$
3. a $7\sqrt{2}$ b $9\sqrt{7}$ c $4\sqrt{3}$ d $4\sqrt{5}$
   e $\sqrt{11}$ f $3\sqrt{3}$ g $-3\sqrt{5}$ h $3\sqrt{2}$
   i $2\sqrt{2}$ j $10\sqrt{2}$ k $20\sqrt{2}$ l $30\sqrt{10}$
   m $\sqrt{6}$ n $4\sqrt{3}$ o 8
   p $2\sqrt{5}$ q 3 r 15
4. a $8 + 5\sqrt{3}$ b $-36 + 13\sqrt{5}$
   c $11 + 6\sqrt{2}$ d $49 - 12\sqrt{5}$
   e $-6 - 6\sqrt{2}$
5. a $\sqrt{2}/2$ b $2\sqrt{3}/3$
   c $12\sqrt{5}/5$ d $\sqrt{30}/9$
   e $\sqrt{2}/2$ f $(\sqrt{3} - 1)$
6. a $\sqrt{13}$ b $2\sqrt{7}$ c $4\sqrt{5}$ d $2\sqrt{3}$
7. a x^7 b z^4 c $12m^2$ d p^4
   e $16x^6$ f $9x^{10}$ g $2x^3$ h $\dfrac{4y^9}{x}$
   i $4x^8$ j $\dfrac{27z^6}{w^3}$ k p^4 l y^{10}
   m $g - 2g^3$ n $\dfrac{4x}{3y^2}$
8. a 4 b 4 c 4
   d 1000 e 32 f 27
9. a $-3x^{1/2} + \dfrac{2}{x^{1/2}} - 5$ b $6t - 15$

   c $p^{17/3} + p^{-10/3} - p^{2/3}$ d $k^2 + 2 + \dfrac{1}{k^2}$

   e $m^2 - \dfrac{1}{m^2}$ f $d^4 - d - \dfrac{6}{d^2}$

Answers to Chapter 18 Page 179

Exercise 18·1 page 179

1. Lou 25 kg 130 cm   Alex 50 kg 140 cm
   Don 20 kg 150 cm   Sam 40 kg 150 cm
   Nick 35 kg 165 cm   Joe 50 kg 160 cm
   Tim 60 kg 170 cm
2. a i Mary ii Toni iii Pat iv Pat
   b Mary (3, 15), Tony(4, 10), Ali(6, 15),
     Mark(8, 20), Tom(9, 25), Shaz(10, 22·5),
     Pat(12, 30)
   c Mark
3. See Scattergraph
4. See Scattergraph
5. See Scattergraph

Exercise 18·2 page 180

1. a i Lou ii Bob iii Bill iv Lee
   b strong
   c Line passing from 3 on y-axis,
     on through Toni & Yan.
   d $y = {}^1/_2x + 3$ (various answers) e 6(ish)
2. a $y = -{}^1/_2x + 12$ b 4 hours
3. a yes - positive b yes - positive
   c yes - positive d no

4. Own Answers
5. a/b/c $y = 2^1/_2x + 28$ (various answers)

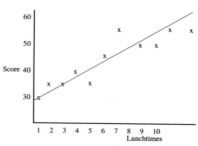

   d 48 (various answers)
6. ab Scattergraph with rising line of best fit.
   c $y = {}^1/_2x + 3$ d $10^1/_2$kg e 9
7. a $y = 2x + 1$ (approx - various answers)
   b $y = -4x + 75$ (various answers) 47 rats
   c $y = {}^4/_3x + 8$ Eng 74 (approx)

Remember Remember Ch 18 page 183

1. See graph
2. Ford $^{200}/_{600}$ Angle 120°
   Vauxhall $^{150}/_{600}$ Angle 90°
   Seat $^{175}/_{600}$ Angle 105°
   Fiat $^{75}/_{600}$ Angle 45°
   Labelled Pie Chart with angles at centre.
3. a yes b 64 g c about 58 g
4. a Scattergraph
   b Generally, the older they got, the
     heavier they became. Positive Corr.
   c Rising Line $y = 5x - 25$ approx.
   d 70 kg approx.
5. a Stem & Leaf diagram with Key !
   b 52 c 45 d 16

Turn off that Calculator 6 page 186

1. a 500 mm b 0·00005 tonne
   c 875 ml d 12500 g
   e 33120 seconds f 0·0004 litre
   g 20 mm
2. £0·45 b 0·33 cmc 1275
   d 1 cm e 0·24 km f £0·96 g153
3. a 16 b 123 c 1360
   d -18000 e -40·5 f -0·05 g1C
4. a 7 b 280000 binks
5. a $a = 4$, $b = 1$
   b A'(4, -3), B'(5, -6), C'(1, -12), D'(0, -9)
6. a 2155 b 1145 c 2110
7. a 40 min b 10 hr 49 min
8. a 300 km/hr b $33^1/_3$ mins
9. 114 cm
10. a $2\sqrt{10}$ b $4\sqrt{2}$ c $8\sqrt{2}$
   d 32 e 8 f 32 g $4^5 = 1024$
11. a $(2n)^2 = 4n^2 = 2 \times 2n^2 =$ even
   b $n + (n + 1) + (n + 2) = 3n + 3 = 3(n + 1)$
     which is a multiple of 3
   c $2n + (2n + 2) + (2n + 4) = 6n + 6 = 6(n + 1)$
     which is a multiple of 6
   d $(n + 1)^2 - n^2 = n^2 + 2n + 1 - n^2 = 2n + 1$
     which is an odd number

Answers to Chapter 19 Page 187

Exercise 19·1 page 187

1. a $y = (x - 3)^2 + 1$ b $y = (x - 6)^2 - 6$
2. $y = (x + 1)^2 + 4$

3.   a $y = (x - 2)^2 + 3$ b $y = (x + 10)^2 - 10$

     c $y = (x - 4)^2 - 21$ d $y = (x + 7)^2 -$

4.   a $y = (x + \frac{3}{2})^2 + \frac{7}{4}$ b $y = (x + \frac{5}{2})^2 + \frac{11}{4}$

     c $y = (x - \frac{1}{2})^2 - \frac{9}{4}$ d $y = (2x + 1)^2 + 4$

Exercise 19·2 page 188

1.   a   3   b   2   c   (3, 2)
     d   sketch of V parabola turning at (3, 2), axis of symmetry $x = 3$.

2.   a   2   b   -1   c   (2, -1)
     d   sketch of parabola turning at (2, -1), axis of symmetry $x = 2$.

3.   a   (-4, -3)   b   (0, 13)
     c   sketch of parabola turning at (-4, -3), crossing y-axis at (0, 13)

4.   a   sketch of parabola turning at (2, 5), crossing y-axis at (0, 9)
     b   sketch of parabola turning at (1, 3), crossing y-axis at (0, 4)
     c   sketch of parabola turning at (-3, 1), crossing y-axis at (0, 10)
     d   sketch of parabola turning at (2, -6), crossing y-axis at (0, -2)
     e   sketch of parabola turning at (-1, -1), crossing y-axis at (0, 0)
     f   sketch of parabola turning at (5, -8), crossing y-axis at (0, 17)
     g   sketch of parabola turning at (-2, -1), crossing y-axis at (0, 3)
     h   sketch of parabola turning at (3, 0), crossing y-axis at (0, 9)

5.   a   (4, 2)   b $y = (x - 4)^2 + 2$

6.   a $y = (x - 5)^2 + 1$, $x = 5$
     b $y = (x - 2)^2 + 5$, $x = 2$
     c $y = (x - 6)^2$, $x = 6$
     d $y = (x + 3)^2 + 2$, $x = -3$
     e $y = (x - 7)^2 - 3$, $x = 7$
     f $y = (x + 2)^2 - 1$, $x = -2$

7.   a $y = (x - 12)^2 - 5$ b   (0, 139)

Exercise 19·3 page 190

1.   a   3   b   5   c   (3, 5)
     d   sketch of upside down parabola turning at (3, 5), axis of symmetry $x = 3$.

2.   a   sketch of upside down parabola turning at (1, 3), axis of symmetry $x = 1$. y intercept at (0, 2)
     b   sketch of upside down parabola turning at (3, 8), axis of symmetry $x = 3$. y intercept at (0, -1)
     c   sketch of upside down parabola turning at (-2, 4), axis of symmetry $x = -2$. y intercept at (0, 0)
     d   sketch of upside down parabola turning at (-1, 1), axis of symmetry $x = -1$ y intercept at (0, 0)
     e   sketch of upside down parabola turning at (3, -2), axis of symmetry $x = 3$. y intercept at (0, -11)
     f   sketch of upside down parabola turning at (4, -1), axis of symmetry $x = 4$. y intercept at (0, -17)
     g   sketch of upside down parabola turning at (-3, -5), axis of symmetry $x = -3$. y intercept at (0, -14)
     h   sketch of upside down parabola turning (5, 0), axis of symmetry $x = 5$. at y intercept at (0, -25)

---

3.   a   (3, 9)   b $y = 9 - (x - 3)^2$
     axis of symmetry $x = 3$

4.   a $y = 3 - (x - 4)^2$, $x = 4$, y-intercept (0, -13)
     b $y = 8 - (x - 2)^2$, $x = 2$, y-intercept (0, 4)
     c $y = 4 - (x + 1)^2$, $x = -1$, y-intercept (0, 3)
     d $y = -2 - (x - 5)^2$, $x = 5$, y-intercept (0, -27)

Exercise 19·4 page 191

1.   a $k = 2$ b $y = 2x^2$

2.   a $k = 5$ b $y = 5x^2$

3.   a $y = 2x^2$ b $y = 4x^2$
     c $y = 4x^2$ d $y = 3x^2$
     e $y = 7x^2$ f $y = 0.5x^2$

4.   a $k = -2$ b $y = -2x^2$

5.   a $k = -3$ b $y = -3x^2$

6.   a $y = -3x^2$ b $y = -4x^2$
     c $y = -11x^2$ d $y = -2x^2$
     e $y = -6x^2$ f $y = -\frac{1}{3}x^2$

Exercise 19·5 page 193

1.   a $a = 1$ $b = 6$ $c = 4$
     b $x = -5.24$ $x = -0.76$
2. $x = -0.26$ $x = -7.74$
3.   a $x = -0.63$ $x = -6.37$
     b $x = -0.76$ $x = -9.24$
     c $x = -2$ $x = -4$
     d $x = -2$ $x = -5$
4.   a $x = -2$ $x = -4$
     b $x = -2$ $x = -5$
5.   a $a = 1$ $b = -4$ $c = 2$
     b $x = 3.41$ $x = 0.59$
6.   a $x = 5.45$ $x = 0.55$
     b $x = 7.32$ $x = 0.68$
     c $x = 6.85$ $x = 0.15$
     d $x = 3$ $x = 5$
7.   a $a = 1$ $b = 3$ $c = -5$
     b $x = 1.19$ $x = -4.19$
8.   a $x = 1.16$ $x = -5.16$
     b $x = 0.32$ $x = -6.32$
     c $x = 4.19$ $x = -1.19$
     d $x = 2.56$ $x = -1.56$
9.   a $a = 3$ $b = 4$ $c = -5$
     b $x = 0.79$ $x = -2.12$
10.   a $x = -1$ $x = -1.5$
     b $x = -0.21$ $x = -3.12$
     c $x = 2.35$ $x = -0.85$
     d $x = 1.18$ $x = -0.43$
11.   Cannot get square root of a negative. Parabola does not cut x-axis.

Exercise 19·6 page 194

1.   a   37   b   0   c   -7   d   1
2.   a   12, 2 real roots   b   -15, no real roots
     c   17, 2 real roots
     d   0, 2 equal roots (1 root)
     e   -16, no real roots f   1, 2 real roots
     g   25, 2 real roots   h   -15 no real roots
     i   0, 2 equal roots   j   -3, no real roots
     k   21, 2 real roots   l   61, 2 real roots
3. $p = 9$
4. $a = -2$

---

5. $b = 10$ or -10
6. $64 + 8p > 0$ $\Rightarrow$ $p > -8$
7. $m = 3$ or -3
8. $36 + 4t < 0$ $\Rightarrow$ $t < -9$

Remember Remember Ch 19 page 195

1.   a $y = (x + 3)^2 + 3$ b $y = (x + 2.5)^2 - 8.25$
2.   a   5   b   3   c   (5, 3)
     d   sketch of parabola turning at (5, 3), axis of symmetry $x = 5$.
3.   a   sketch of parabola turning at (1, 4), crossing y-axis at (0, 5)
     b   sketch of parabola turning at (-2, 5), crossing y-axis at (0, 9)
     c   sketch of parabola turning at (4, -2), crossing y-axis at (0, 14)
     d   sketch of parabola turning at (3, 0), crossing y-axis at (0, 9)
4.   a   sketch of upside down parabola turning at (2, 6), axis of symmetry $x = 2$. y intercept at (0, 2)
     b   sketch of upside down parabola turning at (1, 4), axis of symmetry $x = 1$. y intercept at (0, 3)
     c   sketch of upside down parabola turning at (-3, 5), axis of symmetry $x = -3$. y intercept at (0, -4)
     d   sketch of upside down parabola turning at (-2, -1), axis of symmetry $x = -2$. y intercept at (0, -5)
5.   a $k = 5$ b $y = 5x^2$
6.   a $y = 2x^2$ b $y = 4x^2$ c $y = 4x^2$
7.   a $y = -5x^2$ b $y = -10x^2$ c $y = -9x^2$
8.   a $y = (x - 3)^2 + 6$, $x = 3$
     b $y = (x + 4)^2 + 3$, $x = -4$
     c $y = 5 - (x - 7)^2$, $x = 7$
     d $y = (x - 5)^2$, $x = 5$
8.   e $y = 5 - (x + 2)^2$, $x = -2$
     f $y = -3 - (x - 7)^2$, $x = 7$
9.   a   0, 2 equal roots (1 root)
     b   -3, no real roots
10.   a $x = -0.7$ or $x = -4.3$
     b $x = 5.24$ or $x = 0.76$
     c $x = -0.72$ or $x = -2.78$
     d $x = 1.68$ or $x = -0.48$
11.   A(0·7, 0)   B(4·3, 0)
12.   a $64 - 8n = 0$ $\Rightarrow$ $n = 8$
     b $36 - 12d < 0$ $\Rightarrow$ $d > 3$.

Answers to Chapter 20 Page 196

Exercise 20·1 page 197

1.   a   15·0°   165°   b   210°   330°
     c   85·0°   275°   d   140°   220°
     e   70·0°   250°
2.   a   45·0°   135°   b   22°   158°
     c   87·4°   92·6°   d   46·8°   133·2°
     e   8·00°   172°   f   57·0°   123·2°
     g   45·0°   315°   h   22·0°   338°
     i   78·0°   282°   j   45·0°   225°
     k   8·98°   189°   l   78·5°   258·5°
3.   a   200°   340°   b   240°   300°
     c   186°   354°   d   192°   348°
     e   216°   324°   f   237°   303°
     g   100°   260°   h   160°   200°
     i   97·0°   263°   j   135°   315°
     k   105°   285°   l   100°   280°
     m   126°   306°   n   93·5°   274°
     o   170°   350°

4.
a	30·0° 150°	b	53·1° 127°
c	217° 323°	d	190° 350°
e	7·18° 173°	f	206° 334°

5.
a	60·0° 300°	b	78·5° 282°
c	132° 228°	d	125° 235°
e	124° 236°	f	139° 221°

6.
a	26·6° 207°	b	74·1° 254°
c	174° 354°	d	162° 342°
e	49·8° 230°	f	158° 338°

7. 30·0° 150° 210° 330°

8.
a	30·0° 150°	210° 330°
b	45·0° 135°	225° 315°
c	26·6° 153°	207° 333°

9.
a	69·4° 249°	b	206° 333°
c	48·2° 312°	d	68·2° 248°
e	136° 224°	f	210° 330°
g	146° 214°	h	168° 348°
i	270°		
j	23·6° 156°	204°	336°
k	60·0° 120°	240°	300°
l	80·5° 99·5°	261°	279°
m	30·0° 150°	n	132° 228°
o	78·7° 259°		

10. P(120°,5) Q(240°,5)

11. A(38·7°,-2) Q(141°,-2)

12.
a	60·0° 120°	420°	480°
b	240° 300°	600°	660°
c	19·9° 340°	380°	700°
d	160° 200°	520°	560°
e	30·0° 150°	390°	510°
f	120° 240°	480°	600°

Exercise 20·2 page 200
1. 112°
2. 41·4°
3. 125°
4. 90·0°
5. 92·8°
6. 97·2°
7. a 139° b 041° c 221°

Exercise 20·3 page 201
1. a 0·9 b 0·8 c 0·9 d 0·7
2. a $\frac{4}{5}$ b $\frac{3}{4}$
3. a $\frac{3}{5}$ b $\frac{4}{3}$
4. a $\frac{12}{13}$ b $\frac{12}{5}$
5. a $\frac{12}{13}$ b $\frac{12}{5}$
  c $\frac{4}{5}$ d $\frac{3}{4}$
  e $\frac{33}{56}$
6. a lhs $5\cos^2 A + 5\sin^2 A$
    $= 5(\cos^2 A + \sin^2 A) = 5 \times 1 = 5 =$ rhs
  b - l various methods. Teacher to check
7. a lhs $5\sin^2 A + 3\cos^2 A$
    $= 5\sin^2 A + 3(1 - \sin^2 A)$
    $= 5\sin^2 A - 3\sin^2 A + 3$
    $= 2\sin^2 A + 3 =$ rhs
  b - e various methods. Teacher to check

Remember Remember Ch 20 page 203
1. a 50·0° 130° b 130° 230°
2. a 28·0° 152° b 64·0° 296°
  c 28·0° 208° d 218° 322°
  e 170° 190° f 130° 310°
3. a 30·0° 150° b 115° 245°
  c 166° 346°
  d 44·4° 136° 224° 316°
  e 104° 256° f 16·6° 197°
4. D(199°,5) E(341°,5)

5.
a	45° 135°	405°	495°
b	155° 205°	515°	565°

6. 120°

7. a $\frac{5}{13}$ b $-\frac{5}{12}$

8. a lhs $= 8\cos^2 A = 8(1 - \sin^2 A) = 8 - 8\sin^2 A$
    $=$ rhs
  b - d various methods. Teacher to check

Answers to Chapter 21 Page 204

National 5 Revision - page 204

1. a $2a^2 - 7ab - 15b^2$
  b $9x^2 - 30x + 25$
  c $x^3 - 6x^2 + 12x - 8$ d $2x + 5$
  e $8x^2 - 34x + 12$ f $- 24t + 15$
2. 6 cm
3. Proof. Both $x^2 + 3x$
4. 480 g
5. £136   20%
6. £345   322·05
7. £285
8. a $4\frac{1}{4}$ b $4\frac{1}{2}$ c $\frac{22}{45}$ d $11\frac{1}{8}$
  e $12\frac{4}{15}$ f $\frac{1}{3}$ g $3\frac{7}{12}$ h $3\frac{4}{11}$
9. a $\frac{1}{2}$ b $\frac{7}{36}$ c $9\frac{3}{4}$ d 7
  e $\frac{2}{5}$ f $1\frac{3}{7}$ g $3\frac{3}{4}$ h 6
10. By converse of Pythag, $1\cdot5^2 + 4\cdot2^2 \neq 4\cdot5^2$
  Not a right angled triangle
11. 7·4 cm
12. $2\sqrt{26}$
13. a grad 3 (0,-2) b grad $-\frac{1}{2}$ (0, 2)
  c grad $\frac{3}{2}$ (0,-3) d grad = 4 (0, 0)
14.
15. a $D = 80t$ b $D = -20t + 150$
  c 6 hours altogether from Tolbert
16. a $y = 4x + 2$ b (0,2)
17. 19·1 cm²
18. 75°
19. 149°
20. a 63° b 27·5 km
21. 52°
22. a 220° - 120° = 100°. 180° - 100° = 80°
  b Boat is nearer RY = 362 km
23. a $2x(2x - 3)$ b $\pi rh(r - 2)$
  c $(x + 7)(x - 5)$ d $(x - 6)^2$
  e $(x + 3)(x - 24)$ f $(x + 9y)(x - 8y)$
  g $5(x + 3)(x - 3)$ h $3(3x + 2)(3x - 2)$
  i $(3x - 2)(x - 6)$ j $2(2x + 5)(2x - 1)$
  k $(3y - 2)(2y - 3)$ l $(5 + x)(3 - x)$
24. a $\frac{x+y}{xy}$ b $\frac{7}{2x}$
  c $\frac{3x+1}{x(x+1)}$ d $\frac{x-27}{(x+3)(x-3)}$
  e $\frac{3+2x}{x^2}$ f $\frac{7x-22}{(x-4)(x-2)}$
  g $\frac{3x+7}{(x+1)(x+2)(x+3)}$
  h $\frac{2x+26}{x(x-2)(x+4)}$
  i $\frac{2x+2}{x(x-2)(x+2)}$
25. a $\frac{1}{x}$ b $\frac{x-3}{x}$
  c $\frac{1}{x}$ d $\frac{x+3}{x}$
  e $\frac{x+4}{x+3}$ f $\frac{x-4}{x+5}$

---

26. a $x = \frac{y-b}{a}$ b $n = \frac{P-2m}{2}$
  c $r = \sqrt[3]{\frac{3V}{4\pi}}$ d $V = \frac{1}{6}h$
  e $x = \frac{d-b}{a-c}$ f $G = \frac{L}{4\pi^2 T^2}$
  g $x = \frac{qd+pc}{p-q}$ h $E = \frac{D^2+1}{D^2-1}$
27. a (5,-2) b (3,-4) c (6,-1)
28. £29·70
29. a $3x + 50y = 160$ b $4x + 60y = 204$
  c £30 & £1·40
30. a $4\sqrt{5}$ b $20\sqrt{5}$ c $25\sqrt{5}$ d $6\sqrt{5}$
  e $15\sqrt{2}$ f $6\sqrt{6}$ g $6\sqrt{3}$ h $40\sqrt{3}$
  i $6\sqrt{10}$ j $12 - 3\sqrt{2}$ k 20
  l $20 - 7\sqrt{3}$ m $128 + 10\sqrt{15}$
31. a $6x^7$ b $6a^7$ c $9p^6$ d 1
  e $4x^2 + 4 + \frac{1}{x^2}$ f $9a^2 + 12$
  g $x + x^{-1} + 2$ h $x + x^{-1} + 2$
  i x^{-7} j x^{-12} k $\frac{1}{2m^2}$
  l y m $3y^2$
32. a 5 b $\frac{1}{4}$ c $1\frac{1}{2}$ d $\frac{3}{4}$
  e 3 f $\frac{1}{3}$ g $\frac{1}{16}$ h 2
33. a $\frac{\sqrt{6}}{3}$ b $\sqrt{5}$ c $\frac{\sqrt{6}}{2}$ d $3\sqrt{2}$
34. a $1 : \sqrt{2}$ b Proof using Pythagoras Th.
35. a -6 b -2 c 27 d -1
  e $-8a^3 + 4a + 1$ f $\frac{1}{2}$ g -3
  h 3·5 i 3 j 0, -2, 0.
36.
37. a $\begin{pmatrix}-3\\-6\end{pmatrix}$ b $\begin{pmatrix}-9\\2\end{pmatrix}$ c $\begin{pmatrix}9\\-12\end{pmatrix}$ d $\begin{pmatrix}18\\6\end{pmatrix}$
  e $\begin{pmatrix}18\\-4\end{pmatrix}$ f 5 units
38. a $\begin{pmatrix}3\\-1\\-14\end{pmatrix}$ b $\begin{pmatrix}-9\\9\\-10\end{pmatrix}$ c $\begin{pmatrix}-12\\10\\4\end{pmatrix}$
  d 13 units
39. a $\begin{pmatrix}-1\\-2\end{pmatrix}$ b $\begin{pmatrix}3\\-3\\1\end{pmatrix}$
40. $\begin{pmatrix}1\\-8\\-16\end{pmatrix}$
41. a $\begin{pmatrix}6\\3\\-6\end{pmatrix}\begin{pmatrix}2\\1\\-2\end{pmatrix}$ b L(5,0,0) M(7,1,-2)
42. a $x = 0, x = 4$ b $x = 0, x = 2$
  c $x = 0, x = \frac{2}{3}$ d $x = 3, x = -3$
  e $x = 5, x = -5$ f $x = \frac{4}{3}, x = -\frac{4}{3}$
  g $x = -4, x = -2$ h $x = -2, x = 5$
  i $x = 3, x = -7$ j $x = -\frac{4}{3}, x = 3$
  k $x = -\frac{5}{2}, x = \frac{1}{2}$ l $x = -1, x = 5$
43. a P(-1,0) Q(3,0) R(0,-3)
  b S(-2,0) T(0,4)
  c U(-4,0) V(0,8) W(2,0)

44. a 15 cm   b $56^1/_4$ cm

45. a Median 12   Lower Q 5   Upper Q 15
    b 5
    c
      1   5   12   15   25

46. Mean 4·8 Median 4·5 Mode 3 Range 8
47. Craig is 19 years old
48. a 228   b 6·6
    c Yes, both within limits
49. a 74   b 7   c
                    63 69   74   83   98

50. a max 5   min −5   period 360°
    b max 8   min −8   period 180°
    c max 3   min −3   period 90°
    d max $^1/_2$ min −$^1/_2$ period 120°
    e max Inf   min −Inf   period 90°
    f max 3   min −1   period 360°
    g max 0   min −20   period 360°
    h max 2   min 0   period 360°
    i max 5   min −5   period 180°
    j max 75   min −75   period 60°
    k max 9   min 3   period 90°
    l max 3   min −3   period 720°

51. a   b

52. a $y = 7\sin x°$ b $y = 15\cos 6x°$
    c $y = -0·2\sin x°$ d $y = 4\sin x° + 4$
53. $k = 5$ $b = 2$
54. a 7 metres   b 5 metres
55. a 19·5 cm   b 123 cm²
56. 90°
57. a 279 cm²   b 197 cm²
    c 82 cm²
58. 4535 cm²
59. a 3628 cm²   b 728 cm²
    c 10920 cm³
60. a $y = (x - 3)^2 - 6$ b $y = (x + ^5/_2)^2 + ^7/_4$
61. a $x = -0·81$ $x = -6·19$
    b $x = 3·69$ $x = 0·82$
    c $x = 1·13$ $x = -1·47$
    d $x = 7·16$ $x = 0·84$
62. a $a = 4$ $b = 2$ $x = 4$ (0, 18)
    b $a = 2$ $b = 6$ $x = 2$ (0, 2)
    c $a = -3$ $b = -2$ $x = -3$ (0, 7)
    d $a = 5$ $b = 0$ $x = 5$ (0, −25)
63. a $y = 6x^2$ b $y = -^1/_2 x^2$
64. a 17, 2 real roots b −3, no real roots
    c 25, 2 real roots d 0, equal roots (1)
65. $p = 8$ or $p = -8$
66. $36 + 4a > 0$ $a > -9$
67 A(1·22,0)
68. a 80   b 5°C
69. a/b graph c Yes   d Draw Line
    e $y = ^1/_2 x + 1·8$ approx
    f £3·80 approx
70. a $x = 54·7$ $x = 305·3$
    b $x = 6·87$ $x = 173·2$
    c $x = 194·5$ $x = 345·5$
    d $x = 41·4$ $x = 318·6$
71. a P(90°,1)   b Q(131·4,1·5)
72. a A(90°,0) b B(120°,−0·5) C(240°,−0·5) .